chefs to know
a guide to chefs for chefs

Edited by Antoinette Bruno

Editing contributions from Will Blunt and Heather Sperling

Research assistance by Lindsay Vietor

Design by Zac Overman

Information architecture by Richie Adomako

Photo editing by Vicky Wasik

Cover photo by Antoinette Bruno

Published in the United States by StarChefs.com, Inc.

For information:
StarChefs.com
9 East 19th Street, 9th Floor
New York, NY 10003

Library of Congress Cataloging-in-Publication Data
Chefs to Know: A Guide to Chefs for Chefs / StarChefs.com. -2nd ed.
p. cm.
Includes index.

Library of Congress Control Number: 2008906950

PRINTED IN CHINA

Second Edition

All unaccredited color photography in Chefs to Know was taken with digital SLR cameras - the Nikon D200, D70, and D50 - by StarChefs.com's editorial staff during tastings across the country.

Isabella Shoji

For Isabella and Kendrick,
who put up with a mommy who's always on the road

Acknowledgements

The 2nd edition of Chefs to Know has proven to be no less a labor of love than the first edition. Chefs can be hard to track; with turnover in the culinary industry still averaging over 120% per year, the roster of industry members who have changed their jobs, closed their restaurants, or even left the country is ever-changing. Chefs to Know is a reality thanks to the the diligence and perseverance of those both on and off the StarChefs staff, both paid and unpaid, and the chefs who helped guide us along the way. They have all been critical to its success, and too many pitched in to help to be adequately thanked here.

The StarChefs editorial team tasted and interviewed every chef, sommelier and mixologist on these pages, and the staff worked diligently, badgering chefs for information, searching for photos, googling chefs and restaurants, and calling kitchens in every city across the country. The tireless and industrious Lindsay Vietor came in as an intern, made the project her own, and rocked it out. Heather Sperling helped shape and conceptualize the book, and edited the copy over and over again. The book would not be what it is without her. Jon Proville pitched in when we needed him to help reach the finish line.

Zac Overman lent the book its design and flair, Richie Adomako struggled heroically with the technical aspects of the data, and Vicky Wasik edited hundreds and hundreds of photos. My business partner, Will Blunt, lent a critical eye to the project, and supported and grounded us as we yet again refused to give up on hitting this moving target.

Most of all, I want to thank my husband Ken Shoji and my children, Kendrick and Isabella, for putting up with me working every family vacation, almost every day off, and many, many evenings.

I also want to acknowledge chefs across America (and this year abroad as well) who aren't in this book who should be - we hope to include you in future editions. Whether we've tasted with you and lost touch or we've never met but should have, this book is about celebrating all of you and acknowledging your creativity, passion, and hard work.

Cheers,

Antoinette Bruno

Editor-in-Chief, StarChefs.com

KEY – CHEFS AND PASTRY CHEFS

 Star Chefs are talented, passionate chefs featured on StarChefs.com that have made great contributions to the culinary community over the course of their careers

 StarChefs.com Rising Stars are up-and-coming chefs who have received our national award and represent the vanguard of the contemporary American dining scene

 Accepts Interns/Stages

Seats: # of seats in the restaurant; if a range, it includes dining room and then private dining, patio, bar

Weeknight/Weekend Covers: number of guests served on a weeknight and/or weekend

Check Average: average price spent per diner with/without wine

Tasting Menu: whether the restaurant offers a set tasting menu, and, if so, the price

Kitchen Staff: number of staff in the kitchen (for pastry chefs, refers to pastry kitchen)

Cuisine: personal culinary style, as described by the chefs

Notable Dishes: dishes from StarChefs' most recent tasting

Restaurant Recs: favorite restaurants off the beaten path

Kitchen Tool(s): most indispensable kitchen tool

Interview Question: favorite question to ask a prospective employee

Flavor Combo(s): favorite flavor combinations (of the moment)

Fave Cookbook(s): self explanatory!

Chef to Cook for You: the chef you'd most like to cook for you (alive or dead)

Culinary Travel: where you'd most like to go for culinary travel

Foreword

Chefs to Know is a continuation of StarChefs.com's editorial efforts to identify and feature the best chefs in the industry – not because they are on TV, but because they are talented, innovative, passionate, and driven people who contribute greatly to their culinary community, and are dynamically shaping the identity of American food. StarChefs.com's mission is to be a resource and aid for culinary professionals' success; Chefs to Know is one of the tools that we offer to strengthen and further the culinary industry. At its heart, it's an industry resource and an industry homage – it's a fun, informative, inspiring look at the names and faces behind America's stoves. It's for anyone who wants to learn about the industry - from the tools and the flavors, to chefs' favorite restaurants across the country.

After years of working with chefs, we decided to compile the information from our interviews, gathered on tastings across the country, and put it all in one place. In the same way that our editorial content online is driven by tastings, every chef, mixologist, and sommelier featured in Chefs to Know has met with StarChefs.com's editorial team, prepared a tasting, and invited us to get to know them during an interview.

Having the first book under our belt, we took on the additional challenge this year of recognizing sommeliers, mixologists, and a handful of international chefs we've come across on our travels. We added new chef information: restaurant stats (covers, kitchen size, etc) as well as fun facts – like favorite flavor combinations and culinary travel destinations – to help get your creative juices flowing. The recipes and photos will hopefully inspire you to try new things, and the Restaurants off the Beaten Path index will keep you eating your way through chef haunts across the country.

American cuisine – or, better said, cuisine in America – gets better and better each year. The variety, the talent and the passion is at once astounding and inspiring. The American spirit of rugged individualism and bold risk-taking is at the heart of these chefs' personalities and, in large measure, the reason for their success. What distinguishes these chefs and their approach to cooking is their lack of boundaries: rather than being tied to strict cultural traditions in the kitchen, they are free to interpret cuisines from every country in the world. In this spirit we present the 2nd edition of Chefs to Know, and continue to connect the dots spanning the vast American culinary map.

A

{ Achatz - Ayers }

Grant Achatz
Chef/Owner | Alinea

1723 N. Halsted St. Chicago, IL 60614

Restaurant E-mail: chef@alinearestaurant.com

Phone: (312) 867-0110

RESTAURANT FACTS

Seats: 67 **Weeknight Covers:** 80 **Weekend Covers:** 80 **Check Average (with Wine):** $265 **Tasting Menu:** Yes $140 **Kitchen Staff:** 20

CHEF FACTS

Cuisine: Progressive American **Born:** 1974 **Began Career:** Working at my parent's restaurant when I was around 8 years old, frying eggs and such. I guess that counts! **Culinary School:** The Culinary Institute of America, Hyde Park, NY **Grad Year:** 1994 **Stages:** Chicago, IL: Charlie Trotter's; Yountville, CA: The French Laundry; Spain: el Bulli **Work History:** Grand Rapids, MI: Cygnus; Yountville, CA: The French Laundry; Evanston, Il: Trio; Chicago, IL: Charlie Trotter's **Mentor(s):** Thomas Keller **Protégée(s):** Michael Carlson, Nathan Klingbail **Awards:** 2008 James Beard Foundation Outstanding Chef; 2008, 2007 Restaurant Magazine Top 50 Best Restaurants in the World; 2007 James Beard Foundation Best Chef Great Lakes; 2006 Gourmet Magazine Best Restaurant in America; 2003 James Beard Foundation Rising Star Chef in America; 2002 Food & Wine Best New Chefs **Books Published:** The Alinea Cookbook

NOTABLE DISH(ES): Hot Potato-Cold Potato; Tempura Sweet Potato with Bourbon, Brown Sugar and Smoking Cinnamon

FAST FACTS

Restaurant Recs: Geja's – it's on old-school fondue restaurant. They do it really well. A big menu and a great wine list that's half-price on Mondays. **Kitchen Tool(s):** Offset spatula and French knife - I know they're not exciting, but I couldn't live without them. Also, a pair of sewing scissors that I received as a gift while working at the French Laundry. Functionally they are great in the kitchen. I tell the cooks at Alinea they can borrow them, but if they lose them they might as well walk away. **Interview Question:** I try to scare them away, that's pretty much the tactic I take. I tell them how little money they're going to make, what long hours they're going to work, and how they're going to lose any social life they may have. I want everyone to have a very clear understanding of what they're getting into. After this, I ask: What makes you think you want to work here, as opposed to Trotter's or The French Laundry? **Flavor Combo(s):** Strawberry, niçoise olive and violet **Fave Cookbook(s):** The French Laundry by Thomas Keller; Kaiseki by Yoshihiro Murata; Charmaine Solomon's Encyclopedia of Asian Food **Chef to Cook for You:** Thomas Keller. My 4 years at the French Laundry ended up being the most transformative period in my life. He teaches young cooks much more than cooking. **Culinary Travel:** Number one on my list right now is Japan, followed closely by Morocco

Hugh Acheson
Chef/Owner | Five and Ten

1653 S. Lumpkin St. Athens, GA 30606
Restaurant E-mail: 5and10restaurant@gmail.com
Phone: (706) 546-7300

RESTAURANT FACTS
Seats: 88 **Weeknight Covers:** 110 **Weekend Covers:** 190 **Check Average (with Wine):** $50 **Tasting Menu:** No **Kitchen Staff:** 20

CHEF FACTS
Other Restaurants: The National **Cuisine:** Contemporary American **Born:** 1971 **Began Career:** 1986 – After school I started working doing dishes in a deli, and then got a job cooking on the line in a restaurant in Ottawa. **Stages:** New York, NY: Babbo **Work History:** Quebec, Canada: Henri Burger; San Francisco, CA: Mecca; Gary Danko **Mentor(s):** Rob MacDonald at Henri Burger and Maplelawn Café, for his butchery and stock making. He never takes shortcuts. And Gary Danko at Gary Danko, and Mike Fennelly, formerly of Mecca. **Awards:** 2008 James Beard Foundation Nominee Best Chef Southeast; 2007 StarChefs.com Rising Star Chef Atlanta; 2007 James Beard Foundation Nominee Best Chef Southeast; 2007 Atlanta Journal-Constitution Restaurant of the Year **Affiliations:** JBF, Southern Foodways Alliance **Languages Spoken:** French

NOTABLE DISH(ES): Braised and Crisped Red Wattle Pork Belly with Citrus Salad; Sweetbreads with Succotash, Baked Grits and Tarragon Jus; English Pea Soup with Minted Créme Fraîche, Peekytoe Crab and Julienned Bacon

FAST FACTS
Restaurant Recs: C'om Vietnamese Grill on Buford Highway; Haru-Ichiban for their sushi and light, seasonal salads; Eigensinn Farm outside Toronto **Kitchen Tool(s):** The stove for its versatility **Interview Question:** Where are you going to be in 3 years? I'm looking for dedication to the industry, not a passing interest. **Flavor Combo(s):** Cinnamon and lamb; vanilla and corn **Fave Cookbook(s):** The French Menu Cookbook by Richard Olney **Chef to Cook for You:** Frank Stitt at The Highland Bar and Grill in Birmingham, Alabama **Culinary Travel:** The Basque Country in Spain – the cooking of the Basques is so interesting and the history is so deep

Jody Adams
Chef/Co-Owner | Rialto

One Bennett St., Harvard Square Cambridge, MA 02138

Restaurant E-mail: catherine@rialto-restaurant.com

Phone: (617) 661-5050

RESTAURANT FACTS
Seats: 140 **Weeknight Covers:** 125 **Weekend Covers:** 250 **Check Average (with Wine):** $90 **Check Average (w/o Wine):** $55 **Tasting Menu:** Yes Upon Request **Kitchen Staff:** 10-ish

CHEF FACTS
Cuisine: Italian with New England ingredients **Born:** 1957 **Began Career:** 1984 **Work History:** Boston, MA: Season's Restaurant, Hamersley's Bistro, blu; Cambridge, MA: Michaela's **Mentor(s):** Gordon Hamersley, Nancy Verde Barr, Lydia Shire **Protégée(s):** Carolyn Johnson, Nuno Alves, Tom Fosnot **Awards:** 2004 Gourmet Magazine World's Top Hotel Restaurants; 2003 IACP Best Chefs & Restaurants Cookbook Nominnee; 2000 Nation's Restaurant News Fine Dining Hall of Fame Inductee; 1997 James Beard Foundation Best Chef Northeast; 1996 Bon Appétit Top 25 Hotel Restaurants in the Country; 1993 Food & Wine Best New Chefs; 1992 Esquire Best Young Chefs **Affiliations:** Chefs Collaborative, WCR, SOS, IACP, JBF **Books Published:** In the Hands of a Chef

NOTABLE DISH(ES): Grilled Bluefish with Pomegranate Glaze and Cucumber-Yogurt Sauce; Prune, Plum and Walnut Butter Cake

FAST FACTS
Restaurant Recs: Pomodoro in Brookline for the hospitality **Kitchen Tool(s):** A Microplane – I use it for some of my favorite flavors: Parmigiano Reggiano, lemon zest, garlic paste, and ginger **Interview Question:** What is your favorite thing to eat? **Flavor Combo(s):** Lemon, garlic, fennel, extra virgin olive oil, and chili **Fave Cookbook(s):** Books by Elizabeth David, Claudia Roden and Paula Wolfert **Chef to Cook for You:** It has to be someone fun who doesn't take him/herself too seriously, like Jamie Oliver **Culinary Travel:** India – for the cuisine, the culture and the knowledge

Tammy Alana
Pastry Chef | Alizé at the Top of the Palms Casino Resort

4321 W. Flamingo Rd. Las Vegas, NV 89103

Phone: (702) 245-1263

RESTAURANT FACTS
Seats: 95 **Weeknight Covers:** 80–90 **Weekend Covers:** 160–200 **Check Average (with Wine):** $190 **Check Average (w/o Wine):** $100 **Tasting Menu:** Yes $95/$125 **Kitchen Staff:** 2

CHEF FACTS
Other Restaurants: Andre's at the Monte Carlo Resort **Cuisine:** French desserts **Born:** 1974 **Began Career:** 1998 **Culinary School:** The Culinary Institute of America, St. Helena, CA **Grad Year:** 2000 **Stages:** Las Vegas, NV: Le Cirque, Circo **Work History:** Napa Valley, CA: Domaine Chandon; Yountville, CA: Brix; Las Vegas, NV: The Bellagio Hotel, Tre, Mistral, Andre's Restaurant **Mentor(s):** Linda Bassett, Vincent Pilon, my mother, and my culinary instructors from the CIA **Awards:** 2005 StarChefs.com Rising Star Pastry Chef Las Vegas **Affiliations:** WCR **Languages Spoken:** Little French, little Spanish

NOTABLE DISH(ES): Chocolate and Pandan Leaf Spring Rolls; Strawberry Banana Shortcake with Balsamic Cream

FAST FACTS
Restaurant Recs: Lotus of Siam for coconut sticky rice and duck curry **Kitchen Tool(s):** Six-inch offset spatula **Interview Question:** What can you contribute to the team? **Flavor Combo(s):** Salty sweet; tart and creamy; chocolate with citrus **Fave Cookbook(s):** Grand Livre de Cuisine by Alain Ducasse **Chef to Cook for You:** Chef choice would be Daniel Boulud himself (I've never gotten to experience HIS food) **Culinary Travel:** France – French is my favorite cuisine

Colin Alevras
Consulting Chef

New York, NY

Restaurant E-mail: thetastingroom@msn.com

CHEF FACTS

Cuisine: Seasonal American **Born:** 1971 **Began Career:** 1993 **Culinary School:** Peter Kumps NY Cooking School **Grad Year:** 1993/2004 **Stages:** Paris, France: L'Arpege **Work History:** New York, NY: Petrossian, The Markham, O'Neil's Grand Street, Private Chef to UN Ambassador, Restaurant Daniel, The Tasting Room **Mentor(s):** Thom Scharneccia – a contractor I worked with from the age of 13 until I was 21; Jean Luc Le Du – former sommelier at Restaurant Daniel; Aaron Sanchez – a good friend who helps me keep it all together **Protégée(s):** Many great NYC cooks and chefs have been through our kitchen in the last nine years, including Tina Bourbeau (Fresh Direct) and Alex Raij (Tia Pol/El Quinto Pino) **Awards:** For The Tasting Room: Time Out New York: Best Date Restaurant, Best Wine Bar, Best Small Dishes; New York Magazine: Best of NY Restaurant, Best Haute Barnyard **Affiliations:** We do events with several charitable organizations, including University Settlement House, SOS, City Harvest, Food Bank for New York, and Grand Street Settlement House

NOTABLE DISH(ES): Guinea Hen Terrine; Cinnamon Custard French Toast

FAST FACTS

Restaurant Recs: Saigon Bahn Mi – the Vietnamese sandwich counter in the back of a Chinatown jewelry store **Kitchen Tool(s):** Small wire cake tester that I use as a thermometer **Interview Question:** When was the last time you were arrested and why? First, I want to know if they are a violent felon; second, I want to hear about what kind of mistakes they have made, and how they feel about them. **Flavor Combo(s):** I love the interaction between shellfish and mushrooms and the countless combinations between those two categories, especially when joined by butter **Fave Cookbook(s):** Chado the Way of Tea: A Japanese Tea Master's Almanac by Sasaki Sanmi. This book breaks down the entire year by month, with sections on different foods, serving utensils and decor. There is nothing like this in Western culture. **Chef to Cook for You:** Currently, anyone who will cook me the meal they most want to eat. Historically:Alain Chapel, for having helped create modern food and dying too young, or Carême to see how that food really tasted. **Culinary Travel:** I would love to go to Japan. The reverence and fetishistic attitude towards tools and ingredients is a constant source of wonder, fascination and inspiration.

Mark Allen
Executive Chef | Pine Brook Country Club

42 Newton St. Weston, MA

Phone: (781) 894-3731

RESTAURANT FACTS
Kitchen Staff: 20

CHEF FACTS
Cuisine: Contemporary French **Born:** 1965 **Began Career:** 1989 **Culinary School:** The Culinary Institute of America, Hyde Park, NY **Grad Year:** 1989 **Stages:** Scottsdale, AZ: The Phoenician Resort **Work History:** Scottsdale, AZ: The Phoenician Resort; San Francisco, CA: Inn at the Opera; Boston, MA: The Dining Room at the Ritz-Carlton, Le Soir **Mentor(s):** Mary Elaine, Alessandro Stratta **Protégée(s):** David Frisone **Awards:** 2002-2004 Boston Magazine Best of Boston; 2003 StarChefs.com Rising Star Chef Boston **Affiliations:** Chefs Collaborative **Languages Spoken:** Some French

NOTABLE DISH(ES): Slow Cooked Rabbit Pot Pie; Pan Roasted Whole Monkfish with Carrots, Lardons and Potato Purée

FAST FACTS
Restaurant Recs: Teatro for antipasto; Oleana for deviled eggs **Kitchen Tool(s):** Vita-Prep **Interview Question:** What would you do with the following ingredients: scallops, cucumbers and mushrooms? **Flavor Combo(s):** Capers and tomatoes **Fave Cookbook(s):** The French Laundry Cookbook by Thomas Keller; Art Culinaire Magazine **Chef to Cook for You:** Thomas Keller – for his attention to detail **Culinary Travel:** Barcelona for the intensity of the flavors, food combinations, and availability of products

Zach Allen
Executive Chef | B & B Ristorante

3355 Las Vegas Blvd. South Las Vegas, NV 89109

Restaurant E-mail: zallen@molto.com

Phone: (702)266-9977

RESTAURANT FACTS
Seats: 123 **Weeknight Covers:** 160 **Weekend Covers:** 250 **Check Average (with Wine):** $100 **Tasting Menu:** Yes $99 **Kitchen Staff:** 6–8

CHEF FACTS
Other Restaurants: Enoteca San Marco, Carnevino **Cuisine:** Rustic Italian **Born:** 1977 **Began Career:** 1991 **Culinary School:** Johnson & Wales, Providence, RI **Grad Year:** 1999 **Work History:** New York, NY: La Reserve, Lupa, Otto Enoteca-Pizzeria **Awards:** 2008 StarChefs. com Rising Star Chef Las Vegas **Affiliations:** Slow Food

NOTABLE DISH(ES): Braised Pork with Averna Liqueur and a Cucumber-Ginger Salad; Lobster Crudo Cotto: Lobster Tail Crudo, Lobster Claw Mousse in Zucchini Blossom, Lobster Claw Battered and Fried

FAST FACTS
Restaurant Recs: Sen of Japan – it's unbelievable. I get the mackerel with pickled sheets of sushi. **Kitchen Tool(s):** Blast chiller – we use it for everything **Interview Question:** It is never the same. I like to look over their resume and see what they have done and why they want to move on. **Flavor Combo(s):** Salt and pepper **Fave Cookbook(s):** I like The River Café Cookbook. It is food that speaks for itself – ingredient-focused and simplistic, which is the kind of food that I like to do. **Chef to Cook for You:** Fergus Henderson – I have had dinner with him before, but I've never had him cook for me. I like his complete use of the animal. **Culinary Travel:** Mainly to the Far East. I really like all of the fermented and preserved foods they use. Lots of preserved condiments, dried fish pastes. Things that really bounce off the meal.

Julian Alonzo
Chef | Brasserie 8 1/2

9 W 57th St. New York, NY 10019

Restaurant E-mail: jca@nyc.rr.com

Phone: (212) 829-0812

RESTAURANT FACTS
Seats: 190 **Weeknight Covers:** 120 **Weekend Covers:** 200–250
Check Average (with Wine): $62 **Tasting Menu:** Yes **Kitchen Staff:** 7

CHEF FACTS
Cuisine: American **Born:** 1970 **Began Career:** 1990 **Culinary School:**
French Culinary Institute, New York, NY **Grad Year:** 1990 **Work
History:** New York, NY: Sea Grill, Montrachet, La Caravelle; France:
Guy Savoy **Mentor(s):** Ed Brown **Awards:** 2005 New York Magazine
Top Toque **Affiliations:** FCI, JBF and charity events and fundraisers
Languages Spoken: Spanish, some French

NOTABLE DISH(ES): Hamachi Tartare with Wasabi Whipped Cream

FAST FACTS
Restaurant Recs: Blue Hill – for the raw section of the menu and the bread; Lupa for bucatini pasta
Kitchen Tool(s): Offset spatula **Interview Question:** Can you make an omelette? This tells the difference between a good cook and a bad one. **Flavor Combo(s):** Sweet and salty, like foie gras with strawberries or popcorn with peanut M&M's **Fave Cookbook(s):** Right now I really like Reinventing French Cuisine by Pierre Gagnaire and Clorofilia by Andoni Luis Aduriz **Chef to Cook for You:** Michel Bras – because I find his food so inspiring **Culinary Travel:** I like to go to Spain for inspiration, especially San Sebastian and the Basque country. You have half a dozen three-star Michelin restaurants and local food that is just as good.

Malika Ameen
Executive Pastry Chef/Co-Owner | Aigre Doux

230 W. Kinzie St. Chicago, IL 60610

Restaurant E-mail: malika@aigredouxchicago.com

Phone: (312) 329-9400

RESTAURANT FACTS
Seats: 110 **Weeknight Covers:** 75 **Weekend Covers:** 200 **Check Average (w/o Wine):** $55 **Tasting Menu:** No **Kitchen Staff:** 3

CHEF FACTS
Cuisine: Seasonal contemporary American **Born:** 1974 **Began Career:** 1995 **Culinary School:** French Culinary Institute, New York, NY (baking degree); Peter Kumps, New York, NY (culinary degree) **Grad Year:** 1998 **Work History:** New York, NY: Vong; Cub Room, Balthazar Bakery; Chicago, IL: The Ritz-Carlton; Los Angeles, CA: Chateau Marmont, The Standard **Mentor(s):** Claudia Fleming – I've never worked with her, but she has been a big influence on my pastry style. Her pastry is chef-driven – she thinks things through from a savory perspective first **Affiliations:** Common Threads **Languages Spoken:** Urdu and English

NOTABLE DISH(ES): Crème Fraîche Cheesecake with Saba-Glazed Fig, Concord Grape Sorbet and Pecan Tuile; Sticky Toffee Pudding with Toffee Sauce and Mascarpone Sorbet

FAST FACTS
Restaurant Recs: Tank Noodle – they have the best pho. There's also a Thai dive near Tank Noodle on Hollywood. It has a green awning, and serves really nice Thai catfish and really good noodles. There's a great Pakistani dive called Zaiqa that we go to too. **Kitchen Tool(s):** Microplane – I use it for everything, especially fresh citrus and fresh spices, which I use a lot of **Interview Question:** Do you read? If so, what do you read? And who are your mentors? Why should I hire you? **Flavor Combo(s):** Passionfruit and lavender; pomegranate and lemon; chocolate with very classic things, like caramel, malt, and deep fruits (like cherry). I also like it with some spices – cardamom, especially. **Fave Cookbook(s):** My favorite book is Claudia Fleming's book The Desserts of Gramercy Tavern. I also use Chez Panisse Desserts a lot. And Sherry Yard's new book is fabulous. **Chef to Cook for You:** Jean-Georges Vongerichten – after eating in numerous restaurants during my travels as well as in New York City, Jean-Georges's food is always the food that I remember. His food tingles and excites the palate. Of course no meal could be complete without dessert, and for that I would have Ms. Claudia Fleming, who is the dessert master. Her pastries are timeless and delicious. **Culinary Travel:** France – it's where the master pastry techniques come from. Pastry is really interesting because you can play and create based on where you live.

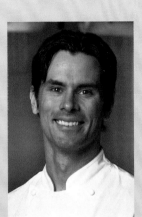

Anthony Amoroso
Executive Chef | Michael Mina at The Bellagio Las Vegas

3600 Las Vegas Blvd. Las Vegas, NV 89109

Restaurant E-mail: aamoroso@bellagioresort.com

Phone: (702) 693-8199

RESTAURANT FACTS
Seats: 150-175 **Weeknight Covers:** 200 **Weekend Covers:** 300
Check Average (with Wine): $152 **Tasting Menu:** Yes $115 **Kitchen Staff:** 10

CHEF FACTS
Cuisine: Contemporary seafood **Born:** 1972 **Began Career:** 1990
Culinary School: Hudson County Community College Culinary Arts
Program, Jersey City, NJ **Grad Year:** 1993 **Stages:** New York, NY:
Picholine, Oceana, RM, Fiamma; Washington, DC: Roberto Donna,
Il Laboratorio **Work History:** New York, NY: RM, Oceana; Las Vegas,
NV: Fiamma **Mentor(s):** Michael Mina, Michael White, Rick Moonen
Protégée(s): Carlos Buscaglia **Awards:** 2008 StarChefs.com Rising Star Chef Las Vegas **Languages Spoken:** Kitchen Spanish

NOTABLE DISH(ES): Pancetta-Wrapped Cavendish Farms Quail, Marcona Almonds, Brown Butter Jus, Almond Milk Foam; Alaskan Halibut with Maine Lobster Tortellini, Roasted Oyster Mushrooms, Lemon and Olive Oil Emulsion

FAST FACTS
Restaurant Recs: Sette Bello for Pizza **Kitchen Tool(s):** My Haziki knife: it's perfectly balanced and holds an edge. And what would we do without the Vita-Prep? How could we do celery root purée? **Interview Question:** What are your activities outside of work? It always tells a lot about a person. **Flavor Combo(s):** Acidic and sweet **Fave Cookbook(s):** Michael Mina by Michael Mina; Culinary Artistry by Karen Page and Andrew Dorenberg **Chef to Cook for You:** My grandmother – for sure **Culinary Travel:** I'd go to Tokyo for sure. I have to see it. I've never been, and I have only heard amazing things and they do nothing but try to be perfect on a regular basis. If for nothing else, to see that.

Mark Andelbradt
Executive Chef | Tao

3355 Las Vegas Blvd. South Las Vegas, NV 89109

Restaurant E-mail: chefmark@taolasvegas.com

Phone: (702) 388-8338

RESTAURANT FACTS
Seats: 400 **Weeknight Covers:** 500+ **Weekend Covers:** 1200 **Check Average (with Wine):** $70 **Tasting Menu:** No **Kitchen Staff:** 17

CHEF FACTS
Cuisine: Contemporary American with Italian and French Influences **Born:** 1973 **Began Career:** 1991 **Culinary School:** Kendall College, Chicago, IL **Grad Year:** 1995 **Stages:** China: Regent Hotel; Italy: Villa Crespi **Work History:** Chicago, IL: Tru; New York, NY: Daniel, Morimoto **Mentor(s):** Rick Tramonto, Daniel Boulud **Protégée(s):** Graham Elliot Bowles, Colby Garrelts **Awards:** 2006 StarChefs.com Rising Star Chef New York; 2002 Bertolli Sous Chef Award **Books Published:** Contributed to Rick Tramonto's books

NOTABLE DISH(ES): Live King Crab with Tomato Sorbet and Fizzy Tomatoes; Skewered Wagyu Beef with Scallion, Mushroom, Spicy Miso

FAST FACTS
Restaurant Recs: In New York: Mercadito Grove, Bar Carerra, and Etats Unis **Kitchen Tool(s):** Japanese mandolin **Interview Question:** Where are your favorite places to eat in the city? **Flavor Combo(s):** I like acid complemented by fat, or a tomato sorbet with fresh sudachi (a small, green, Japanese citrus) juice **Fave Cookbook(s):** The French Laundry Cookbook by Thomas Keller **Chef to Cook for You:** Alain Passard. His food is clean and classic without all the fuss – just a focus on great ingredients and solid technique. **Culinary Travel:** I like Paris – the memorable places are Guy Savoy, L'Arpège and L'Atelier de Joel Robuchon

Paul Anders
Executive Chef | Sweet Basil Restaurant

193 East Gore Creek Dr., Suite 201 Vail, CO 81657

Restaurant E-mail: paul@sweetbasil-vail.com

Phone: (970) 476-0125

RESTAURANT FACTS
Seats: 135 **Weeknight Covers:** 100–300 (depending on season)
Weekend Covers: 100–300 (depending on season) **Check Average**
(with Wine): $75–$80 **Tasting Menu:** No **Kitchen Staff:** 4–7

CHEF FACTS
Cuisine: Ingredient-driven contemporary American **Born:** 1976
Began Career: 1996 **Culinary School:** Johnson & Wales, Norfolk,
VA **Grad Year:** 1998 **Work History:** Hot Springs,VA: The Homestead
Resort; Newport Beach, CA: The Four Seasons Hotel; Denver, CO:
Brown Palace Hotel, Ship Tavern Restaurant, Palace Arms Restau-
rant; Colorado Springs, CO: The Broadmoor Resort **Mentor(s):** Albert
Schnarwyler **Affiliations:** Colorado Restaurant Association and many charity events and causes within
our area. One of our philosophies is to take care of our community, so we frequently donate our time,
gift certificates, special chef dinners, etc. to local charities and auctions.

NOTABLE DISH(ES): Ahi Carpaccio with a Cider Vinaigrette with Chopped Marcona Almonds

FAST FACTS
Restaurant Recs: Phat Thai in Carbondale **Kitchen Tool(s):** My Vita-Prep **Interview Question:** What is
the last thing you cooked for yourself at home? List your five favorite ingredients. What type of cuisine
do you want to cook professionally? **Flavor Combo(s):** Sweet and sour **Fave Cookbook(s):** Simply
French by Joël Robuchon **Chef to Cook for You:** Joël Robuchon, because he is one of the greatest
chefs of the century and has been able to adapt and stay on top of the trends no matter what decade
or country he is cooking in. His technique is amazing and his standards are the absolute highest. **Cu-**
linary Travel: I would love to do a food tour of Southeast Asia, China, Korea and Japan. The philosophies and approaches that these cultures take towards food are really inspiring. Simple and precise
execution of very fresh ingredients. Each region presents something new and equally delicious.

José Andrés
Chef/Owner | minibar by José Andrés

425 8th St. NW, Suite 1130 Washington, DC 20004

Restaurant E-mail: marianac@thinkfoodgroup.com

Phone: (202) 393-0812

RESTAURANT FACTS
Seats: 6 **Weeknight Covers:** 12 **Weekend Covers:** 12 **Check Average (w/o Wine):** $120 **Tasting Menu:** Yes $120 **Kitchen Staff:** 4

CHEF FACTS
Other Restaurants: Washington, DC: Café Atlantico, Jaleo, Zaytinya, Oyamel; Beverly Hills, CA: SLS Hotel **Cuisine:** My cuisine is me, there is no "cuisine" so to speak; I don't like those limitations. It's a blend of Spanish, Nuevo Latino, Eastern Mediterranean, Mexican **Born:** 1969 **Began Career:** 1988 **Culinary School:** Escola de Restauracio i Hostalage, Barcelona, Spain **Stages:** Sapin: el Bulli, Neichel, Cenador del Prado **Work History:** New York, NY: El Dorado Petit **Mentor(s):** Ferran Adriá **Protégée(s):** Katsuya Fukushima **Awards:** 2008 James Beard Foundation Outstanding Chef Nominee; 2005 RAMW Chef of the year; 2005 Food Arts Silver Spoon; 2003 James Beard Foundation Best Chef Mid-Atlantic **Affiliations:** DC Central Kitchen, THINKfoodTANK, StarChefs.com Advisory Board **Books Published:** Tapas: A Taste of Spain in America; Los Fogones de José Andrés **Languages Spoken:** Spanish, Catalan

NOTABLE DISH(ES): New England Clam Chowder; Deconstructed White Wine; Guacamole in a New Way

FAST FACTS
Restaurant Recs: Citronelle, Yanyu, Equinox **Kitchen Tool(s):** Plancha, mortar and pestle, Microplane **Interview Question:** Do you know how to cook everything? Sometimes they say yes but usually after 24 or 48 hours, they'll admit that they don't. If they admit that they don't, it means they are willing to learn from scratch. If you approach me with an attitude that you know everything, you will never open yourself up to learning all that you can. **Flavor Combo(s):** I am very inspired by the classic play of sweet and savory: chocolate and salt; raisins in the classic Catalan spinach; Brussels sprouts with apricot; duck with cherries; watermelon and tomato **Fave Cookbook(s):** That is hard! I collect cookbooks. Recently I bought the 17th century cookbook, very interesting, written by Martinez Montino, the cook to King Philip II of Spain. It was the first cookbook ever written in Spanish. I guess that is my favorite for the moment. **Chef to Cook for You:** I would have a multiple course meal cooked for me by different chefs, cooks and food writers I pay tribute to at my restaurant in the SLS Hotel Beverly Hills. Escoffier, Troisgros brothers, Fredy Girardet, Irma Rombauer, Diana Kennedy, etc. Maybe also the anonymous author of the Libre de Sent Sovi and Rupert de Nola, who wrote the Libre de Coch, early Catalan cookbooks. Maybe Apicius, too. Vatel, La Varenne and Carême too. And why not? Julia Child. And the first guy in history to fry an egg. Think for one moment about the doors that guy opened for other cooks. These people created or documented or refined or made famous dishes that are now classics. **Culinary Travel:** China – I have only been once in my life and only for a few days. I hope to return and really spend the time to try things, eating at restaurants, seeing where the products come from.

Tim Andriola
Executive Chef/Co-Owner | Timō
17624 Collins Ave. Sunny Isles, FL 33160

Restaurant E-mail: comments@timorestaurant.com

Phone: (305) 936-1008

RESTAURANT FACTS
Seats: 120 **Weeknight Covers:** 160 **Weekend Covers:** 200 **Check Average (with Wine):** $53 **Tasting Menu:** No **Kitchen Staff:** 11

CHEF FACTS
Cuisine: Italian, Mediterranean **Born:** 1971 **Began Career:** 1992 **Culinary School:** The Culinary Institute of America, Hyde Park, NY **Grad Year:** 1992 **Stages:** Chicago, IL: Charlie Trotter's; Berkeley, CA: Chez Panisse; San Francisco, CA: One Market Restaurant, Gava, Olives **Work History:** Miami, FL: Chef Allen's; Mark's South Beach **Mentor(s):** Ron Bucher, Mark Militello, Allen Susser **Awards:** 2006 Jerry Halpirin Award for Community Service; 2004 StarChefs.com Rising Star Miami; 1992 CIA Francis L Roth Award **Affiliations:** Project New Born, MOD, Diabetic Foundation, Hope for Vision, SOS, Make-a-Wish Foundation, Catholic Hospice, Women's Emergency Network, Boys and Girls Club, Cancer Society, Alzheimer's Foundation **Languages Spoken:** Some Italian

NOTABLE DISH(ES): Marrow Risotto with Braised Short Ribs; Mediterranean Branzino with Asparagus, Basil and Lemon Confit

FAST FACTS
Restaurant Recs: Yakosan for Japanese **Kitchen Tool(s):** Food mill **Interview Question:** Tell me something funny that's happened to you in the kitchen **Flavor Combo(s):** Lemon and garlic **Fave Cookbook(s):** Cooking by Hand by Paul Bertolli **Chef to Cook for You:** Julian Serrano **Culinary Travel:** San Francisco – people there are more aware of food and its connection to the land. There are many ethnic influences, and it is only 45 minutes from Napa.

Daniel Angerer
Executive Chef/Owner | Klee Brasserie

200 9th Ave. New York, NY 10011

Restaurant E-mail: info@kleebrasserie.com

Phone: (212) 633-8033

RESTAURANT FACTS
Seats: 70 **Weeknight Covers:** 600 **Weekend Covers:** 80 **Check Average (with Wine):** $65 **Check Average (w/o Wine):** $50 **Tasting Menu:** Yes $50/$90 with wine **Kitchen Staff:** 9

CHEF FACTS
Cuisine: American/European stylized comfort food **Born:** 1972 **Began Career:** 1987 **Culinary School:** Landeck Hotel and Restaurant Management School, Tyrol, Austria **Grad Year:** 1991 **Stages:** Italy: Gualtiero Marchesi; France: Chiberta **Work History:** Austria: Restaurant Steirereck, Restaurant Altwienerhof, Hotel Arlberg Hospiz; Germany: Relais & Chateau Hotel Heinz Winkler; France: Joël Robuchon; New York, NY: San Domenico, Jean-Georges, Alouette, Bouley Bakery, Fresh, Shore, Coast **Mentor(s):** Heinz Winkler **Affiliations:** James Beard, Boeg (better hospitality member, Austria) **Languages Spoken:** Native Austrian, German, English, French, Italian, Spanish

NOTABLE DISH(ES): Colorado Lamb Shank poached in Sangria with Citrus Couscous, Sweet-Sour Apricot and Cherry Tomato Chutney

FAST FACTS
Restaurant Recs: Gennaro on the Upper West Side – they have great simple Italian food **Kitchen Tool(s):** My sauce spoon **Interview Question:** I'm looking for character, for someone who is generally interested in cooking. I ask them: what do you think you do really well? **Flavor Combo(s):** Avocado and pineapple **Fave Cookbook(s):** It depends on what I am developing that day, although I love my books by Heinz Winkler **Chef to Cook for You:** Wolfgang Puck – he's from my own country **Culinary Travel:** Provence, France – I've never been but I hear the vegetables are what they are supposed to be

Dominique Ansel
Executive Pastry Chef | Daniel

60 E 65th St. New York, NY 10065

Restaurant E-mail: dansel@danielnyc.com

Phone: (212) 288-0033

RESTAURANT FACTS
Seats: 100-120 **Weeknight Covers:** 180 **Weekend Covers:** 250-270 **Check Average (w/o Wine):** $105 **Tasting Menu:** Yes $105 **Kitchen Staff:** 4-6

CHEF FACTS
Cuisine: French **Born:** 1978 **Began Career:** 1994 **Culinary School:** In the city where I was born: Beauvais in France **Grad Year:** 1996 **Work History:** France: Pâtisserie Peltier, Fauchon **Mentor(s):** Master pastry chef Christophe Adam **Protégée(s):** Raphael Haasz, pastry chef at Café Boulud **Awards:** 2007 Golden Scoop Awards for Best Dessert Menu **Languages Spoken:** French

FAST FACTS
Restaurant Recs: Pylos restaurant **Kitchen Tool(s):** Foamer – because it adds a different dimension to desserts **Interview Question:** Are you single? **Flavor Combo(s):** Hazelnut and lemon; chocolate and caramel **Fave Cookbook(s):** Hervé This: Les Secrets de la Casserole **Chef to Cook for You:** Gordon Ramsay – I think he is a very talented chef. I like the combinations of flavors and textures in his cooking. **Culinary Travel:** Japan – because I think they have a lot of knowledge and they are such perfectionists

David Ansill
Chef/Owner | Ansill Food and Wine

627 South 3rd St. Philadelphia, PA 19147

Restaurant E-mail: david@ansillfoodandwine.com

Phone: (215) 625-2923

RESTAURANT FACTS

Seats: 70 **Weeknight Covers:** 75 **Weekend Covers:** 200 **Check Average (with Wine):** $47 **Tasting Menu:** No **Kitchen Staff:** 3–5

CHEF FACTS

Cuisine: European-influenced **Born:** 1958 **Began Career:** 1987 **Culinary School:** The Restaurant School, Philadelphia PA **Grad Year:** 1987 **Stages:** Philadelphia, PA: Café Nola **Work History:** Miami Beach, FL: Delano Hotel; Philadelphia, PA: Lucy's Hat Shop, Pif **Mentor(s):** Jeff Bramer **Awards:** 2004 StarChefs.com Rising Star Chef Philadelphia **Languages Spoken:** Spanish; some French

NOTABLE DISH(ES): Foie Gras Terrine; Chilled White Asparagus with Truffle Vinaigrette

FAST FACTS

Restaurant Recs: Bar Ferdinand because they've got so many choices **Kitchen Tool(s):** Immersion blender **Interview Question:** Do you have experience with French food? **Flavor Combo(s):** Red wine and chocolate; salt and vinegar **Fave Cookbook(s):** The Babbo Cookbook by Mario Batali **Chef to Cook for You:** Marie-Antoine Carême. I would love to go to one of those Medieval feasts and carry an animal leg over my shoulder. If he had to be living, Eric Ripert. **Culinary Travel:** I like New York because it's so close and there's so much to eat there. I also like San Francisco, Paris, and I love Madrid.

Michael Anthony
Executive Chef | Gramercy Tavern

42 E 20th St. New York, NY 10003

Restaurant E-mail: manthony@gramercytavern.com

Phone: (212) 477-0777

RESTAURANT FACTS
Seats: 130 **Weeknight Covers:** 175 **Weekend Covers:** 200 **Tasting Menu:** Yes **Kitchen Staff:** 28

CHEF FACTS
Cuisine: Contemporary seasonal American **Born:** 1968 **Began Career:** 1991 **Culinary School:** L'Ecole Technique Jean Ferrandi, France **Grad Year:** 1991 **Stages:** France: L'Arpege, L'Astrance, Michel Guerard, Le Prés d'Eugénie, Eugénie les Bains, Antoine Westermann, Le Buerhiesel **Work History:** Japan: Bistro Shima; France: Jacques Cagna, Le Camélia, Le Prés d'Eugénie; New York, NY: Daniel, March, Blue Hill; Pocantico Hills, NY: Blue Hill at Stone Barns **Mentor(s):** Shizuyo Shima, Jacques Cagna, Daniel Boulud, Wayne Nish **Awards:** 2008 James Beard Foundation Best Chef New York City Nominee; 2007 StarChefs.com Rising Star Chef New York; 2002 Food & Wine Best New Chef **Affiliations:** Slow Food **Languages Spoken:** French, Japanese

NOTABLE DISH(ES): Marinated Calamari with Cured Meyer Lemons, Julienne Carrots, Toasted Pine Nuts and Flying Fish Caviar; Hot Smoked Brook Trout with Sunchoke Purée and Pickled Onion Vinaigrette

FAST FACTS
Restaurant Recs: Sushi Yasuda – I always sit in the first 2-4 seats (that's where Yasuda works) – we never walk out without having at least 5 mouthfuls of overwhelmingly delicious sushi. And Al di La Trattoria in Brooklyn – you get a little sense of soul and it's great. **Kitchen Tool(s):** My Nenox Slicer. It's a knife that holds its edge longer than any I have ever used. And a Vita-Prep – I use it for everything. **Interview Question:** How committed are you to achieving your dreams? I ask [prospective employees] to visit the kitchen and I make sure they taste the food. After we spend two days working together, I ask if they found what they expected – I'm curious to hear how people see it from the outside. I also ask about commitment – I ask them to give me at least a year. **Flavor Combo(s):** I like bright acidity. Cauliflower with briny seafood, like lobster or langoustine reduction. **Fave Cookbook(s):** Cooking by Hand by Paul Bertolli, which is beautiful because it's poetic, and The Zuni Café cookbook by Judy Rogers. I especially love Alain Ducasse's Grand Livre de Cuisine – every single page of that book makes me both salivate and dream. It's very technical, too. **Chef to Cook for You:** Michel Troisgros – his style is inventive and true to his region. And I would have Pascal Barbot from L'Astrance in France cook for me as well. He has his own unique style. **Culinary Travel:** Roanne, France, because I'm dreaming of eating at Troisgros. Of all the places in the world, that's where I most want to eat.

Zoi Antonitsas
Consulting Chef

San Francisco, CA

Restaurant E-mail: zflavor@yahoo.com

CHEF FACTS
Cuisine: New American, Californian **Born:** 1977 **Began Career:** 1998
Work History: Seattle, WA: Etta's Seafood; Healdsburg, CA: Bovolo;
San Francisco, CA: Bizou, Presidio Social Club **Mentor(s):** Tom Doug-
las, Loretta Keller, Marcella Hazaan, Julia Child, Mario Batali, to name
a few **Affiliations:** We work with FoodRunners to help feed the home-
less; we are also involved with kids and school lunches, and through
Loretta Keller I am a free-clinic fundraiser at the RC

NOTABLE DISH(ES): Local Dungeness Crab Salad with Belgian En-
dive, Kumquat Vinaigrette and Grapefruit

FAST FACTS
Restaurant Recs: The Slanted Door as I don't cook Asian food. I love
the spring rolls, green papaya salad and the cellophane salad. **Kitchen Tool(s):** My wood-burning
oven for slow roasted meats, whole fish, lamb shanks, fowl, flatbreads, and pizza **Interview Question:**
Where do you see yourself in 3-5 years? **Flavor Combo(s):** The combination of acidity, fattiness and
sweetness really wakes up a palate **Fave Cookbook(s):** The Joy of Cooking; anything by Alice Waters;
anything by Marcella Hazan; Babbo by Mario Batali; Simple French Food by Richard Olney **Chef to
Cook for You:** Marcella Hazan – I grew up on her food, as my mom always used her cookbook. We
have very similar approaches in our food. It would be awesome to go to Venice and have her make me
a meal. **Culinary Travel:** I'd love to go to Cinque Terre in Italy

Joël Antunes
Chef/Owner | The Oak Room

768 Fifth Ave. New York, NY

Restaurant E-mail: erosenthal@susanblondinc.com

Phone: (212) 546-5320

RESTAURANT FACTS
Seats: 210 **Check Average (with Wine):** $65+ **Tasting Menu:** Yes
Kitchen Staff: 15

CHEF FACTS
Other Restaurants: Atlanta, GA: Joël **Cuisine:** French Cuisine with Mediterranean and Asian influences **Born:** 1961 **Began Career:** 1975 **Culinary School:** L'École des Arts & Metiers Culinaire de Flamina, Clermont Ferrand, France **Grad Year:** 1978 **Stages:** France: Ledoyen, Duquesnoy; Thailand: Oriental Hotel's Normandy, Hotel Picardyin; England: Les Saveurs; Atlanta, GA: Ritz-Carlton **Work History:** France: Ledoyen, Duquesnoy, Hotel Negresco, Paul Bocuse, Troisgros, Oriental Hotel's Normandy Restaurant; England: Hotel Picardy, Les Saveurs; Atlanta, GA: Ritz-Carlton Buckhead, Joël **Awards:** 2005–2007 AAA Four Diamonds; 2005 James Beard Foundation Best Chef Southeast **Affiliations:** James Beard Foundation **Languages Spoken:** French

NOTABLE DISH(ES): Sautéed Snails Antiboise, Capers Cappelletti, Niçoise Olives; Sautéed Rouget, Shrimp Ravioli, Red Pepper, Piperade Sauce

FAST FACTS
Restaurant Recs: In Atlanta – Muss and Turner's for their simplicity and quality ingredients **Kitchen Tool(s):** Pasta machine **Interview Question:** What do you eat? **Flavor Combo(s):** I like classic combinations, but one thing that is very important is acidity – it is the key to my cooking **Fave Cookbook(s):** This is very difficult! I must say I do love Donna Hay's books. **Chef to Cook for You:** Pierre Troisgros. He has such passion for cooking and he never takes his success for granted. He cooks with such humor and kindness. I do want to mention as well that there are so many amazing American chefs who have emerged over the last twenty years, and sitting at any of their tables would be great. **Culinary Travel:** I love the street food in Madagascar – any chance to go back there would be great. There is so much diversity in the people and thus in the food.

Nate Appleman
Executive Chef | A16

2355 Chestnut St. San Francisco, CA 94123

Restaurant E-mail: nate@a16sf.com

Phone: (415) 771-2216

RESTAURANT FACTS
Seats: 105 **Weeknight Covers:** 250–300 **Weekend Covers:** 300
Check Average (with Wine): $45 **Tasting Menu:** No **Kitchen Staff:**
5–6

CHEF FACTS
Other Restaurants: SPQR **Cuisine:** Southern Italian **Born:** 1979
Began Career: 1993 **Culinary School:** Culinary Institute of America,
Hyde Park, New York **Grad Year:** 1999 **Work History:** Cincinatti,
OH: Maisonette; Atlanta, GA: The Dining Room at the Ritz-Carlton;
St. Helena, CA: Tra Vigne; San Francisco, CA: Campton Place, A16
Mentor(s): My father, almost every chef I worked for at Maisonette in
Cinncinatti, and Chef Laurent Manrique, who taught me that food is food. **Awards:** 2008, 2007 James
Beard Foundation Rising Star Nominee; 2007 StarChefs.com Rising Star Chef San Francisco **Affiliations:** Slow Food

NOTABLE DISH(ES): House-Made Sausages with Radishes in Salsa Verde; Lamb Crespelle

FAST FACTS
Restaurant Recs: Spices restaurant for Szechuan, Mandarin, Islamic, and Chinese cuisine. Their
cumin lamb, pickled cucumbers and twice-cooked bacon are all great. I think Thai House Express is
the best Thai food outside of Thailand. I get the pork leg stew and pickled turnip greens. Shinto Bui is
good Korean for their fried chicken and pickled turnips. **Kitchen Tool(s):** Rubber spatula; calculator
Interview Question: I don't have a set test, so it depends on the individual. I ask them to make a pizza, too. They have to rise to the occasion and do it all by hand, not using pins. **Flavor Combo(s):** Pistachio and orange **Fave Cookbook(s):** The River Cottage Meat Cookbook by Hugh Fearnley-Whittingstall
Chef to Cook for You: Benedetta Vitali. She has a restaurant outside of Florence called Zibibbo. It is
rustic, country Italian, and I love it. **Culinary Travel:** I would like to go to Morocco – people say it's the
Switzerland of North Africa. But I've been putting it off for three years.

Cathal Armstrong
Chef/Owner | Restaurant Eve

110 S. Pitt St. Alexandria, VA 22314

Restaurant E-mail: meshe@restauranteve.com

Phone: (703) 706-0450

RESTAURANT FACTS
Seats: 100 **Weeknight Covers:** 90 **Weekend Covers:** 130 **Tasting Menu:** Yes $105/$145 **Kitchen Staff:** 10

CHEF FACTS
Other Restaurants: Eamonn's – A Dublin Chipper, The Majestic, PX Social Lounge **Cuisine:** Contemporary American **Born:** 1969 **Began Career:** 1988 **Work History:** Ireland: The Bay Tree; Washington, DC: Bistro Bis, Gabriel, New Heights, Vidalia **Mentor(s):** My mother and father **Protégée(s):** Nathan Beauchamp **Awards:** 2008 James Beard Foundation Best Chef Mid-Atlantic Nominee; 2007 RAMW Chef of the Year; 2006 Food & Wine Best New Chef; 2006 StarChefs.com Rising Star Chef Washington DC; 2005 RAMMY Rising Culinary Star **Affiliations:** JBF, DC Chef's Club, Restaurant Association of Metropolitan Washington (RAMW) **Languages Spoken:** French, German, Irish, Spanish

NOTABLE DISH(ES): "Bacon, Egg and Cheese"; Carolina Black Bass with Orange Braised Fennel

FAST FACTS
Restaurant Recs: Palena – for a BLT **Kitchen Tool(s):** I love my meat grinder. We do a lot of charcuterie in the restaurant and it is one of the most fun branches of cooking. **Interview Question:** Are you ready to devote yourself to your craft? **Flavor Combo(s):** I like the natural affinities of things that grow together **Fave Cookbook(s):** Letters to a Young Chef by Daniel Boulud and The French Laundry Cookbook by Thomas Keller. I make all my staff read Chef Boulud's book. I am grateful to Chef Keller for writing down so many of the rules we use in the kitchen every day. **Chef to Cook for You:** Daniel Boulud because I just like his style of food. It is really natural and earthy. His charcuterie is masterful. **Culinary Travel:** I've been to California twice, which I liked, and I was in Paris, Rome and Barcelona when I was first married

Govind Armstrong
Executive Chef | Table 8

8155 Melrose Ave. Los Angeles, CA 90046

Restaurant E-mail: info@table8la.com

Phone: (323) 782-8258

RESTAURANT FACTS
Seats: 140 **Weeknight Covers:** 120-160 **Weekend Covers:** 300 **Check Average (with Wine):** $60 **Tasting Menu:** Yes Certain Nights **Kitchen Staff:** 8

CHEF FACTS
Other Restaurants: South Beach, Fl: Table 8 **Cuisine:** Market-driven Californian **Born:** 1969 **Began Career:** 1983 **Stages:** Spain: Arzak, Restaurant Akeláre **Work History:** Los Angeles, CA: Pinot Hollywood, Jackson's, Chadwick, City Restaurant, Hotel Bel-Air, Campanile; San Francisco, CA: Postrio; West Hollywood, CA: Spago **Mentor(s):** Wolfgang Puck **Protégée(s):** Andrew Kirschner **Awards:** 2004 StarChefs. com Rising Star Chef Los Angeles **Affiliations:** MCC **Books Published:** Small Bites Big Nights **Languages Spoken:** Spanish

NOTABLE DISH(ES): Poached Tomato with Tuna Confit and Salsa Verde; Duck Breast with Roasted Apple, Hazelnut and Braised Endive

FAST FACTS
Restaurant Recs: Hunan Taste in Los Angeles – a family-owned place. They have the best slippery shrimp in town. **Kitchen Tool(s):** Cryovac vacuum sealer; Berkel vacuum sealer; solid line cooks **Interview Question:** I ask if they are a lifer – if they are completely obsessed with food **Flavor Combo(s):** Salt and pepper **Fave Cookbook(s):** Chez Panisse Cooking by Alice Waters. This book keeps true to the whole California cuisine movement. On Food and Cooking by Harold McGee opened my mind to a completely different level of how I understand food. It has more of a scientific edge. **Chef to Cook for You:** Ferran Adriá – I've never made it to his restaurant **Culinary Travel:** Italy and San Sebastian, Spain. Chefs in Spain are five to ten steps ahead of everyone else in the culinary world. Everyone else has just recently started to take notice, but they've been doing it for many years.

Marc Aumont
Pastry Chef | The Modern

9 W 53rd St. New York, NY 10019

Restaurant E-mail: info@themodernnyc.com

Phone: (212) 333-1220

RESTAURANT FACTS

Seats: 75-80 **Weeknight Covers:** 90-100 **Weekend Covers:** 125-130 **Check Average (with Wine):** $140-$145 **Tasting Menu:** Yes $115/$125

CHEF FACTS

Cuisine: French/Spanish **Born:** 1969 **Began Career:** 1984 **Culinary School:** I apprenticed in France with a master d'apprentissage. After I qualified, I continued on in the education system at a different top school. **Grad Year:** 1998 **Work History:** France: La Gerbe d'Or; New York, NY: Bouley Bakery, Compass **Mentor(s):** My father and mother – they were in the industry of artisanal pastry and chocolate **Protégée(s):** My sous chefs **Awards:** 2005 New York Post Best Dish; 2002 New York Magazine Chef Awards Pastry Star **Affiliations:** CCAP, City Harvest, Food Bank of NY, Share Our Strength. We also have many externs from CIA. **Languages Spoken:** French, Spanish

NOTABLE DISH(ES): Apple Strudel and Caramel Parfait with Mango Ravioli

FAST FACTS

Restaurant Recs: Fleur de Sel **Kitchen Tool(s):** Professional cookbooks **Interview Question:** What do you like about restaurants? **Flavor Combo(s):** It's not about the flavor combinations, it's more about texture and the right equilibrium between fat and acid **Fave Cookbook(s):** Desserts by Pierre Hermé; La Cocina de los Postres by Margaret Malone **Chef to Cook for You:** I'm a lucky person – I've been to many places where the chef has cooked for me. It is difficult to pick one. Why limit ourselves? **Culinary Travel:** Asia, in general. It is not only about the culinary, but the culture as well.

Charlie Ayers
Corporate Consultant/Chef-Founder | Innovative Corporate Well Being

570 El Camino Real #150-429 Redwood City, CA 94301

RESTAURANT FACTS
Seats: 90 **Weeknight Covers:** 180 **Weekend Covers:** 250 **Check Average (with Wine):** $50-$75 **Check Average (w/o Wine):** $35-$50 **Tasting Menu:** No **Kitchen Staff:** 10

CHEF FACTS
Other Restaurants: Palo Alto, CA: Calafia Cafe & Market a Go Go **Cuisine:** Fine food for the fast crowd/California Latin Asian **Born:** 1966 **Began Career:** 1984 **Culinary School:** Johnson & Wales, Providence, RI **Grad Year:** 1988 culinary/1990 business **Work History:** Parsippany & Meadowlands, New Jersey: The Hilton Hotel; Portsmouth, RI: Sea Fare Inn; Providence, RI: Al Forno; Boston, MA: Lafayette Hotel; Watch Hill, RI: Ocean House; San Ramon, CA: Restaurant Enterprises Group; Berkeley, CA: Fourth Street Grill; Palo Alto, CA: Peninsula Fountain and Grille, Left at Albuquerque, Blue Chalk Café; San Rafael, CA: Whole Foods Market; San Francisco, CA: Personal Chef to musicians, thought leaders and artists; Mountain View, CA: Google Inc. **Mentor(s):** Ron Ross, George Karousos, Ken Oringer **Protégée(s):** Kevin Ogle, Sean Thomas, Nate Keller, James Glass, Mirit Cohen, Derek Rupp **Awards:** 2005 Best Corporate Food Service Environment, Menu and Concept **Affiliations:** ChefsforHumanity.Org, RocktheEarth.Org **Books Published:** Food 2.0: Secrets from the Chef Who Fed Google **Languages Spoken:** Kitchen Spanish

FAST FACTS
Restaurant Recs: Bistro Elan in Palo Alto – anything that Abijorn or Barry are cooking that day is fine with me. Of course this is when I'm taking my wife out to eat. If it's just me on the run it would be La Casita Chilanga in Redwood City for really great Mexico City-style street tacos. **Kitchen Tool(s):** My Wolf dual gas range, four burner, French plate, and this really cool steamer my friend's wife brought back for me from India. It makes these wonderful little rice dumplings called Idly. **Interview Question:** The question I ask most is: "why did you get into the business?" **Flavor Combo(s):** Braised pork shoulder with cinnamon, chile, ginger, cumin, paprika, almonds, dried fruit and garlic; lobster stir fry with curry vanilla coconut milk **Fave Cookbook(s):** The Joy of Cooking; Larousse Gastronomique **Chef to Cook for You:** I really love the way Ken Oringer cooks **Culinary Travel:** Spain, West Africa, India

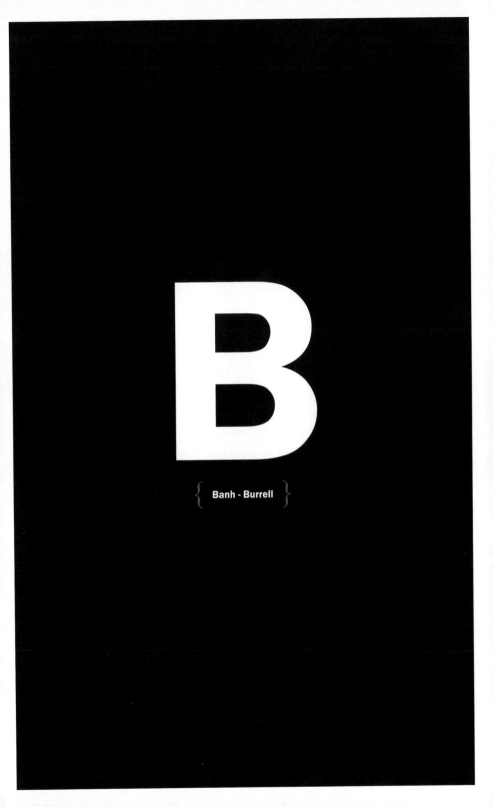

B

{ Banh - Burrell }

B

Eric and Sophie Banh
Chefs/Owners | Monsoon

615 19th Ave. East Seattle, WA 98112

Restaurant E-mail: ericbanh@yahoo.com

Phone: (206) 325-2111

RESTAURANT FACTS
Check Average (w/o Wine): $35 **Tasting Menu:** No

CHEF FACTS
Cuisine: Vietnamese and Chinese **Born:** 1960 **Began Career:**
1998 **Culinary School:** Seattle Central Community College, culinary
program **Grad Year:** 1996 **Work History:** Seattle, WA: ObaChine,
Roy's **Mentor(s):** Jacques Pépin – he's our mentor from afar. We've
read a lot of his work. **Awards:** 2003 StarChefs.com Rising Star Chef
Seattle; Bon Appétit's 2002 Best Neighborhood Restaurants; Wine
Spectator Award **Languages Spoken:** Eric: Vietnamese, Sophie:
Spanish

NOTABLE DISH(ES): Idaho Catfish Clay Pot; Duck Salad with Mint and
Rau Rum; Asian Eggplant in Spicy Coconut Sauce; Five-Spice Roasted
Pork and Organic Sweet Corn

FAST FACTS
Restaurant Recs: Ocean City – for the consistently cooked barbecued duck and pork ribs **Kitchen Tool(s):** The wok – because it's
efficient, practical, quick, and reaches high temperatures **Interview
Question:** Have you washed dishes in a restaurant before? If you
have then you will see everything internally and know how to be
humble, organized and quick. **Fave Cookbook(s):** A Culinary Life by
Susur Lee

Dan Barber
Chef/Owner | Blue Hill

75 Washington Pl. New York NY 10011

Restaurant E-mail: info@bluehillfarm.com

Phone: (212) 539-1776

CHEF FACTS
Other Restaurants: Pocantico Hills, NY: Blue Hill at Stone Barns
Cuisine: Local harvest cuisine **Born:** 1969 **Began Career:** 1993 **Culinary School:** The French Culinary School **Stages:** Berkeley, CA: Chez Panisse; France: Apicius **Work History:** France: Le Clos de la Violette, Michel Rostang; Los Angeles, CA: Campanile, La Brea Bakery; New York, NY: Bouley **Mentor(s):** Eliot Coleman, my dad **Protégée(s):** My nephew **Awards:** 2008 James Beard Foundation Outstanding Chef Nominee; 2008 James Beard Foundation Who's Who of Food and Beverage in America; 2006 James Beard Foundation Best Chef New York City; 2006 New York Times 3 stars; 2005 James Beard Foundation Best New Restaurant Nominee; 2002 Food & Wine America's Best New Chefs; 1999 New York Magazine Rising Star

NOTABLE DISH(ES): Bowl of Tomatoes, Melons, and Homemade Yoghurt in Cantaloupe Melon Broth; Grilled Watermelon with Goat Cheese, Pancetta, and Tomato Water Cloud

FAST FACTS
Restaurant Recs: Lupa – for pasta pomodoro in August or September **Kitchen Tool(s):** A spoon **Interview Question:** Why me? **Flavor Combo(s):** No favorites; new ones come around all the time. I'm fickle. **Fave Cookbook(s):** Much Depends on Dinner: The Extraordinary History and Mythology, Allure and Obsessions, Perils and Taboos, of an Ordinary Meal by Margaret Visser **Culinary Travel:** Morocco – spices are not my strong suit

Karen Barker
Pastry Chef/Owner | Magnolia Grill

1002 9th St. Durham, NC 27705

www.magnoliagrill.net

Phone: (919) 286-3609

RESTAURANT FACTS
Seats: 85–105 **Weeknight Covers:** 110 **Weekend Covers:** 170
Check Average (with Wine): $55–$60 **Check Average (w/o Wine):**
$45 **Tasting Menu:** No **Kitchen Staff:** 1

CHEF FACTS
Cuisine: Seasonal with Southern influences **Born:** 1953 **Began
Career:** 1981 **Culinary School:** The Culinary Institute of America,
Hyde Park, NY **Grad Year:** 1981 **Work History:** Chapel Hill, NC: La
Residence, Fearrington House **Mentor(s):** Paula Wolfert, Madeleine
Kamman **Protégée(s):** Scott Howell, Brett Jennings **Awards:** 2003
The James Beard Foundation Best Pastry Chef; 1999 Bon Appétit
Best Pastry Chef **Affiliations:** Southern Foodways Alliance, Slow Food, National Public Radio, The
Triangle Land Conservancy **Books Published:** Sweet Stuff: Karen Barker's American Desserts

NOTABLE DISH(ES): Butter Almond Cookies

FAST FACTS
Restaurant Recs: Allen and Son's for North Carolina pork bbq **Kitchen Tool(s):** Small offset spatula
Interview Question: What are your top three favorite dessert ingredients? How do you like to use
them? **Flavor Combo(s):** Dark chocolate, roasted almonds and fleur de sel; strawberries and rhubarb;
cherries, black pepper and balsamic vinegar **Fave Cookbook(s):** Anything by Maida Heatter **Chef to
Cook for You:** I've been reading about Victor Arguinzoniz, the chef at Etxebarri in Spain's Basque
country for years. I have never eaten his food but as a real "grill fan" I'd love the chance to dine there.
Everything from the setting to the ingredients to the simple cooking methodology seems right up my
alley. As for dessert, Gina DePalma from Babbo can bake for me anytime! **Culinary Travel:** Spain!
We've never been and have determined that this will be our next trip to Europe. Great wine, food,
architecture and design, history and the coast... a perfect vacation.

Ben Barker
Magnolia Gr

Ben Barker
Chef/Owner | Magnolia Grill

1002 9th St. Durham, NC 27705

www.magnoliagrill.net

Phone: (919) 286-3609

RESTAURANT FACTS
Seats: 85–105 **Weeknight Covers:** 110 **Weekend Covers:** 170
Check Average (with Wine): $55–$60 **Check Average (w/o Wine):**
$45 **Tasting Menu:** No **Kitchen Staff:** 8

CHEF FACTS
Cuisine: Seasonal with Southern influence **Began Career:** 1981
Culinary School: The Culinary Institute of America, Hyde Park, NY
Grad Year: 1981 **Work History:** Chapel Hill, NC: La Residence; Fearrington Village, NC: Fearrington House **Mentor(s):** Maida Heatter
Protégée(s): Phoebe Lawless, Brigid Callinan **Awards:** 1997 James
Beard Foundation Best Chef Southeast **Affiliations:** Southern Foodways Alliance, Slow Food, National Public Radio, The Triangle Land Conservancy **Books Published:**
Not Afraid of Flavor

NOTABLE DISH(ES): Grilled Quail on Vidalia Onion and Country Bacon Spoonbread, Pinot Noir and
Sundried Cherry Jus

FAST FACTS
Restaurant Recs: Allen and Son's for really good Carolina barbecue **Kitchen Tool(s):** 12" black steel
skillet **Interview Question:** Did your family cook at home? This gives me a sense if food memories
were a part of their life and what foods are the base of their palates. **Flavor Combo(s):** Peanut butter
and bacon; lime juice, chilies and mint **Fave Cookbook(s):** The Zuni Café Cookbook by Judy Rodgers
Chef to Cook for You: Todd English at the first (original) Olives location - one of my favorite most fun
meals ever! Or Dominique Le Stanc at La Merenda in Nice, France. It's my fantasy restaurant - casual
market cuisine at it's best. **Culinary Travel:** Spain!

Lidia Bastianich
Chef/Owner | Felidia

243 E 58th St. New York, NY 10022
Restaurant E-mail: lidia@lidiasitaly.com
Phone: (212) 758-1479

RESTAURANT FACTS
Seats: 95–140 **Weeknight Covers:** 160–180 **Weekend Covers:** 250–270 **Check Average (with Wine):** $95–$98 **Tasting Menu:** Yes $55/$65/$85 **Kitchen Staff:** 9–10

CHEF FACTS
Other Restaurants: Felidia, Becco, Del Posto; Pittsburgh, PA: Esca; Kansas City, MO: Lidia's **Cuisine:** Italian **Born:** 1947 **Began Career:** 1971 **Mentor(s):** Julia Child, Lidia Acianti, Paola di Mauro **Protégée(s):** Fortunato Nicotra, Shea Gallante, Jake Addeo **Awards:** 2005 Mother's Day Council Mother of the Year; 2002 James Beard Foundation Outstanding Chef; 2002 IACP Cookbook of the Year; 1999 James Beard Foundation Best Chef New York **Affiliations:** WCR, IACP, JBF **Books Published:** Lidia's Family Table; Lidia's Italian American Kitchen; Lidia's Italian Table; La Cucina Di Lidia **Languages Spoken:** Italian, Croatian, Spanish

NOTABLE DISH(ES): Ossobuco di Capriolo con Spaetzle; Ravioli "Cacio Pepe e Pere"

FAST FACTS
Restaurant Recs: Woo Lae Oak – for the eel on the stone **Kitchen Tool(s):** Wooden spoon; spider to fish out pasta **Interview Question:** Why should I hire you? **Flavor Combo(s):** Today my favorite flavor combination is anchovies, capers and lemon – complex and tangy at the same time **Fave Cookbook(s):** La Covina Regional Italian by Anna Gosetti Della Salda **Chef to Cook for You:** I would have Paola di Mauro, the matriarch of Roman cuisine, cook me bucatini alla Amatriciana. I'd have a bottle of her Colli Picchioni red from the Roman hills, one of the best wines in Lazio. **Culinary Travel:** Lately ever more my curiosity is leading me towards Brazil. I would love to see the country's approach to big meats, and I would love to find out how they keep their beautiful bodies with such big cuts of meats on the table.

Mario Batali
Chef/Owner | Babbo

110 Waverly Pl. New York, NY 10011

Restaurant E-mail: plewy@pastaresources.com

Phone: (212) 674-2044

RESTAURANT FACTS
Seats: 100 **Weeknight Covers:** 257 **Weekend Covers:** 284 **Check Average (w/o Wine):** $69/$119 **Check Average (with Wine):** $75/$125

CHEF FACTS
Other Restaurants: New York, NY: Lupa, Esca, Otto Enoteca Pizzeria, Del Posto, Casa Mono, Bar Jamon, The Spotted Pig; Las Vegas, NV: B&B Ristorante, Enoteca San Marco, Carnevino Italian Steakhouse; Los Angeles, CA: Osteria Mozza, Pizzeria Mozza **Cuisine:** Italian **Born:** 1960 **Began Career:** I began cooking as a child. I collected blackberries and helped my grandmother make pies. **Culinary School:** Le Cordon Bleu, London **Stages:** England: Harvey's **Work History:** San Francisco, CA: Stars **Mentor(s):** Marco Pierre White **Protégée(s):** David Pasternack, Mark Ladner, Tony Liu, Zach Allen, Jason Denton, Anne Burrell **Awards:** 2005 The James Beard Foundation Outstanding Chef in America; 2004 New York Times 3 stars; 2002 The James Beard Foundation Best Chef New York City; 2001 D'Artagnan Cervena Who's Who of Food & Beverage in America; 1999 GQ Magazine Man of the Year in the Chef category; 1998 James Beard Foundation Best New Restaurant **Affiliations:** Heritage Foods, Food Bank for New York City **Books Published:** Italian Grill; Simple Italian Food; Mario Batali Holiday Food; The Babbo Cookbook; Food Men Love **Languages Spoken:** Italian, Spanish, French

NOTABLE DISH(ES): Grilled Prawns with White Beans, Rosemary, Mâche and Mint Oil; Linguine with Manila Clams, Pancetta and Hot Chilies

FAST FACTS
Restaurant Recs: Pearl Oyster Bar, Gray's Papaya **Kitchen Tool(s):** A grill; my Copco enamel-coated cast iron pans; a heavy metal meat mallet **Interview Question:** Where do you like to eat and why? **Flavor Combo(s):** Tomato and basil; chilies and mint; lime, sugar, nam pla, cilantro; brine and acid **Fave Cookbook(s):** Umbria in Bocca by Antonella Santolint **Chef to Cook for You:** Anthony Uglesich and Emeril Lagasse – the cuisine of New Orleans is the most pure and delightful in the world **Culinary Travel:** Southeast Asia – it is constantly surprising

Rick Bayless
Chef /Owner | Frontera Grill

445 North Clark St. Chicago, IL 60610

Restaurant E-mail: jfite@fronteragrill.net

RESTAURANT FACTS
Seats: 70 **Weeknight Covers:** 210 **Weekend Covers:** 280 **Tasting Menu:** No **Kitchen Staff:** 3–4 plus more in the back kitchen

CHEF FACTS
Other Restaurants: Frontera Fresco, Topolobampo **Cuisine:** Mexican **Born:** 1953 **Began Career:** 1987 **Mentor(s):** Julia Child **Protégée(s):** Paul Kahan, Priscilla Satkoff **Awards:** 2002 Bon Appetit Cooking Teaching of the Year; 1998 James Beard Foundation Humanitarian of the Year; 1995 James Beard Foundation National Chef of the Year; 1991 James Beard Foundation Best Chef Midwest **Affiliations:** Chefs Collaborative, Frontera Farmer Foundation **Books Published:** Authentic Mexican: Regional Cooking from the Heart of Mexico; Mexican Kitchen; Salsas that Cook; Mexico One Plate at a Time; Rick and Lanie's Excellent Kitchen Adventures; Mexican Everyday **Languages Spoken:** Spanish

NOTABLE DISH(ES): Grilled Quail in Red Onion Escabeche; Chile-Bathed Fish Grilled in Cornhusks

FAST FACTS
Restaurant Recs: Jane's for really good burgers **Kitchen Tool(s):** Molcajete (mortar and pestle) for grinding spices and making guacamole **Interview Question:** Where have you traveled? **Flavor Combo(s):** I am really into umami at the moment...making dishes that really appeal to all senses... **Fave Cookbook(s):** Too many! I have a library full of them. **Chef to Cook for You:** No way...I'm not touching this one. Too many good cooks... **Culinary Travel:** Mexico – it makes me feel relaxed and I come back to work ready and with fresh ideas

David Bazirgan
Executive Chef | Chez Papa Resto

414 Jessie St. San Francisco, CA 94103

Restaurant E-mail: chezpaparesto@gmail.com

Phone: (415) 546-4134

RESTAURANT FACTS
Seats: 60–120 **Weeknight Covers:** 80–100 **Weekend Covers:** 140
Check Average (with Wine): $60 **Check Average (w/o Wine):** $40
Tasting Menu: Yes **Kitchen Staff:** 6

CHEF FACTS
Cuisine: Provençal cuisine **Born:** 1974 **Began Career:** 1996 **Culinary School:** Cambridge School of Culinary Arts, Cambridge, MA **Grad Year:** 1996 **Stages:** New York, NY: Cafe Boulud, Gramercy Tavern, March **Work History:** Boston, MA: Galleria Italiana, No. 9 Park; Charleston, MA: Olives; San Francisco, CA: Elisabeth Daniel, Baraka, Chez Papa Resto, La Suite **Mentor(s):** Barbara Lynch, Todd English, dad **Protégée(s):** Ed Cotton, Nemo Bolin, Colin Lynch **Awards:** 2005 StarChefs.com Rising Star Chef San Francisco; 2004 San Francisco Chronicle Rising Star **Affiliations:** We just opened but are planning on working with some of the local charities **Languages Spoken:** Kitchen Spanish

NOTABLE DISH(ES): La Belle Farms Foie Gras Torchon with Br,uléed Figs, Ras al Hanout Gastrique; Raw and Cooked Cèpes with Shaved Parmigiano Reggiano, Wild Arugula and Aged Balsamic Vinegar

FAST FACTS
Restaurant Recs: Memphis Minnies for a two-way barbecue combo with ribs, pulled pork, slaw, beans, and cornbread with a Budweiser. **Kitchen Tool(s):** A Japanese mandolin – I use it for fine and really thin layers of cuts. And my mouth, to taste everything and develop the palate. **Interview Question:** Who's your favorite chef in New York and why? I think New York is a mecca. There are just so many chefs to embrace and such great things are happening there. I think all young chefs should spend time in New York – at least go out and eat there. The availability of ingredients is amazing. **Flavor Combo(s):** Sweet, sour, salty **Fave Cookbook(s):** The Making of a Cook by Madeleine Kamman **Chef to Cook for You:** Alain Ducasse. I really admire his style and look up to him as a chef. **Culinary Travel:** I definitely want to go all over Spain but haven't had a chance yet. I'd like to go to Japan, Southeast Asia and the eastern Mediterranean. I want to do expanded travel and research for a while in order to figure out exactly which way I want to take my food.

B

Franklin Becker
Chef | Sheridan Square

138 Seventh Ave. S. New York, NY

Restaurant E-mail: becker.franklin@gmail.com

Phone: (212) 352-2237

RESTAURANT FACTS
Seats: 75 -127 **Weeknight Covers:** 175 **Weekend Covers:** 300 **Tasting Menu:** 5 course, $74; w/wine $120; 7 course, $95; w/wine $150 **Kitchen Staff:** 11

CHEF FACTS
Other Restaurants: Tasca **Cuisine:** New American and modern French **Born:** 1969 **Began Career:** 1993 **Culinary School:** The Culinary Institute of America, Hyde Park, NY **Grad Year:** 1993 **Stages:** Italy: Hotel Siracusa **Work History:** New York, NY: Capitale, Local, Soho Grand Hotel, Tribeca Grand Hotel, Brasserie; Philadelphia, PA: Washington Square **Mentor(s):** Bobby Flay, my mother, Bob Trainor **Protégée(s):** Chris D'Amico, A.J. Bull, Clinton Davis, Michael Jeanty **Awards:** 2006 StarChefs.com Rising Star Chef New York; 2003 Esquire Best New Restaurants in America **Affiliations:** Autism Speaks, JBF, Sustainable Seafood, Slow Food **Books Published:** The Diabetic Chef **Languages Spoken:** Spanglish

NOTABLE DISH(ES): Lamb Chop Caprese Salad; Crisp Duck Breast with Caramelized Endive, Rapini, Apple and Fig Salad

FAST FACTS
Restaurant Recs: Sahara for Turkish Food; Di Fara Pizza in Brooklyn for Sicilian pizza **Kitchen Tool(s):** For me, the Vita-Prep blender by Vita-Mix. I love the variable speed feature that enables me to create smoother purées and cleaner infusions. **Interview Question:** Why do you want to cook? If it's not because they want to make others happy, I do not want them. **Flavor Combo(s):** Sweet and savory together in desserts; crustaceans and creme fraîche; grapefruit and avocado; orange and fennel; rhubarb and fennel; mushrooms and crustaceans; citrus and anything **Fave Cookbook(s):** Essential Cuisine by Michel Bras; The French Laundry Cookbook by Thomas Keller; Fish and Shellfish by James Peterson. These are three of my favorite cookbooks. They all have influenced my style of cooking.
Chef to Cook for You: Michel Bras, because I think he is brilliant, simple yet complex, inspiring, and magical **Culinary Travel:** Australia - because there are ingredients indigenous to the region that have not yet been utilized in the United States. In addition there are a number of chefs, including Tetsuya Wakuda and Justin North of Bécasse, who do simple yet extravagant dishes that inspire those of us who look for the best ingredients to prepare our own dishes.

Noah Bekofsky
Chef | Fairmont Scottsdale Princess

7575 East Princess Dr. Scottsdale, AZ 85255

Restaurant E-mail: noah.bekofsky@fairmont.com

Phone: (480) 585-4848

CHEF FACTS

Other Restaurants: Stone Rose, La Hacienda, The Grill, Sonoran Splash Bar & Grill, LV Bistro, Cabana Café **Cuisine:** Asian-influenced **Born:** 1971 **Began Career:** 1996 **Culinary School:** Culinary Institute of America, Hyde Park **Grad Year:** 1996 **Stages:** San Francisco, CA: Aqua **Work History:** Maui, HI: Kapalua Bay Hotel and Villas; Gleneden Beach, OR: Westin Salishan Lodge and Golf Resort; Chicago, IL: Aria at the Fairmont; Miami Beach, FL; Loews Miami Beach **Mentor(s):** Alain Ducasse **Affiliations:** ACF, SOS, American Liver Foundation, Resort Food Service Committee, James Beard Foundation **Languages Spoken:** Kitchen Spanish

NOTABLE DISH(ES): Lamb Chop Caprese Salad; Crispy Duck Breast with Caramelized Endive, Rapini, Apple and Fig Salad

FAST FACTS

Restaurant Recs: Avec for the goat cheese and truffled focaccia bread **Kitchen Tool(s):** Wooden spoon **Interview Question:** What was the last book you read? It gives me an idea of the candidate's special interests and educational level. It also catches them off-guard and gives me a chance to see how they deal under pressure. **Flavor Combo(s):** Simple high quality organic ingredients that stand out on their own **Fave Cookbook(s):** Mastering the Art of French Cooking by Julia Child, Louisette Bertholle and Simone Beck **Chef to Cook for You:** Julia Child – I would have loved to have her cook me dinner and tell stories of her past and experiences. I'd like to really understand how she really became such a great chef. She is also a great person to have a glass of wine with. **Culinary Travel:** Hong Kong – I have not been to Hong Kong and would love to experience all the wonders it has to offer

Elizabeth Belkind
Chef/Co-Owner | Cake Monkey Bakery

3515 W. Burbank Blvd. unit B Burbank, CA 91505

Restaurant E-mail: info@cakemonkey.com

Phone: (818) 841-0202

CHEF FACTS

Cuisine: Seasonally-driven whimsical yet traditional American sweets
Born: 1972 **Began Career:** 2000 **Culinary School:** California School
of Culinary Arts, Pasadena, CA **Grad Year:** 2000 **Stages:** Los Angeles,
CA: Campanile **Work History:** Los Angeles, CA: Campanile, Grace
Mentor(s): Nancy Silverton, Kim Boyce **Awards:** 2006 StarChefs.com
Rising Star Pastry Chef Los Angeles **Languages Spoken:** Spanish

NOTABLE DISH(ES): Maple-Glazed Doughnuts with Roasted Heirloom
Apples and Apple Cider Ice Cream; Sweet Corn Crème Caramel with
Corn Ice Cream

FAST FACTS

Restaurant Recs: Soy Café – for house-made soybean curd with scallions, ginger and soy sauce
Kitchen Tool(s): Fryer – to quickly turn out amazingly refined, warm desserts finished to order
Interview Question: Are you able to separate your personal life from your professional life? **Flavor
Combo(s):** Brown butter and anything, especially caramel, coconut, huckleberries, vanilla beans;
grapefruit and thyme; red cherries with black pepper; blackberries, sage and brown butter; Meyer
lemon with strawberries and buttermilk **Fave Cookbook(s):** Chocolate Obsession by Michael Recchiuti
Chef to Cook for You: I would be the happiest person on earth if Dan Barber of Blue Hill Restaurant
would cook for me. Ideologically, his cooking can turn any cynic into an ecological optimist. I have
tremendous respect and admiration for his work as a chef and leader in the movement for sustainable, conscientious farming and eating. I am always seeking chefs who allow the true flavors of good
ingredients to shine through in well-executed dishes. Dan's cooking achieves this and so much more
in an inimitable way. **Culinary Travel:** Spain – even as it stands on the forefront of culinary innovation,
it's cuisine is a magnificent amalgam of ancient cultures. I value simplicity in food, and true signs of
something having been made by the hands of another human being. I value the signs of a long history informing the way food is made, and sold, and consumed. Spain exemplifies that for me.

Zach Bell
Chef de Cuisine | Café Boulud

301 Australian Ave. Palm Beach, FL 33480

Restaurant E-mail: zbell@danielnyc.com

Phone: (561) 655-6060

RESTAURANT FACTS
Seats: 300 **Weeknight Covers:** 225 **Weekend Covers:** 300+ **Check Average (with Wine):** $100+ **Check Average (w/o Wine):** $75 **Tasting Menu:** Yes $115 **Kitchen Staff:** 12

CHEF FACTS
Cuisine: French-American **Born:** 1973 **Began Career:** 1991 **Culinary School:** Johnson & Wales, Miami, FL **Grad Year:** 1997 **Stages:** France: Chatêau Du Domaine Saint Martin **Work History:** New York, NY: Le Cirque, Cafe Boulud **Mentor(s):** Daniel Boulud, Andrew Carmellini, Marc Poidevin **Protégée(s):** Scott Quis, Adam Duimstra **Awards:** 2008 StarChefs.com Rising Star Chef South Florida **Affiliations:** Share our Strength, March of Dimes, Daily Bread Food Bank

NOTABLE DISH(ES): Florida Pompano En Croute with Smoked Eggplant Purée, Fennel, Tomato Confit, Meyer Lemon, and Sauce Vierge; Barramundi with Artichoke–New Potato–Basil Nage, Provençal Condiment, Fried Anchovy, and Lemon Aioli

FAST FACTS
Restaurant Recs: Middle Eastern Bakery for shwarma on homemade pita, butter bean salad and chilled roasted cauliflower with tahini and basil **Kitchen Tool(s):** My 3¼-inch Victorinox serrated paring knife. It is nice to have one knife that can trim things down nicely, that doesn't take up a lot of space. And it's cheap! **Interview Question:** Why do you want to work here? It can distinguish between resume builders and those truly looking to learn. **Flavor Combo(s):** I'm a big fan of acidity and sweet. I like acidity with the natural flavors of fish **Fave Cookbook(s):** Le Grand Livre De Cuisine D'Alain Ducasse; Bistro, Brasseries Et Restaurants De Tradition **Chef to Cook for You:** Hands down Jacques Maximum (I never went to his restaurant) **Culinary Travel:** India – to learn more about spices

B

Christophe Bellanca
Executive Chef | Le Cirque

151 E. 58th St. New York, NY 10022

Restaurant E-mail: christophebellanca@hotmail.com

Phone: (212) 644-0202

RESTAURANT FACTS
Seats: 150 **Weeknight Covers:** 180 **Weekend Covers:** 250 **Check Average (with Wine):** $125–$130 **Check Average (w/o Wine):** $90–$95 **Tasting Menu:** Yes $120/$160 with wine **Kitchen Staff:** 12–15

CHEF FACTS
Cuisine: Modern French **Born:** 1972 **Began Career:** 1998 **Culinary School:** L'Ecolier Tain L'Hermitage, France **Stages:** France: L'Hermitage; Spain: Martin Berasategui; Thailand: The Oriental Bangkok **Work History:** France: La Pyramide, Georges Blanc, Pic; Los Angeles, CA: L'Orangerie **Mentor(s):** Anne Sophie Pic **Languages Spoken:** French

NOTABLE DISH(ES): John Dory coated with Coarse Mustard, Braised Fennel and Roasted Root Vegetables

FAST FACTS
Restaurant Recs: Allen and Delancey for the rabbit terrine and the cod **Kitchen Tool(s):** Spoon **Interview Question:** What's your style? **Flavor Combo(s):** Onions and kaffir lime **Fave Cookbook(s):** Côté Crillon and Côté Maison by Jean-François Piege **Chef to Cook for You:** Joël Robuchon, because of his precision and rigor **Culinary Travel:** Thailand for the culture and the produce

Drew Belline
Chef de Cuisine | Floataway Cafe

1123 Zonolite Rd., Suite 15 Atlanta, GA 30306

Restaurant E-mail: floatawaycafe@bellsouth.net

Phone: (404) 892-1414

RESTAURANT FACTS
Seats: 138 **Weeknight Covers:** 175 **Weekend Covers:** 250 **Check Average (with Wine):** $40–45 **Tasting Menu:** No **Kitchen Staff:** 6

CHEF FACTS
Cuisine: Seasonal Rustic **Born:** 1979 **Began Career:** 1999 **Culinary School:** Johnson & Wales University, Providence, RI **Grad Year:** 2002 **Stages:** New York: Nobu, Artisanal, Aureole **Work History:** New York, NY: Craft; Atlanta, GA: Bacchanalia, Quinones **Mentor(s):** Damon Wise; Marco Canora; Anne Quatrano **Awards:** 2007 StarChefs.com Rising Star Chef Atlanta **Languages Spoken:** Kitchen Spanish

NOTABLE DISH(ES): Nantucket Bay Scallops with Celery Root, Celery Leaves, Pickled Celery, Celery Hearts and Burgundy Black Truffles; Seared Diver Scallops in Asparagus-Tarragon Broth with Asparagus and D'Avignon Radishes

FAST FACTS
Restaurant Recs: Watershed for great brunch; Euclid Avenue Yacht Club for the best hot dog ever. **Kitchen Tool(s):** A really good, solid spoon. I have ten of them. I'm a freak for my spoons. They're essential for basting, plating, and sauces. I also love a wood-burning oven and grill; it produces such rustic and wonderful flavor. It's great for making pizza. **Interview Question:** Are you passionate about food? **Flavor Combo(s):** Some great spring combinations we're working with are: ramps, peas and morels; rhubarb and pork fat with English pea risotto **Fave Cookbook(s):** A Return to Cooking by Eric Ripert and The River Café Cookbook by Ruth Rogers **Chef to Cook for You:** Either Jeremiah Towers or Paul Bertolli. I'm very into their food currently and could learn a lot from them. **Culinary Travel:** I'd like to go to San Francisco – I've never been there and this restaurant is that kind of style

Jonathan Benno
Chef de Cuisine | Per Se

10 Columbus Circle New York, NY 10019

Restaurant E-mail: jbenno@perseny.com

Phone: (212) 823-9335

RESTAURANT FACTS
Seats: 64 **Weeknight Covers:** 90 **Weekend Covers:** 90 **Check Average (w/o Wine):** $275 **Tasting Menu:** Yes

CHEF FACTS
Cuisine: French American **Born:** 1969 **Began Career:** 1993 **Culinary School:** The Culinary Institute of America, Hyde Park, NY **Grad Year:** 1993 **Stages:** France: Auberge du Vieux Puits **Work History:** New York, NY: Craft, Daniel, Gramercy Tavern; San Francisco, CA: Aqua; Yountville, CA: The French Laundry **Mentor(s):** Thomas Keller, John Farnsworth **Awards:** 2006 Food & Wine Best New Chef; 2005 StarChefs.com Rising Star Chef New York **Affiliations:** JBF, Slow Food

NOTABLE DISH(ES): Shad Roe Porridge with Persian Lime Salt; Foie Gras en Terrine with Granny Smith Apple "Gelée"

FAST FACTS
Restaurant Recs: Al di La in Park Slope – for malfatti **Kitchen Tool(s):** Small serving spoons for plating **Interview Question:** Why do you want to work here? We look for someone that wants to learn. Those who are building their resume with six months here, six months there, are the least desirable. Culinary school grads should look for a two-year commitment with a restaurant. **Fave Cookbook(s):** The Professional Chef - it's a great resource; Grand Livre de Cuisine by Alain Ducasse **Chef to Cook for You:** My grandmother **Culinary Travel:** San Francisco – I lived there. Also Paris, Barcelona and San Sebastian.

Michelle Bernstein
Chef/Owner | Michy's

6927 Biscayne Blvd. Miami, FL 33138

Restaurant E-mail: michys@bellsouth.net

Phone: (305) 759-2001

RESTAURANT FACTS
Seats: 65 **Weeknight Covers:** 180 **Weekend Covers:** 240 **Check Average (w/o Wine):** $55 **Kitchen Staff:** 7

CHEF FACTS
Other Restaurants: Miami: FL: Social Miami; Los Angeles, CA: Social Hollywood; Delta Airlines Business Class Menus **Cuisine:** Upscale comfort food **Born:** 1970 **Began Career:** 1992 **Culinary School:** Johnson & Wales University, Miami, FL **Grad Year:** 1994 **Stages:** France: Le Feuniere, Rene Summit **Work History:** Miami, FL: Azul at the Mandarin Oriental, Norman's; New York, NY: Alison on Dominic, Le Bernardin; Washington DC: Jean-Louis at the Watergate Hotel **Mentor(s):** Norman Van Aken, Jean Louis Palladin, Steven Raichlen **Protégée(s):** Jason Schaan, Sara Mair, Jon Shook, Vinny Dotolo, Timon Baloo **Awards:** 2008 James Beard Foundation Best Chef South; 2006 Jewish Federation Top 10 Jewish Woman in America; 2006 Breaking the Glass Ceiling; 2005 Jewish Federation Philanthropic Award; 2005 James Beard Foundation Best Chef Southeast Nominee; 2005 Best New Restaurant **Affiliations:** I teach kids how to cook for shelters across America and I volunteer for other charitable organizations **Languages Spoken:** French, Spanish

NOTABLE DISH(ES): Lobster Cappucino with Spanish Sherry

FAST FACTS
Restaurant Recs: Hy Vong for pork rolling cakes **Kitchen Tool(s):** Blender – I make all of my baby soft purées, emulsions, vinaigrettes and marinades. I can't imagine life in the kitchen without it. **Interview Question:** What is the best dish you have ever eaten and why? It gives me an idea of what turns them on with food, if they are really passionate or not. **Flavor Combo(s):** Fish with rye; sea urchin and fennel; cuttlefish and chorizo **Fave Cookbook(s):** Cooking with the Seasons by Jean-Louis Palladin. It was what we used in his kitchen as our bible; he was so ahead of his time. Genius. **Chef to Cook for You:** Joël Robuchon. He's a genius – his food is honest and makes me melt. **Culinary Travel:** Vietnam – the flavors are so alive, clean and perfect

B

Arnaud Berthelier
Executive Chef | The Dining Room at The Ritz-Carlton

3434 Peachtree Rd. Atlanta, GA 30326

Restaurant E-mail: arnaud.berthelier@ritzcarlton.com

Phone: (404) 237-2700

RESTAURANT FACTS

Seats: 60–64 **Weeknight Covers:** 45 **Weekend Covers:** 80 **Check Average (with Wine):** $175 **Tasting Menu:** Yes **Kitchen Staff:** 11

CHEF FACTS

Cuisine: Contemporary French Mediterranean **Born:** 1971 **Began Career:** 1988 **Work History:** Monte Carlo: Le Louis XV; England: Les Saveurs; France: Michel Guerard; Washington D.C.: Lespinasse; Egypt: The Ritz-Carlton; Naples, FL: The Ritz-Carlton; St. Thomas, USVI: The Ritz-Carlton **Mentor(s):** My brother **Affiliations:** SOS, March of Dimes, and other charity events **Languages Spoken:** French, Italian, German, some Spanish

NOTABLE DISH(ES): Vegetable "Bone Marrow" with Cèpes and Red Wine Bordelaise

FAST FACTS

Restaurant Recs: I like to get pizza from the little pizza place next to my home. I think it is called Zucca. **Kitchen Tool(s):** Big tweezers **Interview Question:** Do you know what it takes to work here? **Flavor Combo(s):** Sweet and salty, as well as carrot with lemon; coconut and soy; orange and cilantro **Fave Cookbook(s):** Ma Cuisine by Escoffier, which to me is the bible. I go to it whenever I am not sure of something. Also, the el Bulli cookbooks. **Chef to Cook for You:** Pierre Gagnaire because he has such great technique and is not afraid to make mistakes. I have been twice already and he cooks at such a high level; it is amazing **Culinary Travel:** I would love to go to either China or India do see the different techniques and uses of spices.

Eric Bertoia
Corporate Pastry Chef | The Dinex Group

16 East 40th Street, 4th Floor New York NY 10016

Restaurant E-mail: ebertoia@danielnyc.com

Phone: (212) 327-3434

CHEF FACTS
Other Restaurants: New York, NY: Bar Boulud, Café Boulud, DB Bistro Moderne; Las Vegas, NV: Daniel Boulud Brasserie; Beijing, China: Maison Boulud; Washington, DC – opening October 2008: Daniel Boulud Bistro, Feast & Fétes Catering **Cuisine:** Entremets and cakes **Born:** 1971 **Began Career:** 1990 **Stages:** France: Pâtisserie Marthy **Work History:** New York, NY: Daniel, Cafe Boulud; France: The Ritz, Taillevent, L'Ousteau de Baumaniere, Baux de Provence, Pastry Shop Castagne **Mentor(s):** Yves Thuries **Protégée(s):** Sebastian Bauer **Affiliations:** City-Meals-on-Wheels – Daniel is a Board Member, C-CAP: Careers through Culinary Arts Program, James Beard Foundation **Languages Spoken:** French, Spanish

NOTABLE DISH(ES): Cherry Kriek Beer Ice Cream; Mocha Cake; Hazelnut Praline, Coffee Ice Cream

FAST FACTS
Restaurant Recs: Per Se **Kitchen Tool(s):** Spatula **Interview Question:** What products do you prefer to work with? **Flavor Combo(s):** Chocolate and hazelnut **Fave Cookbook(s):** Pâtisserie Française by Yves Thuries **Chef to Cook for You:** As I am fond of Japanese food, it would be chef Nobuyuki Matsuhisa. His food is exceptional. **Culinary Travel:** Definitely Japan. The Japanese have a culinary culture like in Europe, and they are perfectionists, so you can find a lot of pastry shops with high quality food and with very delicate desserts! That also means "competition" between pastry shops: that is why the pastry level is high.

B

John Besh
Chef/Owner | Restaurant August

301 Tchoupitoulas St. New Orleans, LA 70130

Restaurant E-mail: simone@simonesez.com

Phone: (504) 299-9777

RESTAURANT FACTS
Seats: 100 **Weeknight Covers:** 150 **Weekend Covers:** 150 **Check Average (with Wine):** $110 **Tasting Menu:** Yes $150 per person **Kitchen Staff:** 6

CHEF FACTS
Other Restaurants: Besh Restaurant Group: August, Besh Steak, Lüke, La Provence **Cuisine:** Contemporary Lousiana French **Born:** 1968 **Began Career:** 1992 **Culinary School:** The Culinary Institute of America, Hyde Park, NY **Grad Year:** 1992 **Stages:** France: Alain Assuad; Chez Bruno **Work History:** France: Chateau de Montcaud; Germany: Romantik Hotel Spielweg; New Orleans, LA: Windsor Court Hotel **Mentor(s):** Chris Kerigourgiou, Karl-Josef Fuchs **Protégée(s):** Brandon Sharp, Steven McHugh **Awards:** 2006 James Beard Foundation Best Chef Southeast; 1998 New Orleans Magazine Best Chef; 1999 Food & Wine Best New Chef **Affiliations:** CCC, SFA, SFBM, CCRRP **Books Published:** The New Orleans Program; How to Eat Good; Live Good and Cook Good in Moderation; Ma Louisianne **Languages Spoken:** German, some French

NOTABLE DISH(ES): Cherokee Purple Tomato Terrine with White Asparagus Soup; Salad of White Asparagus and Smoked Foie Gras with Cherries and Summer Truffles

FAST FACTS
Restaurant Recs: Ba Mien for steamed rice flour rolls with grilled pork paste and fried onions with a lemongrass-peanut sauce, charcoal grilled pork on pressed vermicelli with fish sauce and fresh herbs, and combination Pho with lots of tripe, beef tendon, meat balls, fatty brisket and rare flank **Kitchen Tool(s):** Iced tea spoon – I can use it for any number of applications. I taste, stir, plate and quenelle with one. **Interview Question:** What are your favorite foods? What is your favorite restaurant? I like to hear a cook explain his or her passions. I don't care what their favorite foods are, only that they are passionate about an experience or a food. **Flavor Combo(s):** Vietnamese combinations of hot, sour, salty, bitter, and sweet - in the right proportion - make me very happy! **Fave Cookbook(s):** Ma Gastronomie by Fernand Point **Chef to Cook for You:** Chef Clement Bruno of Chez Bruno in Lorgues, France. He works only with local products (the best in the world), creating only one menu daily, with the charisma of a 21-year-old and the soul of a grandmother. **Culinary Travel:** I'm in love with Provence, but I must say that I've not been to many places that I haven't found something to love. The thing I love about Provence is that the food is refined yet approachable, with a focus on terroir.

Jennifer Biesty
Chef | Savage Feasts

San Francisco, CA

Restaurant E-mail: jen@savagefeasts.com

Phone: (415) 307-8516

CHEF FACTS
Cuisine: Cal-Mediterranean **Born:** 1972 **Began Career:** 1992 **Culinary School:** The Culinary Institute of America, Hyde Park, NY **Grad Year:** 1992 **Stages:** England: River Café; France: Amphyclès **Work History:** New York, NY: March, Aquavit; San Francisco, CA: Bizou, Jardinière, Universal Café, COCO 500 **Mentor(s):** Loretta Keller, Mario Batali **Awards:** 2007 StarChefs.com Rising Star Chef San Franciso **Affiliations:** California Culinary Academy **Languages Spoken:** Some French, kitchen Spanish

NOTABLE DISH(ES): Bacon-Wrapped Monkfish with Tomatoes and Broccoli Rabe; Roasted Quail with Liver Toast, Pickled Rhubarb, Kumquats and Quail Eggs

FAST FACTS
Restaurant Recs: Blue Plate for great seasonal food; Front Porch for fried chicken in a bucket **Kitchen Tool(s):** Spoon; spatula **Interview Question:** What cookbooks are you reading? When did you start cooking? Please rate your work ethic on a scale of 1-10. I also have candidates do a trail. **Flavor Combo(s):** I love olive oil and lemon. I also combine aged Italian oak barrel vinegar with sautéed Champagne grapes. And the sweet and salty combination is classic. **Fave Cookbook(s):** The Slow Mediterranean Kitchen: Recipes for the Passionate Cook by Paula Wolfert; cookbooks by Marcella Hazan. **Culinary Travel:** I would love to go to Asia. My dream trip is to go to Laos, Vietnam and then to Australia for two or three months.

Rick Billings
Pastry Chef | L'Atelier de Joël Robuchon

57 East 57th St. New York, NY 10022

RESTAURANT FACTS
Seats: 50 **Weeknight Covers:** 100 **Weekend Covers:** 110–120
Check Average (w/o Wine): $100 **Tasting Menu:** Yes $190 **Kitchen Staff:** 4–7

CHEF FACTS
Cuisine: Modern French pastry **Born:** 1980 **Began Career:** 2001
Culinary School: New England Culinary Institute, Montpelier; VT **Grad Year:** 2001 **Work History:** Boston, MA: L'Espalier, Clio **Mentor(s):** Michel Bras, Oriol Balaguer **Awards:** 2006 StarChefs.com Rising Star Pastry Chef Boston **Languages Spoken:** Spanglish

NOTABLE DISH(ES): Frozen Blood Orange and Amaretto Capsule with Bitter Almond Cream; Salted Caramel Foam with Freeze-Dried Raspberries and Thyme

FAST FACTS
Restaurant Recs: Mike's Deli for a reuben **Kitchen Tool(s):** The Pacojet, because I have a sub-zero (-30°F) deep freezer, I can spin every ice cream to order. With the Pacojet, you can come up with completely new textures, powder, liquids, and get a perfect texture every time. And the Vita-Prep – I have a lot of agar-based sauces, and you need a powerful blender to get the gels to be totally smooth. **Interview Question:** What are you reading? **Flavor Combo(s):** Chicory, violet, and bergamot **Fave Cookbook(s):** Making a Cook by Madeline Kamman **Chef to Cook for You:** Chef Andoni Luis Aduriz from Mugaritz - I've never met anyone who puts so much of their heart on the plate **Culinary Travel:** Sweden – I've been before and the food was unlike anything else I've ever had

Christopher Blobac
Executive Chef

Christopher Blobaum
Chef | River House

476 Mount Pelia Rd. Bluffton, NC 29910
Restaurant E-mail: cblobaum@palmettobluffresort.com
Phone: (843) 706-6535

RESTAURANT FACTS
Seats: 80 **Weeknight Covers:** 80 **Weekend Covers:** 120 **Check Average (with Wine):** $85 **Tasting Menu:** Yes **Kitchen Staff:** 7–8

CHEF FACTS
Cuisine: Local farm-fresh new American **Born:** 1955 **Began Career:** 1979 **Culinary School:** The Culinary Institute of America, Hyde Park, NY **Grad Year:** 1979 **Stages:** New York, NY: Quilted Giraffe **Work History:** New York, NY: Quilted Giraffe; Houston, TX: La Reserve; Chicago, IL: The Dining Room; Beverly Hills, CA: Colette; Santa Monica, CA: Wilshire Restaurant **Mentor(s):** Barry Wine, Ferdinand Gutierrez, Alice Waters, Thomas Keller, Georges Blanc **Awards:** 2004 Orange County Chef of the Year **Affiliations:** AIWF, Chefs Collaborative, Slow Food

NOTABLE DISH(ES): Sea Scallops in Orange-Cardamom Sauce

FAST FACTS
Restaurant Recs: The Hump for omakase or anything the chefs suggests **Kitchen Tool(s):** Benriner Japanese mandolin – a very versatile sharp cutter that travels well and expedites accurate work **Interview Question:** What is your passion outside of work? **Flavor Combo(s):** Truffle, potato, duck fat; honey, chile, lime; fleur de sel, caramel **Fave Cookbook(s):** The French Laundry Cookbook by Thomas Keller; old books from MFK Fisher; I have collected over 3000 cookbooks dating back to the 1700's **Chef to Cook for You:** Michel Bras for his intimate, natural cooking, family and local value. Also, I have always admired Ann Willan, a brilliant cook, teacher and author. **Culinary Travel:** Rural France and Italy for the close connection to seasons, flavor and the farm. Rural China to visit a civilization that has been feeding itself for over 2000 years.

B

Michael B...

Michael Bloise
Consulting Chef

Miami Beach, FL

Restaurant E-mail: michaelbloise@aol.com

CHEF FACTS
Cuisine: Progressive American **Born:** 1975 **Began Career:** 1998
Culinary School: Johnson & Wales, Miami, FL **Grad Year:** 1998 **Work
History:** Miami Beach, FL: The Gaucho Room, Tantra, Wish, 1220
Mentor(s): Feliz Nunez, my father **Protégée(s):** Alejandro Pinero;
Steven Shea **Awards:** 2008 StarChefs.com Rising Star Chef South
Florida; 2005 Restaurant Hospitality Rising Star **Languages Spoken:**
Kitchen Spanish

NOTABLE DISH(ES): Pan-Seared Rougie Foie Gras with Cascabel
Chili, Roasted Banana, Basil, Baby Arugula, Daikon Radish and Black
Pepper Marshmallow; Barbecued Beef Short Ribs with Sushi Rice,
Cilantro, Baby Carrots and Guava Glaze

FAST FACTS
Restaurant Recs: Saigon City for Happy Pancakes **Kitchen Tool(s):** Mortar and pestle **Interview
Question:** I like to ask what they like to eat. Usually the food that people like to eat tells you what kind
of person they are. I ask them what they like to cook – what they actually enjoy cooking, and what
turns them on. That helps me gauge whether they get excited about different ingredients and styles,
or if they're just in it for the paycheck. **Flavor Combo(s):** Peanut butter and jelly; anything with bacon
Fave Cookbook(s): Patricia Yeo: Cooking from A to Z by Patricia Yeo; Morimoto's The New Art of Japanese Cooking; Michel Richard's Happy in the Kitchen **Chef to Cook for You:** Julia Child because she
was a badass! **Culinary Travel:** I'm going to France this year, and I'm probably going to go to Spain
later on in the year. I'd like to go to Brazil and South America, and I'd like to go to China. There's so
much interesting stuff on the other side of the planet that I need to get my hands on.

April Bloomfield
Executive Chef | The Spotted Pig

314 W 11th St. New York, NY 10014
Restaurant E-mail: info@thespottedpig.com

RESTAURANT FACTS
Seats: 100 **Weeknight Covers:** 250+ **Weekend Covers:** 250–350
Check Average (with Wine): $45 **Kitchen Staff:** 7

CHEF FACTS
Cuisine: British/Italian **Born:** 1974 **Began Career:** 1990 **Culinary School:** Birmingham College of Food, Tourism & Creative Studies **Grad Year:** 1991 **Stages:** Berkeley, CA: Chez Panisse **Work History:** England: River Cafe, Bibendum **Mentor(s):** Rose Gray, Ruth Rogers **Awards:** 2008 James Beard Foundation Best Chef New York City Nominee; 2007 Food & Wine Best New Chef; 2006, 2005 Michelin 1 star **Affiliations:** Groove With Me, Food Bank, Grow for Good, and Greenmarket

NOTABLE DISH(ES): Sheep's Ricotta Gnudi with Pesto; Pork Tonnata with Capers, Anchovy and Mayonnaise

FAST FACTS
Restaurant Recs: Thaison on Baxter and Canal for the pho bo **Kitchen Tool(s):** Mortar and pestle **Interview Question:** Why are you here? I want to see if they have researched my menus and want to learn about the food. **Flavor Combo(s):** Lemon and olive oil; garlic and marjoram; fennel seed and chili **Fave Cookbook(s):** The Whole Beast: Nose to Tail Eating by Fergus Henderson; Roast Chicken and Other Stories by Simon Hopkinson **Chef to Cook for You:** Julia Child – she was at the forefront of what she was doing, I loved her TV shows. She's really inspiring. **Culinary Travel:** India – the spices are interesting, and it would be inspiring to see how the items are used together

Dante Boccuzzi
Chef/Owner | Dante

8001 Rockside Rd. Valley View, OH 44125

Restaurant E-mail: danteboccuzzi@danteboccuzzi.com

Phone: (216) 524-9404

RESTAURANT FACTS
Seats: 150 **Weeknight Covers:** 110 **Weekend Covers:** 200 **Check Average (with Wine):** $65 **Tasting Menu:** Yes $75/$115 with wine **Kitchen Staff:** 7

CHEF FACTS
Cuisine: American European **Born:** 1971 **Began Career:** 1991 **Culinary School:** The Culinary Institute of America, Hyde Park, NY **Grad Year:** 1991 **Stages:** England: L'Esgargot Marco Pierre White; France: Les Muscadins Hotel; Italy: L'Albereta **Work History:** Cleveland, OH: Giovanni's; Washington D.C.: Lespinasse; San Francisco, CA: Silks at the Mandarin Oriental; Hong Kong, China: The Mandarin Oriental; Taipei, Taiwan: Lai Lai Sheraton; Milan, Italy: Nobu; New York, NY: Aureole **Mentor(s):** Charlie Palmer **Protégée(s):** Bryan Voltaggio **Awards:** 2006 Michelin Guide 1 star; 2002 StarChefs.com Rising Star Chef New York; 1999, 1998 James Beard Foundation Rising Star Chef Nominee **Affiliations:** JBF **Books Published:** Cooking in Harmony: Notes for the Young Chef **Languages Spoken:** Italian

NOTABLE DISH(ES): Pepper Seared Quail with Cherry Jus; Thyme Baked Artichokes

FAST FACTS
Restaurant Recs: Chuck E. Cheese – for pizza and Pac Man **Kitchen Tool(s):** Miniature tongs **Interview Question:** Do you like Pearl Jam? Good cooks listen to good music. **Fave Cookbook(s):** Italian Cuisine by Tony May

Anthony Bombaci
Executive Chef | Nana Restaurant

2201 Stemmons Fwy. #27 Dallas, TX 75207

Restaurant E-mail: anthony.bombaci@hilton.com

Phone: (214) 761-7475

RESTAURANT FACTS
Seats: 170 **Weeknight Covers:** 90 **Weekend Covers:** 120–200
Check Average (with Wine): 90–100 **Check Average (w/o Wine):**
$60 **Tasting Menu:** Yes $75/$89 **Kitchen Staff:** 12–14

CHEF FACTS
Cuisine: Contemporary European/Mediterranean **Born:** 1964 **Began
Career:** 1988 **Culinary School:** The Culinary Institute of America,
Hyde Park, NY **Grad Year:** 1988 **Stages:** Martin Berasategui's restaurant in Spain; Joël, in Atlanta **Work History:** San Francisco, CA: Gary
Danko; Spain: Hotel Arts, Enoteca Bombaci **Mentor(s):** Gary Danko;
Jose Gutierrez; Joël Antunes; Joan Roca; Ferran Adriá; Jordi Butron
Protégée(s): I am a little too young to have protegées, don't you think? **Awards:** 2007 StarChefs.
com Rising Star Chef Dallas **Affiliations:** March of Dimes, Taste of the Nation, Taste of the World
Languages Spoken: Spanish, A little Catalan

NOTABLE DISH(ES): Seared Venison, Caramelized Bananas, Thai Peanut Sauce, Cilantro; Fresh
Tomato Marmalade, Yogurt Sorbet, Texturized Olive Oil

FAST FACTS
Restaurant Recs: Arcodoro and Pomodoro. The chef's name is Franceso Parra. I really like his food.
Kitchen Tool(s): Microplane; thermocirculator **Interview Question:** What is the first thing you remember eating? What books do you read? Who are your icons? What is your inspiration? **Flavor Combo(s):**
Garlic and parsley; tomatoes and olive oil; coconut with everything; licorice with anything, especially
squash and melon **Fave Cookbook(s):** Asfalto Culinario: El Laboratorio de Arzak by Xabier Gutierrez
Chef to Cook for You: Joan Roca **Culinary Travel:** Japan because I don't know anything about it and
everyone keeps telling me to go

Jean-François Bonnet
Executive Pastry Chef/Owner | Tumbador Chocolates

34 34th St. Brooklyn, NY 11232

Restaurant E-mail: jfbonnet@tumbadorchocolate.com

Phone: (718) 788-0200

RESTAURANT FACTS
Kitchen Staff: 5

CHEF FACTS
Cuisine: French Continental with an American twist **Born:** 1976
Began Career: 1994 **Culinary School:** Apprenticeship program,
France **Grad Year:** 1995 **Stages:** France: L'Hostellerie des Gorges
de Pennafort, La Bastide Saint-Antoine, La Villa Saint-Elme **Work
History:** France: La Bastide Saint-Antoine, L'Hostellerie des gorges
de Pennafort; New York, NY: Atelier Restaurant, Cello, Daniel, Monkey
Bar **Mentor(s):** Philippe Da Silva **Awards:** 2006, 2005 10 Best Pastry
Chefs in America **Affiliations:** We hire people from a program called
Strive **Languages Spoken:** French, Spanish

NOTABLE DISH(ES): Rice Crispy, Peanut Ice Cream, Chocolate Leaves, Condensed Milk Cappuccino

FAST FACTS
Restaurant Recs: Di Fara Pizza in Brooklyn – their parma ham and artichoke pizza does it for me
Kitchen Tool(s): Bread knife, small offset spatula, set of round and square cutters, ruler, wheel cutter,
sugar thermometer, paring knife, citrus grater, bowl scraper, and homemade templates – like the
lid of a bucket **Interview Question:** How do you work with people? Working as a team is the most
important - helping each other out instead of judging each other, and helping the weakest get better
everyday. **Flavor Combo(s):** Pineapple and star anise; chocolate and caramel; raspberry and yuzu;
berries and lime **Fave Cookbook(s):** Fine Chocolates: Great Experience by Jean-Pierre Wybauw **Chef
to Cook for You:** Bertrand Chemel – he is a great friend and he keeps it real **Culinary Travel:** China
and Japan

Scott Boswell
Chef/Owner | Stella!

1024 Chartres St. New Orleans, LA 70116

Restaurant E-mail: chefscottyb@bellsouth.net

Phone: (504) 587-0091

RESTAURANT FACTS
Seats: 85 **Weeknight Covers:** 100 **Weekend Covers:** 140 **Check Average (with Wine):** $100 **Check Average (w/o Wine):** $70 **Tasting Menu:** Yes $95/$150 with wine **Kitchen Staff:** 12

CHEF FACTS
Other Restaurants: Stanley Restaurant, Hoshi **Cuisine:** Local–global – we shop from local markets from around the world **Born:** 1961 **Began Career:** 1995 **Culinary School:** The Culinary Institute of America, Hyde Park, NY **Grad Year:** 1995 **Stages:** Italy: Restaurant Nina; Japan: Chin Kenichi Schezwan Restaurant, La Rochelle, Restaurant Masa; New York, NY: Jean-Georges **Work History:** France: L'Abbaye de St. Croix; Italy: Enoteca Pinchiorri; New Orleans, LA: Windsor Court Grill Room; Big Sky, MT: Rainbow Ranch Lodge **Mentor(s):** Pascal Morel, Kevin Graham, Masahiko Kobe, Hiroyuki Sakai **Protégée(s):** Erik Veney, Nolan Ventura, Gabriella Molina **Awards:** 2004-2006 Wine Spectator Award of Excellence; 2005 DiRoNA Award of Excellence; 2003 StarChefs.com Rising Star Chef New Orleans **Affiliations:** March of Dimes, Breast Cancer Society, New Orleans Ballet and Symphony, SOS, Global Green, etc. **Languages Spoken:** French, some Italian

NOTABLE DISH(ES): Red Snapper with Sesame Lacquered Broccoli Rabe; Heirloom Tomato 4 Ways

FAST FACTS
Restaurant Recs: Le Richelieu for two eggs sunny side up with bacon, grits, and homemade biscuits with a side of crêpes. It's a hidden treasure that serves until 2:00 am. **Kitchen Tool(s):** Vita-Prep – it purées like no other blender out there. I always dreamed of posing for their ad campaign with the chef naked with his blender, but I never got the call. **Interview Question:** Do you love to cook? If not, why don't you change careers? Without love as the main ingredient you can never be great at what you do. I need love and passion in everyone under my roof. The love effect on my guests is magical. **Flavor Combo(s):** Color, crisp, salty, sweet, heat, surprise, and comfort **Fave Cookbook(s):** The French Laundry Cookbook by Thomas Keller **Chef to Cook for You:** Ferran Adriá – I am a go-for-it guy and since I cannot even get a stage there it would be nice for him to cook for me **Culinary Travel:** I will take my travels farther into the Far East this year. I hope to find many treasures and keys to hidden culinary doors.

James Botsacos
Chef/Partner | Molyvos

871 Seventh Ave. New York, NY 10019
Restaurant E-mail: jbotsacos@molyvos.com
Phone: (212) 582-7500

RESTAURANT FACTS

Seats: 220 **Weeknight Covers:** 300 **Weekend Covers:** 450 **Check Average (w/o Wine):** $45 **Tasting Menu:** No **Kitchen Staff:** 4–6

CHEF FACTS

Other Restaurants: Abboccato **Cuisine:** Greek **Born:** 1967 **Began Career:** 1987 **Culinary School:** Johnson & Wales, Providence, RI **Grad Year:** 1988 **Work History:** Palm Beach, FL: Breakers Hotel; New York, NY: 21 Club, Blue Water Grill, Water Club, Park Avalon **Mentor(s):** Alain Sailhac **Protégée(s):** John DeLuci **Affiliations:** Schooling Chefs, American Lamb Board, Taste of the Nation, Meals-on-Wheels **Languages Spoken:** Kitchen Greek and Italian

NOTABLE DISH(ES): Grilled Octopus with Pepper and Olive Salad

FAST FACTS

Restaurant Recs: Blue Ribbon on Sullivan St. for the duck club **Kitchen Tool(s):** Tongs because I use them as an extension of my hand so I don't have to handle the food so much. They are great for picking up sauté pans, food, and hot plates. They're great for working the grill and flipping fish. **Interview Question:** What kind of food do you like to cook? I ask this because I want to know if cooking is really their interest, and if they cook on their own. **Flavor Combo(s):** Anything with garlic **Fave Cookbook(s):** The French Laundry Cookbook by Thomas Keller **Chef to Cook for You:** Either Thomas Keller or Mario Batali. Thomas Keller's attention to detail and use of fine ingredients in whimsical ways is pretty amazing. I think Mario Batali's translation of Italian food is interesting and he has a great way with pasta. **Culinary Travel:** I would go back to Greece to more extensive travel. The changes in the food from island to island and region to region is dramatic.

David Bouley
Chef/Owner | Bouley

120 W Broadway New York, NY 10007

Restaurant E-mail: info@bouleynyc.com

Phone: (212) 964-2525

RESTAURANT FACTS
Seats: 120 **Check Average (with Wine):** $150 **Tasting Menu:** Yes
$90/$160

CHEF FACTS
Other Restaurants: Bouley Restaurant, Danube Restaurant, Bouley
Bakery and Market, Upstairs **Cuisine:** Austrian-inspired modern
French & Japanese **Work History:** New York, NY: Le Cirque, Mon-
strance **Mentor(s):** Roger Verge, Paul Bocuse, Fredy Girardet, Joël
Robuchon, Gaston Lenôtre **Protégée(s):** Shea Gallante, Alex Ureña,
Dan Barber, Anita Lo, Brian Bistrong **Awards:** 2000 James Beard
Foundation Outstanding Chef; 1994 Best Chef New York City; 1991
James Beard Foundation Outstanding Restaurant **Books Published:** East of Paris, The New Cuisines
of Austria and the Danube **Languages Spoken:** French

NOTABLE DISH(ES): Black Sea Bass in a Sea Scallop Crust with 24-Hour Cooked Tomato; Chatham
Cod with Peas, Hon-Shimeji and Porcini Mushrooms

FAST FACTS:
Restaurant Recs: Oriental Garden on Elizabeth Street

Daniel Boulud
Chef/Owner | Daniel

60 E 65th St. New York, NY 10021

Restaurant E-mail: cbilleaud@dinexgroup.com

Phone: (212) 288-0033

RESTAURANT FACTS
Seats: 120–150 **Weeknight Covers:** 1.5 Seatings **Weekend Covers:** 2 Seatings **Check Average (w/o Wine):** $105 **Tasting Menu:** Yes $175 **Kitchen Staff:** 25–35

CHEF FACTS
Other Restaurants: New York, NY: Cafe Boulud, DB Bistro Moderne, Feast & Fetes Catering; Palm Beach, FL: Cafe Boulud; Las Vegas, NV: Daniel Boulud Brasserie at the Wynn Las Vegas Resort; Beijing, China: Maison Boulud **Cuisine:** French **Born:** 1955 **Began Career:** 1969 **Culinary School:** Only very briefly in Lyon, France at the age of 14, but I left early on as I was eager to get into a real kitchen **Grad Year:** 1969 **Stages:** France: Nandron **Work History:** France: La Mère Blanc, Les Pres d'Eugenie, Le Moulin des Mougins; New York, NY: Le Cirque, Le Regence at the Plaza Athenée; Polo Lounge at the Westbury Hotel **Mentor(s):** Roger Verge, Georges Blanc, Michel Guerard **Protégée(s):** Jean François Bruel, Bertrand Chemel, Olivier Muller **Awards:** 2007 StarChefs.com Rising Star Mentor Award New York; 2006 James Beard Foundation Outstanding Restaurateur; 2002-2006 Wine Spectator Grand Award; 2001 New York Times 4 stars; 2001 Gourmet Top 50 Restaurants in America; 1999 Bon Appétit Chef of the Year; 1999 Food & Wine Reader's Poll Favorite US Restaurant ;1999 Esquire One of the Top 25 New Restaurants; 1998 Nation's Restaurant News Fine Dining Hall of Fame; 1994 James Beard Foundation Outstanding Chef of the Year; 1992 James Beard Foundation Best Chef New York City **Affiliations:** StarChefs.com Advisory Board, Citymeals-on-Wheels, NYCCVB, Relais & Chateaux, Tradition & Qualité **Books Published:** Braise – A Journey through International Cuisine; Daniel's Dish – Entertaining at Home with a Four-Star Chef; Letters to a Young Chef; Chef Daniel Boulud: Cooking in New York City; Daniel Boulud's Cafe Boulud Cookbook; Cooking with Daniel Boulud; Elle Decor Magazine bi-monthly column: "Daniel's Dish"; Monthly newsletter: "Easy Cooking with Great Chefs" **Languages Spoken:** French

NOTABLE DISH(ES): Mediterranean Tomato-Lemon Tart; Caramelized Bay Scallops with Clementines and Cauliflower

FAST FACTS

Restaurant Recs: Daisy May's BBQ – Adam Perry has followed his passion and dug deep to focus on making the best barbecue in New York City. Marrema - Cesare Casella's presence is very tangible and personal, and I love the roasted baby goat with a side of farro with mushrooms. **Kitchen Tool(s):** Mortar and pestle for grinding herbs and spices in a way that you simply can't accomplish with a machine. Immersion blender, which replaced traditional blenders and revolutionized the way we work in the kitchen. **Interview Question:** Why do you want to work in the kitchen? I want a real, heartfelt answer so I can learn about what truly motivates them. **Flavor Combo(s):** I would have to choose a different flavor combination for each season. Winter: celery root with chestnut; spring: peas with rosemary; summer: eggplant with cumin; fall: porcini and garlic. **Fave Cookbook(s):** In general I prefer 18th, 19th, and early 20th century French cookbooks by authors like Auguste Escoffier. One of my favorites is Gastronomie Practique by Ali-Bab (the pen name of Henri Babinski) which was first published in 1907 and has been out of print, unfortunately, since the 1950's. **Chef to Cook for You:** It would be impossible for me to choose just one. I must have a whole menu of chefs: two Spanish chefs – Elena and Juan Marie Arzak for tapas. One Danish chef – Jan Hurtigkarl for a first course of Gravlax, to bring back the time we cooked together in Denmark. One American chef – Thomas Keller, for his "Oyster and Pearls." The dish reminds me of my mother's tapioca and milk soup, but Thomas's version is raised to a level of incredible refinement and simplicity. One Italian chef – Nadia Santini of Dal Pescatore Santini for her Pumpkin Ravioli with Amaretto crumbs. One Japanese chef – Tojo, one of the best in Vancouver for a whole freshly caught Pacific snapper or king salmon prepared many ways. One French chef – Michel Troisgros for a Côte de Boeuf Charolais with Marrow. A cheese course of Vieux Comté from Bernard Anthony and St. Marcellin from La Mère Richard. One Pastry chef – Marcus Farbinger of South Africa – out of nostalgia for our days together at Le Cirque. **Culinary Travel:** Laos, Cambodia and India to try their cuisines in their most authentic native versions. I would also like to continue to discover the different regional cuisines of China.

Anthony Bourdain
Consulting Chef | Les Halles

411 Park Ave. New York, NY 10016

Restaurant E-mail: hr@leshalles.net

Phone: (212) 679-4111

CHEF FACTS

Cuisine: Working-class French brasserie **Born:** 1956 **Began Career:** 1978 **Culinary School:** The Culinary Institute of America, Hyde Park, NY **Stages:** New York, NY: Lavins, Rainbow Room, WPA **Work History:** New York, NY: One Fifth Avenue, Supper Club, Sullivan's **Mentor(s):** Fergus Henderson, "Bigfoot" **Books Published:** Anthony Bourdain's Les Halles Cookbook: Strategies, Recipes, and Techniques of Classic Bistro Cooking; non-cookbooks: A Cook's Tour, Kitchen Confidential, No Reservations **Languages Spoken:** Bad French, worse Spanish, can curse in Arabic

NOTABLE DISH(ES): Steak Tartare; Steak Frites

FAST FACTS

Restaurant Recs: Yakitori Totto for the chicken sashimi. It's just like being in Tokyo. There's rarely a gaijin in sight who isn't a chef. Sake Gura, the underground, late night sake place. Prune for the radishes, butter and salt and the sweetbreads with capers and lemon. **Kitchen Tool(s):** Offset serrated knife because it does things easily that a standard chef's knife simply can't. That, and my ridiculously overpriced but eminently useful Gray Kunz spoon. I use it for saucing plates. **Interview Question:** What music do you listen to? I can't work with Dead fans or someone who is going to be turning up the radio if Billy Joel comes on. Also, of course, I look for strength, determination, consistent on-time arrival for work and a sense of humor. I will often ask someone to make me an omelet. If they can do that well, and if they possess the qualities mentioned earlier, the rest I can teach. **Fave Cookbook(s):** The Whole Beast: Nose to Tail Eating by Fergus Henderson

Romeo Bourgault
Chef de Cuisine | Besh Steak

228 Poydras Street New Orleans, LA 70130

Restaurant E-mail: dbourgault@harrahs.com

Phone: (504) 533-6111

RESTAURANT FACTS
Seats: 120 **Weeknight Covers:** 170 **Weekend Covers:** 400 **Check Average (with Wine):** $52 **Tasting Menu:** Yes $180 **Kitchen Staff:** 7

CHEF FACTS
Cuisine: American steakhouse **Born:** 1977 **Began Career:** 1995 **Work History:** New Orleans, LA: La Provence, Artesia, August, Jack Bignon Steakhouse, Lüke; Germany: Romantik Hotel Spielweg **Mentor(s):** John Besh **Affiliations:** The Edible Schoolyard **Languages Spoken:** A little German

NOTABLE DISH(ES): Double Cut Berkshire Pork Chop with Crabmeat and Orzo "Risotto"; Blackened Red Fish with a Ragout of Asparagus, New Potatoes, and Shrimp Butter

FAST FACTS
Restaurant Recs: Stein's deli – it's a great Jewish deli **Kitchen Tool(s):** Spoon – I can do almost anything with it **Interview Question:** I like to see how you move in the kitchen – how you do the dance **Flavor Combo(s):** Saffron and vanilla **Fave Cookbook(s):** Larousse Gastronomique by Prosper Montagne **Culinary Travel:** Paris – the food that I had when I visited was very genuine. It doesn't have to be fancy; it's the real deal.

Graham Elliot Bowles
Chef/Owner | Graham Elliot

217 West Huron St. Chicago, IL 60610

Phone: (312) 624-9975 ext. 877

RESTAURANT FACTS
Seats: 135 **Weeknight Covers:** 250 **Weekend Covers:** 250 **Check Average (with Wine):** $60 **Tasting Menu:** No **Kitchen Staff:** 6–7

CHEF FACTS
Cuisine: Contemporary Avant Garde **Born:** 1977 **Began Career:** 1997 **Culinary School:** Johnson & Wales University, Norfolk, VA **Grad Year:** 1997 **Work History:** Chicago, IL: Charlie Trotter's; Tru; Avenues; Dallas, TX: Star Canyon; The Mansion on Turtle Creek **Mentor(s):** Matthias Merges, Michael Kramer **Awards:** 2008 James Beard Foundation Best Chef Great Lakes Nominee; 2006 Jean Banchet Culinary Excellence; 2006 James Beard Foundation Rising Star Chef Nominee; 2006 Chicago Sun Times 4 stars; 2005 StarChefs.com Rising Star Chef Chicago; 2004 Food & Wine Best New Chef **Languages Spoken:** Kitchen Spanish

NOTABLE DISH(ES): Lobster, Yuzu Caramel and Cucumber Noodles; Pop Rocks-Crusted Foie Lollipop

FAST FACTS
Restaurant Recs: Hot Doug's for an Ace Patrick (corn dog) with duck-fat fries and a coke, and Bijan Bistro for their awesome iceberg wedge with blue cheese. Another is Café Salamera – it's Peruvian – for their little sandwiches and plantains. **Kitchen Tool(s):** Offset spatula **Interview Question:** What is your favorite type of music and why? Whose music are you currently listening to? You can sum up a person from these two questions. **Flavor Combo(s):** I like to juxtapose both high end and lowbrow ingredients: foie and poprocks, bison and cornnuts, lamb and altoids, risotto and Cheez-Its, etc **Fave Cookbook(s):** Ma Gastronomie by Fernand Point **Chef to Cook for You:** Michel Bras **Culinary Travel:** I would like to travel through India and the Middle East to learn about their amazing use of spices

James Boyce
Chef | Studio

30801 Coast Hwy. Laguna Beach, CA 92651

Restaurant E-mail: jimboyce@montagehotels.com

Phone: (949) 715-6420

RESTAURANT FACTS
Seats: 110 **Weeknight Covers:** 85 **Weekend Covers:** 130 **Check Average (with Wine):** $105 **Tasting Menu:** Yes $125/$200 with wine **Kitchen Staff:** 14

CHEF FACTS
Cuisine: Modern French with Mediterranean nuances and Californian influences **Born:** 1963 **Began Career:** 1982 **Culinary School:** The Culinary Institute of America, Hyde Park **Grad Year:** 1988 **Stages:** Washington, DC: Jean-Louis at The Watergate **Work History:** New York, NY: Le Cirque; Scottsdale, AZ: Mary Elaine's at the Phoenician **Mentor(s):** Daniel Boulud, Alan Fuerstman **Protégée(s):** William Bradley, John Cuevas **Awards:** 2006 Zagat America's Top Restaurants; 2003 Food & Wine Top 50 Hotel Restaurants; 2003 Esquire Best New Restaurants in America; 2002 James Beard Foundation Best Chef in the Southwest Nominee **Affiliations:** JBF, Chefs Collaborative

NOTABLE DISH(ES): Pacific Oysters with Frozen Champagne Mignonette

FAST FACTS
Restaurant Recs: La Sirena Grill for a calamari burrito **Kitchen Tool(s):** Peppermill – I like the feel, the texture of pepper it produces and its history in my hands **Interview Question:** Why do you want to work at Studio? The answer will reveal how much the interviewee knows about the restaurant, about me as an executive chef, and about his or her strengths, passion for a career in a high-end restaurant, and work ethic. **Flavor Combo(s):** Tart flavor with creamy texture **Fave Cookbook(s):** Pierre Gagnaire: Reflections on Culinary Artistry by Pierre Gagnaire **Chef to Cook for You:** Jean-Louis Palladin – when I ate at The Watergate in 1989, it was the best and still is the finest meal I have had. Everything was perfect! I have not had anything close since. **Culinary Travel:** Vietnam for the new tastes and flavors. I've never been there and would love to experience it.

B

Thomas Boyce
Chef de Cuisine | Spago Beverly Hills

176 N Canon Dr. Beverly Hills, CA 90210

Restaurant E-mail: thomas.boyce@wolfgangpuck.com

Phone: (310) 385-0880

RESTAURANT FACTS
Seats: 140 **Weeknight Covers:** 220–250 **Weekend Covers:**
250–325 **Check Average (with Wine):** $96 **Tasting Menu:** No
Kitchen Staff: 13–15

CHEF FACTS
Cuisine: California Italian **Born:** 1969 **Began Career:** 1985 **Work History:** St. Helena, CA: Tra Vigne; West Hollywood, CA: Spago **Mentor(s):** Lee Hefter **Affiliations:** JBF, various charities and fund-raisers **Languages Spoken:** Spanish

NOTABLE DISH(ES): Sautéed Monkfish Ragu and Chick Peas, Spinach, Chorizo and Littleneck Clams; Quail Stuffed with Brioche and Herbs, Italian Chestnut Purée, Black and Gold Chanterelle Mushrooms, Cippolini Onions

FAST FACTS
Restaurant Recs: Olympic & Normandy for tofu pork with kimchee hot pot; Suehiro for fried tofu with white miso **Kitchen Tool(s):** Spoons from flea markets; balance **Interview Question:** Why do you want to cook? Where have you worked before? Did you like it? Why or why not? **Flavor Combo(s):** Lately I'm into Kaffir lime with Thai basil and garlic **Fave Cookbook(s):** The Elements of Taste by Gray Kunz and Peter Kaminsky; Cookbooks by Thomas Keller **Chef to Cook for You:** Lee Hefter – I've worked with him for so long yet he still surprises me with his combinations and innovations **Culinary Travel:** Japan – for the aesthetic and the flavors of the cuisine. I would like to see it first-hand.

Jimmy Bradley
Executive Chef/Owner | The Red Cat

227 Tenth Ave. New York, NY 10011

Restaurant E-mail: jimmybradley@theredcat.com

Phone: (212) 242-1122

RESTAURANT FACTS
Seats: 85 **Weeknight Covers:** 160 **Weekend Covers:** 230 **Check Average (with Wine):** $60 **Tasting Menu:** No **Kitchen Staff:** 6–7

CHEF FACTS
Other Restaurants: The Harrison **Cuisine:** Contemporary American with Italian inspiration **Born:** 1967 **Began Career:** 1987 **Protégée(s):** Joey Campanaro, Paul Petersen, David Honeysett, David DuBois, Michael Presnel **Awards:** 2008 James Beard Foundation Outstanding Restaurateur Nominee **Books Published:** The Red Cat Cookbook **Languages Spoken:** Kitchen Spanish

NOTABLE DISH(ES): Sauté of Zucchini with Toasted Almonds and Pecorino

FAST FACTS
Restaurant Recs: Barbuto for squid salad **Kitchen Tool(s):** Serving spoon because I use it to season, taste, manipulate and baste **Interview Question:** Have you ever traveled? Have you seen this food in real life or did you just learn it? **Flavor Combo(s):** Lamb and basil; fish with olive oil and lemon **Fave Cookbook(s):** Ma Gastronomie by Fernand Point **Chef to Cook for You:** I would resurrect Andre Soltner from Lutece to prepare a meal for me because I miss him. **Culinary Travel:** I think Southeast Asia or China. Why not? I've never been.

Gregory Brainin
Chef/Director of Creative Development | Jean-Georges Restaurant Group

1 Central Park W. New York, NY 10012

Phone: (212) 358-0688

CHEF FACTS
Other Restaurants: Jean-Georges Restaurant Group **Cuisine:** Modern French; Modern American; Asian fusion **Born:** 1969 **Began Career:** 1994 **Culinary School:** The Culinary Institute of America, Hyde Park, NY **Grad Year:** 1994 **Work History:** New York, NY: Park Avenue Café, Aja, Alison on Dominick St., 66, Spice Market, Perry Street, Prime Steakhouse **Mentor(s):** Jean-Georges Vongerichten, David Burke **Protégée(s):** Justin Bazdarich, Gregory Gourdet, Josh Roland, Marc Lapico, Wesley Genovart **Awards:** 2006 StarChefs.com Rising Star Chef New York **Affiliations:** We work with a lot of charities **Languages Spoken:** French

NOTABLE DISH(ES): Toasted Organic Egg Yolk with Caviar and Dill; Tuna Sashimi with Wasabi Ice

FAST FACTS
Restaurant Recs: La Esquina for tacos; Zum Schneider for pancake soup; Lan for sukiyaki **Kitchen Tool(s):** My palate, it makes everything taste good **Interview Question:** Why do you want to cook? The answer to this tells you exactly who someone will be in the kitchen, especially if they tell you something they think you want to hear. **Flavor Combo(s):** I love spicy, sour, salty and smoky **Fave Cookbook(s):** Simple Cuisine by Jean-Georges Vongerichten **Chef to Cook for You:** Jean-Georges, because his sense of seasoning, balance, nuance, and layering is so impeccable **Culinary Travel:** Bangkok, and if you've been there then you know exactly why. They have the freshest and most beautiful ingredients brought to life in really elegant dishes. I also like Spain and Hong Kong.

Jeffrey Brana
Private Chef/Consultant

Miami, FL

Restaurant E-mail: jeffreybrana@gmail.com

CHEF FACTS
Cuisine: Contemporary **Born:** 1974 **Began Career:** 1993 **Stages:**
Every stage is important in some respect. I have staged in everything
from a family-run restaurant to a Michelin-starred restaurant, and have
benefited from all in some way. **Work History:** Tampa, FL: Mise en
Place; Coral Gables, FL: Norman's; Coral Gables, FL: Restaurant Brana
Mentor(s): Norman Van Aken **Protégée(s):** When measuring success in
people who have worked under me, I feel I have accomplished my goal
if I have made a difference in their lives or careers, not necessarily by
their rank in the culinary world. **Awards:** 2004 StarChefs.com Rising
Star Chef Miami **Affiliations:** JBF, JLPF, IACP **Languages Spoken:** Some
Spanish, learning Italian

NOTABLE DISH(ES): Foie Gras Croqueta with Creamed Corn Dandelion Greens, Huckleberry; Apala-
chicola Pink Shrimp with Citrus, Avocado and Smoked Trout Roe

FAST FACTS
Restaurant Recs: Hiro's Yakko-San, because it is the late night meeting place for chefs and I've often gone
with my kitchen to celebrate a special event. It's too difficult to choose one favorite dish! **Kitchen Tool(s):**
Chopsticks, because they are used by everyone in the kitchen for everything from cooking to finishing a dish.
They allow us to handle the product with a delicate touch. A farmer takes his or her time and effort to grow,
raise and harvest a particular product, and we should handle that product with the utmost care. **Interview
Question:** What are you reading at the present time? Even the most overworked line cooks can and do find
time to read something. It need not always be a cookbook, though naturally that is what will generally domi-
nate. The process of expanding ones horizons outside of the daily exercise in the kitchen is important. One
must both study about cuisine, but also look down other avenues, which often, when it is least expected,
unlock a door that has been previously closed, either in the process of creativity, culinary technique, or
general thought, all of which are bound together. **Fave Cookbook(s):** Science in the Kitchen and the Art of
Eating Well by Pellegrino Artusi **Chef to Cook for You:** Several years ago, I drove across the country from
California to Florida alone. Though Texas is a bear to drive across, I had the most amazing BBQ in a small
town, barely on the map. I asked a gas station attendant where I could get some good food, and she told me
about her "best friend's daddy" who "owns a BBQ place down the road, behind the tractor and feed store."
I walked up to a smoker filled with brisket, chicken and beef ribs, and was asked to pick out what I wanted.
It was the best meal of a trip in which I sought out the most authentic food I could in each area. So, if I could
have one chef cook for me, it would be the guy who was in charge of that smoker on that day. Not exactly
Thomas Keller, Alain Ducasse or Ferran Adrià, but I would suspect that they would all enjoy the meal as well.
Culinary Travel: I like the San Francisco Bay area. Overseas is great too, but the West Coast is unbelievable.
There is a great attitude, concentrating on the basics of food and wine, including a wonderful diversity.

Sean Brasel
Executive Chef | Touch Restaurant and Lounge

910 Lincoln Rd. Miami Beach, FL 33139

Restaurant E-mail: sbrasel@touchrestaurant.com

Phone: (305) 532-8003

RESTAURANT FACTS
Seats: 180–260 **Weeknight Covers:** Low Season 80-100/High Season 200+ **Weekend Covers:** Low Season 300–400/ High Season 400+ **Check Average (with Wine):** $85 **Tasting Menu:** No **Kitchen Staff:** 12

CHEF FACTS
Other Restaurants: Meat Market, Touch Catering, Touch Kosher Catering, two synagogues **Cuisine:** American-Floridian **Born:** 1968 **Began Career:** 1987 **Stages:** Napa Valley, CA: Auberge du Soleil; New York, NY: Jean-Georges; Chicago, IL: Charlie Palmer **Work History:** Denver, CO: Cliff Youngs, Elios **Mentor(s):** David Query **Affiliations:** I do kosher cooking classes, Dinner in Paradise, and about ten benefits a year **Languages Spoken:** Spanish

NOTABLE DISH(ES): Porcini-Crusted Grouper served on a Goat Cheese Risotto Cake with fresh Baby Clams, Tree Oyster Mushrooms, Baby Tomatoes in a Chipotle Bacon Broth

FAST FACTS
Restaurant Recs: Oshi Thai on Biscayne and 147th **Kitchen Tool(s):** Microplane **Interview Question:** Where have you worked? Where do you want to be in five years? I want chefs who have dreams. **Flavor Combo(s):** Potato and vanilla – it's so diverse **Fave Cookbook(s):** White Heat by Marco Pierre White because it shows how a kitchen really is **Chef to Cook for You:** José Andrés and Katsuya Fukushima – I like they way they are renovating modern Spanish-American cuisine **Culinary Travel:** To China and Vietnam. I like the challenge of taking very cheap ingredients and creating something phenomenal. This is something I strive to do with Mexican-influenced food and would now like to learn how to do with Asian cuisine.

Damien Brassel
Chef/Owner | Knife + Fork

108 E 4th St. New York, NY 10003
Restaurant E-mail: info@knife-fork-nyc.com
Phone: (212) 228-4885

RESTAURANT FACTS
Seats: 36 **Weeknight Covers:** 45–50 **Weekend Covers:** 70–80
Check Average (with Wine): $75–$80 **Tasting Menu:** Yes $45
Kitchen Staff: 1

CHEF FACTS
Cuisine: Modern European **Born:** 1975 **Began Career:** 1989 **Culinary School:** Ballymaloe, Cork, Ireland; The Swiss Hotel Management School, Lucerne, Switzerland **Grad Year:** 1994 **Stages:** England: The Fat Duck **Work History:** Ireland: Peacock Alley; Australia: Tetsuya's **Mentor(s):** Jean-Michel Poulots **Affiliations:** MOW, and other charities **Languages Spoken:** French

NOTABLE DISH(ES): Confit Frog Legs with Squash and Eggplant Purees; Twice Cured Tasmanian Trout with Pickled Cucumber and Wasabi Cream

FAST FACTS
Restaurant Recs: Momofuku – for the veal sweetbreads **Kitchen Tool(s):** Blender – I can't live without it **Interview Question:** I want to know their motivation and ambitions, where do they want to be? **Flavor Combo(s):** Wasabi and white chocolate **Fave Cookbook(s):** Tetsuya by Tetsuya Wakuda **Chef to Cook for You:** Marc Veyrat – his knowledge, inspiration and passion with flavors is unbelievable. He knows how to use herbs on a plate. **Culinary Travel:** I would go to France to go to Michel Bras

Roy Breiman
Culinary Director | Salish Lodge & Spa

6501 Railroad Ave. Snoqualmie, WA 98065

Restaurant E-mail: reservations@salishlodge.com

Phone: (425) 888-2556

RESTAURANT FACTS
Tasting Menu: No **Kitchen Staff:** 21

CHEF FACTS
Cuisine: Season-inspired regional cuisine with French techniques
Born: 1962 **Began Career:** 1985 **Culinary School:** Le Cordon
Rouge, Sausalito, CA **Grad Year:** 1985 **Stages:** France: Les Trois
Marche **Work History:** France: Hotel Nergesco, Chateau Eze, Les
Trois Marche; St. Helena, CA: Meadowood; New York, NY: Maurice
Restaurant **Mentor(s):** Georges Blanc, Dominique Le Stanc, Christian
Delouvrier, Gerard Vie **Protégée(s):** Edward Moro Mirbeau, Chris
Painter **Awards:** 2005 Conde Nast #2 in the USA for Food; 1996 PBS
Rising Star Chef **Affiliations:** Slow Food, Food Lifeline, James Beard Foundation, as well as many local
charities and foundations **Languages Spoken:** French

NOTABLE DISH(ES): Oregon Country Beef Short Ribs with Autumn Fruit Compote

FAST FACTS
Restaurant Recs: Le Pichet for fried eggs with porcini and merguez **Kitchen Tool(s):** Sous-vide machine **Interview Question:** Why do you enjoy cooking? **Flavor Combo(s):** Star anise, vanilla, cinnamon,
and orange zest **Fave Cookbook(s):** The French Laundry Cookbook by Thomas Keller **Chef to Cook
for You:** Fredy Girardet – I've always wanted to eat his food and haven't had the chance **Culinary
Travel:** I've been so many places that as long as it's new it doesn't matter! However, I would like to go
to Australia to explore the indigenous ingredients.

Gabriel Bremer
Chef/Owner | Salts

798 Main St. Cambridge, MA 02139

Phone: (617) 876-8444

RESTAURANT FACTS

Seats: 45 **Weeknight Covers:** 50 **Weekend Covers:** 70 **Check Average (with Wine):** $75 **Tasting Menu:** Yes $110 with wine **Kitchen Staff:** 3

CHEF FACTS

Cuisine: Contemporary French **Born:** 1977 **Began Career:** 1995 **Stages:** Portland, ME: Fore Street; Cambridge, MA: Rialto **Work History:** Portland, ME: Fore Street; Cambridge, MA: Rialto **Mentor(s):** Sam Hayward's executive sous chef, Esau Crosby at Fore Street – he saw that I was a young person at the time who had potential as a gem in the rough. He taught me many things, way more than just technique. **Awards:** 2007 Gayot Rising Chef; 2006 StarChefs.com Rising Star Chef Boston; 2004 Gourmet Magazine Best New Restaurant **Affiliations:** We work with some local charities **Languages Spoken:** Spanish

NOTABLE DISH(ES): Roasted Beet Salad with Goat Cheese Foam and Beet Paper; Sunchoke Soup with Dried Black Olive and Olive Oil

FAST FACTS

Restaurant Recs: Oishi Restaurant for the rock shrimp explosion **Kitchen Tool(s):** The Vita-Prep. I use it for several purees on the menu. I also use it for the soups and some of the emulsions, as well as some herb syrups for pastry. It makes everything absolutely creamy and smooth. **Interview Question:** What made you choose this career? What was your best meal or dining experience that you have had? **Flavor Combo(s):** Savory and sweet **Fave Cookbook(s):** Essential Cuisine by Michel Bras; all the el Bulli books by Ferran Adriá. I just like seeing how we can take those ideas and work them into things here. **Chef to Cook for You:** Albert Adriá because I'm in awe of how unbelievably humble he is about his craft and talent. And we really got along when we hung out! **Culinary Travel:** Spain because there's a large number of people whose food I would love to sample and who I could learn from

B

Stuart Brioza
Executive Chef | Rubicon

558 Sacramento St. San Francisco, CA 94111

Restaurant E-mail: sbrioza@hotmail.com

Phone: (415) 434-4100

RESTAURANT FACTS
Seats: 120 **Weeknight Covers:** 80 **Weekend Covers:** 120 **Check Average (with Wine):** $92 **Tasting Menu:** Yes $82/$152 with wine **Kitchen Staff:** 11

CHEF FACTS
Cuisine: Modern Californian cuisine **Born:** 1974 **Culinary School:** The Culinary Institute of America, Hyde Park, NY **Grad Year:** 1998 **Stages:** France: Michel Rostang **Work History:** Chicago, IL: Park Avenue Café, Savarin; Ellsworth, MI: Tapawingo **Mentor(s):** John Hogan; Harlan "Pete" Peterson; Drew Nieporent; Larry Stone **Protégée(s):** Brett Cooper, Bryce Shuman, Sara Woodward **Awards:** 2005 San Francisco Chronicle Rising Star Chef; 2005 StarChefs.com Rising Star Chef San Francisco; 2003 Food & Wine Best New Chefs **Affiliations:** CUESA

NOTABLE DISH(ES): Cold Terrine Of Guinea Ham with Warm Brioche Butter; Caramelized Garlic Soup with Dungeness Crab, Fennel and Chardonnay Vinegar

FAST FACTS
Restaurant Recs: Great Eastern for minced squab in lettuce cups; Pizzetta 211 for fiore sardo pizza with pine nuts and rosemary. **Kitchen Tool(s):** Vita-Prep for the obvious reasons; saucing spoon because I can and do spend most of my time during service with one in my hand for everything from saucing plate and turning and basting meats, to moving ingredients from pans to the plate, and, most importantly, tasting. **Interview Question:** Tell me, in detail, about the most memorable dish that you have cooked **Flavor Combo(s):** Variatons on butter and vinegar **Fave Cookbook(s):** The Chez Panisse cookbooks for their commitment to understanding ingredients, and Jacques Pépin's Complete Techniques by Jacques Pépin because these were my first cookbooks and I was held accountable for the techniques. I have many favorites and they seem to change a lot. **Chef to Cook for You:** Michel Bras – I really admire his cooking. I ate at his restaurant once and it was amazing; he had the whole family in the kitchen! It was such a great experience, and I would love to repeat it. **Culinary Travel:** Japan – there are certain clean lines to the food and to the way they build a dish with simplicity. I don't know – I don't get it. That's why I want to go, to get it. I want to see how ingredients are dealt with, the minimalism, simplicity, and complexity all at the same time. It is very sincere food.

Chris Broberg
Consulting Pastry Chef

New York, NY 10023

Restaurant E-mail: cwbroberg@yahoo.com

CHEF FACTS
Cuisine: Classics with a twist **Born:** 1962 **Began Career:** 1989 **Culinary School:** Took classes: Cocoa Berry, Pennsauken, NJ; The International School of Confectionary Arts, Gaithersburg, MD; The Culinary School of America, Hyde Park, NY and St. Helena, CA; The French Culinary Institute, New York, NY; The Institute of Culinary Education **Work History:** Philadelphia, PA: Ritz-Carlton, Odeon; Lake Tahoe, NV: Caesars Tahoe; New York, NY: Lespinasse, Petrossian Boutique & Café, The Mark, Café Gray **Mentor(s):** Gary Bachmann, Paula Wolfert, Ian Orr, Phillip Renninger, Francesco Matorelli, Tom Worhach, Gray Kunz **Awards:** 1999, 2000 Pastry Art & Design 10 Best Pastry Chefs **Affiliations:** ACF, JBF, USPA

NOTABLE DISH(ES): Gingerbread House; Pumpkin Cheesecake

FAST FACTS
Restaurant Recs: Sadly to say, I really don't eat out in NYC **Kitchen Tool(s):** Pacojet **Interview Question:** What is your most embarrassing moment professionally? **Flavor Combo(s):** Acids like lemon and kalamansi lime with caramel **Fave Cookbook(s):** Woman's Day Encyclopedia of Cookery by Eileen Tighe **Chef to Cook for You:** This is something I hardly think about as I am so busy with work and family, but I have to say I really would like to try Joël Robuchon's food at his place in Las Vegas **Culinary Travel:** I'd like to go to France again because of the level that they still adhere to culinary tradition

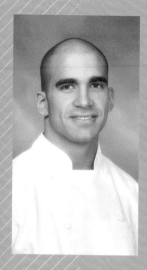

Doug Brown
Chef | Amuse

1326 S. Lamar St. Dallas, TX 75215

Restaurant E-mail: dbrown@foodbeyondthebox.com

Phone: (214) 428-7300

RESTAURANT FACTS
Seats: 70 **Weeknight Covers:** 60 **Weekend Covers:** 120 **Check Average (with Wine):** $50 **Tasting Menu:** No **Kitchen Staff:** 3

CHEF FACTS
Other Restaurants: Beyond the Box Catering, Beyond the Box Weddings **Cuisine:** Italian **Born:** 1973 **Began Career:** 1993 **Culinary School:** The Culinary Institute of America, Hyde Park, NY **Grad Year:** 1995 **Work History:** Miami, FL: Mark's Place, Mark's Las Olas; Dallas, TX: Nana Grill, Landmark Restaurant; Palm Springs, CA: Muriel's Supper Club **Mentor(s):** My mother **Affiliations:** North Texas Food Bank, American Heart Association, March of Dimes

NOTABLE DISH(ES): Salmon Tartare Cones; Osso Bucco with Couscous

FAST FACTS
Restaurant Recs: Vietnam for pho and the amazing $5.60 buffet; Mi Cocina for margaritas **Kitchen Tool(s):** My knife **Interview Question:** What do you want to do? **Flavor Combo(s):** I love to use natural characteristics of fresh fruits with anything to balance out a dish whether it be sweet, acidic or bitter **Fave Cookbook(s):** The French Laundry Cookbook by Thomas Keller; cookbooks by Charlie Trotter **Chef to Cook for You:** My mother – always great, home cooked meals, which is what I crave **Culinary Travel:** I love to go to Napa and Sonoma, so any wine country is great. The focus is all about the food and the wine. It is the entertainment of the day and night.

Frank Brunacci
Executive Chef | Sixteen

401 North Wabash Ave. Chicago, IL 60611

Restaurant E-mail: fbrunacci@trumphotels.com

Phone: (312) 588-8106

RESTAURANT FACTS
Seats: 135 **Weeknight Covers:** 80 **Weekend Covers:** 140 **Check Average (with Wine):** $117 **Tasting Menu:** Yes $82/$110 **Kitchen Staff:** 8–9

CHEF FACTS
Cuisine: Modern American with international accents **Born:** 1970 **Began Career:** 1984 **Culinary School:** William Angliss College, Melbourne, Australia **Grad Year:** 1991 **Work History:** London: Les Saveurs; Atlanta, GA: The Dining Room at the Ritz-Carlton, Buckhead; New Orleans, LA: Victor's; Sedona, AZ: L'Auberge de Sedona; Naples, FL: Caxambas Restaurant **Mentor(s):** Joël Antunes **Awards:** 2003 StarChefs.com Rising Star Chef New Orleans **Affiliations:** St. Jude Children's Hospital **Languages Spoken:** French, a little Spanish

NOTABLE DISH(ES): Duck "Percik," Crisp Polenta, Date & Kumquat Chutney, Black Cumin-Infused Carrot Jus; Diver Scallop, Bang Bang, Fideo, Tomato Gastrique, Sweet Red Onion Heat

FAST FACTS
Restaurant Recs: R&O's in New Orleans, you have to get the Fried Shrimp Po' Boy... delicious **Kitchen Tool(s):** Pasta machine – pasta is a starch that can go on any main course dish I do **Interview Question:** Can you forget everything you have learned and start today on a different journey? **Flavor Combo(s):** Fresh crispy bread and salted butter.... seriously **Fave Cookbook(s):** Essential Cuisine by Michel Bras **Chef to Cook for You:** Michel Bras – I have always been a big fan of his work **Culinary Travel:** Spain, as I have never been. They are combining wonderful flavors right now.

Jeffrey Buben
Chef/Owner | Bistro Bis

15 E St. NW Washington, DC DC 20001
Restaurant E-mail: bis@bistrobis.com
Phone: (202) 661-2700

RESTAURANT FACTS
Seats: 140 **Weeknight Covers:** 175 **Weekend Covers:** 200 **Check Average (with Wine):** $75 **Tasting Menu:** Yes $75 **Kitchen Staff:** 7

CHEF FACTS
Other Restaurants: Vidalia **Cuisine:** Modern American with a Southern accent **Born:** 1958 **Began Career:** 1978 **Culinary School:** The Culinary Institute of America, Hyde Park, NY **Grad Year:** 1978 **Work History:** New York, NY: Le Chantilly, Le Cygne, The Four Seasons Hotel, The Mayflower Hotel, Pierre Hotel, The Sign of the Dove **Mentor(s):** Peter Van Erp **Protégée(s):** RJ Cooper **Awards:** 2002-2007 Washingtonian Magazine Top 100 Restaurants; 1996-2007 Distinguished Restaurants of North America DiRoNA award; 1994-2006 Washingtonian Magazine 4 stars; 2003 Washington Post 3 stars; 2003 The Wine Spectator Award of Excellence; 1999 James Beard Foundation Best Chef Mid-Atlantic; 1996 The Restaurant Association of Metropolitan Washington Chef of the Year; 1993 Bon Appétit Best New Restaurants **Affiliations:** Chef's Alliance, Food & Friends, SOS

NOTABLE DISH(ES): Chesapeake Oyster Toast; Five Onion Soup

FAST FACTS
Restaurant Recs: Taqueria El Michoacano for tongue **Kitchen Tool(s):** Robot-Coupe; sausage maker; hot pan **Interview Question:** How much time are you willing to put into an internship? I ask this because it shows me the applicant's level of dedication and how many sacrifices they are willing to give to further their culinary career. **Flavor Combo(s):** Lemon, butter and thyme **Fave Cookbook(s):** James Beard's American Cookery by James Beard **Chef to Cook for You:** Eric Zeibold – we've worked together so much and I appreciate the combination of wit and groundedness in his food **Culinary Travel:** I'm partial to France – it's just that good. I love the historical aspect of the food, which is so simple yet so difficult.

Thomas Buckley
Executive Chef | Nobu Miami Beach

1901 Collins Avenue Miami Beach, FL 33139

Restaurant E-mail: thomasb@noburestaurants.com

Phone: (305) 695-3232

RESTAURANT FACTS
Seats: 180 **Weeknight Covers:** 250-400 **Weekend Covers:** 450-650 **Check Average (with Wine):** $100 **Tasting Menu:** Yes $110/$150/$200 **Kitchen Staff:** 16-19

CHEF FACTS
Cuisine: Traditional and modern Japanese with Peruvian and European influences **Born:** 1972 **Began Career:** 1990 **Culinary School:** North Yorkshire Coast Technical Institute **Grad Year:** 1990 **Stages:** England: Nobu London; various restaurants in Spain and France **Mentor(s):** Michel Bourdin, Daniel Boulud, Nobu Matsuhisa, and my old French teacher who pushed me to work in France **Affiliations:** Share our Strength, March of Dimes, MOGB Patisserie, Johnson and Wales, AIPT

NOTABLE DISH(ES): Shishito Peppers lightly tempured with Sweet Den Miso Sauce

FAST FACTS
Restaurant Recs: Hiro's Yakko San on 163rd – it's open until 3-4 am. Good, simple, fresh Japanese food. **Kitchen Tool(s):** My voice. Communication is key and with my voice I can guide my team to perform and be extensions of what I want to be achieved. **Interview Question:** Please work a day for free. The proof is in the pudding. It tells me a lot more than any question could. **Flavor Combo(s):** Had dinner at Alinea and there was a dish with lavender and banana – very nice and a new favorite! Usually I stick to classics like coriander seeds with chocolate and caviar with cinnamon (ha)! **Fave Cookbook(s):** Heston Blumenthal's In Search of Perfection – it teaches you to never stop asking why **Chef to Cook for You:** Isabella Beeton – I was introduced to her famous cookbook and it became an instant favorite **Culinary Travel:** I would like to go back to Spain. I've been but I haven't scratched the surface.

David Burke
Executive Chef/Owner | Davidburke & Donatella

131 E 61st St. New York, NY 10021

Restaurant E-mail: david@davidburke.com

Phone: (212) 813-2121

RESTAURANT FACTS
Seats: 110 **Weeknight Covers:** 175 **Weekend Covers:** 225 **Check Average (with Wine):** $100 **Tasting Menu:** Yes **Kitchen Staff:** 8-10

CHEF FACTS
Other Restaurants: Las Vegas, NV: David Burke at Bloomingdale's, David Burke at the Venetian Hotel; Chicago, IL: David Burke's Primehouse; Millburn, NJ: restaurant.mc; Rumson, NJ: The David Burke Fromagerie **Cuisine:** Modern American cuisine **Born:** 1962 **Began Career:** 1982 **Culinary School:** The Culinary Institute of America, Hyde Park, NY; École Lenôtre, France **Grad Year:** 1982 **Stages:** Dallas, TX: Fairmont Hotel, Ratcliff's; Rumson, NJ: La Fromagerie; France: Chez la Mère Blanc, Troisgros Restaurant, Vezelay, L'Esperance **Work History:** Westchester, NY: La CrE-maillere; New York, NY: River Café, Park Avenue Café, Smith & Wollensky Restaurant Group, Daniel Boulud at the Hotel Plaza Athenée **Mentor(s):** Pierre Troisgros, Georges Blanc, Daniel Boulud, Charlie Palmer, Waldy Malouf, Marc Meneau **Protégée(s):** Steve Permaul, Chris Shea, Brad Steelman, Ken Oringer, Joël Reiss, Jason Miller, Scott Ubert, Jerry Hayden, Boy Rob, James Laird, Neil Murphy, John Hogan, Pat Trama, Eric Hara **Awards:** 2006 James Beard Best Chef New York City Nominee, Meilleurs Ouvriers de France, 1998 Chef Magazine of the Year, 1998 The Vatel Club Chef of the year, 1996 and 1997 Robert Mondavi Culinary Award of Excellence, 1995 CIA August Escoffier Award, 1991 Chefs in America Chef of the Year **Affiliations:** RCA **Books Published:** Cooking with David Burke; David Burke's New American Classics

NOTABLE DISH(ES): Salmon Ham; Layer Cake of Lemon Sole

FAST FACTS
Restaurant Recs: Dinosaur BBQ for rubbed ribs with chicken while listening to Sweet Home Alabama **Kitchen Tool(s):** Egg scissors, Himalayan salt blocks **Interview Question:** What was your biggest f*ck up? **Flavor Combo(s):** Sweet and sour; sweet and salty; salt and pepper; zest/aromas; caramelization **Fave Cookbook(s):** Cooking with the Seasons by Jean Louis Palladin **Chef to Cook for You:** Andre Soltner: he is disciplined and classic. I only ate at Lutèce once, and I was a kid. Georges Blanc: I worked for him many years ago and he's a wonderful person and an incredibly talented chef. **Culinary Travel:** I'd like to go to Shanghai and Hong Kong. I never had the opportunity to train there when I was younger. The flavors are so incredibly exotic.

Anne Burrell
Executive Chef | Cento Vinoteca

72 7th Ave. S. New York, NY 10014

Restaurant E-mail: anne@centrovinoteca.com

Phone: (212) 367-7470

RESTAURANT FACTS
Seats: 80 **Weeknight Covers:** 225 **Weekend Covers:** 225 **Check Average (with Wine):** $65–$75 **Tasting Menu:** No **Kitchen Staff:** 5

CHEF FACTS
Other Restaurants: Gusto Ristorante **Cuisine:** Creative Italian **Born:** 1970 **Began Career:** 1989 **Culinary School:** The Culinary Institute of America, Hyde Park, NY **Grad Year:** 1996 **Work History:** Italy: La Taverna del Lupo, La Bottega del'30; New York, NY: Felidia, Savoy, Institute of Culinary Education, Lumi, Italian Wine Merchants **Mentor(s):** Mario Batali, Lidia Bastianich **Awards:** 2008 StarChefs.com Rising Star Chef New York; 2008 Time Out New NY Critic's Choice; 2007 Daily Candy Sweetest Things Taste Winner **Languages Spoken:** Kitchen Spanish, kitchen Italian

NOTABLE DISH(ES): Brined Hampshire Pork Chop Crusted with Fennel Pollen with Bacon, Swiss Chard, Baby Turnips and Crispy Bacon Skin; Braised Oxtail Cakes with Celery Salad and Parmigiano Frico

FAST FACTS
Restaurant Recs: Bone marrow at Blue Ribbon; beef cheek ravioli at Babbo; olive oil gelato at Otto **Kitchen Tool(s):** Wooden spoon **Interview Question:** I ask two questions: what's your favorite cooking technique and what's your favorite ingredient? I like to hear braising and bacon. If they say black pepper, then they don't have a job here. I don't cook with black pepper. **Flavor Combo(s):** Favas and bacon; ramps and bacon, or with anything. Ramps are one of the truly last seasonal things that we have, aside from white truffles. Cheese and anything mushy. And eggs, bacon, and a bit of hot sauce. **Fave Cookbook(s):** I love The Essentials of Classic Italian Cooking by Marcella Hazan; the big Gourmet Cookbook by Ruth Reichl **Chef to Cook for You:** Julia Child **Culinary Travel:** I'm dying to go to Sicily, Tunisia, and Greece for the olive oil cuisine

C

{ Cabrera - Curto-Randazzo }

Alberto Cabrera
Executive Chef | Puro
Miami, FL

Restaurant E-mail: info@albertocabrera.com

CHEF FACTS
Born: 1975 **Began Career:** 1993 **Work History:** Miami: Baleen; Norman's; La Broche; Chispa; Karu & Y **Mentor(s):** Robbin Haas, Norman Van Aken, Angel Palacios **Awards:** 2008 StarChefs.com Rising Star Chef South Florida

NOTABLE DISH(ES): King Crab Salad with Morello Cherry, Fennel, Orange Paper and Cream Cheese Dipping Dots; Boquerones en Escabeche with Heirloom Tomato Tartare, Black Olive Bread Sorbet, Basil Leaves, and Olive Oil Powder

FAST FACTS
Restaurant Recs: Domo Japones – the food and design are great **Kitchen Tool(s):** The Thermomix – it is a great piece of machinery. We use it for everything. **Interview Question:** The simple question is: do you want to cook? Do you want to spend 80 hours a week cooking? It's a simple question. If you aren't prepared to put in the hours, day and night, it's not going to happen. **Flavor Combo(s):** I love the combination of foie gras and coffee. The bitterness and the fattiness go really well together. We get our foie from Hudson Valley Foie Gras, and usually marinate it in Pedro Ximenez. I also like mixing seafood with different charcuteries, like broiled or sous vide cod with Serrano ham. **Fave Cookbook(s):** Clorofilia by Andoni Luis Aduriz; The French Laundry Cookbook; the CIA books; the el Bulli books **Chef to Cook for You:** Ferran Adriá – because you know you're going to see something you've never seen before **Culinary Travel:** Barcelona and Chicago are my two favorite. I also love NYC, but I love it more as a place to eat at small, cultural places. Chicago, to me, is where all the young chefs are and they are doing the most interesting stuff in the country.

Ken Callaghan
Executive Chef | Blue Smoke

116 E 27th St. New York, NY 10016

Restaurant E-mail: kcallaghan@bluesmoke.com

Phone: (212) 447-7479

RESTAURANT FACTS
Seats: 195 **Weeknight Covers:** 400 **Weekend Covers:** 600 **Check Average (w/o Wine):** $40 **Tasting Menu:** No **Kitchen Staff:** 8–10

CHEF FACTS
Other Restaurants: Jazz Standard **Cuisine:** American BBQ **Born:** 1966 **Began Career:** 1986 **Culinary School:** Johnson & Wales, Providence, RI **Grad Year:** 1988 **Work History:** New York, NY: Russian Tea Room, Union Square Café **Mentor(s):** Danny Meyer, Paul Bolles-Beaven, Michael Romano **Affiliations:** SOS, SFA, JBF, Madison Square Park Conservancy, Spoons Across America, Jacob Perlow Hospice Unit, Flatiron Partnership, Jazz at Lincoln Center **Languages Spoken:** Spanish

NOTABLE DISH(ES): Blue Smoke Cole Slaw; Barbecue Ribs

FAST FACTS
Restaurant Recs: Nelly's in Waldwick NJ for the best thin crust pizza **Kitchen Tool(s):** Japanese mandolin **Interview Question:** What unique quality will you bring to the team? This question forces line cooks to think, and usually catches them off-guard. **Flavor Combo(s):** Spicy, sweet and salty – all balanced **Fave Cookbook(s):** Larousse Gastronomique by Prosper Montagne **Chef to Cook for You:** José Andrés – I love his food **Culinary Travel:** Italy – to experience the rustic yet delicious nature of its food. Plus the wines are great!

Joey Campanaro
Chef | Little Owl

90 Bedford St. New York, NY 10014

Restaurant E-mail: joeycampanaro@thelittleowlnyc.com

Phone: (212) 741-4695

RESTAURANT FACTS
Seats: 28 **Weeknight Covers:** 100 **Weekend Covers:** 100 **Check Average (with Wine):** $50–$70 **Tasting Menu:** No **Kitchen Staff:** 3

CHEF FACTS
Cuisine: Seasonal Mediterranean **Born:** 1972 **Stages:** New York, NY: Park Avenue Café **Work History:** New York, NY: The Harrison, Pace, Symphony Café; Los Angeles, CA: Patina, Café Pinot; Universal Studios Executive Dining Room **Mentor(s):** Jonathan Waxman **Affiliations:** Meals-on-Wheels, School Charities **Languages Spoken:** Spanish, Italian, South Philly

NOTABLE DISH(ES): Duck Breast with Arugula, Almonds, Parmesan and Truffle; Potato Gnocchi

FAST FACTS
Restaurant Recs: Decibel – for the wasabi shumai **Kitchen Tool(s):** The hand sink – because my hands are my most important tool and I need to keep them clean **Interview Question:** What was your first job? I look for how long they stayed in each job and what was their reason for leaving. **Flavor Combo(s):** Tomato, pecorino and pork; pork and fennel **Fave Cookbook(s):** The Great American Cook by Jonathan Waxman **Culinary Travel:** Tokyo – I haven't been there yet

Marco Canora
Chef/Owner | Hearth

403 E 12th St. New York, NY 10009

Restaurant E-mail: mcanora@restauarnthearth.com

Phone: (646) 602-1300

RESTAURANT FACTS
Seats: 95 **Weeknight Covers:** 135 **Weekend Covers:** 175 **Check Average (with Wine):** $75–80 **Tasting Menu:** Yes $85 **Kitchen Staff:** 6

CHEF FACTS
Other Restaurants: Insieme, Terroir **Cuisine:** Italian **Born:** 1968 **Began Career:** 1984/1996 **Stages:** Italy: Cibreo **Work History:** New York, NY: Craft, Craftbar, Gramercy Tavern; Martha's Vineyard, MA: La Cucina **Mentor(s):** Fabio Picchi, Tom Colicchio **Awards:** 2005 StarChefs.com Rising Star Chef New York; 2004 James Beard Foundation Best New Restaurant Nominee; 2001 James Beard Foundation Best New Restaurant; 2001 New York Times 3 stars **Affiliations:** We do all sorts of charity events. Children of Bellvue is a big one and we are a part of the Slow Food movement. We just received the "snail of approval," which was pretty cool.

NOTABLE DISH(ES): Fava and Pecorino Salad with Smoked Lamb Tenderloin

FAST FACTS
Restaurant Recs: Al di La for Italian food; Bar Piti for their veal meatballs and bread soup; Café Boulud **Kitchen Tool(s):** Food mill **Interview Question:** I always have them do a trail where I assess knife skills and fundamentals. **Flavor Combo(s):** Rosemary, garlic and lemon **Fave Cookbook(s):** Essentials of Classic Italian Cooking by Marcella Hazan **Chef to Cook for You:** Masa because I love Japanese food and he is the master **Culinary Travel:** Tokyo. I've been there twice. They have a respect for their food that doesn't exist anywhere else. They appreciate subtlety and quality. Also Florence. I love the freshness, the artisan producers.

Homaro Cantu
Chef/Owner | Moto

945 W. Fulton Market Chicago, IL 60607

Restaurant E-mail: hcantu@cantudesigns.com

Phone: (312) 491-0058

RESTAURANT FACTS
Seats: 50–75 **Tasting Menu:** Yes $75/$115/$175 **Kitchen Staff:** 12–16

CHEF FACTS
Cuisine: Post-modern interactive **Born:** 1976 **Began Career:** 1988 **Culinary School:** Le Cordon Bleu, Portland, OR **Grad Year:** 1994 **Stages:** San Francisco, CA: Aqua; Los Angeles, CA: Patina, Citrus; Seattle, WA: Fuller's **Work History:** Chicago, IL: Charlie Trotter's **Mentor(s):** Paul Allen, Stephen Hawking **Awards:** 2005 StarChefs. com Rising Star Chef Chicago; the name "Daddy" **Languages Spoken:** Some Spanish

NOTABLE DISH(ES): Fifty Dollar Maki; Spanish Truffles

FAST FACTS
Restaurant Recs: Sola – for tasty French fries. **Kitchen Tool(s):** Food replicator **Interview Question:** Are you willing to work in both front and back of the house? How do you feel about the job title of gastronomer rather than chef? **Flavor Combo(s):** Pizza, cheeseburger and sushi **Fave Cookbook(s):** The Physiology of Taste by Brillat-Savarin **Chef to Cook for You:** My wife – because she is the greatest cook I know **Culinary Travel:** My backyard, because it doesn't take miles to find good food, and I can enjoy food with my family

Jay Caputo

Chef/Owner | Espuma Restaurant

28 Wilmington Ave. Rehoboth Beach, DE 19971

Restaurant E-mail: jay@espumarestaurant.com

Phone: (302) 227-4199

RESTAURANT FACTS

Seats: 58 **Weeknight Covers:** 50 **Weekend Covers:** 120 **Check Average (with Wine):** $95 **Tasting Menu:** No **Kitchen Staff:** 3

CHEF FACTS

Other Restaurants: Porcini House Bistro **Cuisine:** California-Mediterranean **Born:** 1973 **Began Career:** 1997 **Culinary School:** The Culinary Institute of America, Hyde Park, NY **Grad Year:** 1997 **Stages:** Berkeley, CA: Chez Panisse; Boston, MA: Clio; New York, NY: Union Pacific **Work History:** Boston, MA: Radius; Larkspur, CA: The Lark Creek Inn; San Francisco, CA: Farallon **Mentor(s):** Mark Franz, Christopher Myers, Michael Schlow, Parke Ulrich **Protégée(s):** Chris Conlon, Scott Morozin, Eric Milley **Awards:** 2006 Best of Delaware Best Chef; 2001 DE Today Best New Restaurant on the Beach **Affiliations:** James Beard Foundation **Languages Spoken:** Some Italian, Spanish

NOTABLE DISH(ES): Three-Day Pork with Manchego Fondue, Serrano Ham, Local Green Beans and Whole-Grain Mustard Sauce

FAST FACTS

Restaurant Recs: Prune in New York City for pan-roasted sweetbreads with lemon and capers **Kitchen Tool(s):** Vita-Prep for making the most amazingly textured sauces, soups and purées – sexy food with creamy textures and not all of the fat and cream...not that there is anything wrong with fat and cream! **Interview Question:** Where was the best meal of your life and what made it so spectacular? **Fave Cookbook(s):** The French Laundry Cookbook by Thomas Keller

Floyd Cardoz
Executive Chef | Tabla

11 Madison Ave. New York, NY 10010

Restaurant E-mail: fcardoz@tablany.com

Phone: (212) 889-0667

RESTAURANT FACTS
Seats: 192–264 **Weeknight Covers:** 290/500 **Weekend Covers:** 400–450/750 **Check Average (with Wine):** $45–$92 **Tasting Menu:** Yes **Kitchen Staff:** 7–14

CHEF FACTS
Other Restaurants: Bread Bar **Cuisine:** New Indian **Born:** 1960 **Began Career:** 1986 **Culinary School:** Institute of Hotel Management, India; Taj Hotels Chef-Training Program, India; École Les Roches, Bluche, Switzerland **Grad Year:** 1986 **Stages:** New York, NY: Union Square Café; Gramercy Tavern **Work History:** India: Moghul Room, Kandhar, The Brasserie, Shamiana Restaurant, Rendezvous Restaurant, Tanjore, Taj Mahal Hotel, Orient Express, Casa Medici, Handi Restaurant, Haveli Restaurant; New York, NY: Indian Cafe, Raga, Astor Cour, Beech & Bamboo, Switzerland: Ravis Restaurant, Restaurant Manzinni **Mentor(s):** Gray Kunz **Protégée(s):** Mohan Ismail, Dan Kluger, Ben Pollinger, Andrea Bergquist, Tony Liu, Jason Neroni, Pichet Ong **Awards:** 2004-2007 James Beard Foundation Best Chef New York Nominee; 2000 New York Times 3 stars **Affiliations:** James Beard Foundation **Books Published:** One Spice Two Spice **Languages Spoken:** French, Hindi

NOTABLE DISH(ES): Black Pepper Shrimp with Watermelon and Lime Salad

FAST FACTS
Restaurant Recs: Dosa Hut for mysore masala dosa **Kitchen Tool(s):** Rubbermaid heat resistant spatula because it is great to stir and scrape pots while cooking **Interview Question:** What made you start cooking? This gives them the opportunity to speak about their passion. **Flavor Combo(s):** I love ginger and rosemary **Fave Cookbook(s):** The Cardoz Family Recipes by Beryl Cardoz **Chef to Cook for You:** Gray Kunz. He comes up with the most amazing combinations. **Culinary Travel:** To China. I think Chinese cuisine teaches you to use inexpensive and pedestrian ingredients in creative ways.

Michael Carlson
Chef | Schwa

1466 N. Ashland St. Chicago, IL 60622

Phone: (773) 252-1466

RESTAURANT FACTS
Seats: 26 **Weeknight Covers:** 32 **Weekend Covers:** 32 **Tasting Menu:** Yes $55/$105 **Kitchen Staff:** 4

CHEF FACTS
Cuisine: Contemporary American with Italian influences **Born:** 1974 **Began Career:** 1998 **Culinary School:** The Cooking and Hospitality Institute, Chicago, IL **Stages:** Chicago, IL: Trio; England: The Fat Duck; Italy: San Domenico **Work History:** Chicago, IL: Trio, Spiaggia **Mentor(s):** Grant Achatz **Awards:** 2006 Food & Wine Best New Chef **Languages Spoken:** Some Italian

NOTABLE DISH(ES): Quail Egg Ravioli with Ricotta, Brown Butter, Parmagiano-Reggiano and Sage; Beef in Three Textures – Tartare, Tongue and Short Rib

FAST FACTS
Restaurant Recs: Alinea for the hot and cold potato and just about everything **Kitchen Tool(s):** Dehydrator **Interview Question:** We don't do much hiring, so I can't really think of what question I would ask **Flavor Combo(s):** Talleggio, honey and white truffles **Fave Cookbook(s):** Cookbooks by Michel Bras; cookbooks by Ferran Adriá; The French Laundry Cookbook by Thomas Keller **Chef to Cook for You:** Grant Achatz at Alinea – I just had one of the best meals of my life at his restaurant. I really enjoy his food **Culinary Travel:** Japan, definitely, to see what's going on. Kyoto would be cool.

Andrew Carmellini
Chef | New project in the works for winter 2009

New York, NY

Restaurant E-mail: acarmellini@earthlink.net

CHEF FACTS

Cuisine: Contemporary Italian, but I'm an American Chef who likes food from everywhere. I could work in another kind of restaurant easily, but Italian is my first love. **Began Career:** 1991 **Culinary School:** The Culinary Institute of America, Hyde Park, NY **Grad Year:** 1991 **Work History:** France: L'Arpege; Italy: San Domenico; New York, NY: Café Boulud, La Cirque, A Voce **Mentor(s):** Gray Kunz **Awards:** 2005 James Beard Foundation Best Chef New York City; 2000 Food & Wine Best New Chef; 2000 James Beard Foundation Rising Star **Affiliations:** Some New York cooks and I formed IAFOC (Italian-American Federation of Chefs), but we are only 4 members right now **Books Published:** Urban Italian **Languages Spoken:** French, Italian

NOTABLE DISH(ES): Duck Meatballs

FAST FACTS
Restaurant Recs: Spicy and Tasty for spicy beef tongue, marinated tofu and beans; 300 E 41st St. – I know this restaurant by address not name, and I go here for an amazing authentic Japanese joint with no Eurotech music soundtrack or Sakitinis **Kitchen Tool(s):** Potato masher for the best texture of potatoes, tomatoes, etc. **Interview Question:** Where do you want to be in 5 years? **Flavor Combo(s):** Tomato and chile **Fave Cookbook(s):** La Technique by Jacques Pépin **Chef to Cook for You:** Tough choice. I love to eat and there are a lot of great chefs out there that cook so differently from different parts of the world. There are some various TV "chefs" that call themselves "chefs" that I'd like to see cook a meal. That is what I'd like to see. **Culinary Travel:** I still haven't been to Hokkaido. I'd like to go to Hokkaido and eat some crab.

Edgar Caro
Chef | Baru Bistro

3700 Magazine Street New Orleans, LA 70115

Restaurant E-mail: edgarcaro@hotmail.com

Phone: (504) 895-2225

RESTAURANT FACTS
Seats: 55 **Weekend Covers:** 120 **Check Average (w/o Wine):** $30

CHEF FACTS
Cuisine: Colombian **Born:** 1981 **Began Career:** 2000 **Work History:** New Orleans, LA: Cooter Brown's Tavern, Veracruz, Baru Café **Mentor(s):** My grandmother **Affiliations:** Farmer's markets, and charity events around New Orleans **Languages Spoken:** Spanish

NOTABLE DISH(ES): Grilled Yellowfin Tuna with Sliced Avocado, Tomatoes, Mizuna, and Ginger Vinaigrette

FAST FACTS
Restaurant Recs: Lola's; Rio Mar; Cochon **Kitchen Tool(s):** Tostonera (to make tostones - smashed fried plantains) **Interview Question:** Everyone who interviews gets a trial in the kitchen. The key thing is initiative. I can teach you things, but the willingness to learn is what I want to see. **Flavor Combo(s):** Tuna and avocado; passionfruit and chocolate **Fave Cookbook(s):** Letters to a Young Chef by Daniel Boulud **Chef to Cook for You:** Daniel Boulud – he's one of the chefs who has inspired me to become better and better. I haven't had the chance to meet him. **Culinary Travel:** France, because I want to learn the basics of a the best cuisine

David Andrew Carson
Chef de Cuisine | Quinones at Bacchanalia

1198 Howell Mill Rd. Atlanta, GA 30318

Restaurant E-mail: erin@thereynoldsgroupinc.com

Phone: (404) 365-0410

RESTAURANT FACTS
Seats: 34 **Weeknight Covers:** 32 **Weekend Covers:** 32 **Check Average (with Wine):** $175 **Check Average (w/o Wine):** $125 **Tasting Menu:** Yes **Kitchen Staff:** 4–5

CHEF FACTS
Cuisine: Modern Southern **Born:** 1979 **Began Career:** 1998 **Culinary School:** Johnson & Wales University, Charleston, SC **Grad Year:** 2001 **Stages:** Atlanta, GA: Joël **Work History:** Knoxville, TN: The Orangery; Charleston, SC: Vintage Restaurant; Tristan; Zinc Bistro **Mentor(s):** Anne Quatrano **Languages Spoken:** Some Spanish

NOTABLE DISH(ES): Sweetbread Casserole, Local Beans, House Cured Bacon; Roasted Turkey Consomme, Sage Gnocchi, Shaved Fennel

FAST FACTS
Restaurant Recs: Floataway Café for anything on the menu **Kitchen Tool(s):** Chinois **Interview Question:** Why have you chosen to continue in this profession? **Flavor Combo(s):** Pork and anything **Fave Cookbook(s):** Cooking by Hand by Paul Bertolli **Chef to Cook for You:** Davind Kinch of Manresa because I love Apple Farm **Culinary Travel:** Barcelona to see their style of cuisine

Andrew Carthy
Executive Chef | The Ebbitt Room

25 Jackson St. Cape May, NJ 08204

Restaurant E-mail: acarthy@virginiahotel.com

Phone: (609) 884-5700

RESTAURANT FACTS
Seats: 70 **Weeknight Covers:** 100 **Weekend Covers:** 170 **Check Average (with Wine):** $72 **Check Average (w/o Wine):** $50 **Tasting Menu:** Yes $64 **Kitchen Staff:** 11

CHEF FACTS
Cuisine: Contemporary American **Born:** 1967 **Began Career:** 1996 **Culinary School:** I did not attend culinary school. I learned hands-on. **Work History:** Café at Congress Hall **Mentor(s):** My parents, friends **Protégée(s):** My present staff **Awards:** 2004 American Academy of Hospitality Sciences Four Diamonds; New Jersey Monthly Best of the Best, Top 25 Chefs at the Shore **Affiliations:** JBF, Slow Food, American Heart Association

NOTABLE DISH(ES): Salt-Crusted Muscovy Duck Breast with Dried Cherry and Confit Risotto; Foie Gras and Caramel-Garlic Sauce

FAST FACTS
Restaurant Recs: Blue Pig Tavern for great hamburgers; George's for breakfast **Kitchen Tool(s):** Vita-Prep for smooth purées and soups **Interview Question:** Are you sure you want to do this? **Flavor Combo(s):** I love briny flavors or anything pickled like ramps or carrots – especially when served with a terrine, country bread, and fine Dijon mustard. Oysters are also a favorite. **Fave Cookbook(s):** Anything by Tom Colicchio and Thomas Keller **Chef to Cook for You:** I have always been an admirer of Tom Colicchio's simplistic approach to food and I love the whole Craft concept. And Joël Robuchon, the chef of the century – who else? **Culinary Travel:** Ireland – even though I grew up and lived there until my mid-twenties and I go home every year. I would still like to explore the countryside for its great market towns, restaurants and fresh food. The country has undergone a culinary revolution over the past decade and now hosts some of the finest chefs preparing dishes from some of the highest quality meat, produce and seafood you can get anywhere.

Martin Castillo
Executive Chef/Owner | Limón

524 Valencia St. San Francisco, CA 94110

Restaurant E-mail: martin@limon-sf.com

Phone: (415) 252-0918

RESTAURANT FACTS
Check Average (with Wine): $40 **Tasting Menu:** No

CHEF FACTS
Cuisine: Peruvian **Born:** 1969 **Work History:** Birmingham, AL: Sol y Luna; San Francisco, CA: Rubicon, Pisces **Mentor(s):** My mother **Protégée(s):** Alex Recio **Awards:** 2003 San Francisco Chronicle Rising Star; PromPeru Tourist Bureau Top 40 Peruvian Chefs around the World **Affiliations:** Local Chamber of Commerce **Languages Spoken:** Spanish

NOTABLE DISH(ES): Ceviche Limon; Papa a la Huancaina

FAST FACTS
Restaurant Recs: Slanted Door for the Meyer Ranch shaking beef **Kitchen Tool(s):** Lime squeezer, because many of our food plates have lime and the squeezer facilitates production and better juice extraction **Interview Question:** Are you passionate about food? If they are passionate about food my communication with them is more straightforward, thus we are on the same page when it comes to creating not only a dish, but also an experience. **Fave Cookbook(s):** The Art of Peruvian Cuisine by Tony Custer

C

Anthony Caturano
Executive Chef | Prezza

24 Fleet St. Boston, MA 02113
Restaurant E-mail: hwilson@regancomm.com
Phone: (617) 227-1577

RESTAURANT FACTS
Seats: 98 **Weeknight Covers:** 100 **Weekend Covers:** 200+ **Check Average (with Wine):** $75 **Tasting Menu:** No **Kitchen Staff:** 5

CHEF FACTS
Other Restaurants: Copia **Cuisine:** Italian **Born:** 1973 **Began Career:** 1994 **Culinary School:** The Culinary Institute of America, Hyde Park, NY **Stages:** Charlestown, MA: Olives **Work History:** Charlestown, MA: Olives; Miami, FL: Mark's; Hollywood, CA: Pinot **Mentor(s):** Old chefs that cook simple food from scratch based on tradition **Protégée(s):** All the chefs who have worked in my kitchen, because they put up with me everyday **Affiliations:** We are proud to be affiliated with a number of organizations and charities including: Chefs in Shorts, Dana-Farber Cancer Institute, Greater Boston Food Bank and Franciscan Hospital for Children **Languages Spoken:** Kitchen Spanish

NOTABLE DISH(ES): Arancini

FAST FACTS
Restaurant Recs: Arthur's Deli in Chelsea for a Reuben **Kitchen Tool(s):** Large cooking spoon. When I was working at Olives in Charlestown everyone used it and it was awkward as hell. But once I started using it, I couldn't imagine working without it. I remember using one of those huge kitchen spoons and someone saying "What? This looks like a f***ing cafeteria!" **Interview Question:** Are you fast and can you cook? If they can answer that the right way, usually with a smirk, a simple nod and a yes, then I know I should hire them. **Flavor Combo(s):** My favorite flavor combination is smoke and meat **Fave Cookbook(s):** I have a used cookbook from Piemonte that was written in Dutch. A lot of the pages are missing and I can barely translate it, but the pictures and food look awesome. **Chef to Cook for You:** It would have to be my mom. Her cooking brings me back to my childhood. **Culinary Travel:** I would love to go to Spain because it's similar to Italy, and I haven't been there yet

IAN KITTICHAI

Ian Chalermkittichai
Chef/Owner | Kittichai

60 Thompson St. New York, NY 10012

Phone: (212) 219-2000

RESTAURANT FACTS
Seats: 120 **Weeknight Covers:** 100+ **Weekend Covers:** 300+ **Check Average (w/o Wine):** $62 **Kitchen Staff:** 7-9

CHEF FACTS
Other Restaurants: Barcelona, Spain: Murmuri **Cuisine:** Modern Thai **Born:** 1968 **Began Career:** 1986 **Culinary School:** South East London College; East Sydney Technical School **Grad Year:** 1990 **Stages:** France: George V; Yountville, CA: The French Laundry; Spain: el Bulli; Switzerland: Clinic La Prairie **Work History:** Thailand: Four Seasons; Australia: Claude's **Mentor(s):** My mother **Awards:** 1996 Food Olympics **Affiliations:** Honorary member of the Thai Chefs Association **Languages Spoken:** Thai, Spanglish

FAST FACTS
Restaurant Recs: Street food at the Weekend Market (Chatuchak) in Bangkok **Kitchen Tool(s):** Yanagi knife **Interview Question:** How many hours can you work in a day, a week, and a month? **Flavor Combo(s):** Thai coffee with condensed milk and chili **Chef to Cook for You:** My mother, because I love her food **Culinary Travel:** Japan – this is self-explanatory

Jansen Chan
Pastry Chef | Oceana

55 East 54th St. New York, NY

Restaurant E-mail: jchan@oceanarestaurant.com

RESTAURANT FACTS
Seats: 135 **Weeknight Covers:** 200 **Weekend Covers:** 150 **Check Average (w/o Wine):** $78 **Tasting Menu:** Yes $110 **Kitchen Staff:** 2

CHEF FACTS
Cuisine: Modern American grounded in French technique **Born:** 1975 **Began Career:** 1999 **Culinary School:** Le Cordon Bleu, Paris, France **Grad Year:** 2000 **Work History:** San Francisco, CA: Kuleto's, John Frank, Home, The Fifth Floor, Beaucoup; New York, NY: Essex House, Mix; Las Vegas, NV: Mix**Affiliations:** We participate in numerous fundraisers for groups such as American Cancer Society, SOS, City Harvest, and others

FAST FACTS
Restaurant Recs: When I have time, I enjoy going down to Chinatown to go to such restaurants like Amazing 66 that have very traditional dishes. I also love a good egg custard tart. **Kitchen Tool(s):** Baby offset spatula **Interview Question:** I like to know why each applicant is pursuing a career in pastry. Having good experience in the industry gets you an interview – but I'm looking for more than just a polished resume. I find that passion and drive in your work will overcome any technical weakness. Passion and drive cannot be taught. **Flavor Combo(s):** I think traditional combinations such as rhubarb and strawberry or chocolate and orange are just as interesting as something newer like tarragon and strawberry or chocolate and tea. The problem is traditional combinations are done with less care or forethought than newer ones. Balance and innovation is key. **Fave Cookbook(s):** Le Grand Livre de Cuisine: Desserts and Pastries by Alain Ducasse and Federic Robert **Chef to Cook for You:** I would love to have a dessert created by either Frederic Robert or Nicholas Berger – both worked as Corporate Pastry Chef for all of Alain Ducasse's properties. The inspiration and guidance I had from working at Ducasse was career-altering. **Culinary Travel:** I probably would like to visit East Asian countries to see the different cultures in cooking. It would be a great benefit to learn a different approach to pastry/sweets, using unfamiliar ingredients and philosophy. Learning to make dim sum in Hong Kong or mochi in Tokyo would be an awesome experience.

Richard Chen
Executive Chef | Wing Lei

3131 Las Vegas Blvd. South Las Vegas, NV 89109

Restaurant E-mail: richard.chen@wynnlasvegas.com

Phone: (702) 770-3336

RESTAURANT FACTS
Seats: 120 **Weeknight Covers:** 150 **Weekend Covers:** 220–250
Check Average (with Wine): $145 **Tasting Menu:** Yes **Kitchen Staff:** 12

CHEF FACTS
Cuisine: Asian fusion **Born:** 1964 **Began Career:** 1986 **Culinary School:** The Culinary Institute of America, Hyde Park, NY **Grad Year:** 1986 **Work History:** Chicago, IL: The Ritz-Carlton, Shanghai Terrace at The Peninsula; New York, NY: Vista International Hotel in the World Trade Center **Mentor(s):** Sarah Stegner, Charlie Trotter **Protégée(s):** Gabriel Viti **Awards:** 2005 StarChefs.com Rising Star Chef Las Vegas **Affiliations:** James Beard Foundation **Languages Spoken:** Mandarin Chinese, Taiwanese

NOTABLE DISH(ES): Peking Duck Salad with Orange and Truffle Vinaigrette; Wrapped Bean Curd Sheets with Shiitake Mushrooms

FAST FACTS
Restaurant Recs: Alex's for any of their seafood dishes **Kitchen Tool(s):** Copper pots – for cooking food evenly **Interview Question:** I like to test an applicant for their desire and motivation for the business. **Flavor Combo(s):** I love spicy – spicy with anything **Fave Cookbook(s):** Charlie Trotter's Meat and Game by Charlie Trotter **Chef to Cook for You:** Charlie Trotter – every time I go to his restaurant I am impressed by the consistency and quality of the food **Culinary Travel:** I want to go to New York. It's very competitive. If you are able to survive there you must be doing very well. It's the best of the best.

Alexander Cheswick
Executive Chef/Owner | May Street Market

1132 W Grand Ave. Chicago, IL 60622

Restaurant E-mail: alex@maystreetmarket.com

Phone: (312) 421-5547

RESTAURANT FACTS
Seats: 50–80 **Weeknight Covers:** 60 **Weekend Covers:** 100 **Check Average (with Wine):** $18/$54 **Tasting Menu:** No **Kitchen Staff:** 7–9

CHEF FACTS
Cuisine: Local, seasonal New American **Born:** 1974 **Began Career:** 1995 **Culinary School:** The Culinary Institute of America, Hyde Park, New York **Grad Year:** 1997 **Stages:** Germany: Residenz of Heinz Winkler; Wheeling, Illinois: Le Français; Chicago, Illinois: Tru **Work History:** Germany: Residenz of Heinz Winkler; Wheeling, IL: Le Francais; Chicago, IL: Tru **Mentor(s):** Heinz Winkler, Roland Licioni, Rick Tramonto, Gale Gand **Awards:** 2006 Chicago Tribune; Sun Times; Chicago Social: 3 stars **Affiliations:** We work to support the local farmers and are also involved in Green City Market **Languages Spoken:** German

NOTABLE DISH(ES): Maytag Blue Cheesecake with Rhubarb and Tellicherry Pepper Ragout and Rhubarb Ice; Roasted Venison Medallions in a Pistachio Crust with Chive Spaetzle, Carrot Purée and Lingonberry Sauce

FAST FACTS
Restaurant Recs: Schwa for layered avocado mousse and cauliflower puree, with cauliflower florets and a quenelle of Illinois sturgeon caviar from their tasting menu **Kitchen Tool(s):** My shoes; spoons **Interview Question:** Do you cook on your days off? I want to assess if this person shares the same passion I do. **Flavor Combo(s):** Salty & sweet **Fave Cookbook(s):** Cookbooks by Heinz Winkler **Chef to Cook for You:** Jean-Louis Palladin – I have a signed copy of his book. I am impressed with his free spirit, and there was just something about him that was really cool. **Culinary Travel:** Probably to Peru – the flavors there are really unique and it would be interesting to see how they actually cook there

Gerald Chin
Chef

Las Vegas, NV

Restaurant E-mail: cps98com@hotmail.com

CHEF FACTS
Other Restaurants: Villa Service and private functions **Cuisine:** Market cuisine, seasonal influence with a contemporary twist **Born:** 1980 **Began Career:** 1995 **Culinary School:** The Culinary Institute of America, Hyde Park, NY **Grad Year:** 2001 **Stages:** New York, NY: The Judson Grill **Work History:** Las Vegas, NV: Bradley Ogden, Joël Robuchon at the Mansion MGM Grand; Switzerland: Hotel Intercontinental; Locust Valley, NY: Piping Rock Club; New York, NY: The Judson Grill, Tavern on the Green **Mentor(s):** I have several mentors/teachers that I have had and still have who I can talk to each about different things **Awards:** 2008 StarChefs.com Rising Star Chef Las Vegas; The International Hotel/Motel Restaurant Show Culinary Competition: two 1st place medals **Affiliations:** Right now we have a program set up at The Mansion where we take local culinary school students - they come in for 3 weeks to work in the kitchen, and I work with them one-on-one **Languages Spoken:** Kitchen Spanish and French

NOTABLE DISH(ES): Tonno: Tuna Crudo on Eggplant "Caviar" Tart with Basil Essence; Animelle: Veal Sweetbreads, Morels, Parmesan, Milk Cappuccino, Red Pepper Vinaigrette

FAST FACTS
Restaurant Recs: Lotus of Siam – crispy rice salad is my favorite **Kitchen Tool(s):** Sense of taste because it takes many years of practice to use this "tool" in the kitchen. For a chef, this is one of his/her most valuable tools. **Interview Question:** Where do you see yourself in two years? **Flavor Combo(s):** Sweet and savory **Fave Cookbook(s):** The Food Lover's Companion **Culinary Travel:** I haven't been to Japan, that would be interesting

Vincent Chirico
Chef/Owner | Vincents

225 West 77 St. New York, NY 10023

Restaurant E-mail: info@vincentchirico.com

Phone: (212) 737-7300

RESTAURANT FACTS
Seats: 45 **Check Average (with Wine):** $40 **Tasting Menu:** Yes

CHEF FACTS
Cuisine: Mediterranean **Born:** 1974 **Began Career:** 1995 **Culinary School:** The Culinary Institute of America, Hyde Park, NY **Grad Year:** 1996 **Stages:** France: Georges Blanc **Work History:** France: Georges Blanc; New York, NY: Aquavit, Daniel, Tocqueville, Frederick's **Mentor(s):** Daniel Boulud, Marcus Samuelsson **Protégée(s):** Jimmy Lappalainen **Affiliations:** James Beard Foundation **Languages Spoken:** French, Italian

NOTABLE DISH(ES): King Salmon and Avocado Sushi Roll with Preserved Tomatoes

FAST FACTS
Restaurant Recs: Nino's on Staten Island **Kitchen Tool(s):** Kitchen-Aid **Interview Question:** Why the hell do you want to be in the restaurant business? **Flavor Combo(s):** The contrast of pungent and smooth. For example, soy sauce and great olive oil is a fantastic combination. **Fave Cookbook(s):** The Spirits of Cocktail by Emmanuel Paletz and Rami Rinot **Chef to Cook for You:** My mother – she is the best chef I know **Culinary Travel:** Tuscany

Anthony Chittum
Chef | Vermillion

1120 King St. Alexandria, VA 22314

Restaurant E-mail: manager@vermilionrestaurant.com

Phone: (703) 684-9669

RESTAURANT FACTS
Seats: 90 **Weeknight Covers:** 100–110 **Weekend Covers:** 140
Check Average (with Wine): $62 **Check Average (w/o Wine):** $48
Tasting Menu: Yes $50/$70 with wine **Kitchen Staff:** 7

CHEF FACTS
Cuisine: American Italian **Born:** 1976 **Stages:** New York, NY: Cafe Boulud, Daniel, DB Bistro Moderne; Washington, DC: Galileo **Work History:** San Francisco, CA: Elite Café; Washington, DC: Equinox, Notti Bianchi, Dish **Mentor(s):** Peter McDonuagh showed me that cooking could be a career and Donald Link taught me all about fine dining: how to act in the kitchen, when to talk and when not to, things like that. I worked for Todd Gray for five years and he taught me a lot about the business side of cooking, like watching food costs and the importance of walking through the dining room. He also taught me the importance of proper technique and seasonality. **Awards:** 2006 StarChefs.com Rising Star Chef Washington DC; 2006 RAMW Rising Culinary Star of the Year Nomination; 2005 Washingtonian Best New Restaurant **Affiliations:** SOS; Farm Fresh; DC Central Kitchen **Languages Spoken:** Spanish

NOTABLE DISH(ES): Virginia Rockfish with Celery, Clams and Chowder Froth; Malfatti with Porcini, Mascarpone and Parmesan Cracker

FAST FACTS
Restaurant Recs: I like Sette in DuPont Circle for their prosciutto and arugula pizza and Bistro du Coin for their steak frites **Kitchen Tool(s):** Definitely my fish spatula. It's so versatile. It's slotted so it drains and it's nice and thin so you can get it under things. Donald Link gave it to me. **Interview Question:** What is the best restaurant experience you have had and why? I need to see their passion. **Flavor Combo(s):** I like balance: sweet, sour, salty, and bitter with a little heat. I also like fats with acids. **Fave Cookbook(s):** I like Sauce by James Peterson. He offers techniques for every sauce you can think of and gives shortcuts that don't take away from the final product. **Chef to Cook for You:** Fergus Henderson in London **Culinary Travel:** Spain is blowing up right now!

C

Heather Chittum
Pastry Chef | Hook

3241 M St. NW Washington, DC 20007

Restaurant E-mail: info@hookdc.com

Phone: (202) 625-4488

RESTAURANT FACTS
Seats: 198 **Weeknight Covers:** 200 **Weekend Covers:** 400 **Check Average (with Wine):** $65 **Tasting Menu:** No **Kitchen Staff:** 3

CHEF FACTS
Other Restaurants: Dish and Notti Bianche **Cuisine:** Playful, seasonal American **Born:** 1973 **Began Career:** 2001 **Culinary School:** Fundamentals of Pastry Arts, 20-session program, L' Academie de Cuisine, Gaithersburg, MD **Grad Year:** 2001 **Work History:** Washington, DC: Notti Bianchi, Dish, Equinox, Circle Bistro, Michel Richard Citronelle **Mentor(s):** Lisa Scruggs; Michel Richard **Awards:** 2006 StarChefs.com Rising Star Pastry Chef Washington DC; 2006 Washingtonian Best New Restuarant; 2006 RAMW Pastry Chef of the Year Nomination; 2003 Chaine des Rotisseurs Mid Atlantic Jeune Commis Competition Winner **Affiliations:** SOS **Languages Spoken:** Some Spanish

NOTABLE DISH(ES): Big City S'mores; Goat's Milk Cheesecake with Port Poached Seckel Pears and Almond Florentine

FAST FACTS
Restaurant Recs: Montmartre for any form of their hanger steak **Kitchen Tool(s):** Offset spatula because it is a multitask workhorse. **Interview Question:** What type of desserts do you like better: chocolate or fruit? **Flavor Combo(s):** Caramel and salt **Fave Cookbook(s):** The Last Course by Claudia Fleming **Chef to Cook for You:** Living, it would have to be Thomas Keller – I would love to try his cuisine. Dead, James Beard, for obvious reasons. **Culinary Travel:** I love Italy. Their traditions are very much how I like to eat and cook; with the open markets, the fresh produce, bread and cheese, you can't go wrong.

Kristy Choo
Pastry Chef/Owner | Jin Patisserie

1202 Abbot Kinney Blvd. Venice, CA 90291

Restaurant E-mail: kristy@jinpatisserie.com

Phone: (310) 399-8801

RESTAURANT FACTS
Tasting Menu: No **Kitchen Staff:** 5

CHEF FACTS
Cuisine: Fresh seasonal Kaiseki Japanese cuisine **Born:** 1969 **Began Career:** 1997 **Culinary School:** The California Culinary Academy, San Francisco, CA **Grad Year:** 1997 **Work History:** Singapore: The Raffles Hotel; Malaysia: The Raffles Hotel **Mentor(s):** Kenny Kong **Awards:** 2006 StarChefs.com Rising Star Pastry Chef Los Angeles; 2006 New York, NY Best of Show for Tea Infused Chocolate; 2002 Singapore Hotel Food Asia Silver Medal; 2002 World Cup Culinary Competition **Affiliations:** James Beard Foundation **Languages Spoken:** Mandarin, Cantonese

NOTABLE DISH(ES): Marscapone with Banana and Pistachios; Meringue with Passionfruit Mousse and Mango

FAST FACTS
Restaurant Recs: Manpuku and Torafuku for seaweed salad, prime karubi, kurobuta tonkatsu, and steamed chicken with tofu salad **Kitchen Tool(s):** My palette knife. I use it to level out my mousse, temper my chocolate on a tabletop, and make chocolate garnishes. **Interview Question:** What do you love about making pastries? **Flavor Combo(s):** Sweet and salty; sweet and sour **Fave Cookbook(s):** All cookbooks by Pierre Hermé **Chef to Cook for You:** Joël Robuchon and Gordon Ramsay **Culinary Travel:** Japan – I always love the food, and the ingredients are so fresh. My food has a lot of Japanese influence. Also Paris, of course!

Michael Cimarusti
Executive Chef/Owner | Providence

5955 Melrose Ave. Los Angeles, CA 90038

Restaurant E-mail: michael@providencela.com

Phone: (323) 460-4170

RESTAURANT FACTS
Seats: 90 **Weeknight Covers:** 65–70 **Weekend Covers:** 120 **Check Average (with Wine):** $120 **Tasting Menu:** No $155/$240 with wine **Kitchen Staff:** 8

CHEF FACTS
Cuisine: Modern American **Born:** 1969 **Began Career:** 1990 **Culinary School:** The Culinary Institute of America, Hyde Park, NY **Grad Year:** 1991 **Stages:** France: La Marie **Work History:** New York, NY: An American Place, Le Cirque, Osteria Del Circo; New Hope, PA: The Forager House Restaurant; Los Angeles, CA: Spago **Mentor(s):** My father, Sottah Khunn, Sylvain Portay, Dick Barrows **Protégée(s):** Paul Shoemaker **Awards:** 2006 James Beard Foundation Best New Restaurant Nominee; 2004 StarChefs. com Rising Star Chef Los Angeles **Affiliations:** We work with a lot of charities. We also do a lot with the Beard House and the CIA.

NOTABLE DISH(ES): Foie Gras Torchon with Asian Pear; Terrine of Octopus Infused with Fresh Chamomile with a Chamomile Vinaigrette

FAST FACTS
Restaurant Recs: Cut for the kobe beef rib-eye **Kitchen Tool(s):** Bamix immersion blender **Interview Question:** What is your motivation? What brings you to my door? How do you feel about sweeping and mopping? **Flavor Combo(s):** Burdock and shiso **Fave Cookbook(s):** Essential Cuisine by Michel Bras; The Notebooks of Michel Bras: Desserts by Michel Bras **Chef to Cook for You:** Michel Bras – I've always admired his work **Culinary Travel:** San Sebastian and the Tsukiji fish market in Toyko

Katherine Clapner
Pastry Chef | Stephan Pyles

1807 Rose Ave. Ste. 200 Dallas, TX 75201

Restaurant E-mail: kclapner@stephanpyles.com

Phone: (469) 232-9151

RESTAURANT FACTS
Seats: 160–220 **Weeknight Covers:** 150 **Weekend Covers:** 250
Check Average (with Wine): $100 **Check Average (w/o Wine):** $85
Tasting Menu: No **Kitchen Staff:** 5

CHEF FACTS
Cuisine: Pastry **Born:** 1964 **Began Career:** 1985 **Culinary School:** The Culinary Institute of America, Hyde Park, NY **Grad Year:** 1989 **Stages:** England: The Savoy **Work History:** New Orleans, LA: Windsor Court Hotel; Chicago, IL: Charlie Trotter's, Bread with Appeal; Dallas, TX: Star Canyon, Aquanox, Central Market **Mentor(s):** Shayne Gorring, Stephan Pyles **Awards:** 2007 StarChefs.com Rising Star Pastry Chef Dallas **Affiliations:** We are closely affiliated with Share our Strength, Meals-on-Wheels, and Stephan has his own culinary scholarship program. I was with the Texas Hill Country Wine and Food Festival for several years as well. We also donate to several charities in the city. **Languages Spoken:** Spanish

NOTABLE DISH(ES): Meyer Lemon Pudding with Blackberry Upside Down Cake and Fennel Pollen-Huckleberry Ice Cream; Fresh Ricotta Cheesecake with Brown Butter-Vanilla Pears, Saffron Anglaise, and Black Currant Sorbet

FAST FACTS
Restaurant Recs: York Street for absolutely fantastic food **Kitchen Tool(s):** Silpat; mandolin; small ice-cream scoop – I go nuts if I can't find it **Interview Question:** I like to find out about their personality because skills can be learned, but personality can't **Flavor Combo(s):** Salt and chocolate; yeast and strawberries; corn (Peruvian), cream and fennel pollen; fenugreek or curry and dark berries **Fave Cookbook(s):** New International Confectioner by Wilfred Fance **Chef to Cook for You:** Heston Blumenthal, because his approach is very modern but with a tremendous respect for tradition, which I think is getting lost in the molecular jungle these days **Culinary Travel:** Peru, Spain and Morocco – that needs no explanation

C

Greg Cole
Chef | Cole's Chop House

1122 Main St. Napa, CA 94559

Restaurant E-mail: greg@coleschophouse.com

Phone: (707) 224-6328

RESTAURANT FACTS
Seats: 100–130 **Weeknight Covers:** 140 **Weekend Covers:** 200 **Check Average (with Wine):** $65–$70 **Tasting Menu:** No **Kitchen Staff:** 5

CHEF FACTS
Other Restaurants: Celadon **Cuisine:** Classic American steak and global comfort food **Born:** 1962 **Culinary School:** The Culinary Institute of America, Hyde Park, NY **Grad Year:** 1983 **Stages:** Yountville, CA: Domaine Chandon **Work History:** Reno, NV: Harrah's; Yountville, CA: Domaine Chandon; Sonoma, CA: Piatti **Mentor(s):** Phillipe Jeanty, Roland Henin **Protégée(s):** Jesus Mendez, Marcos Uribe **Awards:** 2006 Wine Spectator Award of Excellence; 2006 Zagat Best Steakhouse in Bay Area **Affiliations:** We support many local charities **Languages Spoken:** Some Spanish

NOTABLE DISH(ES): Fried Calamari with Chipotle Glaze and Pickled Ginger

FAST FACTS
Restaurant Recs: Foothill Cafe for prime rib **Kitchen Tool(s):** Robot Coupe R2, because it is so versatile and dependable **Interview Question:** Why do you cook? What do you love about cooking? **Flavor Combo(s):** Rosemary and pink grapefruit; lemon and tarragon; plums and Pinot Noir **Fave Cookbook(s):** James Beard's American Cookery by James Beard **Chef to Cook for You:** Renée Verdon – he was the White House chef for the Kennedys. I would like to try the food of Camelot. **Culinary Travel:** Vietnam – I've never been and I just love the flavors and the cuisine, and would like to see and taste the colonial French influences

Tyson Cole
Executive Chef | Uchi

801 South Lamar Austin, TX 78704

Restaurant E-mail: info@uchiaustin.com

Phone: (512) 916-4808

RESTAURANT FACTS
Seats: 96 **Weeknight Covers:** 250 **Weekend Covers:** 300+ **Check Average (with Wine):** $120 **Check Average (w/o Wine):** $80 **Tasting Menu:** Yes $200 for two **Kitchen Staff:** 10–13

CHEF FACTS
Cuisine: Modern seasonal Japanese **Born:** 1970 **Began Career:** 1992 **Work History:** Austin, TX: Musashino; New York, NY: Bond Street **Mentor(s):** Takehiko Fuse, Ted Kasuga **Awards:** 2005-2008 Austin Chronicle Best Chef in Austin; 2005 Food and Wine Magazine's Best New Chefs **Languages Spoken:** Japanese, kitchen Spanish

NOTABLE DISH(ES): Japanese Oak Charcoal Grilled Wagyu Flat Iron Steak with Red Miso and Candied Garlic; Bluefin Tuna Collar Sashimi with Golden Currants, White Soy and Marcona Almonds

FAST FACTS
Restaurant Recs: Tam's deli – I get the #36 soft rice noodle with pork; Madam Mam's – for the G4 grilled pork with egg noodles, sugar and Thai fish sauce **Kitchen Tool(s):** Single-edge Japanese blades **Interview Question:** "What's your incentive to do this?" This tells a lot of someone's goals and character. **Flavor Combo(s):** Acidity and fat **Fave Cookbook(s):** Essential Cuisine by Michel Bras **Chef to Cook for You:** Mario Batali. His food is simple, flavorful and delicious. He utilizes acidity in many similar ways as I do. **Culinary Travel:** Europe – I want to go all over the Iberian peninsula to see Spain and Portugal. Catalan cuisine has had a large influence on me lately, but the vast variations of cuisine styles throughout the region is spectacular.

David Coleman
Chef de Cuisine | Toqueville

1 East 15th Street New York, NY 10003

Restaurant E-mail: toqueville15@aol.com

Phone: (212) 675-4908

RESTAURANT FACTS

Seats: 65 **Weeknight Covers:** 75 **Weekend Covers:** 90 **Check Average (with Wine):** $150 **Check Average (w/o Wine):** $75 **Tasting Menu:** No **Kitchen Staff:** 9

CHEF FACTS

Cuisine: French American **Born:** 1972 **Began Career:** 1987 **Culinary School:** The Culinary Institute of America, Hyde Park, NY **Grad Year:** 1992 **Stages:** New York, NY: The Mark **Work History:** New York, NY: The Mark, Union Pacific, Atlas, Kokachin, CT Restaurant; Portland, OR: The Heathman Hotel **Mentor(s):** Gray Kunz, Rocco Di Spirito

NOTABLE DISH(ES): Charred Octopus with Feta, Watermelon and Fresh Watermelon Soup

FAST FACTS

Restaurant Recs: 1492 on Clinton for the bacon-wrapped dates, the croquetas and the gambas with garlic and olives **Kitchen Tool(s):** My Misono knives, especially the carbon steel knife **Interview Question:** For me it is all about their energy. When they trail I see how they handle products and what questions they ask. **Flavor Combo(s):** Sweet and sour; chocolate with mint and foie gras **Fave Cookbook(s):** Cooking with the Seasons by Jean-Louis Palladin **Chef to Cook for You:** My grandmother – I would have her make gefilte fish, chopped liver and matzo pancakes **Culinary Travel:** Vietnam – the food is so clean and light

Tom Colicchio
Chef/Owner | Craft

47 E. 19th St. New York, NY 10003

Restaurant E-mail: tcolicchio@craftrestaurant.com

Phone: (212) 780-0880

RESTAURANT FACTS
Seats: 103 **Weeknight Covers:** 120–160 **Weekend Covers:** 200+
Check Average (with Wine): $100 **Tasting Menu:** Yes $110/$185
with wine **Kitchen Staff:** 10

CHEF FACTS
Other Restaurants: New York, NY: Craftbar, Craft, Craftsteak,
'Wichcraft; Dallas, TX; Craft; Las Vegas, NV: Craftsteak **Cuisine:** New
American cuisine **Born:** 1962 **Began Career:** 1980 **Stages:** France:
Michel Bras **Work History:** New York; NY: The Gotham Bar and Grill,
Mondrian, The Quilted Giraffe, Rakel, Gramercy Tavern **Mentor(s):** No
mentors per se, although I taught myself how to cook from Jacques
Pépin's manuals on French cooking: La Technique and La Méthode **Protégée(s):** Damon Wise, Marco
Canora, Akhtar Nawab, John Schaffer, Jon Benno **Awards:** 2002 Bon Appétit and the Food Network
Chef of the Year; 2000 James Beard Foundation Best Chef New York City; 1991 Food & Wine Best
New Chef **Affiliations:** COB, DOW **Books Published:** Think Like a Chef; Craft of Cooking: Notes and
Recipes from a Restaurant Kitchen

NOTABLE DISH(ES): Seared Tuna with Roasted Tomato Vinaigrette and Fennel Salad

FAST FACTS
Restaurant Recs: Spirito's, an Italian joint in Elizabeth, NJ **Kitchen Tool(s):** Sharp knives **Interview
Question:** Why did you start cooking? **Fave Cookbook(s):** La Technique by Jacques Pépin **Chef to
Cook for You:** Pierre Gagnaire **Culinary Travel:** Southeast Asia – specifically Vietnam and Thailand

Jose

Joseph Comfort
Executive Chef/Managing Partner | Iron Horse

100 South Railroad Ave. Ashland, VA 23005
Restaurant E-mail: ironhorse.ashland@comcast.net
Phone: (804) 752-6410

RESTAURANT FACTS
Seats: 140 **Weeknight Covers:** 100+ **Weekend Covers:** 250+ **Check Average (with Wine):** $35 **Tasting Menu:** No **Kitchen Staff:** 5

CHEF FACTS
Cuisine: Seasonal Southern American brasserie with wild game
Born: 1967 **Began Career:** 1993 **Work History:** Washington, DC:
Poste Moderne Brasserie, Red Sage/Chile Bar, Sutton Place Gourmet, Dean & Deluca; Fredericksburg, VA: Bistro 309 **Mentor(s):** Mark Miller, Bill Phillips, Neal Corman **Protégée(s):** Terrence Sullivan, Blake Bethem **Affiliations:** American Institute of Wine and Food **Languages Spoken:** French, Spanish

NOTABLE DISH(ES): Rabbit Fennel Sausage with Sweet Potato Purée and Apple; Pan Roasted Rockfish with Braised Artichoke-Leek Relish and Olive Oil Cured Olive Tapenade

FAST FACTS
Restaurant Recs: Kuba Kuba for huevos rancheros and tres leches cake. Muy Cubano! **Kitchen Tool(s):** German-made cherry pitter, Microplane, stainless steel truffle shaver, which mostly doesn't shave truffles **Interview Question:** Are you ready for a long-term relationship? You're going to have one with me. Our restaurant is not a one-night stand. Many line cooks I interview say that they are "really eager to learn everything I can" and that is a great quality in an employee. As a chef and culinary mentor I do look for people that I can help to mold and further their knowledge. But, as a businessman, I have to be conscious of return on my investment; line cooks, sous chefs and even executive chefs must be mindful that employers and business partners are looking at the balance sheet and what their employees, as assets, bring to that equation. **Flavor Combo(s):** Lime, basil and cilantro; black pepper and cherry **Fave Cookbook(s):** Cooking by Hand by Paul Bertolli; Paul's sensitivity to process and terroir with regard to food is peerless. **Chef to Cook for You:** Michel Bras – because he's Michel Bras! **Culinary Travel:** The Middle East because as Americans I don't think we're familiar enough with the bitter flavors of that region. We tend to be romanced by sweet and fat.

Tom Condron
Chef | Mimosa Grill

327 Tryon St. Charlotte, NC 28202

Restaurant E-mail: condron@harpers-rest.com

Phone: (704) 343-0700

RESTAURANT FACTS
Seats: 240 **Weeknight Covers:** Lunch: 350 Dinner: 250 **Weekend Covers:** 275 **Check Average (with Wine):** $75 **Check Average (w/o Wine):** $50 **Tasting Menu:** No **Kitchen Staff:** 10

CHEF FACTS
Other Restaurants: Arpa Tapas Bar, Upstream, Zink American Kitchen **Cuisine:** Southern American with an emphasis on seafood **Born:** 1962 **Began Career:** 1988 **Culinary School:** Johnson & Wales University, Providence, RI **Grad Year:** 1988 **Stages:** England: Dorchester Hotel **Work History:** Washington DC: Jean-Louis at The Watergate; New York, NY: Le Cirque; San Francisco, CA: Aqua; Orlando, FL: Peabody Hotel **Mentor(s):** Jean-Louis Palladin **Protégée(s):** Gene Kato **Affiliations:** ACF, SOS, Southern Food Ways, Hospitality Association of Charlotte, Muscular Dystrophy Association **Languages Spoken:** French, Celtic, some Italian

NOTABLE DISH(ES): Smoked Trout with Jumbo Lump Crab Cakes and Cracked Mustard Sauce

FAST FACTS
Restaurant Recs: Illios Noche for roasted whole fish **Kitchen Tool(s):** Japanese mandolin **Interview Question:** What is your passion? **Flavor Combo(s):** Seasonally inspired flavors, like morel mushrooms with fava beans, spring onions and baby carrots **Fave Cookbook(s):** Boulevard by Nancy Oakes **Chef to Cook for You:** Marco Pierre White – his food is spot-on and his passion is intense **Culinary Travel:** India – I love the combination of rich spices and techniques in cooking

Clay Conley
Chef | Azul

500 Brickell Key Dr. Miami, FL 33131

Restaurant E-mail: cconley@mohg.com

Phone: (305) 913-8308

RESTAURANT FACTS
Seats: 120 **Weeknight Covers:** 120 **Weekend Covers:** 140 **Check Average (with Wine):** $100–$110 **Tasting Menu:** Yes $95 **Kitchen Staff:** 8

CHEF FACTS
Cuisine: Asian-influenced Mediterranean **Born:** 1974 **Began Career:** 1988 **Culinary School:** The school of hard knocks, baby! **Stages:** Waterboro, ME: Willy's Pizza **Work History:** Culinary Director of Olives Restaurants - so every Olives around the world **Mentor(s):** Todd English, Michael Mina, Gary Mennie **Awards:** 2008 StarChefs.com Rising Star Chef South Florida **Affiliations:** We do a lot of charity events **Languages Spoken:** Spanish, some Japanese

NOTABLE DISH(ES): Moroccan-Inspired Lamb: Harissa Marinated Loin, Shank Bastilla, Raita, Grilled Chop, Pepper Salad; Orchiette Nero: Turks and Caicos Conch, Hot Italian Sausage, Native Basil and Roasted Tomato

FAST FACTS
Restaurant Recs: Puerto Sagua for ropa vieja **Kitchen Tool(s):** My hands; Japanese steel knives; a large spoon; tasting and plating spoons **Interview Question:** If I called your old kitchen, what would they (not just your boss) say about you? **Flavor Combo(s):** Ginger, sesame, soy, yuzu, and aji amarillo **Fave Cookbook(s):** The French Laundry Cookbook by Thomas Keller; Mediterranean Feast by Clifford Wright **Chef to Cook for You:** I grew up in Maine, and I sometimes miss the food of my youth - so Jasper White would be my chef of choice. I still think about the lobster tamale toast he cooked for me years ago. **Culinary Travel:** Probably Vietnam. I've traveled all through Asia but that's one place I missed. Working in Tokyo influenced my cooking and the way I treat ingredients. They won't serve anything that isn't ripe and at the perfect height of its season. The food is simple and flavorful, and the fish market is fantastic for any chef or anyone in the industry.

Steve Connaughton
Executive Chef | Bar Milano

323 Third Ave. New York, NY 10010

Restaurant E-mail: sconnaughton@gmail.com

Phone: (212) 683-3035

RESTAURANT FACTS
Seats: 90 **Weeknight Covers:** 200 **Weekend Covers:** 200 **Check Average (with Wine):** $60–$70 **Tasting Menu:** Yes $85/$160 with wine **Kitchen Staff:** 8

CHEF FACTS
Born: 1974 **Began Career:** 1999 **Work History:** Washington, D.C: Tabard Inn, Pêche; New York, NY: Atlas, Lupa, 'inoteca **Mentor(s):** David Craig, Mark Ladner, Mario Batali **Affiliations:** We do our usual charities for women's shelters in the Bronx, cancer research, and all the bigger charities **Languages Spoken:** Kitchen Spanish

NOTABLE DISH(ES): Coniglio Fritto: Fried Rabbit with Dried Apricots and Carrots; Borsetti alla Pizzocheri: Potato-Filled Buckwheat Pasta with Cabbage and Speck

FAST FACTS
Restaurant Recs: Café al Portal for cheap Mexican food and margaritas; The Mermaid Inn in the East Village; Curry row in the East Village **Kitchen Tool(s):** A good pair of tongs is underrated **Interview Question:** I look at what the candidate aspires to, what they are looking for, and what they want from the restaurant. A few years from now I want to have people that have come from Bar Milano working in good restaurants. **Flavor Combo(s):** Earthiness and smokiness; buckwheat flour and speck **Fave Cookbook(s):** The Food of Rome and Lazio **Chef to Cook for You:** I'd have Jean-Louis Palladin cook for me. He was one of the early contacts of my career. **Culinary Travel:** Culinarily speaking, China would be a big choice for any cook. I'd like to see what kind of cooking they do over there.

Tony Conte
Chef | The Oval Room

800 Connecticut Ave. NW Washington, DC 20006

Restaurant E-mail: ovalroom@ovalroom.com

Phone: (202) 463-8700

RESTAURANT FACTS

Seats: 90 **Weeknight Covers:** 60–70 **Weekend Covers:** 100 **Check Average (with Wine):** $70 **Tasting Menu:** Yes $75/$115 with Wine **Kitchen Staff:** 7

CHEF FACTS

Cuisine: American **Born:** 1972 **Began Career:** 1992 **Culinary School:** The Culinary Institute of America, Hyde Park, NY **Grad Year:** 1992 **Stages:** New York, NY: wd~50, Bouley, Le Bernardin **Work History:** New York, NY: Jo Jo; Greenwich, CT: Sole e Luna Ristorante; Greenwich Country Club; Belmont, Massachusetts: Belmont Country Club **Mentor(s):** Jean-Georges Vongerichten; Eugene Gerome **Awards:** 2006 StarChefs.com Rising Star Chef Washington DC; 2002 Connecticut Magazine Best New Restaurant **Languages Spoken:** Italian, Kitchen Spanish

NOTABLE DISH(ES): Tuna, Chipotle, Avocado, and Crispy Tapioca; Roasted Baby Beets, Passion Fruit Gelée, Horseradish, and Ice Wine Mignonette

FAST FACTS

Restaurant Recs: Two Amy's for the best pizza in town **Kitchen Tool(s):** Vita-Prep **Interview Question:** I really just want to see them in the kitchen and get a sense for their comfort level **Flavor Combo(s):** Just what feels right in the moment. I also use Thai chiles with everything. **Fave Cookbook(s):** Whatever I'm reading right now. I buy a lot of cookbooks and read them cover to cover but I usually don't look at them again. **Chef to Cook for You:** I have heard nothing but phenomenal things about David Bouley. I have had his food but never actually in Bouley, and I would love to have a meal by him. **Culinary Travel:** I like New York and Boston. San Francisco has great Italian food and I like the Latin influence of cuisine in Miami.

RJ Cooper
Chef | Vidalia

1990 M St. NW Washington, DC 20036

Restaurant E-mail: rjcooper@vidaliadc.com

Phone: (202) 659-1990

RESTAURANT FACTS
Seats: 130 **Weeknight Covers:** 130 **Weekend Covers:** 180 **Check Average (w/o Wine):** $105 **Tasting Menu:** Yes $85 **Kitchen Staff:** 8–12

CHEF FACTS
Other Restaurants: Bistro Bis **Cuisine:** Contemporary American with Southern influence **Born:** 1968 **Began Career:** 1992 **Culinary School:** Kendall College, Evanston, IL **Grad Year:** 1992 **Work History:** Atlanta, GA: The Ritz-Carlton Atlanta, The Ritz-Carlton Buckhead, Brasserie LeCoze; New York, NY: Le Bernardin; Anchorage, AK: Crow's Nest Restaurant; Washington, DC: New Heights, Toka Café **Mentor(s):** Jeff Buben, Eric Ripert **Awards:** 2007 James Beard Best Chef Mid-Atlantic; 2006 StarChefs.com Rising Star Chef Washington DC; 2006 Tom Sietsema Dining Guide 3 stars **Affiliations:** CCAN **Languages Spoken:** Some Spanish

NOTABLE DISH(ES): Truffled Heirloom Potatoes with Crispy Pork Belly, Garlic Cream, Juniper Infused Salt; Beaver Creek Farm Quail with Chestnut, Wild Rice, Apple Stuffing, Boudin Blanc, Brussels Sprouts

FAST FACTS
Restaurant Recs: Ben's Chili Bowl for half smoked with chili and onions **Kitchen Tool(s):** Cryovac® because it keeps a pristine product fresh and the alternative methods are endless **Interview Question:** Which modern chefs are your heroes? This tells me where the cook wants to be in is his career. **Flavor Combo(s):** Huckleberry and horseradish, which is sweet and spicy. I also like plum and mustard and fall fruit with spice. **Fave Cookbook(s):** Happy in the Kitchen: The Craft of Cooking, the Art of Eating by Michel Richard **Chef to Cook for You:** Johnny Monis of Komi. He's doing some really soulful food and really sticking to the concept of local. **Culinary Travel:** China because I've never been and Eric Zeibold keeps teasing me about it

Bill Corbett
Pastry Chef | Michael Mina, Westin St. Francis

335 Powell St. San Francisco, CA 94102

Restaurant E-mail: kmclarty@minagroup.net

Phone: (415) 397-9222

RESTAURANT FACTS
Seats: 100 **Weeknight Covers:** 100–160 **Weekend Covers:** 150–200 **Tasting Menu:** Yes $98/$135 **Kitchen Staff:** 3–4

CHEF FACTS
Cuisine: New American **Born:** 1974 **Began Career:** Started Pastry in 2004 **Stages:** New York, NY: Jean Georges, wd~50 **Work History:** New York, NY: B.R. Guest Restaurants, Dona, wd~50, Anthos **Mentor(s):** Lincoln Carson; Sam Mason; Wylie Dufresne **Awards:** 2007 StarChefs.com Rising Star Pastry Chef New York **Languages Spoken:** French and kitchen Spanish

NOTABLE DISH(ES): Sesame Composition: Sesame Ice Cream, Metaxa Caramel Halva, Black Sesame Pasteli, Tahini Ganache; Bougatza: Goat Cheese Cake with Rhubarb Goat Milk Caramel and Kataifi

FAST FACTS
Restaurant Recs: In New York: Nicky's Vietnamese Sandwiches; Oasis in Williamsburg; Lily Thai for their Panang Curry **Kitchen Tool(s):** Deglon 11-inch offset spatula **Interview Question:** Do you have passion? Do you want to learn? **Flavor Combo(s):** I really like savory spices with chocolate, like curries and earthy Moroccan spices **Fave Cookbook(s):** Au Coeur des Saveurs by Frederic Bau; Essential Cuisine by Michel Bras; Anything by Pierre Hermé **Chef to Cook for You:** Probably Adoni Luis Aduriz because I really like the way he blends the old technique with the new technique while staying grounded and balanced. He really respects the local food and cooking with the seasons. **Culinary Travel:** My sous chef is Thai and I really want to go to Thailand. I'd like to find some new produce over there to use.

Richard J. Corbo
Executive Chef | Ducca

50 Third St. San Francisco, CA 94103

Restaurant E-mail: rcorbo@duccasf.com

Phone: (415) 977-0271

RESTAURANT FACTS
Seats: 100–200 **Weeknight Covers:** 80–120 **Weekend Covers:** 100–180 **Check Average (w/o Wine):** $48 **Tasting Menu:** Yes **Kitchen Staff:** 10

CHEF FACTS
Cuisine: Italian cuisine **Born:** 1978 **Began Career:** 1996 **Culinary School:** Apicius Culinary School, Italy **Stages:** Italy: Bronzino **Work History:** Boston, MA: Tremont 647; New York, NY: Union Square Café; San Francisco, CA: Restaurant Gary Danko, Mecca **Mentor(s):** Joseph Pisacreta, Michael Romano, Sal Chiarella, Gary Danko **Protégée(s):** Benjamin Parks, Orlando Pagan, Jack Lupertino, Benjamin Plung **Awards:** 2008 San Francisco Chronicle Rising Star **Affiliations:** Slow Food **Languages Spoken:** Italian, Spanish

NOTABLE DISH(ES): Tortellone in Brodo; "Uncooked" Tuna Ceviche

FAST FACTS
Restaurant Recs: Shanghai Dumpling King **Kitchen Tool(s):** Wood. There is nothing that I enjoy more than to be able to cook natural, organic and heirloom food products with a natural fuel source, in a wood burning oven, grill, or even a rotisserie. **Interview Question:** Where have you eaten recently? **Flavor Combo(s):** Anise and orange; cocoa and game; truffle and egg; vanilla and saffron... just to name a few **Fave Cookbook(s):** Cucina of Le Marche by Fabio Trabbocchi, and Le Calandre by Massimiliano and Raffaele Alajmo **Chef to Cook for You:** Chef Massimiliano Alajmo of Le Calandre. It seems like he really puts his whole life into his dishes. **Culinary Travel:** My next food trip will be to the southern states of Italy - Puglia and Calabria - and the islands – Sicily, Sardinia, Pantelleria. My cuisine is fundamentally built on my knowledge of regional Italian cuisine and these are the only areas of Italy as of yet personally unexplored.

C

Chris Cosentino
Chef | Incanto

1550 Church St. San Francisco, CA 94131

Restaurant E-mail: chris@incanto.biz

Phone: (415) 641-4500

RESTAURANT FACTS
Seats: 100 **Weeknight Covers:** 120 **Weekend Covers:** 189 **Check Average (with Wine):** $58 **Tasting Menu:** Yes Offal tasting $75 **Kitchen Staff:** 4

CHEF FACTS
Other Restaurants: Oakland, CA: Boccalone Artisan Meats **Cuisine:** Traditional Italian focusing on sustainable eating, and offal cookery **Born:** 1972 **Began Career:** 1994 **Culinary School:** Johnson & Wales University, RI **Grad Year:** 1994 **Stages:** England: La Tante Claire, Passione, St. John Bar and Restaurant, 15 **Work History:** Berkeley, CA: Chez Panisse; Las Vegas, NV: Michael Mina's Aqua group, Nob Hill; Martha's Vineyard, MA: The Coach House; San Francisco, CA: Belon, Rubicon; Washington, DC: Kinkead's, Red Sage **Mentor(s):** Mark Miller; Jean-Louis Palladin **Awards:** 2006 Sante Magazine Sustainability Award; 2005 StarChefs.com Rising Star Chef San Francisco; 2005 Humane Farm Animal Care Certified Humane Restaurant; 2004 Sante Magazine Food and Wine Pairing **Affiliations:** Chefs Collaborative **Languages Spoken:** Bad kitchen Spanish

NOTABLE DISH(ES): Grilled Beef Heart with Roasted Golden Beets and Horseradish; Seared Lamb Kidneys with Spicy Lentils and Mint

FAST FACTS
Restaurant Recs: Pho tu do Noodle House on Clement Street; El Metate Tacqueria; Spices for great Chinese **Kitchen Tool(s):** My pepper mill and my Japaneses knives **Interview Question:** Why are you interested in working at Incanto? What inspires you to cook? What is your most memorable meal and why? What are your goals for the next year? What chef do you look up to and why? What is your favorite cookbook? What do you cook at home? **Flavor Combo(s):** Blood sausage and oysters; juniper and game meats; tripe and clams **Fave Cookbook(s):** The Whole Beast: Nose to Tail Eating by Fergus Henderson; The River Cottage Meat Book by Hugh Fearnley-Whittingstall; The Good Cook Variety Meats by Time Life **Chef to Cook for You:** Each chef is great in their own way. It's impossible to pick just one chef and one meal... **Culinary Travel:** London – everything is a one-hour plane ride away. I could call a farmer and get a 12 pound acorn-fed baby black pig.

Chef Roly

Rolando Cruz-Taura
Executive Chef | The Biltmore Hotel

1200 Anastasia Avenue Coral Gables, FL 33134

Restaurant E-mail: chefroly@fiftyonline.com

Phone: (305) 913-3203

RESTAURANT FACTS
Seats: 70–190 **Weeknight Covers:** 75 **Weekend Covers:** 125 **Check Average (with Wine):** $85 **Tasting Menu:** Yes **Kitchen Staff:** 6

CHEF FACTS
Other Restaurants: The Cellar Club, The Palme d'Or, Fontana **Cuisine:** Progressive American **Born:** 1968 **Began Career:** 1993 **Culinary School:** Florida International University, Miami, FL **Grad Year:** 1993 **Stages:** Miami, FL: Mark's **Work History:** Miami, FL: Hotel Mayfair House, Mark's, Fifty Restaurant and Bar **Mentor(s):** Allen Susser, Mark Militello **Protégée(s):** Agustin Toriz **Awards:** Chaîne des Rotisseurs Certificate of Excellence **Affiliations:** James Beard Foundation; Chaîne de Rotisseurs **Languages Spoken:** French, Spanish

NOTABLE DISH(ES): Short Rib Platter with Brussels Sprout Chow-Chow, White Cheddar Mac & Cheese, Short Rib Galantine and Chipotle Demi; Johnny Cakes with Sunburst Caviar and Crème Fraîche

FAST FACTS
Restaurant Recs: Hy Vong for pork rolling cakes **Kitchen Tool(s):** Chinois – no matter how good a sauce is, it isn't finished if it is not impeccable on the plate **Interview Question:** Tell me about the best night you've ever had on a restaurant line **Flavor Combo(s):** Sweet and sour **Fave Cookbook(s):** La Technique by Jacques Pépin **Chef to Cook for You:** Charlie Trotter, because I think he is a visionary who has changed the way we eat and cook in so many ways **Culinary Travel:** China (all provinces or as many as I can) for the culinary heritage and history

C

Andrea Curto-Randazzo
Chef/Owner | Talula

210 23rd St. Miami Beach, FL 33138

Restaurant E-mail: andrea@talulaonline.com

Phone: (305) 672-0778 and (305) 256-8399

RESTAURANT FACTS
Seats: 70–125 **Weeknight Covers:** 100 **Weekend Covers:** 150–200 **Check Average (with Wine):** $55–$70 **Tasting Menu:** Yes **Kitchen Staff:** 5–7

CHEF FACTS
Other Restaurants: Creative Tastes Catering **Cuisine:** Modern American **Born:** 1970 **Began Career:** 1994 **Culinary School:** The Culinary Institute of America, Hyde Park, NY **Grad Year:** 1996 **Stages:** New York, NY: Park Avenue Café **Work History:** New York, NY: Tribeca Grill, Aja; Coral Gables, FL: The Heights; South Beach, FL: Wish **Mentor(s):** Thomas Keller; Alice Waters; Charlie Palmer **Awards:** 2004 StarChefs.com Rising Star Miami; 2000 Food & Wine Top 10 Chefs; 2000 Esquire John Mariani's List; 2000 Restaurant Hospitality Rising Star **Affiliations:** We support many local charities. March of Dimes is a big one. **Languages Spoken:** English and kitchen Spanish

NOTABLE DISH(ES): Tartare of Ahi Tuna; Shrimp Tamale

FAST FACTS
Restaurant Recs: Timō **Kitchen Tool(s):** Wooden spoon because it is good for everything, and a must for risotto **Interview Question:** Where do you see yourself in the next five years, and then the next ten? **Flavor Combo(s):** I use a lot of citrus zest to finish dishes and brighten them up. I also have a thing for any pork/bacon product. We make our own bacon, sausage, pancetta, and tasso ham at the restaurant. **Fave Cookbook(s):** Of course The French Laundry Cookbook – it is beautiful, insightful and inspiring. Another old favorite – Gotham Bar & Grill Cookbook. **Chef to Cook for You:** Thomas Keller, Charlie Palmer, Eric Ripert. Why? Who wouldn't want that?! **Culinary Travel:** NYC – the pizza, the best chefs... it's just amazing, and so cultural. I also love New Orleans and San Francisco. California has the best produce available to work with.

D'Amico - Duque

Chris D'Amico
Chef | Gemma

335 Bowery New York, NY 10033

Restaurant E-mail: chrisd@bohonyc.com

Phone: (212) 505-9100

RESTAURANT FACTS
Seats: 105 **Weeknight Covers:** 220 **Weekend Covers:** 325 **Check Average (w/o Wine):** $50 **Tasting Menu:** No **Kitchen Staff:** 5–7

CHEF FACTS
Other Restaurants: La Bottega at the Maritime Hotel **Cuisine:** Italian **Born:** 1976 **Began Career:** 1997 **Culinary School:** The Culinary Institute of America, Hyde Park, NY **Grad Year:** 1999 **Stages:** Italy: Il Buco; New York, NY: Café Boulud **Work History:** New York, NY: Cucina, Nino's, Capital, Beacon **Mentor(s):** Franklin Becker, John Delussy, Gabriel Sorgi **Protégée(s):** Angelo Rodriguez, Luis Bravo, Bart Retolatto **Affiliations:** American Culinary Foundation **Languages Spoken:** Italian, some Spanish

NOTABLE DISH(ES): Insalata di Carciofi Crude con Tartufo Nero; Tonno e Fagioli

FAST FACTS
Restaurant Recs: Inoteca for truffled egg toast; Katz's Deli for pastrami **Kitchen Tool(s):** Robot Coupe **Interview Question:** What were the last two places you worked and for how long? **Flavor Combo(s):** Tomato and basil **Fave Cookbook(s):** I really like the Culinara series, particularly those concentrating on European countries, broken down by region; Larousse Gastronomique by Prosper Montagne **Chef to Cook for You:** Andrew Carmellini, because he's a great chef **Culinary Travel:** Either to France or to Turkey. Turkish food sounds very interesting, and I would like to see it. France because their cooking is the foundation of cuisine; it's like going to the Vatican if you are Catholic.

Tim Dahl
Pastry Chef | Blackbird

619 West Randolph St. Chicago, IL 060661

Restaurant E-mail: tim@blackbirdrestaurant.com

Phone: (312) 715-0708

RESTAURANT FACTS
Seats: 65 **Weeknight Covers:** 90 **Weekend Covers:** 150 **Check Average (with Wine):** $80 **Tasting Menu:** Yes $110 **Kitchen Staff:** 3

CHEF FACTS
Other Restaurants: Avec **Cuisine:** French-influenced, seasonal new American **Born:** 1973 **Began Career:** 1991 **Culinary School:** Le Cordon Bleu, Mendota Heights, MN **Grad Year:** 2001 **Work History:** Madison, WI: Restaurant Magnus; Chicago, IL: NoMi, Naha **Mentor(s):** Paul Kahan, my parents **Awards:** 2008 StarChefs.com Rising Star Pastry Chef Chicago; 2007 Jean Banchet Rising Star Pastry Chef **Affiliations:** Slow Food

NOTABLE DISH(ES): Gingerbread with Flavors of Gin, Apples, Juniper, Feta, Cilantro, Sheeps Milk Yogurt and Cider Sorbet; Caraïbe Pave, Caraway Ice Cream, Pickled Roasted Pears, Picholine Olives, Caraway Streusel

FAST FACTS
Restaurant Recs: Kuma's Corner is a heavy metal bar with the best burgers and a great beer selection. Pasticceria Natalina is a really good Italian bakery on Clark. **Kitchen Tool(s):** Either my scale or my TI-86 calculator. My thermometer is important too, but without the scale or calculator, it would be really hard to do my job consistently. **Interview Question:** What do you like to cook. Is there something that you won't eat? **Flavor Combo(s):** Kalamata olives and rhubarb; chestnuts and white truffles; peaches and parmesan; grapefruit and juniper **Fave Cookbook(s):** Au Coeur Des Saveurs by Frederic Bau; Sweet Diversions by Yann Duytsche **Chef to Cook for You:** Fernand Point – his style is the foundation for much of what we do **Culinary Travel:** I'd go back to Italy. My wife and I went there for our honeymoon and worked our way around Emilia Romagna, which was amazing.

D

Elizabeth Dahl
Pastry Chef | Boka

1729 N Halsted Street Chicago, IL 60614

Phone: (312) 337-6070

RESTAURANT FACTS
Seats: 90–130 **Weeknight Covers:** 120 **Weekend Covers:** 190–220
Check Average (with Wine): $80 **Tasting Menu:** Yes **Kitchen Staff:** 1

CHEF FACTS
Cuisine: Seasonal **Born:** 1979 **Began Career:** 1996 **Culinary School:** Kendall College School of Culinary Arts, Chicago, IL **Grad Year:** 2003
Work History: Chicago, IL: Naha, Charlie Trotter's, Campagnola
Mentor(s): Definitely my husband, (pastry chef) Tim Dahl. He's got a great work ethic, great philosophy towards food: the ingredients, the equipment, the industry **Affiliations:** Slow Food, Common Thread

NOTABLE DISH(ES): Cranberry Chestnut Tart with Maple Bourbon Ice Cream, Cranberry Paper Garnish with Orange Zest and Smoked Salt; Oatmeal Stout Panna Cotta with Beer-Battered Apples

FAST FACTS
Restaurant Recs: Spacca Napoli – the owner brought in builders from Naples to build the oven and he gets all of his ingredients imported from Italy. The pizzas are amazing. **Kitchen Tool(s):** Quenelling spoon **Interview Question:** I like to ask what their favorite cookbooks are, who they respect, what restaurants they like to eat at **Flavor Combo(s):** For the fall I really like chocolate and bourbon, maple and chestnut – warm, earthy, smoky flavors. I'm a sucker for liquor in desserts – not to overly booze things up, but it can be underused. **Fave Cookbook(s):** For a good basic technique I go to Bo Friberg's books. Frederic Bau's books are great, and I love what Claudia Fleming did at Gramercy. I'll still pick her book up, even though I think I've gone through it all. **Chef to Cook for You:** My husband. He is such a solid and innovative cook, he knows how to make me things that are new and delicious and how to prepare food I like in ways I wouldn't think of. He just has a talent to put out really great food. **Culinary Travel:** I'd go to the Mediterranean because that encompasses a lot. Spain, France, Italy, Greece, Morocco.

Gary Danko
Chef/Owner | Gary Danko

800 North Point San Francisco, CA 94109

Restaurant E-mail: gary@garydanko.com

Phone: (415) 775-6190

RESTAURANT FACTS
Seats: 65–75 **Weeknight Covers:** 145 **Weekend Covers:** 145 **Check Average (with Wine):** $127.50 **Tasting Menu:** Yes $65/$81/$96 **Kitchen Staff:** 10–12

CHEF FACTS
Cuisine: Californian French **Born:** 1956 **Began Career:** 1977 **Culinary School:** The Culinary Institute of America, Hyde Park, NY **Grad Year:** 1977 **Work History:** San Francisco, CA: The Ritz-Carlton; Napa, CA: Chateau Souverain **Mentor(s):** My mom (Opal), Mabel Cecol, Madeleine Kamman **Protégée(s):** Laurence Josell, Sean O'Brien, Lance Dean Velasquez, Tony Bombaci, Belinda Leong **Awards:** 2007 StarChefs.com Rising Star Mentor San Francisco; 2006 James Beard Foundation Outstanding Service; 2000 James Beard Foundation Best New Restaurant; 1995 James Beard Foundation Best Chef California **Affiliations:** JBF, Slow Food

NOTABLE DISH(ES): Foie Gras Torchon with Duck Prosciutto and Black Mission Figs; Glazed oysters with Osetra Caviar, Zucchini Pearls and Lettuce Cream

FAST FACTS
Restaurant Recs: The Blue Plate for Painted Hills ribeye steak with fries **Kitchen Tool(s):** Joyce Chen scissors because they cut through almost anything **Interview Question:** Do you like to clean? It goes hand in hand with cooking and it is essential to have a clean restaurant. **Flavor Combo(s):** My favorite flavor combinations are the "holy trinity" (mirepoix of carrot, celery and onion) as well as orange, saffron and basil; pistachio, cardamom and vanilla; tuna, anchovies and garlic; red curry, fish sauce and mint **Fave Cookbook(s):** The New Making of a Cook by Madeleine Kamman **Chef to Cook for You:** Madeleine Kamman – she is just an amazing cook – her food is modern yet has the comfort of a grandmother. Her dishes satisfy your palate and your soul. This is what great cooking should do! **Culinary Travel:** Travel is an essential element in a chef's career. I still have many places to visit – Thailand, Egypt, Lebanon, Kashmir, Ireland – I am intrigued by the cultures and the foods of these lands.

Bruno Davaillon
Executive Chef | Mix in Las Vegas

3950Las Vegas Blvd. Las Vegas, NV 89119

Restaurant E-mail: bdavaillon@mrgmail.com

Phone: (702) 632-9500

RESTAURANT FACTS
Seats: 240 **Weeknight Covers:** 250-300 **Weekend Covers:** 450
Check Average (with Wine): $120 **Tasting Menu:** Yes $105/$145
Kitchen Staff: 12-14

CHEF FACTS
Cuisine: Flavorful simplicity **Born:** 1966 **Began Career:** 1984 **Stages:** Monaco: Louis XV; Paris, France: Plaza Athenée **Work History:** France: Ferme Saint Simeon, Jean Bardet, Lasserre **Mentor(s):** Alain Ducasse, Denis Le Cadre **Protégée(s):** Stephane Carrade **Awards:** 2005 American Chefs Association Best French Chef **Affiliations:** James Beard Foundation **Languages Spoken:** French

NOTABLE DISH(ES): Roasted Maine Lobster au Curry, Coconut Basmati Rice; Lobster Salad with Avocado and Osetra Caviar Cream

FAST FACTS
Restaurant Recs: Lotus of Siam for crispy rice Thai salad **Kitchen Tool(s):** Spoon because it's an extension of my hand **Interview Question:** Do you know Alain Ducasse? Where do you see yourself in 10 years? **Fave Cookbook(s):** Grand Livre De Cuisine and Alain Ducasse's Desserts And Pastries by Alain Ducasse **Chef to Cook for You:** I would like to try Ferran Adriá's food at el Bulli because I have heard so much about it. It would be very interesting to see – it is a new world for me. **Culinary Travel:** India, there is a lot going on there right now and I'm not that familiar with the cuisine, but I like it. I am interested in the combinations of spices and different flavors.

Jill Davie
Chef de Cuisine

Jill Davie
Consulting Chef

Santa Monica, CA

Restaurant E-mail: jillianawd@yahoo.com

Phone: (310) 581-9888

CHEF FACTS
Cuisine: California market-driven **Born:** 1971 **Began Career:** 1995
Culinary School: The Culinary Institute of America, Hyde Park, NY
Stages: Chicago, IL: Blackbird, Charlie Trotter's, Tru **Work History:**
San Francisco, CA: LuLu's; Santa Monica, CA: Rockenwagner, Josie
Restaurant **Mentor(s):** Josie Le Balch **Awards:** 2006 Food Network
Hot Chef; 2006 StarChefs.com Rising Star Chef Los Angeles **Affili-
ations:** Chefs Collaborative, Slow Food, Sunkist, California Citrus
Growers **Languages Spoken:** Spanish

NOTABLE DISH(ES): Short Rib Tagine over Toasted Couscous; Grilled
Sepia with Merguez Sausage and Beluga Lentils

FAST FACTS
Restaurant Recs: Papa Christos for grilled octopus; Phillipe's for a French dip sandwich; Soot Bul
Jeep for Korean barbeque; Lare's for mole; Gilbert's for a Fernando burrito; Rae's for cheap eats;
Yabu for monkfish liver; East Wind for tom ka kai **Kitchen Tool(s):** Sieve; spice grinder **Interview
Question:** What do you want to be when you grow up? What is your absolute strength and weakness?
Where do you fit in a line? **Flavor Combo(s):** Sweet and sour – it's a pretty brilliant combination **Fave
Cookbook(s):** The Dean and DeLuca Cookbook by David Rosengarten **Chef to Cook for You:** Paul
Bocuse – just to see how it would be, and also Marco Pierre White **Culinary Travel:** Florence has
amazing Italian cuisine and markets. I love the little cafés. I also like Barcelona for tapas and San
Sebastian. Also, Chicago and New York have an immense amount of talent.

D

Dante De Magistris
Chef/Owner | Dante

40 Edwin H. Land Blvd. Boston, MA 02141

Restaurant E-mail: info@restaurantdante.com

Phone: (617) 497-4200

RESTAURANT FACTS
Seats: 100–160 **Weeknight Covers:** 75 **Weekend Covers:** 125
Check Average (with Wine): $65 **Tasting Menu:** Yes Upon Request
Kitchen Staff: 20

CHEF FACTS
Cuisine: Mediterranean Italian **Born:** 1974 **Began Career:** 1993
Stages: Italy: Enoteca Pinchiorri, Ristorante Don Alfonso **Work
History:** Boston, MA: Pignoli, Café Louis, The Federalist, Blu
Mentor(s): Daniele Baliani, Lydia Shire, Jody Adams, Michael Schlow
Protégée(s): Nathan Chunke **Awards:** 2003 StarChefs.com Rising
Star Chef Boston; 2002 Boston Magazine Up-and-Coming Chef **Languages Spoken:** Italian

NOTABLE DISH(ES): Silky Chestnut and Porcini Mushroom Soup with Mostarda Fruits; Potato Gnocchi
in Celery Broth with Sautéed Fava Beans, Fiddleheads, Asparagus and Pecorino Romano

FAST FACTS
Restaurant Recs: Pizzeria Regina for a small, well-done pizza with anchovies **Kitchen Tool(s):** My
guitarra (chittara pasta maker) – it's a block of wood with guitar strings on it, used to make a certain
shape of spaghetti. I can't get the same shape using a knife or a machine. **Interview Question:** Do
you like cooking? I ask this because it opens up a discussion about their food interests. If they're
enthusiastic, honest and true, I'll be able to tell. If they're brief and lukewarm, then they shouldn't be
working here. It's a way to gauge their passion. **Flavor Combo(s):** A simple yet perfect balance of olive
oil, lemon and salt **Fave Cookbook(s):** Don Alfonso Cookbook – written by the chefs at a restaurant I
worked at in Italy **Chef to Cook for You:** Giada de Laurentiis – I just saw her on TV so she is the first
person that came to mind. It would probably be a lot of fun! **Culinary Travel:** Chile – I've heard a lot of
interesting things about their cuisine

Chris DeBarr
Consulting Chef

New Orleans, LA

E-mail: cdebarr@cox.net

CHEF FACTS:
Born: 1960 **Began Career:** 1976 **Work History:** Athens, GA: The Downstairs, The Commander's Palace, Vincent's Italian, Christian's, The Delachaise **Mentors:** Jamie Shannon, Emmanuel Loubier, Pete Vazquez **Languages:** Kitchen French, menu Vietnamese

NOTABLE DISHES: Tequila Shrimp with Yucca Cake, Crushed Avocado, and Tequila Lime Crema

FAST FACTS:
Restaurant Recs: Casamentos for best fried food in the universe. Phao pau bay for Vietnamese. I like the crushed rice dish. **Favorite Kitchen Tool(s):** Just a good array of knives **Favorite Cookbooks:** For pastry, anything by Nick Malgieri; Cooking Under Wraps by Nicole Routhier **Chef to Cook for You:** Jamie Shannon, that's easy **Culinary Travel:** I would go to Barcelona to see the architecture and eat the food. Then I would move on to San Sebastian

Josh DeChellis
Chef

New York, NY

Restaurant E-mail: jdnyc@gmail.com

CHEF FACTS
Cuisine: Modern Japanese **Born:** 1973 **Began Career:** 1994 **Culinary School:** The Culinary Institute of America, Hyde Park, NY **Grad Year:** 1994 **Stages:** France: L'Arpege, Lucas Carton; Singapore: Raffles Hotel **Work History:** France: L'Arpege; Japan: Sankichi-ya; New York, NY: Bouley, Union Pacific, Sumile, Bar Fry; San Francisco, CA: La Folie **Mentor(s):** Rocco DiSpirito, Alain Passard **Protégée(s):** Christian Schwaiger **Awards:** 2005 StarChefs.com Rising Star Chef New York **Affiliations:** CHS , StarChefs.com Advisory Board

NOTABLE DISH(ES): Poached Hamachi; Oysters with Pineapple Vinegar

FAST FACTS
Restaurant Recs: Pho Nah Trang for the crispy squid **Kitchen Tool(s):** Sharp knives are really important for so many reasons. You can find the perfect piece of fish, but if you don't have a super sharp knife you're going to ruin it. **Interview Question:** What is the best meal you have ever had? This is how I can tell the way a cook connects to food as well as other aspects which make a meal memorable. **Flavor Combo(s):** Nori and pineapple **Fave Cookbook(s):** Cooking by Hand by Paul Bertolli **Chef to Cook for**

You: Pierre Gagnaire because he's the pimp **Culinary Travel:** I'm excited to go back to Japan. I'm going to Tokyo and Okinawa. Apparently Okinawa has food that is completely different form the rest of Japan. I can't even articulate how exited I am. I'm so pumped.

Robert Del Grande
Chef/Owner | Café Annie

1728 Post Oak Blvd. Houston, TX 77056

Restaurant E-mail: robert@cafe-annie.com (but he wants you to know he's slow at responding)

Phone: (713) 840-1111

RESTAURANT FACTS
Seats: 120 **Weeknight Covers:** 200 **Weekend Covers:** 275 **Check Average (with Wine):** $75 **Tasting Menu:** Yes $75–$95 **Kitchen Staff:** 10

CHEF FACTS
Other Restaurants: Bar Annie, Rio Ranch, Café Express, Taco Milagro **Cuisine:** Southwestern **Born:** 1954 **Began Career:** 1981 **Mentor(s):** I've learned something from just about everyone over the years. To have had the opportunity to observe and to have collaborated with so many fine chefs has been a great form of mentoring. **Protégée(s):** Ben and Maryanne Berryhill, Emit Fox **Awards:** 1998 Culinary Award, Chef of the Year; 1992 James Beard Foundation Best Chef Southwest; Who's Who of Cooking in Texas; Food & Wine Honor Roll of American Chefs **Affiliations:** JBF, RCA **Languages Spoken:** Kitchen French, kitchen Spanish

NOTABLE DISH(ES): Texan Pecan Pie; Crispy Striped Bass with Parsley Lemon Butter

FAST FACTS
Restaurant Recs: Good Company BBQ for bbq pork ribs, brisket, jalapeño Czech sausages, bbq turkey, and bbq chicken **Kitchen Tool(s):** Basting brush, pens **Interview Question:** Do you consider yourself lucky? Are you pessimistic or optimistic? **Flavor Combo(s):** I love the combination of spicy flavors with anise related flavors. Shaved fennel and serrano chiles would be a good example – add a little ripe avocado and it's perfect. **Fave Cookbook(s):** Cookbooks by Diana Kennedy **Chef to Cook for You:** I love to watch regional cooks at work – to taste rustic dishes with a long history that are filled with myth and magic and spirit **Culinary Travel:** Any place with a great local cuisine and a great local beach

Karen DeMasco
Consulting Pastry Chef

New York, NY

Restaurant E-mail: ekdemasco@yahoo.com

CHEF FACTS
Cuisine: American **Born:** 1969 **Began Career:** 1993 **Culinary School:** New York Restaurant School, New York, NY **Stages:** New York, NY: Alison on Dominick **Work History:** New York, NY: Chanterelle, Craft, Craftbar, Della Femina, Gramercy Tavern, One If By Land, Two If By Sea, 'Wichcraft; Portland, ME: Fore Street **Mentor(s):** Claudia Fleming **Protégée(s):** Lauren Dawson **Awards:** 2005 James Beard Foundation Outstanding Pastry Chef; 2003 New York Magazine Best Chef

NOTABLE DISH(ES): Hazelnut Hot Chocolate; Lemon Verbena Panna Cotta with Green Apple Jelly

FAST FACTS
Restaurant Recs: A Voce – for lamb ragu **Kitchen Tool(s):** Plastic bowl scraper that fits in my jacket pocket **Interview Question:** What do you like to eat? This lets me know if they have a passion for food.

D

Jody Denton
Chef/Owner | Merenda Restaurant and Wine Bar

900 NW Wall St. Bend, OR 97701

Restaurant E-mail: info@merendarestaurant.com

Phone: (541) 330-2304

RESTAURANT FACTS
Seats: 180 **Weeknight Covers:** 300 **Weekend Covers:** 500 **Check Average (with Wine):** $45 **Tasting Menu:** No **Kitchen Staff:** 6

CHEF FACTS
Other Restaurants: Deep **Cuisine:** Modern Asian, country French, Italian **Born:** 1960 **Began Career:** 1980 **Culinary School:** I apprenticed under German Master Chef Ernst Gruch. I attended classes at El Centro College in Dallas. **Grad Year:** 1980 **Stages:** San Francisco, CA: Postrio **Work History:** Los Angeles, CA: Eureka, Hotel Bel Air; Dallas, TX: The Mansion on Turtle Creek; Washington, DC: Red Sage; San Francisco, CA: LuLu, Azie; Palo Alto, CA: Zibibbo **Mentor(s):** Dean Fearing, Wolfgang Puck **Protégée(s):** Jennifer Jasinski **Awards:** 2006 Wine Spectator Award of Excellence **Affiliations:** James Beard Foundation **Languages Spoken:** Spanish, German

NOTABLE DISH(ES): Roasted Acorn Squash, Pears and Potatoes with Bucheron Cheese; Fig Galette with Raspberries

FAST FACTS
Restaurant Recs: A little Mexican place called Balthazar. I love the queso fundido with chorizo. **Kitchen Tool(s):** Japanese mandolin **Interview Question:** I ask them to tell me about their career. I want to hear them talk about what they've done so that I can assess whether or not they have passion for what they are doing. **Flavor Combo(s):** Garlic and anchovies; truffle and soy; Meyer lemon and rosemary **Fave Cookbook(s):** Cooking by Hand by Paul Bertolli **Chef to Cook for You:** I would choose Mario Batali because I think it would be a hoot. It would definitely be entertaining. **Culinary Travel:** Paris – do you really have to ask why?

Traci Des Jardins
Chef/Owner | Jardiniere

300 Grove St. San Francisco, CA 94102

Restaurant E-mail: traci@jardiniere.com

Phone: (415) 861-5555

RESTAURANT FACTS
Seats: 165 **Weeknight Covers:** 220 **Weekend Covers:** 300 **Check Average (with Wine):** $70 **Tasting Menu:** Yes $125/$190 with wine **Kitchen Staff:** 15

CHEF FACTS
Other Restaurants: Acme Chophouse, Mijita **Cuisine:** French-California **Born:** 1965 **Began Career:** 1983 **Stages:** France: L'Arpege, Louis XV **Work History:** France: Lucas Carton, Troigros; Los Angeles, CA: Patina Restaurant; New York, NY: Montrachet; San Francisco, CA: Rubicon **Mentor(s):** Joachim Splichal, Drew Nieporent **Protégée(s):** Douglas Keane, Richard Reddington, Robbie Lewis **Awards:** 2007 James Beard Foundation Best Chef Pacific; 2003 amfAR Award of Courage; 1995 Food & Wine Best New Chef; 1995 James Beard Foundation Rising Star Chef of the Year **Affiliations:** I am heavily involved with Share Our Strength and on the board of a local organization called La Cocina, which is a business incubator for food entrepreneurs. I am a member of Chefs Collaborative, the James Beard Foundation, and the StarChefs.com Advisory Board. **Languages Spoken:** French, Spanish

NOTABLE DISH(ES): Warm Bread Salad with Baby Artichokes and Marinated Bellwether Farm Crescenza Cheese; Roasted Breast of Squab and Foie Gras Crostini with Local Porcinis, Yellow Peaches and Baby Greens, Thyme Jus

FAST FACTS
Restaurant Recs: Burma Superstar for the most delicious salads I have ever had with great texture and unusual ingredients; Mangosteen for Vietnamese food **Kitchen Tool(s):** Japanese mandolin because it is one of the most useful and expeditious tools to have come along since I have been cooking; different Microplanes are probably one of the most useful things to come along in my career; mortar and pestle because it forces a slow and careful approach when using it **Interview Question:** What are your long-term goals? Why are you getting into the business? If they say that they are doing it because they want to be a star or have a successful restaurant, that is not the right answer. The formation of a chef has to come from a dedication to and passion for food. They must exhibit a thirst for knowledge and not be in a hurry to collect that knowledge. **Flavor Combo(s):** Subtle ones – I love the purity of Japanese food and how the flavors stand alone and are clean and pure **Fave Cookbook(s):** Ma Gastronomie by Fernand Point **Chef to Cook for You:** Gabrielle Hamilton, I think, because her food is clean and delicious but has a very subtle edginess to it **Culinary Travel:** Anyplace new. I have been to France and Italy, of course. I just love exploring new food cultures. I loved going to Japan. I love the food in Mexico. I'm dying to go to Vietnam because I love the food.

Justin Devillier
Executive Chef | La Petite Grocery

4238 Magazine Street New Orleans, LA 70115

Restaurant E-mail: info@lapetitegrocery.com

Phone: (504) 891-3377

RESTAURANT FACTS
Seats: 90 **Weeknight Covers:** 120 **Weekend Covers:** 120 **Check Average (w/o Wine):** $50 **Kitchen Staff:** 5

CHEF FACTS
Cuisine: French with a south Louisiana twist **Born:** 1981 **Began Career:** 1999 **Work History:** Dana Point, CA: Jaxx; Disneyland, CA: Jazz Kitchen; New Orleans, LA: Peristyle **Mentor(s):** Anne Kearney-Sands, Anton Schulte **Affiliations:** Louisiana Restaurant Association, James Beard Foundation

NOTABLE DISH(ES): Grilled Colorado Lamb Tenderloin over Parsnip Purée with Haricot Vert and Braised Lamb Croquette; Roasted Louisiana Oysters with Smoked Bacon and Poblano Butter

FAST FACTS
Restaurant Recs: Pho Tau Bay for the PTB wonton with special egg noodles and char grilled pork **Kitchen Tool(s):** Microplane – my cheater tool. I like to grate garlic on it. Also the Vita-Prep – the best thing ever. You can puree chicken bones in that thing. **Interview Question:** Do you want to be a chef? **Fave Cookbook(s):** Anything by James Peterson. I read all of his books to learn the classic sauces and such. **Chef to Cook for You:** Thomas Keller **Culinary Travel:** Right now Vietnam – they use the freshest ingredients and flavor combinations.

Fabian di Paolo
Executive Pastry Chef | Neomi's

18001 Collins Ave. Sunny Isles Beach, FL 33160

Restaurant E-mail: fdipaolo@trumpsonesta.com

Phone: (305) 692-5600

RESTAURANT FACTS
Seats: 90–170 **Weeknight Covers:** 55–60 **Weekend Covers:** 90–120 **Check Average (with Wine):** $85 **Check Average (w/o Wine):** $65 **Tasting Menu:** Yes $85 **Kitchen Staff:** 5

CHEF FACTS
Cuisine: Modern **Born:** 1968 **Began Career:** 1987 **Culinary School:** Le Cordon Bleu, Argentina **Grad Year:** 1985 **Work History:** Argentina: The Palace Hotel, The Hilton, Restaurant Bice, Caesar Hotel **Mentor(s):** Pascal Pinot **Affiliations:** ACF **Languages Spoken:** Spanish, Italian

NOTABLE DISH(ES): Buffalo Gelato with Olive Oil Cake, Gianduja Croquant, Coconut Froth and Mint Croquette

FAST FACTS
Restaurant Recs: Hiro's Yakko-San for Japanese food – I like the duck liver **Kitchen Tool(s):** Mini offset spatula **Interview Question:** I like to ask, "are you ready to work long hours?" I want to see that they are committed to learning. **Flavor Combo(s):** I like sweet and sour, like chocolate with tonka bean or vanilla with balsamic vinegar **Fave Cookbook(s):** The two books by Paco Torreblanca **Chef to Cook for You:** Albert Adriá, because his mind is so open **Culinary Travel:** Spain – the food there has become the model for the kitchen. Everyone wants to see what's going on there.

John Doherty
Executive Chef | The Waldorf-Astoria

301 Park Ave. New York, NY 10022

Restaurant E-mail: john_doherty@hilton.com

Phone: (212) 872-4866

RESTAURANT FACTS
Kitchen Staff: 85

CHEF FACTS
Other Restaurants: Oscars Brasserie, Bull & Bear Steakhouse, Peacock Alley **Cuisine:** Contemporary French American **Born:** 1958 **Culinary School:** The Culinary Institute of America, Hyde Park, NY **Grad Year:** 1978 **Stages:** Belgium: Hotel Scholpeshof; France: Restaurant George Blanc **Mentor(s):** Roger Souvereyns **Protégée(s):** Neil Gallagher, Carlos Guia, Robert Trainor **Affiliations:** CIA, City Harvest **Books Published:** The Waldorf-Astoria Cookbook

NOTABLE DISH(ES): Seared Scallops with Osetra Caviar and Potato-Chive Mousseline

FAST FACTS
Restaurant Recs: 'ino for truffled egg toast **Kitchen Tool(s):** Thermometer **Interview Question:** Tell me what you did in your last job that made a difference in their business **Flavor Combo(s):** Black truffles, honey and sherry vinegar **Fave Cookbook(s):** The Great Chefs of France by Anthony Blake, Quentin Crewe **Chef to Cook for You:** I would want Gray Kunz to cook for me. He artfully blends spices and textures that only enhance the food that he is serving. His cooking inspires me to think outside the box. **Culinary Travel:** India

Mark Dommen
Chef | One Market Restaurant

1 Market St. San Francisco, CA 94105

Restaurant E-mail: mdommen@onemarket.com

Phone: (415) 777-5577

RESTAURANT FACTS
Seats: 180 **Weeknight Covers:** 200 **Weekend Covers:** 200 **Check Average (with Wine):** $77 **Tasting Menu:** Yes $79 **Kitchen Staff:** 34/28

CHEF FACTS
Cuisine: Californian French **Born:** 1969 **Began Career:** 1989
Culinary School: California Culinary Academy, San Francisco, CA
Grad Year: 1989 **Stages:** France: Louis XV, Monte Carlo; Germany: Schwartzwaldstube; Switzerland: Petermanns Kunststube **Work History:** San Francisco, CA: Fleur de Lys; New York, NY: Lespinasse **Mentor(s):** Hubert Keller; Gray Kunz **Awards:** 2007 StarChefs.com Rising Star Chef San Francisco; 2002 Esquire Best New Restaurant **Affiliations:** Meals-on-Wheels, Make a Wish, Project Open Hand, Tibetan Aid Dinner, Best of the Bay to benefit Family House at UCSF **Languages Spoken:** German

NOTABLE DISH(ES): Beet Carpaccio with Marinated Rock Shrimp; Lightly Smoked Sea Trout 'Mi Cuit'

FAST FACTS
Restaurant Recs: Bistro Jeanty for steak tartare **Kitchen Tool(s):** Gray Kunz spoon **Interview Question:** What are your immediate goals, and where do you see yourself in five years? **Flavor Combo(s):** Nettles and spring garlic; dandelion and apple; lamb and chocolate **Fave Cookbook(s):** Cooking with the Seasons by Jean-Louis Palladin **Chef to Cook for You:** If I could have anyone cook for me, I'd probably have to choose Joël Robuchon **Culinary Travel:** I love all of Europe, but I'd really like to go to Asia because I've never been there. I love the flavors, especially those of Thailand.

Roberto Donna
Chef/Owner | Galileo da Roberto Donna

1110 21st St. NW Washington, DC 20036

Restaurant E-mail: roberto@robertodonna.com

Phone: (703) 412-5077

RESTAURANT FACTS
Seats: 90–170 **Weeknight Covers:** 180 **Weekend Covers:** 220
Check Average (with Wine): $120 **Check Average (w/o Wine):** $85
Kitchen Staff: 14

CHEF FACTS
Other Restaurants: Arlington, VA: Laboratorio del Galileo, Bebo
Trattoria **Cuisine:** Northern Italian **Born:** 1961 **Began Career:** 1978
Culinary School: Instituto Professionale, Italy **Grad Year:** 1978 **Work
History:** Italy: Il Cambio **Mentor(s):** Mario Sobbiar **Protégée(s):** Todd
Gray, Enzo Fargione, Cesare Lanfranconi, Laurie Alleman, Fabrizio
Aielli, Kate Johnson, Carmine Marzano, Mike Nayeri **Awards:** 2004,
1990 Restaurant Association of Metropolitan Washington Chef of the Year; 2001 Immigrant Achievement Award; 1996 James Beard Foundation Best Chef Mid-Atlantic; 1995 Restaurant Association of Metropolitan Washington Restaurateur of the year; 1992 American Culinary Foundation President's Humanitarian Award; 1991 Master Chef's Society The Chef of America Award **Affiliations:** AIWF, JBF, GRI, DC Central Kitchen, SOS and numerous other charitable organizations **Books Published:** Cooking in Piedmont **Languages Spoken:** French, Italian, Spanish

NOTABLE DISH(ES): Chickpea Soup with Sweet Garlic Toasted Bread; Green Risotto with Asparagus and Crispy Artichokes

FAST FACTS
Restaurant Recs: El Paraiso for papusas **Kitchen Tool(s):** Mandolin **Interview Question:** Why did you become a cook? **Flavor Combo(s):** I like very clear and pure flavor, I like to know what I eat. I am not a lover of fusion of flavor; I think nature gave us a gift that we need to preserve, so if I eat a carrot I want to taste the best carrot and not another flavor that will change it or modify it. **Chef to Cook for You:** It would be Pierre Gagnaire – I love his approach to food: clean, pure, inventive and creative, but still in the boundary of pure cooking and not chemistry **Culinary Travel:** I like to go back to Europe - Italy, France and lately to Spain. Going back to my roots brings back the true flavors and cooking styles that I grew up with. Italy for the flavors, France for techniques, and Spain for creativity.

Marika Shimamoto Doob
Pastry Chef | Charles Chocolates

6529 Hollis St. San Francisco, CA 94608

Restaurant E-mail: marika@charleschocolates.com

Phone: (510) 652-4412

RESTAURANT FACTS
Kitchen Staff: 15–25

CHEF FACTS
Cuisine: Clean, familiar, and well-executed pastries **Born:** 1972 **Began Career:** 1996 **Culinary School:** The California Culinary Academy, San Francisco, CA **Grad Year:** 1999 **Work History:** San Francisco, CA: L'Auberge Hotel and Resort, San Francisco's Waterfront Restaurant, Hawthorne Lane, The Fifth Floor **Awards:** 2005 StarChefs.com Rising Star Pastry Chef San Francisco

NOTABLE DISH(ES): Chocolate Velvet Mousse Cake with Brown Sugar Bananas

FAST FACTS
Restaurant Recs: Kirala in Berkeley – it's not quite off the beaten path though. I like the sashimi, especially salmon toro. **Kitchen Tool(s):** My favorite pastry tool in the kitchen is the silicon mat. I can't imagine attempting to make a tuile or do sugar work and decorations without it. Flexible silicon molds are great as well. **Interview Question:** Why should we hire you? What are your strengths and weaknesses? **Flavor Combo(s):** Tahitian vanilla bean and fresh orange zest; Meyer lemon, mint and yogurt; chocolate and anything salty-sweet **Fave Cookbook(s):** The Science of Chocolate and the CIA Chocolates and Confections **Chef to Cook for You:** Jared Doob (chef/husband) because the ingredients are always harmonious and the dishes delicious **Culinary Travel:** Italy for the gelato and Switzerland for the chocolate

D

Shaun Doty
Chef/Owner | Shaun's

1029 Edgewood Avenue NE Atlanta, GA 30307

Restaurant E-mail: shaun@shaunsrestaurant.com

Phone: (404) 577-4358

RESTAURANT FACTS
Seats: 60 **Weeknight Covers:** 80 **Weekend Covers:** 150+ **Check Average (with Wine):** $50 **Tasting Menu:** No **Kitchen Staff:** 4

CHEF FACTS
Cuisine: Modern bistro **Born:** 1969 **Began Career:** 1991 **Culinary School:** Johnson & Wales, Charleston, SC **Grad Year:** 1991 **Stages:** Belgium: Comme Chez Soi, Restaurant Claude Dupont, Restaurant Barbizon; France: Restaurant Bruno, Restaurant Troisgros **Work History:** Dallas, TX: The Grape; Charleston, SC: Restaurant Million; Atlanta, GA: The Ritz-Carlton Buckhead, Mumbo Jumbo, MidCity Cuisine, Table 1280; Beaver Creek, CO: Mirabelle; South Hampton, NY: Savanna's **Mentor(s):** Guenter Seeger **Awards:** 2007 Esquire Magazine Best New Restaurant; 2003 Atlanta Magazine Restaurant of the Year **Affiliations:** Co-Chair of Project Openhand, Believe in Me Foundation, March of Dimes

NOTABLE DISH(ES): Beef Tartare with Romesco, Fennel and Parsley

FAST FACTS
Restaurant Recs: Lotta Frutta, where I get the fruit salad with lime and guajillo pepper **Kitchen Tool(s):** Extra-long bamboo chopsticks from the Asian Market. I go through one set per week. **Interview Question:** Do you have a high tolerance for pain? **Flavor Combo(s):** Citrus and chocolate; rum and bananas **Fave Cookbook(s):** Books by Alain Ducasse; Arabesque by Claudia Roden; Wild Food from Land and Sea by Marco Pierre White; books by Scott Peacock **Chef to Cook for You:** Paul Bocuse – because he's the best ever! **Culinary Travel:** Paris – I know that's boring, but it's the definitive place to go

Tom Douglas
Chef/Owner | Dahlia Lounge

2030 Fifth Ave. Seattle, WA 98121

Restaurant E-mail: office@tomdouglas.com

Phone: (206) 448-2001

RESTAURANT FACTS
Seats: 120-170 **Weeknight Covers:** 200 **Weekend Covers:** 300 **Tasting Menu:** No **Kitchen Staff:** 10

CHEF FACTS
Other Restaurants: Dahlia Bakery, Etta's, Palace Kitchen, Lola, Serious Pie, Tom Douglas Catering & Events, The Palace Ballroom **Cuisine:** Pacific Rim/Northwest American **Born:** 1958 **Began Career:** 1976 **Work History:** Wilmington, DE: Hotel Dupont **Mentor(s):** Restaurant people – I've learned something from every dishwasher, chef, GM, and owner I've ever worked with **Protégée(s):** Those that treat their employees with class and their customers like kings **Awards:** 2008 James Beard Foundation Outstanding Restaurateur Nominee **Books Published:** Tom Douglas' Seattle Kitchen; Tom's Big Dinners; I Love Crab Cakes

FAST FACTS
Restaurant Recs: The Pink Door for lasagna verdi **Kitchen Tool(s):** Wok; bamboo steamer **Interview Question:** What would you make for dinner if you wanted to get lucky? **Flavor Combo(s):** Star anise and orange **Fave Cookbook(s):** China Moon by Barbara Tropp **Chef to Cook for You:** Jacques Pépin – I would have him make me an herb omelet while singing "My Funny Valentine" **Culinary Travel:** Alba – I'm a big fan of Piemontese food

Lissa Doumani
Pastry Chef | Terra

1345 Railroad Ave. St. Helena, CA 94574

Restaurant E-mail: lissasan@terrarestaurant.com

Phone: (707) 963-8931

RESTAURANT FACTS
Seats: 95+ **Weeknight Covers:** 80–100 **Weekend Covers:** 120–150 **Check Average (w/o Wine):** $51 **Tasting Menu:** No **Kitchen Staff:** 6 total in Kitchen

CHEF FACTS
Other Restaurants: Ame **Cuisine:** Pastry **Born:** Before love-ins and after drive-ins **Began Career:** 1975 **Work History:** Los Angeles, CA: Spago, 385 North; Yountville, CA: Vintage 1870 **Mentor(s):** Sally Schmitt, Nancy Silverton, Wolfgang Puck, my two grandmothers, my mother **Awards:** Food and Wine Top 10 New Chefs in America; Ivy Award; Dirona Award; Wine Spectator Award for Wine List; Michelin 1 star **Affiliations:** We are affiliated with many charities, MOW both in San Francisco and Los Angeles, Planned Parenthood, Project Open Hand, SOS, Parkinson's Research, Cancer Research to name a few. There are many others that we work with as we have time. **Books Published:** Terra Cooking from the Heart of the Napa Valley

NOTABLE DISH(ES): Soup Pistou with Goat Cheese Ravioli; Shortcake with Mixed Berries

FAST FACTS
Restaurant Recs: La Luna Market for great tongue or cheek tacos; Maki for all the specials of the day **Kitchen Tool(s):** Torch – something every girl should have! **Interview Question:** Where do you like to eat and why? **Flavor Combo(s):** The flavors I like together are fairly classical. I love the freshness of mint and lemon together. Also noyaux and stone fruit. **Fave Cookbook(s):** Joy of Cooking by Irma S. Rombauer – it was one of the cookbooks that kept me cooking when I was a kid; A Cookbook For Young People by Mildred O. Knopf – another cook book from when I was a kid. Both inspired me.
Chef to Cook for You: Funny enough it would really be my husband Hiro. He and I have similar palates and he always surprises me with the most amazing dishes. If not Hiro, then I would want to gather fishermen that raise Ezo abalone, oysters from everywhere, uni and caviar and have them bring the best that they have and open some beautiful bottles of Sake to go with their choices – all raw, nothing cooked. **Culinary Travel:** Currently I would like to go back to the Middle East and learn more about the differences in the cuisine in each country. I am of Lebanese heritage and can cook what I think are very good Lebanese dishes, but I would like to understand the subtle difference between countries, and regions within the countries. I love the level of flavors that Middle Eastern cooking reaches and the rich warm spices it uses. It is also a cuisine with a lot of history, but the dishes and flavors lend themselves to being used in a more current way.

Celestino Drago
Chef/Owner | Drago

2628 Wilshire Blvd. Santa Monica, CA 90403

Restaurant E-mail: celestino@celestinodrago.com

Phone: (310) 828-1585

RESTAURANT FACTS
Seats: 120 **Weeknight Covers:** 80–90 **Weekend Covers:** 120 **Check Average (with Wine):** $70 **Tasting Menu:** Yes Upon request **Kitchen Staff:** 7

CHEF FACTS
Other Restaurants: Beverly Hills, CA: Enoteca Drago, il Pastaio; Culver City, CA: Dolce Forno **Cuisine:** Authentic contemporary Italian **Born:** 1957 **Began Career:** 1974 **Stages:** Italy: Pierino **Work History:** Italy: Pierino; West Hollywood, CA: Chianti, Cucina, Celestino Steak House; Beverly Hills, CA: Celestino **Mentor(s):** Ignazio Diana, Joachim Splichal (isn't really a mentor but I admire his work greatly) **Awards:** 1993 Food & Wine Best New Chef **Affiliations:** JBF, Wine Masters for Cystic Fibrosis, GRI (Groupo Restaurante Italiano) in New York **Languages Spoken:** Italian, some Spanish and French

NOTABLE DISH(ES): Insalata Di Funghi Porcini e Parmigiano Reggiano (Porcini Mushroom Salad with Parmigiano Reggiano)

FAST FACTS
Restaurant Recs: Tama Sushi for sushi **Kitchen Tool(s):** I love all sorts of gadgets, especially hand mixers **Interview Question:** I like to have them talk about themselves, how they got into the business and why. When I hire someone it depends on their reasons for being in the business. I'm looking for passion, to see if they love what they do, or if they are just in it to make money. **Flavor Combo(s):** I love game, from ducks to venison, combined with fresh and dried fruit and spices. Wild boar, dried figs, cinnamon and star anise. I also love citrus! **Fave Cookbook(s):** Cookbooks by Paul Bocuse **Chef to Cook for You:** Ignacio Diana – the chef I learned from in Tuscany. You can tell the passion in his eyes in his food. **Culinary Travel:** I would like to go to the south of France and Spain to discover new things

D

Jim Drohman
Chef | Le Pichet

1933 1st Ave. Seattle, WA 98101
Restaurant E-mail: j.drohman@gmail.com
Phone: (206) 256-1499

RESTAURANT FACTS
Seats: 38–48 **Weeknight Covers:** 60 **Weekend Covers:** 95 **Check Average (w/o Wine):** $30 **Tasting Menu:** No

CHEF FACTS
Other Restaurants: Cafe Presse **Cuisine:** Traditional regional French **Born:** 1962 **Began Career:** 1977 **Culinary School:** École Superieure de Cuisine, France **Grad Year:** 1990 **Stages:** France: Le Coq de la Maison Blanc, Hotel Bristol **Work History:** France: Le Boudin Sauvage; Seattle, WA: Market Place Caterers/The Ruins, Campagne **Mentor(s):** John McDonnal **Protégée(s):** Tamara Murphy **Affiliations:** Groups we support each year include NW AIDS Foundation, the Lifelong Aids Alliance, UNICEF, Bailey Boushay House, Northwest Film Forum, Pike Place Market Foundation to name a few. We have also hosted events in coordination with the Chefs Collaborative, and I have been involved as a speaker with the American Cheese Society and the culinary arts programs at South Seattle Community College. **Languages Spoken:** French, Spanish

NOTABLE DISH(ES): Pork Belly Confit

FAST FACTS
Restaurant Recs: La Spiga for tagliatelle with truffle butter **Kitchen Tool(s):** Fish palette **Interview Question:** Where have you eaten recently where you had a good or bad experience? **Flavor Combo(s):** My preference in flavor combinations leans towards combinations that have a historical/cultural/regional sense about them. That is to say, I am intrigued by the way that the ingredients of a particular area, when assembled in accord with the traditional recipes of that area and served with the wine of that area, make an almost perfect combination. Several of my favorite examples: garlic, parsley, butter and red Burgundy wine; olives, goats milk cheese and rosé from Bandol; artichokes, apples, buckwheat and cider from Normandy. **Fave Cookbook(s):** La Cuisine du Marché by Paul Bocuse **Chef to Cook for You:** I would choose Eric Frechon, who is currently the chef at the Hotel Bristol in Paris. I have followed his career since he opened his first bistro near the Parc Buttes Chaumont, and believe he is going to be one of the giants. **Culinary Travel:** I would like to return to France. I constantly find inspiration there, not only for dishes for my restaurants, but also for my ideas of living well. Also, no matter how many times I travel in France, and despite the time we lived in Paris, I always find new and surprising parts of France to love. Or to Vietnam. I would love to explore the mingling of French and Indo-Chinese influences there.

Alain Ducasse
Chef/Entrepeneur | Adour

2 East 55th St. New York, NY 10022

Restaurant E-mail: contact@alain-ducasse.com

Phone: (212) 753-4500

RESTAURANT FACTS
Seats: 72-88 **Weeknight Covers:** 120 **Weekend Covers:** 140 **Check Average (w/o Wine):** $140 **Tasting Menu:** Yes $110 **Kitchen Staff:** 25

CHEF FACTS
Other Restaurants: New York, NY: Benoit; Monaco: Benoit, Le Louis-XV, Bar Boeuf & Co.; Paris, France: Alain Ducasse au Plaza Athénée, Au Lyonnais, Benoit, Boulangépicier, Le Jules Verne, Le Relais du Parc, Spoon; London, England: Alain Ducasse at The Dorchester; Moustiers Sainte-Marie, France: La Bastide De Moustiers; La Celle, France: Hostellerie de L'Abbeye de La Celle; Tokyo, Japan: Beige, Benoit; Las Vegas, NV: MIX; Provence, France: Domaind des Andéols **Cuisine:** French-international **Born:** 1956 **Began Career:** 1972 **Culinary School:** Bordeaux Hotel School, France **Stages:** France: Les Pres d'Eugenie; Lenôtre **Work History:** France: Moulin de Mougins, Alain Chapel, l'Amandier, La Terrasse, Le Louis XV-Alain Ducasse, Alain Ducasse au Plaza Athenée **Mentor(s):** Alain Chapel **Protégée(s):** Franck Cerutti, Christophe Moret, Tony Esnault, Didier Elena, Jean-François Piege, Sylvain Portay, David Bellin, David Rathgeber, Frederic Vardon, Benoit Witz, Eric Santalucia, Christian Juilliard, Christophe Martin, Nicola Canuti, Tjaco Van Eijken, Philippe Marc, Romain Corbiere, Pascal Bardet, Stephanie Cole, Dominique Saugnac,Christophe Larrat, Nicolas Berger, Christophe Clarigo, Bruno Davaillon, Baptiste Peupion, Christophe Fiorino, Alain Soulard, Christophe Raoux **Awards:** Groupe Alain Ducasse holds 13 Michelin stars; 2007 James Beard Foundation Award in the Best Cookbook from a Professional Point of View; Bon Appétit 2001 Chef of the Year; Restaurant Magazine best restaurants in the world; Wine Spectator Grand Award **Affiliations:** Châteaux & Hôtels de France **Books Published:** The Grand Livre de Cuisine collection: Mediterrannee; Alain Ducasse's Desserts and Pastries; Spoon Cook Book; La Riviera d'Alain Ducasse; Mediterranées, Cuisine de l'Essential; L'Atelier of Alain Ducasse; Flavors of France; Les recettes de la Rivera; La Bonne Cuisine de Françoise Bernard et Alain Ducasse; La Provençe de Ducasse; Le Dictionnaire Amoureux de la Cuisine **Languages Spoken:** French

FAST FACTS
Restaurant Recs: I have had so many food experiences that I would be unable to only name one. It depends on my appetite, but more recently I really enjoyed Katz's Delicatessen and Daisy May's BBQ in New York City. **Kitchen Tool(s):** Produce – cooking is 60% ingredients, and great cooking is a matter of choosing exceptional ingredients with the best natural qualities. This is where the true savoir-faire begins. The quality of the produce surpasses everything and determines the rest. I follow the maxim: "a turbot without genius is better than a genius without a turbot." **Interview Question:** Ideally, where do you see yourself in 5 years? In 10 years? **Flavor Combo(s):** Simple combinations that highlight the natural and authentic flavors of the ingredients. One of my favorite recipes consists of porcini mushrooms (heads whole, stems cleaned) roasted in chestnut leaves for twenty minutes

with olive oil, shallots, and fleur de sel. The smoke of the chestnut leaves perfumes the whole. **Fave Cookbook(s):** La Cuisine au Pays de Brillat-Savarin by Lucien Tendret **Chef to Cook for You:** Alain Chapel, as he was my mentor **Culinary Travel:** New York continues to inspire me. The city is constantly changing, and there is always something new and different to try.

Wylie Dufresne
Chef/Owner | wd~50

50 Clinton St. New York, NY 10002

Restaurant E-mail: edufresne@earthlink.net

Phone: (212) 477-2900

RESTAURANT FACTS
Seats: 65–72 **Weeknight Covers:** 80 **Weekend Covers:** 120 **Check Average (with Wine):** $110 **Tasting Menu:** Yes $125/$200 with wine **Kitchen Staff:** 8–10

CHEF FACTS
Cuisine: Creative American **Born:** 1970 **Began Career:** 1993 **Culinary School:** The French Culinary Institute, New York, NY **Grad Year:** 1993 **Stages:** France: Guy Savoy, Marc Meneau **Work History:** New York, NY: 71 Clinton Fresh Food, Jean Georges, JoJo; Las Vegas, NV: Prime **Mentor(s):** My parents, Jean-Georges Vongerichten **Awards:** 2008 James Beard Foundation Best Chef New York City Nominee; 2008 New York Times 3 stars; 2007 Johnson and Wales honorary degree of Dr. of Culinary Arts; 2006, 2007 Michelin Guide 1 star; 2005 StarChefs.com Rising Star Chef New York; 2001 Food & Wine Best New Chefs **Affiliations:** IFT, RCA

NOTABLE DISH(ES): Beef Tongue and Fried Mayo; Breast of Squab with Crusty Golden Beets and Sweet Potato Jus

FAST FACTS
Kitchen Tool(s): Vita-Prep **Interview Question:** Our interview process is not really a litany of questions, more an opportunity to get a sense of the person **Flavor Combo(s):** Milk and cookies **Fave Cookbook(s):** I collect cookbooks, so I can't commit to one title. There are so many that provide different angles. Right now, I'm really looking forward to Heston Blumenthal's new book. **Chef to Cook for You:** Escoffier – a cliché, yes, but you'd be guaranteed a good meal **Culinary Travel:** San Sebastian – there's a high concentration of people doing very interesting things, and it's a beach

Greg Dunmore
Executive Chef | Ame

689 Mission St. San Francisco, CA 94105

Restaurant E-mail: greg.dunmore@stregis.com

Phone: (415) 284-4040

RESTAURANT FACTS
Seats: 80 **Weeknight Covers:** 90–110 **Weekend Covers:** 120–160
Check Average (w/o Wine): $60 **Tasting Menu:** Yes $85/$150 with
wine **Kitchen Staff:** 6

CHEF FACTS
Cuisine: New American **Born:** 1976 **Began Career:** 1990 **Culinary
School:** Culinary Institute of America, Hyde Park, NY **Grad Year:** 1996
Stages: San Francisco, CA: Aqua **Work History:** Hudson Valley,NY;
Cascade Mountain Winery & Restaurant; Atlanta, GA: Bacchanalia,
Floataway Café; San Francisco, CA: Terra **Mentor(s):** Every chef/cook
I have ever worked with and my friends and family **Awards:** 2006 San
Francisco Chronicle Bay Area Rising Star **Affiliations:** Meals-on-Wheels

NOTABLE DISH(ES): Carpaccio of Octopus and Castroville Artichokes with Picholine Olives, Mint and
Caper Vinaigrette

FAST FACTS
Restaurant Recs: Swan Oyster Depot – for the Crab Louie **Kitchen Tool(s):** Vita-Prep **Interview
Question:** Where do you dine? Then, because we are union and can't do stages, I have them do
some cooking tests. Onion dice, julienne carrots, etc. **Chef to Cook for You:** Probably Alice Waters. I
love women chefs because I feel like they cook more from within as opposed to men, who cook with
their egos, for the most part. In addition, it would be cool to say Alice Waters cooked for me. **Culinary
Travel:** Everywhere – why not? The world is your oyster.

Kendal Duque
Executive Chef | Sepia

123 N. Jefferson St. Chicago, IL 60661

Restaurant E-mail: kendal@sepiachicago.com

Phone: (312) 441-1920

RESTAURANT FACTS
Seats: 85 **Weeknight Covers:** 100 **Weekend Covers:** 170 **Check Average (w/o Wine):** $40–$50 **Tasting Menu:** No **Kitchen Staff:** 3–4

CHEF FACTS
Cuisine: Inventive American **Born:** 1972 **Culinary School:** Peter Kump's, New York, NY **Grad Year:** 1996 **Work History:** San Francisco, CA: Masa's; Las Vegas, NV: The Bellagio; Chicago, IL: Everest, Tru, Nomi; New York, NY: Union Pacific **Mentor(s):** Julian Serrano **Awards:** 2008 StarChefs.com Rising Star Chef Chicago **Languages Spoken:** Spanish

NOTABLE DISH(ES): Roasted Rabbit Leg with Wisconsin Ricotta Dumplings, Chickpeas and Cherry Tomatoes; Charred Baby Octopus and Toasted Bread with Tomato Sauce

FAST FACTS
Restaurant Recs: La Oaxacana on Milwaukee Ave for the octopus salad and the Torta Tezoatlan; Fonda del Mar on Fullerton Ave for the fish tacos and the cochinita pibil **Kitchen Tool(s):** Sturdy pans – we use a lot of cast iron and black steel. I eschew using tongs unless you work on the grill. I use mostly spoons and forks. I like to handle things as lightly as possible. **Interview Question:** I need to have a balance in my life, so I desperately need to know what they do besides the job. What it is that defines them. Once I know their personality, I know how to approach everyone individually. I like to know them as personally as I can. **Flavor Combo(s):** I use a lot of acid: high herb tones and lemon and limes, with a base of good olive oil and good vinegar. I try to keep my flavors up top, but something has to bring it down. **Fave Cookbook(s):** When I started it was the classical books like Ma Cuisine. Right now it's Mario Batali, Zuni Café, the new Alice Waters book. Those are directing me right now. **Chef to Cook for You:** I would like to have Fredy Girardet cook for me. I feel that maybe I have some insight into what he's gone through in his career. **Culinary Travel:** Japan – it's an aesthetic that I intuitively love and want to experience more

E

{ Eagle - Etchison }

Christopher Eagle
Executive Chef | Cielo

501 East Camino Real Boca Raton, FL 33432

Restaurant E-mail: christophereagle@gordonramsay.com

Phone: (561) 447-3222

RESTAURANT FACTS
Seats: 120 **Weeknight Covers:** 80–90 **Weekend Covers:** 130 **Check Average (with Wine):** $110 **Tasting Menu:** Yes $110 **Kitchen Staff:** 9–10

CHEF FACTS
Cuisine: Modern European with Italian influences **Born:** 1968 **Culinary School:** Johnson and Wales, Charleston **Grad Year:** 1993 **Work History:** Atlanta, GA: Brasserie Le Coze, Fusebox; Aspen, CO: The Ritz-Carlton; Los Angeles, CA: JAAN at Raffles L'Ermitage **Mentor(s):** Troy Thompson, Thomas Keller and Alain Ducasse are mentors in a distant, inspirational sense, and Guenter Seeger **Awards:** 2008 StarChefs.com Rising Star Chef South Florida **Affiliations:** Share our Strength

NOTABLE DISH(ES): Foie Gras Torchon with Quince and Spiced Plum; Peekytoe Crab Cannelloni with Pear, Basil and Lemon

FAST FACTS
Restaurant Recs: Hong Kong Palace in Boca Raton – I like the house fried rice **Kitchen Tool(s):** Vita-Prep **Interview Question:** I ask them what cookbooks they are reading. It says a lot about how dedicated they are. **Flavor Combo(s):** White wine and vanilla beans; brown butter and fish; foie and fruit; duck and fruit – all classical lines. Though I do also appreciate some of the new flavor combinations we are seeing. **Fave Cookbook(s):** Thomas Keller's The French Laundry cookbook, Ducasse's Encyclopedia, Michel Bras Essential Cuisine, and the el Bulli cookbooks. **Chef to Cook for You:** I would like to have Eric Ripert cook for me **Culinary Travel:** Spain, because they are pushing the envelope. It's the epicenter of cuisine today.

Daniel Eardley
Chef | Chestnut

271 Smith St. Brooklyn, NY 11231

Restaurant E-mail: chestnutonsmith@gmail.com

Phone: (718) 243-0049

RESTAURANT FACTS

Seats: 65 (with patio) **Weeknight Covers:** 50 **Weekend Covers:** 80 **Check Average (with Wine):** 60 **Check Average (w/o Wine):** 50 **Tasting Menu:** Yes $60/$85 with wine **Kitchen Staff:** 5

CHEF FACTS

Cuisine: Seasonal, local American **Born:** 1971 **Began Career:** Started working in kitchens at 13 **Culinary School:** The Culinary Institute of America, Hyde Park, NY **Grad Year:** 1996 **Work History:** St. Louis, MO: An American Place; Willamette Valley, OR: Tribona; New York, NY: Washington Park **Mentor(s):** Jonathan Waxman, Larry Forgione **Awards:** 2007 StarChefs.com Rising Star Sustainability Award New York **Affiliations:** American Cancer Society, Share Our Strength, Brooklyn Camp for Kids, Flatbush Development Corporation, many local school auctions, The Cora Dance Company **Languages Spoken:** Spanish, limited French

NOTABLE DISH(ES): Chilled Pea Soup and Smoked Ham Hock and Chive Blossoms; English Pea Pansotti with Mascarpone Foam

FAST FACTS

Restaurant Recs: Castro's Mexican Kitchen on Myrtle **Kitchen Tool(s):** Immersion blender **Interview Question:** Who cooked at home growing up? Did you like their cooking? I'm looking for someone who knows that great food doesn't come without care in all stages of preparation – just like Mom used to make or maybe Grandma. The dishes that stay with you the longest are those that are prepared with love. Someone who recognizes that will have a passion that no school can teach. **Flavor Combo(s):** Sweet, salty and spicy. I really like Chinese 5-spice, but in general, three flavors is all you need. You start with two dominant flavors, like sweet and salty, then add a more subtle flavor to temper the other two. They all end up marrying really well – you get all the multiplicity of flavors without overcomplicating it with too many components. **Fave Cookbook(s):** Lessons in Service by Charlie Trotter; The Greens Cookbook by Deborah Madison; The French Laundry Cookbook by Thomas Keller **Chef to Cook for You:** Escoffier. In an age of preservatives, stabilizers, processing, and artificial ingredients, has food really advanced in a positive direction? I'd like to be able to travel back in time and see if the advent of modern machinery and technique really has advanced the classics. **Culinary Travel:** Japan – the respect for ingredients is so ingrained in the culture that it's like going to Mecca for food purists like myself

Josh Eden
Executive Chef | Shorty's .32

199 Prince St. New York, NY 10021

Restaurant E-mail: info@shortys32.com

Phone: (212) 375-8275

RESTAURANT FACTS
Seats: 32 **Weeknight Covers:** 60–100 **Weekend Covers:** 60–100
Check Average (with Wine): $43–$46 **Tasting Menu:** No

CHEF FACTS
Cuisine: In the spirit of new American **Born:** 1970 **Began Career:**
1986 **Culinary School:** French Culinary Institute, New York, NY **Grad
Year:** 1994 **Stages:** New York, NY: Daniel, Xing, 66, JoJo **Work History:** New York, NY: Daniel, Jean-Georges **Mentor(s):** Jean-Georges
Vongerichten, Tom Valente, Daniel Boulud **Awards:** 2008 StarChefs.
com Rising Star Chef New York **Languages Spoken:** Spanish, a little
French

NOTABLE DISH(ES): Pork Milanese with Pea Shoot and Radish Salad and Passionfruit Beurre Noisette

FAST FACTS
Restaurant Recs: I definitely hit Sushi Samba and Blue Ribbon after service a lot **Kitchen Tool(s):**
The Vita-Prep blender – that thing is a workhorse. I got a new one right before I opened this place.
Interview Question: I like to get to know people first **Flavor Combo(s):** Orange and chocolate – definitely one of my favorites; lemon and parsley; peanut butter and chocolate **Fave Cookbook(s):** Michel
Bras' Essential Cuisine **Culinary Travel:** Spain – I think the culinary industry has really embraced in
Spain. The whole day revolves around food, which is really nice for creative chefs.

Marc Ehrler
Executive Chef | The Ventana Room

7000 North Resort Drive Tuscon, AZ 85750

Restaurant E-mail: mehrler@loewshotels.com

Phone: (305) 604-1601

RESTAURANT FACTS
Seats: 56 **Weeknight Covers:** 50 **Weekend Covers:** 70 **Check Average (w/o Wine):** $103 **Tasting Menu:** Yes Between $85 and $135 **Kitchen Staff:** 8

CHEF FACTS
Cuisine: Open-minded Mediterranean **Born:** 1958 **Began Career:** 1974 **Culinary School:** Académie Culinaire de France, France **Work History:** St. Martin: La Samanna at the Rosewood Hotel, Barbuda K-Club; Miami Beach: Loews; Santa Barbara, CA: The Stonehouse Restaurant at San Ysidro Ranch; Newport Beach, CA: Antoine at Le Meridien; New York, NY: The Westbury Hotel; Maxims; France: La Terrasse at Le Juana, Maxims de Paris, Hotel de Franc **Mentor(s):** Alain Ducasse **Awards:** Master Chef of France **Affiliations:** JBF, Culinaire Philanthropique **Languages Spoken:** French, Spanish

NOTABLE DISH(ES): Crunchy Porcini Truffle Risotto Lollipop; Orange Blossom Banana Dumpling with Coconut Sorbet

FAST FACTS
Restaurant Recs: Hibachi Kama for Japanese **Kitchen Tool(s):** Pacojet; Thermomix; kitchen fork; Peltex fish spatula; Porsche knife; and kitchen towel **Interview Question:** How are you inspired? Where do you get your inspiration from? **Flavor Combo(s):** I always like the simplest combination that will enhance the most amazing main ingredient. Just like a play or good movie, one main actor and an amazing supporting cast that will make the movie shine... **Fave Cookbook(s):** La Riviera d'Alain Ducasse: Recettes au Fil du Temps by Alain Ducasse; Le Guide Culinaire by Auguste Escoffier **Chef to Cook for You:** Chef Hiroyuki Sakai for his respect and passion for food, and his ability to evolve. I have a great affinity for his Japanese approach to French cuisine. **Culinary Travel:** In the US definitely New York. Everything is there. Internationally I would say Japan – I was in Osaka to open the Ritz-Carlton – I'd definitely go back. Spain, Barcelona, the Basque region and the Biarritz area – the food there is very similar to the food from where I come in France – same approach but different ingredients.

E

Michael Ellis
Chef de Cuisine | Dry Creek Kitchen

317 Healdsburg Ave. Healdsburg, CA 95448

Restaurant E-mail: mellis@charliepalmer.com

Phone: (707) 431-0330

RESTAURANT FACTS
Seats: 68–100 **Weeknight Covers:** 100 **Weekend Covers:** 150
Check Average (with Wine): $90 **Tasting Menu:** Yes $74/$119
Kitchen Staff: 6

CHEF FACTS
Other Restaurants: Banquet facilities for the hotel **Cuisine:** Progressive American **Born:** 1977 **Began Career:** 1989 **Work History:** Washington, DC: The Ritz-Carlton, 600 Restaurant at the Watergate Hotel, Charlie Palmer Steak, Ardeo/Bardeo **Mentor(s):** Bryan Voltaggio, Charlie Palmer **Affiliations:** I teach at the local high school and we donate a lot **Languages Spoken:** Kitchen Spanish

NOTABLE DISH(ES): Jumbo Lump Crabcakes with Caper Rémoulade, Toasted Brioche, Arugula, Fennel, Papaya and Matchstick Potatoes

FAST FACTS
Restaurant Recs: Barn Diva for the French onion soup **Kitchen Tool(s):** Vita-Prep – it will purée everything **Interview Question:** What do you want to do with your life? **Flavor Combo(s):** I like Southeast Asian flavor combinations: cilantro, lemongrass, coconut milk and sambal **Fave Cookbook(s):** Barbecue Sauces, Rubs and Marinades by Steve Raichlen; La Cocina de los Postres by Oriol Balaguer; el Bulli 2004-2005 by Ferran Adriá **Chef to Cook for You:** Morimoto – he just kicks ass **Culinary Travel:** Spain – I've always wanted to go, and I've never been out of the country. I want to go to el Bulli.

Josh Eme
Gordon Ra
at The Lo

Josh Emett
Chef | Gordon Ramsay at The London

151 West 54th St. New York, NY 10019

Restaurant E-mail: joshemett@gordonramsay.com

Phone: (212) 468-8888

RESTAURANT FACTS
Seats: 45 **Weeknight Covers:** 80–90 **Weekend Covers:** 80–90
Check Average (with Wine): $200 **Tasting Menu:** Yes $135 **Kitchen
Staff:** 10

CHEF FACTS
Born: 1973 **Began Career:** 1991 **Culinary School:** Waikato Poly-
technic, New Zealand **Work History:** Australia: Waipa Delta, Cin Cin
on Quay, Est Est Est; England: Restaurant Gordon Ramsay, Gordon
Ramsay at Claridge's, The Savoy Grill, Banquette **Awards:** 2008
StarChefs.com Rising Star Hotel Chef New York **Affiliations:** We do
some charity work with City Harvest. We have relationships with culinary schools and done a few classes inside our kitchen. We also teach a lot of stages.

NOTABLE DISH(ES): Saddle of Rabbit Poached in Almond Milk with White Asparagus with La Ratte
Potato and Passion Fruit Vinaigrette

FAST FACTS
Restaurant Recs: Tia Pol for tapas; Public; Ed's Lobster Bar on the corner of Lafayette and Spring
– I love the crab and artichoke dip, the fish, and the lobster **Interview Question:** How long do you
intend to work for us? I want an honest answer, and we expect a minimum of a year out of someone.
Flavor Combo(s): Earthy flavors – Jerusulam artichokes with rabbit; scallop and cauliflower **Fave
Cookbook(s):** The original Michel Bras cookbook **Chef to Cook for You:** Michel Bras – he's got amazing balance and finesse in his cooking **Culinary Travel:** Asia or South America. Somewhere I haven't
been yet. I would like to learn more about the cooking techniques in Asia.

E

Greg Engelhardt
Chef de Cuisine | André's

401 South Sixth St. Las Vegas, NV 890101

Restaurant E-mail: info@andrelv.com

Phone: (702) 385-5016

RESTAURANT FACTS
Seats: 60–70 **Weeknight Covers:** 60 **Weekend Covers:** 60 **Check Average (with Wine):** $160 **Tasting Menu:** Yes Varies **Kitchen Staff:** 10

CHEF FACTS
Cuisine: Classical French **Born:** 1977 **Began Career:** 1993 **Culinary School:** The Culinary Institute of America, Hyde Park, NY **Grad Year:** 2000 **Stages:** Various stages in Norway, Italy and Austria **Work History:** Crystal Cruise Lines **Mentor(s):** Chef Andre Rochat, Trygve Jensen (Norwegian Master Mason), Chef Carlos Guia, "Paddy" Glennon **Awards:** 2008 Starchefs.com Rising Star Chef Las Vegas; Las Vegas "Culinary Cup" Competition at the MGM Grand, First Place; Michelin 1 star

NOTABLE DISH(ES): Cube of Poussin, Black Truffle and Foie Gras with Poussin and Porcini Jus; Caponata-Wrapped Rack of Lamb with Loin, Fondant Potatoes and Natural Lamb Jus with Harissa

FAST FACTS
Restaurant Recs: Vive Mercados for quality inexpensive food and the best margaritas in town. I get the chile relleno chimichanga – an egg-dipped and fried chile relleno stuffed into the burrito before the burrito is deep-fried. The whole thing is served enchilada style (it's not on the menu). I order it with a jarón (big pitcher) of margarita on the rocks. **Kitchen Tool(s):** The pasta machine - I use it every day. Although the Cryovac® is the most important thing in the kitchen. **Interview Question:** Who is Andre Rochat? What cook book are you currently reading? What would you cook for my staff tonight? I have all potential kitchen candidates cook dinner for my staff as their evaluation. They do not know that most of the evaluation falls on the enthusiasm, resourcefulness, cost effectiveness and coordination of the meal – but I base most of my decision on this test. Anyone who wants to cook for guests at a Michelin-starred restaurant should want to cook for the staff of that restaurant too. **Flavor Combo(s):** Lamb and harissa; duck and raspberry; carrot and ginger **Fave Cookbook(s):** Larousse Gastronomique by Prosper Montagne; Cooking with the Seasons by Jean-Louis Palladin; Culinary Artistry by Andrew Dornenburg and Karen Page **Chef to Cook for You:** To cook for me, Escoffier. Absolutely. That would be a big meal, huh? **Culinary Travel:** The Orient – it is one of the last places I haven't been. The spices, the cuisine and the technique are all amazing.

Todd English
Chef/Owner | Olives

201 Park Ave. New York, NY 10003

Restaurant E-mail: tenglish@toddenglish.com

Phone: (212) 353-8345

RESTAURANT FACTS
Seats: 85 **Weeknight Covers:** 100 **Weekend Covers:** 175 **Check Average (w/o Wine):** $54 **Tasting Menu:** No **Kitchen Staff:** 6

CHEF FACTS
Other Restaurants: Boston, MA: Bonfire, Kingfish Hall, Figs; Olives; Charlestown, MA: Olives; Las Vegas, NV: Olives; Washington, DC; Olives; Aspen, CO: Olives; Biloxi, MS: Olives; Uncasville, CT: Tuscany; Seattle, WA: Fish Club; The Queen Mary II: Todd English; Lake Buena Vista, FL: BlueZoo; New Orleans, LA Riche **Cuisine:** Mediterranean **Born:** 1960 **Began Career:** 1975 **Culinary School:** The Culinary Institute of America, Hyde Park, NY **Grad Year:** 1982 **Stages:** Italy: Dal Pescatore; Paraccuchi **Work History:** Cambridge, MA: Michela's; Italy: Dal Pescatore; New York, NY: La Côte Basque **Mentor(s):** Julia Child, Jean Jacques Rachou, various "nonnas" in Italy **Protégée(s):** Suzanne Goin, Barbara Lynch, Marc Ofaly **Awards:** 2001 Bon Appetit Restaurateur of the Year; 1999 Nations Restaurant News Top 50 Tastemaker; 1994 James Beard Foundation Best Chef Northeast; 1991 James Beard Foundation National Rising Star Chef **Affiliations:** Big Brother, Share our Strength, the Anthony Spinazzola Foundation, Community Servings, The Boys and Girls Clubs, City Year, AIWF, IACP, JBF, MCC, StarChefs.com Advisory Board **Books Published:** The Figs Table; The Olives Dessert Table; The Olives Table **Languages Spoken:** French, Italian

NOTABLE DISH(ES): Hot Fiddlehead Fern and Lobster Salad; Parmesan Pudding with Sweet Pea Sauce

FAST FACTS
Restaurant Recs: Louis Luncheonette for burgers **Kitchen Tool(s):** Portable hand blender **Interview Question:** I ask them to dice an onion for me. It shows me their love and passion for cooking. **Flavor Combo(s):** Anchovy, capers and garlic **Fave Cookbook(s):** The Time Life Good Cook Series by Time Life **Chef to Cook for You:** Auguste Escoffier – he was the grandfather of French cuisine so it would really be the ultimate fine dining meal **Culinary Travel:** India – the variety of spices and flavors there really inspires me

E

Tony Esnault
Executive Chef | Adour

2 East 55th Street New York, NY 10022

Restaurant E-mail: tonyesnault@stregis.com

Phone: (212) 753-4500

RESTAURANT FACTS
Seats: 72–88 **Weeknight Covers:** 120 **Weekend Covers:** 140 **Check Average (w/o Wine):** $140 **Tasting Menu:** Yes $110 **Kitchen Staff:** 12

CHEF FACTS
Cuisine: French **Born:** 1971 **Began Career:** 1988 **Culinary School:** Université François Rabelais, France **Grad Year:** 1988 **Work History:** Boston, MA: The Ritz-Carlton; France: Alain Ducasse Restaurant, Auberge de l'Ill, Carré des Feuillants, Le Montparnasse 25, Le Louis XV; San Francisco, CA: The Ritz-Carlton; New York, NY: Essex House **Mentor(s):** Alain Ducasse **Awards:** 2006 StarChefs.com Rising Star Chef New York **Languages Spoken:** French

NOTABLE DISH(ES): Marinated Bay Scallops in Cucumber Vinegar, Romaine, Hearts of Romaine, Caviar, Green Apple Mustard; Foie Gras Tapioca Ravioli, Celery; Sunchoke Broth, Black Truffles

FAST FACTS
Restaurant Recs: Del Posto **Kitchen Tool(s):** Knife sharpener; All-Clad pots **Interview Question:** What is your goal? **Flavor Combo(s):** I like tomato, truffle and basil – the peppery side of basil combined with the acidity of the tomato and the richness of the truffle **Fave Cookbook(s):** The Escoffier Cookbook: and Guide to the Fine Art of Cookery for Connoisseurs, Chefs, Epicures by Auguste Escoffier **Culinary Travel:** I love New York - you can get every ethnic food here, and there is so much energy! Everything seems to start in New York!

Malka Espinel

Malka Espinel
Pastry Chef | Johnny V

625 E Las Olas Blvd. Fort Lauderdale, FL 33301

Restaurant E-mail: info@johnnyvlasolas.com

Phone: (954) 761-7920

RESTAURANT FACTS
Seats: 135 **Weeknight Covers:** 100–150 **Weekend Covers:** up to 300 **Check Average (with Wine):** $75 **Check Average (w/o Wine):** $55 **Tasting Menu:** No **Kitchen Staff:** 2

CHEF FACTS
Cuisine: New American **Born:** 1972 **Began Career:** 1993 **Culinary School:** Cooking and Hospitality Institute of Chicago **Grad Year:** 1994 **Stages:** France: Fauchon; Spain: Hoffman **Work History:** Chicago, IL: Bittersweet; South Beach, FL: Mark's Place, The Tides Hotel, Astor Hotel; Key Biscayne, FL: The Biga Bakery; Palm Beach, FL: Sundy House **Mentor(s):** Hedy Goldsmith, Judy Contino, Chef Richard from CHIC, my grandmother **Awards:** 2008 StarChefs.com Rising Star Pastry Chef South Florida **Affiliations:** We do a lot of charity events as well as Share our Strength and The Newborn Project **Languages Spoken:** Spanish, Italian, a little French

NOTABLE DISH(ES): Spanish Parfait: Layers of Cinnamon Cake, Rhubarb Compote, and Flan Mousse, topped with a Churro; Three Berry Créme Brulée Pot Pie with Macadamia Crust and Seasonal Berries

FAST FACTS
Restaurant Recs: Ice Box Café on Lincoln Road – it's kind of a coffee shop **Kitchen Tool(s):** My Coldelite ice cream machine **Interview Question:** I ask, "What are the most important things that you need to create a new dessert?" **Flavor Combo(s):** I like to use fruits and herbs. Flowers and fruits is another one. **Fave Cookbook(s):** Tropical Desserts by Andrew McFallen **Chef to Cook for You:** I would most like to try Albert Adriá's pastry **Culinary Travel:** Europe for pastry, and specifically Spain

E

Bernardo Espinel
Chef de Cuisine | Bistro One LR

1 Lincoln Rd. Miami Beach FL 33139

Restaurant E-mail: bernardo.espinel@ritzcarlton.com

Phone: (786) 276-4033

RESTAURANT FACTS
Seats: 120 **Weeknight Covers:** 60 **Weekend Covers:** 110 **Check Average (with Wine):** $55–$65 **Tasting Menu:** No **Kitchen Staff:** 5

CHEF FACTS
Cuisine: French Latin **Born:** 1973 **Began Career:** 1994 **Culinary School:** Johnson & Wales University, Miami, FL **Grad Year:** 1996 **Stages:** Spain: The Ritz-Carlton **Work History:** Bal Harbour, FL: The Sheraton; Surfside, FL: The Beach House; Curaçao, NA: Kura Hulanda Hotel; New York, NY: Trust, Alias; Miami, FL: The DiLido Beach Club, Johnny V **Mentor(s):** Rafael Manzano - he taught me hard work and passion. Scott Ehlrich taught me flavor combinations and creative presentation.

NOTABLE DISH(ES): Grapefruit Glazed Duck with Salsify, Escarole and Soy

FAST FACTS
Restaurant Recs: There are a lot of Israelis in Miami so there is good falafel. I especially like Miami Juice for falafel. **Kitchen Tool(s):** Misono knives – they are light, thin and easy to sharpen **Interview Question:** I ask them about their experience and why they started cooking **Flavor Combo(s):** I went to Thailand two years ago and fell in love with their pungent flavors: Thai fish sauce, tamarind, palm sugar and galangal **Fave Cookbook(s):** My Vue: Modern French Cooking by Shannon Bennett **Chef to Cook for You:** Grant Achatz - I think he is the most innovative chef in the country right now **Culinary Travel:** I would love to go to India – when I started cooking I worked in the Caribbean in an Indian restaurant and love Indian spices. I would like to learn more about them.

Duskie Estes and John Stewart
Chefs/Owners | Zazu

3535 Guerneville Rd. Santa Rosa, CA 95401

Restaurant E-mail: deandjs@comcast.net

Phone: (707) 523-4814

RESTAURANT FACTS
Seats: 56-70 **Weeknight Covers:** 50-80 **Weekend Covers:** 80-110
Tasting Menu: No **Kitchen Staff:** 3

CHEF FACTS
Cuisine: American and rustic Northern Italian-inspired **Born:** 1967
Began Career: 1979 **Stages:** In Agliana, Italy and Paris, France
Work History: Providence, RI: Lucky's, Al Forno; Washington, DC: 21
Federal, Kinkead's; San Francisco, CA: Green's; Oakland, CA: Baywolf;
Seattle, WA: Dahlia Lounge; Etta's Seafood, Palace Kitchen, Café
Lago **Mentor(s):** Mario Batali **Awards:** 2003-2005 San Francisco
Chronicle Top 100 Restaurants; 2002 San Francisco Chronicle Top
Ten Best New Restaurant; 2000 City Search Seattle Best Chef **Affiliations:** SOS, Glide Church, DC
Central Kitchen. We give 1% of our profit to local charities. **Books Published:** Duskie was co-author on
Tom Douglas's Seattle Kitchen, which received a James Beard Award in 2001

NOTABLE DISH(ES): Rustichella Bucatini with a Marcona Almond Pistou and Roman Artichokes;
Lavender Fried Rabbit

FAST FACTS
Restaurant Recs: Pho Vietnam; Taylor's Refresher for burgers **Kitchen Tool(s):** Wooden spoons –
they don't beat up pans or ding the rims **Interview Question:** What is the most recent thing that you
have read? As a cook you need to get exposure vicariously. **Flavor Combo(s):** Orange and bay leaf
Fave Cookbook(s): Splendid Table: Recipes from Emilia-Romagna by Lynne Rossetto Kasper **Culinary
Travel:** Umbria to learn. I want to go and eat in all the bistros.

Jenni Etchison
Pastry Chef | Pricci

500 Pharr Rd. Atlanta, GA 30305

Restaurant E-mail: jennietch@hotmail.com

Phone: (212) 546-5320

RESTAURANT FACTS
Seats: 175 **Weeknight Covers:** 100–300 **Weekend Covers:**
300–400 **Check Average (with Wine):** $44 **Tasting Menu:** No
Kitchen Staff: 1

CHEF FACTS
Cuisine: Italian **Born:** 1975 **Began Career:** 1996 **Culinary School:**
Johnson and Wales, Charleston, SC **Grad Year:** 1996 **Work History:** Atlanta, GA: Nava, Two Urban Licks **Mentor(s):** Morten Wulff,
Kirk Parks, Joey Massi **Protégée(s):** Andrea Correa **Affiliations:** Les
Dames d'Escoffier **Languages Spoken:** Spanish

NOTABLE DISH(ES): Mini Nutella Moonpies with Coca Cola Granita

FAST FACTS
Restaurant Recs: La Casita in East Atlanta and Pho 79 on Buford Highway **Kitchen Tool(s):**
Copper pot **Interview Question:** What do you enjoy doing? Hopefully they say they like to cook!
Flavor Combo(s): Hazelnut and chocolate; berries and lemon; fresh cinnamon and vanilla **Fave
Cookbook(s):** Great Italian Desserts by Nick Malgieri **Chef to Cook for You:** Alice Waters – I just think
she started something so amazing with slow food. I have great respect people who pioneer something
new. She is an amazing person. **Culinary Travel:** Italy – as I have been doing a lot of research on Italian desserts and it is what I am really into at the moment

Alexandra Ewald
Executive Chef/Owner | La Tapa

P.O. Box #37 Cruz Bay, St. John, U.S. Virgin Islands

Restaurant E-mail: alex@latapastjohn.com

Phone: (340) 693-77-55

RESTAURANT FACTS
Seats: 65 **Weeknight Covers:** 80 **Weekend Covers:** 140 **Check Average (with Wine):** $65 **Tasting Menu:** No **Kitchen Staff:** 3

CHEF FACTS
Cuisine: Contemporary Mediterranean, rustic **Born:** 1964 **Work History:** Washington, DC: The Four Seasons; France: Bar de Labourd; St. John, Virgin Islands: Fern House Restaurant **Mentor(s):** My father and my staff like Mark Frech (formerly of Mario Batali's Babbo), Gabriel Gabreski (formerly with Daniel Boulud's Daniel) and Roland Czekelius (teacher at CIA in Vermont) **Awards:** Best Wine List Virgin Islands **Languages Spoken:** Spanish, French, German

NOTABLE DISH(ES): La Tapa Filet with Spiced Rum au Poivre; Tuna Tartare Spring Rolls with Passion Soy Glaze

FAST FACTS
Restaurant Recs: Banana Deck, they have very simple food; Hercule's Paté Delight for great local food and the best conch and beef patés **Kitchen Tool(s):** Inexpensive $15 woks – I can do anything and most everything in them, from sauces to paella. When they are worn out, I just buy new ones. **Interview Question:** How flexible are you? **Flavor Combo(s):** Salt, local limes, and olive oil **Fave Cookbook(s):** Bouchon by Thomas Keller and El Gusto de la Diversidad by Santi Santamaria **Chef to Cook for You:** Juan Mari Arzak, because I lived in the Basque country for many years and admire the Basque culture. Juan Mari delivers the simplicity of the Basque food at a very high level. **Culinary Travel:** The Basque Country – I like the simple approach to food, the quality of the ingredients, and the roughness of the country

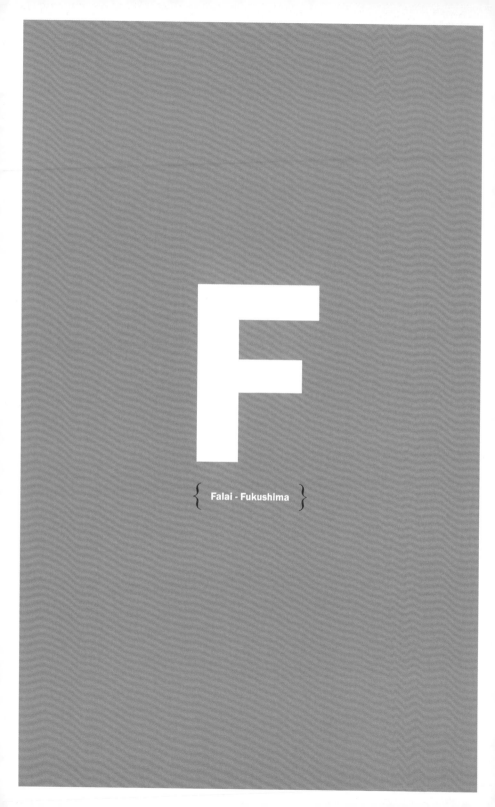

F

{ Falai - Fukushima }

Iacopo Falai
Executive Chef | Falai

68 Clinton St. New York, NY 10002

Restaurant E-mail: iacopofalai@gmail.com

Phone: (212) 253-1960

RESTAURANT FACTS
Weeknight Covers: 50-70 **Weekend Covers:** 70-100 **Check Average (with Wine):** $60 **Check Average (w/o Wine):** $40 **Tasting Menu:** Yes $55 **Kitchen Staff:** 3-4

CHEF FACTS
Other Restaurants: Falai Panneteria, Caffé Falai **Cuisine:** Italian **Born:** 1972 **Began Career:** 1992 **Culinary School:** I.A.P.A.F., Italy **Grad Year:** 1992 **Stages:** France: Lucas Carton, Michel Bras **Work History:** Italy: Enoteca Pinchiorri; New York, NY: Le Cirque 2000, Osteria del Circo, Bread Tribeca **Mentor(s):** Michel Belin, Ricardo Monco **Protégée(s):** Fredrik Berselius, Tom Block **Awards:** 2006 StarChefs. com Rising Star Chef New York **Affiliations:** StarChefs.com Advisory Board **Languages Spoken:** French, Spanish, Italian

NOTABLE DISH(ES): Cocoa Pappardelle with Venison Ragu; Ricotta and Spinach Gnudi; Black Cabbage Bread

FAST FACTS
Restaurant Recs: Acqua in South Street Seaport for focaccia with stracchino **Kitchen Tool(s):** Scale; thermometer **Interview Question:** Why do you want to work for me? Why did you decide to be part of the restaurant business? **Flavor Combo(s):** Parmigiano Reggiano and balsamic **Fave Cookbook(s):** Cookbooks by Michel Bras; el Bulli by Ferran Adriá **Chef to Cook for You:** Wylie Dufresne – no need for explanation **Culinary Travel:** I love Barcelona for its modern and old-fashioned cooking – and I don't just mean el Bulli. I love the concept of tapas.

Elizabeth Falkner
Executive Chef/Owner | Orson

399 Grove St. San Francisco, CA 94102

Restaurant E-mail: elizabeth@citizencake.com

Phone: (415) 861-2228

RESTAURANT FACTS
Seats: 160–190 **Weeknight Covers:** 125–140 **Weekend Covers:** 180–200 **Check Average (with Wine):** $65 **Tasting Menu:** Yes $45/$50/$60/$65 **Kitchen Staff:** 4–5

CHEF FACTS
Other Restaurants: Citizen Cake, Citizen Cupcake **Cuisine:** Modern Californian pastries and desserts **Born:** 1966 **Began Career:** 1990 **Stages:** New York, NY: Daniel; San Francisco, CA: Cypress Club; Holland: Amstel Hotel **Work History:** San Francisco, CA: Rubicon, Masa's **Mentor(s):** Traci Des Jardins, Mary Cech, Julian Serrano, Barbara Tropp, Robert Steinberg **Protégée(s):** Luis Villavelazquez, William Pilz **Awards:** 2003 Women Chefs and Restaurateurs Women Who Inspire; 1999 San Francisco Magazine Pastry Chef of the Year **Affiliations:** CFH, JBF, LDE, WCR

NOTABLE DISH(ES): The Black Island; Steak a la Mode

FAST FACTS
Restaurant Recs: Mijita for the Chilaquiles **Kitchen Tool(s):** Immersion blender **Interview Question:** What kind of food do you like to eat? I learn quickly about a person's palate. **Flavor Combo(s):** Rose, saffron and cardamom; hazelnut and chocolate **Fave Cookbook(s):** Secrets Gourmands by Pierre Hermé **Chef to Cook for You:** I'm a huge fan of Nancy Silverton, Suzanne Goin, Traci Des Jardins, Gabriel Hamilton. They make amazing, delicious, honest and beautiful food. **Culinary Travel:** To Southeast Asia and India – the spice trail. I love the flavors and I've never been to that region of the world.

PUBLIC

Brad Farmerie
Chef | Public

210 Elizabeth St. New York, NY 10012

Restaurant E-mail: brad@public-nyc.com

Phone: (212) 343-7011

RESTAURANT FACTS
Seats: 120–134 **Weeknight Covers:** 130–150 **Weekend Covers:** 225 **Check Average (with Wine):** $70 **Tasting Menu:** No **Kitchen Staff:** 6–7

CHEF FACTS
Other Restaurants: The Monday Room **Cuisine:** Eclectic global fusion **Born:** 1973 **Began Career:** 1996 **Culinary School:** Le Cordon Bleu, England **Grad Year:** 1996 **Work History:** England: The Providores and Tapa Room, Coast, Chez Nico, Sugar Club, Le Manoir aux Quat' Saisons **Mentor(s):** Peter Gordon, Adam Farmerie, my mother **Awards:** 2005 StarChefs.com Rising Star Chef New York **Affiliations:** We aren't directly affiliated with any charities or organizations, but we do tend to support many of the same ones year after year: The Children of Bellevue (where I met my wife!), Publicolor, Taste of the Lower East Side, AIWF Days of Taste, Spoons across America, Project by Project

NOTABLE DISH(ES): Fromage Blanc and Thyme Sorbet; Grilled Kangaroo on Coriander Falafel

FAST FACTS
Restaurant Recs: Dok Suni for bok salad, noodles and deji-bulgogi; Tavern on Jane for burgers; Criff Dogs for any hot dog **Kitchen Tool(s):** Mortar and pestle, food processor **Interview Question:** Where are your favorite places to eat and what dishes do you like to eat there? **Flavor Combo(s):** Fat and acid **Fave Cookbook(s):** Thai Food by David Thompson; The Sugar Club Cookbook by Peter Gordon; On Food and Cooking by Harold McGee **Culinary Travel:** Hanoi and Bangkok. There's just enough western influence to make it available, but they stick to their roots.

F

Dean Fearing
Executive Chef | Fearing's

2121 McKinney Avenue Dallas, TX 75201

Restaurant E-mail: lauren.lapeyre@ritz-carlton.com

Phone: (214) 880-4536

RESTAURANT FACTS
Seats: 235–251 **Weeknight Covers:** 250 **Weekend Covers:** 400 **Check Average (with Wine):** $400 **Check Average (w/o Wine):** $70 **Kitchen Staff:** 16

CHEF FACTS
Cuisine: Southwestern **Born:** 1955 **Began Career:** 1978 **Culinary School:** The Culinary Institute of America, Hyde Park, NY **Grad Year:** 1978 **Stages:** Cincinnati, OH: La Maisonette **Work History:** Cincinnati, OH: La Maisonette; Dallas, TX: The Fairmont Hotel, The Rosewood Mansion on Turtle Creek **Mentor(s):** Wolfgang Puck, Julia Child, Alain Senderen **Protégée(s):** Jody Denton, Jim Mills, Randall Warder **Awards:** 2008 James Beard Foundation Nomination for Best New Restaurant; 2007 Esquire Magazine Restaurant of the Year; 1995-2001 Mobil 5 Star Award; 1994 James Beard Foundation Best Chef Southwest; 1990-present AAA Five Diamond Award **Affiliations:** Chefs for Humanity's Chef Council **Books Published:** The Mansion on Turtle Creek Cookbook; Dean Fearing's Southwest Cuisine **Languages Spoken:** Kitchen Spanish

NOTABLE DISH(ES): Backyard BBQ Chicken

FAST FACTS
Restaurant Recs: Primo's Mexican Restaurant for Eddie's Grandmother's Red Chili Enchiladas; Sonny Bryan's BBQ for everything **Kitchen Tool(s):** Stock pot **Interview Question:** What cook book did you just finish? You learn a lot about a person by what they read. **Flavor Combo(s):** Sweet and spicy – at Fearing's we've done away with rules; our tag line is "Elevated American Cuisine – Bold Flavors, No Borders." We are constantly experimenting in the kitchen to find new flavor combinations that surprise our guests and keep them coming back to see what we will create next. **Fave Cookbook(s):** Out of Kentucky Kitchens by Marion Flexner **Chef to Cook for You:** Alain Chapel is a French chef who I believe was one of the most creative chefs known to man. I had his Foie Gras over Blackened Turnip with Currant Sauce in 1982 and it was so memorable that I can recall every bit of the experience to this day. He passed away in 1990. **Culinary Travel:** I would like to travel to all the major cities because they provide such a diverse, ethnic culinary experience. I was just in New York City and I enjoyed seeing all the new spots and what people were doing, both with design and in the kitchen. It says a lot about where the culinary world is going.

Todd Feitl
Pastry Chef | Vie Restaurant

4471 Lawn Ave. Western Springs, IL 60558

Restaurant E-mail: celebratingvie@yahoo.com

Phone: (708) 246-2082

RESTAURANT FACTS
Seats: around 90 **Weeknight Covers:** 20–60 **Weekend Covers:** 100–160 **Tasting Menu:** Yes **Kitchen Staff:** 1

CHEF FACTS
Cuisine: Contemporary American **Born:** 1982 **Began Career:** 2004 **Culinary School:** CHIC (Cooking and Hospitality Institute of Chicago, affiliated with Le Cordon Bleu) **Grad Year:** 2004 **Work History:** Willow Springs, IL: Courtrights **Mentor(s):** Chef Erika Webb, Chef Paul Virant, Chef Greg Teffs, Chef Mike Salzinsky

NOTABLE DISH(ES): Frozen Honeycrisp Soufflé with Warm Spiced Honeycrisp Compote, Apple Spice Cake and an Apple Chip

FAST FACTS
Restaurant Recs: Kuma's Corner for the Slayer burger **Kitchen Tool(s):** My KitchenAid – never really thought about that until it broke. That and my Carpigiani ice cream machine. **Flavor Combo(s):** Orange and peach **Fave Cookbook(s):** A Chef for all Seaons by Gordon Ramsay – his narratives are great. He tells you what to look for at the markets and he has some really cool recipes. I also like The Silver Spoon and The Joy of Cooking because they're encyclopedias of food. **Chef to Cook for You:** Too many to choose from **Culinary Travel:** Honestly, probably Austria and Germany. I love Bavarian food and beer.

F

Susan Feniger
Co-Chef | Border Grill

1445 4th St. Santa Monica, CA 90401

Restaurant E-mail: susan@bordergrill.com

Phone: (310) 451-1655

RESTAURANT FACTS
Seats: 170 **Weeknight Covers:** 180 **Weekend Covers:** 292 **Check Average (w/o Wine):** $30 **Tasting Menu:** No **Kitchen Staff:** 4–5

CHEF FACTS
Other Restaurants: Las Vegas, NV: Border Grill Mandalay Bay; Los Angeles, CA: Ciudad **Cuisine:** Latin **Born:** 1953 **Began Career:** 1977 **Culinary School:** The Culinary Institute of America, Hyde Park, NY **Stages:** France: L'Oasis **Work History:** Chicago, IL: Le Perroquet; Los Angeles, CA: Ma Maison, City, Border Grill; France: L'Oasis **Mentor(s):** Gus Riedi, Alan Wagner **Protégée(s):** Wendy Brucker, Govind Armstrong **Awards:** 2001 Gourmet Magazine One of the Best Restaurants; 1997 Restaurants & Institutions Magazine IVY Award; 1990 LA Times Forty Best Restaurants; 1988 California Restaurant Writer Chef of the Year **Affiliations:** WCR, Chefs Collaborative, SRF, Share Our Strength **Books Published:** Cooking With Two Hot Tamales; Mesa Mexicana; City Cuisine; Mexican Cooking For Dummies **Languages Spoken:** Some Spanish, some French

NOTABLE DISH(ES): Cochinita Pibil; Coffee Brownies

FAST FACTS
Restaurant Recs: Brentwood for the vegetarian plate; Bombay Café for bhel puri; Peppone's for a steamed artichoke **Kitchen Tool(s):** 8- or 9-inch sauté pan **Interview Question:** Where do you like to go eat? **Flavor Combo(s):** Olive oil, lime and salt; sesame, soy and Pernod **Fave Cookbook(s):** Ethnic books from everywhere about street fare and home-style cuisine **Chef to Cook for You:** Alan Wagner – the most incredible cook from India. Full of passion and great, great taste buds. **Culinary Travel:** Vietnam, Thailand and Singapore – my kind of places. Soulful, full of passion and flavors.

Neil Ferguson
Executive Chef | Allen and Delancey

115 Allen Street New York, NY 10002

Restaurant E-mail: neil@monteverdirestaurant.com

Phone: (212) 253-5400

RESTAURANT FACTS
Seats: 60 **Weeknight Covers:** 110 **Weekend Covers:** 120–130
Check Average (with Wine): $80+ **Tasting Menu:** No **Kitchen Staff:** 7

CHEF FACTS
Cuisine: Tasty **Born:** 1972 **Began Career:** 1988 **Culinary School:** Highbury College of Technology for Professional Cookery, Portsmouth, England **Grad Year:** 1991 **Stages:** England: Le Manoir aux Quat' Saisons; Yountville, CA: The French Laundry **Work History:** England: Le Gavroche, Claridges, Hotel Pied a Terre, La Tante Claire, The Square, Aubergine, Gordon Ramsay, Connaught Hotel; France: L'Esperance, L'Arpege; New York, NY: Gordon Ramsay at The London **Mentor(s):** Alain Passard **Awards:** 2008 StarChefs.com Rising Star Chef New York **Affiliations:** City Harvest, Taste of the Lower East Side, FCI, Union Square Farmers Market **Languages Spoken:** French, a little German and Spanish

NOTABLE DISH(ES): Filet of Cod with Blood Orange, Swiss Chard and Taggiasca Olives; Carmelized Bone Marrow, Caviar, Shallot Puree

FAST FACTS
Restaurant Recs: Taboon on 52nd and 10th for amazing Israeli food – falafel, tatziki, great shellfish, etc. The bread is unbelievable. **Kitchen Tool(s):** Vita-Prep – every single one of my dishes has a purée on it. It makes the food more palatable and concentrates the flavor. **Interview Question:** I like to get a feel for what their aspirations are, what they want to do with their career **Flavor Combo(s):** Apricots and almonds; fennel and pear; hazelnuts and sunchokes; licorice and sage **Fave Cookbook(s):** Great Chefs of France by Anthony Blake and Quentin Crewe from 1977. It is a great, great book. **Chef to Cook for You:** Alain Chapel – he trained Ducasse. Sadly he had a heart attack at 50. **Culinary Travel:** Japan – I've read in Newsweek how well Tokyo has done in the Michelin, and Kyoto has done even better. My food is missing what that food offers.

F

Terence Feury
Executive Chef | Maia Market & Restaurant

789 E. Lancaster Ave. Villanova, PA 19085

Restaurant E-mail: Tfeury@tastenectar.com

Phone: (866)-907-6242

RESTAURANT FACTS
Seats: 200 **Weeknight Covers:** 300 **Weekend Covers:** 450 **Check Average (with Wine):** $65 **Tasting Menu:** No **Kitchen Staff:** 17

CHEF FACTS
Other Restaurants: Maia Cafe, Market and Bistro **Cuisine:** Regional American seafood **Born:** 1967 **Began Career:** 1984 **Culinary School:** Academy of the Culinary Arts, Mays Landing, NJ **Grad Year:** 1988 **Stages:** New York, NY: Le Cirque; Lespinasse **Work History:** New York, NY: Waldorf-Astoria, Le Bernardin, Alison on Domenic; Philadelphia, PA: Striped Bass, The Ritz-Carlton, Fahrenheit **Mentor(s):** Eric Ripert, Laurent Manrique, Dan Silverman **Protégée(s):** Michael Solomonov, Shazad Khan, Mike Daley **Awards:** 2003 StarChefs.com Rising Star Chef Philadelphia; 2001 James Beard Foundation Best Chef Mid Atlantic Nominee; 2000 Restaurants & Institutions Rising Star **Affiliations:** BreastCancer.org, Slow Food, LocalFoodPhilly.org **Languages Spoken:** Spanish

NOTABLE DISH(ES): Spanish Mackerel Tartare with Pickled Kumquats

FAST FACTS
Restaurant Recs: DC Sandwich for Vietnamese pork sandwiches **Kitchen Tool(s):** Silver spoon because I have cooked with it everyday for at least 9 years, except for 2 days a couple of years ago when I lost it in a bucket of butterscotch pastry cream **Interview Question:** What was the best meal you've ever eaten? You can always gauge someone's passion by the way they can recall details of certain meals. **Flavor Combo(s):** I have a lot! Chocolate and mint; fava beans and savory; celery and truffles **Fave Cookbook(s):** Paul Bocuse's Regional French Cooking by Paul Bocuse **Chef to Cook for You:** Joël Robuchon. His restaurant in New York is my absolute favorite. He does very simple food at an extremely high level. **Culinary Travel:** Spain – I have never been and am incredibly curious.

Dirk Flanigan
Executive Chef | The Gage

24Michigan Ave. Chicago, IL 60603
Restaurant E-mail: dflanigan@thegagechicago.com
Phone: (312) 372-4243

RESTAURANT FACTS
Seats: 230 **Weeknight Covers:** 300 **Weekend Covers:** 425 **Check Average (with Wine):** $65 **Check Average (w/o Wine):** $52 **Tasting Menu:** Yes Upon Request **Kitchen Staff:** 8-12

CHEF FACTS
Cuisine: Contemporary American **Born:** 1968 **Began Career:** 1968 **Work History:** Chicago, IL: Blue Water Grill, Blue Plate Catering, Meritage, Echo **Mentor(s):** Carrie Nahabedian, Jeff Jackson, Todd Rogers **Awards:** 2008 Food & Wine Magazine Global Go List; Chicago Tribune 3 Stars; Chicago Magazine Top 21 New Restaurants; Sun Times 2.5 Stars

NOTABLE DISH(ES): Basil-Marinated Escargot, Melted Red Onion, Stickney Hill Goat Cheese Soup; Chicken-Fried Lobster, Frisee, Radish, Blue Cheese Butter, Hot Sauce Vinaigrette

FAST FACTS
Restaurant Recs: I am highly anticipating the opening of Tony Priolo's Piccolo Sogno at Grand and Halstead **Kitchen Tool(s):** The Vita-Prep and the sausage stuffer **Interview Question:** Why should I hire you? Why did you leave your last job? Where do you see yourself in two years? **Flavor Combo(s):** Snails and goat cheese **Fave Cookbook(s):** I am constantly going through my old journals to give my past recipes new life **Chef to Cook for You:** Jean-Louis Palladin, Escoffier – no need to explain why! **Culinary Travel:** I am interested in returning to Italy as well as Spain, because it is a hot bed of what is happening in the culinary world right now. The creativity combined with the new technology is intriguing.

Bobby Flay
Chef/Owner | Boy Meets Grill, Inc.

60 W 23rd St., Suite 630 New York, NY 10010

Restaurant E-mail: bf@bobbyflay.com

Phone: (212) 924-3076

CHEF FACTS

Other Restaurants: New York, NY: Bar Americain, Mesa Grill; Las Vegas, NV: Mesa Grill; Atlantis, Bahamas: Mesa Grill; Atlantic City, NJ: Bobby Flay Steak **Cuisine:** Southwestern **Born:** 1964 **Began Career:** 1983 **Culinary School:** The French Culinary Institute, New York, NY **Grad Year:** 1993 **Stages:** New York, NY: Jams **Work History:** New York, NY: Jam's (with Jonathan Waxman), Miracle Grill **Mentor(s):** Jonathan Waxman, Wolfgang Puck **Protégée(s):** Patricia Yeo, Katie Sparks, Mary Reading **Awards:** 2003 New York Times 3 stars; 1993 James Beard Foundation Rising Star Chef of the Year; 1993 French Culinary Institute Outstanding Graduate Award; 1992 New York Magazine Best Restaurant **Affiliations:** StarChefs.com Advisory Board **Books Published:** Bobby Flay's Bold American Food; From My Kitchen to Your Table; Boy Meets Grill; Bobby Flay Cooks American; Bobby Flay's Boy Gets Grill; The Mesa Grill Cookbook

NOTABLE DISH(ES): Grilled Mushrooms with Hazelnut Gremolata; Spanish Egg Tortilla with Goat Cheese and Charred Peppers

FAST FACTS

Restaurant Recs: Milanes for incredible Cuban sandwiches **Kitchen Tool(s):** Squeeze bottles for sauces and vinaigrettes; tongs; small metal spatula; side towel **Interview Question:** What food publications do you read and why? It's a good barometer of their interest in all aspects of the food world, and I want people who work for me to be tuned in. **Fave Cookbook(s):** The Zuni Café Cookbook by Judy Rodgers

Tom Fleming
Executive Chef | Central 214

5300 E Mockingbird Ln. Dallas, TX 75206

Restaurant E-mail: tom.fleming@central214.com

Phone: (214) 520-7969

RESTAURANT FACTS
Seats: 120 **Weeknight Covers:** 75 **Weekend Covers:** 140 **Check Average (with Wine):** $50 **Tasting Menu:** No **Kitchen Staff:** 3–4

CHEF FACTS
Cuisine: American comfort food **Born:** 1973 **Began Career:** 1990 **Culinary School:** Kendall College, Chicago, IL **Grad Year:** 1990 **Stages:** France: Paul Bocuse, L'Auberge d'Ile **Work History:** Chicago, IL: Everest, Brasserie Jo, Mediterraneo, Rivera, Grapevine, TX:The Old Hickory Steakhouse, Lobster Ranch, Lombardi Mare, Papas Brothers' Steak House **Mentor(s):** Jean Joho, John Hogan, David Holben **Protégée(s):** Bruni Bueno **Affiliations:** We work with numerous charities **Languages Spoken:** Spanish

NOTABLE DISH(ES): Diver Scallops with Rock Shrimp Lentil Ragout; Maryland Crab Cake

FAST FACTS
Restaurant Recs: Amigos for carne asada. As for after-hour places, I have two kids so I don't really get out much! **Kitchen Tool(s):** A really sharp Japanese mandolin and a good knife **Interview Question:** I first ask them to tell me about their three strengths and then explain their three biggest weaknesses. I'm looking for someone who is confident in their ability but who is humble enough to know they always have to constantly learn and improve on what they know to become a better chef. **Flavor Combo(s):** Rosemary and garlic **Fave Cookbook(s):** The Way to Cook by Julia Child **Chef to Cook for You:** Marc Haberline for L'Auberge d'Ile in Alsace. I apprenticed there and I think he is one of the best chefs in the world. **Culinary Travel:** Italy – I've never been and I think the food would be phenomenal

F

Jose Luis Flores
Pastry Chef | Ola

425 Ocean Dr. Miami Beach, FL 33139

Restaurant E-mail: ola_miami@bellsouth.net

Phone: (305) 695-9125

RESTAURANT FACTS
Seats: 95 **Weeknight Covers:** 100 **Weekend Covers:** 220-225
Check Average (with Wine): $65 **Tasting Menu:** No **Kitchen Staff:** 2

CHEF FACTS
Cuisine: Nuevo Latino **Born:** 1973 **Began Career:** 2000 **Culinary School:** Institute of Superior Studies of Pastry, Mexico **Grad Year:** 2001 **Stages:** New York, NY: China Grill **Work History:** New York, NY: Patria, Chicima, Calle Ocho, China Grill; Philadelphia, PA: Deseo, Arizona, Alma de Cuba **Mentor(s):** Douglas Rodriguez, Oriol Balaguer, Jacques Torres, Pierre Hermé **Protégée(s):** Bruni Bueno **Awards:** 2004 StarChefs.com Rising Star Pastry Chef Miami **Affiliations:** We work with many charities **Languages Spoken:** Spanish

NOTABLE DISH(ES): Dulce de Leche Brazo Gitano; Chocolate Bombe with Hazelnut Ice Cream

FAST FACTS
Restaurant Recs: Michy's – I like that the menu is always changing. Michelle makes delicious braised rabbit and wonderful ceviche. **Kitchen Tool(s):** I use a Chinese cleaver to chop chocolate. Also, metal and plastic spatulas, because of the way I work with chocolate. **Interview Question:** Can you work under pressure? I like everything to be perfect especially when it's busy. **Flavor Combo(s):** Chocolate and hazelnut; dulce de leche and fresh bananas **Fave Cookbook(s):** Dessert Cuisine by Oriol Balaguer **Chef to Cook for You:** Chef Juan Marie Arzak because he helped create modern Spanish cuisine. He is a great inspiration. **Culinary Travel:** Spain, especially Madrid, to see all the new big trends

Susanna Foo
Chef/Owner | Susanna Foo

1512 Walnut St. Philadelphia, PA 19102

Restaurant E-mail: shona215@yahoo.com

Phone: (215) 545-2666

RESTAURANT FACTS
Seats: 110–355 **Weeknight Covers:** 100 **Weekend Covers:** 250
Check Average (w/o Wine): $59 **Tasting Menu:** No

CHEF FACTS
Other Restaurants: Suilan (closed), Susanna Foo Gourmet Kitchen
Cuisine: Chinese cuisine with French technique **Born:** 1943 **Began
Career:** 1982 **Culinary School:** The Culinary Institute of America,
Hyde Park, NY **Stages:** China: Mandarin Hotel Thailand, Oriental Ho-
tel **Mentor(s):** Jacob Rosenthal **Protégée(s):** Mike Schulson **Awards:**
1999 Robert Mondavi Culinary Award of Excellence; 1997 James
Beard Foundation Best Chef Mid Atlantic; 1996 James Beard Founda-
tion Best International Cookbook; 1989 Food & Wine Best New Chefs **Affiliations:** IACP, JBF **Books
Published:** Susanna Foo Chinese Cuisine, Susanna Foo New Inspiration **Languages Spoken:** Chinese

NOTABLE DISH(ES): Braised Salmon with Soy and Ginger

Benjamin Ford
Chef | Ford's Filling Station

9531 Culver Blvd. Los Angeles, CA 90232

Restaurant E-mail: chefbenford@fordsfillingstation.net

Phone: (310) 202-1470

RESTAURANT FACTS
Seats: 130 **Weeknight Covers:** 160 **Weekend Covers:** 300 **Check Average (with Wine):** $50 **Check Average (w/o Wine):** $40 **Tasting Menu:** No **Kitchen Staff:** 10

CHEF FACTS
Other Restaurants: Chadwick **Cuisine:** American regional **Born:** 1966 **Began Career:** 1988 **Culinary School:** California Culinary Academy, San Francisco, CA **Grad Year:** 1989 **Work History:** Berkeley, CA: Chez Panisse; Los Angeles, CA: Opus, Campanile, Eclipse, The Farm at Beverly Hills, Chadwick **Mentor(s):** Alice Waters, Paul Bertolli, Jean-Michelle Judy **Protégée(s):** Govind Armstrong **Awards:** 2005 Condé Nast Top 50 Restaurants in the World; 3 stars from the LA Times **Affiliations:** EMA, NDB, Garden Magic Kids, Taste of the Nation

NOTABLE DISH(ES): Braised Kobe Cheeks; Seared Diver Scallop with Hudson Valley Foie Gras and Blood Orange

FAST FACTS
Restaurant Recs: Kiriko for seared toro **Kitchen Tool(s):** Cryovac® machine because it saves time, money and effort **Interview Question:** What inspires you? What sparks your creativity? A strong point of view is the best foundation a young cook can have. **Flavor Combo(s):** Leeks, green garlic and dates **Fave Cookbook(s):** Cooking by Hand by Paul Bertolli **Chef to Cook for You:** Paul Bertolli - he's one of the most rooted chefs when it comes to products. When he cooks something, you know that is how it should be done. **Culinary Travel:** Back to San Sebastian, my old stomping ground

Larry Forgione
Chef/Owner | An American Place

822 Washington Ave. St. Louis, MO 63101

Restaurant E-mail: amy.rossetti@winnlasvegas.com

Phone: (314) 418-5800

RESTAURANT FACTS
Seats: 98 **Weeknight Covers:** 50 **Weekend Covers:** 100 **Check Average (w/o Wine):** $53 **Tasting Menu:** Yes **Kitchen Staff:** 6–7

CHEF FACTS
Other Restaurants: Las Vegas, NV: An American Place at the Wynn Las Vegas; Rhinebeck, NY: Beekman 1776 Tavern, Primo, Above Restaurant, The Grill Room, The Coach House **Cuisine:** Creative American cooking driven by our ingredients **Born:** 1952 **Culinary School:** Culinary Institute of America, Hyde Park, NY **Grad Year:** 1974 **Work History:** England: The Connaught Hotel; France: Michel Guerard; New York, NY: An American Place, Regine, The River Café **Awards:** 1999 James Beard Foundation Award for Best Chef Northeast; 1993 James Beard "Chef of the Year"; Life Magazine "50 Most Influential Baby Boomers"; New York Times 3 stars; James Beard Foundation Best American Cookbook **Affiliations:** American Chefs Tribute to James Beard, City Meals-on-Wheels (Co-founder), American Spoon Foods (Co-founder) **Books Published:** An American Place: Celebrating the Flavors of America (American Place); Heart-Healthy Cooking for All Seasons

FAST FACTS
Kitchen Tool(s): Robot Coupe saves hours that would have been spent laborious tasks **Interview Question:** What do you feel you have contributed to cooking in America? **Culinary Travel:** Italy – to experience the culture and the simplicity of its cuisine

F

Megan Roen Forman
Assistant Pastry Chef | Sucré

3025 Magazine St. New Orleans, LA 70115

Restaurant E-mail: info@shopsucre.com

Phone: 504-520-8311

RESTAURANT FACTS
Tasting Menu: No **Kitchen Staff:** 5

CHEF FACTS
Cuisine: Desserts **Born:** 1973 **Began Career:** 1995 **Culinary School:** New England Culinary Institute, Montpelier, VT **Grad Year:** 1997 **Stages:** New York, NY: Gramercy Tavern; San Francisco, CA: Citizen Cake **Work History:** New York, NY: Park Avenue Café, Payard Pâtisserie and Bistro, The Rhiga Royal Hotel **Mentor(s):** Susan Spicer **Awards:** 2003 StarChefs.com Rising Star Pastry Chef New Orleans **Affiliations:** WCR **Languages Spoken:** French

NOTABLE DISH(ES): Milk Chocolate Mousse Bombe; Apple Pecan Beignets

FAST FACTS
Restaurant Recs: R&O for great oyster po-boys; Nine Roses Vietnamese Restaurant for the caramelized pork **Kitchen Tool(s):** Laser thermometer for checking the accuracy of oven temps and for chocolate tempering – it's less messy than the probe **Interview Question:** I like to ask prospective employees how/when they made the decision to enter the culinary and specifically the pastry business. It's a window into how passionate they are about the industry. **Flavor Combo(s):** Anything salty and chocolate; lychee and vanilla; citrus like kalamansi or yuzu with dark chocolate **Fave Cookbook(s):** The Bakers' Dozen by Fran Gage; Sweet Seasons by Richard Leach **Chef to Cook for You:** Martin Picard from Au Pied de Cochon **Culinary Travel:** Definitely Southeast Asia and India. I love the layering and depth of seasoning, and the fresh and bright notes in dishes.

Yves Fournier
Executive Chef | Andrei's Conscious Cuisine & Cocktails

2607 Main St. Irvine, CA 91614

Restaurant E-mail: yves@andreisrestaurant.com

Phone: (949) 2258-6600 x4731

RESTAURANT FACTS
Seats: 140 **Tasting Menu:** Yes

CHEF FACTS
Cuisine: California cuisine – organic, sustainable, small plates **Born:** 1965 **Began Career:** 1980 **Culinary School:** École Ferandi, France **Grad Year:** 1983 **Stages:** France: Michel Pasquet, Fauchon, Michel Rostang **Work History:** Newport Beach, CA: Hyatt Regency Newport Beach; Irvine, CA: Hyatt Regency Irvine; New York, NY: The Rainbow Room; France: Pitchoune, Le Fer a Cheval, Chez Eugene **Mentor(s):** Alain Passard, Alain Senderens, Michel Bras **Protégée(s):** Arnaud Goubert **Languages Spoken:** French, English

NOTABLE DISH(ES): Three Shots Gazpacho; Humboldt Fog and Chorizo Frittata

FAST FACTS
Restaurant Recs: Marché Moderne in Costa Mesa, CA for the blood sausage risotto and new Caledonia shrimp; Cafe R&D in Newport Beach, CA for a Reuben **Kitchen Tool(s):** Tongs; Japanese mandolin **Interview Question:** Why do you want to be a chef? I want to see if they really have a passion for food. **Flavor Combo(s):** Cheese with fresh herbs, like Humbolt Fog goat cheese with fresh sage;pomegranate glaze with salmon **Fave Cookbook(s):** Your Place or Mine? by Jean-Christophe Novelli; Australian Food Magazines **Chef to Cook for You:** The Pourcel Brothers **Culinary Travel:** Australia

F

Mark Franz
Chef/Owner | Farallon

450 Post St. San Francisco, CA 94102

Restaurant E-mail: mfranz@farallonrestaurant.com

Phone: (415) 956-6969

RESTAURANT FACTS
Seats: 160 **Weeknight Covers:** 200 **Weekend Covers:** 275 **Check Average (w/o Wine):** $85 **Tasting Menu:** No **Kitchen Staff:** 8

CHEF FACTS
Other Restaurants: Nick's Cove, Epic Roast House, Water Bar
Cuisine: Seafood **Born:** 1952 **Began Career:** 1979 **Culinary School:** California Culinary Academy, San Francisco, CA **Work History:** San Francisco, CA: Ernie's, Stars; Berkeley, CA: Sante Fe Bar and Grill
Books Published: The Farallon Cookbook **Languages Spoken:** A little Spanish, kitchen French

NOTABLE DISH(ES): Paprika-Braised Mediterranean Octopus

FAST FACTS
Restaurant Recs: Kabuto – for sushi **Kitchen Tool(s):** All-Clad sauté pan **Interview Question:** Do you really want to do this? **Fave Cookbook(s):** Le Guide Culinaire by Auguste Escoffier

Gabriel Frasca
Chef | Straight Wharf Restaurant

6 Harbor Sq. Nantucket, MA 2554

Restaurant E-mail: gabriel@straightwharfrestaurant.com

Phone: (508) 228-4499

RESTAURANT FACTS
Seats: 100–140 **Weeknight Covers:** 180 **Weekend Covers:** 180
Check Average (with Wine): $85 **Tasting Menu:** No **Kitchen Staff:**
4–8

CHEF FACTS
Cuisine: Seasonal sustainable seafood **Born:** 1974 **Began Career:**
1989 **Stages:** France: L'Abbaye de Saint Croix; Spain: Martin Berasat-
egui; Italy: St. Hubertus; New York, NY: Bouley Bakery **Work History:**
Boston, MA: Hamersley's Bistro, Chez Henri, Aquitaine Bis, Radius,
Spire; Italy: St. Hubertus; New York, NY: Danube **Mentor(s):** Gordon
Hamersley, Jim Becker, Seth Woods, David Bouley, Michael Schlow,
Paul O'Connell **Protégée(s):** Wesley Genovart, William Kovel **Awards:** 2006 StarChefs.com Rising Star
Chef Boston; 2001 Improper Bostonian Rising Star Chef **Affiliations:** JBF **Languages Spoken:** Italian,
Spanish, French

NOTABLE DISH(ES): Chanteney Carrot Gnocchi, Braised Rabbit, Pickled Ramps and Pecorino

FAST FACTS
Restaurant Recs: Nick's Roast Beef – for a large beef with extra sauce on an onion roll **Kitchen
Tool(s):** A Vita-Prep – it allows me to surprise diners by delivering familiar flavors in unexpected ways;
slotted spoon **Interview Question:** What's the last good cookbook you've read? It gives me a good
idea if they're going to like working with us. It's not a prerequisite that they like reading about chefs
with the same culinary background as me, but I'm pretty sure that if they're obsessed with molecular
gastronomy, then it's likely I'm going to bore them to tears. **Flavor Combo(s):** Sweet and salty **Fave
Cookbook(s):** Young Basque Cuisine by Martin Berasategui **Chef to Cook for You:** Martin Berasategui
– a brilliant thinker and an exacting technician **Culinary Travel:** Northern Africa – I'd love to see a
different take on the familiar flavors of the Mediterranean

Neal Fraser
Chef/Owner | Grace

7360 Beverly Blvd. Los Angeles, CA 90036

Restaurant E-mail: neal@gracerestaurant.com

Phone: (323) 934-4400

RESTAURANT FACTS
Seats: 90 **Weeknight Covers:** 60 **Weekend Covers:** 125 **Tasting Menu:** Yes $70-$85; $115-$130 with wine **Kitchen Staff:** 9

CHEF FACTS
Cuisine: New American **Born:** 1969 **Began Career:** 1992 **Culinary School:** The Culinary Institute of America, Hyde Park, NY **Grad Year:** 1992 **Stages:** Los Angeles, CA: Checker's Hotel; New York, NY: Park Avenue Café **Work History:** Los Angeles, CA: Pinot Bistro, Spago, Rox, Boxer, Rix, Grace **Mentor(s):** Octavio Becerra, Thomas Keller, David Burke **Awards:** 2004 StarChefs.com Rising Star Chef Los Angeles **Affiliations:** CIA, SOS, James Beard House, Dirona, Cystic Fibrosis, American Heart Association, Club Culinare, Outstanding in the Field, Slow Food **Languages Spoken:** Some Spanish

NOTABLE DISH(ES): Dungeness Crab Salad with Meyer Lemon Vinaigrette; Skate with Cauliflower and Raisin-Caper Emulsion

FAST FACTS
Restaurant Recs: Yai for duck with chili and garlic **Kitchen Tool(s):** Fish spatula, Vita-Mix, Japanese blender **Interview Question:** I don't have a specific question that I like to ask. I just want to hire people that want to grow. **Flavor Combo(s):** Nettles, sunchokes, raisins and capers; ramps, corn and morel mushrooms; cauliflower and ras al hanout **Fave Cookbook(s):** On Food and Cooking by Harold McGee; Simple Cuisine: The Easy, New Approach to Four-Star Cooking by Jean-Georges Vongerichten **Chef to Cook for You:** Fredy Girardet. He was the one chef on the top level who's food I have never tasted. **Culinary Travel:** Australia for the great produce, great chefs, and great wine. I really want to eat at Tetsuya.

John Fraser
Executive Chef | Dovetail

103 West 77th Street New York, NY 10024

Restaurant E-mail: jfraser@dovetailnyc.com

Phone: (212) 362-3800

RESTAURANT FACTS
Seats: 75–93 **Weeknight Covers:** 150 **Weekend Covers:** 180 **Check Average (with Wine):** $75 **Tasting Menu:** Yes $70 **Kitchen Staff:** 8–10

CHEF FACTS
Cuisine: Creative American **Born:** 1975 **Began Career:** 1993 **Stages:** France: l'Arpege; Los Angeles, CA: Lucques **Work History:** Los Angeles, CA: Cocco Pazzo, Raffles L'Ermitage Beverly Hills; Yountville, CA: The French Laundry; France: Taillevent, Maison Blanche; New York, NY: Snack Taverna, Compass **Mentor(s):** Thomas Keller, my father **Awards:** 2008 StarChefs.com Rising Star Chef New York; 2006 Esquire Magazine Young Chef to Watch; New York Times 3 stars **Languages Spoken:** Kitchen Spanish, kitchen French

NOTABLE DISH(ES): Colossal Crab Ravioli with Chorizo and Chickpeas; Buffalo with Baby Romaine, Sunchokes and Ginger Béarnaise

FAST FACTS
Restaurant Recs: Wonder Siam for the oxtail stew **Kitchen Tool(s):** My fish spatula **Interview Question:** What is your most recent work experience? **Flavor Combo(s):** Sweet and salty **Fave Cookbook(s):** Larousse Gastronomique **Chef to Cook for You:** Jean-Lous Palladin – his cookbook, Cooking with the Seasons, is the reason that I became a chef **Culinary Travel:** Asia – Japan, Thailand, Vietnam. I've never been, and I am curious about elaborate ingredients and styles of cooking which I haven't been exposed to yet.

Amanda Freitag
Chef | The Harrison

355 Greenwich St. New York, NY 10013

Restaurant E-mail: amanda@theharrison.com

Phone: (212) 274-9310

RESTAURANT FACTS
Seats: 80 **Weeknight Covers:** 150 **Weekend Covers:** 215 **Check Average (with Wine):** $140 **Tasting Menu:** No **Kitchen Staff:** 5–6

CHEF FACTS
Cuisine: Italian Mediterranean **Began Career:** 1986 **Culinary School:** The Culinary Institute of America, Hyde Park, NY **Grad Year:** 1989 **Stages:** France: L'Arpege **Work History:** New York, NY: Vong, Verbena, Il Buco, 'Cesca, Lavagna, Dining Room, Gusto Ristorante e Bar Americano, The Harrison **Mentor(s):** Diane Forley, my home economics teacher **Protégée(s):** Saul Montiel **Affiliations:** JBF, CCap and Autism Speaks **Languages Spoken:** Spanish

NOTABLE DISH(ES): Artichoke Heart with Fresh Ricotta, Spring Onions and Sweet Peas; Crispy Skate with Egg and Bacon Salad and Caper Emulsion

FAST FACTS
Restaurant Recs: Al Di La in Park Slope, Brooklyn for braised rabbit leg on soft polenta and pear cake **Kitchen Tool(s):** Microplane **Interview Question:** How long have you been cooking? **Flavor Combo(s):** Sweet and sour **Fave Cookbook(s):** The Silver Spoon Italian Cookbook by Phaidon Press **Chef to Cook for You:** Ferran Adriá, because I know I will never get to his restaurant **Culinary Travel:** Morroco – because I would love to learn about their spice combinations

Ford Fry
Executive Chef | JCT

1198 Howell Mill Rd., Suite 18 Atlanta, GA 30318

Restaurant E-mail: ford@jctkitchen.com

Phone: (404) 355-2252

RESTAURANT FACTS
Seats: 150 **Weeknight Covers:** 100–140 **Weekend Covers:** 300–340 **Check Average (with Wine):** $42 **Tasting Menu:** No **Kitchen Staff:** 18

CHEF FACTS
Cuisine: Classical Bistro with Southern regional influences **Born:** 1969 **Began Career:** 1991 **Culinary School:** New England Culinary Institute, Montpelier, VT **Grad Year:** 1991 **Work History:** Colorado: the Ritz-Carlton, The Ojai Valley Inn & Spa **Mentor(s):** Xavier Saloman, Nick Morfogen, the team at Balthazar **Awards:** 2007 StarChefs.com Rising Star Restaurant Concept Award Atlanta; 5 Star Employee, The Ritz-Carlton, Houston; Leader of the Future, The Ritz-Carlton, Houston; Leader of the Quarter, The Ritz-Carlton Aspen; The Distinguished Graduate Award (NECI) **Affiliations:** Georgia Organics **Languages Spoken:** Spanish

NOTABLE DISH(ES): Shrimps and Grits with Smoked Sausage; Bone-in New York Strip Steak with Turnip Gratin and Onion Rings

FAST FACTS
Restaurant Recs: On Buford Highway, Havana Sandwich Shop for Cuban sandwiches; Ming's BBQ for the roasted pork and Chinese broccoli; Nuevo Laredo is a Tex-Mex joint with good cheese enchiladas; Fritti in The Highlands has great pizza **Kitchen Tool(s):** Aztec wood burning grill **Interview Question:** Tell me a specific time where you went above and beyond to please a guest; I like this question because it shows their passion for service and if they can't give an example of a specific incident or speak vaguely then I know they are full of it. **Flavor Combo(s):** I am currently liking brown butter with everything. Two good combinations are emulsifying it with caramel and using it with pork jus. **Fave Cookbook(s):** The Balthazar Cookbook by Keith McNally **Chef to Cook for You:** Mario Batalli. Everything he does is so simple, authentic, and right on! **Culinary Travel:** New York, Napa, and London – it's the new Paris. Paris hasn't really progressed in the last few years; Napa has grown a ton. New York has such great competition – it keeps things going.

Katsuya Fukushima
Chef | Café Atlantico

405 Eighth St. NW Washington, DC 20004

Restaurant E-mail: katsuyaf@cafeatlantico.com

Phone: (202) 393-0812

RESTAURANT FACTS
Seats: 125 **Weeknight Covers:** 100 **Weekend Covers:** 200–225 **Check Average (w/o Wine):** $45 **Tasting Menu:** Yes $65 **Kitchen Staff:** 5–6

CHEF FACTS
Other Restaurants: minibar by José Andrés **Cuisine:** Nuevo Latino **Born:** 1970 **Began Career:** 1995 **Culinary School:** L'Academie de Cuisine, Gaithersburg, MD **Grad Year:** 1996 **Stages:** Spain: el Bulli **Work History:** Washington, DC: Vidalia, Cashions, The National Press Club, Café Atlantico, Jaleo, kaz sushi bistro; New York, NY: Pipa, Verbena **Mentor(s):** José Andrés, Ann Cashion, Ed Hanson **Protégée(s):** Michael Turner, Edgar Steele, Joe Raffa, Josh Whigham **Awards:** 2006 StarChefs.com Rising Star Chef Washington DC **Affiliations:** CIA, L'Academie de Cuisine, DC Central Kitchen **Languages Spoken:** Japanese, Spanish

NOTABLE DISH(ES): Feta Water Noodles with Tomato Marmalade and Mint; Taste of India Chicken Wing

FAST FACTS
Restaurant Recs: Citronelle **Kitchen Tool(s):** Microplane, my iSi bottles are great for carbonating things and making foams, Vita-Prep **Interview Question:** If a cook wants to learn I'll always give them a trailing day to see how they work with other cooks, how they take directions and how they interact. I can feel right away if they're arrogant and I'm not interested in that. I'm looking for a cook that has respect for all cooks as well as the chef. **Flavor Combo(s):** I like sweet and salty, spicy and sweet, sweet and acidic, and I pretty much love all things with the combination of shoyu. Oh and I can't forget miso combos! **Fave Cookbook(s):** El bulli by Ferran Adriá; On Food and Cooking by Harold McGee; Ma Gastronomie by Fernand Point **Chef to Cook for You:** My boss/mentor José Andrés will be out because he promised to cook for my wedding. Since I only have one choice, I would like to eat the food of no-holds-barred chef Masaharu Morimoto. I think his knowledge and skill combined with his creativity and wit will just absolutely blow me away. I would sit there and take notes just like when he came and ate at minibar. **Culinary Travel:** No particular place right now. If you have an open mind and stomach, you can find unique and wonderful cuisine everywhere! But if I ever felt the need to be inspired for a good decade I would travel through Asia or India. I have no doubt that either one would mesmerize me.

G

{ Gallante - Guerrero }

Shea Gallante
Executive Chef | Cru

24 5th Ave. New York, NY 10011

Restaurant E-mail: shea@cru-nyc.com

Phone: (212) 529-6700

RESTAURANT FACTS
Seats: 55 **Weeknight Covers:** 70–80 **Weekend Covers:** 100+ **Check Average (with Wine):** $100+ **Tasting Menu:** Yes $125/$220 with wine **Kitchen Staff:** 9

CHEF FACTS
Cuisine: Modern European **Born:** 1973 **Began Career:** 1997 **Culinary School:** The Culinary Institute of America, Hyde Park, NY **Grad Year:** 1997 **Work History:** New York, NY: Felidia, Bouley **Mentor(s):** David Bouley; Fortunato Nicotra; Lidia Bastianich **Awards:** 2006 New York Times 3 stars; 2005 StarChefs.com Rising Star Chef New York; 2005 Michelin Guide 1 star; 2005 Food & Wine Best New Chef; 2005 Nestle Brands Rising Star **Affiliations:** We do a lot of donations **Languages Spoken:** Modern European

NOTABLE DISH(ES): Maine Lobster with Turnips, Salsify and Mango Butter

FAST FACTS
Restaurant Recs: Aki, Kanayama, Faicco's **Kitchen Tool(s):** My combi-oven. Nothing can replace it. Best tool any kitchen can have. **Interview Question:** Have you trailed everywhere that you have an interest in? Are you sure that you would like to work for me? **Flavor Combo(s):** Salty and sour **Fave Cookbook(s):** I have hundreds of them. Some of the latest I've acquired are pastry books, one being by Iginio Massari. I just bought Marino Cedrini's sushi book. **Chef to Cook for You:** Fernand Point because he's the godfather of gastronomy **Culinary Travel:** Japan – one of the purest places to eat simple food

Meg Galus
Pastry Chef | Tru

696 N St. Clair St. Chicago, IL 60611

Restaurant E-mail: mgalus@leye.com

Phone: (312) 202-0001

RESTAURANT FACTS
Seats: 60–100 **Weeknight Covers:** 50–80 **Weekend Covers:** 130–180 **Check Average (with Wine):** $150 **Tasting Menu:** Yes $145 **Kitchen Staff:** 4–6

CHEF FACTS
Cuisine: Creative and sumptuous, inspired by and building on the classics **Born:** 1978 **Culinary School:** The French Pastry School, Chicago, IL **Grad Year:** 2005 **Stages:** New York, NY: Jean-Georges **Work History:** Chicago, IL: Vanille **Mentor(s):** My chefs at the French Pastry school were amazing. They're thankfully just a mile away.

NOTABLE DISH(ES): Orange Parfait Float: House Made Ginger Ale, Blood Orange Tapioca; Roasted Pineapple, Coconut Sorbet, Cashew Frangipane, Sourwood Honey

FAST FACTS
Restaurant Recs: Player's Grill on Ashland – it's two blocks from my house, and it's really strange. It's race-car themed and it has tall blonde leggy waitresses, but the food is amazing. It's run by an Eastern European couple and they make heart-friendly whole-grain pastas. **Kitchen Tool(s):** I'm addicted to my pastry guitar. I wander around the pastry kitchen looking for things I can cut into squares. And a really good whisk – I like Matfor whisks. **Interview Question:** Why do you want to work at Tru? I want to hear something that sounds heartfelt. I want to hear that they have an idea about here rather than somewhere else. **Flavor Combo(s):** Chocolate and hazelnut, although, chocolate and peppermint can give it a run for its money **Fave Cookbook(s):** Le Grand Livre de Pâtisserie by Ducasse; Wild Sweets and Wild Chocolates by Dominique and Cindy Duby; the torn and stained 1970s church cookbook which contains most of my late mother's "signature" recipes, like hamburger macaroni casserole and fluffy green Jello **Chef to Cook for You:** Pierre Hermé, for his classic technique paired with unique flavor combinations **Culinary Travel:** Barcelona – because of the innovations taking place both on the savory and pastry sides

Shannon Galusha
Chef | Veil

555 Aloha St. #100 Seattle, WA 98109

Restaurant E-mail: chef@shannongalusha.com

Phone: (206) 216-0600

RESTAURANT FACTS
Seats: 50 **Weeknight Covers:** 40 **Weekend Covers:** 80 **Check Average (with Wine):** $90 **Tasting Menu:** Yes $40 **Kitchen Staff:** 5+

CHEF FACTS
Cuisine: Modern American **Born:** 1975 **Began Career:** 1991 **Stages:** France: Le Petit Boileu **Work History:** France: Michel Rostang; Yountville, CA: The French Laundry **Mentor(s):** Thomas Keller, Michel Rostang **Affiliations:** We support a lot of local charities and have done events with the American Liver Foundation and the Fred Hutch Cancer Society **Languages Spoken:** French, Spanish

NOTABLE DISH(ES): Tricolor Tomato Salad with Lemongrass, Tomato and Basil Oil

FAST FACTS
Restaurant Recs: The taco truck in White Center **Kitchen Tool(s):** A flat spatula **Interview Question:** What percentage of cooking is common sense? **Flavor Combo(s):** Basil Hayden (bourbon) and ice **Fave Cookbook(s):** Mrs. A.B. Marshall's Cookery Book (my great-grandfather's culinary school textbook) **Chef to Cook for You:** Mario Batali comes to mind. I ate at a couple of his restaurants and it is just great food. He has a lot of personality and it would just be fun. **Culinary Travel:** I would head to the Pacific, to Japan. I don't know very much about the cuisine and I like that it is so specific to the region.

Gale Gand
Executive Pastry Chef | Tru

676 N Saint Clair Chicago, IL 60611

Restaurant E-mail: galegand@aol.com

Phone: (312) 202-0001

RESTAURANT FACTS
Seats: 60–100 **Weeknight Covers:** 50–80 **Weekend Covers:** 130–180 **Check Average (with Wine):** $150 **Tasting Menu:** Yes $145 **Kitchen Staff:** 4–6

CHEF FACTS
Other Restaurants: Gale's Coffee Bar, Osteria Di Tramonto, Tramonto's Steak & Seafood, RT Lounge, Nacional 27 **Cuisine:** American with French and English influences **Born:** 1956 **Began Career:** 1984 **Culinary School:** La Varenne, France **Stages:** France: La Pyramid **Work History:** New York, NY: Strathallen Hotel, Jam's with Jonathan Waxman, Gotham Bar & Grill; England: Stapleford Park, Criterion; Highwood, IL: Carlos; Chicago, IL: Charlie Trotter's; Evanston, IL: Trio; Northfield, IL: Brasserie T **Mentor(s):** Moe Brooker, Bob Gand **Protégée(s):** Della Gosset **Awards:** 2004 Chicago Magazine Best Pastry Chef; 2004 Chicago Magazine Best Restaurant; 2004 Wine Spectator Grand Award; 2004 Nation's Restaurant News Fine Dining Hall of Fame; 2003 Restaurants and Institutions IVY Award; 2001 Bon Appétit Top Pastry Chef of the Year; 2001 James Beard Foundation Outstanding Pastry Chef; 2000 James Beard Foundation Best New Restaurant Nominee; 1998 James Beard Foundation Best Chef Midwest Nominee; 1994 Robert Mondavi Award for Culinary Excellence; 1994 Food & Wine Ten Best New Chefs **Affiliations:** IACP, LDE, WDC, JBF, EWG, GCM, Relais & Chateaux **Books Published:** American Brasserie; Butter Sugar Flour Eggs; Gale Gand's Just a Bite; Gale Gand's Short + Sweet; Tru: A Cookbook from the Legendary Chicago Restaurant; Chocolate and Vanilla **Languages Spoken:** French, Italian, some Spanish

NOTABLE DISH(ES): Chocolate Pernod Semi Freddo; Italian Almond-Iced Christmas Cookies

FAST FACTS
Restaurant Recs: Max and Benny's for veal brisket sandwich on challah **Kitchen Tool(s):** Colander – it's good for rinsing, washing, and shocking blanched items **Interview Question:** Do you feel like your hands do what your brain tells then to? This tells me if they are comfortable and confident in their body. Where do you like to eat? This tells me about how into food they are. **Flavor Combo(s):** Berries and cream, like buttermilk panna cotta and flavorful fresh raspberries **Fave Cookbook(s):** Blue Strawberry Cookbook by James Haller. Cooking (Brilliantly) Without Recipes by James Haller **Chef to Cook for You:** Probably Pierre Hermé. I just think he has the best palate and is the most technically sound pastry chef working today. **Culinary Travel:** I've never been to Vienna and I think it would be good for me to see what I consider the motherland (besides France) for pastry

G

Jose Garces
Chef/Owner | Amada

217 Chestnut St. Philadelphia, PA 19106
Restaurant E-mail: melissa.wentzell@amadarestaurant.com
Phone: (215) 625-2450

RESTAURANT FACTS
Seats: 130 **Weeknight Covers:** 200–220 **Weekend Covers:**
280–320 **Check Average (with Wine):** $55 **Tasting Menu:** No
Kitchen Staff: 9–10

CHEF FACTS
Other Restaurants: Philadephia, PA: Tinto, Distrito; Chicago, IL: Mercat a la Planxa **Cuisine:** Spanish Latin Mexican **Born:** 1972 **Began Career:** 1993 **Culinary School:** Kendall College, Chicago, IL **Grad Year:** 1996 **Stages:** Spain: La Taberna del Alabardero **Work History:** New York, NY: The Rainbow Room, Four Seasons, 57/57, Bolivar, Pipa, Chicama; Philadelphia, PA: El Vez, Alma de Cuba **Mentor(s):** Douglas Rodriguez, Waldy Malouf **Protégée(s):** Chad Williams, Tim Spinner, Arthur Cavaliere, Justin Vogel, Michael Isabella **Awards:** 2008 James Beard Foundation Best Chef Mid-Atlantic Nominee; 2004 StarChefs.com Rising Star Chef Philadelphia **Affiliations:** Amada participates in functions for several charities, including Alex's Lemonade Stand and Share Our Strength. **Books Published:** Latin Evolution **Languages Spoken:** Spanish

NOTABLE DISH(ES): Crispy Duck Confit Flautas; Main Lobster and Shrimp Escabache with Fire Roasted Tomato, Pickled Jalapeño and Passion Fruit

FAST FACTS
Restaurant Recs: Sahara Grill for the Middle Eastern combo platter **Kitchen Tool(s):** Microplane zester – it's a great flavor enhancer **Interview Question:** What are the five mother sauces? **Flavor Combo(s):** Pork belly and grits; artichokes and truffles; morels and green asparagus; chestnuts and rabbit; duck and cherry **Fave Cookbook(s):** Arzak Recetas by Juan Mari Arzak **Chef to Cook for You:** Juan Mari Arzak, because I just love his style. He is the master of using innovative techniques without overcomplicating the dish. Arzak knows how to stick to the core of a good, quality meal. **Culinary Travel:** Southeast Asia – I would visit Singapore, Bangkok, Indonesia, and Saigon to start. It's just what I'm into these days.

Ruben García
Director of Research and Development | Think Food Group

425 8th St. NW, Suite 1131 Washington, DC 20004

Restaurant E-mail: rubeng@thinkfoodgroup.com

Phone: (202) 638-1910

CHEF FACTS
Cuisine: Classic-traditional, modern-new techniques, a little bit of everything **Born:** 1978 **Began Career:** 1992 **Culinary School:** Escola Joviat, Barcelona, Spain **Grad Year:** 1997 **Stages:** Spain: Jean Luc Figueras, Martin Berasategui, el Bulli; Germany: Trantris **Work History:** Spain: Jean Luc Figueras, Martin Berasategui, el Bulli **Mentor(s):** Albert Adriá, Ferran Adriá, José Andrés, Martin Berasategui **Languages Spoken:** Spanish and Spanglish

FAST FACTS
Restaurant Recs: New Big Wong for fried rice with dried scallops. Nothing fancy, very gritty. If you didn't know it, you wouldn't dare go in. But trust me, it's worth it. **Kitchen Tool(s):** There is one thing that in this day and age I cannot do without: my computer, and all the information that I have on it **Interview Question:** Do you like to cook? **Flavor Combo(s):** All the ones that make sense and above all TASTE GOOD! **Fave Cookbook(s):** el Bulli collection; Escoffier. Without the past, we don't exist!! **Chef to Cook for You:** Adoni Luis Aduriz, from Mugaritz, is definitely my choice (if I had to pick only one). His cuisine is a living reflection of his passion for cooking. He is a great poet! **Culinary Travel:** Asia – I think it is the big unknown and the most complex and fascinating. It is one of the future challenges that I hope to embark on.

G

Geoff Gardner
Executive Chef | Sel de la Terre

255 State St. Boston, MA 02109

Restaurant E-mail: geoff@seldelaterre.com

Phone: (617) 720-1300

RESTAURANT FACTS
Seats: 140 **Weeknight Covers:** 100 **Weekend Covers:** 200 **Check Average (with Wine):** $45-$50 **Tasting Menu:** No

CHEF FACTS
Other Restaurants: L'Espalier **Cuisine:** French **Born:** 1970 **Began Career:** 1988 **Work History:** Boston, MA: L'Espalier **Mentor(s):** Frank McClelland **Awards:** 2006 StarChefs.com Rising Star Chef Boston; 2005 Boston Magazine Best Bakery Bread; 2005 Condé Nast Traveler Top 100 New Restaurants in the World; 2005 Esquire Top 22 New Restaurants in the Nation

NOTABLE DISH(ES): Pancetta-Wrapped Trout with Arugula and Roasted Red Grapes; Lamb Tenderloin with Fava Beans, Dates and Smoked Bacon

FAST FACTS
Restaurant Recs: CK Shanghai for spicy pork wontons **Kitchen Tool(s):** Fire! How do you define cooking? It's manipulating food. One of the primary ways we manipulate food is by temperature and controlling the fire. I like to think about different kinds of heat and how heat affects the food. **Interview Question:** Tell me about yourself. Did you just go to culinary school? How have you enjoyed working at other restaurants? **Fave Cookbook(s):** Potager: Fresh Garden Cooking in the French Style by Georgeanne Brennan **Culinary Travel:** The restaurant is focused on the cuisine of the South of France, and that's what I have always been particularly drawn toward: rustic, country, Southern French-style cuisine

Jacques Gautier
Chef/Owner | Palo Santo

652 Union St. Brooklyn, NY 11215

Restaurant E-mail: jacques@palosanto.us

Phone: (718) 636-6311

RESTAURANT FACTS
Seats: 40 **Weeknight Covers:** 30–40 **Weekend Covers:** 60–100 **Check Average (with Wine):** $50 **Tasting Menu:** No **Kitchen Staff:** 2-3

CHEF FACTS
Cuisine: Latin American market cooking **Born:** 1978 **Began Career:** 1994 **Culinary School:** Natural Gourmet Cookery School in Manhattan **Grad Year:** 1998 **Stages:** Argentina: Bodega el Cerno **Work History:** New York, NY: Vong, Arioso; San Francisco, CA: Azié, The Brick Oven Gallery; Williamsburg, NY: La Brunette **Mentor(s):** Tim Kelley, Gabriel DiMartino, Kenny Perone **Affiliations:** James Beard Foundation, Green Market, Edible Brooklyn **Languages Spoken:** English, Spanish and a little French

NOTABLE DISH(ES): Rabbit Two Ways: Anticucho and Tostada with Ramps and Spicy Mayo

FAST FACTS
Restaurant Recs: Pio Pio in Jackson Heights for the ceviche and the chicken **Kitchen Tool(s):** I use my serving spoon the most, but I also like my French fork for turning meats on the grill **Interview Question:** I give most people a chance to cook on the line. I look for confidence, professionalism and good knife skills. **Flavor Combo(s):** Lime, chilies and salt **Fave Cookbook(s):** Culinaria the Caribbean by Rosemary Parkinson – it has great pictures **Chef to Cook for You:** Either James Beard or Alice Waters **Culinary Travel:** Japan – I've never been and I'd be interested to go to the fish markets

Wesley Genovart
Executive Chef | Degustation

239 E 5th St. New York, NY 10003

Restaurant E-mail: wesley_genovart@yahoo.com

Phone: (212) 979-1012

RESTAURANT FACTS
Seats: 19 **Weeknight Covers:** 45–50 **Weekend Covers:** 55–60 **Check Average (w/o Wine):** $50–$75 **Tasting Menu:** Yes $50/$75 **Kitchen Staff:** 3

CHEF FACTS
Cuisine: Elaborate Spanish-influenced small plates **Born:** 1979 **Began Career:** 1997 **Culinary School:** Florida Culinary Institute **Stages:** Spain: Mugaritz **Work History:** Boston, MA: Clio; New York, NY: Perry Street **Mentor(s):** Andoni Luis Aduriz, Sergi Arola, Gregory Brainin **Awards:** 2008 James Beard Foundation Rising Star Nominee **Languages Spoken:** Spanish

NOTABLE DISH(ES): Spanish Tortilla with Quail Egg and Shallot Confit; Croquetas with Bacon, Apples, Onions and Pimentón Aïoli

FAST FACTS
Restaurant Recs: Soba-Ya for the monkfish liver with panzo and fried eggplant; Peasant for the suckling pig and octopus **Kitchen Tool(s):** My thermal circulator **Interview Question:** Are you willing to learn? **Flavor Combo(s):** Apples and mackerel **Fave Cookbook(s):** Clorofilia by Andoni Luis Aduriz **Chef to Cook for You:** Fernand Point, because so much of what we do now is based on his cuisine **Culinary Travel:** I would like to go back to Spain to eat at el Bulli, and I also want to eat my way through Japan

Jennifer Giblin
Pastry Chef | Blue Smoke

116 E 27th St. New York, NY 10016

Restaurant E-mail: jgiblin@bluesmoke.com

Phone: (212) 447-7479

RESTAURANT FACTS
Seats: 195 **Weeknight Covers:** 400 **Weekend Covers:** 600 **Check Average (w/o Wine):** $40 **Tasting Menu:** No **Kitchen Staff:** 2

CHEF FACTS
Other Restaurants: Jazz Standard **Cuisine:** Home-Style American desserts **Began Career:** 1997 **Culinary School:** Le Cordon Bleu, England **Grad Year:** 1997 **Work History:** New York, NY: Tabla, Eleven Madison Park **Mentor(s):** Jackie Riely, Nicole Kaplan **Awards:** 2006 StarChefs.com Rising Star Pastry Chef New York **Languages Spoken:** Spanglish

NOTABLE DISH(ES): Chocolate Cake and Milk; Banana Cream Pie; Key Lime Pie

FAST FACTS
Restaurant Recs: Zach's Pizza in Tucson, Arizona – all the pizza they make is great **Kitchen Tool(s):** Microplane, bowl scrapers **Interview Question:** Why do you want to work in this business? I find if people don't have a solid answer to this question, they won't last in this industry. **Flavor Combo(s):** Maple syrup and bacon **Fave Cookbook(s):** The Cake Bible; The Pie Bible by Rose Levy Beranbaum; The Last Course by Claudia Fleming **Culinary Travel:** Austria – I'd love to explore the desserts there

David Gilbert
Chef/Partner | New Project in the works

Dallas, TX

Restaurant E-mail: eauchef@yahoo.com

Phone: (214) 760-9000

CHEF FACTS
Cuisine: New American **Born:** 1977 **Began Career:** 1995 **Culinary School:** Johnson & Wales University, Charleston, SC **Grad Year:** 1997 **Work History:** Holland: Restaurant Vermeer; Atlanta, GA: Ritz-Carlton (Buckhead); St. Thomas, Virgin Islands: Ritz-Carlton; St. Michaels, MD: Orient Express Hotels, The Inn at Perry Cabin; St. Louis, MO: Eau Bistro; Beverly Hills, CA: The Beverly Hilton; Dallas, TX: Luqa **Mentor(s):** My parents, Michael Ganley, Joël Antunes; Xavier Solomon, Stephan Hall, Jack Baum **Awards:** 2007 StarChefs.com Rising Star Chef Dallas; 2004 Best Chef by The St. Louis Riverfront Times; 2001 Silver Medal Chaine des Rotisseurs Junior Commis Competition; 2000 Bronze Medal Chaîne des Rotisseurs Junior Commis Competition **Affiliations:** NTFB

NOTABLE DISH(ES): Fruit Slider with Rosewater and Passion Fruit Curd; Squab "Through a Window," Smoked Bacon, Pearl Onions, Barley Risotto, Apple-Curry Foam

FAST FACTS
Restaurant Recs: Latitude 18 in St. Thomas, USVI – don't miss the burger! **Kitchen Tool(s):** Microplane **Interview Question:** What do you do when you are not working? **Flavor Combo(s):** Tart and sweet; acidic and salty **Fave Cookbook(s):** The Visual Encyclopedia of Food **Chef to Cook for You:** Well, there are so many professional chefs I admire, although, I would prefer the young talent that has come through my kitchens over the years to all get together and have each one of them do a course! That would be ultimate gratification for me. **Culinary Travel:** I have had my eye on Vietnam. I think there is a lot to be said about their simplistic approach to cooking.

Alain Giraud
Chef/Director | Anisette Brasserie

225 Santa Monica Blvd. Los Angeles, CA 90407

Restaurant E-mail: alain@alaingiraud.com

Phone: (310) 395-3200

RESTAURANT FACTS
Seats: 120 **Check Average (with Wine):** $50 **Check Average (w/o Wine):** $40 **Tasting Menu:** No **Kitchen Staff:** 8–10

CHEF FACTS
Cuisine: French Provençal **Born:** 1959 **Began Career:** 1976 **Culinary School:** Nimes Culinary School, France **Grad Year:** 1976 **Work History:** France: Hermitage Meissonnier, Grand Vefour, Hotel de Crillon, Hotel Imperator, Le Reverbere, Leonce; Los Angeles, CA: Citrus, Bastide; Santa Monica, CA: Loews Santa Monica Beach Hotel, Lavande **Mentor(s):** Paul Louis Meissonnier, Michel Richard **Protégée(s):** Cal Stamenov, Robert Curry **Awards:** 2004 France Medaille D'Or du tourisme; 2003 Bon Appétit Chef of the Year; 2003 LA Times 4 stars; 1995 Club Culinaire Français Chef of the Year **Affiliations:** ACDF, Club Culinaire Français of California, The James Beard Foundation **Languages Spoken:** French, some Spanish

FAST FACTS
Restaurant Recs: Spago – for the multi course tasting menu cooked by Lee Hefter team **Kitchen Tool(s):** Small paring knife – I basically do everything with it **Interview Question:** What is your motivation for cooking? **Flavor Combo(s):** Orange and basil **Fave Cookbook(s):** La Grande Cuisine Bourgeoisie by Andre Guillot **Chef to Cook for You:** Antonin Carême, because he set the standard **Culinary Travel:** France – come on, no question! To bring back the memories.

G

Suzanne Goin
Executive Chef | Lucques

8474 Melrose Ave. Los Angeles, CA 90069

Restaurant E-mail: suzanne@lucques.com

Phone: (323) 655-6277

RESTAURANT FACTS
Seats: 110 **Weeknight Covers:** 120 **Weekend Covers:** 220 **Check Average (with Wine):** $65 **Tasting Menu:** No **Kitchen Staff:** 7–9

CHEF FACTS
Other Restaurants: AOC, The Hungry Cat **Cuisine:** Seasonal local Mediterranean **Born:** 1966 **Began Career:** 1984 **Stages:** Los Angeles, CA: Ma Maison; France: L'Arpège, Pain, Adour et Fantasie **Work History:** Los Angeles, CA: Ma Maison, Pinot Bistro, Campanile; Providence, RI: al Forno; Berkeley, CA: Chez Panisse; France: Pain, Adour et Fantasie, Arpege; Boston, MA: Michaela's, Olives **Mentor(s):** George Germon, Johanne Killeen, Alice Waters, David Tanis, Catherine Brandel, Peggy Smith, Nancy Silverton, Mark Peel **Protégée(s):** Corina Weibel **Awards:** 2008 James Beard Foundation Outstanding Chef Nominee; 2005 James Beard Foundation Best Chef California; 2005 James Beard Best Cookbook (From a Professional Viewpoint); 1999 Food & Wine Best New Chefs; 1994 Boston Magazine Best Creative Chef **Affiliations:** JBF, SOS, Chefs Collaborative, Slow Food, Save the Children, Aid for Aids **Books Published:** Sunday Suppers at Lucques **Languages Spoken:** French, kitchen Spanish

NOTABLE DISH(ES): Grilled Chicken with Pancetta, Spinach, Buttermilk Pudding and Currant Relish

FAST FACTS
Restaurant Recs: Tacos Delta for the menudo **Kitchen Tool(s):** Mortar and pestle because nothing else works as well for fresh herb salsas and sauces **Interview Question:** Why do you cook? **Flavor Combo(s):** I have too many to even try to pick a fave! **Fave Cookbook(s):** A Return to Cooking by Eric Ripert **Chef to Cook for You:** David Lentz (my husband) - I love seeing the intense work side of him come out and I never know what he will come up with, but it's always delicious. Maybe he would even join me for dessert. **Culinary Travel:** Everywhere...I would love to spend more time in Asia as well as Europe. I would also love to check out Australia. Why? Because I learn so much and always come back inspired wherever I travel.

Will Goldfarb
Chef/Owner | WillPowder

7217 34th Avenue, 1k Jackson Heights, NY 11372

Restaurant E-mail: spice@willpowder.net

Phone: (212) 941-5405

CHEF FACTS

Other Restaurants: Picnick, Dessert Studio at ABC Carpet and Home **Cuisine:** Experiential **Born:** 1975 **Began Career:** 1998 **Culinary School:** Le Cordon Bleu, France **Grad Year:** 1998 **Stages:** Spain: el Bulli; Australia: Tetsuya's; France: Pierre Gagnaire **Work History:** Spain: el Bulli; France: Gerard Mulot; Australia: Tetsuya's, The Grange; Whitehouse, NJ: The Ryland Inn; New York, NY: Cru, Morimoto, Room 4 Dessert **Mentor(s):** Albert Adriá, Ruben Garcia, Kasper Kurdahl, Davide Scabin, Gerard Mulot **Protégée(s):** Robert Truitt, Pamela Yung, Juan Carlos Pina **Awards:** 2006 StarChefs.com Rising Star Pastry Chef New York; 2006 Pastry Art and Design 10 Best in America; 2006 Time Out New York Best of New York; 2006 New York Magazine Best of New York **Affiliations:** CIA, Experimental Cuisine Collective **Languages Spoken:** French, Catalan

NOTABLE DISH(ES): Voyage to India; White Chocolate Margarita; Apples in Various States

FAST FACTS

Restaurant Recs: Zabb Thai for green papaya salad with raw shrimp **Kitchen Tool(s):** Spoon **Interview Question:** When can you start? **Flavor Combo(s):** Vanilla and anything **Fave Cookbook(s):** Couleurs, Parfums et Saveurs de Ma Cuisine by Jacques Maximin **Chef to Cook for You:** Joël Robuchon – I've never had the chance to taste his food **Culinary Travel:** French Polynesia – so I could take my family

Hedy Goldsmith
Executive Pastry Chef | Michael's Genuine Food & Drink

130 NE 40th St. Miami Beach, FL 33137

Restaurant E-mail: hedygoldsmith@aol.com

Phone: (305) 532-4550

RESTAURANT FACTS
Seats: 140 **Weeknight Covers:** 200 **Weekend Covers:** 400 **Check Average (with Wine):** $56 **Tasting Menu:** No **Kitchen Staff:** 2

CHEF FACTS
Cuisine: Clean, flavorful, unpretentious food oozing with passion **Born:** 1957 **Began Career:** 1985 **Culinary School:** The Culinary Institute of America, Hyde Park, NY **Grad Year:** 1984 **Stages:** New York, NY: The Waldorf Astoria **Work History:** Miami Beach, FL: Mark's Place, Brickell Club, Nemo, Prime, Shoji Sushi; New York, NY: Waldorf Astoria **Mentor(s):** Alice Waters, Bill Reynolds, Maida Heatter, Nancy Silverton **Protégée(s):** Tony Miller **Awards:** 2005 Food Network Iron Chef **Languages Spoken:** Culinary Spanish, culinary Creole

NOTABLE DISH(ES): Bing Cherry and White Chocolate Mousse Napoleon; Pumpkin and Candied Ginger Muffins

FAST FACTS
Restaurant Recs: Michy's for everything **Kitchen Tool(s):** Microplane; 5-quart KitchenAid mixer; Global knives; Silpat **Interview Question:** I want to talk with them to reveal their level of passion for the position. I have to see their experience and enthusiasm and take it from there. If they have no passion I don't delve any further. **Flavor Combo(s):** Bittersweet chocolate and chipotle peppers; anise, goat cheese, and Marcona almonds **Fave Cookbook(s):** Maida Heatter's Book of Great Desserts by Maida Heatter **Chef to Cook for You:** My list is endless! You wouldn't have enough pages in your publication, but if I had to pick one, right now it would be my dear friend Michelle Bernstein because her food is so sexy and we have similar sensibilities. **Culinary Travel:** Morocco and India come to mind – just for the experience of baking and cooking with so many exotic fruits and spices

Carmen Gonzalez
Chef | Working on something new

210 East 22nd St. New York, NY 10010

Restaurant E-mail: chefcarmen08@aol.com

CHEF FACTS

Cuisine: American with Latino flair **Born:** 1958 **Began Career:** 1983
Culinary School: New York Restaurant School, New York, NY **Grad
Year:** 1986 **Stages:** New York, NY: Quilted Giraffe **Work History:**
New York, NY: Quilted Giraffe; Miami, FL: Carmen the Restaurant
Mentor(s): Barry Wine, Lisa Chodosh **Awards:** 2004 StarChefs.com
Rising Star Chef Miami; 2003 Miami New Times Best of Restaurants;
2003 Esquire Best New Restaurants in America **Affiliations:** JBF
Languages Spoken: Spanish

NOTABLE DISH(ES): Key West Shrimp Pionono with Sofrito Sauce;
Slow Roasted Adobo Marinated Niman Ranch Pernil with Sweet Plain-
tain Fufu and Gandules Stew

FAST FACTS

Kitchen Tool(s): Fish spatula **Interview Question:** Why do you like cooking? What's the most important thing when you go out to eat? What is your favorite ingredient? What will you do if an ingredient
is not right in the middle of service? **Flavor Combo(s):** I love clean basic flavors in all cuisines **Fave
Cookbook(s):** Anything by Emily Luchetti **Chef to Cook for You:** Ducasse – I just love his exquisite
combinations and execution of flavors **Culinary Travel:** New York, Paris, and San Francisco, because
of the quality of food and variety of restaurants. In Paris there are so many restaurants, even unknown ones, where you can get great food. In Europe they use different ingredients and techniques
than in the US, and I always learn.

Daisley Gordon
Chef | Campagne

86 Pine St. Seattle, WA 98101

Restaurant E-mail: bonjour@campagnerestaurant.com

Phone: (206) 728-2800

RESTAURANT FACTS
Tasting Menu: No

CHEF FACTS
Other Restaurants: Café Campagne **Cuisine:** Country French **Born:** 1964 **Began Career:** 1994 **Culinary School:** The Culinary Institute of America, Hyde Park, NY **Stages:** France: Le Coq de la Maison Blanche; Dallas, TX: Actuelle **Work History:** Louisville, KY: The Brown Hotel **Mentor(s):** Victor Gielisse CMC

NOTABLE DISH(ES): Calamari Provencal; Buche Maitre Seguin

FAST FACTS
Restaurant Recs: Sea Garden for salt and pepper squid, sauteed spinach in garlic sauce, noodles with green onion and ginger and Alaskan spot prawns **Kitchen Tool(s):** Waring immersion blender **Interview Question:** What is your most memorable meal? This tells me what aspects of the dining experience interest them. For instance, did they notice the food they were eating or was it just the ambiance? Was it the look of the food or the taste and texture or quality of ingredients? This gives me a sense of current development as a cook and if they are attracted to the culinary field for the right reasons. If the food was horrible and they only got excited because they saw the chef or someone famous, their motivation is questionable and they won't last long in my kitchen. **Fave Cookbook(s):** Simply French by Patricia Wells

Mark Gordon
Executive Chef | Terzo

3011 Steiner St. San Francisco, CA 94123

Restaurant E-mail: mark@niceventures.com

Phone: (415) 441-3200

RESTAURANT FACTS
Seats: 100 **Weeknight Covers:** 100 **Weekend Covers:** 150 **Check Average (with Wine):** $49 **Tasting Menu:** No **Kitchen Staff:** 3–5

CHEF FACTS
Cuisine: Pan-Mediterranean **Born:** 1957 **Began Career:** 1992 **Culinary School:** Kendall College Culinary Program, Chicago, IL **Grad Year:** 1994 **Stages:** Berkeley, CA: Chez Panisse **Work History:** Mendocino, CA: Fetzer Winery's Culinary Center; San Francisco, CA: 42 Degrees, Rose's Café **Mentor(s):** Alice Waters **Affiliations:** Meals-on-Wheels, Charity Events, and we support local farmers

NOTABLE DISH(ES): Spaghetti with Pistachio Pesto and Ricotta Salata

FAST FACTS
Restaurant Recs: Dopo in the East Bay for Italian; Aziza for the tagines, chicken pies and couscous **Kitchen Tool(s):** Mortar and pestle, because I like using my hands and breaking things down, using all of the senses **Interview Question:** Why do you want to work here? I want people who want to be here and who want to learn from us. I don't want people who are just looking to make money. **Flavor Combo(s):** Sweet spices in savory dishes, like in Middle Eastern and North African cuisine **Fave Cookbook(s):** Casa Moro by Samantha and Samuel Clark **Chef to Cook for You:** I've been influenced by so many chefs that it is impossible for me to pick just one **Culinary Travel:** Morocco – I would love to go and experience the cuisine

Scott Gottlich
Chef/Owner | Bijoux

5450 W Lovers Ln. Dallas, TX 75209

Restaurant E-mail: scottgottlich@bijouxrestaurant.com

Phone: (214) 350-6100

RESTAURANT FACTS
Seats: 75 **Weeknight Covers:** 35–40 **Weekend Covers:** 80–110 **Check Average (with Wine):** $100 **Tasting Menu:** Yes $95/$145 with wine **Kitchen Staff:** 6

CHEF FACTS
Cuisine: Contemporary French **Born:** 1975 **Began Career:** 2000 **Culinary School:** Johnson & Wales University, Providence, RI **Grad Year:** 2000 **Stages:** New York, NY: Daniel, Aquavit, Oceana, Danube, Jean Georges **Work History:** Newport Beach, CA: Aubergine; Costa Mesa, CA: Troquet; Huntington Beach, CA: Red Pearl Kitchen; New York, NY: Le Bernardin; Dallas, TX: Lola **Mentor(s):** Tim Goodell; Eric Ripert **Awards:** 2007 StarChefs.com Rising Star Chef Dallas **Affiliations:** Le Cordon Bleu **Languages Spoken:** Kitchen Spanish

NOTABLE DISH(ES): Wild Mushroom and Cippolini Onion Soup; Eastern Spotted Skate Wing with Belgian Endive and Citrus Dressing

FAST FACTS
Restaurant Recs: El Camarón for great pupusas **Kitchen Tool(s):** Vita-Prep; Pacojet **Interview Question:** What's the last cookbook you've read? **Flavor Combo(s):** It depends on the season. Right now I like rhubarb and pistachios, which we are serving with foie gras. **Fave Cookbook(s):** Larousse Gastronomique by Prosper Montagne **Chef to Cook for You:** Jean-Louis Palladin. I've read all of his books, and his influence is huge – everybody knew him. **Culinary Travel:** Spain or Italy

Carvel Gould
Chef | Canoe

4199 Paces Ferry Rd. NW Atlanta, GA 30339

Restaurant E-mail: info@canoeatl.com

Phone: (770) 432-2663

RESTAURANT FACTS
Seats: 180 **Weeknight Covers:** 200 **Weekend Covers:** 350 **Check Average (with Wine):** $54 **Kitchen Staff:** 10

CHEF FACTS
Cuisine: Continental American **Born:** 1970 **Began Career:** 1991 **Work History:** Atlanta, GA: Buckhead Diner, 103 West, Che, Pasta de Punchinello **Mentor(s):** Larry Grosshams, Gerry Klaskala **Affiliations:** You name it, I do it! SOS, MOD, The High Museum in Atlanta, American Liver Foundation, Wine Spectator, Les Dames d'Escoffier... **Languages Spoken:** Spanish

NOTABLE DISH(ES): Pan-Seared Hudson Valley Foie Gras, Crab Apple and Mustarda Tarlet, Vanilla-Pomegranate Sauce; Chilled Sunchoke Soup with Lemon Olive Oil, Artichoke, Chips, Basil Oil

FAST FACTS
Restaurant Recs: Ice House for a hamburger **Kitchen Tool(s):** Vita-Prep; my spoon – it's a weathered sterling silver spoon that lost its set many generations ago in my family. It's worn so thin but has a perfect pitch and balance. I grew up tasting and saucing with it. **Interview Question:** Do you prefer Coke or Pepsi? After running a potential line cook through the normal gauntlet of questions, career objectives, ideologies on food, experiences, etc., I like to throw that in as a tension breaker. I am subconsciously looking for "Coke" as the answer. I believe it tells me something about their palate as it relates to me. **Flavor Combo(s):** Fruit and salt **Fave Cookbook(s):** On Food and Cooking by Harold McGee **Chef to Cook for You:** Julia Child – without a doubt. She's one of the pioneering women chefs and she basically created the television movement. **Culinary Travel:** Japan – for the fish! Also because they are such perfectionists, which I admire, and I would love to see the culture that spawned that perfection.

Gregory Gourreau
Pastry Chef | Payard Patisserie & Bistro

3750 Las Vegas Blvd. South Las Vegas, NV 89109

Restaurant E-mail: ggourreau@caesarspalace.com

Phone: (702) 632-9500

RESTAURANT FACTS
Seats: 42 **Weeknight Covers:** 45 **Weekend Covers:** 140 **Check Average (with Wine):** $25 **Check Average (w/o Wine):** $45 **Tasting Menu:** Yes $45 **Kitchen Staff:** 2

CHEF FACTS
Cuisine: French **Born:** 1970 **Began Career:** 1984 **Culinary School:** Jouer les Tours, France **Grad Year:** 1985 **Work History:** France: Lenôtre Patisserie, Negresco Hotel, Roger Verge; New York, NY: Daniel; Las Vegas, NV: Le Cirque, MIX **Mentor(s):** François Payard and Frederic Robert for pastry. For the restaurant business, I have huge respect for Payard and Daniel Boulud. Sylvain Portay taught me about presentation, and what the guests are looking for. **Protégée(s):** Dyan Santos **Awards:** 2002, 2001 Las Vegas Life Magazine Best Pastry Chef **Affiliations:** Meals-on-Wheels **Languages Spoken:** French

NOTABLE DISH(ES): Olive Savory Macaroon, Black Olive Cream Cheese with Gorgonzola Ice Cream

FAST FACTS
Restaurant Recs: Village Steak on Village Square. Chefs go there. One of the managers from the Wynn opened it. **Kitchen Tool(s):** Oven; mixer **Interview Question:** I like to ask how they express themselves with cooking. What do you like about cooking? It helps to differentiate between those who have passion and those who just want to work. 80% of your job in the kitchen is about your passion. **Flavor Combo(s):** I like sour with fat. Exotic fruits can be a bit sour and a bit buttery, for example, pineapple, passion fruit and mango with coconuts. **Fave Cookbook(s):** Encyclopedia of Practical Gastronomy by Ali-Bab – it's a very old book, 100 years old, and it covers everything in the world of cooking. No pictures, all recipes and technique. Very thick. The second book I like is Fusion Chocolate by Frédéric Bau. **Culinary Travel:** China or Switzerland. China for the new fashions in the food industry; Switzerland because I like their artistic design.

Tim Graham
Chef de Cuisine | Tru

676 N. St. Clair St. Chicago, IL 60611

Restaurant E-mail: timgraham_3@hotmail.com

Phone: (312) 202-0001

RESTAURANT FACTS

Seats: 80–149 **Weeknight Covers:** 104 **Weekend Covers:** 128
Check Average (with Wine): $176 **Check Average (w/o Wine):** 120
Tasting Menu: Yes $145 **Kitchen Staff:** 14

CHEF FACTS

Cuisine: New nouveau cuisine **Born:** 1977 **Began Career:** 1996
Culinary School: New England Culinary Institute, Montpelier, VT
Grad Year: 2002 **Stages:** Milwaukee, WI: Sanfords **Work History:**
Milwaukee, WI: Coccette, Sanfords; Rocheport, MO: Les Bourgeois
Mentor(s): Laurent Gras, Rick Tramonto, Jason Robbins **Awards:**
2008 StarChefs.com Rising Star Chef Chicago **Affiliations:** Lettuce
Entertain You

NOTABLE DISH(ES): Scottish Salmon, Daikon, Granny Smith, Thai Long Peppercorn; Alpine Bay Oyster, Tempura Uni, Smoke, Lemon, Bacon

FAST FACTS

Restaurant Recs: Fat Cat – a bar/restaurant that opened on North Broadway. When I get a chance to eat out it's at Lula Café. **Kitchen Tool(s):** My computer for organization and for the rigorous cataloging of recipes **Interview Question:** There's not one question – it's the verbiage of the whole interview. They need to be real with me. I want cooks to make every mistake there is, but only once. **Flavor Combo(s):** I love the bittersweet flavor of turnips cooked in burnt caramel water, and hit with a little lemon juice before being plated. **Fave Cookbook(s):** Le Grand Livre de Cuisine by Alain Ducasse; Essential Cuisine by Michel Bras; Logical Cuisine by Jordi Cruz **Chef to Cook for You:** I would love to eat Fernand Point's food. I would love to try what food was really like back then. **Culinary Travel:** Thailand. There are so many ingredients in their sauces, and yet they end up so balanced – it boggles my mind, and shows me that their cuisine is thousands of years older than French. French sauces are fairly rudimentary compared to Asian sauces.

G

Todd Gray
Chef/Owner | Equinox Restaurant

818 Connecticut Ave NW Washington, DC 20006

Restaurant E-mail: toddgray@equinoxrestaurant.com

Phone: (202) 331-8118

RESTAURANT FACTS
Seats: 100 **Weeknight Covers:** 80 **Weekend Covers:** 120 **Check Average (with Wine):** $95 **Tasting Menu:** Yes $57/$70/$85 **Kitchen Staff:** 7

CHEF FACTS
Other Restaurants: Market Salamander, Salamander Hospitality **Cuisine:** Regional American **Born:** 1964 **Began Career:** 1989 **Culinary School:** The Culinary Institute of America, Hyde Park, NY **Grad Year:** 1989 **Stages:** Washington, DC: The Watergate; Yountville, CA: The French Laundry; Los Angeles, CA: Patina; Italy: Del Cambio, Baltezarre Restaurant **Work History:** Fredericksburg, VA: La Petite Auberge; Los Angeles, CA: L'Orangerie; Washington, DC: Colline, Galileo **Mentor(s):** Christian Renault, Daniel Boulud, Jean-Louis Palladin, Roberto Donna **Protégée(s):** Ethan McKee, Tony Chittum, Brendan Cox **Awards:** 2006 DiRoNA Award for Fine Dining; 2000–2006 Wine Spectator Award of Excellence; 2000–2003 Restaurant Association of Metropolitan Washington Chef of the Year Nominee; 2005 RAMW Fine Dining Restaurant of the Year; 2005 Ivy Awards Fine Dining Nominee; 2002-2005 Washington Post Top 50 Restaurants; 2001-2005 James Beard Foundation Best Chef Mid Atlantic Nominee; 2000-2005 Washingtonian Magazine 100 Very Best Restaurants **Affiliations:** SOS, StarChefs. com Advisory Board, Certified Humane, Slow Food, JBF, DC Chef's Club **Languages Spoken:** Spanish, French, Italian

NOTABLE DISH(ES): Summer Tomato Risotto with Bacon Wrapped Monkfish; Pan Seared Quail with Spaghetti Squash

FAST FACTS
Restaurant Recs: El Paraiso Restaurant for pupusas with marinated cabbage **Kitchen Tool(s):** 8-inch serrated utility knife – it's a great, versatile knife **Interview Question:** If you were a piece of kitchen equipment, what would it be and why? It tests creativity and knowledge of equipment and tells a lot about the candidate. **Flavor Combo(s):** Salty and sweet; sweet and sour; peppercorns and sugar; all things with bacon. **Fave Cookbook(s):** Le Guide Culinaire by Auguste Escoffier **Culinary Travel:** I would like to go to South America to experience all the new developments in sustainable food production as well as all the exciting wine regions scattered throughout the continent. Of course, any trip that includes stops in France, Italy and Spain would be a close second, as these are the countries that have so influenced my cooking style.

Rick Gresh
Executive Chef | David Burke's Primehouse

616 North Rush Chicago, IL 60611

Restaurant E-mail: rgresh@jameshotel.com

Phone: (312) 660-6000

RESTAURANT FACTS
Seats: 165 **Weeknight Covers:** 200 **Weekend Covers:** 350–400
Check Average (with Wine): $100 **Tasting Menu:** No **Kitchen Staff:** 6–9

CHEF FACTS
Other Restaurants: Jbar **Cuisine:** New American steakhouse **Born:** 1975 **Began Career:** 1990 **Culinary School:** The Culinary Institute of America, Hyde Park, NY **Grad Year:** 1995 **Stages:** New York, NY: Le Cirque, Lespinasse **Work History:** Evanston, IL: Trio; Chicago, IL: Celebrity Cafe at the Hotel Nikko, Tsunami, Green Dolphin, Caliterra at the Wyndham, The Saddle and Cycle Club; New York, NY: The Waldorf Astoria **Mentor(s):** Shawn McClain **Awards:** 2006, 2004 Bocuse D'Or Finalist; James Beard Foundation 2001 Rising Star of American Cuisine **Affiliations:** ACF, Common Threads, SOS, Chaine des Rotisseurs

NOTABLE DISH(ES): Seared Hudson Valley Foie Gras with Chanterelles, Peas, Butternut Squash and Pea Shoots

FAST FACTS
Restaurant Recs: Renga Tei on Touhy and Crawford for good Japanese food **Kitchen Tool(s):** My chef's knife because I use it for everything **Interview Question:** What is your favorite food to cook? **Flavor Combo(s):** Tangy and sour; sweet and spicy **Fave Cookbook(s):** The Lutéce Cookbook by Andre Soltner and Seymour Britchky **Chef to Cook for You:** Andre Soltner – I think he is a great chef, his food is classic and I could learn a lot from him **Culinary Travel:** To the Champagne region of France, I love Champagne

Sean Griffin
Executive Chef | Bourbon Steak

7575 E. Princess Dr. Scottsdale, AZ 85255

Restaurant E-mail: sean.griffin@fairmont.com

Phone: (480) 513-6002

RESTAURANT FACTS
Seats: 190–260 **Weeknight Covers:** 110 **Weekend Covers:** 185
Check Average (with Wine): $120 **Tasting Menu:** Yes $55 **Kitchen Staff:** 12

CHEF FACTS
Cuisine: French Californian **Born:** 1972 **Began Career:** 1986 **Stages:** Chicago, IL: Charlie Trotters, Tru, The Ritz-Carlton **Work History:** Beverly Hills, CA: Garden's at the Four Seasons Hotel; Riverside, CA: Mission Inn Hotel; Las Vegas, NV: Neros **Mentor(s):** Connie Anderson, Carrie Nahabedian, Horace Griffin **Protégée(s):** Daniel Waked **Awards:** 2005 StarChefs.com Rising Star Chef Las Vegas **Affiliations:** JBF **Languages Spoken:** Kitchen Spanish

NOTABLE DISH(ES): Kobe Flatiron Steak with Slow Cooked Broccoli; Artichoke Soup with Pine Nuts, Crème Fraîche and Artichoke Chips

FAST FACTS
Restaurant Recs: Lotus of Siam for Spicy Beef Salad with Thai Eggplant, Chili and Lemongrass **Kitchen Tool(s):** Small chef's spoon – because it gives me an artistic and delicate edge that I don't get with squirt bottles or a ladle **Interview Question:** Why are you here? This gives me a glimpse of what motivates their career. **Flavor Combo(s):** Right now I'm into Southwest flavors since I'm new to the area. **Fave Cookbook(s):** The Whole Beast: Nose to Tail Eating by Fergus Henderson expands your horizons; I like the refinement of The French Laundry Cookbook by Thomas Keller **Chef to Cook for You:** Michael Mina – because he's a great chef **Culinary Travel:** Spain – it is the new capital of cooking technology. There are great flavor combinations and great ideas flowing around over there.

Lee Gross
Chef

New York, NY

Restaurant E-mail: danilee14@msn.com

Phone: (212) 228-3100

CHEF FACTS

Cuisine: Modern Vegetarian **Born:** 1974 **Culinary School:** Johnson & Wales University, Providence, RI **Grad Year:** 1996 **Work History:** Boston, MA: Boston Harbor Hotel; Yountville, CA: Domaine Chandon; Providence, RI: Al Forno; New York, NY: Payard Patisserie & Bistro, Broadway East; Los Angeles, CA: Café de Chaya **Mentor(s):** Philippe Jeanty, George Germon, Johanne Killeen, Julie Jordan **Awards:** 2006 StarChefs.com Rising Star Chef Los Angeles; 2006 Angeleno Magazine Runner-Up Best New Chef Los Angeles **Affiliations:** Chefs Collaborative **Languages Spoken:** Kitchen Spanish, kitchen French

NOTABLE DISH(ES): Wild Smoked Salmon Benedict with Tofu and Soy Hollandaise; Scarlet Quinoa with Lotus Root and Sweet Corn Chowder

FAST FACTS

Restaurant Recs: In LA: The Hungry Cat for big-flavored fish, and Inaka for a Zen macrobiotic experience **Kitchen Tool(s):** Suribachi and Surikogi, basically a Japanese mortar & pestle **Interview Question:** What do you like to eat? I listen for the passion in their answer. **Flavor Combo(s):** I have always been big on savory and sweet flavor combinations, but lately I'm really into sour and pungent flavors. I love umeboshi plum, as it is sour, fruity and salty all at once. Using the flesh of the plum, or the salty ume-su (umeboshi vinegar) in conjunction with pungent spring onions, ramps, or garlic chives is really exciting. **Fave Cookbook(s):** The Lima Ohsawa Macrobiotic Cookbook: The Art of Just Cooking by Lima Ohsawa **Chef to Cook for You:** I would love to be cooked for by Jacques Pépin. He is a true master technician and I think he embodies all the best qualities of a professional chef. Above all, he understands that love is the most essential ingredient to good cooking. **Culinary Travel:** Northern California – everything I ate tasted like manna. New York – there's nothing like it for taste and flavors.

G

Alexandra Guarnaschelli
Executive Chef | Butter Restaurant

415 Lafayette St. New York, NY 10003

Restaurant E-mail: chef@butterrestaurant.com

Phone: (212) 253-2828

RESTAURANT FACTS

Seats: 130 **Weeknight Covers:** 100–130 **Weekend Covers:** 300 **Check Average (with Wine):** $60–$100 **Tasting Menu:** Yes $90/$130 with wine **Kitchen Staff:** 11

CHEF FACTS

Cuisine: French American **Born:** 1969 **Began Career:** 1992 **Culinary School:** L'Ecole de Cuisine La Varenne, France **Grad Year:** 1993 **Stages:** France: Restaurant Joël Robuchon, Dusquesne, L' Essential, Jean Michel Bouvier **Work History:** France: Restaurant Guy Savoy; New York, NY: An American Place, Restaurant Daniel; Los Angeles, CA: Patina Restaurant **Mentor(s):** Guy Savoy, Daniel Boulud, Patricia Wells **Affiliations:** Les Dames d'Escoffier, James Beard Foundation, Southern Foodways Alliance **Languages Spoken:** French

NOTABLE DISH(ES): Angel Hair Pasta with Morels, Lemon, and Fingerling Potatoes

FAST FACTS

Restaurant Recs: Forty Carrots for a tuna salad sandwich **Kitchen Tool(s):** Sharp vegetable peeler that costs $2.99, so I don't mind when it winds up in the garbage with the peelings **Interview Question:** Are you going to taste the food? **Flavor Combo(s):** Jerusalem artichokes, chestnut honey and hazelnuts **Fave Cookbook(s):** Simply French by Patricia Wells **Chef to Cook for You:** I would pick Anne-Sophie Pic, France's only female Michelin three-star chef. After seven years cooking in France I am well aware of what a man's world it is over there and what it takes for a woman to succeed. I am in awe and have pure admiration for her shattering the glass ceiling. I'm sure I would feel the same way about her food. **Culinary Travel:** How can you ask a chef to pick just one place? I want to go to Iceland for the fish, to Australia for the products and ingredients, and to Japan for the technique.

David Guas
Pastry Chef | DamGoodSweet Consulting Group, LLC

6011 Chesterbrook Rd. Mclean, VA 22101

Restaurant E-mail: damgoodsweet@aol.com

Phone: (703) 772-1085

CHEF FACTS
Cuisine: Latin, Asian, modern American, Southern (Deep South)
Born: 1975 **Began Career:** 1995 **Culinary School:** Sclafani Cooking School, New Orleans, LA **Grad Year:** 1996 **Stages:** New York, NY: Daniel, Eleven Madison Park; Indonesia: The Ritz-Carlton, The Intercontinental Hotel **Work History:** Washington, DC: Ceiba, TenPenh, Acadiana, DC Coast **Mentor(s):** Jacques Torres **Awards:** 2005, 2004 RAMMY Pastry Chef of the Year Washington DC; 2003 American Culinary Federation Pastry Chef of the Year; 2003 Bon Appétit Eight Dessert Stars **Affiliations:** ACF; CFFA, NCA, SFA **Books Published:** Finishing DamGoodSweet, (Pub: Taunton Press) **Languages Spoken:** English and partial Spanish

NOTABLE DISH(ES): Mexican Hot Chocolate Shooter

FAST FACTS
Restaurant Recs: Café Asia for the calamari **Kitchen Tool(s):** A handheld immersion blender. It is great for emulsification and it gives me the ability to have more control. **Interview Question:** Why do you want to work here? Do you love to eat dessert? I watch facial expressions closely, especially the eyes, which say a lot. I want to hire people who enjoy what they're cooking, and know what it's supposed to taste like. **Flavor Combo(s):** Salt, caramel and chocolate; citrus with fragrant herbs **Fave Cookbook(s):** Desserts by Pierre Hermé **Chef to Cook for You:** Suvir Seran. His cuisine is so unusual with explosive flavors. He is very unique. **Culinary Travel:** Kiawah Island, SC for the mix of Caribbean flavors with African and Spanish influences. These are the flavors I was raised on.

Chad Guay
Pastry Chef | Table 1280

1280 Peachtree St. NE Atlanta, GA 30309

Restaurant E-mail: chad.guay@woodruffcenter.org

Phone: (404) 365-0410

RESTAURANT FACTS
Seats: 125 **Weeknight Covers:** 60–70 **Weekend Covers:** 150–200 **Check Average (with Wine):** $75 **Check Average (w/o Wine):** $50–$55 **Tasting Menu:** No **Kitchen Staff:** 3–6 depending on the season

CHEF FACTS
Other Restaurants: Woodruff Arts Center (catering) **Cuisine:** Modern American **Born:** 1983 **Began Career:** 2001 **Culinary School:** Art Institute of Atlanta, Atlanta, GA **Grad Year:** 2004 **Stages:** Atlanta, GA: The Ritz-Carlton **Work History:** Atlanta, GA: The Ritz-Carlton, Canoe, Concentrics Hospitality, Restaurant Associates **Mentor(s):** Jonathan St. Hilaire, Sam Mason – even though I have never met him **Awards:** 2007 StarChefs.com Rising Star Pastry Chef Atlanta **Affiliations:** Share our Strength

NOTABLE DISH(ES): Smoked Chocolate Tart with Jack Daniel's Ice Cream, Blackberry Sorbet, Smoked Paprika; Stout Cake with Vermont Apple Ice Cream

FAST FACTS
Restaurant Recs: Burma Superstar in San Francisco. They have some of the most amazing food I have ever tasted. **Kitchen Tool(s):** Offset spatula because I always need it. I keep it in my back pocket and it allows me to have a delicate touch. **Interview Question:** Can you quenelle? **Flavor Combo(s):** Golden pineapple and pomegranate; strawberries and white beer; butterscotch with cashews. **Fave Cookbook(s):** Grand Livre de Cuisine: Alain Ducasse's Desserts and Pastries by Alain Ducasse **Chef to Cook for You:** Grant Achatz. I'm leaning towards his style of cooking and I would like to see how far he goes and how he pulls it off. It would be great inspiration. **Culinary Travel:** Spain, for their dairy products like cheese, cream, and butter and San Francisco for their raw, organic produce

Kamel Guechida
Executive Pastry Chef | L'Atelier de Joël Robuchon

3799 Las Vegas Blvd. Las Vegas, NV 89109

Restaurant E-mail: kamel_guechida@lv.mgmgrand.com

Phone: (702) 891-7925

RESTAURANT FACTS
Seats: 55 **Weeknight Covers:** 110 **Weekend Covers:** 110 **Tasting Menu:** Yes $135

CHEF FACTS
Other Restaurants: Joël Robuchon Restaurant, The Mansion Villas at MGM **Cuisine:** French **Born:** 1970 **Began Career:** 1989 **Culinary School:** Le Centre de Formation et d'Aprentissage de Boulazac, France **Grad Year:** 1988 **Stages:** France: Mazi Francis **Work History:** Switzerland: Restaurant de Crissier; Macau: Robuchon à Galera; Japan: Château Restaurant Robuchon; France: L'Atelier de Joël Robuchon; Monte Carlo:Joël Robuchon **Mentor(s):** Fredy Girardet and Joël Robuchon **Awards:** 2007 Bon Appétit Best Pastry Chef **Languages Spoken:** French

NOTABLE DISH(ES): Caramel Crémeux infused with Arabica and a chocolate rice soufflé; Sliced Strawberry in Poppy Syrup with Marshmallow in White Chocolate and Strawberry Sorbet

FAST FACTS
Restaurant Recs: Settebello Pizza. I love the margarita prosciutto pizza. **Kitchen Tool(s):** The apple peeler I have had with me since I was sixteen. **Interview Question:** Do you have passion? **Fave Cookbook(s):** Books by Pierre Hermé

G

Andre Guerrero
Chef | Max Restaurant

13355 Ventura Blvd. Sherman Oaks, CA 91423

Restaurant E-mail: info@maxrestaurant.com

Phone: (818) 784-2915

RESTAURANT FACTS
Seats: 85 **Weeknight Covers:** 55 **Weekend Covers:** 120 **Check Average (with Wine):** $60 **Tasting Menu:** No **Kitchen Staff:** 4

CHEF FACTS
Other Restaurants: Señor Fred's, Oinkster **Cuisine:** Fusion **Born:** 1953 **Began Career:** 1978 **Stages:** Los Angeles, CA: Bernards, Biltmore Hotel **Work History:** Los Angeles, CA: Duet, Link; Santa Monica, CA: Finch **Mentor(s):** My mother and father **Protégée(s):** Robert Lia, Rafael Solorzano, Jason Maddoc **Awards:** 2002 Esquire Best New Restaurant **Affiliations:** We participate in many charities. Savor the Seasons for Break the Cycle (of violence) – I am on the advisory committee; "The Great Chefs of Los Angeles" for the National Kidney Foundation; Bon Appétit's Make a Wish Foundation; Share our Strength; Special Olympics; Project by Project and Aids Project Los Angeles. **Languages Spoken:** Kitchen Spanish

NOTABLE DISH(ES): Butterfish with Ginger, Scallions and Soy Broth

FAST FACTS
Restaurant Recs: Alejandros for Filipino food and bbq mussels **Kitchen Tool(s):** Chinese wok, Alto-Sham smoker, mandolin **Interview Question:** Are you generally interested in food? **Flavor Combo(s):** Garlic and ginger **Fave Cookbook(s):** The Horizon Cookbook. The copyright is 1968. This was my first introduction to cooking. It was a book about the greatest and most popular dishes from around the world – it helped shape my eclectic cooking style. My copy is very tattered and still sits by my desk, and to this day I still read it and use it for reference. **Chef to Cook for You:** Mario Batali, because Mario cooks Italian food the way I would love to cook Italian food. My cooking style is very different and I love having someone cook food that doesn't taste like anything that I might have made. **Culinary Travel:** China, because Chinese is my favorite food. I would think that the caliber of Chinese cooking there is much higher than any other place on earth. In my opinion, it is the most complex cooking style. And the Chinese culture is different than anything I am used to.

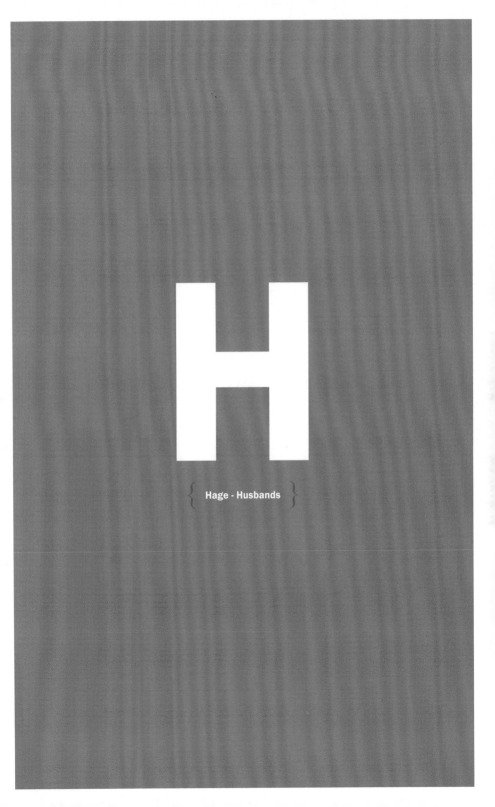

H

{ Hage - Husbands }

H

Sharon Hage
Chef/Owner | York Street

6047 Lewis St. Dallas, TX 75206

Restaurant E-mail: sharon@yorkstreetdallas.com

Phone: (214) 826-0968

RESTAURANT FACTS
Check Average (w/o Wine): $58 **Tasting Menu:** No

CHEF FACTS
Born: 1964 **Culinary School:** The Culinary Institute of America, Hyde Park, NY **Stages:** Dallas, TX: Hotel St. Germain **Work History:** Dallas, TX: Salve!, Hotel St. Germain, Neiman Marcus; New York, NY: Arizona 206, Sam's Cafe **Mentor(s):** Roger Martin, Brendan Walsh **Awards:** 2007 StarChefs.com Rising Star Sustainability Award Dallas **Affiliations:** Farmer's Market

NOTABLE DISH(ES): Crispy Duck Tongue Salad; Grilled Lamb Chops with Couscous

FAST FACTS
Restaurant Recs: Teppo and Tei Tei for Japanese; Yutaka for wonderful fish **Kitchen Tool(s):** Six burner stove; Vita-Prep; spice grinder; ice-cream maker **Interview Question:** Where do you like to eat? What magazines do you subscribe to? Describe the worst shift you have ever had. **Fave Cookbook(s):** All cookbooks by Nancy Silverton and Claudia Fleming **Culinary Travel:** The Far East, because I have never been

Jason Hall
Executive Chef | Anthos

208 East 52nd St. New York, NY 10022

Restaurant E-mail: jason@anthosnyc.com

Phone: (212) 582-6900

RESTAURANT FACTS
Seats: 105 **Weeknight Covers:** 150 **Weekend Covers:** 200 **Check Average (with Wine):** $110 **Kitchen Staff:** 12

CHEF FACTS
Other Restaurants: Mia Dona **Cuisine:** Modern Greek/Mediterranean **Born:** 1979 **Began Career:** 1997 **Culinary School:** Culinary Institute of America, Hyde Park **Grad Year:** 2000 **Stages:** San Francisco, CA: Aqua **Work History:** San Francisco, CA: Fifth Floor; New York, NY: Craft **Mentor(s):** George Morrone, Micheal Psilakis, Marco Canora, Damon Wise, Akhtar Nawab **Affiliations:** We do charity events

NOTABLE DISH(ES): Crispy Rabbit with Cucumber Remoulade; Fricasse of Poularde with Black Truffle, Morels, Leek, Goat Milk, and Cypriot Salad

FAST FACTS
Restaurant Recs: Bar Steak at Raul's **Kitchen Tool(s):** Sharp knife, blue tape, and a black marker **Interview Question:** What do you like to do in life? It tells me what their passions are. **Flavor Combo(s):** Fish and fruit because you can utilize the acidity and change the whole flavor profile **Fave Cookbook(s):** Tout ce que vous devez avoir goûté au moins une fois dans votre vie (Everything That You Must Taste Once In Your Life) by Eric Frechon **Chef to Cook for You:** Bernard Loiseau – the chef who killed himself when he lost his Michelin star **Culinary Travel:** To Greece, to give substance to what I've learned

H

Gordon Hamersley
Chef/Owner | Hamersley's Bistro

553 Tremont St. Boston, MA 02116

Restaurant E-mail: gordon@hamersleysbistro.com

Phone: (617) 423-2700

RESTAURANT FACTS
Seats: 115-165 **Weeknight Covers:** 120 **Weekend Covers:** 200–250 **Check Average (with Wine):** $68 **Tasting Menu:** No **Kitchen Staff:** 7

CHEF FACTS
Cuisine: French-American bistro **Born:** 1951 **Began Career:** 1974 **Work History:** Los Angeles, CA: Ma Maison; Boston, MA: Bostonian Hotel **Mentor(s):** Julia Child, Wolfgang Puck, Lydia Shire **Protégée(s):** Jody Adams, Saul Bolton, Aaron Bashy, Erin McMurrer, Steve Johnson **Awards:** 2004 IACP Chefs and Restaurants Award; 1997 4 stars from the Boston Globe; 1995 James Beard Award Best Chef Northeast; various James Beard Foundation and Food & Wine awards **Affiliations:** We are most identified with Share our Strength and we also do a lot of other local charities **Books Published:** Bistro Cooking at Home

NOTABLE DISH(ES): Coq au Vin; Roast Chicken with Garlic, Lemon and Parsley

FAST FACTS
Restaurant Recs: Charlie's Sandwich Shoppe in South End for poached eggs with sausage **Kitchen Tool(s):** 21-inch cast iron sauté pan **Interview Question:** Tell me about your food history. They start talking about their family and the food they ate as children. **Flavor Combo(s):** Mushrooms and garlic; beef and cinnamon; pork and watermelon **Fave Cookbook(s):** French Provincial Cooking by Elizabeth David **Chef to Cook for You:** Marie-Antoine Carême – I'd like to see if he was as good as history made him out to be **Culinary Travel:** I'd like to go to every major league ballpark in America except Fenway to compare and contrast regional ballpark food. It would be interesting to see different ballpark's approaches to crowd-pleasing food.

Jason Hammel
Chef/Owner | Lula Café

2537 N Kedzie Blvd. Chicago, IL 60647

Restaurant E-mail: eat@lulacafe.com

Phone: (773) 489-9554

RESTAURANT FACTS
Seats: 65–130 **Weeknight Covers:** 130 **Weekend Covers:** 150–175
Tasting Menu: No **Kitchen Staff:** 14

CHEF FACTS
Cuisine: Artisanal, contemporary American **Born:** 1972 **Began Career:** 1999 **Mentor(s):** Alice Waters, Judy Rodgers **Awards:** 2006 Jean Banchet Culinary Excellence; 2005 StarChefs.com Rising Star Chef Chicago **Affiliations:** Chefs Collaborative; Common Threads; Slow Food **Languages Spoken:** Italian, some Spanish

NOTABLE DISH(ES): Parmesan Panna Cotta with Guanciale Croutons; Rainbow Trout with Sunchoke and Winter Radishes

FAST FACTS
Restaurant Recs: Tre Kronor for Swedish home-style food and awesome quiche **Kitchen Tool(s):** Super sharp stainless steel Italian scissors **Interview Question:** What do you do on your day off? **Flavor Combo(s):** Favas and red onions; sweatbreads and maple; nettles and hanger steak **Fave Cookbook(s):** The French Laundry Cookbook by Thomas Keller; The Zuni Café Cookbook by Judy Rogers; Soul of a Chef by Michael Ruhlman **Chef to Cook for You:** Judy Rogers. I'm inspired by her cookbooks **Culinary Travel:** That's easy – Japan

H

Eric Hara
Executive Chef | Davidburke & Donatella

133 E 61st St. New York, NY 10021

Restaurant E-mail: eric@dbdrestaurant.com

Phone: (212) 813-2121

RESTAURANT FACTS
Seats: 110 **Weeknight Covers:** 180–220 **Weekend Covers:** 200–240 **Check Average (with Wine):** $100–$120 **Tasting Menu:** Yes $75 **Kitchen Staff:** 7–10

CHEF FACTS
Cuisine: Modern American **Born:** 1978 **Began Career:** 1995 **Culinary School:** Attended hotel and restaurant school in Santa Barbara **Grad Year:** 1996 **Stages:** Los Angeles, CA: Valentino **Work History:** Santa Barbara, CA: Citronelle, Downey's, Restaurant Mimosa; Dana Point, CA: The Dining Room at The Ritz-Carlton Laguna Niguel; New York, NY: Tao **Mentor(s):** Thomas Keller, Rick Laakkonen, David Burke, Jean-Louis Palladin **Awards:** 2007 StarChefs.com Rising Star Chef New York **Affiliations:** Meals-on-Wheels, Share our Strength **Languages Spoken:** Kitchen Spanish and kitchen Chinese

NOTABLE DISH(ES): "PB&J" Foie Gras Torchon; Seared Diver Scallop with Cauliflower Purée and Tempura of Sea Urchin

FAST FACTS
Restaurant Recs: Noodletown in Chinatown for their lo mein; Trattoria L'incontro in Queens **Kitchen Tool(s):** Vita-Prep **Interview Question:** Are you eager? I look for willingness – I don't care about pedigree. **Flavor Combo(s):** Sweet with sour or really rich savory flavors – foie with french toast or cinnamon buns, like in our PB&J Foie Gras Torchon. I also like pineapple and sumac, and chick peas are great with smoked paprika and garlic. **Fave Cookbook(s):** French Laundry Cookbook by Thomas Keller **Chef to Cook for You:** Jean-Louis Palladin because he was craziness. His style was crazy. He was a great chef. **Culinary Travel:** I think it would be cool to travel around Asia because I don't know a whole lot about it. I'd like to go to Hong Kong and Thailand the most.

Sean Hardy
Director of Food and Beverage | Fairmont Miramar Santa Monica

101 Wilshire Blvd Santa Monica, CA 90401

Restaurant E-mail: sean.hardy@fairmont.com

Phone: (310) 576-7777

CHEF FACTS

Cuisine: Modern American cuisine **Born:** 1970 **Began Career:** 1985
Culinary School: The Culinary Institute of America, Hyde Park, NY
Grad Year: 1991 **Work History:** Beverly Hills, CA: The Belvedere, The
Peninsula; Palm Beach, FL: The Four Seasons Hotel; Montpelier, VT:
The New England Culinary Institute; Lanai City, HI: The Lodge at Koala
Mentor(s): Daniel Boulud **Awards:** 2006 StarChefs.com Rising Star
Chef Los Angeles **Languages Spoken:** Some Spanish

NOTABLE DISH(ES): Spiny Lobster with Corn Pudding and Truffled
Mascarpone; Foie Gras Lollipop with Cherry Vinaigrette

FAST FACTS

Restaurant Recs: Nook for the braised beef short ribs **Kitchen Tool(s):** Hand blender **Interview Question:** Why did you get into this profession? What do you love about it? **Flavor Combo(s):** Sweet and sour; salty and sweet **Fave Cookbook(s):** A Return to Cooking by Eric Ripert **Chef to Cook for You:** Thomas Keller, as he is the modern day American Escoffier and is the most respected chef in America for his high level of standards and commitment to the industry **Culinary Travel:** New York and San Francisco, hands down

Glenn Harris
Executive Chef/Owner | Jane

100 W Houston St. New York, NY 10012

Restaurant E-mail: gharris@janerestaurant.com

Phone: (212) 254-7000

RESTAURANT FACTS
Seats: 115 **Weeknight Covers:** 150 **Weekend Covers:** 250 **Check Average (with Wine):** $37 **Tasting Menu:** No **Kitchen Staff:** 5–6

CHEF FACTS
Other Restaurants: The Neptune Room, The Smith **Cuisine:** American **Born:** 1970 **Culinary School:** The French Culinary Institute, New York, NY **Grad Year:** 1989 **Work History:** New York, NY: Villa Lulu; Vix Café; Rosemaries **Mentor(s):** Marc Meyer, Jonathan Waxman, Larry Forgione, Jacques Pépin **Protégée(s):** Brian Ellis, Julian Hoyas **Awards:** 2005 Time Out New York Best New Seafood Nominee **Affiliations:** We work with lots of charities, such as Unicef, and local schools

NOTABLE DISH(ES): Crispy Artichokes

FAST FACTS
Restaurant Recs: Casa Mono for cockscombs and oyster mushrooms **Kitchen Tool(s):** Microplane, large iron skillet **Interview Question:** How do you make a mayonnaise? **Flavor Combo(s):** Sour and spicy **Fave Cookbook(s):** Culinary Artistry by Andrew Dornenburg and Karen Page **Chef to Cook for You:** Mario Batali – I really like his style of cooking **Culinary Travel:** Spain – the things they are doing are new and exciting and I'd like to learn more about it

Craig Harzewski
Pastry Chef | Naha

500 North Clark Street Chicago, IL 60610

Restaurant E-mail: ikswezrah@aol.com

Phone: (312) 321-6242

RESTAURANT FACTS
Seats: 105 **Weeknight Covers:** 100 **Weekend Covers:** 200 **Check Average (with Wine):** $82 **Tasting Menu:** Yes **Kitchen Staff:** 2

CHEF FACTS
Cuisine: Mediterranean **Born:** 1974 **Began Career:** 1987 **Work History:** New York, NY: Payard, Judson Grill, Le Cirque, Country, San Domenico **Mentor(s):** François Payard – he taught me everything. Beyond just French pastry, he taught me how to challenge myself professionally and make myself better **Languages Spoken:** Kitchen Spanish, French, Italian

NOTABLE DISH(ES): Black Mission Fig Tart of Soft Polenta and Brown Butter with Pistachio Ice Cream and Red Wine Syrup

FAST FACTS
Restaurant Recs: The Grafton for the burger **Kitchen Tool(s):** Small offset spatula, my one chef knife that I keep razor sharp (which is unusual for pastry chefs), and the top of the oven. It holds everything at the right heat. **Interview Question:** I have to see them in action, so I have them stage. It's not necessarily about what they know but how they move and what attitude and motivation they have. If they come with that, I will teach them anything. **Flavor Combo(s):** I like pretty classic and traditional combinations like milk chocolate with hazelnut, and orange and pistachio with cherry **Fave Cookbook(s):** Professional Pastry Chef by Bo Friberg, On Food and Cooking by Harold McGee, and the Ducasse Le Grand Livre line **Chef to Cook for You:** Pastry – Pierre Hermé; savory – Philippe Bertineau: he just makes great food **Culinary Travel:** I can't narrow it down, there are too many places.

Sam Hayward
Chef/Co-owner | Fore Street

288 Fore St. Portland, ME 04101

Restaurant E-mail: sfhay@maine.rr.com

Phone: (207) 775-2717

RESTAURANT FACTS
Seats: 120 **Weeknight Covers:** 175 **Weekend Covers:** 275 **Check Average (with Wine):** $50 **Check Average (w/o Wine):** $36 **Tasting Menu:** No **Kitchen Staff:** 7–8

CHEF FACTS
Cuisine: New England regional cuisine, based upon Maine-grown ingredients **Born:** 1949 **Began Career:** 1974 **Work History:** New York, NY: Regency Hotel; Brunswick, ME: Twenty-Two Lincoln; Freeport, ME: The Harraseeket Inn; Portland, ME: Fore Street **Mentor(s):** Nancy Harmon Jenkins, Gary Clossen **Awards:** 2004 James Beard Foundation Best Chef Northeast **Affiliations:** Chefs Collaborative, Slow Food, SCA, MOFGA **Languages Spoken:** French

NOTABLE DISH(ES): Strawberries with Grilled Pound Cake and Buttermilk Ice Cream

FAST FACTS
Restaurant Recs: Il Nuovo Galeon in Venice for marinated raw seafood from the Lagoon and the Adriatic **Kitchen Tool(s):** Spanish terra cotta cazuela **Interview Question:** Describe your most memorable eating experience **Flavor Combo(s):** Lobster and chanterelles in August. **Fave Cookbook(s):** Ma Gastronomie by Fernand Point; Lulu's Provencal Table by Richard Olney; my mother's copy of the 1946 edition of The Joy of Cooking by Irma S. Rombauer **Chef to Cook for You:** My choice changes with my mood. Today it would be Fredy Girardet. Every bite I had from his stove was an epiphany. **Culinary Travel:** Southeast Asia. The variety of culinary traditions is vast, and it's a part of the world I've not yet seen.

Martin Heierling
Chef | Sensi

3600 Las Vegas Blvd. South Las Vegas, NV 89109

Restaurant E-mail: mheierling@bellagioresort.com

Phone: (702) 693-8800

RESTAURANT FACTS
Seats: 200 **Weeknight Covers:** 300–350 **Weekend Covers:** 350–400+ **Check Average (with Wine):** $50+ **Kitchen Staff:** 12–13

CHEF FACTS
Cuisine: Trans-ethnic **Born:** 1971 **Began Career:** 1990 **Culinary School:** Apprenticeship in Germany near Alsace **Grad Year:** 1990 **Stages:** Germany: Restaurant Schwarzer Adler; Malaysia: Restaurant Jade **Work History:** Germany: Schwarzer Adler; Switzerland: Hummer & Austerbar, Badrutt's Palace; New York, NY: Lespinasse; New Zealand: Essence Restaurant **Mentor(s):** Gray Kunz, Stephen Thompson, my wife **Protégée(s):** Benjamin Bayly, Christophe Schoettle **Awards:** 2005, 2006 Wine Spectator Award of Excellence; 2005 StarChefs.com Rising Star Chef Las Vegas; 2005 Gayot Top 5 Rising Chefs in America; 2005 Condé Nast Best New Restaurants in the World **Affiliations:** CFK, The Epicurean Foundation **Books Published:** Contributed to: Reservations Required: Beef & Lamb Recipes for the New Millennium **Languages Spoken:** French, German, Spanish, Italian

NOTABLE DISH(ES): Halibut with Pickled Onion, Chorogi and Barolo Reduction; Lamb Combo: Tandoori Shortloin, Rogan Josh, Curry Emulsion

FAST FACTS
Restaurant Recs: Joyful House for the special house soup **Kitchen Tool(s):** Gray Kunz spoon, because it is versatile and requires feeling for handling food **Interview Question:** When will you do a stage? How do you think you did during your stage? Shows commitment and willingness to change habits, learn, and be self critical. **Flavor Combo(s):** Hot and sour Asian combinations as well as earthy truffles and root vegetables **Fave Cookbook(s):** Thai Food by David Thompson; Tetsuya by Tetsuya Wakuda; A Culinary Life by Susur Lee **Chef to Cook for You:** Gordon Ramsay – he is brilliant and straight up **Culinary Travel:** China – Shanghai is the new center of the Far East. Singapore is an amazing culinary center. Malaysia, Indonesia and India for the street food.

H

Greg Higgins
Chef-Owner | Higgins Restaurant & Bar

1239 SW Broadway Portland, OR 97205

Restaurant E-mail: higginsrestaurant@comcast.net

Phone: (503) 222-9070

RESTAURANT FACTS
Seats: 85–145 **Weeknight Covers:** 150 **Weekend Covers:** 230
Check Average (with Wine): $50 **Tasting Menu:** No **Kitchen Staff:** 5

CHEF FACTS
Cuisine: Northwest sustainable organic **Born:** 1958 **Began Career:** 1972 **Stages:** France: Les Vosges **Work History:** France: Les Vosges, La Cote d' Or; Seattle, WA: Fullers; Portland, OR: The Heathman Restaurant **Mentor(s):** Joseph Matter, Alice Waters, Michael Wild **Protégée(s):** Scott Dolich, Vito DiLullo, Brad Root, Rich Meyer **Awards:** 2004 DiRoNA Restaurant Hall of Fame; 2001 James Beard Foundation Best Chef Northwest/Hawaii **Affiliations:** Chefs Collaborative, Slow Food **Languages Spoken:** French, Spanish

NOTABLE DISH(ES): Tagine of Alaskan Halibut with Saffron Couscous, Almonds and Harissa

FAST FACTS
Restaurant Recs: Alba Osteria for agnolotti dal plin **Kitchen Tool(s):** Mortar and pestle because it makes great sauces **Interview Question:** What do you know about us? **Flavor Combo(s):** Strong aromatic contrasts with full deep background flavors. For example: seared and roasted wild salmon with a contrasting relish of chilies and aromatic herbs. **Fave Cookbook(s):** Honey from a Weed by Patience Gray **Chef to Cook for You:** Kazumasa Kitajima of Riute Restaurant outside of Fukuoka, Kyushu Japan – incredible organic Inaka-style Keiseki-Ryori all presented on the pottery of Japan's living masters. **Culinary Travel:** My most recent trip was New Zealand, prior to that Extremadura, Alsace, Crete, Apulia, Provence... you get the idea.

Gerald Hirigoyen
Executive Chef/Owner | Piperade

1015 Battery St. San Francisco, CA 94111

Restaurant E-mail: gerald@piperade.com

Phone: (415) 391-2555

RESTAURANT FACTS
Seats: 65 **Weeknight Covers:** 100-120 **Weekend Covers:** 140-150 **Check Average (with Wine):** $50 **Tasting Menu:** No **Kitchen Staff:** 8-10

CHEF FACTS
Other Restaurants: Bocadillos **Cuisine:** Basque **Born:** 1957 **Work History:** San Francisco, CA: Pastis, Fringale, Piperade, Bocadillos, Miro at Bacara **Mentor(s):** My parents **Protégée(s):** Allen Vitti **Awards:** 2006 James Beard Foundation Best Chef California Nominee, 2003 San Francisco Magazine Chef of the Year, 1994 Food & Wine Best New Chefs **Affiliations:** JBF, IACP **Books Published:** The Basque Kitchen **Languages Spoken:** French, Spanish

NOTABLE DISH(ES): Orange Blossom Beignets; Almond and Apricot Tartlet with Crème Chantilly, Gateau Basque and Mango Coulis

FAST FACTS
Restaurant Recs: Yuet Lee for black beans and steamed clams **Kitchen Tool(s):** Grater - because you can do so much with it **Interview Question:** What do you cook at home? Because the answer is always different. **Fave Cookbook(s):** The Cooking of Southwest France by Paula Wolfert

Peter Hoffman
Chef/Owner | Savoy

70 Prince St. New York, NY 10012

Restaurant E-mail: ph@savoynyc.com

Phone: (212) 219-8570

RESTAURANT FACTS
Seats: 65 **Weeknight Covers:** 70 **Weekend Covers:** 120 **Tasting Menu:** No **Kitchen Staff:** 4

CHEF FACTS
Other Restaurants: Back Forty **Cuisine:** Sustainable, seasonal, local, simple cuisine **Born:** 1956 **Began Career:** 1980 **Culinary School:** Madeleine Kamman's Cooking School, France **Grad Year:** 1980 **Stages:** Japan: La Rochelle **Work History:** New York, NY: Huberts, Quilted Giraffe **Mentor(s):** Madeleine Kamman, Richard Olney **Protégée(s):** Caroline Fidanza, Charlie Kiely, Sharon Pachter, John Tucker, Andy Feinberg, Franny Stephens **Awards:** 2005 Organic Styles Power List of 50 Environmental Crusaders **Affiliations:** Chefs Collaborative **Languages Spoken:** French

NOTABLE DISH(ES): Cranberry Bean and Pumpkin Stew with Peach Chutney

FAST FACTS
Restaurant Recs: En Brasserie for homemade tofu **Kitchen Tool(s):** Japanese cooking chopsticks – because they allow you to really precisely place the food **Flavor Combo(s):** Properly raised pork with a pimentón spice rub **Fave Cookbook(s):** The River Cottage Family Cookbook by Hugh Fearnley-Whittingstall **Chef to Cook for You:** The Oaxacan chefs in the open markets. They superbly grill any vegetables you buy in the market alongside their thin sliced meat by the kilo. It's so immediate, essential and Promethean. **Culinary Travel:** Extremadura, Spain to see and taste the Iberico pigs in the Dehesa oak forests

Wesley Holton
Executive Chef | Daniel Boulud Brasserie

3131 Las Vegas Blvd. South Las Vegas, NV 89136

Restaurant E-mail: wesley.holton@wynnlasvegas.com

Phone: (702) 770-3310

RESTAURANT FACTS
Seats: 250 **Weeknight Covers:** 400–600 **Weekend Covers:** 400–600 **Check Average (with Wine):** $89–$105 **Tasting Menu:** Yes upon request **Kitchen Staff:** 12

CHEF FACTS
Cuisine: Modern brasserie fare **Born:** 1977 **Began Career:** 1997 **Culinary School:** Schoolcraft College, Livonia, MI **Grad Year:** 1999 **Work History:** Bloomfield Hills, MI: Oakland Hills Country Club; New York, NY: DB Bistro Moderne, Daniel; Palm Beach, FL: Café Boulud **Awards:** 2008 StarChefs.com Rising Star Chef Las Vegas

NOTABLE DISH(ES): Pan-Roasted Loup de Mer with Cauliflower, Saffron, Grapes and Pine Nuts; Trio of Kurobuta Pork: Roasted Rack with Bacon and Calves' Feet Crust, Pork Sausage with Pine Nuts and Red Currants

FAST FACTS
Restaurant Recs: Sen of Japan – a sushi place by my house **Kitchen Tool(s):** Spoon – we use it to cook, to plate. It's very versatile. **Interview Question:** Do you like to have fun when you cook? I like to read their reaction. **Flavor Combo(s):** Brown butter and thyme; citrus and avocado; pickled vegetables and roasted meats **Fave Cookbook(s):** The Hudson Valley Foie Gras Cookbook because you get to see so many chef's interpretations and recipes **Chef to Cook for You:** Joël Robuchon **Culinary Travel:** France – I haven't been there. That's where it all began. Their level of respect for food is far superior to what we have here.

H

Linton S. Hopkins
Chef/Owner | Restaurant Eugene

2277 Peachtree Rd. Atlanta, GA 30309

Restaurant E-mail: chef@restauranteugene.com

Phone: (404) 355-0321

RESTAURANT FACTS
Seats: 55–85 **Weeknight Covers:** 75 **Weekend Covers:** 125 **Check Average (with Wine):** $90–$130 **Tasting Menu:** Yes $30 Sunday Special **Kitchen Staff:** 7

CHEF FACTS
Other Restaurants: Holeman and Finch Public House, H&F Bread Co. **Cuisine:** Seasonal, New American **Born:** 1966 **Began Career:** 1995 **Culinary School:** The Culinary Institute of America, Hyde Park, NY **Grad Year:** 1995 **Stages:** Atlanta, GA: Taka **Work History:** New Orleans, LA: Mr. B's, Grill Room at Windsor Court; Washington, DC: DC Coast **Mentor(s):** Gerard Maras taught me about foraging for wild goods, treating farmers with respect, putting out quantity and quality. Jeff Tunks taught me about being prepared for service. **Awards:** 2008 James Beard Foundation Best Chef Southeast Nominee; 2007 StarChefs.com Rising Star Chef Atlanta **Affiliations:** SFA, James Beard, Southern Food & Beverage Museum Board, Slow Food, SOS **Languages Spoken:** German, kitchen Spanish

NOTABLE DISH(ES): Metzger Farms Berkshire Black Pork Belly with English Pea and Corn Succotash; Joyce Farms Baby Hen, Pan Roasted Breast, Leg Sous Vide, Heirloom Fingerling Sweet Potatoes, Brussel Sprouts, Chestnut Game Jus

FAST FACTS
Restaurant Recs: Figo Pasta for simple marinara; Taka Sushi; Tasty China for great Chinese food **Kitchen Tool(s):** Thermal circulator; old food mill for its gentleness in breaking down vegetables **Interview Question:** We go through a personal interview, a written test and a practical test: 8 vegetables, 5 methods, 90 minutes **Flavor Combo(s):** Black pepper and fruit; offal with mustard; fleur de sel with fresh raw hamachi **Fave Cookbook(s):** Ma Gastronomie by Fernand Point; White Heat by Marco Pierre White **Chef to Cook for You:** I'm most curious about Fernand Point. I think he had a gift for combinations and for the art of plating. He had a rich appreciation for French cuisine and is sort of a leader in the industry for the twentieth century and going into the twenty-first. **Culinary Travel:** Everywhere, but especially Japan for their culinary sensibility, freshness, and simplicity, and Italy for classic combinations and their passion and vision

Joshua Hopkins
Chef de Cuisine | Bacchanalia
1198 Howell Mill Rd. Atlanta, GA 30318

Restaurant E-mail: joshuathopkins@yahoo.com

Phone: (404) 365-0410

RESTAURANT FACTS
Seats: 65 **Weeknight Covers:** 60 **Weekend Covers:** 130 **Check Average (w/o Wine):** $75 **Tasting Menu:** Yes $75 **Kitchen Staff:** 7-8

CHEF FACTS
Cuisine: American with Southern and French influences **Born:** 1975 **Began Career:** 1996 **Culinary School:** Apprenticeship for French master chef Christian Chemin **Work History:** Atlanta, GA: Capital City Club; Charleston, SC: Slightly North of Broad, High Cotton **Mentor(s):** Christian Chemin, Frank Lee, Jason Scholz, Anne Quatrano, Clifford Harrison

FAST FACTS
Restaurant Recs: Lee's bakery on Buford highway – always nice people with great noodle dishes for cheap **Kitchen Tool(s):** Solid cooks and a Cryovac machine **Interview Question:** Are you a vegetarian and if so can you be persuaded? **Flavor Combo(s):** Pork and fresh organic vegetables **Fave Cookbook(s):** If I had to choose, I would say all of them (thank you Amazon) **Chef to Cook for You:** Fernand Point – not only thought of as a great chef but having read his notebook it seems that he had a great outlook on what it was to be a chef **Culinary Travel:** Spain could easily be a first choice or Italy a second, but I think that I would benefit from going to a country like Japan, where the food and culture are so different than I am used to. I would love to learn how to properly make udon noodles.

H

Mark Hopper
Chef de Cuisine | Bouchon Las Vegas

3355 Las Vegas Blvd. South, #10101 Las Vegas, NV 89109

Restaurant E-mail: mhopper@bouchonbistro.com

Phone: (702) 414-6200

RESTAURANT FACTS
Seats: 200 **Weeknight Covers:** 300 **Weekend Covers:** 400 **Check Average (with Wine):** $75 **Tasting Menu:** No **Kitchen Staff:** 15

CHEF FACTS
Cuisine: Classic French bistro **Born:** 1967 **Culinary School:** Newbury College, Boston, MA **Grad Year:** 1987 **Stages:** New York, NY: Daniel; Chicago, IL: Charlie Trotter's, Park Avenue Café; San Francisco, CA: Rubicon, Silks **Work History:** Yountville, CA: The French Laundry; San Jose, CA: Paolo's **Mentor(s):** My parents, Thomas Keller **Affiliations:** James Beard Foundation, March of Dimes

FAST FACTS
Restaurant Recs: I know it's not quite what you mean, but Tetsuya in Australia is amazing. He is such a gentleman and the food was so memorable I feel like I was there yesterday although it was a year ago. **Kitchen Tool(s):** My spoon (it's a personal thing, we go way back) **Interview Question:** We actually have a questionnaire that asks things like: what do you enjoy about the restaurant industry? What is your favorite food and why? I'm looking for answers that tell me where they are coming from. **Flavor Combo(s):** Olive oil and garlic used as a backdrop of flavors **Fave Cookbook(s):** Simply French by Patricia Wells; The French Laundry Cookbook by Thomas Keller **Chef to Cook for You:** Grant Achatz. We started at French Laundry on the same day in 1996, so we have a long history. I think he is such a well-rounded chef. What he cooks at home for example is equally as impressive as the cuisine he serves at his restaurant. **Culinary Travel:** Probably Spain. I have already done France, Italy and Australia, and it is the one major place I have left to see. I want to learn about the cultural and historical elements of their cuisine.

Craig Hopson
Executive Chef | One if by Land, Two if by Sea

17 Barrow St. New York, NY 10014

Restaurant E-mail: chopson@oneifbyland.com

Phone: (212) 255-8649

RESTAURANT FACTS
Seats: 150 **Weeknight Covers:** 120 **Weekend Covers:** 250 **Check Average (with Wine):** $90 **Tasting Menu:** Yes $75/$95 **Kitchen Staff:** 7

CHEF FACTS
Cuisine: French; Mediterranean **Born:** 1971 **Began Career:** 1987 **Culinary School:** 4 year apprenticeship in Australia **Grad Year:** 1991 **Stages:** France: Alain Ducasse **Work History:** France: Le Lucas Carton, Guy Savoy, Alain Ducasse, Troisgros; Australia: The Grange at the Hyatt; New York: Picholine **Mentor(s):** Alain Senderens, Terrence Brennan **Awards:** 2007 StarChefs.com Rising Star Chef New York **Affiliations:** We do a lot of charity events **Languages Spoken:** French

NOTABLE DISH(ES): Frog Wings Tempura with Celery Kim Chee; Squid Ink Linguini with Calamari, Chorizo Aioli and Paella Broth

FAST FACTS
Restaurant Recs: Wonjo Korean BBQ **Kitchen Tool(s):** Measuring equipment; digital thermometer; digital scale; spoons and cups for consistency **Interview Question:** What do you want to achieve? If they say they want to try new things, it's a step in the right direction. **Flavor Combo(s):** I'm always looking for bright, creative and classic flavors reconfigured – I like to hold on to what's classic but add some sort of surprise twist, like combining chicken with foie gras or truffles. **Fave Cookbook(s):** Any book by Michel Bras and Pierre Gagnaire; Le Repertoire de la Cuisine by Louis Sauliner **Chef to Cook for You:** Escoffier – I would really like to see how he managed back in those days, when everything was done by hand. The carrots were pulled from the ground by hand, the animals were shot and brought to the restaurant. He had no machines but still made incredible food. **Culinary Travel:** Paris – the food there is very exciting. You have to go to Gagnaire. I haven't been there for a year, but I think there's a lot happening there. Japan, too – I've never been, and have always been inspired by the flavors and philosophy of the cuisine.

H

Joel Hough
Chef de Cuisine | Cookshop

156 10th Ave. New York, NY 10011

Restaurant E-mail: joel.hough@gmail.com

Phone: (212) 924-4440

RESTAURANT FACTS
Weeknight Covers: 220–300 **Weekend Covers:** 300–350 **Check Average (with Wine):** $50 **Tasting Menu:** No

CHEF FACTS
Other Restaurants: Hundred Acres **Cuisine:** American with a nod to the Mediterranean **Born:** 1972 **Began Career:** 1996 **Work History:** Washington, DC: Red Sage, Raku, Topeka, The W; New York, NY: Washington Park, Barbuto **Mentor(s):** Jeffrey Olson, Jonathan Waxman **Affiliations:** The local markets, Share our Strength

NOTABLE DISH(ES): Maine Day-Boat Sea Scallops with Sautéed Mustard Greens, Rhubarb Sauce, Pickled Rhubarb, Ginger and Mint Salad

FAST FACTS
Restaurant Recs: I love street food. Its just some guy, not a chef. Dim Sum GoGo – for the variety and dumbed down food in a cafeteria environment. Soup dumplings at Goodies and the Taco Truck on 46/Bliss in Queens. **Kitchen Tool(s):** Mortar and pestle **Interview Question:** "Are you willing to learn?" Trail for one night. The market is so saturated now. **Flavor Combo(s):** I use head to toe, except for cows. Rabbit kidneys and gnocchi is a great combo. **Fave Cookbook(s):** Zuni Café Cookbook – it gives a really comprehensive approach. **Culinary Travel:** I'd go to Tuscany. The Italian touch on food is very restrained and intelligent. There's something very ingenious to me about the simplicity with which Italians approach food. They don't manipulate it – a lot of countries in the Mediterranean have that. I'd like to go to North Africa too. I love dried fruit, nuts, grains – Morocco and Lebanon would be amazing. My wife is from Ethiopia. I use a lot of North African, Central Asian flavors, and I'd like to go check them out and see what they're all about.

Matthew Hoyle
Executive Chef | Nobu 57

40 W 57th St. New York, NY 10019

Restaurant E-mail: matth@noburestaurants.com

Phone: (212) 757-8655

RESTAURANT FACTS
Seats: 200 **Weeknight Covers:** 500 **Weekend Covers:** 500 **Tasting Menu:** Yes $100/$150 **Kitchen Staff:** 27

CHEF FACTS
Cuisine: Japanese **Born:** 1972 **Began Career:** 1994 **Culinary School:** Newcastle College, England **Grad Year:** 1994 **Work History:** England: Nobu London, 21 Queen Street; Greece: Matsuhisa Mykonos **Mentor(s):** Nobu Matsuhisa, Mark Edwards **Affiliations:** NBVN

NOTABLE DISH(ES): Arctic Char Tataki with Spicy Cilantro Sauce; Uni Chawan Mushi

FAST FACTS
Restaurant Recs: Yakitori Totto – for gyutan **Kitchen Tool(s):** Unagi (Japanese eel) knife **Interview Question:** Can you cook? **Flavor Combo(s):** Citrus, spicy and soy **Fave Cookbook(s):** Japanese Cooking: A Simple Art by Shizuo Tsuji **Chef to Cook for You:** Dorothy Hartley – the author of Food in England. I love the way she writes about food: hers sounds really tasty! She has an amazing knowledge of the different regions of England. **Culinary Travel:** Japan for the produce available and the attention to detail. Across a huge range and variety of food and restaurants, the quality is amazing. The simple things are done very well. Eating there is a lot of fun. Plus, unagi is the best.

Joel Huff
Chef de Cuisine | Silks

222 Sansome St. San Francisco, CA 94103

Restaurant E-mail: jhuff@mohg.com

Phone: (415) 986-2020

RESTAURANT FACTS
Seats: 70 **Weeknight Covers:** 40–50 **Weekend Covers:** 40–50
Check Average (with Wine): $125 **Tasting Menu:** Yes $90 **Kitchen Staff:** 3

CHEF FACTS
Cuisine: Californian-Asian **Born:** 1972 **Began Career:** 1988 **Culinary School:** Santa Barbara City College, Santa Barbara, CA **Grad Year:** 1995 **Stages:** Australia: Tetsuya; Los Angeles, CA: Patina **Work History:** Los Angeles, CA: L'Orangerie; Minneapolis, MN: Aquavit; Australia: Restaurant VII; New York, NY: Asiate **Mentor(s):** Tetsuya Wakuda, Masa Takayama **Protégée(s):** Greg Pursell **Languages Spoken:** Spanglish

NOTABLE DISH(ES): Duet of Octopus Ceviche, Red Curry, Lime, Ginger; Yellowfin Sashimi, Ponzu Truffle Vinaigrette, Feta Foam

FAST FACTS
Restaurant Recs: Sushi Sam's for swordfish with black pepper and lemon sauce nigiri **Kitchen Tool(s):** Oroshigane (Japanese grater) **Interview Question:** What do you cook when you are not at the restaurant? I generally prefer to see a cook on the line instead of asking questions. I think it is important to see how they flow with the kitchen. **Flavor Combo(s):** Sour, sweet and spicy: the Thai Trilogy **Fave Cookbook(s):** Total Cooking by Miguel Sanchez; Tetsuya by Tetsuya Wakuda **Chef to Cook for You:** Michel Bras – he's got beautiful food. The guy knows how to cook! **Culinary Travel:** Argentina, because I've never been. I would also go back to Spain – it's been ten years since I was last there, and I need to get back in the loop.

Alan Hughes
Executive Chef | One Ninety Restaurant

26 NW 54th St. Miami, FL 33127

Restaurant E-mail: info@oneninetycatering.com

Phone: (305) 758-7085

RESTAURANT FACTS
Seats: 49 **Weeknight Covers:** 25–49 **Weekend Covers:** 25–49
Check Average (with Wine): $60 **Check Average (w/o Wine):** $40
Tasting Menu: Yes once a month **Kitchen Staff:** 2

CHEF FACTS
Other Restaurants: One Ninety Catering **Cuisine:** European-influenced **Born:** 1968 **Began Career:** 1989 **Culinary School:** The French Culinary Institute, New York, NY **Grad Year:** 1989 **Stages:** Francis Malmann **Work History:** New York, NY: River Café; Key West, FL: SaraBeth's; Miami, FL: Bistro du Nord **Mentor(s):** Chef Francis Mallmann in Argentina – he was the premier chef in Argentina. He opened up all the culinary possibilities – all my horizons **Affiliations:** City Harvest – once a month I feed the homeless **Languages Spoken:** Spanish, Portuguese, Italian, French, kitchen Creole

NOTABLE DISH(ES): Colorado Lamb Loin with Celery Root Purée, Grilled Radicchio and Apples and Lemon Mustard Oil

FAST FACTS
Restaurant Recs: Hy Vong Calle Ocho on 8th Street in Miami downtown for Vietnamese – all the food is great; A&E market on 79th Street does great roti; the Japanese market on 79th Street does great sushi **Kitchen Tool(s):** The grill – I have a simple gas grill **Interview Question:** What is your weakest point? I am looking for honesty, and I also want find out where to supplement them - what they won't be able to provide. **Flavor Combo(s):** Fennel and tomato; olive oil and garlic **Fave Cookbook(s):** Charlie Trotter's cookbooks **Chef to Cook for You:** Charlie Trotter **Culinary Travel:** I would go to Japan. I'm so un-Asian and I want to learn about Japanese cuisine.

H

Daniel Humm
Chef | Eleven Madison Park

11 Madison Ave. New York, NY 10010

Restaurant E-mail: dhumm@elevenmadisonpark.com

Phone: (212) 889-0905

RESTAURANT FACTS
Seats: 116 **Weeknight Covers:** 140 **Weekend Covers:** 180 **Check Average (with Wine):** $145 **Check Average (w/o Wine):** $100 **Tasting Menu:** Yes $145 **Kitchen Staff:** 15–20

CHEF FACTS
Cuisine: Modern French **Born:** 1976 **Began Career:** 1990 **Culinary School:** Three-year apprenticeship in Switzerland **Grad Year:** 1994 **Stages:** New York, NY: Per Se, Restaurant Daniel **Work History:** Switzerland: Hotel Baur au Lac, Gasthaus zum Loewen, Gasthaus zum Gupf, Restaurant le Pont de Brent; San Francisco, CA: Campton Place **Mentor(s):** Gérard Rabaey **Protégée(s):** Thorsten Kissau; Lecham Arlberg; Chris Kostow **Awards:** 2008 Gault Millau Swiss Star Abroad; 2007 Time Out New York Critics Choice Award; 2007, 2005, 2004 James Beard Foundation Rising Star Nominee; 2005 StarChefs.com Rising Star San Francisco; 2005 San Francisco Chronicle 4 stars; 2005 Food & Wine Best New Chef; 2004 Gayot.com Rising Star; 2003 San Francisco Chronicle Rising Star; 2002 Michelin Guide 1 star; 2001 Gault Millau Discovery of the Year **Affiliations:** We align ourselves with Share Our Strength, Citymeals, Bocuse d'Or, and the Madison Square Park Conservancy **Languages Spoken:** German

NOTABLE DISH(ES): California Strawberry Gazpacho with Hawaiian Prawns and Guanciale; Heirloom Tomato Terrine

FAST FACTS
Restaurant Recs: Spotted Pig because the food is good, it's open late, and I always have a good time **Kitchen Tool(s):** A Haake Immersion Circulator – a machine that keeps water at an exact temperature; Hold-o-mat for slow cooking fish **Interview Question:** Why do you want to work here and how long have you stayed in your past positions? Why do you want to cook? **Flavor Combo(s):** Lemon, verbena, and lobster **Fave Cookbook(s):** Le Grand Livre de la Cuisine by Alain Ducasse; El bulli 1998-2002 by Ferran Adriá; Total Cooking by Miguel Sanchez Romera **Chef to Cook for You:** It would have to be Alain Chapel, as I've heard such amazing things about his cuisine but never had a chance to experience it for myself **Culinary Travel:** Barcelona, Spain – they live a great life, eat great food, and it comes from the heart

Todd Humphries
Executive Chef | Martini House

1245 Spring St. St. Helena, CA 94574

Restaurant E-mail: todd@martinihouse.com

Phone: (707) 963-2233

RESTAURANT FACTS
Seats: 109–170 **Weeknight Covers:** 150 **Weekend Covers:** 250 **Check Average (with Wine):** $80 **Tasting Menu:** Yes $85/$131 with wine **Kitchen Staff:** 10

CHEF FACTS
Cuisine: Napa Valley cuisine **Born:** 1959 **Began Career:** 1988 **Culinary School:** Culinary Institute of America, Hyde Park, NY **Grad Year:** 1998 **Stages:** New York, NY: Penninsula Hotel **Work History:** New York, NY: Quilted Giraffe, Lespinasse; San Francisco, CA: Campton Place Hotel **Mentor(s):** Gray Kunz, Jacques Pépin **Protégée(s):** Chris Litts, Larry Finn, Devon Knell **Awards:** 2008 Michelin 1 star; 2003-2005 San Francisco Chronicle Top 100; 2002 Esquire Best New Restaurant; 2002 San Francisco Chronicle 2 stars **Affiliations:** We are affiliated with most local charities in the community related to education, police and fire departments, as well as the local hospital and opera house. We also do Meals-on-Wheels in San Francisco.

NOTABLE DISH(ES): Ginger Braised Shiitake "Lentinus Edodes"

FAST FACTS
Restaurant Recs: Cook for the BLT **Kitchen Tool(s):** Japanese mandolin for great precision **Interview Question:** How do you make a good vinaigrette and simple salad? **Flavor Combo(s):** Olive oil, lemon and black pepper **Fave Cookbook(s):** Le Grand Livre de Cuisine by Alain Ducasse **Chef to Cook for You:** Tim, the owner of Yuet Lee in San Francisco's Chinatown. He always surprises us with lots of great flavor combinations as well as cooking techniques. **Culinary Travel:** Japan to visit the fish market and the food stalls

Robert Hurd
Executive Sous Chef | XYZ at the W hotel

181 Third St. San Francisco, CA 94103

Restaurant E-mail: robert.hurd@whotels.com

Phone: (415) 777-5300

RESTAURANT FACTS
Seats: 90 **Weeknight Covers:** 150–250 **Weekend Covers:** 150–250 **Check Average (w/o Wine):** $40 **Tasting Menu:** Yes $48/$72 with wine **Kitchen Staff:** 6–8

CHEF FACTS
Cuisine: Modern French **Born:** 1978 **Began Career:** 1993 **Culinary School:** Schoolcraft College, Livonia, Michigan **Grad Year:** 1998 **Stages:** France: Ze Kitchen Galerie; New York, NY: Daniel **Work History:** New York, NY: db Bistro Moderne **Mentor(s):** Olivier Muller of db. I met him soon after my return from France, which helped us bond. It's amazing how much he gets done in the kitchen. Michael Golden made my first job at 15 fun – probably why I still do it! **Affiliations:** Meals-on-Wheels, My Tree, and many other charities **Languages Spoken:** Understand French, a little German

NOTABLE DISH(ES): Hamachi with Tea-Soaked Fruit, Granny Smith Apple, Daikon Radish and Riesling Gelée (with Yellow Raisins, Maldon Sel Gris, Fleur de Sel, and Red Clay Salts)

FAST FACTS
Restaurant Recs: Bar Tartine in San Francisco; Suppenkuche for wienershnitzel **Kitchen Tool(s):** Forschner chef knife; 15-year old vegetable peeler – my first tool **Interview Question:** I ask for a preparation of fish and two of meat. I check to see if they are seasoned correctly. **Flavor Combo(s):** Salt and pepper – you can't beat it **Fave Cookbook(s):** The Whole Beast: Nose to Tail Eating by Fergus Henderson **Chef to Cook for You:** Fergus Henderson because I like his style and the fact that he uses the entire animal. He utilizes a lot of underutilized ingredients. **Culinary Travel:** I would go back to France. I lived there for a year and just think they have an amazing culture with food.

Andy Husbands
Chef/Owner | Tremont 647

647 Tremont St. Boston, MA 02118

Restaurant E-mail: andy@tremont647.com

Phone: (617) 266-4600

RESTAURANT FACTS
Seats: 107 **Weeknight Covers:** 70–80 **Weekend Covers:** 180 **Check Average (with Wine):** $60 **Check Average (w/o Wine):** 40 **Tasting Menu:** Yes $40/$60 **Kitchen Staff:** 4–6

CHEF FACTS
Cuisine: American **Born:** 1969 **Began Career:** 1992 **Culinary School:** Johnson & Wales University, Providence, RI **Grad Year:** 1992 **Work History:** Boston, MA: East Coast Grill, Sister Sorel, Rouge **Mentor(s):** Chris Schlesinger **Protégée(s):** Jason Santos; Jamie Bissonnette **Awards:** 2005 New England BBQ Society Team of the Year; 2004 Share Our Strength Chef/Restauranteur of the Year **Affiliations:** SOS **Books Published:** The Fearless Chef

NOTABLE DISH(ES): UFO Social Club BBQ Sauce; Peanut-Crusted Grilled Scallops

FAST FACTS
Restaurant Recs: Miami Café for the Cubano; S&S Deli for chopped liver sandwiches; Tacos El Charo for burritos and tacos; The Busy Bee for breakfast **Kitchen Tool(s):** 6-inch JA Henckels knife **Interview Question:** Where will you be in five years? **Flavor Combo(s):** Salt, hot pepper, and sour **Fave Cookbook(s):** The Flavor Principle by Elizabeth Rozin; The Thrill of the Grill: Techniques, Recipes, & Down-Home Barbecue by Christopher Schlesinger **Chef to Cook for You:** Rick Bayless – I just love his flavor combinations **Culinary Travel:** Thailand and El Salvador

I

Bob Iacovone
Chef | Restaurant Cuvée

322 Rue Magazine New Orleans, LA 70130

Restaurant E-mail: rcho@restaurantcuvee.com

Phone: (504) 587-9001

RESTAURANT FACTS
Seats: 95–115 **Weeknight Covers:** 100 **Check Average (with Wine):**
$88 **Check Average (w/o Wine):** $55 **Tasting Menu:** Yes $70–$80
Kitchen Staff: 7

CHEF FACTS
Cuisine: Contemporary Creole with Spanish and French influences
Born: 1971 **Began Career:** 1991 **Culinary School:** Culinary Institute
of America, Hyde Park, NY **Grad Year:** 1991 **Stages:** Boston, MA:
Windsor Court Hotel; Seasons at Bostonian Hotel **Work History:** Palm
Beach, FL: PGA National; Miami Beach, FL: The Booking Table Café;
New Orleans, LA: The Windsor Court Hotel, Nirvana **Mentor(s):** Bingo
Starr – he is the reason I live here. I learned management technique from him. **Awards:** 2005 Esquire
Chefs to Watch; 2004 New Orleans Magazine Best New Chef; 2003 New Orleans Wine & Food Experi-
ence Best in Show **Affiliations:** We do several charity events every year **Languages Spoken:** Some
Spanish, some French

NOTABLE DISH(ES): Spiced Shrimp Napolean with Crisp Mirliton, Cayenne Beurre Blanc, and Frisée;
Chicken and Waffles with Bacon; Coq au Vin Blanc and Boursain

FAST FACTS
Restaurant Recs: Nirvana Indian Restaurant for all tandoori dishes **Kitchen Tool(s):** Pacojet; pasta
maker **Interview Question:** Where do you see yourself in five years? **Flavor Combo(s):** Sweet and
salty; sweet and spicy **Fave Cookbook(s):** Culinary Artistry by Andrew Dornenburg and Karen Page
Chef to Cook for You: I would like Grant Achatz to cook for me **Culinary Travel:** Spain – it has interesting culture and food

Suzanne Imaz
Corporate Pastry Chef | One Sixty Blue

1400 W. Randolph Chicago, IL 60607

Restaurant E-mail: simaz@cmcichicago.com

Phone: (312) 850-0303

RESTAURANT FACTS
Seats: 120 **Weeknight Covers:** 80 **Weekend Covers:** 175 **Check Average (with Wine):** $94 **Tasting Menu:** No **Kitchen Staff:** 1–2

CHEF FACTS
Other Restaurants: Wave; Uncasville, CT: Mohegan Sun **Cuisine:** Contemporary and seasonally inspired desserts with classic influences **Born:** 1964 **Began Career:** 1988 **Culinary School:** Johnson & Wales University, Providence, RI and Le Ferrandi Centre de Formations Technologique in Paris, France **Grad Year:** 1991 **Stages:** France: Hotel de Crillon; Chicago, IL: Charlie Trotter's **Work History:** Washington, VA: Inn at Little Washington; Washington, DC: Citronelle; St. John's, Antigua: Jumby Bay Resort; Chicago, IL: The Park Hyatt **Mentor(s):** Michel Richard – he's super creative, very playful, very innovative; Patrick O'Connell – he was very much about using local products and ingredients **Awards:** 2007 Jean Banchet Award for Best Rising Pastry Chef **Affiliations:** I'm on the board of Common Threads – I do classes with the kids, and it's amazing how much food knowledge they pick up **Languages Spoken:** Spanish

NOTABLE DISH(ES): Cherry Mascarpone Cannelloni with Poached Ellis Farms' Cherries, Chocolate Cremeux and Sour Cherry Sorbet

FAST FACTS
Restaurant Recs: There are some great Indian places on Devon (around 2200 West) **Kitchen Tool(s):** Paring knife **Interview Question:** I ask for three adjectives that describe them **Flavor Combo(s):** Chocolate and banana; citrus and herbs; citrus and dense, sweet flavors – I use it to cut richness **Fave Cookbook(s):** I would say the Grand Livre de Cuisine d'Alain Ducasse: Desserts et Patisserie. It was a gift from a pastry chef who I respect so it has both sentimental and great practical value. **Chef to Cook for You:** That's a tough question in today's culinary world where there are so many chefs whose work I admire. I would have to say Ferran Adriá. I had the opportunity to meet him and there's a very endearing quality about him. I also greatly admire him as a pioneer of modern culinary technique. **Culinary Travel:** Italy – I've never been. I went every place but Italy when I was in Europe.

Todd Immel
Sous Chef | Bacchanalia

1198 Howell Mill Road Atlanta, GA 30318

Restaurant E-mail: alyssa@thereynoldsgroup.com

Phone: (404) 365-0410

RESTAURANT FACTS
Seats: 65 **Weeknight Covers:** 60 **Weekend Covers:** 130 **Check Average (w/o Wine):** $75 **Tasting Menu:** No **Kitchen Staff:** 8

CHEF FACTS
Cuisine: Seasonal new American **Born:** 1970 **Began Career:** 1990
Culinary School: The Culinary Institute of America, Hyde Park, NY
Grad Year: 1990 **Stages:** New York, NY: Daniel; Atlanta, GA: Seeger's
Work History: New York, NY: Daniel; Los Angeles, CA: Pinot Bistro; Atlanta, GA: Table 1280 **Mentor(s):** Guenter Seeger – for his discipline, fundamentals, everything **Affiliations:** JBF, Les Dames D'Escoffier, SFA **Languages Spoken:** Some Spanish

NOTABLE DISH(ES): Red Wine-Braised Octopus, Ceci Bean Salad; Rabbit Pate, Pickled Cherries, Crosnes, Dijon

FAST FACTS
Restaurant Recs: Pura Vida – a tapas bar for very good empanadas; Joel – a mom and pop Mexican place; Penang – an Indonesian place for scallion pancakes **Kitchen Tool(s):** Mortar and pestle; Vita-Prep **Interview Question:** What book are you reading and what are your favorite restaurants? I think it gauges where someone is or where they want to be as a cook. **Flavor Combo(s):** My favorite flavor combinations are always changing depending on the seasons. Some summer flavors are: peas and morels; tomatoes and cheese; corn and chanterelles; strawberries and balsamico traditionale; plums and star anise; foie gras and peaches; cherries and caramel **Fave Cookbook(s):** Cooking by Hand by Paul Bertolli **Chef to Cook for You:** Guenter Seeger – he was and is a mentor, and always seemed to be ahead of the culinary trends **Culinary Travel:** Italy and Spain – the foods of both countries are so fresh and the styles of cooking are inspirational

Yoshinori Ishii
Omakase (Tasting Menu) Chef | Morimoto

88 10th Ave. New York NY 10011

Restaurant E-mail: tanagokorow@hotmail.com

Phone: (212) 989-8883

RESTAURANT FACTS
Seats: 180 **Weeknight Covers:** 300 **Weekend Covers:** 450 **Check Average (with Wine):** $110 **Tasting Menu:** Yes $120/$200 **Kitchen Staff:** 20

CHEF FACTS
Cuisine: New style Japanese **Born:** 1971 **Began Career:** 1990
Culinary School: Osaka Abeno Tsuji Cooking School, Japan **Grad Year:** 1990 **Work History:** Japan: Higuchi Organic Farms, Arashiyama of Kioto Kitcho Co.; Switzerland: Japanese Embassy; New York, NY: Japanese Embassy **Mentor(s):** Masataka Higuchi (a farmer in Kyoto, Japan), and many great chefs **Awards:** 2008 StarChefs.com Rising Star Chef New York

NOTABLE DISH(ES): Sockeye Salmon, Japanese Sliced Tomato, House Made Orange Vinaigrette; Homemade Yuba, Japanese Uni, Wasabi, and Osetra Caviar

FAST FACTS
Restaurant Recs: I eat at some small Japanese places, but really I like to go to Montauk to go fishing, and make sashimi out of whatever I catch. Recently it was fluke. **Kitchen Tool(s):** Hands **Interview Question:** Do you like jobs? I don't! **Flavor Combo(s):** Sea and firm ground **Fave Cookbook(s):** Arashi-yama Kitcho series by Kunio Tokuoka **Chef to Cook for You:** Hitoshi Ishihara (was chef of Kitcho) – because his dishes are my departure point **Culinary Travel:** Japan – because I can still find new inspiration

Joseph Isidori
Vice President of Food & Beverage/Executive Chef | Trump Hotel Collection

2000 Fashion Show Drive, NE Las Vegas, NV 89109

Restaurant E-mail: jisidori@trumphotels.com

Phone: (702) 369-3117

CHEF FACTS
Cuisine: Modern American **Born:** 1977 **Began Career:** 1999 **Culinary School:** The Culinary Institute of America, Hyde Park, New York **Grad Year:** 2000 **Stages:** Miami, FL: Nemo **Work History:** Miami, FL: Nemo, Shoji Sushi **Mentor(s):** Michael Schwartz **Awards:** 2008 StarChefs.com Rising Star Hotel Chef Las Vegas; American Academy of Hospitality 5 star-diamond chef award from Jean-Georges Vongerichten **Affiliations:** StarChefs

NOTABLE DISH(ES): Chinese Braised Prime Short Rib with Cucumber Yogurt, Parsnip, Cilantro and Candied Mango; South Carolina Squab with Cantonese Black Bean Sauce, Ginger Bok Choy

FAST FACTS
Restaurant Recs: Recently I had a great meal at Fatty Crab in New York City. The watermelon and pork belly was great! **Kitchen Tool(s):** My Winston CVAP! **Interview Question:** What kind of cooking techniques are you currently using in the kitchen? I am looking for a mix of fundamentals and avant garde cooking techniques, and a basic understanding/approach of how certain techniques affect certain proteins. **Flavor Combo(s):** Sweet and sour **Fave Cookbook(s):** The French Laundry Cookbook by Thomas Keller **Chef to Cook for You:** Jean-Georges Vongerichten – I enjoy the flavor profiles of his food immensely **Culinary Travel:** The Mediterranean region – because of my love for seafood

Mohammad Islam
Chef/Owner | Aigre Doux

230 West Kinzie St. Chicago, IL 60610

Restaurant E-mail: mohammad@aigredouxchicago.com

Phone: (312) 329-9400

RESTAURANT FACTS
Seats: 110 **Weeknight Covers:** 75 **Weekend Covers:** 200 **Check Average (w/o Wine):** $55 **Tasting Menu:** No **Kitchen Staff:** 11–14

CHEF FACTS
Other Restaurants: Chateau Marmont **Cuisine:** Simple, local, seasonal cuisine **Born:** 1965 **Began Career:** 1990 **Work History:** Chicago, IL: The Dining Room at The Ritz-Carlton; New York, NY: Mercer Kitchen; Los Angeles, CA: Chateau Marmont **Mentor(s):** Gabino Sotelino, Sarah Stegner, Jean-Georges Vongrichten **Awards:** 2006 StarChefs.com Rising Stars Los Angeles **Affiliations:** Yes **Languages Spoken:** Bengali

NOTABLE DISH(ES): Poached Line Caught Cod, Sushi Rice, Wild Asparagus, Nameko, Mushroom Broth; Sweet Pea and Manchego Ravioli, Asparagus Crudo, Roasted Lemon Vinaigrette

FAST FACTS
Restaurant Recs: Katsu for matsutake soup **Kitchen Tool(s):** Mortar and pestle **Interview Question:** Do you like this profession or love it? **Flavor Combo(s):** Cumin and orange juice **Fave Cookbook(s):** Early cookbooks by Charlie Trotter; Simple French Cooking by Georges Blanc; The Chez Panisse Cookbooks **Chef to Cook for You:** Any of my students who worked with me for long time and became a chef **Culinary Travel:** Any foreign place I am lucky enough to visit. I am always interested in trying something new and learning new techniques.

Johnny Iuzzini
Pastry Chef | Jean-Georges

1 Central Park West New York, NY 10023

Restaurant E-mail: jiuzzini@jean-georges.com

Phone: (212) 299-3900

RESTAURANT FACTS
Seats: 64 **Weeknight Covers:** 110 **Weekend Covers:** 140 **Tasting Menu:** Yes $148 **Kitchen Staff:** 7

CHEF FACTS
Cuisine: Pastry **Born:** 1974 **Began Career:** 1990 **Culinary School:** The Culinary Institute of America, Hyde Park, NY; École DGF du Chocolat et Patisserie, France; International Confectionary School, MD; Valrhona École du Grand Chocolat, France **Grad Year:** 1994 **Stages:** France: La Duree, Hotel Paris, Patisserie Chereau **Work History:** New York, NY: River Cafe, Luxe, Daniel, Payard, Café Boulud, Jean-Georges **Mentor(s):** Francois Payard, Daniel Boulud, Pierre Hermé, Jean-Georges Vongerichten, Thomas Haas **Protégée(s):** Jason Casey, Daniel Skurnick, Melissa Walnock, Emily Wallendjack **Awards:** 2006 NY Times 4 star review; 2006 James Beard Foundation Outstanding Pastry Chef of the Year; 2005 Michelin Guide 3 stars; 2005 Michelin Guide 3 stars; 2004, 2003 Pastry Art and Design 10 Best Pastry Chefs in America; 2002 New York Magazine Best New Pastry Chef **Books Published:** Dessert FourPlay **Languages Spoken:** Some French, some Spanish

NOTABLE DISH(ES): Chilled Sweet Corn Soup with Slated Crisp Corn and Corn Madeleines; Warm Sweet Potato Soufflé with Stewed Cranberries and Date Anglaise

FAST FACTS
Restaurant Recs: Lupa for any pasta dish **Kitchen Tool(s):** Digital scale because it is all about precision. I have a couple of other toys too. **Interview Question:** Are you excited to be here? I'd rather hire someone with a great passion and ambition to learn than with a big résumé or a high-priced education. **Flavor Combo(s):** Any combination where the flavors complement each other while at the same time come together to create a new flavor profile **Fave Cookbook(s):** I have so many. All of Pierre Hermés', Frederic Bau, Michel Bras, Jean-Georges' first book and, not really a cookbook, but Harold McGee's On Food and Cooking. **Chef to Cook for You:** I wish I could have a giant tasting menu with a course cooked by all my talented chef friends **Culinary Travel:** I haven't been through Southeast Asia yet, or to follow the Spice Trail

J

{ Jantz - Jupiter }

Kurtis Jantz
Executive Chef | Neomi's

18001 Collins Ave. Sunny Isles Beach, FL 33160

Restaurant E-mail: kjantz@trumpmiami.com

Phone: (305) 692-5751

RESTAURANT FACTS
Seats: 90–170 **Weeknight Covers:** 55–60 **Weekend Covers:** 90–120 **Check Average (with Wine):** $85 **Check Average (w/o Wine):** $65 **Tasting Menu:** Yes $85 **Kitchen Staff:** 30

CHEF FACTS
Cuisine: Contemporary American/international **Born:** 1969 **Began Career:** 1984 **Culinary School:** Johnson County College, Overland Park, KS **Grad Year:** 1991 **Stages:** France, Switzerland **Work History:** Netherlands Antilles: The Royal Sonesta; New Orleans, LA: The Chateau Sonesta **Mentor(s):** David Cross, Dan Admire, Richard Thompson **Protégée(s):** Michael Marshall, Chad Galiano, Mark Majorie **Awards:** 2008 StarChefs.com Rising Star Hotel Chef Award South Florida; Chaîne des Rotisseurs; Best Dining Experience 2006 Miami Chapter; The Jerry Halpern Award; Project Newborn 2007 **Affiliations:** We work with a lot of local charities and organizations, a few of which are: Le Chaîne de Rotisseurs, The Florida Heart Foundation and Project Newborn **Languages Spoken:** English

NOTABLE DISH(ES): Mulled Pork Belly with Calabaza, Maple Powdered Cracklins, Pumpkin Pickles, and 24–Hour Eggnog; Tw-7 Salmon with Seared Onigiri, Fermented Soy, Enoki, Dashi, Compressed Pea Tendrils

FAST FACTS
Restaurant Recs: Yakko-San; Little Saigon **Kitchen Tool(s):** The Internet – for the knowledge and the amount of possibility. My Shun utility knife, spice grinder, Vita-Prep, immersion circulator...the list goes on! **Interview Question:** Where is your passion for the industry? Are you in it for the long haul? Can you cook an egg? **Fave Cookbook(s):** The el Bulli series; Pierre Gagnaire's books; Reflections on Culinary Artistry; Reinventing French Cuisine; Peru Mucho Gusto **Chef to Cook for You:** I'd love for Marcus Samuelsson or Pierre Gagnaire to cook for me **Culinary Travel:** I would like to go back to Japan, where I was born, to learn more culinary traditions, like Kaiseki

J

Joseba Jiménez de Jiménez
Executive Chef | The Harvest Vine

2701 E Madison St. Seattle, WA 98112

Restaurant E-mail: joseba@harvestvine.com

Phone: (206) 320-9771

RESTAURANT FACTS
Seats: 54 **Weeknight Covers:** 52 **Weekend Covers:** 88 **Check Average (with Wine):** $68 **Tasting Menu:** No **Kitchen Staff:** 6

CHEF FACTS
Other Restaurants: Txori Pintxo Bar **Cuisine:** Southwest French; Basque; regional Spanish **Born:** 1960 **Began Career:** 1979 **Culinary School:** Le Cordon Bleu, Paris, France **Stages:** Spain: Royal Palace, United States Embassy; France: Hotel Palais **Work History:** Spain: El Lando; New York, NY: The Sheraton; Seattle, Washington: Maximiliens, Prego, The Ruins **Mentor(s):** Juan Mari Arzak **Affiliations:** Chaine de Rotisseurs, Academia Gastronomica Espanola, Academi Gastronomique de France **Languages Spoken:** French, Spanish

NOTABLE DISH(ES): Monkfish Liver Terrine; Wild Boar Bacon Smoked in a Broth of Herbs Topped with Trout Caviar

FAST FACTS
Restaurant Recs: Rovers for foie gras **Kitchen Tool(s):** ThermaPrep; foamers **Interview Question:** What do you want to get from your time here? **Flavor Combo(s):** Vanilla bean and tuna belly; olive oil and pimentón; wild boar poached in cocoa beans and roasted onion **Fave Cookbook(s):** Any book by Juan Mari Arzak **Chef to Cook for You:** Arzak because he is my spiritual mentor and a person I respect very much professionally. I would also pick Mikel Zevererio. He is a food and wine writer. He cooked for me one time and it was amazing, you wouldn't believe it. **Culinary Travel:** I would go all around the world! I especially want to see Japan, Western Europe, and of course the Basque Country.

Jenna Johansen
Executive Chef/Owner | Dish Restaurant

56 Edwards Village Blvd. #203 Edwards, CO 81632

Restaurant E-mail: jenna@eatdrinkdish.com

Phone: (970) 926-3433

RESTAURANT FACTS
Seats: 78 **Weeknight Covers:** 75 **Weekend Covers:** 130 **Check Average (with Wine):** $48 **Check Average (w/o Wine):** $30 **Tasting Menu:** Yes $40 **Kitchen Staff:** 4

CHEF FACTS
Cuisine: Daily-changing globally influenced small plates **Born:** 1975 **Began Career:** 1994 **Culinary School:** Johnson & Wales, Vail, Colorado **Grad Year:** 1998 **Stages:** Edwards, CO: Zino Ristorante **Work History:** Orlando, FL: Season's Dining Room at Walt Disney World; Edwards, CO: Zino Ristorante; Denver, CO: Pappadeaux Seafood Kitchen, Ventura Grille, Ocotillo, Great Northern Tavern **Mentor(s):** Peter Hillbeck, Thomas Salamunovich, Alex Seidel **Affiliations:** Slow Food **Languages Spoken:** English, Spanish, Italian

NOTABLE DISH(ES): Grilled Aspen Steak with Crispy Rosemary Garlic Potatoes and Horseradish Cracked Black Pepper Crema

FAST FACTS
Restaurant Recs: Larkburger – for a larkburger, rare **Kitchen Tool(s):** Bare hands, always **Interview Question:** What do you still want to learn? What do you have to teach us? **Flavor Combo(s):** Bacon and just about anything **Fave Cookbook(s):** Culinary Artistry by Andrew Dornenburg and Karen Page **Chef to Cook for You:** Naturally, Julia Child. I know it sounds un-creative, but what she did for female chefs and for the love of beautiful, real, food in general has molded the way I eat, live and feed guests in my restaurant. **Culinary Travel:** Next: Thailand. I want to really immerse myself in the flavors.

Thomas John
Executive Chef | Au Bon Pain

1 Au Bon Pain Way Boston, MA 02111

Restaurant E-mail: chef_thomasjohn@yahoo.com

Phone: (617) 423-2100

CHEF FACTS

Other Restaurants: 250 cafés throughout the US **Cuisine:** South Asian/Indian **Born:** 1965 **Began Career:** 1989 **Culinary School:** Oberoi Culinary School, India **Grad Year:** 1990 **Stages:** India: La Rochelle, Kandhahar **Work History:** Boston, MA: Mantra; India: Meridian Pune, The Oberoi **Mentor(s):** Julian Groom **Protégée(s):** Vinay Jayaraj, Marriott Mumbai, India Vikas Oswal, Park Royal **Awards:** 2003 StarChefs.com Rising Stars Chef Boston; 2002 Food & Wine Best New Chefs **Affiliations:** The culinary arts program at Boston University, Chefs Collaborative **Languages Spoken:** Malayalam, Tamil

NOTABLE DISH(ES): Broiled Lamb Chops with Indian Spices; Crispy Sea Bass with Fava Beans, Rock Shrimp and Mole

FAST FACTS

Restaurant Recs: Toro for paella **Kitchen Tool(s):** Spice grinder – because I don't like to cook with pre-ground spices **Interview Question:** What do you cook at home? It helps me understand someone's passion for cooking, culture. **Flavor Combo(s):** Cumin, cracked black pepper and cilantro; yogurt and stone ground mustard; curry leaf and coconut **Fave Cookbook(s):** White Heat by Marco Pierre White **Chef to Cook for You:** Tetsuya Wakuda or Ananda Solomon **Culinary Travel:** Coastal India or Greece

John Johnson
Executive Chef | The Water Club

1 Renaissance Way Atlantic City, NJ 08401

Restaurant E-mail: jj16912@theborgata.com

Phone: (212) 889-7100

RESTAURANT FACTS
Seats: 20,000 sq. feet of banquet salons and 800 suites **Tasting Menu:** Yes **Kitchen Staff:** 17

CHEF FACTS
Other Restaurants: Leopolds Kafé **Cuisine:** Mediterranean with local, fresh ingredients **Born:** 1974 **Began Career:** 1993 **Culinary School:** Academy of Culinary Arts, Mays Landing, NJ **Grad Year:** 1993 **Stages:** France: L'Arpege **Work History:** New York, NY: Restaurant 44, Patroon, Eight Mile Creek, Town **Mentor(s):** Alain Sailhac **Protégée(s):** Johan Svenson, Chris Lim, Jawn Chasteen **Affiliations:** JBF, C-CAP, ACCC, ACF, CIA, many other charities and organizations **Books Published:** Contributed to: Town & Country Cookbook **Languages Spoken:** Spanish, French

NOTABLE DISH(ES): Minute Cured Shrimp with Spiced Cucumber, Green Tea, Lime Salt

FAST FACTS
Restaurant Recs: New York, NY: Taboon for their mezzes **Kitchen Tool(s):** Alto-Sham combi oven **Interview Question:** Where do you see yourself in five years? **Flavor Combo(s):** Salt and butter; yuzu and honey; black olive and almonds – I tend towards bright and bracing acidity paired with rich sweetness or fats **Fave Cookbook(s):** Essential Cuisine by Michel Bras **Chef to Cook for You:** Phillipe Bertineau and Dieter Scheorner. They are little-known legends in our industry and have influenced my career immensely and they are amazing culinarians. **Culinary Travel:** Anywhere in Italy – it never disappoints and there is always something to discover

Wayne Johnson
Chef | Andaluca

407 Olive Way Seattle, WA 98101

Restaurant E-mail: chefwaj@andaluca.com

Phone: (206) 382-6999

RESTAURANT FACTS
Seats: 73 **Weeknight Covers:** 60 **Weekend Covers:** 110 **Check Average (with Wine):** $60 **Check Average (w/o Wine):** $45 **Tasting Menu:** Yes On occassion **Kitchen Staff:** 4

CHEF FACTS
Cuisine: Hyper-seasonal American **Born:** 1958 **Began Career:** 1998 **Culinary School:** An extended course at The Culinary Institute of America, St. Helena, CA **Grad Year:** 1998 **Work History:** San Francisco, CA: Renaissance Parc 55 Hotel, Veronica; Seattle, WA: Andaluca Restaurant and Bar, Oliver's Lounge; Vail, CO: Windows Restaurant **Mentor(s):** Lula Johnson, Jimmy Gemeniani, Tom Lender, Peter Lee **Protégée(s):** Mariano Lalica, Herbert Ng **Awards:** 2003 StarChefs.com Rising Star Chef Seattle; 2000 James Beard Foundation Regional Cuisine **Affiliations:** CAPC, IACP, Chefs Collaborative

NOTABLE DISH(ES): Lamb Dolmas; Chorizo and Chèvre-Stuffed Duck with Blood Orange Sauce

FAST FACTS
Restaurant Recs: Pan African – for the spicy lamb **Kitchen Tool(s):** Thermometer **Interview Question:** What are your intentions in applying to work here? **Flavor Combo(s):** I really like layers of flavors, so that one ingredient isn't overshadowing another. Most importantly I like to preserve the natural flavor of whatever it is I am cooking. **Fave Cookbook(s):** On Food and Cooking by Harold McGee **Chef to Cook for You:** Right now it would be Ferran Adriá. I don't do much cooking in that style but I am interested in learning more. I'm very curious. **Culinary Travel:** I would like to tour the Mediterranean.

Michael and Wendy Jordan
Chef/Owners | Rosemary's Restaurant

8125 W Sahara Ave. #110 Las Vegas, NV 89117

Restaurant E-mail: info@rosemarysrestaurant.com

Phone: (702) 869-2251

RESTAURANT FACTS
Seats: 110 **Weeknight Covers:** 120-150 **Weekend Covers:** 150-200 **Check Average (with Wine):** $65 **Tasting Menu:** No **Kitchen Staff:** 6

CHEF FACTS
Cuisine: French American **Born:** 1966 **Began Career:** 1989 **Culinary School:** The Culinary Institute of America, Hyde Park, NY **Grad Year:** 1989 **Stages:** New Orleans, LA: Emeril's, Nola; Chicago, IL: Printer's Row **Work History:** New Orleans, LA: Emeril's, Nola; Chicago, IL: Printer's Row **Mentor(s):** Emeril Lagasse, Eric Lindquist **Protégée(s):** Sean Roe **Affiliations:** JBF, SOS, The Leukemia & Lymphoma Society, March of Dimes, and we generally support organizations that work to benefit children and persons with AIDS

NOTABLE DISH(ES): Maytag Blue Cheese-Glazed New York Strip

FAST FACTS
Restaurant Recs: Lotus of Siam for whole fried bass with apple slaw **Kitchen Tool(s):** Chinois and blender – we just couldn't imagine life without them **Interview Question:** Why Rosemary's? **Flavor Combo(s):** Crawfish and andouille; bacon, lettuce and tomato; ham and cheese **Fave Cookbook(s):** Louisiana Real & Rustic by Emeril Lagasse, because it gives a true picture of what Louisiana cooking is all about **Chef to Cook for You:** Antonin Carême – he was the the first superstar "celebrity" chef and, in his time, was a true innovator **Culinary Travel:** Thailand – Thai cuisine is one of our personal favorites that we don't get to do often at Rosemary's Restaurant. The flavor combinations are unique, so flavorful, and we just love the food!

Laurence Jossel
Chef | NOPA

560 Divisadero St. San Francisco, CA 94117

Restaurant E-mail: laurence@nopasf.com

Phone: (415) 864-8643

RESTAURANT FACTS
Seats: 110 **Weeknight Covers:** 280–300 **Weekend Covers:** 400+ **Check Average (with Wine):** $38–$45 **Tasting Menu:** No **Kitchen Staff:** 7–8

CHEF FACTS
Cuisine: Local, sustainable and accessible **Born:** 1969 **Began Career:** 1983 **Work History:** San Francisco, CA: La Folie, Gary Danko, Chow **Awards:** 2007 StarChefs.com Rising Star Sustainability Award San Francisco **Affiliations:** Marin Organic, Slow Food

NOTABLE DISH(ES): White Beans with Feta and Oregano; Calamari with Olives and Capers

FAST FACTS
Restaurant Recs: Firefly for fried chicken; Da Flora in North Beach for great gnocchi and their homemade bread **Kitchen Tool(s):** A rotisserie grill **Interview Question:** Why do you cook? I try to sense their level of intelligence. And I ask: when was the last time you went to the farmer's market? **Flavor Combo(s):** Chili, anchovy and lemon; roasted garlic and thyme; lamb and lavender; cumin, coriander, fennel and black pepper **Fave Cookbook(s):** The Zuni Cafe Cookbook by Judy Rodgers; The Omnivore's Dilemma by Michael Pollan **Chef to Cook for You:** I would love to cook alongside Jacques Pépin. His humility and integrity are contagious. **Culinary Travel:** Italy to learn about rustic cooking

Brian Jupiter
Executive Chef | La Pomme Rouge

108 W Kinzie Chicago, IL 60610

Restaurant E-mail: chefjup@yahoo.com

Phone: (773) 363-7009

RESTAURANT FACTS
Seats: 65 **Weeknight Covers:** 50 **Weekend Covers:** 100-120 **Check Average (w/o Wine):** $60-$78 **Tasting Menu:** No **Kitchen Staff:** 3

CHEF FACTS
Cuisine: Cajun/Creole; innovative soul food **Born:** 1981 **Began Career:** 2003 **Culinary School:** Johnson & Wales University, Miami, Fl **Grad Year:** 2003 **Stages:** I have never staged anywhere. I took my first Executive Chef position on my 22nd birthday. People gave me opportunities at a young age; I ran with it and I have always cooked the food that I felt set me apart from other chefs. **Work History:** Miami, FL: Nobu, Sirena, One Ninety Restaurant; Chicago, IL: Narcisse Champagne & Caviar Salon, The Bella Lounge, Fleur De Lys Bistro **Mentor(s):** My grandmother, although she has never been formally trained, sparked my culinary creativity at the age of eight. Also Leah Chase and John Folse. **Protégée(s):** Curtis McGhee **Affiliations:** C-CAP **Languages Spoken:** Kitchen Spanish

NOTABLE DISH(ES): Caesar Salad with Herbed Polenta Croutons

FAST FACTS
Restaurant Recs: 4 Taste is an appetizer lounge and I always order the same two dishes: Mississippi Quail served with Yukon Gold Potato Hash, Fried Quail Egg, and Black Pepper Molasses Sauce, and Seared Ahi Tuna with Oven-Dried Tomato, Wasabi Cream and Soy Reduction. **Kitchen Tool(s):** Tongs - long tongs! I use tongs as extensions of my hands. Whenever I'm on the line I have a pair of tongs in one hand, moving around hot sauté pans from one burner to another, grabbing hot pans and trays from the oven, turning meat on the grill. You have to be careful though because if you set them down for too long someone else on the line may snatch them up! **Interview Question:** Does cooking make you happy? Working in the restaurant business can be extremely stressful, with long hours and high pressure situations every shift, therefore you must enjoy working in this industry. I don't want cooks that are looking for the next paycheck, I want cooks that enjoy coming to work and share the same passion that I possess for food and the restaurant business. **Flavor Combo(s):** Lemon and thyme **Fave Cookbook(s):** The Encyclopedia of Cajun and Creole Cuisine by John D. Folse **Chef to Cook for You:** John Folse – he's a mentor, and we have similar cooking styles **Culinary Travel:** Probably Mexico – they have really bold flavors and I've always been a fan of the cuisine

K

{ Kagawa - Kunz }

Hitoshi Kagawa
Executive Chef | Donguri

309 E 83rd St. New York, NY 10028

Restaurant E-mail: k.hitoshi@hotmail.com

Phone: (212) 737-5656

RESTAURANT FACTS
Seats: 24 **Weeknight Covers:** 25 **Weekend Covers:** 30 **Check Average (w/o Wine):** $50 **Tasting Menu:** Yes $85-$200 **Kitchen Staff:** 3

CHEF FACTS
Cuisine: Japanese **Born:** 1965 **Began Career:** 1983 **Culinary School:** Tenshin-Gakuen Sakata-Shi Yamagata, Japan **Stages:** Japan: Serina Honten, Shizuoka **Work History:** Japan: Serina Honten; New York, NY: Kai **Mentor(s):** Masaru Kudo **Languages Spoken:** Japanese

NOTABLE DISH(ES): Cold Braised Endive and Cabbage Salad

FAST FACTS
Kitchen Tool(s): Earthenware pots **Interview Question:** I trust my first impression and I look for cleanliness. **Flavor Combo(s):** Bonito broth and chicken broth **Fave Cookbook(s):** Chya-kaiseki by Eiichi Takahashi **Chef to Cook for You:** Chef David Bouley – I want to experience his way of French and Japanese cuisine collaboration **Culinary Travel:** Japan – for the high quality, freshness, and variety of food and seafood

Paul Kahan
Executive Chef | Blackbird

619 W Randolph St. Chicago, IL 60606

Restaurant E-mail: chefpaulkahan@aol.com

Phone: (312) 715-0708

RESTAURANT FACTS
Seats: 62 **Weeknight Covers:** 100 **Weekend Covers:** 140–170
Check Average (with Wine): $90–$100 **Tasting Menu:** Yes **Kitchen
Staff:** 5–7

CHEF FACTS
Other Restaurants: Avec, and a beer hall opening Summer 2008 **Cuisine:** Seasonal American **Born:** 1962 **Began Career:** 1986 **Work History:** Chicago, IL: Metropolis, Frontera Grill, Topolobampo **Mentor(s):** Erwin Dreschler, Rick Bayless **Protégée(s):** Koren Grieveson, Brian Woulfe, Paul Virant, Jeremy Kittleson **Awards:** 2004 James Beard Best Chef Midwest; 1999 Food & Wine Best New Chefs **Affiliations:** Green City Market, SOS, and a zillion others... we do them all! **Languages Spoken:** Spanglish

NOTABLE DISH(ES): Red Kuri Squash and Apple Cider Soup

FAST FACTS
Restaurant Recs: Sunshine Café for pickles and barbecued eel **Kitchen Tool(s):** Duck fat **Interview Question:** With so many great restaurants on your resume, why have you been unable to stay working at any of them for more than one year? **Flavor Combo(s):** Acidic, fatty and salty **Fave Cookbook(s):** Cookbooks by Anne Williams **Chef to Cook for You:** Fergus Henderson from St. John because that is where my brain is at right now. Pig: simple and beautiful. **Culinary Travel:** Asia – I've never spent time there so that's where I would go

Jordan Kahn
Pastry Chef | XIV

8117 Sunset Blvd, West Hollywood, CA 90069

Restaurant E-mail: jkahn23@aol.com

CHEF FACTS
Cuisine: Progressive, dissonant pastry **Born:** 1983 **Began Career:**
2002 **Culinary School:** Johnson & Wales, Charleston, South Carolina
Stages: Yountville, CA: The French Laundry **Work History:** New York,
NY: The Tasting Room, Varietal; Chicago, IL: Alinea; Yountville, CA: The
French Laundry; Charleston, SC: The Charleston Grill; San Francisco,
CA: Michael Mina **Mentor(s):** Thomas Keller, Sebastian Rouxel, Vin-
zenz Aschbacher **Languages Spoken:** Spanish

NOTABLE DISH(ES): Lime Flower Sabayon, Wolfberry, Broken Maca-
roons, Kecap Manis; Absinthe, Pear, Black Sesame; Liquid Sable

FAST FACTS
Restaurant Recs: New York, NY: Mandoo Bar in Midtown for dump-
lings. It's a great, clean cafe where a couple of old ladies make everything by hand; it's cheap too.
Kitchen Tool(s): Acetate for everything that doesn't get cooked: dehydrating, setting mousses. It helps
create glass-like desserts that look inedible, but aren't. **Interview Question:** Ideally, how many hours
would you like to work? I'm looking for someone who will work as many hours as the job takes and
won't complain about being tired. **Flavor Combo(s):** Gianduja, kalamansi, plantain, gula jawa (palm
sugar), triple cream, and sunflower seed **Fave Cookbook(s):** The Physiology of Taste by Brillat-Savarin
Chef to Cook for You: Jacques Pépin **Culinary Travel:** Japan

K

Nicole Kap

Nicole Kaplan
Executive Pastry Chef | The Plaza Hotel

Fifth Ave. at Central Park South New York, NY 10019

Restaurant E-mail: nicole.kaplan@fairmont.com

Phone: (212) 759-3000 ext 3584

RESTAURANT FACTS
Seats: 110 **Weeknight Covers:** 240 **Weekend Covers:** 350 **Check Average (w/o Wine):** $100 **Tasting Menu:** No **Kitchen Staff:** 6

CHEF FACTS
Cuisine: French American desserts **Began Career:** 1996 **Culinary School:** Peter Kumps, New York, NY **Stages:** France: Laboratoire of Pierre Hermé **Work History:** New York, NY: Sign of the Dove, Osteria del Circo, Eleven Madison Park, Del Posto **Mentor(s):** Patrice Caillot, Pierre Hermé, Frederic Bau **Protégée(s):** Jennifer Giblin, Robert Fitzhenry **Awards:** 2006, 2003 Pastry Art and Design Top 10

NOTABLE DISH(ES): Raspberry Millefeuille with Ice Wine Granité and Litchi Sorbet; Apple Spice Cake with Cheddar Bacon Crumble and Maple Pecan Ice Cream

FAST FACTS
Restaurant Recs: Menkuitei for miso ramen **Kitchen Tool(s):** Spoon – I have a favorite one for perfect quenelles and scooping from containers **Interview Question:** Where have you eaten recently? **Flavor Combo(s):** Chocolate, chocolate, chocolate **Fave Cookbook(s):** Paco Torreblanca:The Book by Paco Torreblanca **Chef to Cook for You:** My husband because after ten years he almost knows what I like to eat **Culinary Travel:** Spain and Austria are at the top of my list. I haven't been to either country.

Ravi Kapur
Chef de Cuisine | Boulevard

One Mission St. San Francisco, CA 94105

Restaurant E-mail: boulevardrestaurant@gmail.com

(415) 543-6084

RESTAURANT FACTS
Seats: 175 **Weekend Covers:** 290+ **Check Average (with Wine):** $90 **Tasting Menu:** No **Kitchen Staff:** 14

CHEF FACTS
Cuisine: French-influenced new American **Born:** 1976 **Began Career:** 1998 **Culinary School:** California Culinary Academy, San Francisco, CA **Grad Year:** 1999 **Stages:** Chicago, IL: Alinea **Work History:** Santa Fe, NM: Coyote Café, The Compound; San Francisco, CA: Redwood Park **Mentor(s):** Nancy Oakes, Pam Mazzola, Matthew Dickson **Affiliations:** Meals-on-Wheels, Slow Food **Languages Spoken:** Broken kitchen Spanish

FAST FACTS
Restaurant Recs: Kimchee tofu soup with stone pot rice at My Tofu House **Kitchen Tool(s):** Ittosai chef's knife **Interview Question:** What's your favorite restaurant and why? Why do you want to work in the kitchen? **Flavor Combo(s):** Sour, sweet, earthy **Fave Cookbook(s):** Ingredienti by Faith Wilinger and La Calandre by Massimiliano e Raffaele Alajmo **Chef to Cook for You:** Marco Pierre White at Harvey's – he had unparalleled passion for the craft at the time and place where he was **Culinary Travel:** Morocco, Turkey – they're parts of the world I haven't been to yet. They are fascinating places where food is an integral part of daily life.

Gene Kato

Executive Chef | Japonais

600 W Chicago Ave. Chicago, IL 60610

Restaurant E-mail: gene@japonaischicago.com

Phone: (312) 822-9600

RESTAURANT FACTS
Seats: 300 **Weeknight Covers:** 200–400 **Weekend Covers:** 600–700 **Check Average (w/o Wine):** $75 **Tasting Menu:** No **Kitchen Staff:** 10–12

CHEF FACTS
Other Restaurants: Las Vegas, NV: Japonais; New York, NY: Japonais **Cuisine:** Japanese-French **Born:** 1977 **Began Career:** 1995 **Culinary School:** Central Piedmont Community College in Charlotte, NC **Grad Year:** 1998 **Work History:** Charlotte, NC: Mimosa Grill; Charleston, SC: Upstream; Chicago, IL: Ohba **Mentor(s):** Joël Robuchon, Jeff LaBerge **Awards:** 2005 StarChefs.com Rising Star Chef Chicago **Affiliations:** SOS, Meals-on-Wheels **Languages Spoken:** Japanese

NOTABLE DISH(ES): Fluke Carpaccio; Japanese Cheese Puffs

FAST FACTS
Restaurant Recs: Cho Sun Ok for Korean sliced beef on the stone and kimchi **Kitchen Tool(s):** My mind – without it I have no vision or creative process to prepare my own style of food **Interview Question:** What do you think characterizes great food? It helps me see where they are mentally with food. **Flavor Combo(s):** Japanese curry and chocolate **Fave Cookbook(s):** I don't get inspiration from cookbooks - I get my inspiration from what's in season and new plateware. **Chef to Cook for You:** Robuchon – he has a sensibility for simplicity which he balances with elegance **Culinary Travel:** I'm going back to Japan to get back in touch with traditional tastes and flavors. I'd love to go to Spain and France – I've never been.

Elizabeth Katz
Corporate Pastry Chef | BR Guest Restaurant Group

206 Spring St. New York, NY 10012

Restaurant E-mail: ekatz@brguestinc.com

Phone: (212) 529-0900

CHEF FACTS
Other Restaurants: New York, NY: Atlantic Grill, Blue Fin, Blue Water Grill, Dos Caminos, Fiamma, Isabella's, Level V, Ocean Grill, Primehouse, Ruby Foo's, Vento, Wildwood; Chicago, IL: Blue Water Grill, David Burke's Primehouse; Las Vegas, NV: Dos Caminos, Fiamma **Cuisine:** Simplicity using fresh ingredients **Born:** 1975 **Began Career:** 1995 **Culinary School:** The Culinary Institute of America, Hyde Park, NY **Grad Year:** 1995 **Stages:** New York, NY: Daniel **Work History:** New York, NY: Daniel, Fiamma **Awards:** 2006, 2005 Pastry Art & Design 10 Best Pastry Chefs **Affiliations:** Our company is very involved with many charities: City Harvest, Share our Strength, AIWF, Days of Taste **Books Published:** Contributed to: Fiamma: The Essence of Contemporary Italian Cooking

NOTABLE DISH(ES): Steamed Pumpkin Budino

FAST FACTS
Kitchen Tool(s): Gelato machine – for the simplicity of making a pure, well-infused gelato base and then serving a freshly spun, creamy, airy gelato. There's nothing like it! **Flavor Combo(s):** Fresh herbs with fruits such as farmer's strawberries with basil. I also love orange zest with bittersweet chocolate. **Fave Cookbook(s):** Martha Stewart's Baking Handbook by Martha Stewart – it goes back to the basics and the photographs are wonderful **Culinary Travel:** Italy – for freshness of ingredients, purity of cooking techniques, simple flavor profiles and combinations

Gavin Kaysen
Chef de Cuisine | Café Boulud

20 E 76th St. New York, NY 10021

Restaurant E-mail: gkaysen@danielnyc.com

Phone: (212) 772-2600

RESTAURANT FACTS
Seats: 95 **Weeknight Covers:** 175 **Weekend Covers:** 175 **Check Average (with Wine):** $85-$105 **Tasting Menu:** Yes **Kitchen Staff:** 11

CHEF FACTS
Cuisine: Fanatically seasonal French fare with a definite American twist **Born:** 1979 **Began Career:** 1994 **Culinary School:** New England Culinary Institute, Montpelier, VT **Grad Year:** 2001 **Stages:** New York, NY: Daniel; Switerzland: Phillipe Rochon; Chicago, IL: Alinea **Work History:** San Diego, CA: El Bizcocho; Switzerland: L'Auberge de Lavaux; England: L'Escargot **Awards:** 2008 James Beard Foundation Rising Star Chef; 2008 StarChefs.com Rising Star Chef New York; 2007 Food & Wine Magazine Best New Chef; 2007 USA Bocuse d'Or Representative; 2002 National Trophy of Cuisine and Pastry Winner; Académie Culinaire of France third in the world **Languages Spoken:** French, some Swedish

NOTABLE DISH(ES): Spaghetti Nero with Squid and Shrimp; Kona Kampach Sashimi, Butternut Squash Puree Ponzu and Daikon

FAST FACTS
Restaurant Recs: Gusto in the west village – I had a good pork belly sandwich; Hundred Acres – it's very market-driven and the prices are awesome. It's nice to get properly seasoned beet greens with garlic. **Kitchen Tool(s):** Spoon – because you can use it for everything, and for cooking fish and meats with plenty of butter basted on top. I steal spoons. That's my thing. When I eat in a restaurant I take a spoon. Some are framed and some are in flowerpots. The best that I took was from Paul Bocuse when I was eating dinner with him in his kitchen in France – I took it right in front of him. It says PB! I save every significant guest's tickets too. **Interview Question:** I don't really interview people that heavily. I prefer to have them work one day in the kitchen and see the way they move, and how confident they are in plating. **Flavor Combo(s):** Corn and tomatoes with ricotta or burrata; corn with lobster; farfalle, corn petits pois and lobster foam. **Fave Cookbook(s):** Michel Bras – it's beautiful. If you don't read the book but just look at it, it's amazing. I cooked for him once for lunch and I was so nervous. **Chef to Cook for You:** I would love to have tasted and cooked with Fredy Girardet. I have his book and go back to it and see the similarities between my cuisine and his. I would have loved to have tasted his food. **Culinary Travel:** Asia – I would love to travel to all different areas and just see and be inspired

Doug Keane
Executive Chef | Cyrus

29 North St. Healdsburg, CA 95448

Restaurant E-mail: dougkeane@cyrusrestaurant.com

Phone: (707) 433-3311

RESTAURANT FACTS
Seats: 66 **Weeknight Covers:** 85 **Weekend Covers:** 85 **Check Average (with Wine):** $155 **Tasting Menu:** Yes $130 **Kitchen Staff:** 11

CHEF FACTS
Cuisine: Contemporary luxury **Born:** 1971 **Began Career:** 1988 **Culinary School:** Cornell University School of Hotel Administration, Ithaca, NY **Grad Year:** 1993 **Work History:** New York, NY: The Four Seasons, Lespinasse; San Francisco, CA: Jardinière, Gary Danko; Napa Valley, CA: Market an American Restaurant **Awards:** 2002 San Francisco Chronicle Rising Star; Michelin Guide 2 stars; San Francisco Chronicle 4 stars; Gourmet Magazine Top Fifty Restaurants; Esquire Magazine Chef of the Year; 2007 Food & Wine Best New Chef **Affiliations:** Relais & Châteaux, tons of events and fundraisers **Languages Spoken:** A little better than kitchen Spanish

FAST FACTS
Restaurant Recs: Sushi Hana in Rohnert Park **Kitchen Tool(s):** Spoon **Interview Question:** Why do you want to be in this business? I want to know if it just something they saw on TV, or if the grew up with food. Basically, whether there is a reason. **Flavor Combo(s):** Ginger and lime **Fave Cookbook(s):** La Technique by Jacques Pépin **Chef to Cook for You:** Fredy Girardet – I've read and heard great things about him and something about his food speaks to me **Culinary Travel:** Tokyo – Japanese flavors really excite me. They are clean, fresh, crisp and yet still rich. I also really enjoy umami, which is very prevalent in the cuisine.

Danielle Keene
Pastry chef | BLT Steak

8720 Sunset Blvd. West Hollywood, CA 90069

Restaurant E-mail: daniellekeene@juno.com

Phone: (310) 360-1950

RESTAURANT FACTS
Seats: 200–235 **Weeknight Covers:** 180 **Weekend Covers:** 280
Check Average (w/o Wine): $80 **Tasting Menu:** No **Kitchen Staff:** 3

CHEF FACTS
Cuisine: American classic desserts with unique combinations **Born:** 1980 **Began Career:** 1999 **Culinary School:** Los Angeles Culinary Institute, Encino, CA **Grad Year:** 1999 **Stages:** Los Angeles, CA: Campanile **Work History:** Los Angeles, CA: Water Grill, AOC, Campanile **Mentor(s):** Nancy Silverton, Kim Boyce **Awards:** 2005 Los Angeles Magazine Best Bread Pudding **Affiliations:** I participate in many charity events but I don't specifically belong to any organizations **Languages Spoken:** Some Spanish

NOTABLE DISH(ES): Chai Hot Chocolate; Bread Pudding

FAST FACTS
Restaurant Recs: Dona Rosa's in Pasadena for sopes **Kitchen Tool(s):** Offset spatula, because it has so many uses: frosting a cake, cutting something, cleaning a work surface... **Interview Question:** What type of money are you looking to make? It helps weed out all the people that think they are going to make tons of money. **Flavor Combo(s):** Chocolate, vanilla and coffee. My all-time favorite combo is fresh mint with pretty much anything, because the flavor is so clean and refreshing. **Fave Cookbook(s):** In the Sweet Kitchen by Regan Dealy **Chef to Cook for You:** I would have Suzanne Goin cook for me because her food is so delicious and simple but amazing at the same time. I also have a great deal of respect for her because she is a great chef, a nice person, and a wife and mother. **Culinary Travel:** I love going to San Francisco. I think it is the best food city because they have so many local ingredients and the people are so into the food and service. I would really like to travel to Asia to eat because I can eat any Asian food and never get sick of it. I would like to try all their specialties, street food, fine dining...anything!

Christine Keff
Chef/Owner | Flying Fish

2234 1st Ave. Seattle, WA 98121

Restaurant E-mail: anna@flyingfishseattle.com

Phone: (206) 728-8595

RESTAURANT FACTS
Seats: 100 **Weeknight Covers:** 170 **Weekend Covers:** 250 **Check Average (with Wine):** $50 **Tasting Menu:** No **Kitchen Staff:** 6

CHEF FACTS
Cuisine: Seafood with Asian flavors **Born:** 1953 **Began Career:** I've been in the business 25 years **Stages:** New York, NY: The Four Seasons **Work History:** New York, NY: Four Seasons; Seattle, WA: Hunt Club **Mentor(s):** Seppi Renggli **Protégée(s):** Stephanie Meiers **Awards:** 2001 Robert Mondavi Award of Culinary Excellence; 1999 James Beard Foundation Best Chef Northwest/Hawaii **Affiliations:** JBF, LDE, IACP, WCR **Languages Spoken:** Spanish

NOTABLE DISH(ES): Sister-in-Law Mussels, Sea Scallops in Thai Curry

FAST FACTS
Restaurant Recs: Lark for carpaccio of yellowtail **Kitchen Tool(s):** Wooden spoon **Interview Question:** I let them talk as much as possible and I just listen. A person will hang themselves pretty quickly if they're going to. I never hire anyone who bad-mouths a former employer. If they left with bad feelings, it means they're not very good at working things out. **Flavor Combo(s):** I love Asian and Latin flavors **Fave Cookbook(s):** It Rains Fishes: Legends, Traditions and the Joys of Thai Cooking by Kasma Loha-Unchi **Chef to Cook for You:** I would love to have Pete Boyd, who has worked in my kitchen for years, cook for me. His food is simple and always perfectly cooked. I'd like him to be my personal chef when I retire. **Culinary Travel:** I would love to return to Mexico and master the food from Oaxaca. I love Mexican regional cooking and find Oaxacan food particularly intriguing.

Thomas Keller
Chef/Owner | The French Laundry

6640 Washington St. Yountville, CA 94599

Restaurant E-mail: tkpress@prconsulting.net

Phone: (831) 626-7880

RESTAURANT FACTS
Seats: 62 **Weeknight Covers:** 70 **Weekend Covers:** 70 **Check Average (w/o Wine):** $240 **Tasting Menu:** Yes $240 **Kitchen Staff:** 10–12

CHEF FACTS
Other Restaurants: Napa, CA: Ad Hoc; Beverly Hills, CA: Bouchon Bistro; New York, NY: Bouchon Bakery, Per Se; Las Vegas, NV: Bouchon **Cuisine:** French-influenced contemporary American **Born:** 1955 **Began Career:** 1974 **Stages:** France: Taillevent, Guy Savoy, Michael Pasquet, Gerard Besson, Le Toit de Passey, Chiberta, Le Pré Catelan **Work History:** New York, NY: Raoul's, La Reserve, Raphael, Rakel; Los Angeles, CA: Checkers Hotel; Yountville, CA: The French Laundry **Mentor(s):** Roland Henin **Protégée(s):** Jonathan Benno, Corey Lee, Jeff Cerciello, Mark Hopper, Josh Schwartz, Eric Ziebold, Grant Achatz, Gregory Short, Stephen Durfee, Ron Siegel, John Fraser **Awards:** 2007 Michelin Guide 3 stars; 2006-2007 AAA Five Diamonds; 2006 James Beard Foundation Outstanding Restaurant Award; 2005-2006 Restaurant Magazine Best in Americas; 2006-1999 Mobil Travel Guide 5 stars; 2006 Grand Prix Académie Internationale de la Gastronomie De L'Art de la Cuisine; 2004 Readers' Digest Best Chef; 2003, 2004 Restaurant Magazine #1 in The World's 50 Best Restaurants; 2003-2004 James Beard Foundation Best Service; 1998-2002 Zagat Guide to the Bay Area #1Top Food; 2002 San Francisco Magazine Best Wine Director; 2001 Time Magazine America's Best Chef; 2001 Wedgewood World Master of Culinary Arts Award; 2001 James Beard Foundation Outstanding Wine Service; 2000 Food & Wine Restaurant Experts Poll Favorite Inductee; 2000 Wine Spectator Top Restaurant for Food; 1999 Nation's Restaurant New Fine Dining Hall of Fame; 1998 Bon Appétit Chef of the Year **Affiliations:** James Beard Foundation, Share-Our-Strength **Books Published:** The French Laundry Cookbook; The Bouchon Cookbook; Under Pressure **Languages Spoken:** French

NOTABLE DISH(ES): Oysters and Pearls; White Truffle Custard with Perigord Black Truffle Ragout

FAST FACTS
Restaurant Recs: Bouchon – for roasted chicken **Kitchen Tool(s):** Spoon **Interview Question:** There's not one question, I'm afraid. The interview process for a line cook is to have them become part of the team for a day, and then see how that interaction goes. **Flavor Combo(s):** My favorite flavor combinations are classic in nature – things that are recognizable, if you will. Take potatoes and beef, for example. I strive to use these ordinary, everyday items in an extraordinary way to get extraordinary results. Peas and carrots are another example. So are coffee and doughnuts. We strive to put together flavor combinations and flavor profiles that have reference points to us that we can then refine and modernize in a way that is going to make them even better than what we have in our immediate memory. **Fave Cookbook(s):** Ma Gastronomie by Fernand Point **Chef to Cook for You:** Without question it would be Fernand Point, because he represented a departure from a classic standpoint

of a chef. He was willing to go out of his way to inspire, and very willing to give to the chefs that work for him the support that they needed to become great chefs – as they have now become. **Culinary Travel:** Japan is a wonderful place to go for culinary travel, and I would love to experience its different regional cuisine. I'd like to travel throughout Asia, actually. China would be a wonderful place to go. I like to go places that do not have an immediate connection to what I do.

Matthew Kelley
Pastry Chef | Bin 36

339 N Dearborn St. Chicago, IL 60610

Restaurant E-mail: mkelley@bin36.com

Phone: (312) 755-9463

RESTAURANT FACTS
Seats: 100+ **Weeknight Covers:** 80 **Weekend Covers:** 180–200 **Tasting Menu:** Yes **Kitchen Staff:** 2–3

CHEF FACTS
Other Restaurants: Bin Wine Café, Amano **Cuisine:** Contemporary American pastry with strong French influence **Born:** 1975 **Began Career:** 2003 **Culinary School:** Seattle Culinary Academy, Seattle, WA **Grad Year:** 2004 **Work History:** Seattle, WA: Le Fournil; Snoqualmie, WA: Salish Lodge; Chicago, IL: Seasons **Mentor(s):** Regis Bernard, Kriss Harvey **Languages Spoken:** Kitchen Spanish

NOTABLE DISH(ES): Chocolate and Caramel with Espresso Granité; Dark Chocolate Rosemary Ganache in Filo with Rosemary-Pine Nut Ice Cream

FAST FACTS
Restaurant Recs: Ditka's Steakhouse for meatloaf **Kitchen Tool(s):** Immersion blender – because it fixes and finishes just about anything **Interview Question:** What are your favorite flavor pairings? It gives me an idea of their style and creativity. **Flavor Combo(s):** Goat cheese, lemon and port wine **Fave Cookbook(s):** Wild Sweets: Exotic Dessert and Wine Pairings by Dominique Duby **Chef to Cook for You:** Albert Adriá – the Spanish pastry chefs are really taking off. It would be interesting to see what he would come up with. **Culinary Travel:** France – I've been wanting to go for a long time. It is the birthplace of pastry.

K

Chris Kidder
Chef | New project in the works

Los Angeles, CA

Restaurant E-mail: chriskidder1@yahoo.com

CHEF FACTS
Cuisine: Rustic Californian **Born:** 1969 **Began Career:** 1992 **Work History:** New York, NY: Zoe; San Francisco, CA: Zuni Café; Los Angeles, CA: Campanile, Literatti II **Mentor(s):** Stephen Levine, Judy Rodgers, Nancy Silverton, Mark Peel **Protégée(s):** Matt Molina **Affiliations:** JBF

FAST FACTS
Restaurant Recs: Sushi Nozawa – for yellowtail sushi **Kitchen Tool(s):** Timer – it saves a lot of money **Interview Question:** Why did you move to LA? **Flavor Combo(s):** Citrus, avocado and onion; almond and cheese **Fave Cookbook(s):** The Zuni Café Cookbook by Judy Rodgers **Chef to Cook for You:** I would like to have Julia Child – she put a lot of love into her food, had a lot of fun and was very classic **Culinary Travel:** I would like to go through Spain – there is so much history and so many quality products and interesting combinations, and I haven't spent that much time there

Maura Kilpatrick
Pastry Chef | Oleana

134 Hampshire St. Cambridge, MA 02139

Restaurant E-mail: info@oleanarestaurant.com

Phone: (617) 661-0505

RESTAURANT FACTS
Seats: 80–130 **Weeknight Covers:** 120 **Weekend Covers:** 160
Check Average (with Wine): $65 **Tasting Menu:** Yes $42 **Kitchen Staff:** 1–2

CHEF FACTS
Cuisine: Mediterranean with Arabic and Turkish influences **Began Career:** 1994 **Culinary School:** California Culinary Academy, San Francisco, CA **Grad Year:** 1993 **Work History:** Cambridge, MA: High Rise Bakery, La Ettola, Casablanca, Eight Holyoke **Mentor(s):** Ana Sortun, Pierre Hermé **Awards:** 2008 James Beard Foundation Outstanding Pastry Chef Nominee; 2002 Boston Magazine Best Pastry Chef **Affiliations:** We participate pretty heavily in various charities

NOTABLE DISH(ES): Walnut Steamed Pudding with Figs

FAST FACTS
Restaurant Recs: B&G Oysters for the lobster roll **Kitchen Tool(s):** Plastic bowl scrapers **Interview Question:** What was your favorite dessert out at a restaurant? **Flavor Combo(s):** Cocoa bean or chocolate with sherry and dates **Fave Cookbook(s):** A Passion for Ice Cream: 95 Recipes for Fabulous Desserts by Emily Luchetti; Desserts by Nancy Silverton **Chef to Cook for You:** Pichet Ong – I recently ate at P*ONG and the experience got me thinking how many ways you can combine and refine simple flavors **Culinary Travel:** Istanbul – there are so many flavors and the city has the friendliest people. I love the style of the food and the charm of the city.

Bill Kim
Executive Chef | Le Lan

749 N Clark St. Chicago, IL 60610

Restaurant E-mail: bkim@lelanrestaurant.com

Phone: (312) 280-9100

RESTAURANT FACTS

Seats: 67–127 **Weeknight Covers:** 50–60 **Weekend Covers:** 150–160 **Check Average (with Wine):** $75 **Check Average (w/o Wine):** $55 **Tasting Menu:** No **Kitchen Staff:** 6–9

CHEF FACTS

Other Restaurants: Soul, Urban Belly **Cuisine:** Classic French with Pan-Asian offerings **Born:** 1968 **Began Career:** 1988 **Culinary School:** School of Culinary Arts at Kendall College, Chicago, IL **Grad Year:** 1993 **Stages:** New York, NY: Cello **Work History:** Chicago, IL: Charlie Trotter's, Ben Pao, Trio; Philadelphia, PA: Susanna Foo, The Inn on Blueberry Hill; New York, NY: Bouley Bakery **Mentor(s):** Charlie Trotter, David Bouley and Pierre Pollin – he taught me life balance **Awards:** 2008 StarChefs.com Rising Star Chef Chicago **Languages Spoken:** Korean, kitchen Spanish

NOTABLE DISH(ES): Wagyu Beef Carpaccio with Marinated Jicama and Trout Roe and a Sesame Pancake; Dumplings with Wild Mushrooms, Mirin-Dashi Broth, and Parmigiano Reggiano

FAST FACTS

Restaurant Recs: A Japanese grocery store called Matsuya – we get the special pork ramen; I get Korean food at San Soo Gap San – short ribs and marinated beef **Kitchen Tool(s):** Vita-Prep – we purée a lot of things. It almost intensifies the flavor of whatever you're making because you're blending all of the product and focusing the flavor in that dollop of purée. It's the essence, in a spoonful. **Interview Question:** I see if they have a dream for themselves. Where do they see themselves 5 years from now? That's my favorite question, because it means they're thinking about the next step and motivated to get there. **Flavor Combo(s):** Coconut and lime; curry and squash; chorizo, Brussels sprouts and mole **Fave Cookbook(s):** Nina Simon's Noodle - she's not a chef, but it's the first Asian cookbook I bought **Chef to Cook for You:** My nephews – if they ever become chefs. Alain Ducasse would be great, too. **Culinary Travel:** I would go to Hong Kong, which I'm probably going to do next year. I spent 14 days in Shanghai and Korea with a writer from the Tribune. We ate at 60 restaurants in 14 days. I hadn't been there for 20 years.

Kathryn King
Pastry Chef | Aria

490 E. Paces Ferry Rd. Atlanta, GA 30305

Restaurant E-mail: info@aria-atl.com

Phone: (404) 233-7673

RESTAURANT FACTS
Seats: 80 **Weeknight Covers:** 60 **Weekend Covers:** 140 **Check Average (with Wine):** $85 **Tasting Menu:** No **Kitchen Staff:** 6

CHEF FACTS
Cuisine: Modern American **Born:** 1958 **Began Career:** 1992 **Stages:** San Francisco, CA: Hawthorne Lane **Work History:** Atlanta, GA: Alon's Bakery, We're Cookin', Hedgerose, Canoe, The Occidental Grand Hotel **Mentor(s):** Gerry Klaskala **Affiliations:** SOS, Atlanta's Table, The Food Bank, The American Liver Foundation, The Southern Foodways Alliance, and many others.

NOTABLE DISH(ES): Lemon Panna Cotta, Tangerine Sorbet, Tangerine Gelée and Almond Shortbread

FAST FACTS
Restaurant Recs: Penang, a Malaysian/Thai restaurant here in Atlanta. I love their Roti Canai, Satay with Peanut Sauce, Lady Finger Belacan, and the service is terrific. **Kitchen Tool(s):** I hardly use tools, but I do think the Microplane is a terrific invention **Interview Question:** Where do you want to be in a few years? What do you read? Where do you eat? I'm looking to see if they have a life, if they're interested in the industry, or if they're just looking for a job. **Flavor Combo(s):** Orange with vanilla; ginger with apricots; caramel and chocolate **Fave Cookbook(s):** The Joy of Cooking – it's great if I'm looking for a good classic recipe **Chef to Cook for You:** The only chef for me is Gerry Klaskala at Aria **Culinary Travel:** Italy as I've never been. It has incredible traditional food.

K

David Kinkead
Chef | Sibling Rivalry

525 Tremont St. Boston, MA 02116

Restaurant E-mail: siblingrivalry525@hotmail.com

Phone: (617) 338-5338

RESTAURANT FACTS
Seats: 157 **Weeknight Covers:** 165 **Weekend Covers:** 245 **Check Average (with Wine):** $68 **Tasting Menu:** No **Kitchen Staff:** 7

CHEF FACTS
Cuisine: Japanese **Born:** 1965 **Began Career:** 1986 **Work History:** Chicago, IL: Everest; New York, NY: Park Ave Café; Boston, MA: Biba; Nantucket, MA: 21 Federal **Mentor(s):** Jean Joho, Bob Kinkead **Protégée(s):** Jake Smith **Affiliations:** Massachusetts Restaurant Association **Languages Spoken:** Spanish

NOTABLE DISH(ES): Crispy Rare Tuna with Nori; Tempura-Fried Long Beans

FAST FACTS
Restaurant Recs: Bangkok Bistro for green duck curry **Kitchen Tool(s):** Japanese mandolin **Interview Question:** Where was the last great dinner you had? **Flavor Combo(s):** Peaches and Virginia ham; curry and coconut milk; black bean, tomatoes and tomatillos **Fave Cookbook(s):** The French Laundry Cookbook by Thomas Keller **Chef to Cook for You:** David Burke – he's always doing something new **Culinary Travel:** France – it's still the best

Bob Kinkead
Chef | Kinkead's
2000 Pennsylvania Ave. NW Washington, DC 20006

Restaurant E-mail: chef@kinkead.com

Phone: (202) 296-7700

RESTAURANT FACTS
Seats: 240 **Weeknight Covers:** 250 **Weekend Covers:** 350–360
Check Average (with Wine): $77 **Kitchen Staff:** 10

CHEF FACTS
Other Restaurants: Colvin Run, VA: Colvin Run Tavern; Boston, MA: Sibling Rivalry **Cuisine:** American seafood **Born:** 1952 **Began Career:** 1967 **Work History:** Cambridge, MA: The Harvest; Chillingsowrth, MA: Joseph's; Boston, MA: Sheraton Commander Hotel, Twenty-One Federal **Protégée(s):** Jeff Black, Scott Bryan, Chris Cosentino, Ris Lacoste, Tracy O'Grady, Chris Schlesinger **Awards:** 1999-2007 Zagat Most Popular Restaurant in DC; 2006 IFMA Silver Plate; 2005 Food Arts Silver Spoon; 2000 Ivy Award; 1995 James Beard Award for Best Chef Mid-Atlantic; Nation's Restaurant News Fine Dining Hall of Fame Inductee **Affiliations:** Sullivan College's National Center for Hospitality Studies Board of Directors, AIWF, JBF, IACP, Council of Independent Restaurant Owners President **Books Published:** Kinkead's Cookbook

NOTABLE DISH(ES): Chocolate Crème Brulée; Cod Cheeks with Parsley Shallot Sauce

FAST FACTS
Restaurant Recs: Four Sisters for good Vietnamese food like noodle soups and shaking beef; The Supper Club for traditional Indian food, especially the bread and curry; Picco in Boston for their pizza **Kitchen Tool(s):** Blenders and high quality sauté pans **Interview Question:** How many cookbooks do you own? What food magazines do you subscribe to? **Fave Cookbook(s):** The Good Cook Series by Time Life Books **Chef to Cook for You:** Guy Savoy. He's a good friend and one of the best cooks in the world. **Culinary Travel:** France because I always enjoy it and it has the best food

Steve Klc
Pastry Chef/Owner | PastryArts.com

Washington, DC 20004

Restaurant E-mail: chef@pastryarts.com

Phone: (202) 638-1910

CHEF FACTS
Began Career: 1982 was when I bought my first cookbook and talked my way into a professional kitchen for the very first time.
Culinary School: L'Académie de Cuisine's part-time professional pastry program, Gaithersburg, MD **Grad Year:** 1994 **Work History:** Washington, DC: Jaleo, Café Atlantico, Zaytinya **Mentor(s):** Jacques Torres, François Joneaux, Philippe Conticini, José Andrés **Awards:** 2005-2007, Three-Time "Best Pastry Chef" nominee by the Restaurant Association of Metropolitan Washington; 2003 StarChefs.com Rising Star Pastry Chef Washington DC **Languages Spoken:** Kitchen Spanish

NOTABLE DISH(ES): Casta Diva: Tahitian Vanilla Gelatin with Lemon Granita and Summer Berry Salad

FAST FACTS
Restaurant Recs: Minh's – a Vietnamese restaurant in our Arlington, VA neighborhood, for Bo La Lot: ground beef seasoned with garlic and lemongrass and wrapped in la lot leaves, then grilled **Kitchen Tool(s):** A freezer that gets down to -5; Indian spice grinder; Microplane **Interview Question:** Why do you want to become a pastry chef, when the position in most restaurants is well on its way to becoming extinct? **Fave Cookbook(s):** The first book about desserts to transcend everything previously written about the subject – Los Postres de el Bulli by Albert Adriá

Eric Klein
Executive Chef | Spago Las Vegas

3500 Las Vegas Blvd. South, Suite G-1 Las Vegas, NV 89109

Restaurant E-mail: eklein@bellagioresort.com

Phone: (702) 693-8400

RESTAURANT FACTS
Seats: 150 **Tasting Menu:** Yes $100 **Kitchen Staff:** 8–10

CHEF FACTS
Other Restaurants: Spago Café Las Vegas **Cuisine:** Simple Alsatian cuisine **Born:** 1973 **Began Career:** 1991 **Culinary School:** Jean Michel Storck, Alsace, France **Grad Year:** 1991 **Stages:** Switzerland: Les Iris, Chernex, La Petite Auberge **Work History:** Las Vegas, NV: Chinois, SW Steakhouse, Fix, SW; Beverly Hills, CA: Spago, Maple Drive; France: Schillinger; Germany: Holzschope Gasthaus **Mentor(s):** Wolfgang Puck, Lee Hefter **Protégée(s):** Yianni Koufodontis **Awards:** 2005 StarChefs.com Rising Star Chef Las Vegas; 2004 Food & Wine Best New Chefs **Languages Spoken:** French, Spanish, German, Alsatian

NOTABLE DISH(ES): Maryland Blue Crab Salad with Avocado; Foie Gras Terrine "Speck"; Plum Purée and Brioche

FAST FACTS
Restaurant Recs: Pho Kim Long – I order the number 11 **Kitchen Tool(s):** Spoon **Interview Question:** What makes you think that you are the best grill cook, or whatever the opening is for? What is your dream? What makes you happy? What drives you? Who do you think is the best chef right now? What can you bring to the restaurant? It doesn't matter where they worked before, I need to get a feel for their drive as a chef. **Fave Cookbook(s):** Secrets of Baking by Sherry Yard; Larousse Gastronomique by Prosper Montagne; Junior League cookbooks because they really gave me a good idea of American food when I first came to America from Europe **Chef to Cook for You:** Lee Hefter, because he is my mentor **Culinary Travel:** Asia, because they have been cooking for so many thousands of years

Eric Kleinman
Chef/Owner | inoteca

98 Rivington St. New York, NY 10002

Restaurant E-mail: erock2112@gmail.com

Phone: (212) 614-0473

RESTAURANT FACTS
Seats: 75 **Tasting Menu:** No **Kitchen Staff:** 5

CHEF FACTS
Other Restaurants: Ino, Bar Milano **Cuisine:** Rustic Italian **Born:** 1975 **Began Career:** 1990 in front of the house; 1994 back of house **Stages:** San Francisco, CA: Bix, Fog City Diner; St. Helena, CA: Tra Vigne **Work History:** San Francisco, CA: Caffe Museo, Bix, Grand Café, Modern Catering, Gordon's House of Fine Eats; New York, NY: Lupa Osteria **Mentor(s):** Gordon Drysdale and Mark Ladner **Protégée(s):** Mike Beradino, Marlon Manty **Awards:** 2004, 2005 Time Out New York Best Small Plates and Best Winebar; 2004 Gourmet Magazine's 50 Top Restaurants in America; 2004 50 Hottest Restaurants **Languages Spoken:** Spanish (spanglish)

NOTABLE DISH(ES): House Smoked Trout with Charred Ramps and Fried Egg

FAST FACTS
Restaurant Recs: Momofuku Noodle Bar for Berkshire pork buns **Kitchen Tool(s):** My sous chef, Heavy Henckels knives **Interview Question:** Do you love cooking? **Flavor Combo(s):** Flavor combos change as seasons change. For spring: earthy mushrooms (Morels, Chanterelles, Porcinis) with ramps, asparagus and peas, or favas **Fave Cookbook(s):** Chez Panisse Vegetables by Alice L. Waters; Cookbooks by Joyce Goldstein. **Chef to Cook for You:** Gordon Drysdale out of San Francisco because he was my mentor in San Francisco for eight years **Culinary Travel:** Somewhere I haven't been in Italy – Alto Adige or the Amalfi Coast. Most of what I cook professionally is Italian.

Michael Kornick
Chef/Owner | MK

868 N Franklin St. Chicago, IL 60610

Phone: (312) 482-9179

RESTAURANT FACTS
Seats: 150 **Weeknight Covers:** 125 **Weekend Covers:** 250–260
Check Average (with Wine): $90 **Tasting Menu:** Yes $79 **Kitchen Staff:** 11

CHEF FACTS
Other Restaurants: Chicago, IL: N9NE Steakhouse; Las Vegas, NV: N9NE Steakhouse, Nove Italiano; Dallas, TX: N9NE Steakhouse, Nove Italiano **Cuisine:** Provençal French and regional Italian-influenced American **Born:** 1962 **Began Career:** 1982 **Culinary School:** The Culinary Institute of America, Hyde Park, NY **Grad Year:** 1982 **Stages:** France: Alain Chapel; Berkeley, CA: Chez Panisse; Hollywood, CA: Stars, Spago; San Francisco, CA; Regent Hotels: Hong Kong; Bangkok; Malaysia; Hyatt Hotels: Hong Kong; Singapore; Bangkok **Work History:** New York, NY: Nick's Fish market; Quilted Giraffe; New Orleans, LA: Windsor Court Hotel; Boston, MA: Four Seasons Hotel; Chicago, IL: Marche, Vivo, Red light, Nine Group **Mentor(s):** Richard Melman, Barry Wine **Protégée(s):** Douglass Anderson, Barry Dakake **Awards:** 2001-2007 AAA Four-Diamonds; 5 Time James Beard Foundation Best Chef Midwest Nominee **Affiliations:** James Beard Foundation, CIRA, Chefs Collaborative

NOTABLE DISH(ES): Lamb Noisettes with Garlic and Roquefort Potato Croquettes

FAST FACTS
Restaurant Recs: In Vegas: Lotus of Siam for spicy shrimp with chorizo oil. In Chicago: Lula Cafe for steak tartare and Phoenix Restaurant for sticky rice with dried shrimp and Chinese sausage. **Kitchen Tool(s):** Non-stick sauté pan because I can use less oil and fat to achieve caramelization **Interview Question:** What are your short term goals at this job? How will you accomplish them as part of our team? Why did you choose our restaurant to pursue them? This line of questioning allows you to find out what someone knows about their own interests and themselves, what they know about your business, your training and development style, and whether or not they identify with being part of a team or organization greater than the themselves. **Flavor Combo(s):** Shellfish, Chiles, and Lemon; Mint, Tomato and Lamb; Chocolate and Orange. **Fave Cookbook(s):** Chez Panisse Menu Cookbook by Alice Waters. This book set the tone for American owned and operated restaurants cooking an original style based on sound technique. It is a beautiful historical reference to the birth of the connection between American-trained, chef-driven restaurants and American-published cookbooks **Chef to Cook for You:** Keith Korn – because I miss him dearly **Culinary Travel:** Tokyo, to witness the Japanese art of perfection. You can also get the best Kaiseki and sushi experience.

Nicole Krasinski
Pastry Chef | Rubicon

558 Sacramento St. San Francisco, CA 94111

Restaurant E-mail: painperdu3@hotmail.com

Phone: (415) 434-4100

RESTAURANT FACTS
Seats: 120 **Weeknight Covers:** 80 **Weekend Covers:** 120 **Check Average (with Wine):** $92 **Tasting Menu:** Yes $82/$152 with wine **Kitchen Staff:** 3

CHEF FACTS
Cuisine: Modern American **Born:** 1976 **Began Career:** 1996 **Work History:** Chicago, IL: Red Hen Bread; Ellsworth, MI: Tapawingo; San Francisco, CA: Rubicon **Mentor(s):** Nancy Carey **Awards:** 2007 StarChefs.com Rising Star Pastry Chef San Francisco; 2005 San Francisco Magazine Best Pastry Chef; 2005 San Francisco Chronicle Rising Star Chef

NOTABLE DISH(ES): Pistachio-Rose Petal Meringue, Honeycomb, Dates, Yogurt Sorbet; Aged Pecorino and Walnut Cake, Roasted Clementine Jam, Arbequina Olive Oil Ice Cream

FAST FACTS
Restaurant Recs: Pizzetta 211 for pizza **Kitchen Tool(s):** Calculator because without it I'd be out of a job. There is so much math in the pastry kitchen. **Interview Question:** Tell me your favorite dishes when you go out to eat. You can tell a lot about someone from their answer, their details and the way they speak. **Flavor Combo(s):** Peanuts with chocolate and seven-year-aged balsamic; strawberries and star anise; chestnut honey and blue cheese **Fave Cookbook(s):** The Last Course: The Desserts of Gramercy Tavern by Claudia Fleming **Chef to Cook for You:** Pierre Hermé – to have him make something special for me would be pretty incredible **Culinary Travel:** Japan – I have a really strong desire to go see what is going on there

Gabriel Kreuther
Executive Chef | The Modern

9 W 53rd St. New York, NY 10019

Restaurant E-mail: gkreuther@themodernnyc.com

Phone: (212) 333-1220

RESTAURANT FACTS
Seats: 75-80 **Weeknight Covers:** 90-100 **Weekend Covers:** 125-130 **Check Average (with Wine):** $140-$145 **Tasting Menu:** Yes $115/$125 **Kitchen Staff:** 18

CHEF FACTS
Cuisine: Contemporary and classic French **Born:** 1969 **Began Career:** 1987 **Culinary School:** L'École Hôtelière, France **Grad Year:** 1987 **Stages:** Washington, DC: Le Caprice **Work History:** Washington, DC: Le Caprice, Colmar; France: Le Fer Rouge; Switzerland: L'Ermitage de Bernard Ravet; New York, NY: La Caravelle, Jean Georges, L'Atélier at The Ritz-Carlton Central Park **Mentor(s):** My uncle, Bernard Ravet, and Jean-Georges Vongerichten **Awards:** 2006 James Beard Foundation Best New Restaurant; 2006 James Beard Foundation Best Chef New York Nominee; 2006 Michelin 1 star; 2003 Food & Wine America's Best New Chefs; 2002 StarChefs.com Rising Star Chef New York **Affiliations:** James Beard Foundation **Languages Spoken:** French, German

NOTABLE DISH(ES): Pan-Seared Sea Bass in a Lemon Verbena Broth; Peasant Flour Soup with Florida Frog Legs and Scallions

FAST FACTS
Restaurant Recs: Katz's Deli for a pastrami sandwich **Kitchen Tool(s):** Rubber spatula; spoon **Interview Question:** What are your long and short term culinary goals and how are you positioning yourself to achieve them? I want to get a sense for how committed and focused on their profession a potential candidate really is. **Flavor Combo(s):** Some combinations I have been using lately are: scallops, vanilla bean, lime zest, and toasted buckwheat; cauliflower panna cotta with orange vinaigrette and caviar; roasted trout with rhubarb emulsion. **Fave Cookbook(s):** Larousse Gastronomique and Le Repertoire de la Cuisine by Louis Saulnier– they are two very comprehensive and classic culinary guides that provided me with a solid knowledge of cooking **Chef to Cook for You:** A guy in France: Jean Georges Klein. I like the way he thinks about food. He has an interesting perspective as he began in the front of house before he started cooking. His food is very flavorful. **Culinary Travel:** I think it would be intriguing to spend time time in Japan. I would like to get a closer look at their techniques and to see traditional way of cooking and the way they use their products.

Gray Kunz
Chef/Owner | Grayz

13-15 West 54th St. New York, NY 10019

Restaurant E-mail: grayzinfo@grayz.net

CHEF FACTS

Cuisine: Modern French with Asian and Eastern European influences **Born:** 1955 **Began Career:** 1975 **Grad Year:** 1975 **Work History:** Switzerland: Beau Rivage Palace, Restaurant Girardet, Baur au Lac in Zurich; Hong Kong: Plume; New York, NY: The Adrienne, Lespinasse, Café Gray, Spice Market **Mentor(s):** Fredy Girardet **Protégée(s):** Floyd Cardoz, Andrew Carmellini, Sammy DeMarco, Todd Humphries, Troy Dupuy, Brian Bistrong **Awards:** 2006 James Beard Foundation Who's Who of Food & Beverage Inductee; 2005 Michelin 1 star; 2005 Mobil Four Diamonds; 2004 New York Times 2 stars; 2004 New York Times 3 stars (Spice Market); 2002 IACP Cookbook Awards Nominee; 2002 The Culinary Institute of America Restaurant Hall of Fame Inductee; 1996-1998 James Beard Foundation Outstanding Chef Nominee; 1995 James Beard Foundation Best Chef in New York City; 1993-1995 Zagat Survey NYC Restaurant Guide #1 Best Overall Restaurant (Lespinasse); 1993 The New York Times 4 stars (Lespinasse); 1993 Food & Wine Best New Chef **Books Published:** The Elements of Taste **Languages Spoken:** French, German, Cantonese

NOTABLE DISH(ES): Kalamansi-Cured Kampachi with Soba Noodles and Flying Fish Roe; Skate Schnitzel with Cucumber Potato Salad, Pumpkin Seeds and Brown Butter

FAST FACTS

Restaurant Recs: Sammy's Roumanian for chicken liver with onions **Kitchen Tool(s):** Gray Kunz spoon. It's a simple tool, but its size and shape help me spoon the right amount of liquid onto a plate, and it feels great in your hand. One spoonful gives you just the right amount of sauce for any dish. **Interview Question:** What are your long term goals? It gives me a good sense of the person and I am able to discover something I wouldn't normally learn. **Fave Cookbook(s):** Larousse Gastronomique by Prosper Montagne

L

{ Lagasse - Lyman }

L

Emeril Lagasse
Chef | Emeril's New Orleans

800 Tchoupitoulas St. New Orleans, LA 70130

Restaurant E-mail: jeff.hinson@emerillagasse.com

Phone: (504) 528-9393

RESTAURANT FACTS
Seats: 150 **Kitchen Staff:** 8

CHEF FACTS
Other Restaurants: Las Vegas, NV: NOLA, Emeril's Delmonico, Emeril's New Orleans Fish House, Delmonico Steakhouse; Orlando, FL: Emeril's Tchoup Chop, Emeril's Orlando; Atlanta, GA: Emeril's Atlanta; Miami, FL: Emeril's Miami Beach **Cuisine:** New Orleans cuisine: Creole, Cajun, French **Born:** 1959 **Began Career:** 1978 **Culinary School:** Johnson & Wales University, Providence, RI **Grad Year:** 1978 **Stages:** Paris; Lyon; New York; Boston; Philadelphia; New Orleans **Work History:** New Orleans, LA: Commander's Palace **Mentor(s):** My mother, Ella Brennan, Julia Child **Protégée(s):** Thomas Wolfe, David McCelvey, Bernard Carmouche, Chris Wilson **Awards:** 2006 Nation's Restaurant News Menu Masters; 2005 Wine Spectator Distinguished Service Award; 2004 Restaurant and Institutions Magazine Executive of the Year; 2004; 1991 Wine Spectator Grand Award; 2002 Las Vegas Life Magazine Best Steakhouse; 1999 People Magazine 25 Most Intriguing People of the Year; 1998 GQ Chef of the Year; 1993 Esquire Best New Restaurant; 1991 James Beard Foundation Best Chef Southeast; 1990 Johnson & Wales Honorary Doctorate; 1990 Esquire Restaurant of the Year **Affiliations:** The Emeril Lagasse Foundation, JBF **Books Published:** Emeril's Delmonico; Emeril's There's a Chef in My World; Louisiana Real and Rustic; Emeril's Creole Christmas; Emeril's TV Dinners; Every Day's A Party; Prime Time Emeril; Emeril's There's A Chef in My Soup; From Emeril's Kitchens; Emeril's There's A Chef in My Family; Emeril's Potluck

NOTABLE DISH(ES): Emeril's Eggplant and Shrimp Beignets; Steamed Mussels in a Fennel Pernod Broth

FAST FACTS
Restaurant Recs: La Crepe Nanou for great crêpes with a variety of fillings, including crawfish; R&O Pizza Place for boiled crawfish; Central Grocery Company for muffaletta **Kitchen Tool(s):** All-Clad pans **Interview Question:** What inspired you to become a cook? **Fave Cookbook(s):** The Cooking of Southwest France by Paula Wolfort

Mourad Lahlou
Chef/Owner | Aziza

5800 Geary Blvd. San Francisco, CA 94121

Restaurant E-mail: mourad@aziza-sf.com

Phone: (415) 752-2222

RESTAURANT FACTS
Seats: 128 **Weeknight Covers:** 180 **Weekend Covers:** 225 **Check Average (with Wine):** $70 **Tasting Menu:** Yes $49 **Kitchen Staff:** 8

CHEF FACTS
Cuisine: New Moroccan **Born:** 1968 **Began Career:** 1996 **Work History:** San Rafael, CA: Kasbah Restaurant **Mentor(s):** Paula Wolfert **Awards:** 2007 StarChefs.com Rising Star Chef San Francisco; 2007 Citysearch.com Best Mediterranean Cuisine; 1998-2008 San Francisco Chronicle by Michael Bauer Top 100 Restaurants; 2006 San Francisco Magazine 50 Very Best Restaurants; 2002 San Francisco Weekly Best New Restaurant; 2002 San Francisco Chronicle Top 10 New Restaurants; 1998 San Francisco chronicle by Michael Bauer Rising Star Chef **Affiliations:** Chef's Club, Slow Food, CUESA **Languages Spoken:** Moroccan, Arabic, French, and a little Spanish

NOTABLE DISH(ES): Roasted Root Vegetable Couscous, Braised Beef Cheeks, Chickpeas, Golden Raisins and Harissa; Moroccan Spiced Carrot Soup with Blood Orange Foam

FAST FACTS
Restaurant Recs: Chez Panisse; Thai Express for Pad Thai and egg noodle soup; Pizetta for margarita pizza and anchovy and radicchio pizza **Kitchen Tool(s):** Note pad and pen because I like to write down what I am thinking **Interview Question:** What are your other interests? It lets me know something else about them. I want someone who has other interests besides cooking. **Flavor Combo(s):** Mushrooms and squab; peanut butter and green olives **Fave Cookbook(s):** Couscous and Other Good Food from Morocco by Paula Wolfert; The Zuni Cafe Cookbook by Judy Rodgers **Chef to Cook for You:** Paula Wolfert. She understands Moroccan food better that any Moroccan. People who live in the culture take it for granted – what she has done is to look at the food from a Western perspective, taking the best of the cuisine and making sense of it **Culinary Travel:** I'd like to go to China. I think what they are doing is great. I've always been intrigued by their flavors. Spain comes in a close second.

Joël Lahon
Pastry Chef | Nobu Miami Beach

1901 Collins Ave Miami, FL 33139

Restaurant E-mail: joëll@noburestaurants.com

Phone: (305) 695-3232

RESTAURANT FACTS
Seats: 180 **Weeknight Covers:** 250–400 **Weekend Covers:**
400–650 **Check Average (with Wine):** $100 **Tasting Menu:** Yes
$110/$150/$200 **Kitchen Staff:** 3

CHEF FACTS
Cuisine: Japanese/Peruvian **Born:** 1970 **Began Career:** 1995
Culinary School: Bordeaux Academy, Pau, France **Grad Year:** 1996
Stages: I staged around Europe in France, Switzerland and England
Work History: England: L'Escargot, Nobu London; Japan: Nobu Japan
Mentor(s): Oriol Balanguer, Stephane Glacier, Michel Bras, Pierre
Gagnaire **Awards:** 2008 StarChefs.com Rising Star Pastry Chef
South Florida **Languages Spoken:** French, English, kitchen Japanese

NOTABLE DISH(ES): Thai Jewels: Coconut Tapioca, Thai Tea Foam, Lemongrass Ice Cream, and Kaffir
Lime Emulsion; Carpaccio: Fresh Mango, Chocolate Caviar, Yuzu Cake, Fresh Grapefruit, Raspberry
Foam

FAST FACTS
Restaurant Recs: I like to go to this small Peruvian fish restaurant called Pachamamma in Sunny
Isles **Kitchen Tool(s):** Oven; ice cream machine **Interview Question:** I like to ask them if they want to
be a pastry chef, what their favorite dessert is, and also what book they last read. I look for a combination of passion and skill. **Flavor Combo(s):** Yuzu and raspberry; apricot and curry; red miso and
chocolate milk **Fave Cookbook(s):** Albert Adriá's first book in '99 broke a lot of boundaries and introduced new textures **Chef to Cook for You:** Pierre Gagnaire – I would like him to make my daughter's
wedding cake **Culinary Travel:** I love Asia, particularly Japan. It is amazing and it's another culture
close to food. Chefs honor their craft and respect tradition.

Hichem Lahreche
Pastry Chef | Sixteen

330 N Wabash Ave. Chicago, IL 60611

Restaurant E-mail: hlahreche@trumphotels.com

Phone: (312) 588-8030

RESTAURANT FACTS
Seats: 120 **Weeknight Covers:** 75 **Weekend Covers:** 120 **Check Average (with Wine):** $117 **Tasting Menu:** Yes $82/$110 **Kitchen Staff:** 2–4

CHEF FACTS
Cuisine: Modern French **Born:** 1969 **Began Career:** 1993 **Culinary School:** L'Academie de Cuisine, Gaithersburg, MD; International School of Confectionary Arts, Gaithersburg, MD **Grad Year:** 1998 **Stages:** Washington, DC: Citronelle **Work History:** Washington DC: Citronelle, The Willard Room in The Intercontinental Hotel, Red Sage, Colvin Run Tavern, Kinkead's **Mentor(s):** Olivier Bajard, Laurent L'Huilier, Michel Richard, Bob Kinkead **Awards:** 2006 StarChefs.com Rising Star Pastry Chef Washington DC **Affiliations:** St. Jude Children's Hospital **Languages Spoken:** French, Arabic, Spanish

NOTABLE DISH(ES): Pineapple Tatin with Lemon Chibouste; Hazelnut Suprême

FAST FACTS
Restaurant Recs: In Washington, DC: Bistrot Du Coin for great moules frites and beer; Pollo Rico for spicy chicken **Kitchen Tool(s):** Offset spatula; paring knife **Interview Question:** Are you sure this is what you want to do? Because it's going to be hard. **Flavor Combo(s):** Coconut, passion fruit and mango; chocolate and mint; all the different combinations of hazelnut and chocolate **Fave Cookbook(s):** Kinkead's Cookbook: Recipes from Washington DC's Premier Seafood Restaurant by Bob Kinkead **Chef to Cook for You:** Frank Brunacci – I think he is amazing, which is why I came to work for him. The details and the flavors in his food are incredible; he really appreciates what he does. He cares so much and is so present, and you see that in his food. **Culinary Travel:** Perpignan, France – to L'École Internationale de Pâtisserie to see my mentor Olivier Bajard

L

Michael Laiskonis
Pastry Chef | Le Bernardin

155 W 51st St. New York, NY 10019

Restaurant E-mail: mlaiskonis@le-bernardin.com

Phone: (212) 554-1515

RESTAURANT FACTS
Seats: 90 **Weeknight Covers:** 175 **Weekend Covers:** 250 **Check Average (with Wine):** $175 **Check Average (w/o Wine):** $107 **Tasting Menu:** Yes $180/$320 with wine **Kitchen Staff:** 4–5

CHEF FACTS
Cuisine: Contemporary treatments of classical flavors and techniques with a touch of science **Born:** 1972 **Began Career:** 1993 **Work History:** Northville, MI: Emily's; Farmington Hills, MI: Tribute **Mentor(s):** Eric Ripert, Takashi Yagihashi, Rick Halberg **Protégée(s):** Eric Voigt, Monica Glass **Awards:** 2007 James Beard Foundation Outstanding Pastry Chef; 2006 StarChefs.com Rising Star Pastry Chef New York; 2004 Bon Appétit Pastry Chef of the Year; 2003, 2002 Pastry Art & Design Top Ten **Affiliations:** James Beard Foundation, City Harvest, Jean Louis Palladin Foundation **Languages Spoken:** Some French

NOTABLE DISH(ES): Chocolate Passion Fruit Fondue; Rose-Raspberry Tart with Almond, Lychee and Pistachio

FAST FACTS
Restaurant Recs: Lassi for the frequently changing specials on their takeout menu **Kitchen Tool(s):** Scales. While I like spontaneity, I also love precise measurement. **Interview Question:** What do you like to eat? What chefs inspire you the most? It doesn't matter what the answer is, just as long as they have an answer. I like to know I'm dealing with someone with a certain degree of passion. **Flavor Combo(s):** Acid and bitter; salty and sweet; and a combination of all four. **Fave Cookbook(s):** With hundreds of books in my library it is difficult to even narrow it down to a top ten, though of late, I very much respect Desserts by Pierre Hermé **Chef to Cook for You:** Fernand Point because he is so influential in bringing modern cuisine into it's day. He was a bridge between the days of Escoffier and the beginning of nouvelle cuisine. **Culinary Travel:** All over Southeast Asia, not only for the food but also the culture

Lanny Lancarte, II
Chef/Owner | Lanny's Alta Cocina Mexicana

3405 W 7th St. Fort Worth, TX 76107

Restaurant E-mail: lanny@lannyskitchen.com

Phone: (817) 850-9996

RESTAURANT FACTS
Seats: 64–90 **Weeknight Covers:** 40 **Weekend Covers:** 100–120 **Check Average (w/o Wine):** $60 **Tasting Menu:** Yes $60/$100 with wine **Kitchen Staff:** 2–4

CHEF FACTS
Cuisine: Mediterranean with Mexican ingredients **Born:** 1975 **Began Career:** 2002 **Culinary School:** The Culinary Institute of America, Hyde Park, NY **Grad Year:** 2002 **Stages:** Chicago, IL: Topolobampo, Frontera Grill **Work History:** Chicago, IL: Frontera Grill, Topolobampo; Fort Worth, TX: Cafe Modern **Mentor(s):** Rick Bayless, Diana Kennedy **Awards:** 2007 StarChefs.com Rising Star Chef Dallas **Affiliations:** IACP, ACF, Chefs Collaborative **Languages Spoken:** Spanish

NOTABLE DISH(ES): Elk Loin with Mole Colorado; Lobster Ravioli with Brussels Sprouts and Foie Gras Butter

FAST FACTS
Restaurant Recs: M+M Steakhouse for chicken fried steak; Esperanzas for chorizo and eggs **Kitchen Tool(s):** Immersion Circulator **Interview Question:** We promote from within. We haven't hired anyone with outside experience. **Flavor Combo(s):** I think pork and fish work well together, like braised pork belly with scallops, or braised oxtail with halibut **Fave Cookbook(s):** Grand Livre de Cuisine by Alain Ducasse **Chef to Cook for You:** I love how tried and true Thomas Keller's dishes are; he really executes the classics well. I would really like him to cook for me. **Culinary Travel:** It changes weekly but I'd have to say Spain because I have never been. I would also like to go to Japan.

L

David Larkworthy
Executive Chef/Co-Owner | 5 Seasons Brewing

5600 Roswell Rd. NE Atlanta, GA 30342

Restaurant E-mail: chefdave5@gmail.com

Phone: (404) 255-5911

RESTAURANT FACTS
Seats: 340 **Weeknight Covers:** 200–700 **Weekend Covers:** 400–700 **Check Average (with Wine):** $37 **Tasting Menu:** No **Kitchen Staff:** 6

CHEF FACTS
Other Restaurants: 5 Seasons North **Cuisine:** Local, seasonal and sustainable Modern American **Born:** 1968 **Began Career:** At age 12. I used to take a bus an hour away to Westport, Connecticut to work with my dad at his restaurant. **Work History:** Atlanta, GA: The Gourmet Grill, Buckhead Bread Co, Pano & Paul's; Tallahassee, FL: Jack Shoop **Mentor(s):** My mother and father, Thomas Keller (via his work), Jean Banchet for his effective handling of everything, Julia Child (from afar) **Awards:** 2007 StarChefs.com Rising Star Chef Sustainability Award Atlanta **Affiliations:** Slow Food, Georgia Organics, and dozens of charities **Languages Spoken:** Spanish

NOTABLE DISH(ES): Buffalo Quail with Baby Carrot and Celery Slaw, Buffalo Froth and Blue Cheese; Strawberry Soup with Sweetgrass Dairy Chèvre Mousse, Pea Shoots, Chipotle-Glazed Berries and Lemon Oil

FAST FACTS
Restaurant Recs: Little Bangkok; Penang; Nuevo Laredo **Kitchen Tool(s):** It's more important to be adaptable than to rely on tools. You need to be able to improvise. **Interview Question:** Why are you here? Do you know how challenging this is? **Flavor Combo(s):** I love acids and vinegar and how both play off round, fatty tastes. I'm more inclined to sour than sweet. I like pairing lime with pork belly and smoked chili peppers with strawberries. **Fave Cookbook(s):** On Food and Cooking by Harold McGee; I taught myself with the CIA book and I grew up with The Joy of Cooking **Chef to Cook for You:** I would love to have dinner with Jaques Pépin **Culinary Travel:** China has some of the most interesting food on the planet. I'd love to go to some 4000-year-old restaurant.

Ken Larsen
Pastry Chef | Brasserie

100 E. 53rd St. New York, NY 10022

Restaurant E-mail: kenlarsen76@yahoo.com

Phone: (212) 750-3645

RESTAURANT FACTS
Seats: 225 **Weeknight Covers:** Lunch: 400 **Weekend Covers:** Lunch: 400 **Check Average (with Wine):** $65 **Tasting Menu:** No **Kitchen Staff:** 2–3

CHEF FACTS
Cuisine: French **Born:** 1976 **Began Career:** 1997 **Culinary School:** Culinary Institute of America, Hyde Park, NY **Grad Year:** 2000 **Work History:** New York, NY: Park Avenue Café, Gotham Bar and Grill, Fresh, Bistro du Vent, I Trulli **Mentor(s):** Richard Leach, Joseph Murphy

NOTABLE DISH(ES): Raspberry Trio: Vanilla-Raspberry Coupe, Sorbet and Crisp Rice Pudding

FAST FACTS
Restaurant Recs: Al di La in Brooklyn; Shabu Tatsui on 10th between 2nd and 3d Avenues **Kitchen Tool(s):** The Vita-Prep **Interview Question:** The first thing that makes an impression with me is their demeanor. I tend not to hire people who are insecure or introverted because I don't believe that they can handle the scrutiny of the kitchen culture. So first I look for someone who is confident and from there I simply trust my instincts. Of course, they have to have some skills. **Flavor Combo(s):** I love chèvre goat cheese and figs in the fall because the tang and richness of the goat cheese balances well with the acidity and sweetness of the fig. I also love chocolate and banana. **Fave Cookbook(s):** Baking and Pastry: Mastering the Art and Craft by The Culinary Institute of America **Chef to Cook for You:** Last year I went to Le Bernardin and it was the most memorable meal I have ever had. To have Eric Ripert cook for me personally so that I could pick is brain would be the ultimate experience. **Culinary Travel:** I would like to go back to Thailand and visit the rest of Southeast Asia. The produce and spices are incredible and the food carts in Bangkok have the most amazing yet simple delicacies. I would like to spend a significant amount of time there and immerse myself in the culture and culinary scene.

Christine Law
Pastry Chef | FullBloom Baking Co.

205 Constitution Dr. Menlo Park, CA 94025

Restaurant E-mail: christinel@fullbloom.com

Phone: (650) 325-6200

RESTAURANT FACTS
Kitchen Staff: 100+

CHEF FACTS
Cuisine: Upscale American-style desserts **Born:** 1970 **Began Career:** 1994 **Culinary School:** The Culinary Institute of America, Hyde Park, NY **Grad Year:** 1994 **Stages:** San Francisco, CA: Postrio **Work History:** San Francisco, CA: Postrio; Palo Alto, CA: Spago; Santa Monica, CA: Shutters on the Beach **Mentor(s):** Janet Rikala Dalton, Emily Luchetti **Protégée(s):** Chenoa Bol **Awards:** 2005 StarChefs.com Rising Star Pastry Chef San Francisco **Affiliations:** The Bakers Dozen **Languages Spoken:** Some French, some Spanish

NOTABLE DISH(ES): Chilled Peach and Prosecco Soup with Lavender Short Cake Biscuits; Poached Pear Baba with St. Andre and Black Pepper Ice Cream

FAST FACTS
Restaurant Recs: Town Hall **Kitchen Tool(s):** Mini offset spatula – just about anything in pastry can be done with this tool. I don't leave home without it! **Interview Question:** Can you start tonight? Obviously I want them to give notice, but I want to see their enthusiasm. **Flavor Combo(s):** It's hard to name a "favorite" flavor combination because I'm always looking for something new. My specialty is ice cream, so I guess I'd choose either olive oil ice cream or pink and black peppercorn ice cream with macerated strawberries. **Fave Cookbook(s):** The Secrets of Baking by Sherry Yard **Chef to Cook for You:** I would have Suzanne Goin of Lucques and AOC cook for me. I admire her as a successful female chef and restaurateur, and find her dishes sophisticated and elegant, while providing an element of comfort food for me. I wish I lived closer to her restaurants so I could visit them more often! **Culinary Travel:** Argentina – they have fabulous ice cream, and that's what I love

Josie Le Balch
Chef/Owner | Josie Restaurant

2424 Pico Blvd. Santa Monica, CA 90405

Restaurant E-mail: josie@josierestaurant.com

Phone: (310) 581-9888

RESTAURANT FACTS
Seats: 100 **Weeknight Covers:** 40-80 **Weekend Covers:** 150 **Check Average (with Wine):** $75 **Tasting Menu:** No **Kitchen Staff:** 5-6

CHEF FACTS
Cuisine: Californian French **Born:** 1957 **Began Career:** 1969 **Stages:** Los Angeles, CA: Ma Maison, L'Hermitage **Work History:** Los Angeles, CA: Saddle Peak Lodge, Remi, The Beach House **Mentor(s):** Gregorie Le Balch, Jivan Tabibian **Protégée(s):** Jill Davie, Jennifer Naylor, Suzanne Goin **Affiliations:** Les Dames d'Escoffier, FCS **Languages Spoken:** French, some Spanish

NOTABLE DISH(ES): Melanzana with Heirloom Tomato; Grilled Lamb Chops with Curried Couscous and Romesco Sauce

FAST FACTS
Restaurant Recs: Saddle Peak Lodge – for brunch **Kitchen Tool(s):** White asparagus peeler from Germany; spoon **Interview Question:** What are your weaknesses and strengths? **Fave Cookbook(s):** The Zuni Café Cookbook by Judy Rodgers and any cookbooks by Auguste Escoffier

Richard Leach
Pastry Chef | Park Avenue

100 East 63 St. New York, NY 10021

Restaurant E-mail: leachr22000@yahoo.com

Phone: (212) 644-1900

RESTAURANT FACTS
Seats: 220 **Weeknight Covers:** 250 **Weekend Covers:** 325 **Check Average (w/o Wine):** $85 **Tasting Menu:** No **Kitchen Staff:** 3-4

CHEF FACTS
Cuisine: Architectural desserts **Born:** 1965 **Began Career:** 1987 **Culinary School:** The Culinary Institute of America, Hyde Park, NY **Grad Year:** 1987 **Stages:** Brooklyn, NY: The River Café **Work History:** New York, NY: Aureole; One Fifth Avenue; Symphony Café; Lespinasse; Le Côte Basque **Mentor(s):** Charlie Palmer, Peter Bracero **Protégée(s):** Joe Murphy, Deborah Radicot, Ryan Butler **Awards:** 1997 James Beard Pastry Chef of the Year; 1997, 1995 Chocolatier Magazine 10 Best Pastry Chefs in America **Affiliations:** JBF, multiple charitable events throughout the year **Books Published:** Sweet Seasons

FAST FACTS
Restaurant Recs: Kitchen Ubols for Thai food and BBQ pork **Kitchen Tool(s):** Heat gun **Interview Question:** What are you looking to do in the future? **Flavor Combo(s):** Pineapple and basil; licorice root and tangerine; malted milk and kinako; coconut and curry; chocolate and Earl Grey tea **Fave Cookbook(s):** Sweet Seasons **Culinary Travel:** I think that Thai and Mexican cuisine can be very exciting with their refreshing, bright flavors, so I wouldn't mind taking a trip to either one

Edgar Leal
Chef | Cacao Restaurant

141 Giralda Ave. Coral Gables, FL 33134

Restaurant E-mail: edgarleal@cacaorestaurant.com

Phone: (305) 445-1001

RESTAURANT FACTS
Seats: 90 **Weeknight Covers:** 50–80 **Weekend Covers:** 130 **Check Average (with Wine):** $84 **Check Average (w/o Wine):** $62 **Tasting Menu:** Yes $75 **Kitchen Staff:** 5

CHEF FACTS
Other Restaurants: Beijing, China: The Garden of Delights **Cuisine:** South American **Born:** 1969 **Began Career:** 1987 **Culinary School:** The Culinary Institute of America, Hyde Park, NY **Grad Year:** 1995 **Stages:** New York, NY: Daniel; Spain: el Bulli; France: Café de Paris **Work History:** Venezuela: Restaurant ARA **Mentor(s):** Miro Popic, Pierre Blanchard **Protégée(s):** Daniel Urdaneta, David Posner, Gabrielle Lamantia, Gamal Fadlala **Awards:** 2004 StarChefs.com Rising Star Chef Miami **Affiliations:** Easter Seals **Languages Spoken:** Spanish

NOTABLE DISH(ES): Reina Pepiada Arepa Chips; Venezuelan Chicken Chupe

FAST FACTS
Restaurant Recs: Ouzo in Miami Beach for the octopus **Kitchen Tool(s):** Silpat **Interview Question:** Who are the chefs you most admire, and who do you want to become? **Flavor Combo(s):** Cilantro with avocados and chilies **Fave Cookbook(s):** Nobu Now by Nobuyuki Matsuhisa **Chef to Cook for You:** Joël Robuchon – I have always considered him my favorite chef **Culinary Travel:** South America – Lima, and Sao Paulo, and Santiago, Chile. Amazing restaurants and places to party.

Dennis Leary
Chef | Canteen

817 Sutter St. San Francisco, CA 94109

Restaurant E-mail: dennisleary@earthlink.net

Phone: (415) 928-8870

RESTAURANT FACTS

Seats: 22 **Weeknight Covers:** 66 **Weekend Covers:** 100+ **Check Average (with Wine):** $40-$50 **Tasting Menu:** Yes Tuesdays **Kitchen Staff:** 2-3

CHEF FACTS

Other Restaurants: The Sentinel **Cuisine:** American **Work History:** Scottsdale, AZ: Boulders Resort; San Francisco, CA: Rubicon **Mentor(s):** Alain Rondelli, Drew Nieporent and Hubert Keller **Awards:** 2005 StarChefs.com Rising Star Chef San Francisco

NOTABLE DISH(ES): King Salmon with Sauce Soubise, Pickled Artichokes and Ham; Halibut Ceviche with Green Tomato and Avocado

FAST FACTS

Restaurant Recs: Hon's Wun Tun House; La Bergerie; Francesci's Restaurant – for food that reminds me of old east coast beach places in Ipswich and the Jersey shore **Kitchen Tool(s):** Plastic bowl scrapers **Interview Question:** How much pot do you smoke when you wake up? **Fave Cookbook(s):** Charcuterie and French Pork Cookery by Jane Grigson; The Futurist Cookbook by Filippo Marinetti; The Foods of France by Waverly Root **Culinary Travel:** New York and Paris

Chris Lee
Chef | Gilt

455 Madison Ave. New York, NY 10022

Restaurant E-mail: clee@nypalace.com

Phone: (212) 891-8100

RESTAURANT FACTS

Seats: 50 **Weeknight Covers:** 50 **Weekend Covers:** 90 **Check Average (with Wine):** $125 **Tasting Menu:** Yes $110/$175 with wine $140/$215 with wine **Kitchen Staff:** 7

CHEF FACTS

Cuisine: New American **Born:** 1975 **Began Career:** 1994 **Culinary School:** California Culinary Academy, San Francisco, CA **Grad Year:** 2000 **Work History:** New York, NY: Daniel, Oceana, Jean-Georges; San Francisco, CA: Bruce Hill, The Fifth Floor; Philadelphia, PA: The Striped Bass **Mentor(s):** Alex Lee, Daniel Boulud, Neil Gallagher, Alfred Portale **Awards:** 2007 StarChefs.com Rising Star Chef New York; 2005 James Beard Foundation Rising Star Chef **Affiliations:** We support all culinary schools and do as much charity work as we can **Languages Spoken:** Kitchen Spanish, French

NOTABLE DISH(ES): Sea Bass with Piperade, Garlic Aïoli and Saffron Mussel Broth; Maine Diver Sea Scallop Ceviche with Sea Urchin, Shiitake Mushrooms, Fresh Wasabi and Yuzu-Carrot Caviar

FAST FACTS

Restaurant Recs: I love the pasta at Lupa and the gyro stand up the street from here is pretty great **Kitchen Tool(s):** Vita-Prep, F. Dick sausage stuffer **Interview Question:** Are you willing to learn – not just from me, but from everyone else? If they want to be a sous chef they have to commit 3 years to "the program." **Flavor Combo(s):** My favorite flavors vary by season. I look for balance and global flavors. Right now: guinea hen with foie-Guinness sauce; sweet pea purée and carrot essence; Lychee-based ceviche with scallops. **Fave Cookbook(s):** Sauces: Classic and Contemporary Sauce Making by James Peterson **Chef to Cook for You:** Charlie Trotter – I have always admired his style, books, and overall theories **Culinary Travel:** Italy – I would love to get lost there for a year. I'm really into Italian wines. After Italy, I'd go to Japan or China.

L

Jamie Leeds
Chef/Owner | Hank's Oyster Bar

1624 Q St. NW Washington, DC 20009

Restaurant E-mail: jleeds@hanksdc.com

Phone: (202) 462-4265

RESTAURANT FACTS
Seats: 60–80 **Weeknight Covers:** 140–280 **Weekend Covers:** 350–450 **Check Average (with Wine):** $33 **Tasting Menu:** No **Kitchen Staff:** 3

CHEF FACTS
Other Restaurants: Alexandria, VA: Hanks Oyster Bar; Washington, DC: CommonWealth (to open in summer 2008) **Cuisine:** Seafood **Born:** 1961 **Began Career:** 1985 **Stages:** France: Hotel Negresco, Pain Adour et Fantaisie, Gascogne and Hostellerie du Cerf, Marienheim **Work History:** New York, NY: Union Square Café, Tribeca Grill; Washington, DC: Hank's Oyster Bar, 15 Ria **Mentor(s):** Danny Meyer, Michael Bonadies, Rich Melman **Protégée(s):** Maria Hines **Awards:** 2003 StarChefs.com Rising Star Chef Washingon DC **Affiliations:** WCR, AIWF Board Member, RAMW Board Member, Les Dames d'Escoffier **Languages Spoken:** Kitchen Spanish

NOTABLE DISH(ES): Molasses Braised Short Ribs; Crispy Oven Fried Pecan Chicken with Jalapeño Hush Puppies

FAST FACTS
Restaurant Recs: Minh's for fried shrimp and sweet potato cakes **Kitchen Tool(s):** Squeeze bottles **Interview Question:** How do you make mayonnaise? If they've been in a kitchen that makes their own mayo then you know they've been exposed to making things from scratch. **Flavor Combo(s):** Mediterranean flavors: tomato, basil, olive oil and garlic **Fave Cookbook(s):** Cookbooks by Chris Schlesinger **Chef to Cook for You:** Julia Child, because it would be a legendary and incredible experience. You know everything would be amazing, real and honest. **Culinary Travel:** London – I was there on a recent trip researching for my new gastropub and had great food experiences

Ludovic Lefebvre
Executive Chef | Lavo

3325 S. Las Vegas Blvd. Las Vegas, NV 89101

Restaurant E-mail: ludo.lefebvre@lavolv.com

Phone: (702) 607-7777

RESTAURANT FACTS
Seats: 200–100 **Check Average (with Wine):** $60 **Tasting Menu:** Yes Upon Request **Kitchen Staff:** 80

CHEF FACTS
Cuisine: Mediterranean-influenced **Born:** 1971 **Began Career:** 1985 **Culinary School:** Dijon Academy, Dijon, France **Grad Year:** 1987 **Stages:** France: L'Esperance **Work History:** France: L' Espérance, Pierre Gagnaire, L' Arpege, Le Grand Vefour; Los Angeles, CA: L'Orangerie, Bastide **Mentor(s):** Pierre Gagnaire, Alain Passard **Protégée(s):** Frank Otte **Awards:** 2006 StarChefs.com Rising Stars Los Angeles; 2006 Mobile Travel Guide 5 Star Award at Bastide; 2001 James Beard Rising Star Chef; 1997-1999 Mobile Travel Guide Five Star Award at L'Orangerie; 1998 Worlds 50 Greatest Chefs by Relais & Chateau **Books Published:** Crave: A Feast of the Five Senses **Languages Spoken:** French

NOTABLE DISH(ES): Fried Vermicelli, Langoustines and Clams with Cinnamon Butter; Deconstruction of Bloody Mary

FAST FACTS
Restaurant Recs: Bin 8945 for jerk chicken **Kitchen Tool(s):** My Pacojet for ice creams, sorbets, and mousses **Interview Question:** Why have you decided to be a chef? I want to see if they have passion and love. **Flavor Combo(s):** Citrus with fish **Fave Cookbook(s):** Ma Gastronomie by Fernand Point **Chef to Cook for You:** Pierre Gagnaire – I worked for him for four years. I love his creativity and the way he puts together flavors. The way he builds his plates is totally surprising. While he uses so many techniques he never forgets the most important thing, the ingredients. **Culinary Travel:** I loved traveling through China. I loved the ingredients and the spices. I love to use unusual spices and surprise people.

David LeFevre
Executive Chef | The Water Grill

544 South Grand Ave. Los Angeles, CA 90071

Restaurant E-mail: dlefevre@kingsseafood.com

Phone: (213) 891-0900

RESTAURANT FACTS
Seats: 140 **Weeknight Covers:** 180 **Weekend Covers:** 220 **Check Average (w/o Wine):** $87 **Tasting Menu:** Yes $95/$150 with wine **Kitchen Staff:** 30

CHEF FACTS
Cuisine: Contemporary American seafood **Born:** 1972 **Began Career:** 1993 **Culinary School:** The Culinary Institute of America, Hyde Park, NY **Grad Year:** 1995 **Stages:** Spain: el Bulli, Restaurant Martín Berasategui; England: The Fat Duck; Australia: Tetsuya's; France: Roger Verge, Michel Trama, La Cote D'Or, Jean Bardet **Work History:** Chicago, IL: Charlie Trotter's; Las Vegas, NV: Charlie Trotter's; France: La Cote D'Or, Restaurant Jean Bardey, Le Moulin de Mougins **Mentor(s):** Charlie Trotter **Awards:** 2006 StarChefs.com Rising Star Chef Los Angeles **Affiliations:** We work with a ton of charities **Languages Spoken:** French, Spanish

NOTABLE DISH(ES): Seared Scallops with Kuri Squash Soup; Wasabi Marinated Tuna with Red Radish Purée and Shiso

FAST FACTS
Restaurant Recs: Panchos in Manhattan Beach **Kitchen Tool(s):** Masamoto and Aritsugu knives; shark skin wasabi grater **Interview Question:** Why do you like to cook? Why did you leave your last job? **Flavor Combo(s):** Sweet, sour, salty **Fave Cookbook(s):** The Joy of Cooking by Irma S. Rombauer; The Moosewood Cookbooks by Mollie Katzen; cookbooks by Charlie Trotter **Chef to Cook for You:** I would want to have a tasting of all the chefs I've worked under, each one cooking one course. Charlie Trotter would have to do the red wine and vegetable course. **Culinary Travel:** Singapore and Chiang Mai are awesome for great cultural food, but San Sebastian is probably my favorite city of where I have visited

Jonnatan Leiva
Chef | Jack Falstaff

598 2nd St. San Francisco, CA 94107

Restaurant E-mail: j_leiva@plumpjack.com

Phone: (415) 836-9239

RESTAURANT FACTS
Seats: 120 **Weeknight Covers:** 60–80 **Weekend Covers:** 110–120
Check Average (with Wine): $60 **Tasting Menu:** Yes Upon Request
Kitchen Staff: 4–5

CHEF FACTS
Cuisine: Modern American **Born:** 1979 **Began Career:** 1997 **Culinary School:** The California Culinary Academy, San Francisco, CA **Grad Year:** 1999 **Work History:** Coral Gables, FL: La Palme d'Or at the Biltmore Hotel; France: Apicius, Les Elyssees Hotel Vernet; New York: Union Pacific; San Francisco, CA: The Fifth Floor, Boulevard, Incanto **Mentor(s):** Donna Winter, George Morrone **Awards:** 2008 San Francisco Chronicle Rising Star **Languages Spoken:** Spanish, some French

NOTABLE DISH(ES): Hamachi Crudo; Chantenay Carrot Soup

FAST FACTS
Restaurant Recs: La Corneta Taqueria for prawn and beef quesadillas; Pho Vietnamese Ocean for great pho on Sundays **Kitchen Tool(s):** Microplane **Interview Question:** Do you cook at home? I want to know if they enjoy cooking. I also ask them to make me an omelet. **Flavor Combo(s):** I like offal with unique, vibrant and fresh ingredients. For example: bone marrow and scallops, or sweetbreads with watermelon. **Fave Cookbook(s):** Cookbooks by Julia Child **Chef to Cook for You:** Escoffier – to see the classics. I'm curious to know what the true cuisine was back then. **Culinary Travel:** Japan – it is a culture where they live and breath food and respect it for what it is. It is not just a commodity.

L

David Lentz
Chef and Owner | The Hungry Cat

1535 N Vine St. Hollywood, CA 90028

Restaurant E-mail: davidlentz@thehungrycat.com

Phone: (323) 462-2155

RESTAURANT FACTS
Seats: 80 **Weeknight Covers:** 120–140 **Weekend Covers:** 200–240 **Check Average (w/o Wine):** $42 **Tasting Menu:** No **Kitchen Staff:** 4–5

CHEF FACTS
Other Restaurants: Santa Barbara, CA: The Hungry Cat **Cuisine:** Seafood **Born:** 1972 **Began Career:** 1992 **Stages:** Berkeley, CA: Chez Panisse; England: Cliveden **Work History:** Sparks, MD: The Milton Inn; San Francisco, CA: The Heights; Miami Beach, FL: The Blue Door at the Delano; Las Vegas, NV: China Grill; Los Angeles, CA: Campanile; Studio City, CA: Firefly **Mentor(s):** Joe O'brien, Luke Rinaman, Jimmy Buffet, and Richard Branson **Awards:** 2006 StarChefs.com Rising Star Chef Los Angeles **Affiliations:** We participate in a lot of charity events **Languages Spoken:** Some Spanish

NOTABLE DISH(ES): Hawaiian Marlin, Salsa Verde, Cranberry Beans, House-Cut Pappardelle Noodles and Braised Leeks; Baked Maine Oysters, Black Kale, Applewood Smoked-Bacon and Clarified Butter

FAST FACTS
Restaurant Recs: Urasawa – the tasting menu is always different every day. Ammo for brunch - I especially like the poached egg with roasted beets. **Kitchen Tool(s):** Spoon – it's very versatile. It's good for tasting, basting and plating **Interview Question:** What's your goal? To be a chef, a restaurant owner, or to just pay the bills? I also like to ask why they want to work at my restaurant – is it because of the ad on Craigslist, or because they like what we are doing here? **Flavor Combo(s):** I believe in clean flavors and letting the ingredients speak for themselves **Fave Cookbook(s):** Sunday Suppers at Lucques by Suzanne Goin and Teri Gelber **Chef to Cook for You:** Joël Robuchon

Belinda Leong
Executive Pastry Chef | Restaurant Gary Danko

800 North Point St. San Francisco, CA 94109

Restaurant E-mail: information@garydanko.com

Phone: (415) 749-2060

RESTAURANT FACTS
Seats: 65–75 **Weeknight Covers:** 145 **Weekend Covers:** 145 **Check Average (with Wine):** $127.50 **Tasting Menu:** Yes $96/$161 with wine **Kitchen Staff:** 4

CHEF FACTS
Other Restaurants: San Diego, CA: Arterra Restaurant **Cuisine:** California French **Born:** 1977 **Began Career:** 2000 **Culinary School:** City College of San Francisco, San Francisco, CA **Grad Year:** 2000 **Stages:** San Francisco, CA: Michael Mina; New York, NY: Café Boulud, Aureole **Work History:** San Francisco, CA: Aqua **Mentor(s):** Gary Danko, Thomas Haas, Eric Bertoia, Florian Bellanger, Bill Yosses **Awards:** 2007 StarChefs.com Rising Star Pastry Chef San Francisco; 1999-2005 Mobil 5 star; 2002-present Relais and Chateau; 2000 James Beard Foundation Best New Restaurant **Affiliations:** Relais & Châteaux/Relais Gourmand **Languages Spoken:** Cantonese, kitchen Spanish

NOTABLE DISH(ES): Ants on a Log; Blueberry French Toast with Salted Almond Ice Cream and Maple Foam

FAST FACTS
Restaurant Recs: Delfina, Quince **Kitchen Tool(s):** Small offset spatula **Interview Question:** What is your style of desserts? **Flavor Combo(s):** My favorite flavor combinations are usually tropical flavors. I like pairing banana, lime, passionfruit and coconut together. I also like chocolate with tropical flavors (chocolate and passionfruit.) **Fave Cookbook(s):** Paco Torreblanca: The Book, Volume 1 by Paco Torreblanca **Chef to Cook for You:** If I could have any chef cook for me (for dessert, that is), I would say Paco Torreblanca. I just really like his work. **Culinary Travel:** I would like to go to Spain. There are some chefs that I would really like to work with out there because they are just doing some really interesting things: Paco Torreblanca, Jordi Cruz, Oriol Balaguer, Ramon Morato, and Carme Ruscalleda, just to name a few.

L

Peter Levine
Chef | Troiani Ristorante

1001 Third Ave. Seattle, WA 98104

Restaurant E-mail: plevine@troianiseattle.com

Phone: (206) 624-4060

RESTAURANT FACTS
Seats: 200 **Weeknight Covers:** 70 **Weekend Covers:** 90 **Check Average (with Wine):** $65 **Tasting Menu:** No **Kitchen Staff:** 4

CHEF FACTS
Cuisine: Simple Italian with French influences **Born:** 1964 **Began Career:** 1987 **Culinary School:** California Culinary Academy, San Francisco, CA **Grad Year:** 1987 **Stages:** Washington, DC: Jean-Louis at the Watergate **Work History:** San Francisco, CA: Blue Fox; Washington, DC: Jean-Louis at the Watergate **Mentor(s):** Roberto Gerometta, Gordon Ramsey, Thomas Keller, my father **Protégée(s):** All of my cooks! **Affiliations:** NRA, WRA **Languages Spoken:** Spanish

FAST FACTS
Restaurant Recs: Del Rey – for BBQ pork sliders **Kitchen Tool(s):** Tongs; fish spatula **Interview Question:** Do you really want to be a chef? **Flavor Combo(s):** Basil, Italian parsley and green onion; Chinese red braise; cumin, chili powder and chipotle powder **Fave Cookbook(s):** Gastronomy of Italy by Anna del Conte **Chef to Cook for You:** Marco Pierre White – I love his style and stamina **Culinary Travel:** Any coastal village in the world (except for in the United States). I love fresh-from-the-dock seafood.

Robbie Lewis
Executive Chef | Bacar

448 Brannan St. San Francisco, CA 94107

Restaurant E-mail: robbie@bacarsf.com

Phone: (415) 904-4100

RESTAURANT FACTS
Seats: 180 **Weeknight Covers:** 160 **Weekend Covers:** 230 **Check Average (with Wine):** $75 **Tasting Menu:** Yes $89 **Kitchen Staff:** 10

CHEF FACTS
Cuisine: Modern American **Born:** 1969 **Began Career:** 1990 **Culinary School:** California Culinary Academy, San Francisco, CA **Stages:** Berkeley, CA: Chez Panisse; San Francisco, CA: Stars **Work History:** San Francisco, CA: Rubicon, Boulevard, 42 Degrees, The Village Pub, Jardinière **Mentor(s):** From Traci Des Jardins I learned technique and refinement. From James Moffat of the Slow Club and 42 Degrees, I learned composition and freestyle. **Awards:** 2005 StarChefs.com Rising Star Chef San Francisco **Affiliations:** JBF, Meals-on-Wheels

NOTABLE DISH(ES): Foie Gras Torchon with Pain d'Épice and Tulare Cherries; Suckling Pig: Loin Confit, Sweetbread-Stuffed Trotter and Coppa di Testa

FAST FACTS
Restaurant Recs: INO Sushi in Japantown and Burma Super Star **Kitchen Tool(s):** I'm a fiend for spoons. I mine flea markets and estate sales looking for them. They make the best Christmas presents for cooks. **Interview Question:** Do you know what you're getting yourself into? What is your favorite cookbook? **Flavor Combo(s):** Fennel, lemon and niçoise olives **Fave Cookbook(s):** Flavors of the Riviera by Coleman Andrews **Chef to Cook for You:** Michel Bras – I feel that his work is the origin of new style cuisine **Culinary Travel:** Rural Japan – I am ignorant of the cuisine of that region, and I like its complex simplicity and its aesthetic. I've lived and worked in Italy and it really clarified the concept of "less is more."

L

Jason Licker
Consulting Pastry Chef | Nobu San Diego

207 Fifth Ave. San Diego, CA 92101

Restaurant E-mail: lickerjason@hotmail.com

Phone: (619) 814-4124

CHEF FACTS
Cuisine: Global fusion pastry **Born:** 1976 **Began Career:** 1998
Culinary School: The French Culinary Institute, New York, NY;
French Pastry School, Chicago, IL **Grad Year:** 1999 **Work History:**
New York, NY: Union Square Café, Jean Georges, Metrazur, Fives
at The Peninsula Hotel; Miami, FL: The Shore Club featuring Nobu
Miami; China: The Westin Bund Center **Mentor(s):** Eric Hubert, Kim
O'Flaherty **Protégée(s):** Steven Jiang and Martin Xu – they would
both be famous pastry chefs anywhere else **Awards:** 2004 StarChefs.
com Rising Stars Pastry Chef New York **Languages Spoken:** Some
Spanish, some Mandarin

NOTABLE DISH(ES): Dulce de Leche Chocolate Tart with Banana Five Spice Ice Cream; Almond cake
with Rhubarb, Peaches and Truffle Oil Sorbet

FAST FACTS
Restaurant Recs: John's Pizza on Bleecker in New York **Kitchen Tool(s):** Silpat; sugar thermometer;
offset spatula; Flexi-pan of any shape **Interview Question:** Why do you want to work in pastry? I'm
looking for someone with passion, who loves what they do. **Flavor Combo(s):** Bitter chocolate and
passion fruit; cherries and smoked cedar wood; white chocolate with sake and yuzu; any stone fruit
with herbs and spices **Fave Cookbook(s):** The Last Course by Claudia Fleming **Chef to Cook for You:**
Jean-Georges. What he's done is just crazy! For a chef to accomplish what he has on such a large
scale is ridiculous. **Culinary Travel:** Tokyo – the Japanese culture is introverted and built upon respect, and you can really see that in their pastry. Being part of that as an American is difficult. I think
it would be a good test for me to go work alongside all the big boys there and see their technique and
work ethic.

Jeremy Lieb
Executive Chef | Trois

1180 Peachtree St. Atlanta GA 30309

Restaurant E-mail: jlieb@trois3.com

Phone: (404) 815-3337

RESTAURANT FACTS

Seats: 140–340 **Weeknight Covers:** 150–250 **Weekend Covers:** 250–300 **Check Average (with Wine):** $75 **Check Average (w/o Wine):** $50 **Tasting Menu:** Yes Varies **Kitchen Staff:** 6

CHEF FACTS

Cuisine: Modern French **Born:** 1972 **Began Career:** 1992 **Culinary School:** Milwaukee Area Technical College, Milwaukee, Wisconsin **Grad Year:** 1992 **Work History:** Lake Buena Vista, Fl: Disney's Yacht and Beach Club Resort; France: La Cote d'Or; Cincinnati, OH: The Maisonette; New York, NY: Daniel, Café Boulud; Las Vegas, NV: The Mansion at MGM Grand, Restaurant Medici, Le Cirque **Mentor(s):** Daniel Boulud, Alex Lee, Jean Francios Bruel **Awards:** 2007 Esquire Magazine Critic John Mariani "one of the country's best new restaurants"; 2005 StarChefs.com Rising Star Chef Las Vegas **Affiliations:** I do about 10-12 charity events a year **Books Published:** none yet **Languages Spoken:** French

NOTABLE DISH(ES): Sugpiaq Salmon "Ravioli" with Osetra Caviar; Braised Beef Oxtail with Roasted Scallop and Corn Fondue

FAST FACTS

Restaurant Recs: Pearl and Joyful House (in Vegas) for Chinese. The Chinese food in Las Vegas is Hong Kong style. **Kitchen Tool(s):** My knife is very, very important. I have handmade Nenox knives from Japan. I really think knives have a personality. There's an ancient Japanese story about a sword and a sword maker – the sword salivates for the blood of an enemy. My knife salivates to cut vegetables. **Interview Question:** In order to be great at what you do, you have to have it here (head), here (heart) and here (hands). I start a conversation about their life and food in order to determine where their head and heart are. **Flavor Combo(s):** Brown butter and asparagus; sous vide eggs and tuna **Fave Cookbook(s):** Larousse Gastronomique by Prosper Montagne; On Food and Cooking by Harold McGee; Grand Livre de Cuisine by Alain Ducasse **Chef to Cook for You:** Alex Lee – he was a very big mentor (while I was at Daniel). He taught me the basic respect for the kitchen. **Culinary Travel:** Spain, but not necessarily el Bulli. I want to go to the small towns and eat what the locals eat. The coast, the farms, the fish. I'd like to work in a good Spanish restaurant with some classical influence.

L

Paul Liebrandt
Chef/Partner | Corton

239 West Broadway New York, NY 10013

Restaurant E-mail: paul@paulliebrandt.com

Phone: (212) 219-2777

RESTAURANT FACTS
Seats: 60 **Tasting Menu:** Yes **Kitchen Staff:** 12

CHEF FACTS
Cuisine: Modern European **Born:** 1976 **Began Career:** 1992 **Culinary School:** University of London, London, England **Grad Year:** 1994 **Stages:** France: Pierre Gagnaire **Work History:** England: Le Manoir aux Quat Saisons; Marco Pierre White; France: Pierre Gagnaire; New York, NY: Bouley Bakery, Atlas, Papillon, Gilt **Mentor(s):** Pierre Gagnaire **Awards:** 2006 StarChefs.com Rising Star Chef New York; 2006 New York Times 3 stars; 2002 Esquire Best and Brightest **Languages Spoken:** English

NOTABLE DISH(ES): Peekytoe Crab Salad, Sea Herb Glass; Black Cod with Beet-Hibiscus Purée and Glazed Petit Butterball Potatoes

FAST FACTS
Restaurant Recs: Bar Masa for uni fried rice **Kitchen Tool(s):** Small offset spatula; plating tweezers **Interview Question:** Does this person have the tenacity and passion to succeed? **Flavor Combo(s):** Coffee and cardamom; green tea and strawberries **Fave Cookbook(s):** Alain Chapel Laffon series; White Heat by Marco Pierre White **Chef to Cook for You:** Antoine Carême **Culinary Travel:** Japan – the sensibility of Japanese cuisine is just beautiful, absolutely beautiful

Kelly Liken
Chef/Owner | Kelly Liken

12 Vail Road, # 100 Vail, CO 81657

Restaurant E-mail: kelly@kellyliken.com

Phone: (970) 479-0175

RESTAURANT FACTS
Seats: 72 **Weeknight Covers:** 100-150 **Weekend Covers:** 180
Check Average (with Wine): $100-$150 **Tasting Menu:** Yes **Kitchen Staff:** 6-7

CHEF FACTS
Other Restaurants: Rick and Kelly's American Bistro **Cuisine:** Seasonal American cuisine **Born:** 1976 **Began Career:** 1997 **Culinary School:** Culinary Institute of America, Hyde Park, NY **Grad Year:** 2002 **Work History:** Washington, VA: The Inn at Little Washington: Beaver Creek, CO: Splendido at the Château**Languages Spoken:** Kitchen Spanish

NOTABLE DISH(ES): Colorado Wildflower Honey Glazed Duck Breast with Cornmeal Crêpes, Duck Confit, and Braised Collard Greens

FAST FACTS
Restaurant Recs: Moe's Original Barbecue for the 'Bama-style pork sandwich **Kitchen Tool(s):** My hands **Interview Question:** I ask why they cook. I think it is really important. I'm looking for someone who is passionate and interested in learning. **Flavor Combo(s):** Bacon and onions – they were born to be together. **Fave Cookbook(s):** The Joy of Cooking has stood the test of time. I'm also enjoying Frank Stitt's The Southern Table **Chef to Cook for You:** Bernard Loiseau – his food is amazing and he really helped to revolutionize French cooking by lightening everything up and staying 100% true to flavor. It is how I learned to cook and he has always been a huge influence. **Culinary Travel:** The American Southeast and Mid-Atlantic. I love the food from that region and would really like to learn more about that style of cooking.

L

Donald Link
Chef/Proprietor | Herbsaint Bar and Restaurant

701 St. Charles Ave. New Orleans, LA 70130

Restaurant E-mail: link@herbsaint.com

Phone: (504) 524-4114

RESTAURANT FACTS
Seats: 100 **Weeknight Covers:** 150 **Weekend Covers:** 200 **Check Average (with Wine):** $50 **Tasting Menu:** No **Kitchen Staff:** 15

CHEF FACTS
Cuisine: French-Cajun **Born:** 1969 **Began Career:** 1984 **Culinary School:** The California Culinary Academy, San Francisco, CA **Grad Year:** 1995 **Stages:** San Francisco, CA: Rubicon, Flying Saucer **Work History:** San Francisco, CA: Cha Cha Cha, Flying Saucer, Jardinière, The Elite Café; Palo Alto, CA: Mojo; New Orleans, LA: Bayona **Mentor(s):** Albert Tordjman, Susan Spicer **Protégée(s):** Kelly Hartman, Ryan Prewitt, Kyle Waters **Awards:** 2007 James Beard Foundation Best Chef South; 2006 James Beard Foundation Best Chef Southeast Nominee; 2006 New Orleans Magazine People to Watch; 2003 StarChefs.com Rising Star Chef New Orleans; 2002 New Orleans Magazine Chef of the Year **Books Published:** Real Cajun (to be released in spring of 2009) **Languages Spoken:** Kitchen Spanish

NOTABLE DISH(ES): Short Ribs on Potato Cake with Dijon Horseradish Sour Cream; Coconut Cream Pie

FAST FACTS
Restaurant Recs: Pho Tau Bay for pork, wonton, and noodle soup **Kitchen Tool(s):** Fish spatula – it's thin, versatile and doesn't tear up food **Interview Question:** Why do you want to be a line cook? **Flavor Combo(s):** Pork, smothered onions and black eyed peas; bacon and lima beans **Fave Cookbook(s):** The Zuni Café Cookbook by Judy Rodgers **Chef to Cook for You:** Fernand Point

Scott Linquist
Chef | Dos Caminos

373 Park Ave.New York, NY 10016

Restaurant E-mail: slinquist@brguestinc.com

Phone: (212) 294-1000

RESTAURANT FACTS
Seats: 240 **Weeknight Covers:** 350 **Weekend Covers:** 350 **Check Average (with Wine):** $48 **Tasting Menu:** No **Kitchen Staff:** 12-15

CHEF FACTS
Other Restaurants: New York, NY: Dos Caminos; Las Vegas, NV: Dos Caminos **Cuisine:** Mexican **Born:** 1966 **Began Career:** 1993 **Culinary School:** The Culinary Institute of America, Hyde Park, NY **Grad Year:** 1993 **Stages:** France: L'Ésperance **Work History:** New York, NY: Gotham Bar and Grill, Lespinasse, Lutèce; San Francisco, CA: Boulevard; Santa Monica, CA: Border Grill, City Restaurant **Mentor(s):** Rick Bayless, Alfred Portale, Susan Feniger, Mary Sue Milliken **Affiliations:** We are members of the Green Restaurant Association, among many others. We do many events and work with too many charities to list. **Languages Spoken:** Spanish

FAST FACTS
Restaurant Recs: Santa Clarita for carnitas, al pastor tacos, sopas and cold beer **Kitchen Tool(s):** Tortilla press **Interview Question:** How much money do you expect? What shift would you like to work? **Flavor Combo(s):** Guajillo chiles, toasted garlic and epazote; cajeta (goats milk dulce de leche) and roasted bananas **Fave Cookbook(s):** Zarela's Veracruz by Zarela Martínez and Anne Mendelson; Food From My Heart by Zarela Martinez **Chef to Cook for You:** Fernand Point – because he was the pioneer of nouvelle cuisine. He was very generous with his knowledge and he has so many great quotes like: "the duty of a good cusinier is to transmit to the next generation everything he has learned and experienced." He is not only a great chef but a great philosopher. Dinner with him would be incredibly interesting! **Culinary Travel:** My next trip will be a food and wine tour of Spain. From Madrid and north, through the wine country, to San Sebastian, then to Barcelona and down the coast to Sevilla, finishing in Portugal.

L

Tony Liu
Executive Chef | Morandi

211 Waverly Pl. New York, NY 10014

Phone: (212) 627-7575

RESTAURANT FACTS
Tasting Menu: No **Kitchen Staff:** 4

CHEF FACTS
Cuisine: Pan-European **Born:** 1974 **Began Career:** 1998 **Culinary School:** The Culinary Institute of America, Hyde Park, NY **Grad Year:** 1997 **Stages:** Spain: Restaurant Martin Berasategui **Work History:** Honolulu, HA: Roy's; New York, NY: Lespinasse, Daniel, Tabla, Babbo, August **Mentor(s):** Floyd Cardoz, Alex Lee, Mario Batali **Awards:** 2006 StarChefs.com Rising Star Chef New York **Affiliations:** Days of Taste **Languages Spoken:** Spanish

NOTABLE DISH(ES): Paffenroth Farm Beet and Blood Orange Salad; Grilled Baby Leeks with Romesco

FAST FACTS
Restaurant Recs: Sunset Park for dim sum and Mexican food; Red Hook ball fields for Central American grub under tents **Kitchen Tool(s):** Wood burning oven – it imparts great flavor and has great heat **Interview Question:** What do you like to eat? **Flavor Combo(s):** Salty and sweet; sweet and sour **Fave Cookbook(s):** I love cookbooks! The Chez Panisse Cookbooks; The Zuni Café Cookbook by Judy Rodgers; Cooking by Hand by Paul Bertolli; cookbooks by Alain Ducasse **Chef to Cook for You:** The Troisgros brothers – they have so much history and tradition imbedded in their cuisine yet they can also be very contemporary. Also when I think of food I think of it as something very nurturing and familial. I love the way they have their whole family involved. **Culinary Travel:** San Francisco – I love places like Zuni Café because the food is so straightforward and so flavorful. I also recently traveled around Italy – it was great eating in Rome because the recipes are so classical and are so much a part of the foundation for a lot of what we eat today.

Jesse Llapitan
Executive Chef | The Palace Hotel

2 New Montgomery St. San Francisco, CA 94105

Restaurant E-mail: jesse.llapitan@luxurycollection.com

Phone: (415) 512-1111

RESTAURANT FACTS
Kitchen Staff: 100

CHEF FACTS
Other Restaurants: Garden Court, Maxfields, Kyoya, Pied Piper **Cuisine:** Cal-Asian **Born:** 1965 **Began Career:** 1980s **Culinary School:** The California Culinary Academy, San Francisco, CA **Grad Year:** 1989 **Stages:** France: Le Cordon Bleu **Work History:** Houston, TX: The Houstonian Club & Spa; Los Angles, CA: The St. Regis; Vail, CO: Vail Cascade Resort; Chicago, IL: Whitehall Hotel; San Francisco, CA: Fleur De Lys; The Palace Hotel; The Hyatt Regency; The Grand Hyatt Wailea Resort; The Ritz-Carlton San Francisco **Mentor(s):** Yuki Igimia **Protégée(s):** Jason Rogers, Kelly Armetta, Ben Paula **Awards:** 2002 AIWF Distinguished Chef Award **Affiliations:** Professional Chefs Association, San Francisco, CA **Languages Spoken:** Kitchen Spanish

NOTABLE DISH(ES): Jumbo Lump Crab Cakes; Seared Scallops with Pancetta Scallion Vinaigrette

FAST FACTS
Kitchen Tool(s): Passion **Interview Question:** If you had to throw a party for 50 people what would you serve? Oh, and there is an unlimited budget. I am very amused with some of the unbelievable answers. **Flavor Combo(s):** Truffles, Kobe beef and yuzu salt **Fave Cookbook(s):** Art of Aureole by Charlie Palmer **Chef to Cook for You:** I would have Jacques Pépin because I admire his style. His way of thinking is very classical, not a lot of fuss. **Culinary Travel:** Japan because it seems so regimented and disciplined and I would like to be around that sort of stringent environment. They also have a lot of exotic products that are not easily available over here.

Anita Lo
Chef/Owner | Annisa

13 Barrow St. New York, NY 10014

Phone: (212) 741-6699

RESTAURANT FACTS
Seats: 45 **Weeknight Covers:** 50 **Weekend Covers:** 80 **Check Average (with Wine):** $75 **Tasting Menu:** No **Kitchen Staff:** 4

CHEF FACTS
Other Restaurants: Rickshaw Dumpling Bar, Bar Q **Cuisine:** Contemporary American **Born:** 1965 **Began Career:** 1988 **Culinary School:** École de la Gastronomie Ritz Escoffier, France **Grad Year:** 1990 **Stages:** France: Michel Rostang, L'Espadon **Work History:** New York, NY: Bouley, Chanterelle **Mentor(s):** David Waltuck **Protégée(s):** Sohui Kim **Awards:** 2006 Michelin 1 star; 2004 WCR Golden Whisk; 2002 NY Magazine Culinary Wizards; 2001 Food & Wine Best New Chefs **Affiliations:** WCR, Les Dames d'Escoffier **Languages Spoken:** French, Some Italian

NOTABLE DISH(ES): Oysters with Three Root Vegetables; Seared Foie Gras with Foie Gras Soup Dumplings

FAST FACTS
Restaurant Recs: Aki on W 4th Street for uni mousse **Kitchen Tool(s):** Plastic quart containers – they're watertight, reusable and disposable **Interview Question:** Do you have any food aversions? I need to know if they are adventurous and if they're interested in this type of cuisine. **Flavor Combo(s):** Shiso and fatty fish **Fave Cookbook(s):** The Joy of Cooking by Irma S. Rombauer **Chef to Cook for You:** Taka Yoneyama was a great sushi chef who is no longer working. I was a regular at her place. **Culinary Travel:** Japan, because I love Japanese cuisine

Michael Lomonaco
Executive Chef/Managing Partner | Porter House New York

10 Columbus Circle 4th Floor New York, NY 10019

Restaurant E-mail: mlomonaco@porterhousenewyork.com

Phone: (212) 823-9500

RESTAURANT FACTS
Seats: 140 **Weeknight Covers:** 300 **Weekend Covers:** 425 **Check Average (with Wine):** $82 **Check Average (w/o Wine):** $65 **Tasting Menu:** No **Kitchen Staff:** 12

CHEF FACTS
Cuisine: New American/modern steakhouse **Born:** 1955 **Began Career:** 1984 **Culinary School:** New York City College of Technology – Restaurant Hospitality Program, New York, NY **Grad Year:** 1984 **Stages:** New York, NY: Le Cirque **Work History:** New York, NY: Le Cirque, '21' Club, Windows on the World, Wild Blue, Noche **Mentor(s):** Daniel Boulud, Julia Child, Patrick Clark, Alain Sailhac **Protégée(s):** Jim Botsacos, Michael Ammirati, Jesse Davis, Mark Lippman **Awards:** 2008 NYIT Professional Excellence in Culinary-Quarterly Review of Wines; 2008 Alumni of the Year-NYC College of Technology; 2002 Ivy Award Winner **Affiliations:** SOS, City Harvest, Co-founder of Windows of Hope Family Relief Fund **Books Published:** Nightly Specials – 125 Recipes for Spontaneous Creative Cooking at Home; The "21" Cookbook **Languages Spoken:** English, French, Italian, Spanish

NOTABLE DISH(ES): Chili-Rubbed Pork Tenderloin with Peach Fritters; Michael's '21' Burger; Whitefish Fillets with Morels and Asparagus

FAST FACTS
Restaurant Recs: Tommaso's in Dyker Heights, Brooklyn for a special bottle of Barolo, gnocchi with pesto, roasted fresh-harvested squab, and budino al cioccolato **Kitchen Tool(s):** 8-inch Wusthof chef's knife – it's a versatile tool that I use to prepare anything. I've been using this non-stop for years despite all the other knives I have added to my kit. **Interview Question:** When you're off from work and you dine out, what's your favorite restaurant? **Flavor Combo(s):** Roasted fresh sardines stuffed with pine nuts, dried currants, toasted bread crumbs, and lemon zest. It's sea-salty, briny, sweet, savory, and tart all in one bite. **Fave Cookbook(s):** It's a tie: The Art of Eating by M.F.K. Fisher; James Beard's American Cookery by James Beard; Between Meals: An Appetite for Paris by A. J. Liebling; The Food of Italy by Waverly Root **Chef to Cook for You:** Fernand Point – he so revolutionized classic French cooking and inspired generations of chefs. He may have been the first true, original, creative chef, and the spark that lit the fire. **Culinary Travel:** Buenos Aires, Argentina for the beef, the Malbec, and the tango

L

Christina Longo
Pastry Chef | Barking Frog

14582 NE 145th St. Woodinville, WA 98072

Restaurant E-mail: christina.longo@barkingfrog.org

Phone: (425) 424-2999

RESTAURANT FACTS
Seats: 70–130 **Weeknight Covers:** 50–70 **Weekend Covers:** 100–120 **Check Average (w/o Wine):** $75–$100 **Kitchen Staff:** 2

CHEF FACTS
Cuisine: Pastry **Born:** 1973 **Began Career:** 1993 **Culinary School:** Seattle Central Community College Pastry Program **Grad Year:** 2000 **Stages:** France: Patisserie Grandin **Work History:** Snoqualmie, WA: The Salish Lodge and Spa; Seattle, WA: Dahlia Lounge **Mentor(s):** Claudia Fleming **Awards:** 2003 StarChefs.com Rising Star Pastry Chef Seattle **Affiliations:** I'm affiliated with Chefs Collaborative and Slow Food. The Barking Frog participates in many charity fundraisers and auctions, namely FareStart and Share Our Strength.

NOTABLE DISH(ES): Friar Plum Beignets with Pistachio Ice Cream and Poached Apricots

FAST FACTS
Restaurant Recs: Le Gourmand is a Seattle institution, but not as hyped lately, so it's a bit under the radar. Sara Naftaly's creme brulée with brandied raspberries is a dish this pastry chef will trek across town for! **Kitchen Tool(s):** An offset serrated knife, tournet knife **Interview Question:** Where do they see themselves a year out? **Flavor Combo(s):** Strawberries and goat cheese; cherries and sheep's milk cheeses; rhubarb, honey, and lavender; chocolate and blueberries, to name a few summer seasonal favorites **Fave Cookbook(s):** I have been enjoying Georges Blanc's books for seasonal flavor inspirations and spins on French classics **Chef to Cook for You:** I'd have to say Mario Batali because I love his food and I feel we've got some common ground to chat about. Something casual rather than a dining event. It would be even better if he invited Michael Stipe along for the meal! **Culinary Travel:** Norway and other parts of Scandinavia because it is a part of the world I haven't seen, with different ingredients and style of cuisine. Plus, my husband's roots are Norwegian, and we'd both like to explore there.

Mark LoRusso
Executive Chef | Tableau

3131 Las Vegas Blvd. Las Vegas, NV 89109
Restaurant E-mail: mark.lorusso@wynnlasvegas.com
Phone: (702) 770-3330

RESTAURANT FACTS
Seats: 120 **Weeknight Covers:** 85 **Weekend Covers:** 150 **Check Average (with Wine):** $110 **Tasting Menu:** Yes **Kitchen Staff:** 11

CHEF FACTS
Cuisine: American seafood **Born:** 1968 **Began Career:** 1990 **Culinary School:** The Culinary Institute of America, Hyde Park, NY **Grad Year:** 1990 **Work History:** Los Angeles, CA: Checkers; San Francisco, CA: Aqua, The Cyprus Club; New York, NY: Aureole, Jean-Georges; Las Vegas, NV: Aqua at the Bellagio **Mentor(s):** Jerry Comfort **Protégée(s):** BJ Patel

NOTABLE DISH(ES): Maine Lobster Salad with Heirloom Tomatoes, Sweet Melon and Frisée; Alaskan Wild Salmon and Summer Corn Pudding with Chanterelles

FAST FACTS
Restaurant Recs: Lotus of Siam for the green papaya salad **Kitchen Tool(s):** Japanese mandolin – it's portable, light, efficient, and great for shaving thin vegetables **Interview Question:** What was the last cookbook you read? **Flavor Combo(s):** I like Mediterranean flavors **Fave Cookbook(s):** The Chez Panisse cookbooks **Chef to Cook for You:** I would have Lidia Bastianich cook for me. Her food is comforting and it reminds me of the food I grew up with. **Culinary Travel:** To Italy for the interesting food and rustic character

Dewey Losasso
Executive Chef | North One Ten

11052 Biscayne Blvd. North Miami, FL 33161

Restaurant E-mail: north110dl@aol.com

Phone: (305) 893-4211

RESTAURANT FACTS
Seats: 105 **Weeknight Covers:** 100 **Weekend Covers:** 175-200
Check Average (w/o Wine): $38 **Tasting Menu:** Yes **Kitchen Staff:** 3

CHEF FACTS
Cuisine: New American **Born:** 1963 **Began Career:** 1976 **Culinary School:** Culinary Institute of America, Hyde Park, NY **Grad Year:** 1983 **Stages:** I staged at some fish houses on the Jersey Shore growing up and have done various stages in Italy over the years **Work History:** Miami, FL: The Foundlings Club, Personal Chef to Donatella Versaci, Tuscan Steak; New York, NY: The Hudson Hotel **Mentor(s):** Alice Waters, Danny Meyers **Affiliations:** Slow Food **Languages Spoken:** Very bad Italian

FAST FACTS
Restaurant Recs: Pacific Time in the design district. I like the asparagus with prosciutto, egg Milanese and parmesan. I also love to go to Michael's Genuine Food and Drink for the crispy hominy.
Kitchen Tool(s): My soul **Interview Question:** We first give them and hour and a half to cook an entree and an appetizer. After that I ask what kind of music they listen to. We can't have any arguing over the iPod. **Flavor Combo(s):** I love citrus in all desserts, as in our pine nut tart with rosemary and lemon olive oil. I also like basil with vanilla ice cream and cherries. **Fave Cookbook(s):** The Chez Panisse Cookbook by Alice Waters **Chef to Cook for You:** I saw Daniel Boulud cook when I was a guest on a cooking program and it was amazing, like going back to school. He has such integrity in his dishes. Mario Batali is another chef I greatly admire; they are my two favorites. **Culinary Travel:** I would like to go to Paris as I haven't spent much time there. I have been all over Italy and southern France but need to make a it up a little farther north.

Willis Loughhead
Executive Chef | Country

90 Madison Ave. New York, NY 10016

Restaurant E-mail: willisl@countryinnewyork.com

Phone: (212) 889-7100

RESTAURANT FACTS
Seats: 70 **Weeknight Covers:** 50–60 **Weekend Covers:** 80–110 **Check Average (with Wine):** $125 **Tasting Menu:** Yes $75/$89/$135 **Kitchen Staff:** 6

CHEF FACTS
Cuisine: European American **Born:** 1971 **Began Career:** 1986 **Culinary School:** Continuing Education at The Culinary Institute of America, Hyde Park, NY **Stages:** Spain: Restaurant Abac **Work History:** Santa Monica, CA: Schatzi on Main; Key West, FL: Palm Grill; South Beach, FL: Pacific Time; Miami, FL: Tantra, Bizcaya Grill; Coconut Grove, FL: The Ritz-Carlton; New York, NY: The Modern **Mentor(s):** Roberto Holz, Marco Selva **Protégée(s):** Atala Olmos, Orlando Paquin, Ari Bokovska **Awards:** 2003 StarChefs.com Rising Star Chef Miami **Affiliations:** Share our Strength and I do a lot with the culinary schools **Languages Spoken:** Spanish, some Italian

NOTABLE DISH(ES): Asparagus Spiked Loin of Tuna with Shaved Foie Gras and Sautéed Spinach; Sautéed Quail with Chanterelles and Warm Potato Vinaigrette

FAST FACTS
Restaurant Recs: Restaurant Picasso for tapas **Kitchen Tool(s):** Sauce spoon; cake tester; extra virgin olive oils to finish dishes **Interview Question:** What do you like to cook at home? Do you read cookbooks? **Flavor Combo(s):** Sour, vinegary, lemony, salty and olive oil-y **Fave Cookbook(s):** Nueva Cocina Catalana: de La Tradicion a la Innovacion by Angel Salvador Esplugas; La Bonne Cuisine de Madame E. Saint-Ange: The Original Companion for French Home Cooking by Madame Evelyn Saint-Ange and Paul Aratow **Chef to Cook for You:** I would want a full on blow-out Chinese meal prepared by my girlfriend's grandmother **Culinary Travel:** I would go back to Tunisia, to a place called Djerba where I had a great street food experience. Also Cambodia for the street food.

Emily Luchetti
Executive Pastry Chef | Farallon

450 Post St. San Francisco, CA 94102

Restaurant E-mail: cdurie@farallonrestaurant.com

Phone: (415) 834-1605

RESTAURANT FACTS
Seats: 160 **Weeknight Covers:** 200 **Weekend Covers:** 275 **Check Average (w/o Wine):** $85 **Tasting Menu:** No **Kitchen Staff:** 2–3

CHEF FACTS
Other Restaurants: WaterBar **Cuisine:** Classic American and European desserts with a twist **Began Career:** 1979 **Culinary School:** New York Restaurant School, New York, NY **Grad Year:** 1979 **Stages:** France: Pangauds **Work History:** New York, NY: Silver Palate; San Francisco, CA: Farallon Restaurant, Stars Restaurant **Mentor(s):** Jeremiah Tower, Lois Murphy, Sheila Lukins **Awards:** 2004 James Beard Foundation Best Pastry Chef **Affiliations:** JBF, Bakers Dozen, WCR **Books Published:** Stars Desserts; Four Star Desserts; A Passion for Desserts; A Passion for Ice Cream **Languages Spoken:** Some French, some Italian

NOTABLE DISH(ES): Red Berry White Chocolate Trifles; Black Forest Brownies with Mocha Ganache

FAST FACTS
Restaurant Recs: Sweet Ginger in Sausalito for sushi **Kitchen Tool(s):** Rubber spatula **Interview Question:** If you weren't baking what would you be doing? **Flavor Combo(s):** Caramel and vanilla; ginger and lemon; peanut butter and chocolate **Fave Cookbook(s):** Mastering the Art of French Cooking by Julia Child, Louisette Bertholle, and Simone Beck **Chef to Cook for You:** Escoffier for both savory and sweet. I would like to see how things were originally prepared. **Culinary Travel:** Paris – as far as pastry goes they are doing a lot of new and different things, and they still do all the traditional pastry really well

Amanda Lydon
Chef/Owner | Straight Wharf Restaurant

6 Harbor Square Nantucket Island, MA 02554

Restaurant E-mail: straightwharfrestaurant@gmail.com

Phone: (508) 228-4499

RESTAURANT FACTS
Seats: 100–140 **Weeknight Covers:** 180 **Weekend Covers:** 180
Check Average (with Wine): $85 **Tasting Menu:** No **Kitchen Staff:**
4–8

CHEF FACTS
Cuisine: Seasonal sustainable seafood **Born:** 1971 **Began Career:**
1991 **Stages:** Spain: Martin Berasategui; France: L'Abbaye de Sainte
Croix **Work History:** Boston, MA: Straight Wharf Restaurant, Chez
Henri, Truc, Radius, Upstairs on the Square, Ten Tables **Mentor(s):**
Deborah Hughes, Mary Catherine Diebel **Awards:** 2006 StarChefs.
com Rising Star Chef Boston; 2000 Food & Wine Best New Chefs;
2000 Boston Magazine Best New Chefs; 2000 James Beard Foundation Rising Star Nominee **Languages Spoken:** Enough French to order a good dinner

NOTABLE DISH(ES): Chantenay Carrot Gnocchi, Braised Rabbit, Pickled Ramps and Pecorino; Pistachio Financier, Tarragon Ice Cream and Apricot

FAST FACTS
Restaurant Recs: Jumbo Seafood where they fish the eel out of the tank for you; Café D; City Feed and Supply for sandwiches **Kitchen Tool(s):** Japanese mandolin; meat grinder; pasta machine **Interview Question:** Whose food do you love? What do you read for inspiration/instruction? **Flavor Combo(s):** Too many to list, but off the top of my head and our menu at the moment: pear, celery, lemon and parmesan salad; marsala pot de crème with shaved bitter chocolate and pine nut biscotti; artichoke and potato ravioli with green almonds; wood-grilled duck with a rhubarb tartine; swordfish with smoked shiitakes and ginger **Fave Cookbook(s):** A Return to Cooking by Eric Ripert; Sunday Suppers at Lucques by Suzanne Goin; The Zuni Café Cookbook by Judy Rodgers. **Chef to Cook for You:** Alain Passard – I love the idea of his going all-vegetarian, but making an exception for squab **Culinary Travel:** I love Asian food, and I'm dying to go Vietnam, Thailand, or Cambodia just for pure joy! India too.

L

Stephen Lyle
Chef/Owner | Village

62 W 9th St. New York, NY 10011

Restaurant E-mail: udaymonia@aol.com

Phone: (212) 505-3355

RESTAURANT FACTS
Seats: 130 **Weeknight Covers:** 130 **Weekend Covers:** 180+ **Check Average (with Wine):** $75 **Tasting Menu:** No **Kitchen Staff:** 5

CHEF FACTS
Cuisine: French American bistro **Born:** 1959 **Began Career:** 1976
Culinary School: L'École Hoteliere of Nice, France **Grad Year:** 1977
Stages: France: Le Homard a la Crème **Work History:** France:
Oustaou de Baumanieres; New York, NY: Le Plaisir, Restaurant
Leslie **Mentor(s):** Leslie Revsin, Masataka Kobayashi, Gerard Ferri
Protégée(s): Josh Rosenstein, David Ferraro **Awards:** All to be awarded posthumously, I'm sure **Affiliations:** Chefs From Hell **Languages Spoken:** French, Spanish

NOTABLE DISH(ES): Pan Roast of Oysters with Poblano Chiles on Toasted Cornbread

FAST FACTS
Restaurant Recs: Katz's Deli for pastrami sandwiches **Kitchen Tool(s):** Soup spoon; palate – food must taste good before it looks good **Interview Question:** Where do you see yourself in five years? It lets me know how serious they are. **Flavor Combo(s):** Salt, lemon juice and olive oil (on almost anything); raw beef with truffles **Fave Cookbook(s):** Bistro Cooking by Patricia Wells **Chef to Cook for You:** Michel Guerard, because he invented modern cuisine **Culinary Travel:** Anywhere I can learn something new that I love – Queens is a good place to start

Matthew Lyman
Chef/Co-Owner | Tender Greens

9523 Culver Blvd. Culver City, CA 90232

Restaurant E-mail: matt@tendergreensfood.com

Phone: (310) 842-8300

RESTAURANT FACTS
Seats: 100 **Weeknight Covers:** 600–800 **Weekend Covers:** 600–800 **Check Average (w/o Wine):** $13 **Kitchen Staff:** 6

CHEF FACTS
Cuisine: Modern American/French **Born:** 1969 **Began Career:** 1991 **Culinary School:** L'Académie de Cuisine Gaithsburg, Maryland **Grad Year:** 1990 **Work History:** Atlanta, GA: Seeger's, Dining Room at The Ritz-Carlton, Pentagon City; Santa Monica, CA: Shutters on the Beach Hotel, Hotel Casa del Mar **Mentor(s):** Guenter Seeger, Gerard Panguad, Jean Banchet **Languages Spoken:** Spanish

NOTABLE DISH(ES): House-Smoked Salmon with Warm Hush Puppies; Free Range Chicken Cooked Two Ways

FAST FACTS
Restaurant Recs: Korean BBQ **Kitchen Tool(s):** Chinese mandolin **Interview Question:** Where do you see yourself in five years?

{ MacPherson - Myers }

Grant MacPherson
Culinary Director and Head Chef | Sandy Lane

St. James, Barbados, West Indies BB24024

Restaurant E-mail: gmac@sandylane.com

Phone: 1 (246) 444-2000

RESTAURANT FACTS
Seats: 60 **Weeknight Covers:** 80 **Weekend Covers:** 80 **Check Average (w/o Wine):** $130 **Tasting Menu:** No **Kitchen Staff:** 40

CHEF FACTS
Other Restaurants: Bajan Blue, Spa Cafe, Country Club **Cuisine:** Modern French with Asian influence **Born:** 1962 **Began Career:** 1983 **Culinary School:** Niagara Rainbow Centre, Niagara Falls, Canada **Grad Year:** 1982 **Stages:** Singapore: Raffles Hotel; Malaysia: The Datai Hotel **Work History:** Las Vegas, NV: Wynn, Bellagio Hotel, Raffles Hotel, The Datai Hotel, The Regent; Hawaii: The Ritz-Carlton Hotel, Big Island of Hawaii; Malaysia: The Regent of Kualapur; Australia: The Regent; Canada: Sheraton Centre, The Four Seasons; England: The Four Seasons **Mentor(s):** Serge Dansereau; Manvinder Puri; Jean-Louis Palladin, Hishum Johari **Protégée(s):** Louis Tay, Ewart Wardhaugh, David Snyder **Awards:** 1999 Gourmet Games Las Vegas First Place; 1992 Culinary Olympics Gold Medal **Affiliations:** Jean-Louis Palladin Foundation, James Beard Foundation **Languages Spoken:** Basic French and basic Malay

NOTABLE DISH(ES): Braised Shank of Pauillac Lamb with Caramelized Veal Sweetbreads and Roast Artichoke Jus

FAST FACTS
Restaurant Recs: Archi Thai Kitchen for som tam salad **Kitchen Tool(s):** Gray Kunz spoon; fish slicer **Interview Question:** What are your hobbies? Do you play sports? I like to see if someone's a team player – if they'll get along well with everyone. **Flavor Combo(s):** Tomato, basil and garlic; soya sauce and ginger **Fave Cookbook(s):** Les Routiers Cookbook by Raymond Blanc **Chef to Cook for You:** Joël Robuchon, because he is the best chef in the world **Culinary Travel:** South America, because it is interesting and one of the few places I have not visited

Pino Maffeo
Chef

Boston, MA

CHEF FACTS

Cuisine: Heavy protein and Asian **Born:** 1970 **Began Career:** 1991
Culinary School: Newbury Culinary College **Grad Year:** 1991 **Work
History:** New York, NY: AZ, Pazo; Boston, MA: Restaurant L, Boston
Public; San Francisco, CA: Café Katie, Molhern and Shackern, San
Francisco's Inn at the Opera **Mentor(s):** My mother and Joël Robu-
chon **Awards:** 2006 Boston StarChefs.com Rising Star Chef Boston;
2006 Food & Wine Best New Chef **Affiliations:** A lot **Languages
Spoken:** Italian, Spanish, Portuguese, kitchen French

NOTABLE DISH(ES): Bruléed Hudson Valley Foie Gras with Barbecued
Japanese Eel and Balsamic Reduction

FAST FACTS

Restaurant Recs: Santoria Pizza **Kitchen Tool(s):** Syringes and Japanese knives **Interview Question:**
Are you married? Do you love to cook from your heart? You have to really love it. It's a lifestyle. You
can feel it when they do; you can see it in their eyes. **Flavor Combo(s):** Today it is sauternes and red
bull, but in general sour and sweet **Fave Cookbook(s):** That question is almost impossible for me
to answer since I read everything. I find that many books have something I can use, whether it be
Betty Crocker or one of those new great books coming from Spain. I actually collect super traditional
old-school cookbooks from the 1800's and 1900's. **Chef to Cook for You:** Besides my mother...I
think mothers and grandmothers make the most soulful food, which I need to be brought back down
to earth. If I had to pick a professional it would be Pierre Gagnaire. He is by far the best chef on the
planet. **Culinary Travel:** New York – it's the modern-day Rome and the culinary capital of the world. It
encompasses all cultures. You can't beat New York City. Next in line would be Paris, then London, and
Italy.

Kenny Magana
Director of Pastry | Wolfgang Puck Fine Dining Group

Las Vegas Blvd. South Ste. G-1 Las Vegas NV 89109

Restaurant E-mail: kenny.magana@wolfgangpuck.com

CHEF FACTS
Other Restaurants: Spago, Chinois, Postrio, Wolfgang Puck American Grill, Trattoria del Lupo, Wolfgang Puck Bar and Grill, CUT Las Vegas **Cuisine:** Pastry **Born:** 1971 **Began Career:** 1989 **Culinary School:** Joliet Junior College, Joliet, IL **Grad Year:** 1995 **Work History:** Chicago, IL: Spago; Las Vegas, NV: Renoir, Postrio, Sensi at the Bellagio, Wolfgang Puck; Atlantic City, New Jersey: American Grille **Mentor(s):** Sherry Yard, Christophe Ithurritze, David Robins, John Lagrone **Protégée(s):** Melissa Zahnter **Awards:** 2005 StarChefs.com Rising Star Pastry Chef Las Vegas; 2003 Las Vegas Life Epicurean Award Best Desserts; 2002 Raisin Dessert Competition Third Place; 2002 ACF International Hotel and Restaurant Show Gold Medal in Showpiece Competition; 2002 International Hotel and Restaurant Show Best of Show Patisserie Section **Affiliations:** Too many to count! And the Humane Society **Languages Spoken:** Kitchen Spanish

NOTABLE DISH(ES): Drinkable Apple Pie à la Mode with Brandied Apples and Ice Cream; SENSI's PB&J: Grape Gelée, Peanut Butter Wafer, Chocolate Mousse

FAST FACTS
Restaurant Recs: Drazil for their organic small plates: mashed potatoes with minced carrots, chives and herbs **Kitchen Tool(s):** Offset serrated knife – it cuts really crisp, and makes a lot of things easier **Interview Question:** I bring a piece of parchment paper cut into a triangle to the interview and I ask them, usually at the end of the interview, to make me a pastry bag. This does a couple of things: first, because it's unexpected, it shows me how well a person works under pressure; second, from my experience, the way a potential pastry cook makes the bag is directly related to their level of experience. **Flavor Combo(s):** I like combining sweet and savory. Balsamic, basil and strawberries; lemon and thyme; pineapple and cilantro. **Fave Cookbook(s):** Grand Livre de Cuisine by Alain Ducasse **Chef to Cook for You:** I really like José Andrés. He's really innovative and has a lot of techniques that are pretty cutting edge. I had lunch at one of his restaurants and it was amazing to have him cook me dinner would be pretty great. **Culinary Travel:** There are a lot of Spanish influences right now, so I suppose Spain would be a great place to go to. There are so many hidden, local places with bold and simple food.

Waldy Malouf
Chef/Owner | Beacon

25 W 56th St. New York, NY 10019

Restaurant E-mail: reservations@beaconnyc.com

Phone: (212) 332-0500

RESTAURANT FACTS
Seats: 200 **Weeknight Covers:** 200 **Weekend Covers:** 200 **Check Average (with Wine):** $65 **Tasting Menu:** Yes $85 **Kitchen Staff:** 7

CHEF FACTS
Cuisine: Regional; seasonal American; classic French **Born:** 1954 **Began Career:** 1975 **Culinary School:** The Culinary Institute of America, Hyde Park, NY **Grad Year:** 1975 **Stages:** France: Hotel de France **Work History:** France: The Four Seasons, La CrE-maillere; New York, NY: La Côte Basque, The Hudson River Club, The Rainbow Room, Beacon Restaurant & Bar **Mentor(s):** Bruno Elmer, Hermen Flekinstein, Charles Goodwich, Albert Cumin **Protégée(s):** David Burke **Awards:** 2001 Food & Wine Featured Chef; 1997 New York Times 3 stars; 1992 Cointreau Recipe Contest Winner **Affiliations:** The Culinary Institute of America Alumni Association Board of Directors, Windows of Hope Family Relief Fund, SOS, Taste of the Nation, God's Love We Deliver, City Meals-on-Wheels, JBF, Green Chimneys **Books Published:** High Heat: Grilling and Roasting Year-Round with Master Chef Waldy Malouf; The Hudson River Valley Cookbook: A Leading American Chef Savors the Region's Bounty **Languages Spoken:** Kitchen Spanish, French

NOTABLE DISH(ES): Baby Eggplant with Harissa, Mint and Roasted Root Vegetables

FAST FACTS
Restaurant Recs: The Burger Joint and The Parker Meridian – both for burgers **Kitchen Tool(s):** Tongs; self-designed rolling cutting board table with a garbage can hooked to the side **Interview Question:** How would you poach 36 eggs for use later in the day? **Flavor Combo(s):** In no particular order: lemon and butter; garlic and black pepper; red wine and onion; cumin and coriander seed; nutmeg and cream; ginger and lime **Fave Cookbook(s):** Le Repertoire De La Cuisine by L. Saulnier **Chef to Cook for You:** Antoine Carême – I would have enjoyed seeing his piéces montées and his techniques **Culinary Travel:** Southeast Asia, because I have never been there and I am very interested in the products and unfamiliar cooking techniques

Steve Mannino
Executive Chef | The Presidential Golf Club

45120 Waxpool Rd. Dulles, VA 20166

Restaurant E-mail: stevem@thepresidential.com

Phone: (703) 230-2000

RESTAURANT FACTS
Seats: 72 **Check Average (w/o Wine):** $65 **Tasting Menu:** Yes
Kitchen Staff: 22

CHEF FACTS
Cuisine: Mediterranean **Born:** 1973 **Began Career:** 1988 **Culinary School:** The Culinary Institute of America, Hyde Park, NY **Grad Year:** 1995 **Stages:** New York, NY: Aureole, Gotham Bar and Grill; Yountville, CA; The French Laundry; Chicago, IL: Spiaggia; Spain: el Bulli **Work History:** Chicago, IL: Les Nomads; Washington, DC: Olives; Las Vegas, NV: Olives; Boston, MA: Olives; San Francisco, CA: Brasserie Savoy **Mentor(s):** David Burke, Todd English **Protégée(s):** Seth Eldridge, Robert Decoste **Awards:** 2005 StarChefs.com Rising Star Chef Las Vegas

NOTABLE DISH(ES): Wild Mushroom and Quail Egg Ravioli; Risotto with Heirloom Tomato Salad

FAST FACTS
Restaurant Recs: La Chozita Grill Leesburg, Virginia – the best roasted chicken I've had in my life **Kitchen Tool(s):** A saucier spoon to put food on the plate **Interview Question:** That's easy: do you know exactly what you're getting into? I think too many cooks walk into a position either thinking they know it all or thinking that they can handle any situation. **Flavor Combo(s):** Sweet, salt; hot, cold **Fave Cookbook(s):** Molto Italiano by Mario Batali but, honestly, I'm more of a culinary magazine man **Culinary Travel:** Culinary travel is important to me. I'm headed to Rome this fall and I can't wait, but I'd also love the chance to travel more extensively and work in Spain.

M

Tony Mantuano
Chef/Partner | Spiaggia

980 N Michigan Ave. Chicago, IL 60611

Restaurant E-mail: tmantuano@levyrestaurants.com

Phone: (312) 280-2750

RESTAURANT FACTS
Seats: 90 **Weeknight Covers:** 110–120 **Weekend Covers:** 160
Check Average (with Wine): $95 **Tasting Menu:** Yes $165/$255
with wine **Kitchen Staff:** 12

CHEF FACTS
Other Restaurants: Mangia Restaurant **Cuisine:** Italian **Born:** 1954
Began Career: 1977 **Stages:** Italy: Dal Pescatore, Cannetto Sull'
Oglio, Da Romano, Viareggio, Albergo Del Sole, Maleo, Trattoria La
Mora, Lucca **Work History:** Italy: Dal Pescatore, Cannetto Sull' Oglio,
Da Romano, Viareggio, Al Bersagliere, Trattoria La Mora **Mentor(s):**
Nadia Santini, Massimo Ferrari, Franco Colombani **Protégée(s):**
Missy Robbins **Awards:** 2005 James Beard Foundation Best Chef Midwest; 2004 Chicago Tribune
Good Eating Award **Affiliations:** JBF **Books Published:** The Spiaggia Cookbook, Wine Bar Food

NOTABLE DISH(ES): Mediterranean Tuna Tartare

FAST FACTS
Restaurant Recs: Silver Seafood for whole fried pomfrit **Kitchen Tool(s):** Chitarra – it is a very old way
of making pasta from the Abruzzo region of Italy. The square spaghetti that it produces is always a hit
on our restaurant's menu, and when demonstrating its use, our guests are always fascinated by it. **Interview Question:** Describe your most memorable restaurant meal. Their answer shows their passion
for food and awareness of the total dining experience. **Flavor Combo(s):** Olive oil, garlic, tomato, and
basil **Fave Cookbook(s):** Right now it is Wine Bar Food, our new cookbook. It just came out! **Chef to
Cook for You:** Alain Ducasse – because he understands the soul of Mediterranean cooking **Culinary
Travel:** Italy, to see all the different regional cuisine. Each region has such passion for their ingredients; it is exciting and interesting.

Zarela Martinez
Owner | Zarela Restaurant

953 2nd Ave. New York, NY 10022

Restaurant E-mail: zarela@zarela.com

Phone: (212) 644-6740

RESTAURANT FACTS
Seats: 80 **Weeknight Covers:** 160 **Weekend Covers:** 200+ **Kitchen Staff:** 4–5

CHEF FACTS
Cuisine: Regional Mexican **Born:** 1947 **Began Career:** 1976 **Work History:** New York, NY: Cafe Marimba **Mentor(s):** Paul Prudhomme **Protégée(s):** Aaron Sanchez, Gary Jacobson **Awards:** 2006 The Coalition for Hispanic Family Services "The Orgullo de la Comunidad" Award **Affiliations:** IACP, IWF, JBF **Books Published:** Food from My Heart; The Food and Life of Oaxaca; Zarela's Veracruz **Languages Spoken:** Spanish

NOTABLE DISH(ES): Pan Del Dia de los Muertos

FAST FACTS
Restaurant Recs: Sripraphai for drunken noodles **Kitchen Tool(s):** Molcajete; electric spice grinder for grinding Mexican cuisine's many spices **Interview Question:** What do you do for fun? **Flavor Combo(s):** Chipotle, garlic and olive oil; poblano, onion and garlic; canela, cloves and cumin; cilantro with anything; hoja santa, garlic and jalapeño **Fave Cookbook(s):** I have basically cooked my through all of Peggy Knickerbocker's books **Chef to Cook for You:** There is a chef named Ali in Queens at The Kabob Cafe. He always remembers my likes and dislikes and constantly surprises me. Still there is nothing more special than when my son Aaron cooks for me. He does it with so much love. **Culinary Travel:** Mexico – the regional cooking is so distinct that is always exciting to see the different styles and flavors; China for this same reason.

Sam Mason
Executive Chef | Tailor

525 Broome St. New York, NY 11206

Restaurant E-mail: samasonnyc@gmail.com

Phone: (212) 477-2900

RESTAURANT FACTS

Seats: 45 **Weeknight Covers:** 45 **Weekend Covers:** 95 **Check Average (with Wine):** $65 **Tasting Menu:** Yes $95 **Kitchen Staff:** 5

CHEF FACTS

Cuisine: Pastry with savory influences **Born:** 1974 **Began Career:** 1994 **Culinary School:** Johnson & Wales, Providence, RI **Grad Year:** 1994 **Stages:** France: Ladurée **Work History:** New York, NY: Park Avenue Café, Palladin, Union Pacific, Atlas, wd~50 **Mentor(s):** Jean-Louis Palladin **Awards:** 2005 StarChefs.com Rising Star Pastry Chef New York; 2005 Pastry Art & Design Top Ten Pastry Chefs **Affiliations:** French Culinary Institute Instructor

NOTABLE DISH(ES): Caramelized Apple with Miso Ice Cream; Banana-Cocoa Ravioli with Coffee Soil and Mustard Ice Cream

FAST FACTS

Restaurant Recs: Momofuku for great noodle dishes; Peasant for amazing rustic Italian fare **Kitchen Tool(s):** Immersion circulator; radio; ice cream machine; Pacojet; Vita-Prep **Interview Question:** We hire based on many criteria: attitude, enthusiasm, willingness to learn. We rarely hire someone solely in regard to their experience. **Flavor Combo(s):** Foie gras and peanut butter; black olives and cherries **Fave Cookbook(s):** Michel Bras' Cookbooks **Chef to Cook for You:** Jean-Louis Palladin, because he is my mentor and I miss him to death. And, he would have to let me watch. **Culinary Travel:** I'm kind of a spice fanatic. So, Morocco for the spices and then Asia for the produce.

Hemant Mathur
Chef/Owner | Dévi

8 18th St. New York, NY 10003

Restaurant E-mail: contact@devinyc.com

Phone: (212) 691-1300

RESTAURANT FACTS
Seats: 70 **Weeknight Covers:** 75 **Weekend Covers:** 120 **Check Average (with Wine):** $65 **Check Average (w/o Wine):** $45 **Tasting Menu:** Yes $65/$110 with wine **Kitchen Staff:** 10

CHEF FACTS
Other Restaurants: New Delhi, India: Veda **Cuisine:** Indian (Tandoor) **Born:** 1967 **Began Career:** 1984 **Culinary School:** Institute of Hotel Management, Catering and Nutrition, India **Grad Year:** 1984 **Stages:** New York, NY: Tamarind; India: Bukhara **Work History:** New York, NY: Diwan, Tamarind; India: Sonar Goan, Rambagh Palace Taj Hotel, Bukhara; Germany: Seeterson, Kashmir Palace **Mentor(s):** Arvind Bhargava **Protégée(s):** Rajendra Rana **Affiliations:** Citymeals-on-Wheels, Taste of the Nation, Feast of Many Moons, Share our Strength, City Harvest and others. **Languages Spoken:** Hindi, Spanish

NOTABLE DISH(ES): Tandoori Prawns; Falooda

FAST FACTS
Restaurant Recs: Sripraphai – a Thai restaurant in Woodside, Queens, for the duck **Kitchen Tool(s):** Tandoor **Interview Question:** What is mis en place?

Nobu Matsuhisa
Chef/Owner | Nobu New York

105 Hudson St. New York, NY 10013

Restaurant E-mail: junef@noburestaurants.com

Phone: (212) 219-0500

CHEF FACTS

Other Restaurants: New York, NY: Nobu Next Door, Nobu Fifty Seven; London, England; Ubon by Nobu, Nobu Berkeley St.; Beverly Hills, CA: Matsuhisa; Tokyo, Japan: Nobu, Las Vegas, NV: Nobu; Malibu, CA: Nobu; Milan, Italy: Nobu; Miami Beach, FL: Nobu; Dallas, TX: Nobu; Nassau, Bahamas; Nobu; Kowloon, Hong Kong: Nobu; Waikiki, HI: Nobu; Melbourne, Australia: Nobu; San Diego, CA; Nobu; West Hollywood, CA: Nobu; Aspen, CO: Matsuhisa; Mykonos, Greece: Matsuhisa **Cuisine:** New style Japanese **Born:** 1949 **Work History:** Japan: Matsuei; Beverly Hill, CA: Matsuhisa **Awards:** 1999-2006, 1997 James Beard Foundation Outstanding Chef nomination; 2002 James Beard Foundation Who's Who of Food and Beverage in America; 1998 Los Angeles Times Magazine Rising Star Southern California; 1995 New York Times 3 stars; 1989 Food and Wine Magazine Best New Chef **Books Published:** Nobu the Cookbook; Nobu Now; Japanese Finger Food- Nobu Style; Nobu West **Languages Spoken:** Japanese

NOTABLE DISH(ES): Yellowtail Sashimi with Jalepeno and Ponzu; Broiled Black Cod with Miso; Rock Shrimp Tempura with Creamy Spicy Sauce

FAST FACTS

Restaurant Recs: Kokekokko – a yakitori place in Los Angeles **Kitchen Tool(s):** Sashimi knife **Interview Question:** How much do you love this job? **Flavor Combo(s):** Soy sauce with anything **Fave Cookbook(s):** Any seafood book **Chef to Cook for You:** Mara Martin of Da Fiore in Venice – this is my favorite restaurant! **Culinary Travel:** I have been fortunate enough to travel around the world, but I would like to take some time to travel along the coast of Japan from the northern tip of Hokkaido to the southern tip of Okinawa to appreciate all the local produce and seafood

Ignacio Mattos
Chef | il Buco

47 Bond St. New York NY 10012

Restaurant E-mail: jamiekohen@gmail.com

Phone: (212) 533-1932

RESTAURANT FACTS
Weeknight Covers: 160 **Weekend Covers:** 200 **Check Average (with Wine):** $80 **Tasting Menu:** No **Kitchen Staff:** 5

CHEF FACTS
Born: 1979 **Began Career:** 1998 **Culinary School:** One year at a culinary school in Montevideo, Uruguay **Stages:** I did an internship with Michel Kerever, he was a mentor of Alan Passard. **Work History:** Uruguay: Los Negros; Argentina: Francis Mallman 1884, Patagonia Sur; Brazil: Figueira Rubaiyat; Spain: Martin Berasategui; Italy: il Cesare; San Francisco, CA: Chez Panisse; New York, NY: Spotted Pig **Mentor(s):** Francis Mallman **Affiliations:** James Beard Foundation, Slow Food, Food Bank for NYC, The We Campaign – part of The Alliance for Climate Protection, UNICEF, NYC Food Film Festival, Degustibus, Institute for Culinary Education **Languages Spoken:** Spanish

NOTABLE DISH(ES): Colorado Rack of Lamb with Baby Artichokes, Garlic Nougatine, and Citrus Confit

FAST FACTS
Restaurant Recs: Nicky's Vietnamese sandwiches **Kitchen Tool(s):** Where I came from, you don't have that much. You just need a knife and a match. **Interview Question:** I try to understand the background of the guy – what he's doing, where he's coming from. I don't follow an ABC routine of questions. Where do you like to eat? What kind of cooking? What kind of music? **Flavor Combo(s):** I am not sure if I would call it a "combination" but I'm a lemon fanatic, and also dry chilies. I use them in everything, same as a great salt. With great quality and just the right pinch of these ingredients, I could create a bigger impression in pretty much any dish I create. **Fave Cookbook(s):** Elizabeth David – any of her books; Julia Child – any of her books **Chef to Cook for You:** Gilbert Pilgram – he used to be the Chef at Chez Panisse; Russell Moore – he also used to be at Chez Panisse and is opening Camino in Oakland; Santiago Garat – he owns Standard in Buenos Aires. The great thing is that all of them have already cooked for me at their houses. And those have been my favorite meals. **Culinary Travel:** I would love to take a flight tomorrow to Turkey and Lebanon and spend some good time eating there. I keep trying to figure out why that kind of food is so special to me. Most people have an obsession with other types of food, but for me, Turkish and Lebanese food are so simple, fresh and charming, while at the same time very pleasant, full of flavor and very rounded. I love Mediterranean food but here is that great mix of the Middle East with the Mediterranean.

Jeff Mauro
Consulting Chef

Chicago, IL

Restaurant E-mail: ccmhockeyman@hotmail.com

Phone: (773) 477-5845

CHEF FACTS

Cuisine: Innovative American **Born:** 1977 **Began Career:** 1997 **Culinary School:** Johnson & Wales University, Providence, RI **Grad Year:** 1997 **Stages:** Boston, MA: Back Bay Brewing Company **Work History:** Philadelphia, PA: Opus 251, Susanna Foo; Chicago, IL: Charlie Trotter's, North Pond, Powerhouse; Las Vegas, NV: Bradley Ogden **Mentor(s):** Sven Mede, Bill Kim, Bradley Ogden **Languages Spoken:** Kitchen Spanish

NOTABLE DISH(ES): Pan Roasted Amish Chicken with Foie Gras Chicken Thigh Tortellini

FAST FACTS

Restaurant Recs: Gino's East – for deep-dish cheese and sausage pizza **Kitchen Tool(s):** Fish spatula **Interview Question:** Who is your favorite chef idol? **Flavor Combo(s):** Fennel and fish **Fave Cookbook(s):** The Food Lover's Companion by Sharon Tyler Herbst; Charcuterie by Michael Ruhlman and Brian Polcyn; Art Culinaire Magazine **Chef to Cook for You:** Raymond Blanc – I did an event with him many years ago during which I realized that his passion and knowledge have helped inspire me to become a better, more focused chef **Culinary Travel:** Germany – I haven't been yet, and my grandfather is from there so it would be interesting to see

Tony Maws
Chef/Owner | Craigie Street Bistrot

5 Craigie Circle Harvard Sq. Cambridge, MA 02138
Restaurant E-mail: tmaws@craigiestreetbistrot.com
Phone: (617) 497-5511

RESTAURANT FACTS
Seats: 49 **Weeknight Covers:** 60–70 **Weekend Covers:** 80–90
Check Average (with Wine): $86 **Tasting Menu:** Yes $80/$115
Kitchen Staff: 5–6

CHEF FACTS
Cuisine: French **Born:** 1970 **Began Career:** 1985 **Stages:** New York, NY: wd~50 **Work History:** Cambridge, MA: East Coast Grill; San Francisco, CA: La Folie, Postrio; Santa Fe, NM: Coyote Cafe **Mentor(s):** Chris Schlesinger, Roland Passot, Ken Oringer **Awards:** 2006 StarChefs.com Rising Star Chef Boston; 2006 Boston Magazine Best French Restaurant; 2006 Boston Magazine Best Chef 2006; 2006 Wine Enthusiast Best in Fine Dining; 2005 Food & Wine Best New Chefs **Affiliations:** JBF, Chefs Collaborative **Languages Spoken:** French

NOTABLE DISH(ES): Fried Clams with Purple Potato Chips and Ramp Salsa; Red Chile Marinated Skirt Steak

FAST FACTS
Restaurant Recs: Rod Dee, a tiny little dive Thai place in Brookline. Usually I get the Larb, a traditional Thai dish of ground pork, chilies and lime. **Kitchen Tool(s):** Either the plastic board scraper or the "spoonula" from William Sonoma. The one they make is the perfect size for working the line. **Interview Question:** If you've quit a job, what made you quit? What's the definition of a bad boss? What are your ambitions? If you come work for me, what position do you want? **Flavor Combo(s):** We have something here called the Craigie Street Trinity: fennel seed, coriander seed and dried New Mexican chilies **Fave Cookbook(s):** The New Making of a Cook: The Art, Techniques, and Science of Good Cooking by Madeleine Kamman **Chef to Cook for You:** Michel Bras because he's freaking brilliant! He mixes technology and nature like no other chef, his food looks like food and tastes even better. **Culinary Travel:** I would either go back to Singapore, a place I've already been, or go to Japan, as I have been dying to go

Dean Max
Executive Chef | 3030 Ocean

3030 Holiday Drive Fort Lauderdale, FL 33316

Restaurant E-mail: deanjamesmax@yahoo.com

Phone: (954) 765-3130

RESTAURANT FACTS
Seats: 110 **Weeknight Covers:** 175 **Weekend Covers:** 225 **Check Average (with Wine):** $70 **Tasting Menu:** Yes **Kitchen Staff:** 7–8

CHEF FACTS
Other Restaurants: Columbus, OH: Latitude 41; Grand Cayman: The Brasserie; Baltimore, MD: Water Table **Cuisine:** Modern American seafood **Born:** 1967 **Began Career:** 1988 **Stages:** Washington, DC: Dining Room at the Ritz-Carlton Pentagon City **Work History:** Atlanta, GA: Dining Room at The Ritz-Carlton; San Francisco, CA: Savoy Hotel; Washington, DC: Dining Room at The Ritz-Carlton Pentagon City **Mentor(s):** Gerard Pangaud, Guenter Seeger, my mom **Protégée(s):** Peter Rudolph, Andrew DeGroot, Paula DaSilva, Garrett Gooch, Stephen Johnston **Awards:** 2006 National Restaurant Association Best Chef South Florida; 2005 Boca Magazine Best Chef South Florida **Affiliations:** AIWF, The Florida Restaurant Association, The Advisory Committee for the State of Florida Department of Seafood and Aquaculture **Books Published:** A Life By the Sea

NOTABLE DISH(ES): Roasted Lamb, Potatoes and Asparagus

FAST FACTS
Restaurant Recs: Las Fajitas **Kitchen Tool(s):** Fish knife **Interview Question:** Why do you want to be a chef? The answers are endless. **Flavor Combo(s):** Bacon and vinegar **Fave Cookbook(s):** White Heat by Marco Pierre White **Chef to Cook for You:** Probably Georges Blanc because I like his simple style and would like to see how he handles the product **Culinary Travel:** India – for the spices, and because I have never been

Kevin Maxey
Chef | Craft, Dallas

2440 North Houston St. Dallas, TX 75219

Restaurant E-mail: info@craftdallas.com

Phone: (214) 397-4111

RESTAURANT FACTS
Seats: 130 **Weeknight Covers:** 100 **Weekend Covers:** 200 **Check Average (with Wine):** $85 **Tasting Menu:** No **Kitchen Staff:** 7

CHEF FACTS
Cuisine: Modern American with Italian influences **Born:** 1973 **Began Career:** 1994 **Stages:** New York, NY: Le Bernardin **Work History:** Seattle, WA: Rover's; New York, NY: Gramercy Tavern **Mentor(s):** Tom Collichio, John Schafer **Awards:** 2007 StarChefs.com Rising Star Chef Dallas **Affiliations:** SOS, North Texas Food Bank **Languages Spoken:** Kitchen Spanish, Italian

NOTABLE DISH(ES): Jumbo Lump Crab Risotto with Baby Sorrel and Lemon Confit; Japanese Squash Tortellini with Chestnut Honey and Sage; Juniper-Crusted Wild Boar with Dried Fruit

FAST FACTS
Restaurant Recs: Cuquita's for Mexican food like chicken mole and enchiladas; Kuby's for beer and sausage **Kitchen Tool(s):** Gray Kunz spoon; meat fork **Interview Question:** How do you define sauté? How do you braise short ribs? **Flavor Combo(s):** I like citrus and poultry or citrus and game together, like blood orange and guinea hen or tangerine and rabbit **Fave Cookbook(s):** Cookbooks by Mario Batali and by Julia Child **Chef to Cook for You:** My great grandmother. There are so many dishes that inspire me from my grandmother, so I would like to go back to the woman who taught her and see the originals. **Culinary Travel:** I like to go to Vietnam because everything here is so Americanized that it's hard to figure out what is authentic

M

Juan Mario Maza
Chef | Alta Cocina

5837 Sunset Drive Pinecrest, Fl 33143

Restaurant E-mail: mariomaza@altacocinarestaurant.com

Phone: (305) 662-7435

RESTAURANT FACTS
Seats: 74–110 **Weeknight Covers:** 50 **Weekend Covers:** 140 **Check Average (with Wine):** $50 **Tasting Menu:** Yes **Kitchen Staff:** 4

CHEF FACTS
Cuisine: Fusion: Caribbean, Latin, American **Born:** 1982 **Began Career:** 2002 **Culinary School:** Johnson & Wales University **Grad Year:** 2006 **Stages:** Miami, FL: Azul at the Mandarin Oriental **Work History:** Miami, FL: Azul at the Mandarin Oriental, Café Sambal, Michy's **Mentor(s):** Vani (my wife), Jason Schaan, Michelle Bernstein **Languages Spoken:** Spanish

NOTABLE DISH(ES): Fusion dell Rabo: Homemade Gnocchi Gorgonzola Sauce with Braised Oxtail pulled from the bone

FAST FACTS
Restaurant Recs: Panya Thai - we've been going there for four years. I always have the same thing: crispy duck. **Kitchen Tool(s):** The cutting board **Interview Question:** Have you attended culinary school and if yes, can you work mornings, nights, weekends, and holidays? **Flavor Combo(s):** Sweet and spicy **Chef to Cook for You:** Probably Emeril: I just love that guy and he was a big influence in my decision to go to Johnson and Wales **Culinary Travel:** Asia – I really admire the respect Asian chefs show to food and to the profession

Vicky McCaffree
Chef | Yarrow Bay Grill

1270 Carillon Point Kirkland, WA 98033

Restaurant E-mail: grillinfo@ybgrill.com

Phone: (425) 889-9052

RESTAURANT FACTS
Seats: 100 **Weeknight Covers:** 80 **Weekend Covers:** 100+ **Check Average (with Wine):** $70+ **Tasting Menu:** No **Kitchen Staff:** 4

CHEF FACTS
Cuisine: Local Northwest cuisine **Born:** 1956 **Began Career:** 1986ish **Work History:** Seattle, WA: The Surrogate Hostess, Rosselinni's **Mentor(s):** Barbara Tropp, Joyce Goldstein, Alice Waters, Deborah Madison **Protégée(s):** Jessica Campbell, Don Devan, Scott Samuel **Awards:** 1996 Columbia Crest Premier Chef's Competition **Affiliations:** The Children's Hospital and other local charities **Languages Spoken:** Kitchen Spanish

NOTABLE DISH(ES): Sake King Salmon; Berry Sorbet Terrine

FAST FACTS
Restaurant Recs: Monsoon in Seattle – a wonderful upscale Vietnamese restaurant **Kitchen Tool(s):** Tongs – they are an extension of my hand every time I cook **Interview Question:** Who are your favorite celebrity chefs and/or do you follow what's happening in the culinary world? This tells me how serious a potential cook is about the culinary business, or if it's just a job. **Flavor Combo(s):** I like the classic spicy, sweet and salty combination **Fave Cookbook(s):** Chez Panisse Menu Cookbook by Alice Waters is my favorite, but I have all of her books and reference them constantly **Chef to Cook for You:** Alice Waters. My whole career I have considered her a mentor. I've always been inspired by her approach to food. There are also so many great young chefs around these days doing such amazing things who are on my list as well. **Culinary Travel:** Thailand

Shawn McClain
Chef/Owner | Green Zebra

1460 W Chicago Ave. Chicago, IL 60622

Restaurant E-mail: shawn@springrestaurant.net

Phone: (312) 243-7100

RESTAURANT FACTS
Seats: 60 **Weeknight Covers:** 80 **Weekend Covers:** 120 **Check Average (with Wine):** $40 **Tasting Menu:** Yes $55/$90 with wine **Kitchen Staff:** 5

CHEF FACTS
Other Restaurants: Custom House, Spring **Cuisine:** New American **Born:** 1967 **Began Career:** 1985 **Culinary School:** Kendall College, Evanston, IL **Grad Year:** 1990 **Work History:** Chicago, IL: The Boulevard at the Intercontinental, Les Plumes Restaurant; Wilmette, IL: Betise; Evanston, IL: Trio **Mentor(s):** Henry Adaniya from Trio definitely had the biggest impact, both as someone who has a great palate and as a business owner and friend **Awards:** 2008 StarChefs.com Rising Star Restaurateur Chicago; 2006 James Beard Foundation Best Chef Midwest; 2004 Jean Banchet Awards Celebrity Chef; 2001 Esquire Chef of the Year; 2001 James Beard Foundation Rising Star Chef **Affiliations:** We work with a lot of charities. Anything to do with hospice, MOD, SOS, market charities and the American Heart Association to name a few.

NOTABLE DISH(ES):
Filet of Beef with Braised Oxtail, Wild Mushrooms, and Sweet Soy; Hawaiian Blue Prawn with Lemongrass and Coconut Broth

FAST FACTS
Restaurant Recs: I love the food at Le Colonial, which is not off the beaten path, but I get the shrimp beignets, the bo satay tenderloin and the sweet potato on rice. I also like Sushi from Bob San, Mirai, and Kamehachi, and San Soo Gap San - a 24-hour Korean BBQ place. **Kitchen Tool(s):** Vita-Prep – because, unlike traditional bar blenders, it's a serious workhorse. For sauces, purées, and finishing soups, nothing comes close. **Interview Question:** Why will my restaurant make you a better cook and how will it get you closer to your goals? This question forces applicants to focus on the future, as well as the present. **Flavor Combo(s):** Anything with caramel **Fave Cookbook(s):** Essential Cuisine by Michel Bras **Chef to Cook for You:** Pierre Gagnaire **Culinary Travel:** Japan – I haven't had a chance to go yet. I incorporate a lot of Japanese ingredients in my cooking and I would like to see the food first hand.

Jason McClain
Chef | East Hampton Point

295 Three Mile Harbor Rd. East Hampton, NY 11937

Restaurant E-mail: chefjason@atlanticbb.net

Phone: (631) 329-2800

RESTAURANT FACTS
Seats: 200 **Weeknight Covers:** 100–150 **Weekend Covers:** 400–600 **Check Average (with Wine):** $75 **Tasting Menu:** Yes **Kitchen Staff:** 10–15

CHEF FACTS
Cuisine: Creative global cuisine **Born:** 1973 **Began Career:** 1988 **Culinary School:** Culinary Institute of America, Hyde Park, NY **Grad Year:** 1994 **Work History:** Philadelphia, PA: The Fountain Room at the Four Seasons; New York, NY: Fifty-Seven at the Four Seasons; Miami Beach, FL: Sirena at the Shore Club, Nikki Beach, Pearl Restaurant, 8 1/2, Jason's at The Harrison; Chicago, IL: Narcisse **Mentor(s):** Martin Hammond **Awards:** The Sun Post Best New Chef; The Sun Post Best New Restaurant

FAST FACTS
Restaurant Recs: In Miami: A little Mexican place on Calle Ocho called La Mexicana for the chicken enchiladas or chorizo tacos **Kitchen Tool(s):** The immersion blender, because it is great for emulsifying **Interview Question:** Will you listen to me? Obviously I want them to say yes! You need to listen to learn. **Flavor Combo(s):** Oxtail, tamarind and pickled papaya; duck confit, brown butter and sage; truffles and lemon **Fave Cookbook(s):** The French Laundry Cookbook by Thomas Keller **Chef to Cook for You:** Alfred Portale – I just like that his food is clean, well-presented and straightforward. The food speaks for itself. **Culinary Travel:** Italy. I've done Barcelona and France, and I love the simplicity of Italian food; when it's done right it is so good.

M

South Florida

Jeff McInnis
Chef de Cuisine | The DiLido Beach Club

1 Lincoln Road Miami Beach, FL 33139

Restaurant E-mail: jeffrey.mcinnis@ritzcarlton.com

Phone: (786) 276-4000

RESTAURANT FACTS
Seats: 140 **Weeknight Covers:** 225 **Weekend Covers:** 350 **Check Average (with Wine):** $50 **Tasting Menu:** Yes upon request **Kitchen Staff:** 4

CHEF FACTS
Cuisine: Southeast Mediterranean **Born:** 1978 **Began Career:** 1993 **Culinary School:** Johnson and Wales, Charleston, SC **Grad Year:** 1998 **Work History:** Charleston, SC: Atlanticville; St. John, VI: Asolare; San Francisco, CA: Azie; Charlottesville, VA: Five Star Orient Express Hotel **Mentor(s):** Jody Denton, Phil Corr, Thomas Connell, my father, and my grandfather **Awards:** 2008 StarChefs.com Rising Star Chef

NOTABLE DISH(ES): Melons and Cucumber with Lemon, Mint, and Yogurt Sorbet; Lemon and Apricot Roasted Chicken with Sardinian Couscous "Risotto," Pistachio, Manchego, and Arugula

FAST FACTS
Restaurant Recs: Liberty Grill serves great blood sausage. The Abbey is a total dive bar that is open 365 days a year and is a local spot; they make their own brews, which are great. **Kitchen Tool(s):** I like my Pacojet - it allows me to make quick small batches of sorbets. We also keep a tank of liquid nitrogen on hand in the kitchen. Between these two pieces of equipment we are able to make some interesting and original items like parmesan ice cream, goat cheese sorbet, and cucumber sorbet. **Interview Question:** Why are you passionate about the cooking industry? What drives you? **Flavor Combo(s):** I love sweet and spicy, like Chinese char siu pork. Umame and sour is another one. Also, I like using texture combinations that are not flavors but still excite everyone. Crispy and soft, hot and cold. **Fave Cookbook(s):** Of course the el Bulli books are blowing everyone's mind right now. I still pick up the French Laundry Cookbook for French inspiration, and The Joy of Cooking is great for a solid, tested recipes that you can depend on. Recently I was given Ana Sortun's book Spice, which has made a difference in the way I think and cook. Arabesque has also been a favorite of mine. **Chef to Cook for You:** It would be nice to pick Auguste Escoffier's brain to determine what drove him to succeed. But later this month I've got a reservation at The French Laundry, so Corey Lee and Thomas Keller will do just fine for now. **Culinary Travel:** I'd really like to visit Lebanon. My favorite places to eat are in Spain, especially Madrid, Malaga, and Mallorca, and I really enjoy Istanbul, Turkey. These places are saturated in history and culture, and it shows in their food. Also most of these places design their menus around seafood.

Ethan McKee
Chef | Rock Creek

5300 Wisconsin Ave NW Washington, DC 20015

Restaurant E-mail: info@rockcreekrestaurant.com

Phone: 202-966-7625

RESTAURANT FACTS
Seats: 160 **Weeknight Covers:** 80 **Weekend Covers:** 200 **Check Average (with Wine):** $50 **Tasting Menu:** No **Kitchen Staff:** 4–6

CHEF FACTS
Cuisine: Conscious cuisine **Born:** 1977 **Began Career:** 1998 **Culinary School:** L'Academie de Cuisine, Gaithersburg, MD **Grad Year:** 1998 **Stages:** Arlington, VA: Carlyle Grand Café **Work History:** Vail, CO: The Left Bank; Washington, DC: Equinox **Mentor(s):** Todd Gray, Luc Myer, Ris Lacoste **Languages Spoken:** Spanish

NOTABLE DISH(ES): Chanterelle Risotto with Corn and Crispy Sweetbreads; Sautéed Soft Shell Crab with Roasted Shiitake Vinaigrette and Pickled Ramps; Terrine of Beet-Cured Salmon, Sweet Melon Soup, Pickled Cherry with Foie Duck Prosciutto

FAST FACTS
Restaurant Recs: Dolce Vita for pizza; Yoko for sushi **Kitchen Tool(s):** Pasta machine **Interview Question:** Are you willing to work everyday? **Flavor Combo(s):** Garlic, onion, chilies and citrus **Fave Cookbook(s):** Charcuterie by Michael Ruhlman and Brian Polcyn; The French Laundry Cookbook by Thomas Keller **Chef to Cook for You:** Thomas Keller – because I still haven't had a chance to get out to Napa and I would really like to try his food **Culinary Travel:** Thailand - since I have been getting into a more healthy style of cooking, going to Thailand could bring a lot of inspiration. I can't use butter or cream in my dishes so I could learn a lot from the style and ingredients used in Thai cuisine.

NOBHILL
Sven Mede

Sven Mede
Chef | Nobhill

MGM Grand Las Vegas, NV 89109

Restaurant E-mail: sven_mede@lv.mgmgrand.com

Phone: (702) 891-7337

RESTAURANT FACTS
Seats: 125 **Weeknight Covers:** 150 **Weekend Covers:** 250 **Check Average (with Wine):** $130 **Tasting Menu:** Yes $125 **Kitchen Staff:** 12

CHEF FACTS
Cuisine: New American **Born:** 1972 **Began Career:** 1996 **Culinary School:** Bad Reichenhall, Germany **Grad Year:** 1989 **Stages:** England: Aubergine **Work History:** England: Le Manoir aux Quat' Saisons; Las Vegas, NV: Bradley Ogden; Chicago, IL: Charlie Trotter's **Mentor(s):** Raymond Blanc, Charlie Trotter, Bradley Ogden **Protégée(s):** Jeff Mauro **Awards:** 2005 StarChefs.com Rising Star Chef Las Vegas **Affiliations:** JBF **Languages Spoken:** German

NOTABLE DISH(ES): Marinated Tuna with Sea Urchin; English Pea Risotto with Gazpacho Sauce

FAST FACTS
Restaurant Recs: Lotus of Siam for deep fried catfish **Kitchen Tool(s):** Microplane zester to give dishes an incredible final touch **Interview Question:** What is your favorite dish and why? I want to find out about their passion for food. **Flavor Combo(s):** Olive oil, garlic and lemon **Fave Cookbook(s):** Art Culinaire; Nobu the Cookbook by Nobu Matsuhisa; Tetsuya by Tetsuya Wakuda **Chef to Cook for You:** I would have my grandmother cook for me. Her food is what I remember as a kid as the greatest. **Culinary Travel:** Japan, for the sense of respect and techniques. Their culture really shows in their food.

Julian Medina
Chef/Owner | Toloache

251 West 50th St. New York, NY 10019

Restaurant E-mail: chefmedina@gmail.com

Phone: (212) 581-1818

RESTAURANT FACTS
Seats: 90 **Weeknight Covers:** 150–180 **Weekend Covers:** 200–220 **Check Average (with Wine):** $45–$50 **Tasting Menu:** No **Kitchen Staff:** 5

CHEF FACTS
Cuisine: Contemporary Mexican **Born:** 1975 **Culinary School:** The French Culinary Institute, New York, NY **Grad Year:** 1999 **Stages:** Mexico City, Mexico: Hacienda de los Morales **Work History:** Mexico: Les Celebrites; New York, NY: Pampano, Maya, Sushi Samba, Zócalo; Miami, FL: Sushi Samba **Mentor(s):** Alban Du Temple, Richard Sandoval **Affiliations:** JBF, City Harvest **Languages Spoken:** Spanish

NOTABLE DISH(ES): Trio of Guacamole con Granada y Rojo; Seared Sea Scallops with Honshimeji Mushrooms, Avocado Fries with Meyer Lemon-Chili Vinaigrette

FAST FACTS
Restaurant Recs: El Paso Taqueria for Pancita (tripe soup with chilie guajillo) **Kitchen Tool(s):** Molcajete to grind my spices and salsas **Interview Question:** Why did you leave your last job? I'm looking for a responsible cook, not necessarily one with a lot of experience. **Flavor Combo(s):** Citrus and chili pepper **Fave Cookbook(s):** Nobu the Cookbook by Nobu Matsuhisa **Chef to Cook for You:** Masaharu Morimoto, because I love Japanese food **Culinary Travel:** To Peru for the variety of chilies, seafood, and meats

M

Ron Mendoza
Executive Pastry Chef | Bouchée Restaurant and Bar

7th Ave. & Monte Verde Carmel, CA 93921

Restaurant E-mail: ronmendozapastry@yahoo.com

Phone: (831) 626-7880

RESTAURANT FACTS
Seats: 24–30 **Weeknight Covers:** 40 **Weekend Covers:** 40 **Check Average (with Wine):** $200 **Check Average (w/o Wine):** $130 **Tasting Menu:** Yes $115 **Kitchen Staff:** 5

CHEF FACTS
Other Restaurants: L'Auberge Carmel; Bouchée Bistro; Cantinetta Luca **Cuisine:** Contemporary American pastry **Born:** 1973 **Began Career:** 1999 **Culinary School:** The California School of Culinary Arts, Pasadena, CA **Grad Year:** 2000 **Work History:** Los Angeles, CA: Patina Restaurant, Boule Patisserie, Sona Restaurant, Ortolan; Beverly Hills, CA: Jaan Restaurant at L'Hermitage Hotel; Yountville, CA: The French Laundry **Mentor(s):** Michelle Myers, David Myers **Protégée(s):** Robert Tarlow, Elizabeth Gottfried, Miho Travi, Karen Yoo, Alison Roman **Awards:** 2006 StarChefs.com Rising Star Pastry Chef Los Angeles

NOTABLE DISH(ES): Milk Confit Cake with Grapefruit Sorbet and Pistachio Ice Cream; Smoked White Chocolate Mousse with Meyer Lemon Granita and Shiso Ice Cream

FAST FACTS
Restaurant Recs: Tito's Tacos in Los Angeles. I can eat about eight at a time. **Kitchen Tool(s):** Matfer plastic bench scraper; Pacojet; an open mind **Interview Question:** What are your favorite bands? **Flavor Combo(s):** I really like something creamy mixed with herbs, it's a very refreshing and natural combination. I just did a yogurt parfait with a Thai basil ice cream which was really nice. **Fave Cookbook(s):** Dessert Cuisine by Oriol Balaguer because it's technical, yet inspirational. The el Bulli Cookbook by Ferran and Albert Adriá for the beauty of the plated dish. There should be a museum with those photos. **Chef to Cook for You:** I would love to get all my pastry friends who I have worked with in the past together to cook for each other. It would be great to see the new ideas they've taken from new jobs and to see each others' evolution. **Culinary Travel:** I would love to go to the south of France to go to Michel Bras, as well as to check out the produce and flavors of the region. Also San Sebastian.

Marc Meyer
Chef/Restaurateur | Cookshop

156 Tenth Ave. New York, NY 10011

Phone: (212) 924-4440

RESTAURANT FACTS
Weeknight Covers: 220–300 **Weekend Covers:** 300–350 **Check Average (with Wine):** $50 **Tasting Menu:** No

CHEF FACTS
Other Restaurants: Hundred Acres, Five Points **Cuisine:** American with a nod to the Mediterranean **Work History:** New York, NY: The Odeon, Vix, Consulting Chef for ARK Restaurants, Five Points; St. Louis, MO: An American Place; San Francisco, CA: Brasserie Savoy **Mentor(s):** Patricia Clark, Larry Forgione **Books Published:** Brunch: Recipes from Five Points

FAST FACTS
Restaurant Recs: Franny's in Brooklyn for pizza and charcuterie; Kang Suh on 32nd for Korean cold noodles, mackerel cooked in chilies with turnips, and squid stew **Kitchen Tool(s):** A good chef's knife. I like Misono – the Japanese knives without a bolster **Interview Question:** How do you make a mayonnaise? What do you believe it takes to do the job? **Flavor Combo(s):** Anchovies infused in oil; lemon zest and breadcrumbs

M

Sandro Micheli
Pastry Chef | Adour

2 East 55th St. New York, NY 10022

Restaurant E-mail: sandro.micheli@stregis.com

Phone: (212) 753-4500

RESTAURANT FACTS
Seats: 72–88 **Weeknight Covers:** 120 **Weekend Covers:** 140 **Check Average (w/o Wine):** $140 **Tasting Menu:** Yes $110 **Kitchen Staff:** 3

CHEF FACTS
Cuisine: Classic French **Began Career:** 1996 **Culinary School:** Poligny, France **Grad Year:** 1996 **Work History:** France: Restaurant Paul Bocuse, Michel Guérard, Restaurant Les Crayéres; New York, NY: Restaurant Daniel, Alain Ducasse at the Essex House **Mentor(s):** Stephane Klein – probably the best pastry chef in sugar show piece **Awards:** 2008 StarChefs.com Rising Star Pastry Chef New York **Affiliations:** CCAP, Meals-on-Wheels **Languages Spoken:** French

NOTABLE DISH(ES): Contemporary Vacherin with Mango Marmalade, Coconut, and Passion Fruit Emulsion

FAST FACTS
Restaurant Recs: Soba-Ya for soba and tempura **Kitchen Tool(s):** Baby offset spatula – I never had this in France. It's very convenient, practical, and can fit in my pocket. **Interview Question:** What do you want to be in three years? I'm looking for: I want to be a chef. **Flavor Combo(s):** Strawberries and vanilla **Fave Cookbook(s):** PH10 by Pierre Hermé **Chef to Cook for You:** Michel Bras

Tracy Miller
Chef/Owner | LOCAL

2936 Elm St. #A Dallas, TX 75226

Restaurant E-mail: local@airmail.net

Phone: (214) 752-7500

RESTAURANT FACTS
Seats: 75 **Weeknight Covers:** 50 **Weekend Covers:** 125 **Check Average (with Wine):** $65 **Tasting Menu:** Yes $70–$100 **Kitchen Staff:** 2–3

CHEF FACTS
Cuisine: Modern American **Began Career:** 1990 **Work History:** Dallas, TX: 1717 **Mentor(s):** Danny Meyer, Thomas Keller, Alice Waters, Jean-Georges Vongerichten, and Donna Hay – all from afar **Awards:** 2007 StarChefs.com Rising Star Chef Dallas **Affiliations:** We do a lot of charity events

NOTABLE DISH(ES): Cream of Celery Root Soup with Crispy Leeks; Grilled Double Lamp Chop with Lavender-Madeira Sauce, Fingerling Potato, Pearl Onion Roast and a Broccoli Sauté

FAST FACTS
Restaurant Recs: Teppo for sushi with soft shell crab, smoked salmon, spicy tuna; Avila's for tamales, and a pork and chicken enchilada **Kitchen Tool(s):** KitchenAid mixer **Interview Question:** What are you looking for? What type of food inspires you? Are you clean, reliable and dependable? Can you work with a small staff in a small kitchen? What is your focus? **Flavor Combo(s):** Tawny port with lavender and Madeira. I'm a huge sweet person. Chocolate and ice cream are a naturally perfect match. I like grapefruit and rosemary a lot too. **Fave Cookbook(s):** Cookbooks by Donna Hay **Chef to Cook for You:** Thomas Keller, because he is so serious about what he does, and the details and refinement of his food demonstrate his fundamental expertise **Culinary Travel:** I always find inspiration on my trips to New York. Paris and Australia are both beautiful and inspiring as well.

Mark Miller
Consulting Chef/Partner | Coyote Cafe

132 W Water St. Santa Fe, NM 87501

Restaurant E-mail: morechiles@aol.com

Phone: (505) 983-1615

CHEF FACTS

Other Restaurants: Consultant for over forty companies as a consumer researcher and concept analyst **Cuisine:** Traditional, ethnic-inspired with modern Latin and Asian influences **Born:** 1949 **Began Career:** 1977 **Work History:** Berkeley, CA: Chez Panisse; Santa Fe, NM: Coyote Café; Las Vegas, NV: Coyote Café; Washington, DC: Red Sage; Australia: Wildfire (I've owned 13 restaurants) **Mentor(s):** While not mentors specifically, these people are certainly inspiring: Paula Wolfert, Craig Claiborne, Richard Olney, Diana Kennedy, James Beard, Charlie Trotter, Thomas Keller **Protégée(s):** Paul Bertoli, Chris Cosentino, Jesse Perez **Awards:** 1996 James Beard Best Chef Southwest; Esquire Magazine Ivy Award; James Beard Foundation Who 's Who **Affiliations:** Chefs Collaborative, Meals-on-Wheels **Books Published:** Mark Miller's Indian Market Cookbook: Recipes from Santa Fe's Famous Coyote Cafe; Coyote's Pantry: Southwest Seasonings and at Home Flavoring Techniques; Tamales; Flavored Breads: Recipes from Mark Miller's Coyote Cafe; The Great Salsa Book; The Great Chile Book; The Great Chile Book; The Neglected Art of Being Interviewed; Red Sage; Cool Coyote Cafe Juice Drinks

FAST FACTS

Restaurant Recs: Les Vinum – a small restaurant outside of Tokyo. They serve western game and combine the best ingredients from Europe with modern Japanese techniques. The menu changes daily but an example of something they would have is Alfredo Romano with wild Scottish pheasant. **Kitchen Tool(s):** Electric spice mill; KitchenAid **Interview Question:** I have them pull a cookbook off the shelf in my library and open to a random page. I ask them to look at the recipe and tell me why it works, and then give me three variations on it: a southwest variation, their own interpretation, and one that is appropriate for the restaurant they are applying for. They need to be able to conceptualize and modify recipes correctly. **Flavor Combo(s):** I like things with chilies – corn and chilies; Asian dishes with yuzu; combinations of wild mushrooms with wild herbs like epazote and hoja santa **Fave Cookbook(s):** That's a hard question to answer considering I have over 6,000! For reference I really like Mark Bittman's books. For Latin food I like Patricia Quintana. An all-time favorite would be Paula Wolfert and others like her who know cultural traditions in depth. **Chef to Cook for You:** Jean-Louis Palladin – he did the most amazing, inspired and spontaneous cooking that I know. He used incredible combinations of flavors that seemed mis-defined but were always satisfying. **Culinary Travel:** I travel to about 30 countries a year! Next in line is Tbilisi, Georgia. The cuisine and culture is an interesting cross of the Mediterranean, spice routes, Balkan, and Eurasian. It is one of the few areas I haven't lived in or traveled to.

Mary Sue Milliken
Co-Chef | Border Grill

1445 4th Street Santa Monica, CA 90071

Restaurant E-mail: marysue@bordergrill.com

Phone: (310) 451-1655

RESTAURANT FACTS
Seats: 170 **Weeknight Covers:** 180 **Weekend Covers:** 292 **Check Average (w/o Wine):** $30 **Tasting Menu:** No **Kitchen Staff:** 4–5

CHEF FACTS
Other Restaurants: Las Vegas, NV: Border Grill Mandalay Bay; Los Angeles, CA: Ciudad **Cuisine:** Latin-Mexican **Born:** 1958 **Began Career:** 1978 **Culinary School:** Washburn Trade School, Chicago, IL **Stages:** France: Restaurant D'Olympe **Work History:** France: Restaurant D'Olympe, Maxines of Paris, Le Perroquet; Chicago, IL: Let Them Eat Cake; Santa Monica, CA: City Café **Mentor(s):** Jovan Treboyevic, Alice Waters **Protégée(s):** Govind Armstrong, Wendy Brecker, Monique King **Affiliations:** WCR, SOS, AIFF, Les Dames d'Escoffier, Chefs Collaborative, JBF **Books Published:** Cooking with Two Hot Tamales: Recipes & Tips From TV Food's Spiciest Cooking Duo; Mesa Mexicana; Mexican Cooking for Dummies; Cantina: The Best of Casual Mexican Cooking; City Cuisine **Languages Spoken:** French, kitchen Spanish

NOTABLE DISH(ES): Cochinita Pibil; Red Roasted Chicken

FAST FACTS
Restaurant Recs: Isazoi for salted squid guts or anything from the "specials" menu **Kitchen Tool(s):** Ceramic ginger grater; mortar and pestle **Interview Question:** What do you do in your spare time? **Flavor Combo(s):** I will eat just about anything and love discovering new and exotic flavors, especially from different parts of the world. In our restaurants we strive to find the perfect balance on each plate: salty, cold, sour, crunchy, warm, smooth, sweet, spicy. **Fave Cookbook(s):** Nose to Tail and its sequel by Fergus Henderson; all three of the Moro cookbooks by Sam and Sam Clark; anything by Paula Wolfert; The Art of Baking by Paula Peck **Chef to Cook for You:** I'm terribly fond of Japanese food and when Masa was in LA I would have my birthday dinner at his restaurant. His food is always a joy and I miss him now that he's moved to NYC. **Culinary Travel:** EVERYWHERE!!! I love traveling to find new foods and ways of cooking. On my list this year are sailing the Croatian coast and cycling in Laos, Burma and Northern Thailand, and a weekend in rural Holland. In the next few years I hope to explore Portugal and New Zealand.

M

Michael Mina
Executive Chef/CEO Mina Group | Restaurant Michael Mina

335 Powell St. San Francisco, CA 94102

Restaurant E-mail: mmina@minagroup.net

Phone: (415) 359-0791

RESTAURANT FACTS
Seats: 100 **Weeknight Covers:** 100–160 **Weekend Covers:** 150–200 **Tasting Menu:** Yes $98/$135

CHEF FACTS
Other Restaurants: Las Vegas, NV: Michael Mina, Nobhill, StripSteak, Seablue; Scottsdale, AZ: Bourbon Steak; Miami, FL: Bourbon Steak; San Jose, CA: Arcadi; Dana Point, CA: Stonehill Tavern; Detroit, MI: Bourbon Steak, Saltwater **Cuisine:** Modern American **Born:** 1968 **Began Career:** 1987 **Culinary School:** The Culinary Institute of America, Hyde Park, NY **Grad Year:** 1988 **Stages:** Los Angeles, CA: Hotel Bel Air **Work History:** New York, NY: Aureole, Tribeca Grill; San Francisco, CA: Charles Nob Hill; Las Vegas, NV: Aqua at the Bellagio, Nob Hill **Mentor(s):** Charlie Palmer, Don Pintabono, George Morrone **Protégée(s):** Chris L'Hommedieu, Jay Wetzel, Mark LoRusso, Jeffrey Lloyd **Awards:** 2005 Bon Appetit Chef of the Year; 1997 James Beard Foundation Rising Star Chef; 2002 James Beard Foundation Best Chef California; 2005 San Francisco Magazine Chef of the Year **Affiliations:** The Andre Agassi Charitable Foundation, which does really good work with under-served kids. Andre is great friend of mine and he has put together an incredible foundation that has started a not-for-profit, free, co-educational private preparatory school in Las Vegas for kids who couldn't otherwise afford it. **Books Published:** Michael Mina: The Cookbook by Michael Mina **Languages Spoken:** Egyptian

NOTABLE DISH(ES): Tomato Soup with Minted Scallops; Pancetta-Wrapped Atlantic Cod; Lobster Pot Pie

FAST FACTS
Restaurant Recs: Bodega Bistro for the green papaya and dried beef salad **Kitchen Tool(s):** Potato ricer **Interview Question:** What can you contribute to the success of this restaurant? It's a question that most potential applicants are unprepared for, so it makes them think. So many young cooks are just looking for a stepping stone to their next job – I want cooks who seek to contribute to the greatness of a restaurant, not just to put another name on their resume. **Flavor Combo(s):** I like bold, clean flavors. Typically I go for classic flavor combinations and try to make them really stand out through a new or interesting technique. **Fave Cookbook(s):** The French Laundry Cookbook by Thomas Keller **Chef to Cook for You:** There are so many, but the late Jean-Louis Palladin stands out in my mind. He was an incredible cook and good friend, who cooked with a sensitivity and depth of knowledge that is still almost unrivaled. **Culinary Travel:** I'd love to go to Japan again. The purity of the flavors and the quality of the ingredients are breathtaking.

Mike Minor
Executive Chef | Border Grill

3950 Las Vegas Blvd. South Las Vegas, NV 89119

Restaurant E-mail: bglvechef@bordergrill.com

Phone: (702) 632-7403

RESTAURANT FACTS
Seats: 300 **Weeknight Covers:** 200–400 **Weekend Covers:** 300–500 **Check Average (with Wine):** $34 **Tasting Menu:** No **Kitchen Staff:** 9

CHEF FACTS
Cuisine: Modern Mexican **Born:** 1972 **Began Career:** 1989 **Work History:** Las Vegas, NV: Z'Tejas, The Hard Rock Café, Wolfgang Puck Enterprises **Mentor(s):** Susan Feniger and Mary Sue Milliken **Awards:** 2008 StarChefs.com Rising Star Sustainability Award Las Vegas **Affiliations:** Rick Moonen and I just taught a class at Le Cordon Bleu on sustainability. I have students come in here and work for credit and learn what we do with sustainability. **Languages Spoken:** Spanish – in between kitchen and fluent

NOTABLE DISH(ES): New Zealand Green Lip Mussels with Ancho Chiles, Garlic and Chorizo; Hawaiian Ceviche Napolean: Opa with Mango and Cherries on a Spicy Taro Chip

FAST FACTS
Restaurant Recs: Sushi Loca – the chefs are really outgoing and fun and the rolls all have crazy names. It's a fun place. **Kitchen Tool(s):** My 8 inch chefs knife. It can do any job; I use it for everything **Interview Question:** I'm a huge music guy so I first ask what music they're listening to at the moment. Then I ask them what their absolute favorite dish to make is. These questions help me out a lot, it tells me what they're all about. **Flavor Combo(s):** Sweet and sour **Fave Cookbook(s):** Boy Meets Grill by Bobby Flay **Chef to Cook for You:** Emeril Lagasse - I love all the different ingredients he uses. He puts his heart and soul into his food. **Culinary Travel:** Napa Valley because it's close to me, the French Laundry is there, and it has very unique characteristics like Mexico.

Mariana Montero de Castro
Pastry Chef | Cacao Restaurant

141 Giralda Ave. Coral Gables, FL 33134

Restaurant E-mail: marianamontero@cacaorestaurant.com

Phone: (305) 445-1001

RESTAURANT FACTS
Seats: 90 **Weeknight Covers:** 50–80 **Weekend Covers:** 130 **Check Average (with Wine):** $84 **Check Average (w/o Wine):** $62 **Tasting Menu:** Yes $75 **Kitchen Staff:** 1–2

CHEF FACTS
Cuisine: Venezuelan-French cuisine **Born:** 1978 **Began Career:** 1998 **Culinary School:** Centro de Estudios Gastronomicos CEGA Caracas, Venezuela; École Superieure de Cuisine Française ESCF-Ferrandi Paris, France **Grad Year:** 2001 **Work History:** Venezuela: Centro Estudios Gastronomicos "CEGA"; France: L'Astor, Laurent **Mentor(s):** Jose Rafael Lovera, Edgar Leal **Protégée(s):** Ana Carolina Estevez **Awards:** 2004 StarChefs.com Rising Star Pastry Chef Miami **Affiliations:** Easter Seals **Languages Spoken:** Spanish, French

NOTABLE DISH(ES): Milk Chocolate Tower; Miniature chocolates, parfaits and espumas

FAST FACTS
Restaurant Recs: Nobu in Miami Beach for miso black cod **Kitchen Tool(s):** Scale – it is absolutely necessary for precision in pastry **Interview Question:** What is your favorite cookbook? What are you reading now? **Flavor Combo(s):** Chocolate with tonka beans **Fave Cookbook(s):** The Physiology of Taste by Jean-Anthelme Brillat-Savarin **Chef to Cook for You:** Thomas Keller **Culinary Travel:** Italy – I haven't had the chance to go yet

Rick Moonen
Chef/Owner | Restaurant RM

3930 Las Vegas Blvd. South Las Vegas, NV 89119

Restaurant E-mail: chefmoonen@rmseafood.com

Phone: (702) 632-9300

RESTAURANT FACTS

Seats: 80 **Weeknight Covers:** 75 **Weekend Covers:** 75 **Check Average (with Wine):** $125 **Tasting Menu:** Yes **Kitchen Staff:** 6

CHEF FACTS

Other Restaurants: R Bar Café, RM Seafood **Cuisine:** Seafood **Born:** 1956 **Began Career:** 1974 **Culinary School:** The Culinary Institute of America, Hyde Park, New York **Grad Year:** 1978 **Work History:** Hillsdale, NY: L'Hostellerie Bressane; New York, NY: La Côte Basque, Le Cirque **Mentor(s):** Eugene Bernard, Jean Jacques Rachou, Jean-Louis Palladin **Protégée(s):** Brian Rae, Anthony Amoroso **Awards:** 1993 Chefs in America Chef of the Year Northeast **Affiliations:** StarChefs.com Advisory Board, Chef's Coalition, Ecofish, Seafood Choices Alliances, SOS, French Culinary Institute Board of Advisors **Books Published:** Fish Without a Doubt

NOTABLE DISH(ES): Sea Scallops with Apple, Ginger and Lemon; Pan Seared Orata with Roasted Garlic and Gnocchi

FAST FACTS

Restaurant Recs: Honey Pig for Korean barbecue - it is a hole in the wall and is very good **Kitchen Tool(s):** Microplane – when it comes to seafood and citrus, it plays a vital role in brightening up the flavor **Interview Question:** If I am interviewing a potential hire and they are presently working, I ask them if they can start next week. If they answer yes, I will not hire them. If they don't have the respect to give the proper notice to their present employer it says a lot about the trajectory of their career. **Flavor Combo(s):** Fennel and orange; lemon and dill **Fave Cookbook(s):** Dorie Greenspan's Baking at Home - the recipes really work **Chef to Cook for You:** Jean-Louis Palladin – he had such respect for high quality products. I had an amazing time hunting and foraging with him and then going back to cook with our found ingredients. **Culinary Travel:** I've never been to an Asian country. I would love to visit Thailand and Japan.

Frank Morales
Executive Chef | Rustico

827 Slaters Ln. Alexandria, VA 22314

Restaurant E-mail: frankm@restucorestaurant.com

Phone: (703) 224-5051

RESTAURANT FACTS
Seats: 160 **Weeknight Covers:** 360 **Weekend Covers:** 360 **Check Average (w/o Wine):** $31.49 **Tasting Menu:** No **Kitchen Staff:** 7

CHEF FACTS
Cuisine: American **Born:** 1967 **Began Career:** 1995 **Culinary School:** The Culinary Institute of America, Hyde Park, NY **Stages:** New York, NY: An American Place, Le Bernardin, Daniel **Work History:** New York, NY: Le Cirque, An American Place, Union Pacific; Washington, DC: Zola **Mentor(s):** Sottha Khunn, Larry Forgione, Rocco DiSpirito **Languages Spoken:** Spanish

NOTABLE DISH(ES): Chicken Liver Terrine with Corn Salt; Summer Melon and Elderflower Soup with Shrimp and Hearts of Palm

FAST FACTS
Restaurant Recs: Hank's Oyster Bar for lobster rolls; Florida Avenue Grill for grits and fried apples **Kitchen Tool(s):** Cryovac® machine **Interview Question:** Where do you see yourself in five years? The answer gives you a better impression of the employee. If their goals are unrealistic, then they are an unrealistic employee. **Fave Cookbook(s):** Simply French by Patricia Wells

Vernon Morales
Consulting Chef | Lombardi Family Concepts

3100 Monticello Ave., Ste. 325 Dallas, TX 75205

Restaurant E-mail: viniciovm@hotmail.com

Phone: (214) 748-5566

CHEF FACTS
Other Restaurants: Sangria Tapas Bar; La Cubanita **Cuisine:** Modern American **Culinary School:** California Culinary Academy, San Francisco, CA **Stages:** Spain: el Bulli, Martín Berasategui **Work History:** Philadelphia, PA: Salt; San Francisco, CA: Winterland Restaurant and Lounge; New York, NY: Daniel, Peacock Alley in the Waldorf Astoria **Mentor(s):** Laurent Gras **Awards:** 2004 StarChefs.com Rising Star Chef Philadelphia **Languages Spoken:** Spanish

NOTABLE DISH(ES): Young Rabbit Escabeche; Snail Croquettes and Spring Garlic Aioli

FAST FACTS
Restaurant Recs: In Philly: Melograno for simple, rustic Italian food; Morimoto **Kitchen Tool(s):** Probe thermometer; digital scale **Interview Question:** I don't have a generic question; I usually just get a feeling. But it's important to ask whether or not they enjoy cooking. It's important to like what you do. At the end of the day, you have to feel fortunate that you're doing something you like. **Flavor Combo(s):** Bitter and sweet. For example: romaine lettuce soup with white chocolate mousse or corn and huitlacoche. **Fave Cookbook(s):** La Cocina Vasca en Bizkaia by Andra Mari; The Elements of Taste by Gray Kunz; Dessert Cuisine by Oriol Balaguer **Chef to Cook for You:** Ferran Adriá – his tasting menus are fantastic – like thoughts on plates **Culinary Travel:** I love Barcelona, Paris, San Sebastian, Madrid, and Sevilla

M

Marco Moreira
Chef/Owner | Tocqueville

1 E 15th St. New York, NY 10003

Restaurant E-mail: tocqueville15@aol.com

Phone: (212) 647-1515

RESTAURANT FACTS

Seats: 65 **Weeknight Covers:** 70 **Weekend Covers:** 90 **Check Average (with Wine):** $150 **Check Average (w/o Wine):** $75 **Tasting Menu:** No **Kitchen Staff:** 9

CHEF FACTS

Other Restaurants: 15 East Sushi Bar and Restaurant **Cuisine:** Modern American with French and Japanese influences **Born:** 1965 **Began Career:** 1983 **Stages:** France: Amphyclaise **Work History:** New York, NY: The Quilted Giraffe, Bouley, The Mark Hotel **Mentor(s):** Barry Wine, Phillip Boulot **Protégée(s):** George Mendes, Vincent Chirico **Awards:** 2006 Distinguished Restaurants of America Award; 2004 Star Diamond Award **Affiliations:** JBF, DiRoNa **Languages Spoken:** Portuguese, Spanish

NOTABLE DISH(ES): Young Garlic and Almond Gazpacho; Creamy Parmesan Grits with Black Truffles and Veal Bacon

FAST FACTS

Restaurant Recs: Oriental Garden for the #1 Chicken Soup **Kitchen Tool(s):** Ziploc bags **Interview Question:** Where do you see yourself in two years? You can tell how serious and realistic someone is about the profession, what kind of motivation they have, and if they will have any longevity. **Flavor Combo(s):** Egg and anything onion; sea urchin and egg; banana and lime; banana and chocolate **Fave Cookbook(s):** Paul Bocuse's French Cooking by Paul Bocuse **Chef to Cook for You:** Alain Ducasse, because he is the master of classic cuisine **Culinary Travel:** The Brazilian countryside to learn about an area of Brazilian cuisine I'm not very familiar with, or Japan because of the integrity of the ingredients

Masaharu Morimoto
Owner/Chef | Morimoto

88 Tenth Ave. New York, NY 10011

Restaurant E-mail: mstone@infoclear.com

Phone: (215) 413-9070

RESTAURANT FACTS
Seats: 180 **Weeknight Covers:** 300 **Weekend Covers:** 450 **Check Average (with Wine):** $110 **Tasting Menu:** Yes $120 **Kitchen Staff:** 20

CHEF FACTS
Other Restaurants: Philadelphia, PA: Morimoto; Tokyo, Japan: Morimoto-XEX; Mumbai, India: Wasabi by Morimoto **Cuisine:** Japanese **Born:** 1955 **Began Career:** 1973 **Work History:** Japan: Sushi; New York, NY: The Sony Club, Nobu **Mentor(s):** Rokusaburo Michiba, Barry Wine **Awards:** 2008 IACP Cookbook Award for Chefs and Restaurants **Affiliations:** Iron Chef, Iron Chef America **Books Published:** Morimoto: The New Art of Japanese Cooking **Languages Spoken:** Japanese

NOTABLE DISH(ES): Miyazaki Wagyu Beef Tartare; Braised Black Cod

FAST FACTS
Restaurant Recs: I don't know many restaurants in Philadelphia because I go to my restaurant to work, then go to a bar after work, and just go home. I don't have the time to go to a restaurant. **Kitchen Tool(s):** The cutting board – it is a sacred tool and should be kept clean because we cut raw fish on the cutting board and serve the sliced raw fish directly over the counter to the customers **Interview Question:** It would be easier if there were such a question. Just as people have different tastes, people are all different in terms of personality, experience, etc. I change questions depending on the person I am interviewing. **Fave Cookbook(s):** Rosanjin (in Japanese) **Chef to Cook for You:** Hanaya Yohei – he was the founder of Edo-style sushi, the closest thing to what today we call nigiri sushi **Culinary Travel:** Vietnam – I've never been. I love Vietnamese cuisine and want to experience local ingredients and styles of cooking in the place where they originate.

Bill Morris
Executive Chef | Rainier Club

820 4th Ave. Seattle, WA 98104

Restaurant E-mail: bill@therainierclub.com

Phone: (206) 296-6913

RESTAURANT FACTS
Seats: 150, up to 600 with private rooms **Weeknight Covers:** 150 **Weekend Covers:** 200 **Check Average (w/o Wine):** $50–$55 **Tasting Menu:** Yes **Kitchen Staff:** 5-7

CHEF FACTS
Cuisine: Regional Pacific Northwest **Born:** 1965 **Began Career:** 1985 **Culinary School:** South Seattle Community College, Seattle, WA; California Culinary Academy, San Francisco, CA; Culinary Institute of America, Hyde Park, NY **Stages:** Rovers Restaurant **Work History:** Seattle, WA: Sorrentos Hotel, Rover Restaurant, Salish Lodge at Snoqualmie Lodge **Mentor(s):** David Kellaway, Thierry Rautureau **Protégée(s):** Mayra Melka, Scott Megargle, Tyler Anderson **Awards:** 1994, 2005 Local ACF Chapter Chef of the Year; 2004 Puget Sound Business Journal "40 under 40" Business Leaders in Seattle **Affiliations:** SOS, March of Dimes, Farestart, Childrens Hospital (Auction of Washington Wines), various others

FAST FACTS
Restaurant Recs: Crush for a foie gras and savory waffle with wild huckleberries **Kitchen Tool(s):** German egg topper **Interview Question:** What kind of cookbooks do you read? What kind of music do you listen to? **Flavor Combo(s):** There are really quite a few, but some of the most recent combinations I enjoy are: fennel, ginger, radish, togarashi; dark chocolate, praline, foie gras, Pedro Ximenez; truffle, asparagus, morel (or wild mushroom); Marcona almond, rhubarb, roasted strawberry, fennel, anise, hyssop; smoked paprika, olive oil, smoked ham. As I mentioned, I could on and on. **Fave Cookbook(s):** The French Laundry Cookbook by Thomas Keller **Chef to Cook for You:** A collaborative line up of Thomas Keller, Ferran Adriá, Louis Outhier, Freddy Giradet, Joël Robuchon, Oriol Balaguer, Frederic Bau, Marco Pierre White, Kiyomi Mikuni and Michel Richard. That being said, although she was not a chef proper, yet an accomplished cook, I would give anything to have my late, great mother cook for me one last time. **Culinary Travel:** Spain – although almost cliché, I enjoy the new, vibrant flavors coming out of there right now by the many great chefs. I would like to return to the many places in Italy and France that I visited in my past to reconnect to the culture, terroir and food scene to see how it has evolved.

Harrison Mosher
Executive Chef | Alta

64 West 10th St. New York, NY 10011

Restaurant E-mail: hmosher@nyc.rr.com

Phone: (212) 505-7777

RESTAURANT FACTS
Seats: 150 **Weeknight Covers:** 150–200 **Weekend Covers:** 300+
Check Average (with Wine): $50 **Tasting Menu:** No **Kitchen Staff:** 7

CHEF FACTS
Cuisine: Mediterranean small plates **Born:** 1961 **Began Career:**
1990 **Stages:** France: Auberge du Père Floranc **Work History:** New
York, NY: Bouley, Danube, Payard, Oceana, Daniel, 71 Clinton Fresh
Food **Mentor(s):** David Bouley, Mario Lohninger **Languages Spoken:**
Some French and Spanish

NOTABLE DISH(ES): Caramelized Cauliflower with Clams, Chorizo and
Golden Raisins

FAST FACTS
Restaurant Recs: Aburiya Kinnosuke **Kitchen Tool(s):** Salt shaker, and various pepper mills – if it
isn't seasoned, it doesn't taste like anything! **Interview Question:** What are your long-term goals and
how do they relate to working here? Is this a job or a passion or both? **Flavor Combo(s):** I've been
working with a lot of fun combinations lately. Tamarind and membrillo; slow-cooked tomatoes and
cocoa; afuega 'l pitu cheese with beets tossed in Tunisian spices **Fave Cookbook(s):** The el Bulli cookbooks by Ferran and Albert Adriá **Chef to Cook for You:** Joan Roca **Culinary Travel:** North Africa

Lynn Moulton
Consulting Pastry Chef

Boston, MA

Restaurant E-mail: birde_802@yahoo.com

Phone: (617) 375-8550

CHEF FACTS

Cuisine: Pastry **Born:** 1976 **Began Career:** 2000 **Culinary School:** New England Culinary Institute, Montpelier, Vt **Grad Year:** 1999 **Stages:** France: Helene Darroze **Work History:** Boston, MA: Radius, blu; Edgartown, MA: L'Etoile; Cambridge, MA: Rialto **Mentor(s):** Paul Connors, Jody Adams **Awards:** 2006 StarChefs.com Rising Star Pastry Chef Boston **Affiliations:** Greater Boston Food Pantry, Virginia Thurston Healing Garden, Community Servings **Languages Spoken:** French

NOTABLE DISH(ES): Chocolate Pots de Créme with Coriander Madeleines and Amaretto Milk; Lemon Tart with Orange Flower Cream

FAST FACTS

Restaurant Recs: Delux for their current variation of a grilled cheese sandwich **Kitchen Tool(s):** Kuhn Rikon peeler; Best whisk; KitchenAid coffee grinder with removable metal canister; Pacojet **Interview Question:** I haven't found the perfect, insightful, guarantees-a-great-employee question. The most important point for me in an interview is to determine if an applicant will be enthusiastic and responsive to criticism; all the other aspects of the job can be taught. **Flavor Combo(s):** Sour cherry, honey and rose; mango, chevre and black pepper; yogurt and cornmeal; olive oil, lemon and mint **Fave Cookbook(s):** The Last Course by Claudia Fleming and The Joy of Cooking by Irma S. Rombauer as a reference for the how's and why's of classic American baked goods **Chef to Cook for You:** The chef whose creative process I'd most like to be able to watch would be Pierre Hermé; he's a design genius **Culinary Travel:** France – the general attitude towards food is so incredible, and the sensitivity to quality is evident in everyday life

Sara Moulton
Executive Chef | Gourmet Magazine

4 Times Square New York, NY 10036

Restaurant E-mail: sara_moulton@condenast.com

Phone: (212) 286-4355

CHEF FACTS
Other Restaurants: Gourmet Magazine Executive Dining Room
Cuisine: American **Born:** 1952 **Began Career:** 1977 **Culinary School:**
The Culinary Institute of America, Hyde Park, NY **Grad Year:** 1977
Stages: New York, NY: La Tulipe; France: Henri Quatre **Work History:**
Cambridge, MA: The Harvest **Mentor(s):** Julia Child, Jacques Pépin,
Jean Anderson **Protégée(s):** Lori Powell **Awards:** 2003 James Beard
Foundation General Cookbook for Everyday Nominee; 2002 James
Beard Foundation Who's Who in American Food & Wine Inductee;
2002 More Magazine 50 Turning 50; 2001 Culinary Institute of
America Chef of the Year **Affiliations:** IACP, WCR, NYWCA **Books Pub-
lished:** Sara Moulton Cooks at Home; Sara's Secrets for Weeknight
Meals **Languages Spoken:** French, more or less

FAST FACTS
Restaurant Recs: La Taza de Oro; Cabo Rojo – for yellow rice, black beans and roast chicken **Kitchen
Tool(s):** Fish spatula – I use it for turning all sorts of items over from fish to pancakes. It has the best
design. **Interview Question:** What are your goals? I'm hoping they will say, they just want to learn and
will do anything – work crazy hours, and do whatever it take to accomplish this. **Flavor Combo(s):**
Salty and sweet; chile and sugar; fried anything; creamy with citrus (basically any variation on the
creamsicle); raspberry and chocolate; sauternes and Roquefort **Fave Cookbook(s):** Cookbooks by
Marcella Hazan, Madhur Jaffrey and Eileen Yin Fei Lo **Chef to Cook for You:** I'm really into Indian food
right now so I'd pick Madhur Jaffrey **Culinary Travel:** India – the cuisine is so exciting with so many
layers of flavors. I also love Latin food, so a South American tour would be interesting as well.

Seamus Mullen
Chef | Boqueria

53 W 19th St. New York, NY 10011

Restaurant E-mail: seamus@boquerianyc.com

Phone: (212) 255-4160

RESTAURANT FACTS
Seats: 65 **Weeknight Covers:** 160 **Weekend Covers:** 220 **Check Average (with Wine):** $50 **Tasting Menu:** No **Kitchen Staff:** 5

CHEF FACTS
Other Restaurants: Suba **Cuisine:** Market-driven, rustic-traditional Spanish **Born:** 1974 **Began Career:** 1996 **Stages:** Spain: Mugaritz, Abac, Alkimia **Work History:** San Francisco, CA: Mecca; New York, NY: Tabla, Crudo, Brasserie 8 1/2 **Mentor(s):** Jordi Vila **Affiliations:** We do many charity events **Languages Spoken:** Spanish, Gibberish

NOTABLE DISH(ES): Sepia y Guisantes (Cuttlefish and Peas)

FAST FACTS
Restaurant Recs: Bacaro on the lower east side for the squid ink risotto **Kitchen Tool(s):** My spoon – it is the most versatile tool out there. It's great for tasting, basting and making a point! **Interview Question:** Where is the last place you ate dinner? Can you turn an artichoke? Then I have them show me. **Flavor Combo(s):** Basil and apple; lavender and foie **Fave Cookbook(s):** Baccalao by Andoni Luis Aduriz **Chef to Cook for You:** Vittorio **Culinary Travel:** To India – Indian food has always been challenging for me. I think if I went there, though, I would find some that I really liked.

David Mullen
Chef de Cuisine | Bourbon Steak

19999 West Country Club Dr. Miami, FL 33180

Phone: (786) 279-6600

CHEF FACTS

Cuisine: Modern American **Born:** 1970 **Began Career:** 1997 **Culinary School:** California Culinary Academy, San Francisco, CA **Grad Year:** 1997 **Stages:** France: L'Epi Dupin **Work History:** San Francisco, CA: Masa's, Picasso, The Fifth Floor; New York, NY: 71 Clinton Fresh Food, Daniel; Palm Beach, FL: Angle at the Ritz-Carlton **Mentor(s):** Wylie Dufresne, Kim Canteenwalla **Awards:** 2008 StarChefs.com Rising Star Chef South Florida

NOTABLE DISH(ES): Barramundi with Wild Forest Morels, English Peas, Ramps and Madeira Jus; Hamachi with Apple Gelée, Jicama and Coriander Rice Cracker

FAST FACTS

Restaurant Recs: Cucina is a great little Italian restaurant that converts to a club after the evening's customers finish eating. It's also open until into the middle of the night, which is good for a working chef. **Kitchen Tool(s):** Vita-Prep – I blend a lot of varied ingredients and would not be able to get the results I demand without it **Interview Question:** What are you reading? Where did you last eat and why? What flavors or spices do you like and why? What cooking references do you read? I am looking for honest and natural responses that come from the heart. If they have to think about it too long or if the answers seem rehearsed, then I know it isn't the right fit. **Flavor Combo(s):** I love acidity - citrus and vinegar **Fave Cookbook(s):** Art Culinaire; anything from the Alain Ducasse series; Thomas Keller's books **Chef to Cook for You:** If Escoffier wanted to cook me dinner, that would be great. But for it to be perfect, I would love for us to dine together and talk about food. **Culinary Travel:** New York is one of the most inventive and exciting culinary destinations in the world. You can travel a few blocks in any direction and find authentic cuisine from any region.

Matt Murphy
Chef | Mélange

921 Canal St. New Orleans, LA 70112

Restaurant E-mail: matt.murphy@ritzcarlton.com

Phone: (504) 524-1331

RESTAURANT FACTS
Seats: 120–132 **Weeknight Covers:** 75 **Weekend Covers:** 130–140
Check Average (with Wine): $58 **Tasting Menu:** No **Kitchen Staff:** 12

CHEF FACTS
Other Restaurants: 5 beverage outlets within The Ritz-Carlton **Cuisine:** French country cuisine **Born:** 1969 **Began Career:** 1992 **Culinary School:** Cathal Brugha Street Culinary College, Dublin, Ireland **Grad Year:** 1992 **Stages:** England: The Restaurant at Hyde Park Hotel; New York, NY: Daniel **Work History:** Ireland: Ashford Castle, Dromoland Castle, Ayumi-Ya, La Stamp, La Tavola; England: The Canteen; Hawaii: Plantation House, Jameson's; Boston, MA: East West; New Orleans, LA: Commander's Palace, Victor's New Orleans **Mentor(s):** My grandfather, Dennis Lenahan, Jim Bowe, Eddie Sheraton, Paul Flynn **Protégée(s):** Kevin Nashan, Javier Lopez, Eric Aldis **Affiliations:** We work with a local training café for at-risk youths called Café Reconcile. We help train kids that come from difficult backgrounds how to be cooks and, hopefully, to become chefs.

NOTABLE DISH(ES): Duck Gumbo; Louisiana Crabcakes with Picante Sauce and Fennel Stew

FAST FACTS
Restaurant Recs: Jacques Imo's for alligator cheesecake **Kitchen Tool(s):** 10" French scalloped slicer knife. I can use it in many different areas in the kitchen. It is thin enough to do precise work, but also very easy to chop with. **Interview Question:** What do you think the job you are applying for entails? It's a kind of a question that tells you whether you have a winner or not. **Flavor Combo(s):** Duck and blackberry, but warm blackberry (like in a sauce); a nice piece of white fish with butter (a Plugra-type butter) **Fave Cookbook(s):** Ma Gastronomie by Fernand Point **Chef to Cook for You:** Julia Child – she was a one of the most real and learned people in food. She tasted things for what they were and had no preconception, no borders and no set limitations on her food preparation and ideas. She is one of the most famous pioneering chefs of our day. **Culinary Travel:** India, big time, because of the culture. The food is based on a lot of different religions that use a vast variety of ingredients. Our palates are used to the traditional French flavors. The flavors Indians can get out of food is crazy.

Tamara Murphy
Executive Chef | Brasa

2107 Third Ave. Seattle, WA 98121

Restaurant E-mail: seattle@brasa.com

Phone: (206) 728-4220

RESTAURANT FACTS
Seats: 170 **Weeknight Covers:** 125–150 **Weekend Covers:** 150–225 **Check Average (with Wine):** $65 **Kitchen Staff:** 4–6

CHEF FACTS
Cuisine: Mediterranean **Born:** 1961 **Began Career:** 1976 **Work History:** Seattle, WA: Dominique's, Campagne **Mentor(s):** Dominique Place **Protégée(s):** Mary Lokar, James Dromman, Daisley Gordon **Awards:** 2000 Food and Wine Magazine Seattle's Best Restaurant; 2002, 2001 Mobil Guide 4 stars; 1995 James Beard Foundation Best Chef Pacific Northwest; 1994 Food & Wine Best New Chefs **Affiliations:** WCR, Chefs Collaborative **Languages Spoken:** Spanish, Italian, Thai

NOTABLE DISH(ES): Ricotta Gnocchi with Peas and Pancetta; Caramelized Flan

FAST FACTS
Restaurant Recs: Chiso for kasu cod **Kitchen Tool(s):** Plastic wrap **Interview Question:** How do you make a soup? This question allows me to see inside a cook. What techniques would they use? What's their creativity/resourcefulness level? **Flavor Combo(s):** Smokey and citrus **Fave Cookbook(s):** I have so many cookbooks and I like them for so many reasons. There is not one book that I go to for everything. **Chef to Cook for You:** I guess Ferran Adriá to try molecular gastronomy – if you're going to try it it might as well be from the best. It would be fun to see things I've never seen before. **Culinary Travel:** To Morocco to see the traditional ways of using tagines and making couscous. A lot of this food is on my menu, so to see the culture behind it would be really interesting.

David Myers
Chef/Owner | Sona

401 N La Cienega Blvd. Los Angeles, CA 90048

Restaurant E-mail: info@sonarestaurant.com

Phone: (310) 659-7708

RESTAURANT FACTS
Seats: 90 **Tasting Menu:** Yes $95/$169

CHEF FACTS
Other Restaurants: Boule, Comme Ça **Cuisine:** Modern French, seasonally spontaneous **Born:** 1974 **Began Career:** 1993 **Work History:** Chicago, IL: Charlie Trotter's; France: Les Crayeres; New York, NY: Daniel; Los Angeles, CA: Patina; Beverly Hills, CA: JAAN **Mentor(s):** Charlie Trotter, Daniel Boulud **Protégée(s):** Nathan McCall, Michael David **Awards:** 2005 Angeleno Best Restaurant; 2004 StarChefs.com Rising Star Chef Los Angeles; 2004 Angeleno Magazine Chef of the Year; 2004 James Beard Foundation Rising Star Nominee; 2003 Food & Wine Best New Chefs **Affiliations:** DiRona, James Beard Foundation. We donate to multiple local, regional, and national charities every month, but have a particular interest in non-profits that focus on the protection and conservation of beaches, such as Surfrider.

NOTABLE DISH(ES): Hamachi with Edamame Purée, Spicy Grapefruit and Watermelon Radish Salad; Braised Licorice Root Lamb Shoulder with Cardamom-Infused Yogurt

FAST FACTS
Restaurant Recs: Neptune's Net, which is up past Malibu, for live Dungeness crab **Kitchen Tool(s):** Sous vide machine, because it has infinite possibilities **Interview Question:** What book are you reading? **Flavor Combo(s):** I don't like sweet; so anything salty, sour, or bitter. I Really like salted plums as well as the brightness and bitterness of lovage. **Fave Cookbook(s):** Cookbooks by Charlie Trotter **Chef to Cook for You:** If I were in Japan, it would be the chef of Umi. In Paris – Pierre Gagnaire. In Chicago – Charlie Trotter. In New York - Daniel Boulud. And in Napa – Thomas Keller. These guys are so in the zone with what they are doing, it's sure to be an experience on the highest level. **Culinary Travel:** I like Malibu for its natural resources. I'd like to go to Kyoto because it is very creative and modernized.

{ Nahabedian - Nusser }

N

Carrie Nahabedian
Chef/Co-Owner | Naha

500 N Clark St. Chicago, IL 60610

Restaurant E-mail: mnnaha@att.net

Phone: (312) 321-6242

RESTAURANT FACTS
Seats: 105 **Weeknight Covers:** 100 **Weekend Covers:** 200 **Check Average (with Wine):** $82 **Tasting Menu:** Yes **Kitchen Staff:** 10

CHEF FACTS
Cuisine: Seasonal American with Mediterranean influence **Began Career:** 1976 **Work History:** Pittsburgh, PA: Le Perroquet; Chicago, IL: Le Français, The Park Hyatt, The Four Seasons; Lake Forest, IL: Sinclair's; Beverly Hills, CA: The Four Seasons Hotel Los Angeles **Awards:** 2008 James Beard Foundation Best Chef Great Lakes **Affiliations:** Board member of Les Dames d'Escoffier, Board member of Green City Market, Common Threads, Slow Food, Vital Bridges, the Armenian Community, and we donate a lot to cancer and diabetes organizations

NOTABLE DISH(ES): Roasted Quail with American Prosciutto, Coddled Quail Eggs Benedict, Chanterelle Mushrooms, Potatoes, Spinach, and Tarragon

FAST FACTS
Restaurant Recs: Bacchanalia – a traditional Italian restaurant in Little Italy that has been around forever. I like the Chicken Vesuvio. **Kitchen Tool(s):** My hemostats (medical scissors with a clamp instead of a blade) – I have an attachment to them. My surgeon gave them to me 25 years ago when I had jaw surgery, and they have been with me ever since. **Interview Question:** Have you ever dined in my restaurant? If not, what restaurants have you eaten in in this city? It shows a lot about a person. **Flavor Combo(s):** I love sweet and savory combinations, especially when I do roasted birds **Fave Cookbook(s):** I love the first edition of The Inn at Little Washington Cookbook. I like Harry's Bar from Venice. Another good one is Gourmet's France - it is an incredible journey through France. I like anything from Alain Ducasse and I like Ma Gastronomie, of which I have multiple copies and give out as gifts. **Chef to Cook for You:** Fernand Point, because of the excess **Culinary Travel:** I am probably the only chef in the free world who has yet to go to Spain, so Spain is one place. I also want to do an in-depth exploration of Northern Africa and of Greece.

Elissa Narow
Pastry Chef | Custom House

500 Dearborn St. Chicago, IL 60605

Restaurant E-mail: elissa@customhouse.cc

Phone: (312) 523-0200

RESTAURANT FACTS
Seats: 120 **Weeknight Covers:** 80-100 **Weekend Covers:** 150-200 **Check Average (with Wine):** $80 **Tasting Menu:** No **Kitchen Staff:** 1-2

CHEF FACTS
Other Restaurants: Spring **Cuisine:** Modern American Desserts **Born:** 1971 **Began Career:** 1996 **Culinary School:** Cooking and Hospitality Institute of Chicago, Chicago, IL **Grad Year:** 1996 **Work History:** Evanston, IL: Trio Restaurant; Chicago, IL: Blackbird, Avec **Mentor(s):** Della Gossett **Protégée(s):** Tara Lane **Awards:** 2008 StarChefs.com Rising Star Pastry Chef Chicago; 2004 Jean Banchet Rising Star Pastry Chef **Languages Spoken:** Some Spanish

NOTABLE DISH(ES): Meyer Lemon Cheesecake with Lemon Beurre Blanc and Lemon Rosemary Sorbet Soda; Chocolate Caramel Crunch Cake with Green Tea Cream, Coconut Sorbet, and Chocolate Crispies

FAST FACTS
Restaurant Recs: Lao Sze Chuan for hot pots **Kitchen Tool(s):** Small square spatula that is the perfect size for so many things. I'd really like a confectionary guitar. **Interview Question:** Why do you want to be in the business? I want to know about their passion for working with food. **Flavor Combo(s):** At Spring I'm doing a miso butterscotch and green tea cream. I wouldn't do green tea at Custom House, but I would do other teas. I love using tea in desserts. **Fave Cookbook(s):** I still love going to Fannie Farmer for classics because it's absolutely beautiful. Oriol Balaguer's book is visually stunning and I also like the el Bulli books. **Chef to Cook for You:** I'd like Claudia Fleming to cook for me **Culinary Travel:** I'd go to Spain because of all of the new techniques that are coming out of Spain. Everything that I've ever heard about the food there is phenomenal.

Daryl Nash
Executive Chef | Otom

951 W Fulton Market Chicago, IL 60607

Restaurant E-mail: dnash@otomrestaurant.com

Phone: (312) 491-5804

RESTAURANT FACTS
Seats: 90–140 **Kitchen Staff:** 6–8

CHEF FACTS
Cuisine: Contemporary American **Born:** 1973 **Began Career:**
1991/2001 **Culinary School:** Johnson County Community College,
Overland Park, KS **Grad Year:** 1994 **Work History:** Chicago, IL: Moto
Mentor(s): Homaru Cantu

NOTABLE DISH(ES): Braised Pork Belly with Puffed Barley-Turnip
Hash, Beets and Rosemary

FAST FACTS
Restaurant Recs: Vie Restaurant in Western Springs, IL is cool. Paul Virant is totally into micro-seasonal stuff. Cures, pickles and handcrafted sausages. The last time I was there was early spring, and I had braised rabbit thigh, seared loin, English peas, bacon and jus. Mmm... good. **Kitchen Tool(s):** Vita-Prep blender **Flavor Combo(s):** I really dig "salty/sweet" combos in savory applications. A hint of sweet salinity is often as effective in seasoning as acid. **Fave Cookbook(s):** The French Laundry Cookbook by Thomas Keller **Chef to Cook for You:** José Andrés' attitude about food is just awesome. I heard him once in an interview say something like "being happy is easy... so easy." Food is his joy, as is mine. I would be psyched to "eat light" with him or to sit down with him for a tasting. **Culinary Travel:** I would spend two weeks in France kicking around in bistros and staging

Akhtar Nawab
Executive Chef | Elettaria

33 West 8th St. New York, NY 10011

Restaurant E-mail: anawab@msn.com

Phone: (212) 677-3833

RESTAURANT FACTS
Seats: 75 **Weeknight Covers:** 120 **Weekend Covers:** 160 **Check Average (with Wine):** $50 **Tasting Menu:** No **Kitchen Staff:** 4

CHEF FACTS
Cuisine: Eclectic American **Born:** 1972 **Began Career:** 1992 **Culinary School:** The California Culinary Academy **Grad Year:** 1992 **Stages:** San Francisco, CA: Jardiniere; Chicago, IL: Charlie Trotter's **Work History:** New York, NY: Craft Bar, The E.U.; San Francisco, CA: Bizou **Mentor(s):** Loretta Keller, Tom Colicchio **Awards:** 2007 StarChefs.com Rising Star Chef New York **Affiliations:** Green Restaurant Association **Languages Spoken:** Spanish

NOTABLE DISH(ES): Pickled Beef Tongue with Porcinis and Marcona Almonds

FAST FACTS
Restaurant Recs: Oriental Garden on Elizabeth and Canal; Nikki's on 2nd and B for Vietnamese sandwiches; Mary's Fish Camp on Charles and W 4th **Kitchen Tool(s):** Cake tester; Winston Cvap Cook and hold oven **Interview Question:** Will you be here everyday and doing your best? **Flavor Combo(s):** Asparagus and morels; pickled cherries and Szechuan peppers; cêpes and marcona almonds **Fave Cookbook(s):** Grand Livre de Cuisine by Alain Ducasse; Essential Cuisine by Michel Bras **Chef to Cook for You:** Fredy Girardet – I was too young when he was doing his thing, but he made some food that was really inspiring **Culinary Travel:** India – as I get older, I find the food more and more exciting. The regional cuisine is different in very subtle ways. They take a lot of care in their flavoring and execution. Sicily reflects those values as well.

Uyen Nguyen
Executive Pastry Chef | Restaurant Guy Savoy

3570 Las Vegas Blvd. South Las Vegas, NV 89109

Restaurant E-mail: unguyen@harrahs.com

Phone: (702) 731-7286

RESTAURANT FACTS
Seats: 75 + private rooms **Weeknight Covers:** 40 **Weekend Covers:** 60 **Check Average (with Wine):** $250-$300 **Tasting Menu:** Yes **Kitchen Staff:** 2

CHEF FACTS
Cuisine: Modern French **Born:** 1979 **Began Career:** 2000 **Culinary School:** École Lenôtre, Paris, France **Grad Year:** 2001 **Stages:** A pastry shop in Versailles, France **Work History:** France: Pâtisserie Gaulupeau; Las Vegas, NV: Le Cirque at the Bellagio; Fleur de Lys at Mandalay Bay **Mentor(s):** Gaston Lenôtre, my mom **Awards:** 2008 StarChefs.com Rising Star Pastry Chef Las Vegas **Languages Spoken:** French, Vietnamese

NOTABLE DISH(ES): Fresh Dates with Fromage Blanc Sorbet; Citrus Salad with Hot Chamomile Tea Steam

FAST FACTS
Restaurant Recs: Sette Bello for the pizza; Harbor Palace for the dim sum **Kitchen Tool(s):** Robot Coupe **Interview Question:** Who is your favorite pastry chef and why? **Flavor Combo(s):** I like everything salty. We like to add a subtle amount of salt to our pastry, it just brings it out. Also fruit and herbs – basil goes with everything; it's everyone's best friend. When it's used correctly, it can be great. **Fave Cookbook(s):** Dessert Cuisine by Oriol Balaguer **Chef to Cook for You:** Gaston Lenôtre – he is a pioneer in pastry, and I went to his school **Culinary Travel:** Bologna, Italy because I want to learn gelato. It's totally different from French or American ice cream. It's all about texture and consistency.

Fortunato Nicotra
Executive Chef | Felidia

243 East 58th St. New York, NY 10022

Restaurant E-mail: info@lidiasitaly.com

Phone: (212) 758-1479

RESTAURANT FACTS
Seats: 95–140 **Weeknight Covers:** 160–180 **Weekend Covers:** 250–270 **Check Average (with Wine):** $95–$98 **Tasting Menu:** Yes $55/$65/$85 **Kitchen Staff:** 9–10

CHEF FACTS
Cuisine: Italian **Born:** 1962 **Began Career:** 1981 **Culinary School:** Scuola Alberghiera di Torino, Italy **Grad Year:** 1981 **Stages:** Italy: Villa Esperanza, Villa Marchese **Work History:** Italy: Villa Marchese, Villa Esperanza, Pigna d'Oro **Mentor(s):** Lidia Bastianich **Protégée(s):** Shea Gallante **Awards:** 2006 New York Times 3 stars **Affiliations:** JBF, Taste of the Nation, and we try to do everything possible charity-wise **Languages Spoken:** Italian

NOTABLE DISH(ES): Lobster and Mango Butter; Felidia Polenta with Duck in Guazzetto

FAST FACTS
Restaurant Recs: Ama Restaurant for rhum baba **Kitchen Tool(s):** Tongs **Interview Question:** How do you organize and clean your station? This is a major challenge in a small kitchen. **Flavor Combo(s):** I just like simple combinations, only 3-4 ingredients on a plate. I like to be able to taste the main ingredient and use the rest to enhance. **Fave Cookbook(s):** Le Ricette Regionali Italiane by Della Salda and Anna Gosetti **Chef to Cook for You:** Lidia not included and my mother not included, I would pick one of two sushi chefs in New York right now – the chef from 15 East or the chef from Soto. I just had amazing meals at both places, and lately Japanese is my favorite food. **Culinary Travel:** I've never been to Australia and I am fascinated by it. Great food, great wine and great chefs, like Tetsuya, whose food I was lucky enough to try one time here in New York.

Wayne Nish
Consulting Chef

New York, NY

Restaurant E-mail: marchone@aol.com

CHEF FACTS

Cuisine: East-West fusion **Born:** 1951 **Began Career:** 1983 **Culinary School:** New York Restaurant School, New York, NY **Grad Year:** 1983 **Stages:** Vero Beach, FL: The Quilted Giraffe **Work History:** New York, NY: Gramercy Tavern, Country, Onera, Varietal, March **Mentor(s):** Barry Wine, Craig Claiborne **Protégée(s):** Michael Anthony, Doug Psaltis, Steve Koutsoumbaris **Awards:** 2006 Michelin 1 star; 1992-2006 Forbes Magazine 4 stars; 1997, 1995,1992, 1988 New York Times 3 stars **Books Published:** Simple Menus for the Bento Box

NOTABLE DISH(ES): Savory Oyster Panna Cotta with Pernod; Stirred Eggs with White Truffles and Baby Potatoes

FAST FACTS

Restaurant Recs: Jing Fong for dim sum **Kitchen Tool(s):** Benriner Japanese mandolin **Interview Question:** Where do you want to be in 5 years? That tells me what ambitions they have and whether they will be in for the long-haul or if they just want to add restaurants to their resume. **Flavor Combo(s):** Olive oil and soy sauce; lobster and mentaiko; roast tomatoes and black figs; salted black beans with chili; pork and shellfish; buttered baguettes, ham and cornichons; sauerkraut and sausages with mustard. I could go on and on. **Fave Cookbook(s):** Simple French Food by Richard Olney **Chef to Cook for You:** The late Richard Olney. He wrote what I still consider to be the finest cookbook ever written in the English language, "Simple French Food." **Culinary Travel:** The two best countries in the world to eat in are Japan and Spain. They both simply have the most abundant high-quality food of anywhere I can think of.

Martial Noguier
Executive Chef | 160 Blue Chicago

1400 W Randolph St. Chicago, IL 60607

Restaurant E-mail: mnoguier@onesixtyblue.com

Phone: (312) 850-0303

RESTAURANT FACTS
Seats: 120–174 **Weeknight Covers:** 60–80 **Weekend Covers:** 150–200 **Check Average (with Wine):** $85 **Tasting Menu:** No **Kitchen Staff:** 6–9/9–11

CHEF FACTS
Other Restaurants: Cornerstone Restaurant Group **Cuisine:** Contemporary **Born:** 1964 **Began Career:** 1978/1982 **Culinary School:** Jean Ferrandi, Paris, France **Grad Year:** 1984 **Stages:** Monaco: Le Louis XVI under Alain Ducasse **Work History:** France: Diamond Vert; Los Angeles, CA: Citrus, Patina; Santa Barbara, CA: Citronelle; Washington, D.C.: Citronelle; Antigua: Jumby Bay Resort; Chicago, IL: The Pump Room **Mentor(s):** Joachim Splichal, Michel Richard **Awards:** 2008 James Beard Foundation Best Chef Great Lakes Nominee

NOTABLE DISH(ES): Peekytoe Crab Salad with Apple Jelly, Piquillo Pepper Purée, Lime, Watermelon Radish, Citrus Vinaigrette and an Apple Sheet Garnish

FAST FACTS
Restaurant Recs: Ricardo Trattoria; Sapore de Napoli pizza (Alex Yanuk's restaurant) on Belmont – they have the best pizza. He has a beautiful Moretti Forni oven. **Kitchen Tool(s):** The Japanese mandolin **Interview Question:** How did you hear about us? I want to check to see if the person knows about the restaurant. **Flavor Combo(s):** Truffle, basil and tomato **Fave Cookbook(s):** Marvelous Recipes by Regis Marcon **Chef to Cook for You:** I would like Jean-Louis Palladin to cook for me. **Culinary Travel:** Thailand – I love the cooking and the sweet and sour flavors. Everything is always so fresh, and there is always something a bit different to discover.

Nils Noren
Vice President of Culinary Arts | The French Culinary Institute

462 Broadway New York, NY 10013

Restaurant E-mail: nnoren@frenchculinary.com

Phone: (888) 324-2433

CHEF FACTS
Cuisine: Contemporary Scandinavian **Born:** 1967 **Began Career:** 1987 **Culinary School:** AMU Culinary School, Sweden **Grad Year:** 1987 **Stages:** Singapore: Mezzanine; Chicago, IL: Charlie Trotter's; England: The Fat Duck; Australia: Tetsuya's **Work History:** New York, NY: Aquavit; Sweden: Restaurant KB **Mentor(s):** Melker Andersson, Örjan Klein **Protégée(s):** Joël Harrington, Lee Anne Wong **Awards:** Contemporary Scandinavian **Affiliations:** James Beard Foundation, Gohan Society, Philanthropique **Languages Spoken:** Swedish

NOTABLE DISH(ES): Smoked Yellow Tomato Soup, Goat Cheese and Shrimp

FAST FACTS
Restaurant Recs: Nyonya for roti canai **Kitchen Tool(s):** Blender for everything from making purées to grinding spices **Interview Question:** Are you willing to work every station in the kitchen? **Flavor Combo(s):** Apple and fennel (from my Swedish side); scotch and peanuts; cheddar cheese and pickled onions **Fave Cookbook(s):** A cookbook from Hotel Nanjing (from Nanjing, China) – it's a compilation of food/dishes you normally would not see in Chinese cookbooks that have been translated into English. A second favorite is the Time Life Book: Foods of the World Series, especially the one on Scandinavian cooking. **Chef to Cook for You:** I would like to have all the chefs that worked for me who are now running their own kitchens to prepare the meal. I've been fortunate to have some extremely talented people on my team, and this would be great way to see where they are now. **Culinary Travel:** Kazakhstan – where the apple and other fruits/nuts originated

Christopher Nugent
Executive Chef | Les Nomades

222 East Ontario St. Chicago, IL 60611

Restaurant E-mail: chef@lesnomades.net

Phone: 312-649-9010

RESTAURANT FACTS
Seats: 80 **Weeknight Covers:** 65 **Weekend Covers:** 105 **Check Average (with Wine):** $170 **Tasting Menu:** No

CHEF FACTS
Cuisine: Classic French with a twist **Born:** 1973 **Began Career:** 1985 **Culinary School:** Johnson & Wales University Providence, RI **Grad Year:** 1994 **Stages:** Boston, MA: Radius; Chicago, IL: Tru, Grace, Zealous **Work History:** Chicago, IL: Prairie, Mid-American Club, MK, Park Avenue Café **Mentor(s):** John Daly, Michael Kornick, Dan Mcgee **Awards:** 2008 StarChefs.com Rising Star Chef Chicago **Affiliations:** Common Threads Chef Advisory Board **Languages Spoken:** Working on Brazilian Portuguese – my wife is from Brazil

NOTABLE DISH(ES): Torchon of Rabbit and Squab, Smoked Bacon, Quinoa, and Sauce D'Épice; Roasted Veal Sweetbread, Spanish Chorizo, Smoked Paprika, and Potato

FAST FACTS
Restaurant Recs: Dan Magee – it's a great, simple, well-designed place that gets to the heart of good cuisine. I'm a huge fan of Hot Chocolate too. **Kitchen Tool(s):** Bamix immersion blender **Interview Question:** One of the most important questions is why do you want to come cook HERE? I want to know why they want to do classical French. We're modern, but for the public I keep the descriptions simple, so people don't necessarily know what we do. **Flavor Combo(s):** I'm from upstate New York, and we're a fall-driven community. I love roasted vegetables, so I think of squash with cinnamon and nutmeg. Foie gras and capers are great to finish certain sauces and reductions, along with some red wine. Preserved lemons and olive oil makes a perfect sauce. I use it on a scallop dish here. **Fave Cookbook(s):** Essential Cuisine by Michel Bras **Chef to Cook for You:** Charlie Trotter **Culinary Travel:** Toss up between France and Italy. France because I love French food; I'm very passionate about the food and the technique, which is the foundation for many elements and types of cuisine. Italy brings me back to being at home.

Andy Nusser
Chef/Owner | Casa Mono

52 Irving Pl. New York, NY 10003

Restaurant E-mail: anusser@casamononyc.com

Phone: (212) 253-2773

RESTAURANT FACTS
Seats: 42 **Weeknight Covers:** 175 **Weekend Covers:** 250 **Check Average (with Wine):** $50 **Tasting Menu:** No **Kitchen Staff:** 3

CHEF FACTS
Other Restaurants: Bar Jamón **Cuisine:** Spanish **Born:** 1960 **Began Career:** 1995 **Culinary School:** The Culinary Institute of America Hyde Park, New York **Stages:** Spain: Casa Nun (dishwasher) **Work History:** New York, NY: Po, Babbo **Mentor(s):** My father, William Nusser **Protégée(s):** My son, William Nusser **Awards:** 1999 James Beard Foundation Best New Restaurant **Affiliations:** Hastings on Hudson Eating Society and many local charities **Languages Spoken:** Spanish

NOTABLE DISH(ES): Pumpkin and Goat Cheese Croquettes; Razor Clams; Fried Artichokes

FAST FACTS
Restaurant Recs: Bongo Seafood Lounge for lobster rolls **Kitchen Tool(s):** Jade Plancha for its speed and the color it gives ingredients **Interview Question:** What inspires you? **Flavor Combo(s):** Sweet, savory and acidic **Fave Cookbook(s):** Les Diners de Gala by Salvador Dali **Chef to Cook for You:** Julia Child circa 1963 in a hotel suite with a kitchen in Paris - just the two of us over a weekend **Culinary Travel:** Barcelona and San Sebastian

O

{ O'Connell - Ouattara }

Liz O'Connell
Consulting Pastry Chef

Boston, MA

Restaurant E-mail: lizard8280@yahoo.com

CHEF FACTS
Cuisine: Pastry **Born:** 1980 **Began Career:** 2001 **Culinary School:** Johnson & Wales, Providence, RI **Grad Year:** 2001 **Work History:** England: Mosimann's Club; Boston, MA: Harvest **Mentor(s):** Molly Hanson **Languages Spoken:** I try my hardest to speak Spanish

NOTABLE DISH(ES): Irish Soda Bread; Guinness Cake

FAST FACTS
Restaurant Recs: Casablanca for Sari's lamb **Kitchen Tool(s):** Offset spatula – I use it for everything **Interview Question:** What is your ultimate goal? I think you can find out if they are passionate and if they will be dedicated and hard working. **Flavor Combo(s):** Anything salty and sweet together **Fave Cookbook(s):** The Last Course by Claudia Fleming **Chef to Cook for You:** If I could pick anyone, it would be Julia Child. She was unbelievable in the kitchen and will always be a great inspiration. **Culinary Travel:** Spain – I love Spanish food, Spanish wine and practicing speaking

Patrick O'Connell
Chef/Co-Owner | The Inn at Little Washington

Middle and Main St. Washington, VA 22747

Restaurant E-mail: washington@relaischateaux.com

Phone: (540) 675-3800

RESTAURANT FACTS
Seats: 70–110 **Check Average (w/o Wine):** $148–$168 **Tasting Menu:** Yes **Kitchen Staff:** 12–20

CHEF FACTS
Cuisine: de terroir **Began Career:** Age 15 **Awards:** 2001 James Beard Foundation Chef of the Year; 1993 James Beard Foundation Restaurant of the Year; Mondavi Award for Culinary Excellence **Affiliations:** Relais & Châteaux, Five and Alive, Food and Friends **Books Published:** Patrick O'Connell's Refined American Cuisine: The Inn at Little Washington; The Inn at Little Washington: A Consuming Passion

NOTABLE DISH(ES): Pan-Roasted Maine Lobster with Rosemary Cream

FAST FACTS

Restaurant Recs: Helmand (an Afghani restaurant in Baltimore) – the Blissful Braised Pumpkin appetizer is delicious **Kitchen Tool(s):** Chinois – it improves the texture of almost everything **Flavor Combo(s):** I never met a flavor I didn't like **Fave Cookbook(s):** Cuisine Naturelle by Georges Blanc **Chef to Cook for You:** Edna Lewis – ain't nothing like southern food when you're drunk or feeling down **Culinary Travel:** Vietnam – the intriguing juxtaposition of cooked and raw ingredients has always fascinated me

Jeff O'Neill
Executive Chef | Mar-A-Lago Club

1100 South Ocean Blvd. Palm Beach FL 33480

Restaurant E-mail: joneill@maralagoclub.com

Phone: (561) 832-2600

RESTAURANT FACTS

Seats: 170 **Weeknight Covers:** 110 plus multiple private events daily **Weekend Covers:** 140 plus multiple private events **Check Average (with Wine):** $100 **Check Average (w/o Wine):** $70 **Tasting Menu:** Yes $95 **Kitchen Staff:** 35

CHEF FACTS

Cuisine: Modern American **Born:** 1972 **Began Career:** 1985 **Culinary School:** The Culinary Institute of America, Hyde Park, NY **Grad Year:** 1992 **Stages:** France: L'Ami Louis, Léon de Lyon, and just about every restaurant in New York City **Work History:** New York, NY: Aureole, Daniel, Le Bernardin; Palm Beach, FL: L'Escalier **Mentor(s):** Eric Ripert, Daniel Boulud, Charlie Palmer and Matthias Radits **Awards:** 1995-1998 Five Diamond AAA Award; 1995-1997 5 stars Mobil Travel Guide **Languages Spoken:** Spanish, Kitchen French

NOTABLE DISH(ES): Korean-Style Kumamoto Oysters with Kim Chi Mignonette and Kaffir Lime; Crispy Rougie Duck Confit with Cashew Butter, Tamarind, Candied Lime, Banana Brulée; Frozen Black Plum, Heirloom Tomato, Yuzu Emulsion, Micro Coriander, Chili Oil Powder

FAST FACTS

Restaurant Recs: Little Moir's Fish Shack in Jupiter Beach, Florida. I like the Cuban Crab Cakes with Caribbean Fruit Salsa **Kitchen Tool(s):** The Immersion Blender or Vita-Prep for stabilization **Interview Question:** Do you know what ramps are? Do you know how to cook fish? **Flavor Combo(s):** Sweet and sour; floral and spicy; sweet and savory **Fave Cookbook(s):** Elements of Taste by Gray Kunz; Nobu: The Cookbook by Nobuyuki Matsuhisa **Chef to Cook for You:** Fredy Girardet – they say he's the best cook that ever lived. **Culinary Travel:** Spain – because I haven't been and I can't stop hearing about it

Jonah Oakden
Chef | The Blue Plate

3218 Mission St. San Francisco, CA 94110

Phone: (415) 282-6777

RESTAURANT FACTS
Seats: 72-92 **Weeknight Covers:** 80-120 **Weekend Covers:** 120-190 **Tasting Menu:** No **Kitchen Staff:** 4

CHEF FACTS
Cuisine: Modern seasonal, American **Born:** 1977 **Began Career:** 1994 **Culinary School:** California Culinary Academy, San Francisco, CA **Work History:** San Francisco, CA: Postrio, Gabrielle Café, Wildwood **Mentor(s):** Cory Obenour, Cory Schreiber, Dustin Clark **Awards:** 2007 StarChefs.com Rising Star Chef San Francisco **Languages Spoken:** Kitchen Spanish

NOTABLE DISH(ES): Housemade Pastrami with Rye Croutons and Seared Scallops; Cornbread and Pecorino-Stuffed Pork Chop with Fried Sage

FAST FACTS
Restaurant Recs: Brothers Korean BBQ; Boulevard; La Taqueria **Kitchen Tool(s):** Gray Kunz plating spoon – I hate it when I can't find it **Interview Question:** Are you getting a job where you love the food you'll be serving? **Flavor Combo(s):** I like any surf and turf combinations, like fried oysters and braised bacon, clams and chicken, and scallops with pastrami **Fave Cookbook(s):** Anything by Michel Bras **Chef to Cook for You:** Fergus Henderson. I'd really be interested in trying his food. He takes it to another level. **Culinary Travel:** To the UK- there is a really cool, young culinary and restaurant scene going on, and lots of good products. I want to go to St. John (Fergus Henderson's restaurant) and eat some meat!

Nancy Oakes
Chef/Owner | Boulevard

1 Mission St. San Francisco, CA 94105

Restaurant E-mail: richardc@boulevardrestaurant.com

Phone: (415) 543-6084

RESTAURANT FACTS
Seats: 175 **Weekend Covers:** 290+ **Check Average (with Wine):** $90 **Tasting Menu:** No **Kitchen Staff:** 14

CHEF FACTS
Cuisine: French-influenced new American **Born:** 1951 **Began Career:** 1978 **Work History:** San Francisco, CA: L'Avenue, Barnacle, Alexis on Nob Hill **Mentor(s):** My peers who are using incredible ingredients to make really simple food. I was just up in Portland, Oregon, at Nostrana with Cathy Whims, and she made the most beautiful pasta dough. **Awards:** 2004, 2002 James Beard Foundation Outstanding Service; 1997-2001 James Beard Foundation Best Chef California Nominee; 1998-2000 San Francisco Chronicle Reader's Poll Number 1 Restaurant; 1997 Wine Spectator Top 7 San Francisco Restaurants **Affiliations:** We have a strong tie with the charity Meals-on-Wheels of San Francisco, although we also do a number of other charities every year. Organizations include WCR, Les Dames d'Escoffier and James Beard Foundation. **Books Published:** Boulevard

NOTABLE DISH(ES): Butternut Squash and Wild Mushroom Bread Pudding; Sweet Potato, Pecan and Tangerine Relish

FAST FACTS
Restaurant Recs: Pizzaiolo in Oakland for crisp pizzas and fresh preparations **Kitchen Tool(s):** Japanese mandolin – for ease of preparation **Interview Question:** What was the last serious thing you cooked for yourself and/or friends and when? This shows passion, dedication and creativity. **Flavor Combo(s):** I tend to think in terms of balance and texture, like flake salt and butter or beefy richness with horseradish cream, or crispy sticky braised bacon and high acid tomatoes. **Fave Cookbook(s):** Mangoes & Curry Leaves: Culinary Travels Through the Great Subcontinent by Jeffrey Alford and Naomi Duguid **Chef to Cook for You:** Joël Robuchon **Culinary Travel:** I would like to return to Sicily. There is a lot going on there right now, with chefs returning home and opening up places after working abroad, and all of the great locally grown, biodynamic products.

Cory Obenour
Chef/Owner | The Blue Plate

3218 Mission St. San Francisco, CA 94110

Phone: (415) 282-6777

RESTAURANT FACTS
Seats: 72–92 **Weeknight Covers:** 80–120 **Weekend Covers:** 120–190 **Tasting Menu:** No **Kitchen Staff:** 4

CHEF FACTS
Cuisine: American **Born:** 1970 **Began Career:** 1993 **Work History:** Santa Cruz, CA: Gale's Bakery, Gabriella Café; San Francisco, CA: The Moa Room, Pauline's Pizza Kitchen **Mentor(s):** My mentors are around me everyday, right here **Affiliations:** We do a lot of charity events throughout the year

NOTABLE DISH(ES): Pork Chops stuffed with Tasso Ham and Pecorino with Meyer Lemon and Fried Sage

FAST FACTS
Restaurant Recs: Joe's Shanghai in New York for the soup dumplings and the radish cakes **Kitchen Tool(s):** My Gray Kunz spoon – I like the way it feels in my hand **Interview Question:** I ask what they like to eat, I ask about ingredients, and what they are in it for... Why are you here? I'm looking for someone who sounds inspired and creative. Someone who is really into the products and ingredients we use, and who is not just looking to pay the bills. **Flavor Combo(s):** Lemon, olive oil, and parsley **Fave Cookbook(s):** The Whole Beast: Nose to Tail Eating by Fergus Henderson **Chef to Cook for You:** My friend Ravi Kapur from Boulevard. He has a knack for always sending out surprising and clever dishes whenever I eat at his restaurant. **Culinary Travel:** Sardinia – it is so close to Italy yet also very different and unique.

Mihoko Obunai
Executive Chef/Co-Owner | Repast

620 N Glen Iris Dr. Atlanta, GA 30308

Restaurant E-mail: mobunai@repastrestaurant.com

Phone: (404) 870-8707

RESTAURANT FACTS
Seats: 60–155 **Weeknight Covers:** 50–80 **Weekend Covers:** 150+
Check Average (with Wine): $50–$60 **Tasting Menu:** No

CHEF FACTS
Cuisine: American-Japanese **Born:** 1969 **Began Career:** 1996
Culinary School: The French Culinary Institute, New York, NY **Grad Year:** 1996 **Work History:** New York, NY: La Caravelle, Bayard, Club Guastavino **Mentor(s):** Daniel Orr **Awards:** 2007 StarChefs.com Rising Star Chef Atlanta; 2006 Esquire Best New Restaurants **Affiliations:** Slow Food, WCR **Languages Spoken:** Japanese, Spanish

NOTABLE DISH(ES): Steamed Halibut, Shiitake Mushrooms, Soy Onion Vinaigrette; Braised Pork Belly, Braised Daikon, Hot Mustard; Macrobiotic Composition

FAST FACTS
Restaurant Recs: Pho 96 for pho **Kitchen Tool(s):** Vita-Prep **Interview Question:** Why do you want to work for me? **Flavor Combo(s):** Sea salt and fish, especially shrimp **Fave Cookbook(s):** Nobu Now by Nobuyuki Matsuhisa; The French Laundry Cookbook by Thomas Keller **Chef to Cook for You:** James Beard **Culinary Travel:** Buenos Aires – because I love the culture

Bryan Ogden
Executive Chef | Apple Restaurant

665 North Robertson West Hollywood, CA 90069

Restaurant E-mail: bryflyog@aol.com

Phone: (310) 358-9191

RESTAURANT FACTS
Seats: 96 **Check Average (w/o Wine):** $70

CHEF FACTS
Cuisine: Contemporary American cuisine **Born:** 1977 **Began Career:** 2000 **Culinary School:** The Culinary Institute of America, Hyde Park, NY **Grad Year:** 2001 **Stages:** Berkeley, CA: Chez Panisse **Work History:** San Francisco, CA: Aqua; Santa Barbara, CA: Citronelle; Chicago IL: Charlie Trotter's; Las Vegas, NV: Bradley Ogden **Mentor(s):** Felicien Cueff, Paul Frank, Martin Frei, Michel Richard, Bradley Ogden **Awards:** 2005 StarChefs.com Rising Star Chef Las Vegas; 2004 James Beard Foundation Best New Restaurant **Languages Spoken:** Some Spanish

NOTABLE DISH(ES): Fluke Sashimi with Citrus Sponge Puffed Rice and Soy Vinaigrette; Sweet Corn Soup with Butter Poached Lobster

FAST FACTS
Restaurant Recs: Joyful House for the salt and pepper shrimp **Kitchen Tool(s):** The Microplane – I love using zest in my food. It's great for truffles, horseradish, wasabi, and apple **Interview Question:** Why do you want to work here? If they don't know about us or our food, the interview's over. **Flavor Combo(s):** Anything with balance and contrast. It is all about elevating the ingredient, herbs, acid, salt, spices. You have to know how to use those things. **Fave Cookbook(s):** Notebooks of Michel Bras: Desserts by Michel Bras **Chef to Cook for You:** Ferran Adriá, the most creative chef I have ever seen. I have eaten there three times and it is always inspiring. **Culinary Travel:** Every year we take a trip to Spain and France for eight days to just eat. Mugaritz, Arzak, El Bulli, Restaurant Martin Berasategui, Troisgros, and Marc Veyrat are some of my favorites.

Makoto Okuwa
Executive Chef and Partner | SASHI sushi and sake lounge

451 Manhattan Beach Blvd. #234 Manhattan Beach, CA 90266

Restaurant E-mail: morimakoto@sashimb.com

Phone: (858) 259-0176

RESTAURANT FACTS
Seats: 44–160

CHEF FACTS
Cuisine: Japanese **Born:** 1975 **Began Career:** 1990 **Work History:** Washington, DC: Sushi Taro; Philadelphia, PA: Morimoto; New York, NY: Morimoto **Mentor(s):** Masaharu Morimoto **Awards:** 2006 StarChefs.com Rising Star Chef New York **Languages Spoken:** Japanese

NOTABLE DISH(ES): Warm Spring-Style Salad of Fresh Bamboo Shoot, Japanese Water Eggplant, Pickled Ramps and Azuki Hata (Japanese Grouper); Prosciutto Di Parma-Wrapped Shikaimaki

FAST FACTS
Restaurant Recs: New York, NY: Ushiwakamaru for really good sushi; Momofuku Noodle Bar **Kitchen Tool(s):** Nenox knife – it's made of great material and looks good too, though it's very expensive **Interview Question:** How long have you worked with sushi? What do you want to learn here? **Flavor Combo(s):** Yuzu or any kind of Cutlass and Saikyo miso (Japanese sweet white miso) because Cutlass brings out a clear miso flavor. Also lemongrass and coconut milk. **Fave Cookbook(s):** Alfred Portale Simple Pleasures: Home Cooking from the Gotham Bar and Grill's Acclaimed Chef by Alfred Portale and Andrew Friedman **Chef to Cook for You:** Ferran Adrià because I've never had his food before. I believe he is one of the best chefs in the world. **Culinary Travel:** I like to go to Spain to see new techniques and flavors, and I really want to go to England to eat at The Fat Duck

Nick Oltarsh
Executive Chef | TWELVE Atlantic Station

361 17th St. Atlanta, GA 30363

Restaurant E-mail: noltarsh@ctrxhs.com

Phone: (404) 961-7370

RESTAURANT FACTS
Seats: 150 **Weeknight Covers:** 100–150 **Weekend Covers:** 200–300 **Check Average (with Wine):** $30–$50 **Tasting Menu:** No **Kitchen Staff:** 10

CHEF FACTS
Other Restaurants: Room at Twelve; TWELVE Centennial Park; Concentrics Restaurants **Cuisine:** Contemporary American **Born:** 1968 **Began Career:** 1990 **Culinary School:** The Culinary Institute of America, Hyde Park, NY University of Pennsylvania, Philadelphia, PA **Grad Year:** 1992 **Stages:** Italy: Trattoria Cesarina **Work History:** New York, NY: Huberts, Aquavit, Lespinasse, Gramercy Tavern, Eleven Madison Park **Mentor(s):** Tom Colicchio, Gray Kunz **Protégée(s):** Sarah Schafer **Awards:** 2007 StarChefs.com Rising Star Hotel Chef Atlanta **Affiliations:** SOS, March of Dimes, American Liver Foundation **Books Published:** Atlanta Cooks at Home, Murphy's **Languages Spoken:** French, Kitchen Spanish

NOTABLE DISH(ES): Pulled Braised Lamb, Crème Fraîche, Grilled Bread; Local Georgia Trout, Almond Brown Butter, Lemon, Capers

FAST FACTS
Restaurant Recs: Pho Number One for pho; Chef Liu for salty soy bean milk and leek pie; China Delight for dim sum; Hae Woon Dae for Korean seafood pancakes and jap chae **Kitchen Tool(s):** A pocket-sized spiral notebook for writing down menu ideas, production and staffing issues, food ordering notes, observations, etc. I am useless without it. **Interview Question:** What kind of food do you love? I look for any kind of interest or passion for food. **Flavor Combo(s):** I love vinegar and butter. I'm also very fond of shiso. **Fave Cookbook(s):** The Taste of France by Robert Freson and Jacqueline Saulnier **Chef to Cook for You:** Jean-Georges Vongerichten – he is incredible **Culinary Travel:** Singapore and Thailand – I plan on going for my fortieth birthday

Pichet Ong
Executive Chef | P*ONG

150 West 10th St. New York, NY 10014

Restaurant E-mail: pichet@p-ong.com

Phone: (212) 929-0898

RESTAURANT FACTS
Seats: 28 **Weeknight Covers:** 35 **Weekend Covers:** 69 **Check Average (with Wine):** $49 **Tasting Menu:** Yes $28-$107 **Kitchen Staff:** 2

CHEF FACTS
Other Restaurants: Batch Bakery **Cuisine:** Savory and pastry **Born:** 1968 **Began Career:** 1991 **Work History:** Berkeley, CA: Chez Panisse; San Francisco, CA: La Folie; Charlestown, MA: Olives; New York, NY: Cello, Jean-Georges, Patron, Perry Street, RM, Sono, Tabla, Spice Market **Mentor(s):** Jean-Georges Vongerichten **Awards:** 2008 James Beard Foundation Outstanding Pastry Chef Nominee; 2005 StarChefs.com Rising Star Pastry Chef New York **Affiliations:** I have regular classes at the Institute of Culinary Education, The CIA Greystone and Hyde Park. I also work with The French Culinary Institute; and I participate regularly with the James Beard Foundation. **Books Published:** The Sweet Spot; Sugar & Salt: Blurring the Line Between Sweet and Savory (to be released at the end of 2008) **Languages Spoken:** Two dialects of Chinese, Thai

NOTABLE DISH(ES): Thai Jewels; Ovaltine™ Kulfi with Banana and Spiced Chocolate; Warm Rice Pudding with Passion Fruit Seeds

FAST FACTS
Restaurant Recs: Bolo; Josephs Citarella; Mesa Grill; wd~50; all for desserts **Kitchen Tool(s):** Excluding my hands, a KitchenAid Mixer and spatulas **Interview Question:** They must be hands-on. Their answers must show passion about cuisine and pursuit of better lifestyle through better food. **Flavor Combo(s):** My signature flavor combination falls somewhere between sweet and salty. For optimum flavor experience, I also like sour, bitter, and spicy. **Fave Cookbook(s):** I love The Joy of Cooking and The Best of Cook's Illustrated. But my most-used of all time is the Fanny Farmer Cookbook. **Chef to Cook for You:** Any chef or cook who became one, like myself, because they love to eat **Culinary Travel:** Anywhere and everywhere around the world. This past year, it was China and Australia. For the coming year, my choice would be Norway, Sweden, India, and Korea.

Tadashi Ono
Executive Chef/Partner | Matsuri

369 W 16th St. New York, NY 10011

Restaurant E-mail: tadashi@themaritimehotel.com

Phone: (212) 243-6400

RESTAURANT FACTS
Seats: 300 **Weeknight Covers:** 200 **Weekend Covers:** 500 **Check Average (with Wine):** $50 **Check Average (w/o Wine):** $40 **Tasting Menu:** No **Kitchen Staff:** 20

CHEF FACTS
Cuisine: Japanese **Born:** 1962 **Began Career:** 1980 **Work History:** Los Angeles, CA: La Petite Chaya, L'Orangerie; New York, NY: La Caravelle, Sono **Mentor(s):** Kitaoji Rosanjin **Protégée(s):** Ruyji Irie **Affiliations:** Gohan Foundation **Languages Spoken:** Japanese, Spanish

NOTABLE DISH(ES): Braised Yellowtail Collar

FAST FACTS
Restaurant Recs: Omen for everything **Kitchen Tool(s):** Chopsticks **Interview Question:** What is your favorite ingredient? **Flavor Combo(s):** Steamed white rice and miso **Fave Cookbook(s):** Cooking Kingdom by Kitaoji Rosanjin **Culinary Travel:** Japan

Marc Orfaly
Chef | Pigalle

75 Charles St.Boston, MA 02114

Restaurant E-mail: marc@pigalleboston.com

Phone: (617) 423-4944

RESTAURANT FACTS
Seats: 48 **Weeknight Covers:** 40 **Weekend Covers:** 80–90 **Check Average (with Wine):** $75 **Tasting Menu:** Yes $110/$165 both with wine **Kitchen Staff:** 4

CHEF FACTS
Other Restaurants: Marco Cucina Romana **Cuisine:** Contemporary French **Born:** 1969 **Began Career:** 1990 **Culinary School:** Johnson & Wales, Providence, RI **Grad Year:** 1990 **Stages:** New York, NY: Mondrian, Union Pacific **Work History:** Los Angeles, CA: Campanile, Patina; Charlestown, MA: Olives; Providence, RI: Al Forno; New York, NY: Coco Pazzo **Mentor(s):** Todd English, Nancy Silverton, Joachim Splichal **Protégée(s):** Matt Abdoo **Awards:** 2005-2006 James Beard Foundation Best Chef Northeast Nominee; 2004 Food & Wine Best New Chefs; 2003 StarChefs.com Rising Star Chef Boston; 2002 Boston Magazine Best Upscale Romantic Restaurant **Affiliations:** SOS, Dana Farber Cancer Institute, NEC, CIA **Languages Spoken:** Kitchen Spanish

NOTABLE DISH(ES): Foie Gras Crème Brulée; Lobster à la Thai

FAST FACTS
Restaurant Recs: Santarpio's Pizza for lamb kebobs and spicy pork sausage **Kitchen Tool(s):** Multi-vac sealing machine because meats and seasonings can be sealed for marinating and then slowly cooked sous vide **Interview Question:** Have you dined at my restaurant? You should love the place and the food if you want to work here. **Flavor Combo(s):** A really great combo I whipped up for my staff recently was fried sweetbreads with Frank's hot sauce. On the menu something that turned out really well was lobster with foie gras served with quark and fromage blanc tortellini. The foie fat mixed with the tangy cheeses was really interesting. **Fave Cookbook(s):** Larousse Gastronomique by Prosper Montagne **Chef to Cook for You:** David Bouley – he has taken a lot of European technique and mixed it with his own style, creating a great range of classic and modern dishes. Every you time you eat his food it is a surprise. **Culinary Travel:** Malaysia – Kuala Lumpur is a huge melting pot of Asian culture and food. There is Indian, Cantonese, Singaporean and Malaysian cuisine... the options are endless. I love the whole culture.

Kenneth Oringer
Executive Chef | Clio

370 Commonwealth Ave. Boston, MA 2215

Restaurant E-mail: koringer@cliorestaurant.com

Phone: (617) 536-7200

RESTAURANT FACTS
Seats: 65 **Weeknight Covers:** 70 **Weekend Covers:** 100 **Check Average (with Wine):** $125 **Tasting Menu:** No **Kitchen Staff:** 6–7

CHEF FACTS
Other Restaurants: Toro, Uni **Cuisine:** Contemporary French and Asian **Born:** 1965 **Began Career:** 1987 **Culinary School:** The Culinary Institute of America, Hyde Park, NY **Grad Year:** 1989 **Stages:** Spain: el Bulli **Work History:** New York, NY: The River Café; Providence, RI: Al Forno; Boston, MA: Le Marquis de Lafayette; Greenwich, CT: Terra; San Francisco, CA: Silks; Hingham, MA: Tosca **Mentor(s):** Michel Bras, David Burke, Jean-Georges Vongerichten **Protégée(s):** Alex Stupak, Todd MacDonald, Tony Maws **Awards:** 2001 James Beard Foundation Best Chef Northeast **Affiliations:** Autism Speaks, Michael J Fox Foundation **Languages Spoken:** Some French

NOTABLE DISH(ES): Sea Urchin with Green Apple and Wasabi Foam in Nori Croquant; Foie Gras Terrine with Citrus Textures and Flavors

FAST FACTS
Restaurant Recs: Sapporo Ramen, Tacos El Charo, Taiwan Café **Kitchen Tool(s):** Thermomix blender **Interview Question:** What separates you from the hundreds of other people we have coming in? **Flavor Combo(s):** Anything salty, sour, hot, and sweet **Fave Cookbook(s):** La Methode: An Illustrated Guide to the Fundamental Techniques of Cooking by Jacques Pépin **Chef to Cook for You:** Michel Bras – I love his connection to nature and his region **Culinary Travel:** Japan for the seasonality of food and the interest in tradition

Louis Osteen
Executive Chef | Louis's at Pawleys

10880 Ocean Hwy., #19 Pawleys Island, SC 29858

Restaurant E-mail: louisosteen@louislasvegas.com

Phone: (843) 237-8757

RESTAURANT FACTS
Seats: 125 **Weeknight Covers:** 60 **Weekend Covers:** 60-125 **Check Average (with Wine):** $90 **Tasting Menu:** No **Kitchen Staff:** 3-7

CHEF FACTS
Other Restaurants: Louis's To Go, The Fish Camp Bar **Cuisine:** Foods of the Southern Low Country **Born:** 1941 **Work History:** Atlanta, GA: Le Versailles, Midnight Sun **Mentor(s):** François Delcros **Protégée(s):** Tyler Florence, Michael Keogh **Awards:** 2004 James Beard Foundation Best Chef Southeast; 1997 Restaurant & Institutions Ivy Award; 1994 Nation's Restaurant News Fine Dining Hall of Fame Inductee **Affiliations:** JBF, AIFW, SFA **Books Published:** Louis Osteen's Charleston Cuisine: Recipes from a Low Country Chef

FAST FACTS
Restaurant Recs: Nora's (the one on Flamingo; an old fashion Italian red sauce-style place) for pizzas, pastas and meatballs **Kitchen Tool(s):** Chinois, because it's one of the last steps of refinement **Interview Question:** What are the last three cookbooks you bought and read? I put an emphasis on bought because I want to know if they are putting their money where their mouth is. **Fave Cookbook(s):** Mastering the Art of French Cooking, Volume I by Julia Child **Chef to Cook for You:** Fredy Girardet – he opened and closed before I got there. He was considered the finest chef in the world. **Culinary Travel:** Spain

Chris Otten
Chef | Nine One Five

915 Duval St. Key West, FL 33040

Restaurant E-mail: chrisotten@bellsouth.net

Phone: (305) 296-0669

RESTAURANT FACTS
Seats: 100 **Weeknight Covers:** 100 **Weekend Covers:** 180 **Check Average (with Wine):** $200 **Tasting Menu:** Yes $150 **Kitchen Staff:** 4

CHEF FACTS
Cuisine: International **Born:** 1978 **Began Career:** 1996 **Mentor(s):** Claire Archibold, Martha Hubbard **Languages Spoken:** Spanish

NOTABLE DISH(ES): Sizzling Thai Whole Yellow Tail Snapper with Sizzling Chili-Garlic Sauce, Steamed Basmati Rice and Chinese Cabbage

FAST FACTS
Restaurant Recs: Ambrosia for the uni sashimi **Kitchen Tool(s):** Strainers – I liked everything strained. The final product is more refined and smoother. **Interview Question:** What is the most recent cookbook you have read? It tells me what they are into and if they are in fact reading cookbooks, which I think is very important. **Flavor Combo(s):** I really like jalapeño, cilantro and lime as a base for ceviche and also for sauces **Fave Cookbook(s):** Any Chez Panisse cookbook. I like her food and I like her books. **Chef to Cook for You:** Alice Waters, because the food is fresh, organic and simple **Culinary Travel:** Vietnam – the flavors are fresh and the use of herbs is fantastic

Morou Ouattara
Chef/Owner | Farrah Olivia by Morou

600 Franklin St. Alexandria, VA 22314

Restaurant E-mail: morou@farraholiviarestaurant.com

Phone: (703) 778-2233

RESTAURANT FACTS
Seats: 65–85 **Weeknight Covers:** 60 **Weekend Covers:** 120 **Check Average (with Wine):** $75 **Check Average (w/o Wine):** $50 **Tasting Menu:** Yes $65/$75/$125 **Kitchen Staff:** 4

CHEF FACTS
Other Restaurants: Sprigz, coming fall 08 **Cuisine:** Creative American **Born:** 1966 **Began Career:** 1988 **Work History:** Washington, DC: Ricchi, Red Sage, Signatures Restaurant **Mentor(s):** Francesco Ricchi, Mark Miller **Protégée(s):** Eddie Marine, Leon Baker, Noriaki Yasutake **Awards:** 2006 Leukemia Society's Man of the Year Host Chef; 2003 StarChefs.com Rising Star Chef Washington DC; 3 RAMW nominations **Affiliations:** RAMW **Books Published:** I am currently writing one **Languages Spoken:** French, African dialect

NOTABLE DISH(ES): Smoked Pears, Wasabi, Black Salt; Caramelized Maine Lobster with Madagascar Vanilla, Truffled Tapioca Risotto, Fennel Confit, and Olive Oil Foam

FAST FACTS
Restaurant Recs: Makoto in DC **Kitchen Tool(s):** Spice grinder **Interview Question:** Why here, why now? Because you can only keep an employee if their expectations are met at your establishment at a specific time in their career. **Flavor Combo(s):** Sweet and sour; foie gras and dates; escargot and palm nut pulp; nutty and smoky **Fave Cookbook(s):** Essential Cuisine by Michel Bras **Chef to Cook for You:** Michel Bras – an amazing chef and a great artist **Culinary Travel:** I love ethnic food. I'd like to take a tour through Asia, eating traditional food in small hidden villages and towns.

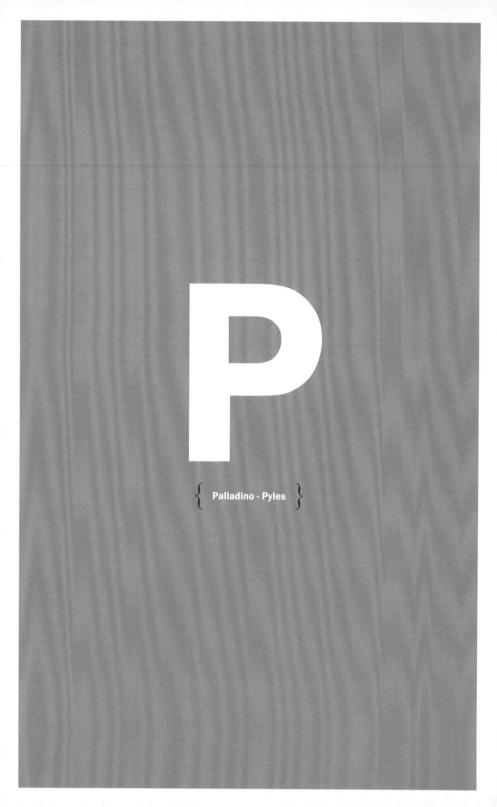

P

{ Palladino - Pyles }

Luke Palladino
Chef | Ombra

404 Stockbridge Ct. Absecon, NJ 08205

Restaurant E-mail: luke@lukepalladino.com

Phone: (609) 385-2875

RESTAURANT FACTS
Seats: 160 **Weeknight Covers:** 170 **Weekend Covers:** 400 **Check Average (with Wine):** $60 **Check Average (w/o Wine):** $45 **Tasting Menu:** Yes $85 **Kitchen Staff:** 14

CHEF FACTS
Other Restaurants: Pompano Beach, FL: Bragozzo; Biloxi, MI: Specchio, Risi Bisi, Bragozzo **Cuisine:** Italian **Born:** 1969 **Began Career:** 1989 **Culinary School:** The Culinary Institute of America, Hyde Park, NY **Grad Year:** 1989 **Stages:** Italy: Al Covo, Osteria Boccondivino, Da Romea, Al Fornello da Ricci, Francu U Piscaturi **Work History:** Italy: Al Covo, Osteria Boccondivino, Da Romea, Al Fornello da Ricci, Francu U Piscaturi; San Francisco, CA: Stars, J.T.'s Bistro, Oliveto; Aspen, CO: Olives **Mentor(s):** Cesare Benelli, Al Covo **Protégée(s):** Jason Rogers **Awards:** 2003-2008 Casino Player Best Italian Restaurants; Best New Restaurants: Atlantic City, South Florida, Biloxi **Affiliations:** Slow Food, Chefs Collaborative **Books Published:** My Fish Only Speak Italian **Languages Spoken:** Italian

FAST FACTS
Restaurant Recs: Dock's Oyster House in Atlantic City for pommes soufflé **Kitchen Tool(s):** Wüsthof straight carving fork because it's great for twirling pasta, sautéing, and turning meats on the grill **Interview Question:** Are you sure you want to do this? I ask this because too many young people think that the road to success in restaurants comes quickly when it really takes decades of experience. **Flavor Combo(s):** "Agro-dolce" (sweet and sour) **Fave Cookbook(s):** Il Talismano Della Felicita by Ada Boni **Chef to Cook for You:** Paul Bertolli – few people are in tune with the true soul of Italian cuisine, but Paul certainly is **Culinary Travel:** Italy of course! My heritage, love and passion for food and wine lie there.

P

Charlie Palmer
Chef | Aureole

34 E 61st St. New York, NY 10021

Restaurant E-mail: agouras@charliepalmer.com

Phone: (212) 319-1660

RESTAURANT FACTS

Seats: 80 **Weeknight Covers:** 90-100 **Weekend Covers:** 150 **Check Average (with Wine):** $165 **Check Average (w/o Wine):** $105 **Tasting Menu:** Yes $115/$195 with wine **Kitchen Staff:** 10–13

CHEF FACTS

Other Restaurants: Las Vegas, NV: Astra, Metrazur, Aureole, Charlie Palmer Hotel, Charlie Palmer Steak; Healdsburg, CA: Dry Creek Kitchen, Lime Stone; Washington, DC: Charlie Palmer Steak; Dallas, TX: Charlie Palmer at the Joule; Reno, NV: Charlie Palmer Steak; Costa Mesa, CA: Charlie Palmer at Bloomingdales **Cuisine:** Progressive American **Began Career:** 1979 **Culinary School:** The Culinary Institute of America, Hyde Park, NY **Grad Year:** 1981 **Stages:** France: Georges Blanc **Work History:** New York, NY: La Côte Basque; The River Café **Mentor(s):** Jean-Jacques Rachou **Protégée(s):** David Burke, Gerry Hayden, Michael Mina **Awards:** 1998 James Beard Foundation Who's Who of Food & Beverage in America; 1997 James Beard Foundation Award Best Chef New York; 1997 Restaurant & Institutions IVY Award; 1997 Relais & Châteaux New Member; 2000-2002 Wine Spectator Award of Excellence; 2000-2002 Wine Spectator Grand Award; 2003 Food Arts Silver Spoon for Outstanding Service **Affiliations:** CMW, CIA board **Books Published:** Great American Food; Charlie Palmer's Casual Cooking; The Art of Aureole; Charlie Palmer's Practical Guide to the New American Kitchen

NOTABLE DISH(ES): Mushroom Velouté Soup; Dried Fruit and Nut Bread Stuffing

FAST FACTS

Restaurant Recs: Pinch for pizza by the inch. My kids love the pizza and I love their braised dishes. **Kitchen Tool(s):** Surgical tweezers for accuracy when plating **Interview Question:** Why do you want to cook? **Flavor Combo(s):** Pork and Pinot Noir **Fave Cookbook(s):** Larousse Gastronomique by Prosper Montagne **Culinary Travel:** To France, especially to Leon. I am very interested in wine – I actually have a vineyard in Healdsburg, CA. I am very interested in the winemaking history and techniques in France and I try to go annually.

Ron Paprocki
Pastry Chef | Gordon Ramsay at The London

151 W. 54th St. New York, NY 10019

Restaurant E-mail: ronpaprocki@gordonramsay.com

Phone: (212) 468-8888

RESTAURANT FACTS
Seats: 45 **Weeknight Covers:** 80 **Weekend Covers:** 100 **Check Average (with Wine):** $200 **Tasting Menu:** Yes $135 **Kitchen Staff:** 11

CHEF FACTS
Other Restaurants: Maze, room service, and all other hotel operations for The London **Cuisine:** Modern French **Born:** 1970 **Began Career:** 2002 **Culinary School:** The Elisabeth-Knipping Schule, Kassel, Germany **Grad Year:** 2004 **Work History:** Germany: Café Alheit; New York, NY: Financier Pâtisserie, Sascha Bakery/Restaurant **Mentor(s):** Wolfgang Alheit **Languages Spoken:** German

NOTABLE DISH(ES): Pineapple Soufflé with Hand-Ground Thai Curry Ice Cream

FAST FACTS
Restaurant Recs: Dinosaur Bar-B-Que in Harlem – I get the full-rack of pork ribs with cucumber-tomato salad and a Genesee Cream Ale **Kitchen Tool(s):** The scraper – I use it for everything, including picking up fragile things **Interview Question:** What inspired you to want to work in pastry? **Flavor Combo(s):** Strawberry and pistachio; cherries and dark chocolate – I like classic combinations **Fave Cookbook(s):** The Fannie Farmer Cookbook **Chef to Cook for You:** Julia Child would steal my heart if she made me meatloaf with a side of mashed potatoes. She was the ultimate inspiration. **Culinary Travel:** Spain – with pastry chefs like Enric Rosich, Paco Torreblanca and Roman Moroto coming from Spain, it increases my curiosity about what else lies within the region

P

Kirk Parks
Pastry Chef | Rathbun's

112 Krog St., Suite R Atlanta, GA 30307

Restaurant E-mail: info@rathbunsrestaurant.com

Phone: (404) 524-8280

RESTAURANT FACTS
Seats: 150 **Weeknight Covers:** 175-200 **Weekend Covers:** 350-400
Check Average (with Wine): $55 **Tasting Menu:** No **Kitchen Staff:** 7

CHEF FACTS
Other Restaurants: Krog Bar, Kevin Rathbun Steak **Cuisine:** Southwestern Pacific Rim melting pot **Born:** 1958 **Began Career:** 1976 **Culinary School:** Art Institute of Atlanta **Grad Year:** 2001 **Stages:** Dallas, Texas: Baby Routh's **Work History:** Houston, TX: Brennan's; Dallas, TX: Baby Routh's; Calistoga, CA: All Seasons; Antigua: Jumby Bay Resort; Atlanta, GA: NAVA **Mentor(s):** Kevin Rathbun, Cliff Bramble, Stephan Pyles **Protégée(s):** Rebecca Weil **Awards:** 1993 James Beard Foundation Baker of the Year **Affiliations:** SOS, MOD, JBF and many other events, charities and fundraisers **Books Published:** Contributed to New Texas Cuisine **Languages Spoken:** Kitchen Spanish

FAST FACTS
Restaurant Recs: Floataway Café – for the double bone pork chop with parsnips **Kitchen Tool(s):** Microplane for citrus and ginger, which add flavor to anything! It reminds me of a rasp in woodworking. **Interview Question:** What do you read? What is your favorite fruit? What is your favorite cuisine? How do you deal with stress? And where do you want to be in 5-10 years? **Flavor Combo(s):** Vanilla bean and ginger; raspberry and Chambord; Jack Daniel's and butterscotch; Tabasco and strawberries **Fave Cookbook(s):** Bread Alone by Daniel Leader. It is a great great book and I recommend it to anyone who loves to bake bread. **Chef to Cook for You:** Michel Richard – he is a pastry chef and an executive chef. His food is stellar. **Culinary Travel:** I would love to go to Hong Kong and Singapore to check out the street food. I really love spicy, sticky and sweet combinations, and I hear the food is amazing.

Maria Passaris
Pastry Chef | Maria Passaris Cakes

P.O. Box 5564 Novato, CA 94948

Restaurant E-mail: maria@mariapassariscakes.com

Phone: (415) 572-9977

CHEF FACTS
Cuisine: Greek **Born:** 1979 **Began Career:** 2001 **Culinary School:** Culinary Institute of America, Greystone, CA **Grad Year:** 2000 **Stages:** San Francisco, CA: Kokkari **Work History:** San Francisco, CA: Postrio, Town Hall **Mentor(s):** Jacques Torres **Languages Spoken:** Greek

FAST FACTS
Restaurant Recs: Cha Cha Cha for the Cajun shrimp appetizer. It's simple and delicious! **Kitchen Tool(s):** Spatula – always the perfect tool! **Interview Question:** Why did you choose this path? What brought you into the industry? **Flavor Combo(s):** Simple, basic and delicious – like vanilla bean, caramel and a smooth, bold chocolate **Fave Cookbook(s):** The Professional Pastry Chef: Fundamentals of Baking and Pastry by Bo Friberg **Chef to Cook for You:** Thomas Keller – his work amazes me. His flavor combinations and creativity inspire me. **Culinary Travel:** Italy – never been and find it fascinating. I have traveled Greece many times and hope to travel to different parts of Europe in the near future. I love their passion for food. The food is fresh and so tasty and the beautiful atmosphere helps too!

P

Daniel Patterson
Executive Chef | Coi

373 Broadway San Francisco, CA 94133

Restaurant E-mail: coikitchen@gmail.com

Phone: (415) 393-9000

RESTAURANT FACTS
Seats: 29-49 **Weeknight Covers:** 30-40 **Weekend Covers:** 40+
Check Average (with Wine): $120 **Tasting Menu:** Yes $120 **Kitchen Staff:** 9

CHEF FACTS
Cuisine: Contemporary American **Born:** 1968 **Began Career:** 1982
Work History: Sonoma, CA: Babette's; San Francisco, CA: Elisabeth Daniel, Frisson **Affiliations:** We do lots of events and fundraisers

FAST FACTS
Restaurant Recs: Aziza – I love everything, especially the couscous **Kitchen Tool(s):** The knife. It is the most intimate tool that a chef uses. It says a lot about who you are as a chef and how you approach your work. **Interview Question:** I like to watch how they work – I can usually tell what I need to know that way. I also like to ask what their goals are. In our kitchen the people who do well are driven and clear about the quality and level of food they want to work with. **Fave Cookbook(s):** The Cooking of Southwest France by Paula Wolfert **Chef to Cook for You:** Alain Chapel – he passed away before I could go to his restaurant. From what I've read, his cooking seems pretty thrilling. He had amazing attention to detail, precision, and focus on perfection. **Culinary Travel:** Japan – I think it has the greatest food culture on the planet

François Payard
Chef/Owner | Payard Patisserie & Bistro

1032 Lexington Ave. New York, NY 10021

Restaurant E-mail: Francois@payard.com

Phone: (212) 717-5252

RESTAURANT FACTS
Seats: 110 **Weeknight Covers:** 150 **Weekend Covers:** 200 **Check Average (with Wine):** $65 **Tasting Menu:** Yes $72/$112 with wine **Kitchen Staff:** 7

CHEF FACTS
Cuisine: French desserts and pastries **Born:** 1966 **Began Career:** 1982 **Culinary School:** Apprenticeship in France **Grad Year:** 1984 **Work History:** France: La Tour d'Argent, Lucas Carton; New York, NY: Daniel, Le Bernardin **Mentor(s):** Charles Ghignone, Alain Senderens **Protégée(s):** Lincoln Carson, Gregory Gourreau, Johnny Iuzzini **Awards:** 1998 Bon Appétit Pastry Chef of the Year; 1995 James Beard Foundation Outstanding Pastry Chef of the Year **Affiliations:** JBF, RDI **Books Published:** Bite Size: Elegant Recipes for Entertaining; Simply Sensational Desserts **Languages Spoken:** French, Spanish

NOTABLE DISH(ES): Rose Petal Sorbet and Crystallized Rose Petals

FAST FACTS
Restaurant Recs: L'Atelier de Joël Robuchon **Kitchen Tool(s):** Silpat **Interview Question:** It's not really a question, but I am looking for passion and dedication to the field. This is more important to me than a resume. **Flavor Combo(s):** Chocolate and caramel **Fave Cookbook(s):** Secrets Gourmands by Pierre Hermé **Chef to Cook for You:** Masaharu Morimoto – he is very creative, and I love Japanese food. **Culinary Travel:** Back to Spain. It has changed so much in the past five years. I also always love to go to Japan.

Scott Peacock
Chef/Owner | Watershed

406 West Ponce De Leon Ave. Decatur, GA 30030

Restaurant E-mail: friends@watershedrestaurant.com

Phone: (404) 378-4900

RESTAURANT FACTS
Seats: 99 **Weeknight Covers:** 130 **Weekend Covers:** 180–200 **Tasting Menu:** No **Kitchen Staff:** 5+

CHEF FACTS
Cuisine: Southern **Born:** 1962 **Began Career:** 1987 **Work History:** Atlanta, GA: Former Executive Chef for two Georgia governors, Horseradish Grill **Mentor(s):** Edna Lewis **Protégée(s):** Steven Satterfield **Awards:** 2007 James Beard Foundation Best Chef Southeast **Affiliations:** SFA, Slow Food, Georgia Organics, City Meals-on-Wheels, Project Open Hand, Chefs Collaborative, Georgia Restaurant Asssociation **Books Published:** The Gift of Southern Cooking

NOTABLE DISH(ES): Fried Chicken; Garlic and Thyme Roasted Pork; Pimento Cheese

FAST FACTS
Kitchen Tool(s): Microplane; Silpat; dough scraper – I don't know how anyone cooks without one **Interview Question:** Where do you like to eat in Atlanta? **Flavor Combo(s):** Simple and balanced **Fave Cookbook(s):** The Alice B. Toklas Cookbook by Alice B. Toklas **Chef to Cook for You:** Edna Lewis – for obvious reasons **Culinary Travel:** Southern Italy and India, because I'm intrigued by the commonalities with the American South

Mark Peel
Executive Chef/Owner | Campanile

624 South La Brea Los Angeles, CA 90036

Restaurant E-mail: info@campanilerestaurant.com

Phone: (323) 938-1447

RESTAURANT FACTS

Seats: 200 **Weeknight Covers:** 75-150 **Weekend Covers:** 175-350
Check Average (with Wine): $75 **Check Average (w/o Wine):** $56
Tasting Menu: No **Kitchen Staff:** 8

CHEF FACTS

Cuisine: Californian urban rustic **Born:** 1954 **Began Career:** 1975
Stages: Los Angeles, CA: Ma Maison; France: La Tour d'Argent,
Moulin de Mougins **Work History:** Los Angeles, CA: Michael's
Restaurant, Spago, La Brea Bakery; New York, NY: Maxwell's Plum
Mentor(s): Wolfgang Puck **Awards:** 1997 DiRoNA Distinguished Res-
taurant of North America; 1996 Nation's Restaurant News Fine Din-
ing Award; 1996, 1995, 1990 James Beard Best Chef California Nominee; 1995 Southern California
Restaurant Writers Restaurateur of the Year and Restaurant of the Year; 1989 Food & Wine Best New
Chefs **Affiliations:** We support a number of them: Meals-on-Wheels, Vintage Hollywood, etc. **Books
Published:** Mark Peel and Nancy Silverton at Home: Two Chefs Cook for Family and Friends; Mark
Peel and Nancy Silverton: The Food of Campanile

FAST FACTS

Restaurant Recs: Café Verona for their Italian French toast **Kitchen Tool(s):** Mortar and pestle,
because they create a chunkier texture for things like pesto without incorporating air or heating
anything up, and they preserve color, flavor and texture. It might take a little more time and muscle,
but the results are worth it. **Interview Question:** Where have you worked? How long were you there?
If someone's been to six places in two years, that's not a good sign. I also look for intelligence,
energy and apparent dedication. **Flavor Combo(s):** Lemon and thyme **Fave Cookbook(s):** Larousse
Gastronomique by Prosper Montagne **Chef to Cook for You:** Marie-Antoine Carême – he was the
beginning of it all! **Culinary Travel:** Thailand because I don't know much about it

P

Zak Pelaccio
Chef | Fatty Crab

643 Hudson St. New York, NY 10014

Restaurant E-mail: ryan@nyrsg.com

Phone: (212) 352-3592

RESTAURANT FACTS
Seats: 32 **Weeknight Covers:** I don't know, but the place takes some serious abuse.... **Check Average (with Wine):** $37 **Tasting Menu:** No **Kitchen Staff:** 3–4

CHEF FACTS
Other Restaurants: New York: Fatty 'Cue, Borough; London, England: Suka **Cuisine:** Malaysian, American **Born:** 1973 **Began Career:** 1997 **Culinary School:** The French Culinary Institute, New York, NY **Grad Year:** 1997 **Stages:** Thailand: Thai Restaurant at Westin Chiang Mai **Work History:** Yountville, CA: The French Laundry; New York, NY: Union Pacific, Daniel, Chickenbone Café **Mentor(s):** My parents **Protégée(s):** My son **Awards:** 2006 StarChefs.com Rising Star Chef New York **Affiliations:** Slow Food, Heritage Foods **Languages Spoken:** Some Italian

NOTABLE DISH(ES): Pork Belly and Watermelon Salad; Chili Crab

FAST FACTS
Restaurant Recs: Chao Thai for clams with chili **Kitchen Tool(s):** Telephone for calling my purveyors **Interview Question:** What are you reading now? **Flavor Combo(s):** They're always changing, evolving **Fave Cookbook(s):** I like Royal Thai Family Favorites, which I picked up in Northern Thailand in 1995, and I like Thai Seafood, which I also got there. Zarina's Home Cooking is great too, with Indonesian and Indian influences. **Chef to Cook for You:** David Thompson because he cooks Thai food better than most Thais. Thai cuisine is so incredibly dynamic and has a great range of flavors. **Culinary Travel:** All of Malaysia is great, but Kuala Lumpur is my favorite city

Luciano Pellegrini
Executive Chef | Valentino Restaurant

3355 Las Vegas Blvd.Las Vegas, NV 89109

Restaurant E-mail: chefvlv@lvcoxmail.com

Phone: (702) 414-3000

RESTAURANT FACTS
Seats: 150-260 **Weeknight Covers:** 300-350 **Weekend Covers:** 400-450 **Check Average (with Wine):** $45-$100 **Tasting Menu:** Yes $70/$95/$105 **Kitchen Staff:** 6-10

CHEF FACTS
Other Restaurants: Giorgio **Cuisine:** Italian **Born:** 1964 **Began Career:** 1978 **Culinary School:** San Pellegrino Hotel School, Italy **Stages:** Italy: Dal Pescatore **Work History:** Italy: Locanda Dell'Angelo; Los Angeles, CA: Primi, Posto **Mentor(s):** Pierangelo Cornaro, Piero Selvaggio **Awards:** 2004 James Beard Foundation Best Chef Southwest **Affiliations:** Meals-on-Wheels, Share our Strength, March of Dimes, and various local charities **Languages Spoken:** Italian, Spanish

FAST FACTS
Restaurant Recs: Andre's Downtown for everything they make **Kitchen Tool(s):** Tongs – because some things are just too hot! **Interview Question:** How much line experience do you have? What kind of cuisine have you worked with, and in what kind of volumes? This tells me whether or not a cook can have an immediate impact on the line. **Flavor Combo(s):** Chocolate with anything **Fave Cookbook(s):** I don't read cookbooks **Chef to Cook for You:** I would choose any of the 3-star French chefs, because I've never had the pleasure **Culinary Travel:** Definitely the Orient, because I've never been

P

Melissa Perello
Chef | New Project in the works

San Francisco, CA

Restaurant E-mail: mperello@mac.com

CHEF FACTS

Cuisine: Market-driven American **Born:** 1976 **Began Career:** 1994
Culinary School: The Culinary Institute of America, Hyde Park, NY
Grad Year: 1996 **Work History:** San Francisco, CA: Aqua, Charles Nob
Hill, Fifth Floor **Mentor(s):** Ron Siegel, Michael Mina **Awards:** 2005
StarChefs.com Rising Star Chef San Francisco; 2003-2005 James
Beard Award Rising Star Chef of the Year Nominee; 2004 Food &
Wine Best New Chef **Affiliations:** James Beard, WCR

NOTABLE DISH(ES): Pan Roasted Maple Leaf Farms Duck Breast,
Duck Confit, Fingerling Potato Hash with Plum Gastrique and Plum
Salad

FAST FACTS

Restaurant Recs: Tacos from the El Tonayense Truck, usually parked on Harrison near Division. The
lengua and the el pastor are great. **Kitchen Tool(s):** Immersion blender - it's small enough to keep
on your station during service, convenient, and quick to clean. It comes in handy for emulsifying or
aerating sauces, or puréeing soups and vegetables. **Interview Question:** Where do you see yourself in 5 and 10 years? What do you expect from those you work with and from me? This helps me
determine how they will fit into my team. **Flavor Combo(s):** Salt with sweet – salty caramel; chocolate
covered pretzels and peanut butter; bacon with honey **Fave Cookbook(s):** Roger Vergé's Vegetables
in the French Style by Roger Vergé **Chef to Cook for You:** I grew up watching Julia Child on PBS but
never had a chance to meet her; I think it would be pretty amazing to have a meal cooked by her. Just
something very simple. I think it might be most interesting for the conversation alone. **Culinary Travel:**
I would love to see more of Italy, as I've only had the opportunity to visit Umbria and Tuscany. I also
would like to visit Croatia, Portugal, India, and Southeast Asia.

Joshua Perkins
Chef | The Globe
75 Fifth St. NW Atlanta, GA 30308

Restaurant E-mail: josh@globeatlanta.com

Phone: (404) 541-1487

RESTAURANT FACTS
Seats: 75–110 **Weeknight Covers:** 175–225 **Weekend Covers:** 160–175 **Tasting Menu:** No **Kitchen Staff:** 5

CHEF FACTS
Cuisine: Global Cuisine **Born:** 1973 **Began Career:** 1988 **Stages:** Italy: La Locunda Di Piero **Work History:** Memphis, TN: Bistro 122, Jarrett's, Season's at the White Church, The Grove Grill; Atlanta, GA: Di Paolo, Brasserie Le Coze **Mentor(s):** Eric Ripert, Rinnato Rizzardi **Affiliations:** Green Market, The Liver Foundation, SOS, Camp Twin Lakes, anything that helps children **Languages Spoken:** Italian, some French, Spanish

NOTABLE DISH(ES): Striped Bass with Sweet Potato Gnocchi, Lardon, Medjool Dates and Citrus Butter

FAST FACTS
Restaurant Recs: Moro in London – the menu is constantly changing so I can't recommend one specific dish. In two days I ate through the entire menu! **Kitchen Tool(s):** The Vita-Prep – everything goes through it **Interview Question:** I want to know who they are and what their personal aspirations are. I want someone who wants to learn. **Flavor Combo(s):** I like extreme opposites: sugar and spring lemon; balsamic and port **Fave Cookbook(s):** White Heat by Marco Pierre White; A Return to Cooking by Eric Ripert and Michael Ruhlman; books by Ducasse **Chef to Cook for You:** Eric Ripert: I had to do so many tastings for him when I worked for him that it seems fair to have him cook for me. I have so much respect for him and love for his food – he has been the major influence in my cooking. **Culinary Travel:** Morocco, because it is so influential to my food now. The cuisine there is still pretty honest.

Ralph Perrazzo
Chef/Owner | Rare Concepts

Las Vegas, NV

Restaurant E-mail: perrazzo79@hotmail.com

CHEF FACTS
Cuisine: Market cuisine **Born:** 1979 **Began Career:** 2001 **Culinary School:** The Culinary Institute of America, Hyde Park, NY **Grad Year:** 2001 **Stages:** New York, NY: Jean-Georges **Work History:** New York, NY: Jean-Georges; Las Vegas, NV: Bradley Ogden, Social House, Pure Management Group **Mentor(s):** Eric Hubert **Awards:** 2005 StarChefs. com Rising Star Pastry Chef Las Vegas

NOTABLE DISH(ES): Milk Chocolate Panna Cotta, Liquid Butterscotch, Guiness Cotton Candy; Golden Watermelon Water, Tapioca, Bloomed Basil Seeds, Citrus Sorbet

FAST FACTS
Restaurant Recs: Lotus of Siam for Thai beef jerky **Kitchen Tool(s):** Rubber bowl scraper – I keep it in my back pocket; food injector - it's basically a syringe. I use it for homemade ice pops. **Interview Question:** Tell me about yourself **Flavor Combo(s):** Beer and chocolate **Fave Cookbook(s):** On Food and Cooking: The Science and Lore of the Kitchen by Harold McGee **Chef to Cook for You:** Michel Bras – he is the creator of a lot of things that are done now **Culinary Travel:** Italy because that's where it all started

Georges Perrier
Chef/Owner | Le Bec-Fin

1523 Walnut St. Philadelphia, PA 19102

Restaurant E-mail: lebecfin@aol.com

Phone: (215) 567-1000

RESTAURANT FACTS
Seats: 80 **Weeknight Covers:** 80 **Weekend Covers:** 150 **Check Average (with Wine):** $175 **Tasting Menu:** Yes $140/$210 with wine **Kitchen Staff:** 7

CHEF FACTS
Other Restaurants: Wayne, PA: Brasserie Perrier, Café Perrier at Boyd's, Table 31, Georges; Atlantic City, NJ: Mia **Cuisine:** Modern French **Born:** 1943 **Began Career:** 1959 **Stages:** France: La Pyramide **Work History:** France: L'Oustau de Baumanière à Les Baux de Provence **Mentor(s):** Paul Bocuse **Protégée(s):** Marcus Haight **Affiliations:** L'Académie de Cuisine. We are involved in numerous charities. We also give back to our culinary "community" by promoting young chefs through internships, sending our new sommeliers to Napa Valley to donate their time to vineyards, and hosting the French and cooking classes of our local high schools. **Books Published:** Georges Perrier Le Bec-Fin Recipes **Languages Spoken:** French

FAST FACTS
Restaurant Recs: Au-Père Claude Rotisserie in Paris. I love it all! I could spend a whole afternoon there! **Kitchen Tool(s):** Hand, knives **Interview Question:** What are their plans for the future? Marriage? Children? **Flavor Combo(s):** Curry and fresh green apples **Fave Cookbook(s):** New York Times Cookbook by Craig Claiborne **Chef to Cook for You:** I have had the honor of dining with so many chefs over the years that I could not choose. I love to experience the culinary artistry of great chefs. **Culinary Travel:** South of France. I love the simplicity of Mediterranean cuisine.

John Peters
Chef

Chicago, IL

CHEF FACTS
Cuisine: Classic American in a modern style **Born:** 1974 **Began Career:** 1990 **Culinary School:** Culinary Institute of America, Hyde Park, NY **Grad Year:** 1990 **Work History:** Dallas, TX: Steak and Ale, Bob Steak and Chop House, The Mansion at Turtle Creek; New Orleans, LA: The Palace Café; Chicago, IL: Vong Chicago, Trio, Alinea, Naha, Powerhouse **Mentor(s):** Michael Morabito, Dean Fearing, Grant Achatz**Languages Spoken:** Spanish

NOTABLE DISH(ES): Cervena Venison Loin, Wild Rice and Dried Fruit, Spinach, Glazed Chestnuts, and Huckleberry Reduction; Slow Roasted Chicken Thigh, Farro, Winter Root Vegetables, and Thyme Chicken Jus

FAST FACTS
Restaurant Recs: Spoon Thai – they have great peanut sauce and red coconut curry **Kitchen Tool(s):** Small offset spatula **Interview Question:** I usually like to know what they love about cooking or why they are getting into cooking. What drives them? **Flavor Combo(s):** I have a Mexican mirepoix I use a lot, which is jalapeño, onion, garlic and poblano. I also like olive, orange, fennel and saffron and mint and zucchini, cherries and lamb. **Fave Cookbook(s):** Culinary Artistry by Andrew Dornenburg and Karen Page **Chef to Cook for You:** Jacques Pépin – I used to watch him cook with Julia Child on PBS and it seemed that everything he touched turned to gold. He has flawless execution and a graceful personality. A true master at what he does. **Culinary Travel:** I would definitely go to Italy. I would love to see the variety of regional cuisine first hand and work on my Italian.

Charles Phan
Chef/Owner | The Slanted Door

1 Ferry Building #3 San Francisco, CA 94111

Restaurant E-mail: charles@slanteddoor.com

Phone: (415) 861-8032

RESTAURANT FACTS
Seats: 150-204 **Weeknight Covers:** 500 a day **Weekend Covers:** 500 a day **Check Average (w/o Wine):** $46 **Tasting Menu:** No

CHEF FACTS
Other Restaurants: Out the Door **Cuisine:** Vietnamese **Born:** 1962 **Began Career:** 1995 **Awards:** 2004 James Beard Foundation Best Chef California **Affiliations:** JBF **Languages Spoken:** Vietnamese, Cantonese

NOTABLE DISH(ES): Manila Clams with Thai Basil, Crispy Pork Belly and Fresh Chilies; Shaking Beef; Grapefruit and Jicama Salad

FAST FACTS
Restaurant Recs: Happy Café – for shaved pig's ear **Kitchen Tool(s):** Wood-burning hearth – there are no substitutes **Interview Question:** What is your favorite restaurant? It tells you where his or her heart is.

P

King Phojanakong
Chef/Owner | Kuma Inn

113 Ludlow St., 2nd. Fl. New York, NY 10002

Restaurant E-mail: kumainn@hotmail.com

Phone: (212) 353-8866

RESTAURANT FACTS
Seats: 32 **Weeknight Covers:** 50 **Weekend Covers:** 88 **Check Average (w/o Wine):** $30 **Tasting Menu:** Yes **Kitchen Staff:** 3

CHEF FACTS
Other Restaurants: Rainmaker Management, Talay **Cuisine:** Filipino and Thai **Born:** 1968 **Began Career:** 1998 **Culinary School:** The Culinary Institute of America, Hyde Park, NY **Grad Year:** 1998 **Stages:** New York, NY: Restaurant Daniel, Jean-Georges, Le Bernardin **Work History:** New York, NY: Restaurant Daniel, Bouley Bakery, Danube, The Grocery **Mentor(s):** David Bouley, Daniel Boulud, Alex Lee **Protégée(s):** Jeanette Arcillas **Awards:** 1997 Aspen CO Top Ten Student Chefs **Affiliations:** AmFAR, Grand Street Settlement, AIWF Spoons Across America, Time Out for Hunger, TAP Project **Books Published:** New Asian Cuisine **Languages Spoken:** Tagalog, kitchen Spanish

FAST FACTS
Restaurant Recs: 69 Bayard for beef and bitter melon over egg fried rice **Kitchen Tool(s):** Spoon; fish fork; fish spatula to taste and plate everything I cook **Interview Question:** Have you ever tried balut? **Flavor Combo(s):** Soy and vinegar; Thai chilies, garlic and fish sauce; peanut butter and jelly **Fave Cookbook(s):** Thai Food by David Thompson **Chef to Cook for You:** Marco Pierre White – I've read so much about him but I'd love to see him in action. I'd also like to hear his input on my kitchen and food. **Culinary Travel:** I love traveling to Thailand. I always see, taste, and learn something new while I'm there.

Laurent Pillard
Corporate Chef | Burger Bar
3950 Las Vegas Blvd. South Las Vegas, NV 89119

Restaurant E-mail: lpillard@gmail.com

Phone: (702) 632-7777

RESTAURANT FACTS
Seats: 140 **Weeknight Covers:** 800-900 **Weekend Covers:** 900-1500 **Check Average (with Wine):** $22 **Tasting Menu:** No **Kitchen Staff:** 7

CHEF FACTS
Other Restaurants: St. Louis, MO: Burger Bar, Sleek; San Francisco, CA: Burger Bar **Cuisine:** Modern French **Born:** 1966 **Began Career:** 1982 **Culinary School:** Centre de Formation Apprentissage, France **Grad Year:** 1984 **Stages:** France: Troisgros **Work History:** France: Lucas Carton, Troisgros; England: Les Saveurs; Australia: Mietta's; Atlanta, GA: Ritz-Carlton Buckhead **Mentor(s):** Joël Antunes **Protégée(s):** Frank Brunacci **Languages Spoken:** French

FAST FACTS
Restaurant Recs: Shibuya MGM for the Kurobuta pork – crisp, braised pork in brick leaf and nihon glaze **Kitchen Tool(s):** Spoon for tasting **Interview Question:** What motivates you to be a chef? Why are you interested in working in my kitchen? **Flavor Combo(s):** Basil and pineapple **Fave Cookbook(s):** Bras: Laguiole, Aubrac, France by Michel Bras **Chef to Cook for You:** The Chef from Shibuya in Las Vegas. He is one of my best friends and I love what he is cooking. He has a very different approach to Japanese food. **Culinary Travel:** To Thailand because I love Asian food. I especially like the flavorful herbs and fruits they have over there.

P

Odessa Piper
Cook/Writer

Madison, WI

Restaurant E-mail: odessa@execpc.com

CHEF FACTS

Born: 1952 **Began Career:** 1970 **Stages:** I learned about sourcing and growing ingredients while working at a farm in New England and a farm in Wisconsin prior to becoming a chef **Work History:** Madison, WI: Ovens of Brittany, L'Etoile **Mentor(s):** JoAnna Guthrie **Protégée(s):** Tory Miller, current Chef/Proprietor of L'Etoile **Awards:** 2001 James Beard Foundation Best Chef Midwest **Affiliations:** Guest lecturer at the University of Wisconsin, CIA and NECI, co-chair of the scholarship committee of Women Chefs and Restaurateurs, on the Board of Friends of Dane County Farmers' Market, Slow Food, Chefs Collaborative, IACP, International Women's Forum

FAST FACTS

Kitchen Tool(s): This is not very glamorous, but it's my toaster oven. Since I became a home cook, I use it in combination with my large stove to brown, finish or hold - jobs of more sophisticated equipment I took for granted at the restaurant. **Interview Question:** I ask people what they love to eat. Then I ask them why, and encourage them to take the answer where ever they want it to go. **Flavor Combo(s):** Anise hyssop used with a variety of other ingredients: watermelon; pear and proscuitto; fresh goat cheese; apricot biscotti and anise seed **Fave Cookbook(s):** The one I hope to write **Chef to Cook for You:** The morning after a wonderful meal at the three star L'Arnsbourg in northern Alsace, a cheerful man came into the breakfast room of the small hotel. He had a loaf of freshly baked bread under one arm, and a ham under the other. It was Chef George Klien, who oversaw our meal the night before. He is simply one of the hottest three-star chefs on the planet. All I know is that he inspires in his staff and his guests the belief that nothing is too small or too unimportant to do wholeheartedly and that makes for an incomparable meal. **Culinary Travel:** For me, it would be somewhere completely new. I'm intrigued by all the cuisines of the Far East and would love to study the interplay of ingredients and techniques with the body's subtle energies. I know that to even begin to understand them I would need to live there and enter the culture.

Paul Piscopo
Executive Chef | XYZ at the W hotel

181 Third St. San Francisco, CA 94103

Restaurant E-mail: paul.piscopo@whotels.com

Phone: (415) 777-5300

RESTAURANT FACTS
Seats: 90 **Weeknight Covers:** 150–250 **Weekend Covers:** 150–250
Check Average (w/o Wine): $40 **Tasting Menu:** Yes $48/$72 with
wine **Kitchen Staff:** 6–8

CHEF FACTS
Cuisine: Market cuisine **Born:** 1970 **Began Career:** 1996 **Culinary
School:** The Culinary Institute of America, Hyde Park, NY **Grad Year:**
1994 **Stages:** San Francisco, CA: Aqua; New York, NY: Aureole **Work
History:** San Francisco, CA: Aqua, Charles, Nob Hill, Masa's, XYZ;
Oakland, CA: Oliveto Restaurant **Mentor(s):** Ron Siegel **Protégée(s):**
Robert Hurd – my right hand **Awards:** 2005 StarChefs.com Rising
Star Chef San Francisco; runner-up for SF Hotel Hero **Affiliations:** Lots of local charities and fund rais-
ers **Languages Spoken:** Not fluent, but kitchen Spanish is a must

NOTABLE DISH(ES): Stuffed Provencal Sardines; Pan-Roasted Sonoma Squab

FAST FACTS
Restaurant Recs: Coffee from Blue Bottle in Hayes Valley; a ham and cheese croissant from Tartine
bakery; breakfast at Dottie's **Kitchen Tool(s):** Vita-Prep **Interview Question:** Can you commit for a
year? Commitment is imperative. Also, for a sous chef or manager I ask, "Do you want my job?" That
is someone who is going to be a strong candidate. You can usually tell by the amount of focus and
energy they put into the interview. **Flavor Combo(s):** Cured pork product with just about anything!
Brown butter, thyme and fresh lemon. **Fave Cookbook(s):** White Heat by Marco Pierre White **Chef to
Cook for You:** The Swedish Chef from the Muppets. Who doesn't like the Muppets? **Culinary Travel:**
I've visited Europe, mostly France and Italy. Spain would be the next. It's a cuisine that I am not very
familiar with, so I would love to travel and see it.

P

Nicole Plue
Pastry Chef | Redd Restaurant

6480 Washington St. Yountville, CA 94559

Restaurant E-mail: info@reddnapavalley.com

Phone: (707) 944-2222

RESTAURANT FACTS
Seats: 90 **Weeknight Covers:** 150 **Weekend Covers:** 200 **Tasting Menu:** Yes $70/$110 with wine **Kitchen Staff:** 2

CHEF FACTS
Cuisine: Plated desserts **Began Career:** 1991 **Culinary School:** California Culinary Academy, San Francisco, CA **Stages:** San Francisco, CA: Masa's **Work History:** San Francisco, CA: One Market, Hawthorne Lane; New York, NY: Eleven Madison Park; Napa Valley, CA: Julia's Kitchen **Mentor(s):** David Gingrass, my family **Awards:** 2008 James Beard Foundation Outstanding Pastry Chef Nominee; San Francisco Magazine Pastry Chef of the Year; San Francisco Chronicle Rising Star

NOTABLE DISH(ES): Sweet Corn Fritters with Cherries and Vanilla Bean Ice Cream; Peanut Buttermilk Chocolate Gianduja Parfait with Honey Vanilla Cream

FAST FACTS
Restaurant Recs: Jack London Saloon in Glen Ellen for pulled pork sandwiches **Kitchen Tool(s):** Immersion blender for emulsifying **Fave Cookbook(s):** Fannie Farmer Baking by Marion Cunningham

Ryan Poli
Chef de Cuisine | Perennial Restaurant

1800 North Lincoln Ave. Chicago, IL 60614

Restaurant E-mail: ryanpoli@hotmail.com

Phone: (312) 981-7070

RESTAURANT FACTS
Check Average (w/o Wine): $31–$50 **Tasting Menu:** No **Kitchen Staff:** 10

CHEF FACTS
Cuisine: Modern American **Born:** 1977 **Began Career:** 1995 **Stages:** Various restaurants around Spain **Work History:** Yountville, CA: The French Laundry; Wheeling, IL; Le Français; Chicago, IL: Butter **Mentor(s):** Thomas Keller, Jean Banchet

NOTABLE DISH(ES): Squab and Foie Gras with Red Cabbage Perogi; Mascarpone Truffle Angolotti, Black Trumpet Mushrooms, Chestnuts and Celery Root Froth

FAST FACTS
Restaurant Recs: Lao Sze Chuan for the empress crab, flash-fried, and served in an amazing spicy sauce **Kitchen Tool(s):** Joyce Chen scissors – strong enough to cut fish and lamb bones, delicate enough to cut herbs **Interview Question:** What makes you different? Why should we hire you? I want to hear that they're dependable. **Flavor Combo(s):** I enjoy using ginger quite a bit. I love the freshness it brings to enhance other flavors. Right now I am using it with a crab salad dish with avocados and I also have it in a dessert on the Perennial menu with white chocolate, passionfruit, pumpkin seeds, lemon and orange. Chocolate, extra virgin olive oil and sea salt are a combination that I absolutely adore. **Fave Cookbook(s):** Cookbooks by Alfred Portale; cookbooks by Thomas Keller; Sous Vide Cuisine by Joan Roca is a geyser of information **Chef to Cook for You:** People who I have cooked with in the past who are good friends and are running their own restaurants such as John Fraser of Dovetail in New York, Eric Ziebold of CityZen in DC, and Lachlan MacKinnon-Patterson at Frasca Food and Wine in Boulder. I am just really happy for all of them and it's good to see people you worked with and have learned from doing their own thing and living their dreams. **Culinary Travel:** I always love Spain. I had the opportunity to stage and work there again for most of 2007 and it's just such a great place. The people are so friendly, the food is amazing. For me, it's a place of inspiration, both personally and professionally. I love it there.

Ben Pollinger
Executive Chef | Oceana

55 E 54th St. New York, NY 10022

Restaurant E-mail: bpollinger@optonline.net

Phone: (212) 759-5941

RESTAURANT FACTS
Seats: 110 **Weeknight Covers:** 140 **Weekend Covers:** 175 **Check Average (w/o Wine):** $85 **Tasting Menu:** Yes $110 **Kitchen Staff:** 6–8

CHEF FACTS
Cuisine: Global seafood **Born:** 1971 **Began Career:** 1990 **Culinary School:** The Culinary Institute of America, Hyde Park, NY **Grad Year:** 1997 **Stages:** A full-year stage at Le Louis XV Monte-Carlo, Monaco **Work History:** New York, NY: Tabla, Union Square Café; Lespinasse; La Côte Basque, Les Celebrités; Monaco: Le Louis XV **Mentor(s):** Floyd Cardoz, Michael Romano, Christian Delouvrier, Alain Ducasse **Awards:** New York Times 3 stars; 1 Michelin star **Affiliations:** Les Amis d'Escoffier, Slow Food, James Beard Foundation **Languages Spoken:** Spanish, French

NOTABLE DISH(ES): Squid Ink Potato Gnocchi with Manilla Razor Clams, Calamari, Meyer Lemon and Basil

FAST FACTS
Restaurant Recs: Woo Chon for the scallion pancake and the tiny dried little fish; Yakitori Totto for the grilled chicken skin skewers **Kitchen Tool(s):** Your nose – your sense of smell is one of the most important things you use as a chef **Interview Question:** What makes you happy? **Flavor Combo(s):** Deep earthy flavors accented with fresh herbs **Fave Cookbook(s):** La Riviera d'Alain Ducasse **Chef to Cook for You:** Alain Chapel – I would like to be able to go back and explore the roots of contemporary cookery **Culinary Travel:** India – Indian spices and ingredients, and having learned how to use them properly, have forever changed the way I think and feel about food. They have opened the door to a whole new world for me that I now cannot imagine cooking without.

Michelle Polzin
Pastry Chef | Range

842 Valencia St. San Francisco, CA 94110

Restaurant E-mail: michelle@rangesf.com

Phone: (415) 282-8283

RESTAURANT FACTS
Seats: 70 **Weeknight Covers:** 120 **Weekend Covers:** 160 **Check Average (w/o Wine):** $46 **Tasting Menu:** No **Kitchen Staff:** 2

CHEF FACTS
Cuisine: New American **Born:** 1969 **Began Career:** 1992 **Stages:** Berkeley, CA: Chez Panisse **Work History:** San Francisco, CA: Delfina, Californian Culinary Academy, Bacar **Mentor(s):** Kevin Farmer, Julia Stockton, Kathy Edwards **Awards:** 2006 San Francisco Magazine Best Pastry Chef **Affiliations:** Bicycle Coalition

NOTABLE DISH(ES): Coconut Bavarian with Tangelo Sorbet and Tapioca; Bittersweet Chocolate and Bergamot Tea Soufflé with Earl Grey Ice Cream

FAST FACTS
Restaurant Recs: I love to ride my bike to Pizzetta 211 and order everything but the calzone **Kitchen Tool(s):** My hands and my copper bowl KitchenAid attachment **Interview Question:** Are you sure you want to do this? **Flavor Combo(s):** Peach and coconut; plum and cardamom. Mostly I love fruit and fruit, and more fruit. Also with fruit. **Fave Cookbook(s):** The Edna Lewis Cookbook and The Omnivore's Dilemma, which is not really a cookbook, but had a powerful impact on my cooking **Chef to Cook for You:** Edna Lewis, of course. She cooked for some of the great minds of the 20th century. Obviously eating her food makes you smarter. Maybe Mary Francis Kennedy could be my dining companion? **Culinary Travel:** I would love to see the rest of the world, but the taste of Italian cooking is so simple, and pure, that I seem to end up there. I love simple food not because I'm incapable of outlandish thoughts, but because I love the way things taste - not totally plain, but dressed very simply. I like to taste the things in things, not to make things taste like things besides the things they are (also, I have a new conspiracy theory about Italy, that they're keeping all of the good stuff for themselves, and I need many more meals to prove that theory).

Alfred Portale
Chef Owner | Gotham Bar & Grill

12 E 12th St. New York, NY 10003-4428

Restaurant E-mail: gothamgm@gothambarandgrill.com

Phone: (212) 620-4020

RESTAURANT FACTS
Seats: 165 **Weeknight Covers:** 280 **Weekend Covers:** 320 **Check Average (with Wine):** $110 **Tasting Menu:** Yes **Kitchen Staff:** 16

CHEF FACTS
Other Restaurants: Miami, FL: Gotham Steak; Las Vegas, NV: Gotham Bar and Grill **Cuisine:** Modern American **Born:** 1956 **Began Career:** 1978 **Culinary School:** Culinary Institute of America, Hyde Park, NY **Grad Year:** 1981 **Work History:** New York, NY: Michel Guerard; France: Michel Guerard, Troisgros, Jacques Maxim **Awards:** 2006 James Beard Outstanding Chef; 2002 James Beard Outstanding Restaurant; 1993 James Beard Foundation Best Chef New York; 1989 Who's Who in Food and Beverage in America **Books Published:** The Gotham Bar and Grill Cookbook; The Twelve Seasons Cookbook; Alfred Portale Simple Pleasures

FAST FACTS
Restaurant Recs: Tomasso's in Bensonhurst – he does a great roast baby lamb and has an extensive selection of Italian wine. And he sings opera! **Kitchen Tool(s):** Lately it is the potato ricer **Interview Question:** I ask them what are the last five cookbooks they bought or read **Flavor Combo(s):** I like salty and sweet with a little heat, like mango with limes, piquillo peppers, and sea salt **Fave Cookbook(s):** The River Café Cookbook by Ruth Rogers **Chef to Cook for You:** Jacques Maxim – I worked with him twenty years ago and he was one of the most brilliant chefs in the world. I would love to see what he's doing now. **Culinary Travel:** To Northern Italy – I've never been and I know that the cuisine is extraordinary and that the wine is fantastic

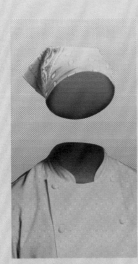

Sylvain Portay
Corporate Chef | Alain Ducasse

The Hotel at Mandalay Bay Las Vegas, NV 89119

Restaurant E-mail: sylvainportay@yahoo.com

Phone: (702) 632-9500

RESTAURANT FACTS
Tasting Menu: Yes $95/$135

CHEF FACTS
Other Restaurants: Groupe Alain Ducasse **Cuisine:** Contemporary French **Born:** 1961 **Began Career:** 1976 **Stages:** Italy: Enoteca Pinchiorri **Work History:** France: Negresco Hotel, Le Louis XV; New York, NY: Le Cirque; San Francisco, CA: The Ritz-Carlton **Mentor(s):** Alain Ducasse **Protégée(s):** Sean O'Toole **Affiliations:** James Beard Foundation **Languages Spoken:** French

NOTABLE DISH(ES): Fedelini with Summer Truffle; Roasted Scallops with Fresh Almond Salad, Arugula, Tomato Confit, Balsamic Reduction

FAST FACTS
Restaurant Recs: Restaurant Fish for fish and chips **Kitchen Tool(s):** My brain **Interview Question:** What are you ready to sacrifice for your job? **Fave Cookbook(s):** Grand Livre De Cuisine by Alain Ducasse

Boris Portnoy
Pastry Chef | Candybar

1335 Fulton St. San Francisco CA 94117

Restaurant E-mail: info@candybarsf.com

Phone: (415) 673-7078

RESTAURANT FACTS
Seats: 50 **Weeknight Covers:** 60 **Weekend Covers:** 85 **Check Average (with Wine):** $40 **Tasting Menu:** Yes **Kitchen Staff:** 2

CHEF FACTS
Cuisine: Modern eclectic pastry **Born:** 1976 **Began Career:** 2001 **Stages:** Spain: Mugaritz **Work History:** San Sebastian, Spain: Restaurant Mugaritz; Philadelphia, PA: Deux Cheminees, Restaurant Salt; San Francisco, CA: Cru, Winterland, Campton Place **Mentor(s):** Fritz Blank, a chef and a former microbiologist, was the first person to expose me to the chemistry of food **Awards:** 2005 StarChefs.com Rising Star Pastry Chef San Francisco

NOTABLE DISH(ES): Avocado Parfait, Coconut-Carrot Ravioli, Carrot-Cardamom Nage and Tangerine Sorbet; Licorice Salad with Coriander-Raspberry Sorbet, Raspberry Jelly Beans and a Tarragon Veil; White Coffee Parfait, Coffee Earth and Fig Gastrique

FAST FACTS
Restaurant Recs: The tamales lady in my neighborhood – she has great sauces **Kitchen Tool(s):** A digital thermometer and a scale **Interview Question:** I ask why they come looking for a job here - it gives me a gauge of their expectations and level of maturity. I want to see honesty and the level of their motivation. **Flavor Combo(s):** Sweet with bitter; warm liquids with dry crumb **Fave Cookbook(s):** Right now, A Cocinar. It has a million and one recipes. That's value! **Chef to Cook for You:** My grandmother - I'd want her to make her Rugelach, because she is losing her memory **Culinary Travel:** I would like to travel back in time to go and see Roman feasts - to taste European food before new world ingredients like tomatoes and potatoes arrived

Gavin Portsmouth
Chef

CHEF FACTS
Cuisine: Asian and French-inspired American **Born:** 1976 **Began Career:** 1997 **Culinary School:** Highbury College, England **Grad Year:** 1995 **Stages:** England: Connaught Hotel; The Langsbough Hotel **Work History:** England: Connaught Hotel; New York, NY: An American Place, Sapa; AZ: Compass; Los Angeles, CA: Zax **Mentor(s):** Michael Bourdin and Larry Forgione **Protégée(s):** Christian Lomas, Douglas Silverberg **Awards:** 1997 National Student Chef of the Year (England) **Affiliations:** The Restaurant Association **Languages Spoken:** Some Spanish

NOTABLE DISH(ES): Steamed Bao, Smoked Chicken with a Pomegranate Hoisin Sauce; Slow Poached Duck Breast, Confit 5 Spice Drumstick, Ramps, Garlic-Chive Purée

FAST FACTS
Restaurant Recs: Knife and Fork in the East Village **Kitchen Tool(s):** Japanese mandolin **Interview Question:** Why did you start cooking? Why this restaurant? **Flavor Combo(s):** Yuzu and shiso; lychee and strawberry; Chinese black vinegar and Asian pear **Fave Cookbook(s):** Cookbooks by Charlie Trotter **Chef to Cook for You:** Escoffier, even though his food his outdated. The old classic French cuisine is what I first learned to cook, and you don't see it any more. **Culinary Travel:** I've been to Japan, Korea and Singapore, and I would love to go to Vietnam and Thailand

P

Vincent Pouessel
Chef | Aureole Las Vegas

3950 Las Vegas Blvd. Las Vegas, NV 89119

Restaurant E-mail: vpouessel@mrgmail.com

Phone: (702) 632-7401

RESTAURANT FACTS
Seats: 360–525 **Weeknight Covers:** 250 **Weekend Covers:** 350
Check Average (with Wine): $135 **Tasting Menu:** Yes $95/$105
Kitchen Staff: 8

CHEF FACTS
Cuisine: French **Born:** 1971 **Began Career:** 1989 **Culinary School:** Lycée Hotelier Notre Dame, France **Grad Year:** 1989 **Work History:** France: Le Jules Verne; Las Vegas, NV: The Mansion at MGM Grand **Mentor(s):** Charlie Palmer **Awards:** 2005 StarChefs.com Rising Star Chef Las Vegas **Affiliations:** CPG **Languages Spoken:** French

NOTABLE DISH(ES): Citrus Grilled Escolar with Watercress Emulsion and Balsamic Vinegar; Zucchini Blossoms Stuffed with Pesto-Infused Ahi Tuna

FAST FACTS
Restaurant Recs: Lotus of Siam for the coconut mussel soup **Kitchen Tool(s):** Soup spoon – I always have one on me **Interview Question:** Do you like to eat? What food do you like and why? Would you rather enjoy a slice of country pâté with cornichons or an In n' Out burger? **Flavor Combo(s):** Sweet and salt **Fave Cookbook(s):** Le Répertoire de la Cuisine by Louis Sauliner, it's the little book that every apprentice in France starts to work with. I love it because it's small, complete, and easy to use. **Chef to Cook for You:** Anthony Bourdain – he is a great guy, humble, with a low key approach to cooking that I enjoy **Culinary Travel:** I have always wanted to go to Asia; I have never been. The end of April I am attending the World Gourmet Summit in Singapore; it will fulfill a lifetime dream.

Nora Pouillon
Chef/Owner | Restaurant Nora

2132 Florida Ave. NW Washington, DC 20008

Restaurant E-mail: nora@noras.com

Phone: (202) 462-5143

RESTAURANT FACTS

Seats: 170 **Weeknight Covers:** up to 200 **Weekend Covers:** up to 300 **Check Average (with Wine):** $85 **Check Average (w/o Wine):** $70 **Tasting Menu:** Yes $70 **Kitchen Staff:** 8–10

CHEF FACTS

Cuisine: Certified organic new American **Born:** 1943 **Began Career:** 1972 **Work History:** Ran cooking school 1972-1976; Washington DC: Tabard Inn Restaurant **Mentor(s):** My parents and later Elizabeth David, and James Beard **Protégée(s):** All my former chefs who I inspired to continue seasonal, organic cooking **Awards:** The American Tasting Institute Chef of the Year; International Association of Culinary Professionals Award of Excellence; Organic Trade Association; New Hope Natural Media, American Horticultural Society, Campaign for Better Health **Affiliations:** On the Board of Directors for: Environmental Film Festival, Amazon Conservation Team, Earth Day Network, Wholesome Wave, Fresh Farm Markets **Books Published:** Cooking with Nora: Seasonal Menus from Restaurant Nora **Languages Spoken:** German, French

NOTABLE DISH(ES): Asian Caesar Dressing; Marinated Tofu with Shiitake Stuffing

FAST FACTS

Restaurant Recs: Makoto; 2 Amy's for pizza **Kitchen Tool(s):** Japanese mandolin **Interview Question:** Do you know what organic means? Do you know how to cook without butter and cream? **Flavor Combo(s):** Of course everything must be organic. My favorite flavor combination would be dark sourdough bread with delicious farm butter and a sprinkle of sea salt and finally a ripe slice of tomato on top, but only if it's in season. **Fave Cookbook(s):** Cookbooks by Jamie Oliver and Nigella Lawson **Chef to Cook for You:** Nigela Lawson or Jamie Oliver. They both cook in the style that I like to eat. **Culinary Travel:** Turkey or Greece – I love the flavors and Mediterranean food

Liz Prueitt and Chad Robertson
Pastry Chefs/Owners | Tartine Bakery

600 Guerrero St. San Francisco, CA 94110

Restaurant E-mail: tartinebakerysf@earthlink.net

Phone: (415) 487-2600

RESTAURANT FACTS
Seats: 27 **Kitchen Staff:** 14

CHEF FACTS
Other Restaurants: Bar Tartine **Cuisine:** French-influenced baking and pastry **Culinary School:** The Culinary Institute of America, Hyde Park, NY **Grad Year:** 1993 **Stages:** France: Boulangerie Artisinale des Maures (Chad and Liz), Patrick Leport (Chad) **Work History:** New York, NY: Montrachet; Lenox, MA: Canyon Ranch; Point Reyes Station, CA: Bay Village Bakery **Awards:** 2008 James Beard Foundation Outstanding Pastry Chefs; 2003 San Francisco Magazine Critics' Choice Pastry Chef of the Year

NOTABLE DISH(ES): Brioche Bread Pudding with Strawberries Cooked in Caramel

FAST FACTS
Restaurant Recs: Eiji is a Japanese restaurant that we recently discovered. It's most notable for it's freshly made Tofu. They make three different types of tofu to order, served with an array of accompaniments – shiso leaf, sesame, freshly grated daikon. The restaurant is tiny, always full, and has an ever-changing blackboard of specials. Most recently lightly smoked cold duck breast, roast eggplant with a walnut crust, and a raw tuna salad with mountain yam. **Kitchen Tool(s):** Liz: my cake knife that my Chad gave me years ago (serrated, but different from a serrated bread knife). Chad: my chocolate cutting knife. **Interview Question:** What book (non-culinary) are you reading right now? **Flavor Combo(s):** Young coconut with fresh berries or fruit of the season. It is uncanny how well coconut goes with everything from blueberries to nectarines. **Fave Cookbook(s):** Larousse Gastronomique – you can find absolutely everything in it you are looking for, and you can learn a lot just by flipping through the pages at random **Chef to Cook for You:** More than a particular chef, it would be fascinating to travel to a particular time. Say, the era of Shakespeare, to see and taste a feast of the day with all of the game birds they used, the wine of the time, and to taste whole roast animals before we bred the flavor out of them. **Culinary Travel:** We're dying to go to Morocco to eat. Chad and I once stayed with a young Moroccan woman in Paris who was there for University. Her family's cook would send packages of freshly made Bistella once a week, which we were lucky enough to have her share with us. It was extraordinary, even considering the transit from Morocco to Paris.

Doug Psaltis
Executive Chef | Elizabeth

265 Elizabeth St. New York, NY

Restaurant E-mail: dpsalt@gmail.com

Phone: (212) 334-2426

CHEF FACTS

Cuisine: Eclectic modern American **Born:** 1974 **Began Career:** 1993 **Work History:** New York, NY: March, Bouley Bakery, Alain Ducasse at the Essex House, Mix, Country at the Carlton Hotel; Yountville, CA: The French Laundry; France: Le Louis XV **Mentor(s):** My grandfather and Alain Ducasse **Awards:** 2007 StarChefs.com Rising Star Hotel Chef New York **Books Published:** The Seasoning of a Chef: My Journey from Diner to Ducasse and Beyond **Languages Spoken:** I struggle through French

NOTABLE DISH(ES): Lobster Carpaccio with Cornichon, Gribiche and Caviar; Lamb Shish Kebab, Tzatziki, Hummus and Rosemary

FAST FACTS

Restaurant Recs: Land; Katz's deli **Kitchen Tool(s):** A tiny little hot dog fork. I've been fortunate enough to have had the same tools for the last 10 years. **Interview Question:** I want to know why they want the job. I look for simple answers. I also look for someone who knows without question why they want to be a chef. **Flavor Combo(s):** Garlic with oil and lemon; black pepper and blue cheese; yogurt and berries **Fave Cookbook(s):** Recipes and Memories by Sophia Loren **Chef to Cook for You:** All the people who have worked with me before. It would be great to see how far they have come. **Culinary Travel:** Paris for the bakeries, the shops, and the chocolate

P

Michael Psilakis
Executive Chef/Owner | Anthos

36 West 52nd St. New York, NY 10019

Restaurant E-mail: michael@anthosnyc.com

Phone: (212) 582-6900

RESTAURANT FACTS
Seats: 105 **Weeknight Covers:** 150 **Weekend Covers:** 200 **Check Average (with Wine):** $110 **Kitchen Staff:** 12

CHEF FACTS
Other Restaurants: Mia Dona, Kefi **Cuisine:** Exploration of Greek food **Born:** 1968 **Began Career:** 2000 **Work History:** Long Island, NY: Ecco; New York, NY: Onera, Dona **Mentor(s):** My dad **Affiliations:** We work with so many charities – it is non-stop! I am a big advocate of charity work. **Languages Spoken:** Greek

FAST FACTS
Restaurant Recs: Celeste – a tiny Italian restaurant close to where I work. They have a wood burning oven and the chef is from Bologna. He makes stick-to-your-ribs style traditional food. **Kitchen Tool(s):** A knife **Interview Question:** I have one question: What do you love to do? If they don't say cook, that's not a good sign. You really need to love what you are doing if you're going to be spending 15 hours a day at it. **Flavor Combo(s):** Flavor profiles are the most important things and we're always experimenting with new ones. One I really like is cinnamon when combined with something in a savory sense. **Fave Cookbook(s):** Books by Michel Bras **Chef to Cook for You:** Michel Bras – he just captures the soul of what Mediterranean food is about even though he is first considered a French chef. His flavors, ingredients and focus reminds me of why I do what I do. **Culinary Travel:** I would like to set up camp in Michel Bras' kitchen and just learn. He captures the identity of what food can be.

Wolfgang Puck
Executive Chef | Spago

100 N Crescent Dr., Suite 100 Beverly Hills CA 90210

Restaurant E-mail: sgratz@wpwmail.com

Phone: (714) 542-5232

RESTAURANT FACTS
Seats: 140 **Weeknight Covers:** 220-250 **Weekend Covers:** 250-325 **Check Average (with Wine):** $96 **Tasting Menu:** No **Kitchen Staff:** 13-15

CHEF FACTS
Other Restaurants: Atlantic City, NJ: Wolfgang Puck American Grille at the Borgata; Beverly Hills, CA: Spago; Beaver Creek, CO: Spago; Las Vegas, NV: Postrio, Spago, Chinois, Trattoria del Lupo at Mandalay Bay, Wolfgang Puck Bar and Grill at the MGM Grand, CUT; Maui, HI: Spago; Detroit, MI: Wolfgang Puck Grille at the MGM Grand; Santa Monica, CA: Chinois; San Francisco, CA: Postrio; Los Angeles, CA: CUT; Washington, DC: The Source by Wolfgang Puck, Wolfgang Puck Catering, Wolfgang Puck Worldwide Inc., Wolfgang Puck Express, Wolfgang Puck Bistro **Cuisine:** California Italian **Born:** 1949 **Began Career:** 1963 **Work History:** Indianapolis, IN: La Tour; Los Angeles, CA: Ma Maison **Awards:** James Beard Award Outstanding Chef of the Year; James Beard Award Outstanding Restaurant of the Year (Spago); James Beard Award Outstanding Service Award (Spago) **Affiliations:** HSUS, The Seafood Watch Program, Puck-Lazaroff Charitable Foundation, MOW **Books Published:** Wolfgang Puck Makes it Easy, Modern French Cooking for the American Kitchen

P

Stephan Pyles
Chef/Owner | Stephan Pyles

1807 Ross Ave. Dallas, TX 75201

Restaurant E-mail: spyles@stephanpyles.com

Phone: (469) 232-9151

RESTAURANT FACTS
Seats: 160 **Weeknight Covers:** 200 **Weekend Covers:** 300 **Check Average (with Wine):** $75 **Tasting Menu:** No **Kitchen Staff:** 11

CHEF FACTS
Cuisine: Southwestern **Born:** 1952 **Began Career:** 1979 **Culinary School:** Gaston Lenôtre Pastry School, France **Grad Year:** 1981 **Work History:** Dallas, TX: Routh Street Café, Baby Routh, Star Canyon; Minneapolis, MN: Goodfellow's, Tejas **Mentor(s):** Alain Chapel, Michel Guerard, Pierre Troisgros, Julia Child **Protégée(s):** Mark Kiffin, David Garrido, Tim Anderson, Lynn Saathoff, Matthew Dunn **Awards:** 2007 StarChefs.com Rising Star Mentor Award Dallas; 1998 Share Our Strength's Humanitarian of the Year; 1994 Nation's Restaurant News Fine Dining Award; 1992-present AAA Five Diamonds Award;1991 James Beard Foundation Best Chef Southwest **Affiliations:** Share Our Strength, North Texas Food Bank, The National Culinary Advisor's Board of The Art Institutes **Books Published:** The New Texas Cuisine; Tamales; New Tastes from Texas; Southwestern Vegetarian **Languages Spoken:** Spanish

NOTABLE DISH(ES): Coriander-Cured Black Buck Antelope with Olive Llapingacho; Crab Tamale Tart with Sea Bass in Hoja Santa

FAST FACTS
Restaurant Recs: Cuquita's for Pozole **Kitchen Tool(s):** Blender, because it eliminates the need for the molcajete that so much of Southwestern Mexican food relies on for grinding and puréeing **Interview Question:** What is your level of passion for cooking? I would rather have a cook who is passionate about food than one who is skilled but has no fire. **Flavor Combo(s):** Generally chilies and fruits. Specifically, aji mirasol and passionfruit. I also like fennel and vanilla. **Fave Cookbook(s):** James Beard American Cookery by James Beard **Chef to Cook for You:** I would have Escoffier and Ferran Adriá make me a joint meal. I would love to see the interaction between the two, as they are both groundbreaking and non-conventional chefs of their day. **Culinary Travel:** I would go back to Peru, India, or Spain. I'm most happy in these places.

Q

{ Quatrano - Quinones }

Q

Anne Quatrano
Executive Chef/Owner | Star Provisions

1198 Howell Mill Rd. Atlanta, GA 30318

Restaurant E-mail: aquatrano@eatoutoften.net

Phone: (404) 365-0410

RESTAURANT FACTS
Seats: 80 **Weeknight Covers:** 80 **Weekend Covers:** 125 **Check Average (with Wine):** $75 **Check Average (w/o Wine):** $105 **Tasting Menu:** No **Kitchen Staff:** 8

CHEF FACTS
Other Restaurants: Bacchanalia, Quinones, Floataway Café **Cuisine:** Modern American with country Italian **Born:** 1959 **Began Career:** 1986 **Culinary School:** California Culinary Academy, San Francisco, CA **Grad Year:** 1986 **Stages:** San Francisco, CA: Zuni Café **Work History:** San Francisco, CA: Zuni Café; Nantucket, MA: 21 Federal; New York, NY: La Petite Ferme **Mentor(s):** Judy Rodgers, Alice Waters **Protégée(s):** Greg Dunmore, Brandon McGlammery, Drew Belline, Josh Hopkins **Awards:** 2007 StarChefs.com Atlanta Rising Stars Mentor Award, 2001 James Beard Foundation Best Chef Southeast; 1995 Food & Wine Best New Chef **Affiliations:** WCR, SFA

FAST FACTS
Restaurant Recs: Tasty China for fiery hot northern Chinese cuisine, specifically for eggplant with Sichuan peppercorns **Kitchen Tool(s):** Peppermill – it is a required chef tool in our kitchens **Interview Question:** Where do you want to be professionally in five years? **Flavor Combo(s):** Sour and salty **Fave Cookbook(s):** Taste of Country Cooking by Edna Lewis **Chef to Cook for You:** Helene Darroze – her food is both interesting and pure **Culinary Travel:** Next stop is Italy. It has been many years and I love the simplicity.

Ernie Quinones
Executive Chef | The University of Massachusetts Club

225 Franklin St. Boston, MA 02110

Restaurant E-mail: contactus@umassclub.com

Phone: (617) 287-3030

RESTAURANT FACTS
Seats: 250+ **Weeknight Covers:** Lunch: 150–200 **Weekend Covers:** Closed **Check Average (with Wine):** $30-$35 **Tasting Menu:** No **Kitchen Staff:** 12

CHEF FACTS
Cuisine: Pastry **Born:** 1970 **Began Career:** 1981 **Culinary School:** The Culinary Institute of America, Hyde Park, NY **Grad Year:** 1996 **Stages:** Pasadena, CA: Abiento **Work History:** Boston, MA: Mantra Restaurant **Mentor(s):** Paul Muller, Randy Gehman **Awards:** 2003 StarChefs.com Rising Star Pastry Chef Boston **Affiliations:** ClubCorp, UMass Scholarship Fund, Employees Partner Fund, MDA **Languages Spoken:** Spanish

NOTABLE DISH(ES): Strawberry Rhubarb Tart with Banyuls Sorbet and Vanilla Tuiles

FAST FACTS
Restaurant Recs: Sage **Kitchen Tool(s):** Tongs – because they are an extension of my hand **Interview Question:** Where do you see yourself in the next three years? **Flavor Combo(s):** I like combinations of Asian and South American spice blends **Fave Cookbook(s):** The Professional Chef by The Culinary Institute of America **Chef to Cook for You:** Lydia Shire - she is one of Boston's best known chefs. She has a great handle on traditional New England cooking. **Culinary Travel:** Mexico – to see more of my heritage through the cuisine. India – to learn more about traditional Indian cooking.

R

{ Rae - Rudolph }

Brian Rae
Chef de Cuisine | Rick Moonen's RM Seafood

3930 Las Vegas Blvd. South, 134 Las Vegas, NV 89119

Restaurant E-mail: brae@rmseafood.com

Phone: (702) 795-7155

RESTAURANT FACTS
Seats: 65 **Weeknight Covers:** 50–60 **Weekend Covers:** 100 **Check Average (with Wine):** $150 **Tasting Menu:** Yes **Kitchen Staff:** 7

CHEF FACTS
Cuisine: Fine dining seafood **Born:** 1976 **Began Career:** 1994 **Culinary School:** The Culinary Institute of America, Hyde Park, NY **Grad Year:** 1997 **Work History:** Nantucket, MA: Straight Wharf; Richfield, CT: The Elm's Inn, The Bernard's Inn **Mentor(s):** Steve Cavagnaro, Rick Moonen **Awards:** 2008 StarChefs.com Rising Star Chef Las Vegas **Affiliations:** Slow Food, charity events and fundraisers

NOTABLE DISH(ES): Pan-Seared Abalone, Slow-Cooked Araucana Egg, Toasted Brioche with Brown Butter and White Balsamic; Butter-Poached Lobster, Porcini, Favas, Toasted Gnocchi, and Grand Marnier Monte

FAST FACTS
Restaurant Recs: Naked Fish for sushi; Lotus of Siam; there's this little hot dog store called Big Al's in southwest. I also like going to Nora's Wine Bar – they have one of those enomatic machines so you can have wines by the glass, and their sweet and sour meatballs are off the charts. **Kitchen Tool(s):** My spoons; blue steeled French cast iron pans that we sauté all of our fish in;Vita-Prep – it's so powerful. I've worked in restaurants with bar mixers but you can't do half the stuff. **Interview Question:** I ask people what they cook at home, and what kind of music they like. I'm just looking for an honest and unique answer. If you say you don't cook at home but that you have 5000 different condiments that you do something with, well that's interesting. **Flavor Combo(s):** Lemon, olive oil and fennel pollen; grains of paradise and powdered yuzu on cobia; carrot and olive; anything spicy and sweet. I'm using Piment d'E'spelette powder a lot these days. **Fave Cookbook(s):** Culinary Artistry – I use it so much the pages are falling out **Chef to Cook for You:** I'd really like to go to el Bulli and see what they're doing there. And to go home to Mom and Grandma. **Culinary Travel:** I'd go back to Torino (Turin), Italy; it's just a really great food city and of course it's right in the heart of Piedmont so it's got great wine, truffles, chocolate. It's a half Italian, half French style of cooking.

César Ramirez
Consulting Chef

New York, NY

E-mail: cesarramirez7@mac.com

CHEF FACTS
Cuisine: Seasonal, with the best products I can find **Born:** 1972 **Began Career:** 1991 **Stages:** Spain: Arzak, Aquilare, Mugaritz, Comerç 24 **Work History:** Chicago, IL: Le Français, The Ritz-Carlton, Tru; New York, NY: Danube, Bouley, Bar Blanc **Mentor(s):** Jean Banchet, my mother, my grandmother **Languages Spoken:** Spanish

NOTABLE DISH(ES): Gently-Cooked Salmon with Herb Pasta, Preserved Tomatoes and White Wine Sauce; Seared Black Cod, Wilted Arrowleaf Spinach, Roast Burdock, Squid Ink, Saffron Mussel Sauce

FAST FACTS
Restaurant Recs: Franny's in Brooklyn – it is very simple and clean. Nothing special, but they really care about what they're doing there. Lan on 3rd Ave and 10th street – they do an amazing job on consistency there. The menu might not change so much but they're really good at consistency. **Kitchen Tool(s):** Definitely the Rational. I can't work anywhere without it. I've worked with it for 10–12 years. You can sous vide, you can steam, you can dry. It's a Bentley of ovens. That, and the Pacojet. **Interview Question:** I look for people with a lot of excitement, and when I do, I tell them that I'm willing to put them to work. You have to sacrifice a lot to be in the kitchen. **Flavor Combo(s):** I like very clean combinations. If you cook a vegetable, it's got to taste like a vegetable. I reinforce it with reductions of the same vegetable, like finishing carrot with reduced carrot juice. **Fave Cookbook(s):** Roger Vergé's Entertaining in the French Style, The Gran Livre from Ducasse and La Gastronomique. Great reference books. **Chef to Cook for You:** I'd want my grandmother to cook for me. She had great seasonings and really loved cooking. There was a famous bullring where I was born, and when I was little, famous matadors from Spain would come over to my house and she would cook for them. **Culinary Travel:** Japan – because there is so much tradition and love and honor in what they do.

Gordon Ramsay
Executive Chef | Gordon Ramsay at The London

151 West 54th St. New York, NY 10019

Phone: (212) 468-8888

RESTAURANT FACTS
Seats: 45 **Weeknight Covers:** 80 **Weekend Covers:** 100 **Check Average (w/o Wine):** $100 **Tasting Menu:** Yes $135/$230 with wine **Kitchen Staff:** 10

CHEF FACTS
Other Restaurants: London, England: Petrus, Restaurant Gordon Ramsay, Gordon Ramsay at Claridge's, Foxtrot Oscar, Sloane Street, York & Albany, Murano, The Narrow, The Devonshire,The Warrington, Boxwood Café, Maze, The Maze Grill; Heathrow Airport, England: Plane Food; New York, NY: Maze; Prague, Czech Republic: Maze; West Hollywood, CA: Gordon Ramsey at The London; Boca Raton, FL: Cielo by Angela Hartnett; Versailles, France: La Veranda, Gordon Ramsay au Trianon; Tokyo, Japan: Gordon Ramsay at The Conrad; Dubai, UAE: Verre; County Wicklow, Ireland: Gordon Ramsay at Powerscourt **Cuisine:** French, British **Born:** 1966 **Began Career:** 1989 **Culinary School:** North Oxon Technical College, Great Britain **Grad Year:** 1987 **Stages:** England: Harvey's; France: Joël Robuchon, Guy Savoy **Work History:** England: La Gavroche, Aubergine **Mentor(s):** Albert Roux, Joël Robuchon, Guy Savoy **Protégée(s):** Mark Sargeant, Josh Emmet, Angela Hartnett, Jason Atherton **Awards:** 9 Michelin stars; 2008, 2007 Restaurant Magazine 50 Best Restaurants in the World (Restaurant Gordon Ramsay); 2007 Restaurant Magazine Breakthrough Restaurant Award (Maze); 2001-2006 Harden's Guide Best Fine Dining Restaurant; 2000 Chef of the Year Award at the Cateys **Affiliations:** Womens' Aid **Books Published:** Humble Pie; Roasting in Hell's Kitchen; Gordon Ramsay Makes it Easy; Gordon Ramsay: A Chef for All Seasons; Gordon Ramsay's Kitchen Heaven; Gordon Ramsay;s Passion for Flavour; Gordon Ramsay's Just Desserts; Gordon Ramsay's Secrets; Gordon Ramsay's Passion for Seafood; Gordon Ramsay's Sunday Lunch; Gordon Ramsay's Fast Food; Gordon Ramsay, 3 Star Chef **Languages Spoken:** French

FAST FACTS
Restaurant Recs: I love Benares, an Indian restaurant on Berkeley Square in Mayfair, London for Atul Kochhar's amazing Indian curry **Kitchen Tool(s):** Sharp knives are always essential. I love Bourgeat pans from France, but since working with Royal Doulton to design an exclusive range for the kitchen and home, I naturally prefer the new collection. At the restaurants, we highly favor copper pans as they're one of the best conductors of heat. **Interview Question:** I don't really go by CVs with all the carefully gathered work experience. I ask all of my potential line chefs to cook something from a selection of scraps and leftovers that I give them. That's a great way of finding out what the raw talent of that particular individual is like. **Flavor Combo(s):** I like to cook with few but flavorful ingredients – simple flavors without pretense **Fave Cookbook(s):** 1080, the Spanish cookbook by various contributors (published by Phaidon); Kitchen Confidential by Anthony Bourdain; The French Laundry Cookbook by Thomas Keller **Chef to Cook for You:** Alain Ducasse – he's someone that I truly admire and would be honored to have him prepare a meal for me **Culinary Travel:** New York continues to be a source of inspiration for me, and I've also been spending a lot of time in Los Angeles, having just opened a restaurant in West Hollywood. The quality of produce available out there is fantastic.

Frank Randazzo
Chef | Talula

210 23rd St. Miami Beach, FL 33139

Restaurant E-mail: frank@talulaonline.com

Phone: (305) 672-0778 and (305) 256-8399

RESTAURANT FACTS
Seats: 125 **Weeknight Covers:** 100 **Weekend Covers:** 150–200
Check Average (with Wine): $55–$70 **Tasting Menu:** Yes $79/$140
with wine **Kitchen Staff:** 9

CHEF FACTS
Other Restaurants: Creative Tastes Catering & Event Production **Cuisine:** New American and Italian **Born:** 1971 **Began Career:** 1992 **Culinary School:** Johnson & Wales University, Providence, RI **Grad Year:** 1992 **Work History:** New York, NY: Tribeca Grill; Miami Beach, FL: The Heights **Mentor(s):** Daniel Boulud, Thomas Keller **Protégée(s):** My wife, Andrea Curto-Randazzo **Awards:** 2004 StarChefs.com Rising Star Chef Miami **Affiliations:** JBF

NOTABLE DISH(ES): Tartar of Ahi Tuna; Shrimp Tamale

FAST FACTS
Restaurant Recs: Doraku for Japanese; Ortanique; Rosinella for dive-y Italian; Pub Haus for German food **Kitchen Tool(s):** Hot sauté pan; chefs' knife; tongs; really good quality grill **Interview Question:** Why do you want to be a chef? **Flavor Combo(s):** I have many combinations that I absolutely love using, however I must go back to my upbringing to answer this question: garlic and olive oil. They're pretty much the two items that remind me of my family when I was growing up and my present family and home. I love garlic and olive oil. **Fave Cookbook(s):** The French Laundry Cookbook by Thomas Keller **Chef to Cook for You:** My wife Andrea (Curto- Randazzo). She is an awesome cook, which makes her an incredibly talented chef. **Culinary Travel:** NYC – it's the best in the world, you can find it all. Very diverse, quality food,fanfare, international cuisine, and the best chefs all at your fingertips.

Kevin Rathbun
Chef/Owner | Rathbun's

112 Krog St., Suite R Atlanta, GA 30307

Restaurant E-mail: kevin.rathbun@rathbunsrestaurant.com

Phone: (404) 524-8280

RESTAURANT FACTS
Seats: 150 **Weeknight Covers:** 175–200 **Weekend Covers:** 350–400 **Check Average (with Wine):** $55 **Tasting Menu:** No **Kitchen Staff:** 7

CHEF FACTS
Other Restaurants: Krog Bar, Kevin Rathbun Steak **Cuisine:** Southwestern Pacific Rim melting pot **Born:** 1962 **Began Career:** 1983 **Culinary School:** Johnson County Community College, Kansas City, KA **Grad Year:** 1983 **Stages:** New Orleans, LA: Mr. B's; Dallas, TX: Routh Street Café; Minneapolis, MN: Goodfellows **Work History:** Kansas City, KS: American Restaurant; Dallas, TX: Baby Routh; New Orleans, LA: Commander's Palace; Atlanta, GA: Nava, Bluepointe, Buckhead Diner **Mentor(s):** Bradley Ogden, Emeril Lagasse, Stephen Pyles, Pano Karratossos, Ella Brennan **Protégée(s):** Marc Cassel, Clark McDaniel, Jason Gorman, Scott Serpas, Matt Harris **Awards:** 2007 StarChefs.com Rising Star Restaurateur Atlanta; 2006 Creative Loafing Best Chef; 2006-2007 Mobil Travel Guide 3 stars; 2006 Georgia Trend Magazine Silver Spoon Award; 2006 Atlanta AOL Guide Atlanta Best Restaurant; 2005 Bon Appétit Hot 50; 2005 Atlanta Magazine Best American Bistro; 2004 Travel and Leisure Magazine Best New American Restaurants; 2004 Esquire Best New Restaurant; 2002 Share Our Strength Southeast Chef of the Year **Books Published:** Featured: Atlanta Cooks **Languages Spoken:** Kitchen Spanish

NOTABLE DISH(ES): Hickory Smoked Beef Short Rib with White Balsamic Butter and Garlic Chips; Lobster-Cauliflower Bisque with Wisconsin SarVecchio and Tarragon Oil

FAST FACTS
Restaurant Recs: Floataway Café for Gorgonzola Pizza; LC'S Kansas City BBQ **Kitchen Tool(s):** Asian mandolin – it travels every where and it's not too pricey **Interview Question:** Tell me what teams you've worked with and what position you held. Did you ever climb to a head position on a sports team, a school club or for a charity? **Flavor Combo(s):** Citrus and butter; bacon and potatoes; banana and peanut butter **Fave Cookbook(s):** The Silver Palate Cookbook by Julee Rosso and Sheila Lukins; Happy in the Kitchen by Michel Richard **Chef to Cook for You:** I would have to say James Beard because of his gregariousness and his thoughts on food **Culinary Travel:** I'd like to go to Asia – all parts. I love the cuisine and the different styles, and I've never been there. I have had so much of their cuisine here that I would like to go and see the difference between what is brought over what is truly their style.

Kent Rathbun
Chef/Owner | Abacus

4511 McKinney Ave. Dallas, TX 75205

Phone: (214) 559-3111

RESTAURANT FACTS
Seats: 160 **Weeknight Covers:** 170 **Weekend Covers:** 275 **Check Average (with Wine):** $115 **Tasting Menu:** Yes $90/$115 with wine **Kitchen Staff:** 9

CHEF FACTS
Other Restaurants: Jasper's **Cuisine:** Southwest American **Born:** 1961 **Began Career:** 1976 **Stages:** Kansas City, MO: La Bonne Auberge **Work History:** New Orleans, LA: Mr. B's; Kansas City, MO: American Restaurant, Milano; Dallas, TX: Mansion on Turtle Creek, Landmark; Thailand: Dusit Thani **Mentor(s):** Jim Mills, Robert Hoffman **Protégée(s):** Tre Wilcox **Awards:** Mobil Four Star and AAA Four Diamond awards for Abacus; 2002-2004 James Beard Foundation Best Chef Southwest Nominee; 2001 Bon Appétit's Best of the Year **Affiliations:** American Cancer Society, March of Dimes, Zoo to Do, the North Texas Food Bank and the American Heart Association

NOTABLE DISH(ES): Wisconsin Mobay and Hudson Valley Foie Gras Grilled Cheese Sandwich

FAST FACTS
Restaurant Recs: Green Papaya Vietnamese; 1st Chinese BBQ for the dim sum, dumplings and ducks feet; Bubba's for fried chicken **Kitchen Tool(s):** An extremely sharp knife because a great knife in the right hands can speed up any process **Interview Question:** My number one question is: "What do you feel your weaknesses are and where do you want to see improvement?" The answer I'm looking for is simple and honest. I want to know that I'm hiring someone who is humble and who wants to learn. **Flavor Combo(s):** Sweet and salty **Fave Cookbook(s):** The French Laundry Cookbook by Thomas Keller **Chef to Cook for You:** My mom was such an amazing chef and I know that her mother taught her everything, so I'd love to have the opportunity to learn some of my grandmother's skills and recipes now that I'm older and appreciate the art of cooking. THAT would be an experience of a lifetime. **Culinary Travel:** Definitely China, and I say China because I think that it's a Mecca of dining –meaning you can find food and products from all over the world. I would love to experience the cuisine, from the small villages and towns to the upscale and renowned restaurants.

Thierry Rautureau
Owner | Rover's

2808 E Madison St. Seattle, WA 98112

Restaurant E-mail: thierry@rovers-seattle.com

Phone: (206) 325-7442

RESTAURANT FACTS
Seats: 50 **Weeknight Covers:** 45 **Weekend Covers:** 65 **Check Average (with Wine):** $150 **Check Average (w/o Wine):** $100 **Tasting Menu:** Yes $90–$140 **Kitchen Staff:** 7–9

CHEF FACTS
Cuisine: Northwest Cuisine with a French accent **Born:** 1959 **Began Career:** 1974 **Work History:** France: Le St Michel; Chicago, IL: La Fontaine; Los Angeles, CA: The Regency Club,The 7th Street Bistro **Mentor(s):** Laurent Quenioux, Fred Halpert **Protégée(s):** Bill Morris, Viljo Basso, Adam Hoffman, Branden Karow **Awards:** 1998 James Beard Foundation Best Chef Pacific Northwest; Seattle Magazine Best Restaurant; Seattle Magazine Best Chef **Affiliations:** JBF, IACP, Slow Food, Chefs Collaborative **Books Published:** Rover's: Recipes from Seattle's Chef In The Hat!!! **Languages Spoken:** French, Spanish, English

NOTABLE DISH(ES): Clear Tomato Soup with Herb Crèpes; Strawberry Pizza with Almond Cream

FAST FACTS
Restaurant Recs: Catfish Corner for fried filet of catfish with their homemade sauce **Kitchen Tool(s):** Fish spatula, because I can use it to flip just about anything **Interview Question:** What is your favorite dish to cook at home? That will tell me if they cook outside of work. **Flavor Combo(s):** Sweet and sour; yin and yang **Fave Cookbook(s):** The Way to Cook by Julia Child **Chef to Cook for You:** Daniel Boulud – cooking a traditional braised dish **Culinary Travel:** Vietnam, Thailand, China, West Africa

R

Richard Reddington
Executive Chef/Owner | Redd Restaurant

6480 Washington St. Yountville, CA, 94599

Restaurant E-mail: info@reddnapavalley.com

Phone: (707) 944-2222

RESTAURANT FACTS
Seats: 90 **Weeknight Covers:** 150 **Weekend Covers:** 200 **Tasting Menu:** Yes $70/$110 with wine **Kitchen Staff:** 7-9

CHEF FACTS
Cuisine: Napa Valley cuisine **Born:** 1965 **Stages:** France: Moulin de Mougins, Pierre Orsi **Work History:** San Francisco, CA: La Folie, Rubicon, Jardinière; New York, NY: David Burke's Park Avenue Café, Daniel; France: L'Arpege, Moulin de Mougins; Beverly Hills, CA: Spago; Napa Valley, CA: Auberge du Soleil **Mentor(s):** Daniel Boulud, Roland Passot, Alain Passard **Protégée(s):** Robert Leva, Eric Webster, Scott Pikey **Awards:** 2006 Esquire Top New Restaurants; 2003 San Francisco Magazine Best Rising Chef **Languages Spoken:** French, Spanish

NOTABLE DISH(ES): Sautéed Diver Scallops with Cauliflower, Capers and Almonds

FAST FACTS
Restaurant Recs: Angele in Napa Valley for hamburgers **Kitchen Tool(s):** Peltex fish spatula **Interview Question:** Why do you want to work here? **Fave Cookbook(s):** The Art of Eating Well by Pellegrino Artusi

Jennifer Reed
Consulting Pastry Chef | The Sugar Monkey

Miami, FL

Restaurant E-mail: jennifer@thesugarmonkey.com

Phone: (561) 252-8400

CHEF FACTS

Cuisine: Modern American with a twist **Born:** 1972 **Began Career:** 1990 **Culinary School:** The Culinary Institute of America, Hyde Park, New York **Grad Year:** 1999 **Work History:** New York, NY: Beacon, Café Boulud **Mentor(s):** Remy Funfrock **Languages Spoken:** Kitchen Spanish, a little French

NOTABLE DISH(ES): Chocolate Fondant with Cocoa Almond Streusel; Biscuit Sacher and Earl Grey Ice Cream

FAST FACTS

Restaurant Recs: Middle Eastern bakery (on Dixie and West Palm) for great shwarma, falafel and homemade pitas **Kitchen Tool(s):** Scraper-spatulas are hard to come by. I always have one in my back pocket. **Interview Question:** Do you know who Daniel Boulud is? Most of the times if they say no then I know its probably not going to work out. **Flavor Combo(s):** I like fromage blanc with apples; chocolate and Meyer lemon **Fave Cookbook(s):** The Ducasse pastry book **Chef to Cook for You:** Michel Richard – because he knows pastry and savory **Culinary Travel:** We just went to California – they have the best farmers markets and that makes for great food. We love to go to NYC. We plan our trips around going to restaurants.

Michael Regrut
Executive Chef | Restaurant Avondale

126 Riverfront Ln. Avon, CO 81620

Restaurant E-mail: mregrut@avondalerestaurant.com

Phone: (970) 790-6000

RESTAURANT FACTS
Seats: 85 **Tasting Menu:** Yes **Kitchen Staff:** 10

CHEF FACTS
Cuisine: New American elegant seasonal cuisine **Born:** 1969 **Began Career:** 1994 **Culinary School:** Johnson & Wales, Vail, CO **Grad Year:** 1999 **Stages:** New York, NY: Daniel, Le Bernardin; La Jolla, CA: Georges at the Cove; Chapel Hill, NC: Fearrington House **Work History:** Clearwater, FL: Felice's Italian Pork Shop; Tampa, FL: Oyster Catchers; Frisco, CO: Uptown Bistro; Vail, CO: Sweet Basil, Michael's American Bistro, Larkspur **Mentor(s):** Bruce Yim **Affiliations:** We do events and fundraisers

NOTABLE DISH(ES): Veal Scaloppini with Twice Baked Potatoes and Creamed Spinach; House Smoked Atlantic Salmon

FAST FACTS
Restaurant Recs: Moe's BBQ for the pulled pork sandwich, cornbread and a tall boy of PBR **Kitchen Tool(s):** Vita-Prep **Interview Question:** Show me five ways to thicken a sauce **Flavor Combo(s):** Right now I have a fix for tarragon, so anything with tarragon **Fave Cookbook(s):** Bouchon by Thomas Keller **Chef to Cook for You:** Eric Ripert – he's one of the best chefs out there right now – his food is amazing. It's too good. He is a great, great chef. **Culinary Travel:** I have family in Vienna so I would like to go there and see what the traditional food is like. I would like to visit the small places and get a feel for the local cuisine.

E. Michael Reidt
Chef/Owner | EMR/Lantana

3000 West Olympic Blvd. Santa Monica, CA 90404

Restaurant E-mail: emreidt@aol.com

Phone: (310) 449-4026

RESTAURANT FACTS
Seats: 130 **Weeknight Covers:** 110 **Weekend Covers:** 225 **Check Average (with Wine):** $70 **Check Average (w/o Wine):** $55 **Tasting Menu:** Yes $85 **Kitchen Staff:** 11

CHEF FACTS
Cuisine: Modern American **Born:** 1970 **Began Career:** 1987 **Culinary School:** The Culinary Institute of America, Hyde Park, NY **Grad Year:** 1993 **Work History:** Washington, VA: Inn at Little Washington; Maui, HI: HailE-maile General Store; Miami, FL: Wish; Boston, MA: OLIVES, Bomboa; Santa Barbara, CA: Sevilla, Penthouse **Mentor(s):** Todd English, Charlie Trotter, Alan Wong **Awards:** 2005 Esquire Best New Restaurant; 2003 StarChefs.com Rising Star Chef Miami; 2001 Food & Wine Best New Chef; 2000 Best New Chef Boston Phoenix **Languages Spoken:** Portuguese, Spanish

NOTABLE DISH(ES): Braised Short Ribs Churrasco

FAST FACTS
Restaurant Recs: Lily's Taqueria on lower Chapala for the veal cheek tacos **Kitchen Tool(s):** Vita-Prep, because everything can become a silky purée or soup **Interview Question:** Do you like to cook? This way I get the bullshit out of the way right off the bat. **Flavor Combo(s):** Bacon and anything **Fave Cookbook(s):** Simple Cuisine: The Easy New Approach to Cooking from Jean-Georges by Jean-Georges Vongerichten **Chef to Cook for You:** Giada de Laurentis – do you have to ask why? **Culinary Travel:** The southern coast of Chile

Cyril Renaud
Chef/Owner | Fleur de Sel

5 East 20th Street New York, NY 10003

Restaurant E-mail: contact@fleurdeselnyc.com

Phone: (212) 460-9100

RESTAURANT FACTS
Seats: 45 **Weeknight Covers:** 35–40 **Weekend Covers:** 70 **Check Average (with Wine):** $100 **Tasting Menu:** Yes $89/$145 with wine/$125 **Kitchen Staff:** 4

CHEF FACTS
Cuisine: Simple and flavorful **Born:** 1969 **Began Career:** 1981 **Work History:** France: Le Villard, L'Escalier du Palais Royal; Belgium: La Villa Lorraine; England: London Hilton; New York, NY: Cellar in the Sky at Windows on the World, Bouley, La Caravelle **Mentor(s):** David Bouley **Affiliations:** We do a lot of charity events **Languages Spoken:** French

NOTABLE DISH(ES): Yellow and Green Bean Salad with Tomato Confit; Goat Cheese Artichoke Ravioli

FAST FACTS
Restaurant Recs: Provence en Boite for the opera cake dessert **Kitchen Tool(s):** Wooden spatula **Interview Question:** Do you cook with a smile? For me one of the most important things about the new people that I bring into my team is their attitude and if they have a smile on their face while they're cooking. It helps to build a better work environment. **Flavor Combo(s):** Peas and mint **Fave Cookbook(s):** Couleurs, Parfums et Saveurs de Ma Cuisine by Jacques Maximin **Chef to Cook for You:** William Schutz – I just love his passion for food and life **Culinary Travel:** Brazil and Argentina – I really like the way they think of food in these cultures

Kate Rench
Chef/Owner | Cafe Diva

1855 Ski Times Sq. Steamboat, CO 80487

Restaurant E-mail: chefkvr@comcast.net

Phone: (970) 871-0508

RESTAURANT FACTS
Seats: 60 **Weeknight Covers:** 100 **Weekend Covers:** 120 **Check Average (with Wine):** $100 **Check Average (w/o Wine):** $50 **Tasting Menu:** No **Kitchen Staff:** 4

CHEF FACTS
Other Restaurants: Mohagony Ridge Pub and Brewery **Cuisine:** Eclectic American **Born:** 1972 **Began Career:** 1996 **Culinary School:** French Culinary Institute, New York, NY **Grad Year:** 1998 **Stages:** New York, NY: Jean-Georges **Work History:** Boulder, CO: Mountain Sun Pub and Brewery, New York, NY: Jean-Georges, Balducci's; Westport, CT: Hay Day Country Market **Mentor(s):** My mom, Jean-Georges Vongerichten, Josh Eden, Wylie Dufresne, Mark Urwand **Protégée(s):** Andrew King **Awards:** 1999 French Culinary Institute Jacques Pépin Award **Books Published:** My recipes are in various Colorado cookbooks **Languages Spoken:** Some Italian

NOTABLE DISH(ES): Asian Duck Confit Wonton Tacos; Balsamic Chestnut-Glazed Pheasant with Baby Brussel Sprouts and Mushroom Leek Bread Pudding

FAST FACTS
Restaurant Recs: Tequilas for the fresh squeezed margaritas and a chipotle vegetable burrito; Mountain Sun Pub and Brewery for a large plate of nachos **Kitchen Tool(s):** Burr mixer because it can purée things in half the time, and I can walk away from it; a juicer for my reductions **Interview Question:** Do you have any drug problems! **Flavor Combo(s):** Corn and bacon; heirloom tomatoes, lobster and verjus; pork belly and peanut butter **Fave Cookbook(s):** Donna Hay's books because they are clean, simple and fresh; White Heat by Marco Pierre White; Nuevo Latino by Douglas Martinez **Chef to Cook for You:** Marco Pierre White – White Heat inspired me to become a chef **Culinary Travel:** My husband and I love to travel to Latin American Countries, like Costa Rica and Mexico, for the soul behind their food, the love and energy they put into it, and for the history behind it

David Reynoso
Executive Chef | Al Forno

577Main St. Providence, RI 02903

Restaurant E-mail: dreynoso@alforno.com

Phone: (401) 273-9760

RESTAURANT FACTS
Seats: 150 **Weeknight Covers:** 150–170 **Weekend Covers:** 290–315 **Check Average (with Wine):** $65 **Tasting Menu:** No

CHEF FACTS
Cuisine: Italian **Born:** 1971 **Began Career:** 1990 **Culinary School:** Washburne Culinary Institute, Chicago, IL **Grad Year:** 1990 **Stages:** Italy: La Chiusa **Work History:** Italy: Antica Osteria del Ponte **Mentor(s):** Johanne Killen, George Germon, Tony Mantuano **Protégée(s):** Phil Niosi **Awards:** 2006 StarChefs.com Rising Star Chef Boston **Languages Spoken:** Spanish, Italian

NOTABLE DISH(ES): Venison with Mole and Tamale Stuffed with Shiitake Mushrooms

FAST FACTS
Restaurant Recs: Mike's Kitchen for polenta and meatballs **Kitchen Tool(s):** Rubber spatula **Interview Question:** Do you want to be a star? **Flavor Combo(s):** Cloves with rabbit **Fave Cookbook(s):** Chez Panisse Café Cookbook by Alice Waters **Chef to Cook for You:** Julia Child – I love her spirit **Culinary Travel:** Chicago – my brother lives there and has a taqueria place. My favorite Mexican restaurant is on Milwaukee Ave. It's run by a kid who used to work for Rick Bayless.

Evan Rich
Executive Chef | Quince

1701 Octavia St. San Francisco, CA 94109

Restaurant E-mail: info@quincerestaurant.com

Phone: (415) 775-8500

RESTAURANT FACTS
Seats: 45 **Weeknight Covers:** 80 **Weekend Covers:** 110 **Check Average (with Wine):** $80 **Tasting Menu:** Yes $90/$145 with wine **Kitchen Staff:** 5

CHEF FACTS
Cuisine: American-inspired Japanese **Born:** 1980 **Began Career:** 1996 **Culinary School:** Culinary Institute of America, Hyde Park, NY **Grad Year:** 2000 **Stages:** New York, NY: Danube, Restaurant David Drake **Work History:** Scotch Plane, NJ: Stage House Inn; Japan: SumileTokyo; New York, NY: Bouley, Jovia, Sumile Sushi **Mentor(s):** David Bouley, Josh Dechellis **Affiliations:** JBF, Slow Food, Local Farms, any organization that promotes sustainability **Languages Spoken:** Spanish

NOTABLE DISH(ES): 24-Hour Roasted Pork Loin with Ramps, Pea Shoots, Sunchoke Purée and Foie Gras Mousse Foam; Cherry-Glazed Anago Handroll with Arugula and Foie Gras

FAST FACTS
Restaurant Recs: Il Posto Accanto for the oxtail ravioli **Kitchen Tool(s):** CVap combi-oven **Interview Question:** What was the last cookbook you bought? It shows their willingness to spend money on their craft. **Flavor Combo(s):** Sweet and salty **Fave Cookbook(s):** Lust auf Genuss by Hans Haas **Chef to Cook for You:** My friend Pete Serpico from Ko. We have a lot of work history together and a competitive nature between us. I've cooked for him and I want to give him a chance to reciprocate. **Culinary Travel:** Japan – because they look at food in such a different way. They have so much respect for the ingredients.

R

Michel Richard
Chef/Owner | Michel Richard Citronelle

3000 M St. NW Washington, DC 20007

Restaurant E-mail: citronelledc@ihrco.com

Phone: (202) 625-2150

RESTAURANT FACTS
Seats: 90 **Weeknight Covers:** 100 **Weekend Covers:** 110 **Check Average (w/o Wine):** $100 **Tasting Menu:** Yes $95 /$175/$225 **Kitchen Staff:** 12

CHEF FACTS
Other Restaurants: Washington, DC: Central; Los Angeles, CA: Citrus at Social; Carmel, CA: Citronelle at Carmel Valley Ranch **Cuisine:** American-French **Born:** 1948 **Began Career:** 1962 **Work History:** France: Lenotre; San Francisco, CA: Bistro M; Santa Barbara: Citronelle **Mentor(s):** Gaston Lenôtre, Jean-Louis Palladin **Protégée(s):** Robert Curry, Auberge de Soliel, Cal Stamenov **Awards:** 2008 James Beard Foundation Best New Restaurant (Central); 2008, 2007 Washingtonian Magazine #1 Restaurant in Washington, DC; 2007 Zagat Award of Distinction; 2007 James Beard Foundation; Outstanding Chef and Outstanding Wine Program; 2007 Gayot Top 40 Restaurants in USA; 2007 American Immigration Law Foundation Immigrant Achievement Award; 2006 Food Arts Silver Spoon; 2004 Nation's Restaurant News Fine Dining Hall of Fame; 2002 Restaurant Association of Metropolitan Washington; Best Chef of The Year and Best Fine Dining Restaurant; 2002-present Traditions and Qualité Les Grandes Tables du Monde; 2002-present Exxon Mobile Four Star Award; 2001-present AAA Four Diamond Award; 2001 Wine Spectator Award of Excellence; 1991 Restaurants & Institutions Ivy Award; Restaurant Association of Los Angeles Best Restaurant & Best Chef; French Government Médaille Agricole and Mérite National; Maîtres Cuisiniers de France **Affiliations:** St. Jude Children's Research Hospital, Les Maîtres Cuisiniers, Tradition & Qualité, Les Grande Tables du Monde, DC CHEFS Magazine, JBF Who's Who in America **Books Published:** Happy in the Kitchen; Home Cooking with a French Accent **Languages Spoken:** French, Spanish

FAST FACTS
Restaurant Recs: Normandie Restaurant for brunch. We take the kids, who feel like they are in France and they can eat as much as they want. **Kitchen Tool(s):** Pots and pans because grilling is only good for a picnic. You must be able to make sauces and be able to sauté. **Interview Question:** What do you eat? I need to know if they love food. **Flavor Combo(s):** Garlic and parsley; garlic and basil; garlic and ginger. I am French, I love garlic. Garlic and parsley with escargot, and my mother's garlic and parsley chicken. The smell is so good. **Fave Cookbook(s):** Gastronomie Practique by Ali-Bab (Henri Babinski). The recipes are impeccable and precise. It was published in 1907, and it was the first book I ever got excited about. **Chef to Cook for You:** My wife – she knows what I love. Everything she cooks is so good. She is my perfect petite chef. **Culinary Travel:** Morocco – I love the food. I love the smell of the tagines and the sweet and spicy flavor.

James Richardson
Chef | Nook

11628 Santa Monica Blvd. Los Angeles, CA 90025

Restaurant E-mail: james@nookbistro.com

Phone: (310) 207-5160

RESTAURANT FACTS
Seats: 48 **Weeknight Covers:** 95 **Weekend Covers:** 130 **Check Average (w/o Wine):** $25 **Tasting Menu:** No **Kitchen Staff:** 3–4

CHEF FACTS
Cuisine: Southern-inspired, market-driven neo-Americana **Born:** 1969 **Began Career:** 1997 **Stages:** Tampa, FL: Boca **Work History:** Tampa, FL: Boca, Atomic Café, Bern's Steakhouse; Santa Monica, CA: Bergamot Café **Mentor(s):** Jean Pierola **Protégée(s):** My daughter - Bailey **Awards:** 2006 StarChefs.com Rising Star Chef Los Angeles **Languages Spoken:** Some French, some Spanish

NOTABLE DISH(ES): Jumbo Shrimp with Sweet Corn Succotash; Kurobuta Pork Belly with Tomatillo, Shiitake and Black-Eyed Peas

FAST FACTS
Restaurant Recs: Cobras and Matadors for fried lentils; Allegria for Mexican carnitas **Kitchen Tool(s):** Microplane **Interview Question:** What was your favorite dish at your previous restaurant, and please describe to me how it's made. It's not their answer I am concerned with, I want to hear that they have some passion about what they do. **Flavor Combo(s):** Tangy and earthy – like cherries and bacon fat, or tomatillos and shiitakes **Fave Cookbook(s):** Sheila Lukins All Around the World Cookbook by Sheila Lukins; cookbooks by Julia Child and Jacques Pépin **Chef to Cook for You:** Auguste Escoffier – for the chance to have a conversation with someone who transformed the culinary arts as we know them **Culinary Travel:** San Francisco and New York. There are so many great chefs in each of those cities. New Orleans because my family is from there. It has memories and comfort food.

Matthew Ridgway
Chef | The Oak Room at The Plaza

768 Fifth Ave. New York, NY

Restaurant E-mail: matt@theoakroomny.com

Phone: (212) 546-5320

RESTAURANT FACTS
Seats: 210 **Check Average (with Wine):** $65+ **Tasting Menu:** Yes
Kitchen Staff: 15

CHEF FACTS
Cuisine: Modern Italian-French **Born:** 1975 **Began Career:** 1996
Culinary School: Johnson & Wales University, Providence, RI **Grad
Year:** 1996 **Stages:** Sonoma, CA: The Eastside Oyster Bar and Grill;
France: George V, Relais St. Victoire Aix **Work History:** Philadelphia,
PA: LaCroix at the Rittenhouse, The Fountain Room in The Four Sea-
sons Hotel; Atlanta, GA: Joël **Mentor(s):** Martin Hamman, Jean Marie
Lacroix, Joël Antunes **Protégée(s):** Chris Agneau, Shawn Gaules, Josh
Taggert **Awards:** 2004 StarChefs.com Rising Star Chef Philadelphia; 2003 Esquire Restaurant of the
Year **Affiliations:** Meals-on-Wheels, Autism Foundation **Languages Spoken:** French, Spanish

NOTABLE DISH(ES): Lobster en Gelée with Cauliflower Chaud Froid, Sauce Morna; Marinated Boston
Mackerel Basquaise with Smoked Uni Soup

FAST FACTS
Restaurant Recs: Canton House for crispy fried black bass with ginger and lime **Kitchen Tool(s):** I
can't live without my French omelet pan. If you can't make a good omelet, then you can't cook food
like foie gras or beef. The first thing a chef should learn is how to make a proper omelet. **Interview
Question:** I like to hear that they are well rounded and that they read other books than just culinary,
like Joyce or Tolstoy. **Flavor Combo(s):** Meat and sea – for example, using a meat sauce on a seafood
dish. Acidity is also very important to me in all aspects of my cooking. **Fave Cookbook(s):** Cooking
With the Seasons by Jean-Louis Palladin **Chef to Cook for You:** Jean-Louis Palladin – he was one of
the first French chefs to marry American cuisine with the a delicate French aesthetic. His food was
simple yet amazing. **Culinary Travel:** New York and San Francisco. New York is refined technically and
San Francisco has some of the best products in the country. San Francisco also has great markets
and everything is impeccably fresh. Both cities have a great food culture and great appreciation of
food.

Eric Ripert
Chef/Owner | Le Bernardin

787 7th Ave. New York, NY 10019

Phone: (212) 554-1515

RESTAURANT FACTS
Seats: 90 **Weeknight Covers:** 175 **Weekend Covers:** 250 **Check Average (with Wine):** $175 **Check Average (w/o Wine):** $107 **Tasting Menu:** Yes $135 or $180/$220 or $320 with wine

CHEF FACTS
Other Restaurants: Washington, DC: Westend Bistro **Cuisine:** Seafood **Born:** 1965 **Culinary School:** Perpignan, France **Work History:** France: La Tour D'Argent, Jamin; Washington DC: Jean-Louis at The Watergate **Mentor(s):** Gilbert Le Coze, Jean-Louis Palladin **Awards:** 2005 Michelin Guide 3 stars; 2003 James Beard Foundation Outstanding Chef Award; 1999 James Beard Foundation Outstanding Service Award; 1998 James Beard Foundation Outstanding Restaurant of the Year and Best Chef New York City; 1995 The New York Times 4 stars **Affiliations:** CHFC, JLPF **Books Published:** A Return to Cooking **Languages Spoken:** French

NOTABLE DISH(ES): Wild Alaskan and Smoked Salmon; Apple, Celery and Baby Watercress; Jalapeño Emulsion; Braised Baby Octopus; Black Trumpet-Truffle Purée; Herb de Provence Infused Red Wine-Ink Sauce

FAST FACTS
Restaurant Recs: Baraonda; Spigolo for Italian food; Balthazar for lunch **Kitchen Tool(s):** My knives – without knives you cannot cook precisely. The cut is essential for liberating the right amount of flavors and creating the right consistency. **Interview Question:** When I interview I follow my instinct, and I don't have anything pre-set. It's always an open discussion, and at the end of it I have my opinion.

R

Philippe Rispoli
Chef | Project on the way...

Las Vegas, NV

Restaurant E-mail: phillipe@philliperispoli.com

CHEF FACTS

Cuisine: French **Born:** 1973 **Began Career:** 1987 **Culinary School:** L'Aubergade du Pont DeJonc, France **Grad Year:** 1989 **Stages:** France: Georges Blanc; Italy: Don Alfonso **Work History:** France: Les Eaux Vives, Villa Florentin, Paul Bocuse; New York, NY: Daniel; Las Vegas, NV: The Mansion at MGM Grand, Aureole, Daniel Boulud Brasserie **Mentor(s):** Daniel Boulud **Awards:** 2005 StarChefs.com Rising Star Chef Las Vegas **Affiliations:** LAES **Languages Spoken:** French, Italian

NOTABLE DISH(ES): Millefeuille with Saffron Poached Tomatoes, Goat Cheese and Serrano Ham; Lamb Pastilla with Eggplant Caviar, Braised Fennel and Taggiasca Olives

FAST FACTS

Restaurant Recs: Nobu for sushi; Charlie Palmer for steak **Kitchen Tool(s):** My paring knife – I don't have a special one, but I can do everything with it **Interview Question:** What do you want to be in two or three years? I want them to say a chef or owner of a restaurant. I'm looking for people who want to work. I also have to see them working. I put them to work a bit before I hire them. **Flavor Combo(s):** Ginger and lemongrass **Fave Cookbook(s):** The French Laundry Cookbook by Thomas Keller; cookbooks by Alain Ducasse **Chef to Cook for You:** Charlie Palmer **Culinary Travel:** I like to go to Italy – specifically to Naples, to see my father's family and for pizza and pasta

Missy Robbins
Chef | Spiaggia

980 North Michigan Ave. Chicago, IL 60611

Restaurant E-mail: mrobbins@levyrestaurants.com

Phone: (312) 280-2750

RESTAURANT FACTS
Seats: 100 **Weeknight Covers:** 60 **Weekend Covers:** 150 **Check Average (with Wine):** $100 **Tasting Menu:** Yes $165/$255 with wine **Kitchen Staff:** 9-11

CHEF FACTS
Cuisine: Italian, seasonal, Mediterranean **Born:** 1971 **Began Career:** 1994 **Culinary School:** Peter Kump's New York School of Cooking **Grad Year:** 1995 **Stages:** New York, NY: March Restaurant **Work History:** Italy: Agli Amici; New York, NY: March, Arcadia, The Lobster Club, SoHo Grand Hotel **Mentor(s):** Wayne Nish, Anne Rosenzweig, Tony Mantuano **Awards:** 2005 StarChefs.com Rising Star Chef Chicago **Affiliations:** The James Beard Foundation **Languages Spoken:** Italian

NOTABLE DISH(ES): Guinea Hen Wrapped in Pancetta with Creamy Yukon Gold Potatoes and Umbrian Black Truffle Sauce; Wood-roasted Filet of Turbot with Sunchoke Purée, Trumpet Royale Mushrooms and Mushroom Veal Reduction

FAST FACTS
Restaurant Recs: Lao Sze Chuan – an amazing Chinese restaurant in Chinatown with very spicy food. Twice cooked pork is my favorite dish (pork belly braised and then done in the wok with chilies and leeks). **Kitchen Tool(s):** Our amazing custom-built wood burning ovens **Interview Question:** How did you get into cooking? I think it gives an opportunity for a potential line cook to show why they are passionate about cooking and why they want to be in the business. **Flavor Combo(s):** Lemon and marjoram; fresh cheese (like ricotta) with honey; roasted mushrooms and rosemary, brown butter and Parmigiano Reggiano **Fave Cookbook(s):** The River Café series by Rose Gray and Ruth Rogers; Cooking the Roman Way by Michel Bras; Chocolate Desserts by Pierre Hermé **Chef to Cook for You:** Nadia Santini from Dal Pescatore in Italy – simple, amazing, authentic **Culinary Travel:** I want to go to Asia to learn and experience Asian food. It is just so different. I will continue to go to Italy once a year to stage at restaurants there.

R

Nick Roberts
Chef/Owner | Beechwood

822 Washington Blvd. Venice, CA 90292

Restaurant E-mail: info@beechwoodrestaurant.com

Phone: (310) 448-8884

RESTAURANT FACTS
Seats: 70–220 **Weeknight Covers:** 120 **Weekend Covers:** 350 **Check Average (with Wine):** $30 **Tasting Menu:** No **Kitchen Staff:** 3–5

CHEF FACTS
Cuisine: American bistro **Born:** 1978 **Began Career:** 2000 **Culinary School:** California Culinary Academy, San Francisco, CA **Grad Year:** 1999 **Stages:** San Francisco, CA: Masa's; New York, NY: Union Pacific, Bouley **Work History:** New York, NY: Union Pacific, Café Boulud; Carmel, CA: Highlands Inn; Los Angeles, CA: Zax; Venice, CA: Amuse Café **Mentor(s):** Burt Cutino, Phil Baker, John Gerber **Awards:** 2004 StarChefs.com Rising Star Chef Los Angeles **Languages Spoken:** Spanglish

NOTABLE DISH(ES): Fig, Prosciutto, and Cabrales Tart; Roasted Tomato and Red Pepper Soup with Lemon Aïoli and Steamed Mussels

FAST FACTS
Restaurant Recs: Hinano's for beer and burgers **Kitchen Tool(s):** Fish spatula; spoons **Interview Question:** Where have you worked and for how long? **Flavor Combo(s):** Savory and sweet **Fave Cookbook(s):** The Making of a Cook by Madeline Kamman **Chef to Cook for You:** Thomas Keller just because he has been so innovative and such great part of the culinary world **Culinary Travel:** San Sebastian, Spain – the whole city is centered on food and they have such phenomenal cuisine. I'm inspired by chefs like Arzak and Ferran Adría.

Joël Robuchon
Executive Chef/Owner | L'Atelier de Joël Robuchon

57 East 57th St. New York, NY 10022

Phone: (212) 350-6658

RESTAURANT FACTS
Seats: 50 **Weeknight Covers:** 100 **Weekend Covers:** 110–120
Check Average (w/o Wine): $100 **Tasting Menu:** Yes $190 **Kitchen Staff:** 12

CHEF FACTS
Other Restaurants: Paris, France: L'Atelier; Las Vegas, NV: Joël Robuchon, L'Atelier; London, England: L'Atelier, Le Bar de Joël Robuchon, La Cuisine de Joël Robuchon; Tokyo, Japan: L'Atelier, Salon de Thé de Joël Robuchon; Monaco: Joël Robuchon; Macau: Joël Robuchon **Cuisine:** Modern French **Born:** 1945 **Began Career:** 1960 **Culinary School:** Apprenticeship at Relais de Poitiers **Work History:** France: Berkely Restaurant, Hôtel Concorde Lafayette, Hôtel Nikko, Restaurant Jamin, Restaurant Laurent, Restaurant Joël Robuchon, Restaurant l'Astor; Japan: Château Restaurant Taillevent-Robuchon **Awards:** 1994 International Herald Tribune Best Restaurant in the World; 1990 Gault Millau Chef of the Century; 1988 Vermeil Medal of City of Paris; 1987 Chef of the Year; 1986 Michelin 3-stars; 1985 Hachette Prize; 1984 Michelin 3-stars; 1979 Silver Medal of the Société des Cuisiniers de Paris; 1976 Meilleur Ouvrier de France; 1972 Trophée National de l'Académie Culinaire de France; 1969 Prosper Montagné Prize; 1969 Sévres Vase bestowed by the President of the French Republic; Pudlowski Guide Three Plates; Bottin Gourmand 4 stars; Gault Millau Guide 4 toques **Books Published:** La Cuisine de Joël Robuchon; L'Atelier of Joël Robuchon: The Artistry of a Master Chef and His Protegées; Cooking Through the Seasons; Tout Robuchon **Languages Spoken:** French

NOTABLE DISH(ES): Gelée de Caviar a la Crème de Chou-Fleur

FAST FACTS
Restaurant Recs: Paris: Le Pre Catalan; Le Bristol

R

Andre Rochat
Chef/Owner | Andre's

401Sixth St. Las Vegas, NV 89101

Restaurant E-mail: andre@andrelv.com

Phone: (702) 385-5016

RESTAURANT FACTS
Seats: 60–100 **Weeknight Covers:** 45–150 **Weekend Covers:** 45–150 **Check Average (with Wine):** $125 **Tasting Menu:** Yes Upon Request **Kitchen Staff:** 5

CHEF FACTS
Other Restaurants: Andre's Monte Carlo, Alizé at the Palms **Cuisine:** French **Born:** 1944 **Began Career:** 1958 **Stages:** France: Leon de Lyon, The Club of Industry and Commerce, Hotel du Mont Blanc, Les Reflet **Work History:** France: The Club of Industry and Commerce, Hotel du Mont Blanc, Les Reflet; Washington, DC: The Madison; Lake Tahoe, NV: King's Castle; Las Vegas, NV: Sands Regency Room **Mentor(s):** Fernand Point, Paul Bocuse, Roger Verge **Protégée(s):** Eric Patterson, Michael Njorge. John Guyer, Steven Geddes **Affiliations:** NTS, NRA, JLPF, JBF, WCR, Nevada Restaurant Association **Languages Spoken:** French, Spanish

FAST FACTS
Restaurant Recs: Rosemary's for everything; Mayflower Cuisinier for everything **Kitchen Tool(s):** Fresh products **Interview Question:** Why do you want to cook? **Flavor Combo(s):** French cooking is all about sauces. Using different products is the challenge to make the right combination of flavor. **Fave Cookbook(s):** Art Culinaire and Thuries are both great magazines that are current and keep me in touch with cooking trends from around the world **Chef to Cook for You:** Chef Jean-Louis Palladin – he was a purist. He always used the freshest products to create fine sauces to enhance the natural flavor of the product. **Culinary Travel:** Vietnam for its history and French influence combined with traditional Vietnamese cooking

Ben Roche
Pastry Chef | Moto

945 W Fulton Mkt. Chicago, IL 60607

Restaurant E-mail: broche@motorestaurant.com

Phone: (312) 491-0058

RESTAURANT FACTS
Seats: 50–75 **Tasting Menu:** Yes $75/$155/$175 **Kitchen Staff:** 1.5

CHEF FACTS
Cuisine: I like to deliver a bit of the "huh?... Wow!" factor **Born:** 1982 **Began Career:** 2002 **Culinary School:** Johnson & Wales University, Providence, RI **Grad Year:** 2002 **Stages:** England: Tylney Hall **Work History:** Chicago, IL: Houston's, Charlie Trotter's **Mentor(s):** Homaro Cantu, Scott Stegman, Matthias Merges, Salvador Dalí **Protégée(s):** Andreas Exharos, Lee Wolen **Affiliations:** Taste#, Poptech!, many charities **Languages Spoken:** Basic Spanish

NOTABLE DISH(ES): Doughnut Forms; Dessert Nachos

FAST FACTS
Restaurant Recs: Sushi Tanoshii for fish and chips, but only when Chef Mike crushes it with his hands **Kitchen Tool(s):** Food replicator – to initiate the ability to sustainably feed in space **Interview Question:** Do you have anything to lose? If the answer is no, then this chef is willing to devote themselves fully. **Flavor Combo(s):** Juniper, quinine and carbonic acid, with a hint of lime. These flavors are plentiful year-round and always delicious. **Fave Cookbook(s):** Get in the Van by Henry Rollins – it's not exactly about cooking, but it is inspirational for life **Chef to Cook for You:** Charlie Trotter – it would probably be a most excellent and tasty experience **Culinary Travel:** The Food Development Division of NASA because I believe they offer the most (and literally!) intergalactic dining experience this side of the milky way

Hans Röckenwagner
Chef | 3 Square Café & Bakery

1121 Abbott Kinney Blvd. Venice, CA 90291

Restaurant E-mail: hrockenwagner@aol.com

Phone: (310) 399-6504

RESTAURANT FACTS
Seats: 50 **Weeknight Covers:** 200 all day **Weekend Covers:** 250 all day **Check Average (w/o Wine):** Lunch: $18 Dinner: $30 **Tasting Menu:** No **Kitchen Staff:** 4-5

CHEF FACTS
Cuisine: German **Born:** 1961 **Began Career:** 1981 **Culinary School:** Hotel Villingen Schwenningen, Black Forrest, Germany **Grad Year:** 1981 **Stages:** Germany: Zum Adler **Work History:** Los Angeles, CA: Rock, Röckenwager **Mentor(s):** Theor Strauss **Protégée(s):** Trey Foshee, Neal Fraser **Awards:** 1994 Robert Mondavi Award for Culinary Excellence; 1993 GQ Golden Dish Award; 1992 James Beard Foundation Rising Star Chef **Affiliations:** SOS, Cure Autism Now **Books Published:** Röckenwagner **Languages Spoken:** German, French

FAST FACTS
Restaurant Recs: Dong il Jang on 8th St. in Koreatown for the chap jae **Kitchen Tool(s):** My 70-year-old Berkel slicer **Interview Question:** What do you like to eat? I like to get them to talk about food to see what their interest level is. **Flavor Combo(s):** Sweet and sour **Fave Cookbook(s):** The Natural Cuisine of Georges Blanc **Chef to Cook for You:** Fredy Girardet **Culinary Travel:** Vietnam for the great heritage of French and Asian flavors

Douglas Rodriguez
Executive Chef | Ola at Sanctuary

1745 James Ave. Miami, FL 33139

Restaurant E-mail: info@chefdouglasrodriguez.com

Phone: (305) 673-5455

RESTAURANT FACTS
Seats: 80 **Weeknight Covers:** 80–100 **Weekend Covers:** 200 **Check Average (with Wine):** $100+ **Tasting Menu:** No **Kitchen Staff:** 6–8

CHEF FACTS
Other Restaurants: Scottsdale, AZ: Deseo; Coral Gables, FL: Ola Steak & Tapas; Philadelphia, PA: Alma de Cuba; Chicago, IL: De La Costa; New York, NY: Nuela **Cuisine:** Nuevo Latino **Born:** 1965 **Began Career:** 1985 **Culinary School:** Johnson & Wales University, Providence, RI **Grad Year:** 1985 **Stages:** Washington DC: Jean-Louis at the Watergate **Work History:** Miami, FL: Wet Paint Café, Yuca; New York, NY: Ola, Patria, Chicama, Pipa **Mentor(s):** Julia Child, Felipe Rojas, Mark Miller **Protégée(s):** José Garces, Aaron Sanchez, Aaron May, Michael Crossti, Victor Scargle **Awards:** 1995 James Beard Foundation Rising Star **Books Published:** Nuevo Latino: Recipes That Celebrate the New Latin American Cuisine; Latin Ladles: Fabulous Soups & Stews from the King of Nuevo Latino Cuisine; Douglas Rodriguez's Latin Flavors on the Grill **Languages Spoken:** Spanish

NOTABLE DISH(ES): Ecuadorian Shrimp Ceviche; Patria Pork

FAST FACTS
Restaurant Recs: Hot Doug's in Chicago for a foie gras hotdog **Kitchen Tool(s):** The stick blender and a food processor **Interview Question:** Do you want to be a chef, and why? **Flavor Combo(s):** Any contrasting combination. Sweet and sour; spicy and bitter. **Fave Cookbook(s):** The Art of South American Cooking by Felipe Rojas Lombardi **Chef to Cook for You:** Felipe Rojas Lombardi – my mentor although I never met him. He passed away in 1999. He was the father of tapas in America and the chef/owner of Ballroom in New York City. **Culinary Travel:** Korea, as it is my favorite cuisine

Gerdy Rodriguez
Executive Chef | One Bleu

10295 Collins Ave. Bal Harbour, FL 33154

Restaurant E-mail: grodriguez@regentexperience.com

Phone: (305) 455-5400

RESTAURANT FACTS
Seats: 106 **Weeknight Covers:** 60-70 **Weekend Covers:** 106 **Check Average (with Wine):** $100 **Tasting Menu:** Yes $125 **Kitchen Staff:** 10

CHEF FACTS
Other Restaurants: View Bar **Cuisine:** New Spanish **Born:** 1975 **Began Career:** 1991 **Stages:** Miami, FL: La Broche **Work History:** Miami, Fl: La Broche, Norman's, Café Sambal, Mandarin Oriental **Mentor(s):** Sergi Arola, Angel Palacios **Awards:** 2005-2007 AAA Four Diamonds; 2006 AIWF People's Choice Award; 2001 South Florida Gourmet Best Young Chef **Affiliations:** Easter Seals, Kampong, March of Dimes, SOS, Taste of the Nation, Transplant Foundation, Diabetes Research **Languages Spoken:** Spanish

FAST FACTS
Restaurant Recs: Francesco – a tiny Peruvian restaurant in the gables – for a great parihuela and ceviche **Kitchen Tool(s):** Thermomix; Pacojet; mini spatula; digital scale **Interview Question:** When/why did you decide to become a chef? What are your career goals? Do you consider yourself a dedicated person? Are you willing to give this job your all? **Flavor Combo(s):** Potato with vanilla, anise, and mollusk **Fave Cookbook(s):** All the el Bulli cookbooks by Ferran Adriá and Albert Adriá; Essential Cuisine by Michel Bras; cookbooks by Nobu Matsuhisa **Chef to Cook for You:** Ferran Adriá because I know that I will see and taste something that I've never experienced before **Culinary Travel:** I would go back to Spain – they have such a wealth of small privately owned restaurants with great food and product

Michael Romano
Executive Chef | Union Square Café

21 E 16th St. New York, NY 10003

Restaurant E-mail: info@unionsquarecafe.com

Phone: (212) 243-4020

RESTAURANT FACTS
Seats: 130 **Weeknight Covers:** 250 **Weekend Covers:** 300+ **Check Average (with Wine):** $60-$70 **Tasting Menu:** No **Kitchen Staff:** 12

CHEF FACTS
Other Restaurants: Japan: Union Square Café Tokyo **Cuisine:** American with Italian soul **Born:** 1953 **Began Career:** 1969 **Culinary School:** New York City Technical, Brooklyn, NY **Grad Year:** 1974 **Stages:** France: Eugenie-les-bains, Le Chapon Fin, The Bristol Hotel **Work History:** France: Michel Guerard, Eugenie les Bains; New York, NY: La Caravelle **Mentor(s):** Michel Guerard, Roger Fessague, Pierre Franey **Protégée(s):** Ken Callaghan, Terry Harwood, Scott Fratangelo, Sandro Romano **Awards:** 2001 James Beard Foundation Best Chef New York City **Affiliations:** Chefs Collaborative, SOS, City Harvest, and numerous others **Books Published:** The Union Square Café Cookbook; Second Helpings from Union Square Café **Languages Spoken:** French, Spanish, Italian

NOTABLE DISH(ES): Pumpkin Bread Pudding; Roast Turkey with Apple Cider Gravy

FAST FACTS
Restaurant Recs: Rao's for Chicken Scarpariello **Kitchen Tool(s):** Plastic scraping card – I use it every time I cook to clear off the cutting board **Interview Question:** It's now three months after your hire date. You wake up every morning and are really happy to come to work. Why? **Flavor Combo(s):** My palate has been taking a turn towards Japanese flavors lately. I really like flavors like ume, shiso, and different types of miso and sake. **Fave Cookbook(s):** Le Ricette Regionali Italiane by Milan Solares **Chef to Cook for You:** I am most curious about Fernand Point. When I was learning to cook he was such a legendary figure, his legacy seemed to loom above everything chefs at that time were doing. He was the teacher of so many chefs who began contemporary French cuisine. A dinner with him would be amazing. **Culinary Travel:** These days it would be Japan. I go three to four times a year. I am amazed by the cuisine and the brilliance of it.

R

Sebastien Rouxel
Executive Pastry Chef | Thomas Keller Restaurant Group

10 Columbus Circle, 4th floor New York, NY 10019

Restaurant E-mail: sebastien@perseny.com

Phone: (212) 245 6078 x15

CHEF FACTS
Other Restaurants: Thomas Keller Restaurant Group **Cuisine:** Classic technique with modern presentation **Born:** 1974 **Culinary School:** France: La Chambre des Metiers a Sainte Luce sur Loire **Grad Year:** 1994 **Stages:** France: Les Jardins de la Forge, Le Peché Mignon **Work History:** France: Mess de l'Elysse, Restaurant Le Grand Vefour; Los Angeles, CA: Restaurant L'Orangerie; New York, NY: Restaurant Lutèce, Per Se; Yountville, CA: The French Laundry **Mentor(s):** Pierre Hermé, Guy Martin, Gaston Lenôtre, Michel Bras **Protégée(s):** Richard Capizzi **Awards:** 2006 Pastry Art and Design 10 Best Pastry Chefs; 2005 StarChefs.com Rising Star Pastry Chef New York **Affiliations:** City Harvest **Languages Spoken:** French, Spanish

NOTABLE DISH(ES): Yuzu Bavarois et Son Gateau

FAST FACTS
Restaurant Recs: Blue Ribbon Sushi **Kitchen Tool(s):** Spoons – I use them to taste, measure, check consistency, plating, etc **Interview Question:** Why are you here with us? What is your goal in life? Their answer gives you a sense of who they are as a person and as a professional as well as their future. **Flavor Combo(s):** My favorites are the ones that remind me of my childhood **Fave Cookbook(s):** Le Gout du Pain by Professor Raymond Calvel **Culinary Travel:** Italy – the country has a great food history and I haven't had the chance to go there yet

Rhonda Ruckman
Pastry Chef/Owner | Doughmonkey

6708 Snider Plaza Dallas, TX 75205

Restaurant E-mail: rhonda@doughmonkey.com

Phone: (214) 890-1300

RESTAURANT FACTS
Kitchen Staff: 3

CHEF FACTS
Cuisine: Pastry **Born:** 1972 **Began Career:** 1996 **Work History:** Baton Rouge, LA: Jubans, Drakes; Naples, FL: Ritz-Carlton; Los Angeles, CA: Four Seasons **Mentor(s):** Norman Love **Awards:** 1996 International Herb Growers and Marketers Association Competition Gold Medal **Affiliations:** James Beard Foundation, Slow Food USA, various charity events

NOTABLE DISH(ES): Strawberries and Cream; Double Chocolate Cookies

FAST FACTS
Restaurant Recs: Zanata for great pizzas; 2900 for braised short ribs ravioli **Kitchen Tool(s):** Spoon **Interview Question:** The first question would be, "Do you enjoy eating dessert after a meal?" The second is, "What is your favorite dessert?" The answer is only important for the first question. **Flavor Combo(s):** Tahitian vanilla bean with 70% Madagascar chocolate from Patric Chocolate, an American micro-batch chocolate maker who uses cocoa beans from the Sambirano Valley in Madagascar **Fave Cookbook(s):** The Professional Pastry Chef by Bo Friberg; Pâtisserie of Pierre Hermé by Pierre Hermé **Chef to Cook for You:** I would be thrilled to have Ferran Adrià of el Bulli cook for me because he is formulating groundbreaking techniques that elevate food to a higher level, which in turn trickles down and raises the bar for all of us **Culinary Travel:** I would like to go to Costa Rica with Steve DeVries, owner of DeVries Chocolate, to watch the specific production of the Costa Rican Trinitario cocoa bean. Steve DeVries hand crafts amazing chocolate from bean to bar, currently with beans from Costa Rica and the Dominican Republic.

Peter Rudolph
Consulting Chef

San Francisco, CA

Restaurant E-mail: phrudolph@gmail.com

Phone: (415) 673-7078

CHEF FACTS
Cuisine: California coastal cuisine **Born:** 1970 **Began Career:** 1993
Culinary School: California Culinary Academy, San Francisco, CA
Grad Year: 1995 **Work History:** Atlanta, GA: The Ritz-Carlton Buckhead; Los Angeles, CA: Jer-ne; Half Moon Bay, CA: Navio; San Francisco, CA: Campton Place **Mentor(s):** Joël Antunes, Guenter Seeger, Troy Thompson, Xavier Salomon **Awards:** 2007 StarChefs.com Rising Star Chef San Francisco

NOTABLE DISH(ES): Roast American Lamb with Pistachio Purée; Striped Bass with Ginger-Foie Gras Sauce and Black Radish; Sweetbreads with Pappardalle in Chicken Broth

FAST FACTS
Restaurant Recs: Brother's Korean BBQ for gal-bi **Kitchen Tool(s):** Scale, because it ensures consistency **Interview Question:** What are your weaknesses? **Flavor Combo(s):** Milk and olive oil; citrus and chile; anything umame **Fave Cookbook(s):** One Day at Mugaritz Restaurant by Andoni Luis Aduriz **Chef to Cook for You:** Michel Troisgros because when I ate there it was the first meal that completely opened my eyes to the limitlessness of cuisine **Culinary Travel:** The Italian countryside – I want to eat through all the little places on the side of the road. I love the authenticity of the national cuisine.

Slade Rushing
Executive Chef | Mila

817 Common Street New Orleans, LA 70112

Restaurant E-mail: slade.rushing@renaisaancehotels.com

Phone: (504) 412-2580

RESTAURANT FACTS
Seats: 80 **Weeknight Covers:** 50 **Weekend Covers:** 70 **Check Average (with Wine):** $150 **Check Average (w/o Wine):** $100 **Tasting Menu:** Yes $65 **Kitchen Staff:** 4-6

CHEF FACTS
Cuisine: Nouvelle southern cuisine **Born:** 1974 **Culinary School:** Johnson & Wales, Providence, RI **Grad Year:** 1992 **Stages:** San Francisco, CA: Jardiniere **Work History:** San Francisco, CA: Rubicon; Abita Springs, LA: Longbranch, New York, NY: Daniel, Jack's Luxury Oyster Bar **Mentor(s):** Cyril Renaud from Fleur de Sel and Bruce Hill from San Francisco **Languages Spoken:** Kitchen Spanish

NOTABLE DISH(ES): Porcini-Dusted Monkfish on Asparagus Purée, Braised with Coffee Glaze, Confit Shallot, and Aspargus

FAST FACTS
Restaurant Recs: We don't eat out much; we're into late night cooking at home. **Kitchen Tool(s):** A little sausage fork **Interview Question:** Do you have a sense of urgency? Are you willing to push yourself? **Flavor Combo(s):** Caramel and pepper **Fave Cookbook(s):** Mark Veyrat's books **Chef to Cook for You:** Alain Chapel – I would have him cook me something in a pigs bladder **Culinary Travel:** Germany because I like the precision of German chefs. I would love to stage with Heinz Beck.

S

Salter - Syhabout

Mark Salter
Executive Chef | Sherwood Landing

308 Watkins Ln. St. Michaels, MD 21663

Restaurant E-mail: info@perrycabin.com

Phone: (410) 745-2200 or (866) 278-9601

RESTAURANT FACTS
Seats: 80 **Weeknight Covers:** 50-60 **Weekend Covers:** 100 **Check Average (with Wine):** $100 **Tasting Menu:** Yes $85 **Kitchen Staff:** 4-5

CHEF FACTS
Cuisine: Modern classical with an emphasis on lightness **Born:** 1962 **Began Career:** 1981 **Culinary School:** Colchester Institute, England **Grad Year:** 1981 **Stages:** Germany: Steglitz International **Work History:** Switzerland: Montreaux Palace Hotel; Germany: Brenner's Park Hotel, The Brenner's Stephanie Clinic; France: Eden Roc Restaurant; Scotland: Cromlix House **Mentor(s):** Malcolm Long, Frans Wild **Awards:** 2007 ACF Gold Medal; 2006 ACF Silver Medal; 2005 Wine Spectator Award of Excellence **Affiliations:** Master Chefs of Great Britain, ACF, Meals-on-Wheels, SOS, Food for Friends, numerous others **Languages Spoken:** French, German

FAST FACTS
Restaurant Recs: Scosa – where I like to get their antipasti and cheese platter with a nice glass of Italian red wine and some breadsticks **Kitchen Tool(s):** My tongue – I need it to taste the food I am preparing **Interview Question:** I usually ask them to prepare a menu using local ingredients from the Chesapeake Bay **Flavor Combo(s):** Sweet and sour **Fave Cookbook(s):** Quaglino's by Terence Conran **Chef to Cook for You:** Jean-Georges Vongerichten – I admire the way he cooks so simply with such fresh flavors **Culinary Travel:** Japan – because I have very little knowledge of their food. All of the raw products intrigue me and it would be interesting to learn how to utilize them to their best.

Abraham Salum
Chef/Owner | Salum Restaurant

4152 Cole Ave. #103 Dallas, TX 75204

Restaurant E-mail: abraham@salumrestaurant.com

Phone: (214) 252-9604

RESTAURANT FACTS
Seats: 86 **Weeknight Covers:** 60–80 **Weekend Covers:** 100–150
Check Average (with Wine): $65 **Tasting Menu:** No **Kitchen Staff:** 4

CHEF FACTS
Cuisine: Eclectic American **Born:** 1967 **Began Career:** 1987 **Culinary School:** New England Culinary Institute, Montpelier, VT **Grad Year:** 1991 **Stages:** France: Ousteau de Baumaniere **Work History:** Mexico: Camino Hotel, Xcaret; Belgium: Café des Artistes **Mentor(s):** Michel Le Borgne, my advisor from school **Affiliations:** ACF, Dallas Opera, Dallas AIDS Resource Center, Katy Trail Foundation **Languages Spoken:** English, Spanish, French and Portuguese

NOTABLE DISH(ES): Hush Puppy Shrimp with Onion Rings, Cilantro Oil and Cole Slaw

FAST FACTS
Restaurant Recs: Arc en Ciel in Arlington for the dim sum; Babe's for fried chicken **Kitchen Tool(s):** My mandolin and my fish spatula **Interview Question:** I would list some ingredients and ask what would you make for dinner. It gives me some insight on who they are. **Flavor Combo(s):** Sweet and savory **Fave Cookbook(s):** La Cuisine de Georges Blanc and the el Bulli cookbooks **Chef to Cook for You:** Ferran Adriá, as I've never seen what he does and they say he is the best chef in the world **Culinary Travel:** Mainland China for the food and culture

Marcus Samuelsson
Chef/Co-Owner | Aquavit

65 E 55th St. New York, NY 10012

Restaurant E-mail: msamuelsson@aquavit.org

Phone: (212) 307-7311

RESTAURANT FACTS
Seats: 55–137 **Weeknight Covers:** 100 **Weekend Covers:** 150
Check Average (w/o Wine): $95 **Tasting Menu:** Yes $115/$195

CHEF FACTS
Other Restaurants: New York, NY: Riingo, Merkato 55; Chicago, IL: C-House **Cuisine:** Swedish **Born:** 1970 **Began Career:** 1988 **Culinary School:** Culinary Institute of Gotheburg, Sweden **Grad Year:** 1988 **Stages:** France: Georges Blanc; New York, NY: Aquavit **Work History:** France: Georges Blanc; New York, NY: Riingo **Mentor(s):** Hakan Swahn, my grandmother **Protégée(s):** I have a lot of protégées that are successful on different levels. Success is a long journey and it's about executing the mission you have for yourself. **Awards:** 2003 James Beard Foundation Best Chef New York City; 2001 New York Times 3 stars; 1995, 2001 New York Times 3 stars; 1999 James Beard Foundation Rising Star Chef **Affiliations:** I'm a Goodwill Ambassador for UNICEF and a supporter of the TAP project. I also sit on the board for CCAP, and I'm a member of the StarChefs.com Advisory Board. **Books Published:** En Smakresa: Middagstips Från Marcus Samuelsson; Aquavit and The New Scandinavian Cuisine; The Soul of a New Cuisine: A Discovery of the Foods and Flavors of Africa **Languages Spoken:** Swedish, German

NOTABLE DISH(ES): Swedish Meatballs with Mashed Potatoes and Lingonberries

FAST FACTS
Restaurant Recs: Fatty crab for the chili crab **Kitchen Tool(s):** Paint brush; pots; pans; a good oven **Interview Question:** How do you work in a group? How much respect do you have for yourself? I follow my gut feeling. I also have candidates do a trail to see what the person is about. They do three trails at different stations. **Flavor Combo(s):** Contrast is important. Something spicy with something cooling, such as a hot sambal on watermelon. A couple other of my favorite combinations is monkfish liver and Riesling, and milk and strawberries. **Fave Cookbook(s):** White Heat by Marco Pierre White; vintage cookbooks from the 30's and 40's **Chef to Cook for You:** I really appreciate a talented sushi chef. I love to watch Chef Yasuda (of Sushi Yasuda in New York City). **Culinary Travel:** In Ethiopia, cooking is a humble experience. There's a lot to learn from watching simple cooking techniques.

Richard Sandoval
Chef/Owner | Modern Mexican Restaurants

307 E 44th St., Suite F New York, NY 10017

Restaurant E-mail: richard@modernmexican.com

Phone: (646) 285-0796

CHEF FACTS
Other Restaurants: Las Vegas, NV: Isla, Zengo; Denver, CO: La Sandia, Tamayo; McClean, VA: La Sandia; New York, NY: Maya, Pampano; Washington DC: Zengo; Mexico City, Mexico: Pampano; San Francisco, CA: Maya; Dubai, UAE: Maya; Acapulco, Mexico: Madeiras **Cuisine:** Modern Mexican **Born:** 1967 **Began Career:** 1996 **Culinary School:** The Culinary Institute of America, Hyde Park, NY **Grad Year:** 1993 **Stages:** Newport, CA: Pascal Restaurant **Work History:** New York, NY: Savanna **Mentor(s):** Diana Kennedy, my father **Protégée(s):** Julian Medina **Awards:** 2006 Bon Appétit Restaurateur of the Year; 2005 Crain's NY Business 40 under 40; 2003 Esquire Magazine Best New Restaurant in America; 2003 New York Magazine Best Chef; 1997 Hispanic Magazine 50 Best Hispanic Restaurants **Affiliations:** Capital Food Fight of DC Central Kitchen, Taste of the Summer of Central Park Conservancy, A Slice of Latin American of Hispanic Children and Families, etc. **Books Published:** Modern Mexican Flavors **Languages Spoken:** Spanish

FAST FACTS
Restaurant Recs: Sushi Seki for all of their sushi **Kitchen Tool(s):** Hand blender – it's essential to my cooking **Interview Question:** Where do you see yourself in three years? It will tell me a lot about their personality and it will also help me determine his/her potential. **Flavor Combo(s):** I take great care to balance flavors and try to combine contrasting but complimentary flavors in each bite (spicy/sweet/sour). As for specific flavors, I like the incredible variety of spicy Mexican chilies, and use lime juice to add zest. **Fave Cookbook(s):** Nobu the Cookbook by Nobu Matsuhisa **Chef to Cook for You:** Nobu – he was a pioneer in combining Japanese and Latin ingredients and I appreciate his vision **Culinary Travel:** My favorite cuisines are Asian and Mexican. I was born and raised in Mexico so I would travel to Asia, specifically to Vietnam and Thailand.

Hector Santiago
Chef | Pura Vida

656 N Highland Ave. NE Atlanta, GA 30306

Restaurant E-mail: hector@puravidatapas.com

Phone: (404) 870-9797

RESTAURANT FACTS

Seats: 100 **Weeknight Covers:** 80 **Weekend Covers:** 200 **Check Average (with Wine):** $35 **Tasting Menu:** No **Kitchen Staff:** 12

CHEF FACTS

Cuisine: Latin American tapas **Born:** 1968 **Began Career:** 1993 **Culinary School:** CIA **Grad Year:** 1993 **Stages:** Washington, DC: Jaleo, Zaitinya, Café Atlantico, Mini Bar; New York, NY: wd~50; Spain: Mugaritz **Mentor(s):** Giovanna Huyke, Sam Hazen **Awards:** 2007 StarChefs.com Rising Star Chef Atlanta **Affiliations:** James Beard Foundation, Share our Strength, The Liver Foundation, and we work with a lot of local charities **Languages Spoken:** Spanish

NOTABLE DISH(ES): Agnolotti de Malanga al Huitlacoche Epazote Brown Butter, Huitlacoche "Truffle" Shavings; Green Mango-Cured Salmon Wrapped in Jicama

FAST FACTS

Restaurant Recs: Kool Korner is my favorite place to have Cuban sandwiches. Taqueria Los Rayas in Claremont, and Hong Kong Harbor on Cheshire Bridge has great Hunan style food. Salsa con Sabor for Puerto Rican and Peruvian. **Kitchen Tool(s):** Chinois; super bag **Interview Question:** I always look to see if they're really passionate about food, detail-oriented, and willing to learn. It doesn't matter if you're a seasoned cook or not – when you walk in the door, you're in Latin America and not everyone knows about our cuisine so everyone has to be willing to learn. **Flavor Combo(s):** Sweet, salty, sour and spicy. Spicy should not be the first flavor. As soon as you put it in your mouth you can feel the flavor all over your mouth, not just the spice – it's the flavor that you can taste and feel. That's why I want to be able to tame the heat of chilies: because I want you to be able to taste it. **Fave Cookbook(s):** Clorofilia by Andoni Luis Aduriz **Chef to Cook for You:** Quique Dacosta from El Poblet in Spain. To me his food is amazing – it encompasses all the new Spanish techniques and is still very original and personal. He uses lots of local ingredients and stays very true to Spain and to the whole movement. **Culinary Travel:** El Salvador – I've never been. My goal is to hit every Latin American country. There are 27 of them... I need to embrace Central America. I was in Costa Rica 15 years ago and the cuisine was surprising – very mezo-American: tortillas and an interesting pico de gallo ceviche.

Chris Santos
Chef/Owner | The Stanton Social

99 Stanton St. New York, NY 10002

Restaurant E-mail: chris@thestantonsocial.com

Phone: (212) 995-0099

RESTAURANT FACTS
Seats: 130–180 **Weeknight Covers:** 250–350 **Weekend Covers:**
400–550 **Check Average (with Wine):** $70 **Check Average (w/o
Wine):** $48 **Tasting Menu:** No **Kitchen Staff:** 12–14

CHEF FACTS
Cuisine: Whimsically updated multicultural classics **Born:** 1971
Began Career: 1993 **Culinary School:** Johnson & Wales University,
Providence, RI **Grad Year:** 1993 **Work History:** New York, NY: Suba,
Rue 57, Time Café, Wyanoka; Boston, MA: Cranebrook Restaurant
and Tearoom **Awards:** 2007 StarChefs.com Rising Star Restaurant
Concept Award New York **Affiliations:** City Harvest **Books Published:**
Social Dining (currently being written) **Languages Spoken:** Spanglish

NOTABLE DISH(ES): French Onion Soup Dumplings; Maine Crabcake Corn Dogs

FAST FACTS
Restaurant Recs: Franny's for pizza; Bahn-Mi at Saigon No #1; Cafecito for anything. **Kitchen Tool(s):**
Dynamic hand blender; electric spice grinder; Microplane graters **Interview Question:** Do you drink
alcohol, smoke cigarettes or marijuana? Do you have a significant other? If they answer no to all four,
it's probably not going to work out, because they're either straight-up lying to me or they simply won't
have the means outside of work to decompress from the stress and strain that our busy restaurant
will deliver to them night after night. If they say yes to all four then it definitely won't work out. Something is going to get the better of them eventually and before you know it they won't know how to
come in on time and stay focused. But if they answer yes to one or two questions, they are generally
hired if they appear to be motivated, educated and sincere. **Flavor Combo(s):** Chilies and ginger, nori
and sesame, and dates with thyme and lavender honey. I'm also very into Latin flavors right now. **Fave
Cookbook(s):** I don't actually look at cookbooks. I buy them and put them on the shelf but I rarely
open them up. The Charlie Trotter books are incredibly gorgeous though. **Chef to Cook for You:** François Vital. He was so incredibly passionate about food that he took his life for it. I would love to have
someone with that much passion cook a meal for me. **Culinary Travel:** I traveled all around Europe for
inspiration – I went to Naples and the Amalfi Coast in Italy, Prague, and a bunch of other places. I'd
like to go to Guatemala, Honduras and Brazil for the street food.

Suvir Saran
Chef/Owner | Dévi

8 E 18th St. New York, NY 10003

Restaurant E-mail: chef@suvir.com

Phone: (212) 691-1300

RESTAURANT FACTS
Seats: 70 **Weeknight Covers:** 75 **Weekend Covers:** 120 **Check Average (with Wine):** $65 **Check Average (w/o Wine):** $45 **Tasting Menu:** Yes $65/$110 with wine

CHEF FACTS
Other Restaurants: Berkeley, CA: American Masala; New Delhi, India: Veda **Cuisine:** Pan-Indian **Born:** 1972 **Began Career:** 1994 **Culinary School:** Self-taught **Stages:** Homes of friends and family members, and with our family chef of 60-plus years **Work History:** India: Veda; New York, NY: NYU Department of Food and Nutrition **Mentor(s):** Julia Child, Jacques Pépin, Alain Sailhac, Shanti Bhardwaj, Sunita Saran, Devi Prasad Pandey **Protégée(s):** Hemant Mathur, Surbhi Sahni, Nyle Kanda **Awards:** 2008, 2007 Michelin one star; New York Magazine three stars; New York Times two stars **Affiliations:** JBF, IACP, anothersubcontinent.com, eGullet.com, The Culinary Institute of America, City Meals-on-Wheels, SOS **Books Published:** Indian Home Cooking: A Fresh Introduction to Indian Food, with More Than 150 Recipes and American Masala: 125 New Classics From My Home Kitchen **Languages Spoken:** English, Hindi, Punjabi, Urdu

NOTABLE DISH(ES): Manchurian-Style Cauliflower; Crispy Fried Okra

FAST FACTS
Restaurant Recs: Di Fara's for square pizza pie; Tanoreen for all the eggplant dishes and the rice dishes **Kitchen Tool(s):** Mortar and pestle; spice grinder/coffee grinder; spice mill **Interview Question:** Are you a professional chef? I ask that because I like to find those that love food, not just those looking at it as a profession. One has to have the mix of both passion and education. **Flavor Combo(s):** Being Indian, from a young age, my palate has been trained to look for sour, salt, sweet and bitter. To enjoy even a small bite, I look to experience some of all of this. Also, I find myself always hoping for a textural contrast in a dish. That is what makes a dish take on new heirs, without fuss. Temperature contrasts help as well. **Fave Cookbook(s):** Mastering the Art of French Cooking by Julia Child **Chef to Cook for You:** Cathal Armstrong in Washington DC; Maricel Presilla in New Jersey; Gary Danko and Elizabeth Falkner in San Francisco. They are willing to experiment with other cuisines from around the globe. For excellent desserts, David Guas, whose creations are always a great mix of the traditional and the adventurous. **Culinary Travel:** All across the many countries of Europe and Asia. And more importantly, into the homes of the locals. Trying out dishes that extol the virtues of simple, local, regional and seasonal fare. That is often not shared at restaurants.

Guy Savoy
Chef/Owner | Restaurant Guy Savoy

3570 Las Vegas Blvd.Las Vegas, NV 89109

Phone: (702) 731-7286

RESTAURANT FACTS
Seats: 75 + Private Rooms **Weeknight Covers:** 40 **Weekend Covers:** 60 **Check Average (with Wine):** $250-$300 **Tasting Menu:** Yes

CHEF FACTS
Other Restaurants: France: Restaurant Guy Savoy, Les Bouquinistes, Atelier Maitre Albert, Le Chiberta, La Butte Chaillot **Cuisine:** Classic French **Born:** 1955 **Stages:** France: Troisgros **Work History:** France: Troisgros, La Barrière de Clichy **Mentor(s):** My mother, Troisgros **Protégée(s):** Richard Ekkebus, Gordon Ramsay, Damien Dulas **Awards:** 2002 Michelin Guide 3 stars; 2000 Legion d' Honneur **Books Published:** Guy Savoy: Simple French Recipes for the Home Cook; La Cuisine de mes Bistrots; 120 Recettes Comme à la Maison

Languages Spoken: French

FAST FACTS
Restaurant Recs: Sardegna a Tavola for baby pig and baby goat **Kitchen Tool(s):** Spoon for tasting; fourchette diapason (fork with two prongs) – it is my third hand for turning poultry, meat and fish **Interview Question:** What is your passion outside of the kitchen? Everyone has an outside passion, and I want to understand them.

Victor
Execut

Victor Scargle
Executive Chef | Go Fish

641 Main St. St. Helena, CA 94574

Restaurant E-mail: vscargle@patinagroup.com

Phone: (707) 963-0700

RESTAURANT FACTS
Seats: 160-260 **Weeknight Covers:** 150 **Weekend Covers:** 300
Check Average (w/o Wine): $45 **Tasting Menu:** No **Kitchen Staff:** 8

CHEF FACTS
Cuisine: French-Californian from our 3.5-acre garden **Born:** 1972
Began Career: 1986 **Stages:** New York, NY: Lespinasse, Park Avenue
Café, Aureole **Work History:** San Francisco, CA: Aqua, Jardinière;
New York, NY: Patria; Napa, CA: Julia's Kitchen **Mentor(s):** Traci des
Jardins, Michael Mina **Awards:** 2000 SF Chronicle Rising Star Chef
Affiliations: Samantha Foundation, National Ability Center

FAST FACTS
Restaurant Recs: Ramen Club for chicken karaage udon **Kitchen Tool(s):** Robot Coupe for blending purées, chopping and emulsifying **Interview Question:** Are you afraid of hard work? It lets them have an idea of what is to come. **Flavor Combo(s):** Acid and sweet **Fave Cookbook(s):** Cooking With the Seasons by Jean-Louis Palladin **Chef to Cook for You:** Jean-Louis Palladin – I have much respect for him and was able to meet him on a couple of occasions. He had a great sense of humor and unparalleled passion. **Culinary Travel:** Japan for the tradition and clean bright flavors

Brian D. Scheehser
Executive Chef | Trellis

220 Kirkland Ave. Kirkland, WA 98033

Restaurant E-mail: bscheehser@trellisrestaurant.net

Phone: (425) 284-5800

RESTAURANT FACTS
Seats: 68 **Weeknight Covers:** 120 **Weekend Covers:** 120 **Check Average (with Wine):** $41 **Tasting Menu:** No **Kitchen Staff:** 6

CHEF FACTS
Cuisine: Pacific Northwest **Born:** 1956 **Began Career:** 1975 **Culinary School:** The Culinary Institute of America, Hyde Park, NY **Grad Year:** 1977 **Stages:** Chicago, IL: L'Escargot **Work History:** Chicago, IL: L'Escargot, Hotel Nikko, Chicago Sheraton, The Bakery; Seattle, WA: The Hunt Club at the Sorrento Hotel **Mentor(s):** Lucien Verge, James Verville, Louie Szathmarie **Protégée(s):** Carlos Estrada, Bennett Holberg, Nick Devine **Awards:** 2003 StarChefs.com Rising Star Chef Seattle; 2003 Preferred Hotels Worldwide Chef of the Year **Affiliations:** Fred Hutch Cancer Research, Liver Foundation, local YWCA **Languages Spoken:** Spanish

NOTABLE DISH(ES): Lemon and Mint Grilled Trout; Seared Wild Salmon with Sautéed Apples

FAST FACTS
Restaurant Recs: Café Campagne for pâté **Kitchen Tool(s):** Japanese slicer because it is sharp, inexpensive, and does all types of cuts. **Interview Question:** Can you cook? If they are not a really good cook they will hesitate when the question is asked. A good cook will answer immediately and say "of course!" **Flavor Combo(s):** Tomatoes and mint **Fave Cookbook(s):** Food Lovers Companion by Sharon Tyler Herbst **Chef to Cook for You:** Alice Waters – she was a pioneer in farm to table philosophy **Culinary Travel:** Lyon, France – the first chef I apprenticed with was from Lyon. I loved his country fresh cuisine.

Francesco Schintu
Chef | Zeffirino at the Venetian Hotel and Casino

3355Las Vegas Blvd. Las Vegas, NV 89109

Restaurant E-mail: fschintu@zeffirinolasvegas.com

Phone: (702) 414-3500

RESTAURANT FACTS
Seats: 435 **Weeknight Covers:** 400 **Weekend Covers:** 1200 **Check Average (with Wine):** $90 **Check Average (w/o Wine):** $68 **Tasting Menu:** No **Kitchen Staff:** 14

CHEF FACTS
Other Restaurants: Las Vegas: Tintoretto Trattoria, Pizzeria da Enzo Le Golosita' Italian Gastronomia **Cuisine:** Italian **Born:** 1967 **Began Career:** 1982 **Culinary School:** Instituto Arti Culinarie Etoile, Sottomarina di Chioggia, Venice, Italy **Grad Year:** 1984 **Stages:** Italy: Hotel Cenobio dei Dogi, La Villa Manuelina, Zeffirino **Work History:** Italy: Hotel Park Concordia, Hotel li Cuncheddi, Hotel La Rotonda, la Villa Manuelina, Hotel Cenobio dei Dogi, Zeffirino **Mentor(s):** My brother-in-law **Awards:** 2006 Maitre du Gout; 2006 Las Vegas Best Top 100; 2005 Best Italian Chef of the Year **Affiliations:** ACF and Federazione Cuochi Italiana **Languages Spoken:** Spanish, Italian, some French

NOTABLE DISH(ES): Chocolate Lasagna with Pesto

FAST FACTS
Restaurant Recs: Japanese for sashimi **Kitchen Tool(s):** Pasta machine, creativity, humility **Interview Question:** Do you know how to cook pasta? Because pasta often comes into restaurants pre-made, when I ask to cook or make pasta from scratch they don't know how. **Flavor Combo(s):** Seafood and poultry **Fave Cookbook(s):** Le Ricette Regionali Italiane by Anna Gosetti della Salda **Chef to Cook for You:** Mario Batali – because from what I've seen his food is close to the real thing **Culinary Travel:** I am going to go back to Italy to a school called Etoile, which is close to Venice where I am planning on studying more of the different styles and techniques of Italy's many regions.

Chris Schlesinger
Chef/Owner | East Coast Grill

1271 Cambridge St. Cambridge, MA 02139

Restaurant E-mail: egrill@aol.com

Phone: (617) 491-6568

RESTAURANT FACTS
Seats: 100 **Weeknight Covers:** 150 **Weekend Covers:** 300 **Check Average (with Wine):** $35 **Tasting Menu:** No **Kitchen Staff:** 7

CHEF FACTS
Other Restaurants: All Star Sandwich Bar **Cuisine:** Grilling **Born:** 1955 **Began Career:** 1977 **Culinary School:** The Culinary Institute of America, Hyde Park, NY **Grad Year:** 1977 **Work History:** Cambridge: The Harvest **Mentor(s):** Jimmy Burke, Bob Kinkead **Protégée(s):** Andy Husbands, Pat Sullivan **Awards:** 1996 James Beard Foundation Best Chef Northeast **Affiliations:** Big Brothers, Shelter Inc., Somervile Homeless Coalition, East End House **Books Published:** License to Grill: Achieve Greatness At The Grill With 200 Sizzling Recipes; The Thrill of the Grill: Techniques, Recipes, & Down-Home Barbecue; How to Cook Meat; Big Flavors of the Hot Sun: Recipes and Techniques from the Spice Zone; Salsas, Sambals, Chutneys, and Chowchows; Lettuce in Your Kitchen; Quick Pickles: Easy Recipes for Big Flavor; Co-author: Let the Flames Begin: Tips, Techniques, and Recipes for Real Live Fire Cooking **Languages Spoken:** Kitchen Spanish

NOTABLE DISH(ES): Grilled Delmonico Steak Adobo; Grilled Peaches with Blue Cheese and Balsamic

FAST FACTS
Restaurant Recs: Santarpios for the combination lamb skewer and sausage **Kitchen Tool(s):** Tongs **Interview Question:** Are you willing to work hard for not much money? Can you commit to this restaurant for a year? **Flavor Combo(s):** Lime, chilies and fish sauce **Fave Cookbook(s):** Barbecue with Beard: Outdoor Recipes from a Great Cook by James Beard **Chef to Cook for You:** Fernand Point because I'd like to taste his food **Culinary Travel:** Hanoi – the food and the art is great

Michael Schlow
Chef/Owner | Radius

8 High St. Boston, MA 02110

Restaurant E-mail: michael@radiusrestaurant.com

Phone: (617) 426-1234

RESTAURANT FACTS
Seats: 110–170 **Tasting Menu:** Yes $80/$115

CHEF FACTS
Other Restaurants: Via Matta, Great Bay Restaurant **Cuisine:** Modern French; Italian **Born:** 1964 **Began Career:** 1986 **Culinary School:** The Academy of Culinary Arts, England **Grad Year:** 1986 **Stages:** Washington, DC: Jean-Louis at the Watergate **Work History:** New York, NY: Le Madri; Chicago, IL: Coco Pazzo; Whitehouse, NJ: Ryland Inn **Mentor(s):** Craig Shelton, Jean-Louis Palladin, Pino Luongo **Protégée(s):** Brian Reimer, Adam Plitt, Gabriel Frasca, Amanda Lydon, Jeremy Sewall **Awards:** 2001 Santé Magazine Chef of the Year; 2000 James Beard Foundation Best Chef Northeast; 2000 Robert Mondavi Culinary Award of Excellence; 2000 Food and Wine Best New Chefs; 1999 Boston Magazine Best Chef; 1999 Esquire Best New Restaurants **Affiliations:** JBF **Books Published:** It's About Time – Great Recipes for Everyday Life **Languages Spoken:** Italian

NOTABLE DISH(ES): Maine Crab Tart with Avocado, Tomato, Cucumber

FAST FACTS
Restaurant Recs: Pho Republique for crispy tofu with spicy dipping sauce **Kitchen Tool(s):** The Vita-Prep blender – it's incredibly versatile for everything from purées to smoothies **Interview Question:** Tell me about the greatest meal you have ever eaten and why it gets that distinction **Flavor Combo(s):** One underlying thing I like is a balance of acid, salt and chile **Fave Cookbook(s):** Simply French by Patricia Wells **Chef to Cook for You:** Joël Robuchon – I've always been a fan of his meticulous behavior and great flavor combinations. **Culinary Travel:** Italy – it is my favorite place to visit and I also go for validation of the food I make

Jimmy Schmidt
Chef/Owner | Rattlesnake Club

300 River Pl. Detroit, MI 48207

Restaurant E-mail: info@rattlesnakeclub.com

Phone: (313) 567-4400

RESTAURANT FACTS
Seats: 130+ **Weeknight Covers:** 150 **Weekend Covers:** 250+ **Check Average (with Wine):** $105 **Check Average (w/o Wine):** $70 **Tasting Menu:** No **Kitchen Staff:** 10

CHEF FACTS
Other Restaurants: Palm Desert, CA: Rattlesnake Club **Cuisine:** Contemporary American **Born:** 1964 **Began Career:** 1975 **Culinary School:** Luberon College, France; Modern Gourmet, Boston, MA **Grad Year:** 1978 **Work History:** Detroit, MI: Rattlesnake Restaurant; The London Chophouse **Mentor(s):** Madeleine Kamman **Protégée(s):** Scott Campbell, Jan Birnbaum **Affiliations:** American Institute of Food & Wine; American Culinary Federation; Chefs Collaborative Founder; James Beard Foundation; Research Chefs Association; SOS **Books Published:** Jimmy Schmidt's Cooking Class: Seasonal Recipes from a Chef's Kitchen; Heart-Healthy Cooking for All Seasons; Cooking for All Seasons **Languages Spoken:** French

NOTABLE DISH(ES): Blue Cheese Cheeseburger with Grilled Pineapple

FAST FACTS
Restaurant Recs: Annam for garlicky catfish cooked in an earthen crock **Kitchen Tool(s):** Vacuum chamber **Interview Question:** What do you like to eat? **Flavor Combo(s):** Chilies and chocolate; ginger and sweet corn; vanilla and lobster **Fave Cookbook(s):** The Making of a Cook by Madeleine Kamman **Chef to Cook for You:** Madeleine Kamman – she was my mentor and she rocked **Culinary Travel:** South America – either Argentina or the Amazon. There are lots of nutritious native ingredients.

Ian Schnoebelen
Chef | Iris Restaurant

8115 Jeannette St. New Orleans, LA 70118

Restaurant E-mail: irisrest@yahoo.com

Phone: (504) 862-5848

RESTAURANT FACTS
Seats: 35 **Weeknight Covers:** 20–30 **Weekend Covers:** 50–70
Check Average (with Wine): $60 **Tasting Menu:** No **Kitchen Staff:**
2–3

CHEF FACTS
Cuisine: Contemporary American **Born:** 1970 **Began Career:** 1986
Work History: England: Gidleigh Park, Le Manoir aux Quat' Saisons,
Red Room; New Orleans, LA: Lilette **Mentor(s):** John Harris who
taught me simplicity and Michael Caine who taught me about fresh-
ness of ingredients **Awards:** 2007 Food & Wine Best New Chefs
Languages Spoken: Some Spanish

NOTABLE DISH(ES): Scallops with Braised Vietnamese Greens and Grapefruit Butter

FAST FACTS
Restaurant Recs: Tan Dinh for the short ribs. Que Crawl – a BBQ truck parked outside of Tipitinas
Kitchen Tool(s): My Japanese knife **Interview Question:** How long have you cooked professionally?
Flavor Combo(s): Garlic, olive oil and thyme **Fave Cookbook(s):** Books by Escoffier **Chef to Cook for
You:** Masaharu Morimoto – I love sushi **Culinary Travel:** Italy – I've never been. I'm most interested in
learning about the techniques and the flavors they use.

Adam Schop
Executive Chef | Nuela

43 West 24th Street New York, NY 10010

Restaurant E-mail: amike80@hotmail.com

CHEF FACTS
Cuisine: Coastal-Inspired Latin cuisine **Born:** 1975 **Began Career:** 1991 **Culinary School:** The Culinary Institute of America, Hyde Park, NY **Work History:** Scottsdale, AZ: Zinc Bistro, Michael's at the Citadel, Lon's at the Hermosa Inn; Chicago, IL: De La Costa **Mentor(s):** Michael De Maria, Matt Carter, Christopher Gross, Douglas Rodriguez, James McDevitt, Bob Lynn **Affiliations:** We do a lot of charity events

NOTABLE DISH(ES): Salmon Belly Quiche with Key Lime, Horseradish, Green Apple and Sage Salt

FAST FACTS
Restaurant Recs: Hot Doug's – but be sure to call. He's closed like every 14th day. **Kitchen Tool(s):** Vita-Prep **Interview Question:** I ask them what their favorite meal was. Were they paying attention? Do they have a favorite meal? Is it on line with what I think their favorite meal should be? If they can talk about 14 courses that they had then you get a clue about who they are and what they're into. **Flavor Combo(s):** I like grapefruit, duck fat and artichokes (or fava beans) **Fave Cookbook(s):** French Laundry Cook Book by Thomas Keller **Chef to Cook for You:** Daniel Boulud – the stuff he cooks on After Dark is awesome. He makes great ingredient-driven cuisine with a high level of execution. **Culinary Travel:** Spain – I love what they're doing, not just in the high-concept places, but just going to La Boqueria in Spain and sitting at the Pintxo bar and having chipirones and pulpo at 10am, then a coconut drink at the juice bar and some ham – seeing produce at that level is amazing. The monkfish is perfectly white and the razor clams are impeccable. When we get them here, we have to send 30% of them back.

Anton Schulte
Executive Chef | Bistro Daisy

5831 Magazine St. New Orleans, LA 70195

Phone: (504) 899-6987

RESTAURANT FACTS
Seats: 60 **Weeknight Covers:** 60 **Check Average (with Wine):** $55
Tasting Menu: No **Kitchen Staff:** 4

CHEF FACTS
Cuisine: French Creole **Born:** 1968 **Began Career:** 1990 **Culinary School:** Delgado Community College, New Orleans, LA **Work History:** New Orleans, LA: Clancy's, Emeril's **Mentor(s):** Ann Kearney **Affiliations:** We donate to different causes locally, and I do demos at high schools **Languages Spoken:** A little French

NOTABLE DISH(ES): Louisiana Crawfish and Mascarpone Ravioli with Wilted Leeks; Louisiana Oysters in a Bacon, Mushroom and Truffle Cream over a Caramelized Onion Crépe

FAST FACTS
Restaurant Recs: Iris; a little tapas restaurant called Vega in Metairie **Kitchen Tool(s):** I have 30 different chefs knives. Most of them are handmade knives, and they all maintain a razor edge. Glestain (japanese) are probably the most functional of any knife I've ever used. **Interview Question:** What's your favorite food? What do you most like to eat? **Flavor Combo(s):** Duck confit and raisins; fennel, orange and Pastis; crab and horseradish **Fave Cookbook(s):** Early cookbooks by Jeremiah Tower; The French Laundry Cookbook; Cooking with Claudine by Jacques Pépin **Chef to Cook for You:** Thomas Keller or Mario Batali **Culinary Travel:** Either New York, San Francisco or Napa. There are so many options in New York – that would be my first stop.

Michael Schwartz
Executive Chef/Owner | Michael's Genuine Food & Drink

130 NE 40th St. Miami Beach, FL 33137

Restaurant E-mail: info@michaelsgenuine.com

Phone: (305) 573-5550

RESTAURANT FACTS
Seats: 140 **Weeknight Covers:** 200 **Weekend Covers:** 400 **Check Average (with Wine):** $56 **Tasting Menu:** No **Kitchen Staff:** 5–9

CHEF FACTS
Cuisine: New American **Born:** 1964 **Began Career:** 1979 **Stages:** Los Angeles, LA: Patina **Work History:** Los Angeles, CA: Chinois on Main; New York, NY: Andiamo; Vail, CO: L'Hostellerie; Miami Beach, FL: Nemo **Mentor(s):** Wolfgang Puck, Frank Crispo **Languages Spoken:** Spanish

NOTABLE DISH(ES): Jumbo Lump Crab Cakes with Carrot Butter Sauce

FAST FACTS
Restaurant Recs: Enriqueta's for great Cuban food, especially on Fridays **Kitchen Tool(s):** Japanese mandolin **Interview Question:** What about cooking do you like most? **Flavor Combo(s):** While not exactly flavors, what is important to me in a dish in the combination of temperature and texture **Fave Cookbook(s):** The Rose Pistola Cookbook: 140 Italian Recipes from San Francisco's Favorite North Beach Restaurant by Reed Hearon, Peggy Knickerbocker; The Zuni Café Cookbook by Judy Rodgers **Chef to Cook for You:** Alice Waters – I shouldn't have to elaborate on that **Culinary Travel:** If I pick somewhere I haven't been, I would pick Spain. With all the hype and the emerging chefs I'm very curious. If I could pick some place I've already been, I would say the south of France for the pure, simple approach to flavor and taste and the unpretentious presentation.

Warren Schwartz
Chef

Restaurant E-mail: warrenschwartz@gmail.com

CHEF FACTS
Cuisine: Modern American **Born:** 1969 **Began Career:** 1991 **Culinary School:** California Culinary Academy, San Francisco, CA **Grad Year:** 1996 **Work History:** Larkspur, CA: Lark Creek Inn; Los Angeles, CA: Patina; Calabasas, CA: Saddle Peak Lodge; Santa Monica, CA: Whist **Mentor(s):** Joachim Splichal **Affiliations:** We do a lot of charity events

NOTABLE DISH(ES): Lemon and Parsley Roasted Chicken; Penne Pasta With Heirloom Tomatoes and Summer Squash

FAST FACTS
Restaurant Recs: Palms Thai restaurant for soups; Zip Fusion Sushi for sushi and tuna rolls; Felipe's for a great wine list and a roast beef sandwich with hot mustard **Kitchen Tool(s):** Japanese knife with a fine blade **Interview Question:** How bad do you really want this? **Flavor Combo(s):** I would have to say a ribeye steak grilled over wood with a glass of Napa Cabernet **Fave Cookbook(s):** Backyard Bistros, Farmhouse Fare: A French Country Cookbook by Jane Sigal **Chef to Cook for You:** Escoffier – so much of what we do has its origins with Escoffier. Wouldn't it be amazing to dine on his cuisine, and then sit back after dinner with a bottle of Bordeaux and ask him 5000 questions? **Culinary Travel:** South America, Peru and Chile. As American chefs, we look so much to Europe, but have and incredibly diverse cuisine south of us on our own continent.

Chad Scothorn
Chef | The Cosmopolitan

300 W San Juan Ave., PO Box 3587 Telluride, CO 81435

Restaurant E-mail: chad@telluridecolorado.net

Phone: (970) 728-1292

RESTAURANT FACTS
Seats: 115 **Weeknight Covers:** 150 **Weekend Covers:** 190 **Check Average (with Wine):** $65 **Tasting Menu:** Yes **Kitchen Staff:** 6

CHEF FACTS
Other Restaurants: Durango, CO: The Cosmopolitan **Cuisine:** Creative American comfort food **Born:** 1959 **Began Career:** 1983/1995 **Culinary School:** Oklahoma State Restaurant Management School, Stillwater, OK; The Culinary Institute of America, Hyde Park, NY; Ecole Lenôtre, France **Grad Year:** 1983 **Work History:** Argentina: Hotel Pisces; Oklahoma City, OK: Cafe 501; Salt Lake City, UT: Log Haven; Beaver Creek, Colorado: Chadwicks, Beano's Cabin **Mentor(s):** Ferdinand Metz, Wolfgang Puck **Languages Spoken:** Spanish

FAST FACTS
Restaurant Recs: La Marmotte for hanger steak **Kitchen Tool(s):** Immersion hand blender by Robot Coupe; Hobart soup strainer **Interview Question:** I like to watch them cook **Flavor Combo(s):** I have been doing a lot of combinations with smoke lately, specifically with acids and with salads **Fave Cookbook(s):** The French Laundry Cookbook by Thomas Keller – it really motivates you **Chef to Cook for You:** Gaston Lenôtre. I went to his school and learned to admire how precise he was and what a perfectionist he was. While I originally thought it was all a little contrived, the recipes were right-on and when you ate the food it really worked. **Culinary Travel:** Thailand – I haven't been yet

Kerry Sear
Chef/Proprietor | Cascadia Restaurant

2328 1st Ave. Seattle, WA 98121

Restaurant E-mail: cascadia@cascadiarestaurant.com

Phone: (206) 448-8884

RESTAURANT FACTS
Seats: 76 **Weeknight Covers:** 75-125 **Weekend Covers:** 75-125
Tasting Menu: Yes $75/$125 with wine **Kitchen Staff:** 5-6

CHEF FACTS
Other Restaurants: Cascadia Catering **Cuisine:** Regional Pacific
Northwest cuisine **Born:** 1958 **Began Career:** 1977 **Culinary School:**
Stratford Upon Avon Culinary College, Warwickshire, England **Work
History:** Hong Kong: Le Plume, Hong Kong Regent Hotel; Japan: Four
Seasons; Vancouver, CN: Four Seasons; New York, NY: Four Seasons;
Seattle, WA: Four Seasons, Regent Hotel Auckland **Mentor(s):** Alfons
Konrad, John Williams **Protégée(s):** Rod Butters, Andrew Springett,
Brook Vosika, Gavin Stephenson **Awards:** 2002 Frankfurt Culinary Olympics Gold Medal **Affiliations:**
JBF

NOTABLE DISH(ES): Spiced Copper River Salmon

FAST FACTS
Restaurant Recs: Food stalls in Pike Place Market **Kitchen Tool(s):** Plastic wrap because it has unlimited uses – slicing, rolling, sausages, etc. **Interview Question:** How do you make mayonnaise? It's an important basic. **Fave Cookbook(s):** A Culinary Life by Susur Lee

Barton Seaver
Chef | www.bartonseaver.org/

Washington DC

info@bartonseaver.org

CHEF FACTS
Cuisine: Seasonal with a focus on sustainable seafood **Born:** 1979 **Began Career:** 1998 **Culinary School:** Culinary Institute of America, Hyde Park, NY **Grad Year:** 2001 **Stages:** Chicago, IL: TRU; Lucaniña, Spain: Venta del Museo **Work History:** Chicago, IL: The Ritz-Carlton; Croton Falls, NY: Finch Tavern; Spain: Venta del Museo; Washington, DC: Greenwood, Jaleo, Café Saint-Ex, Bar Pilar, Hook, Tackle Box **Mentor(s):** José Andrés, Corky Clark, Thomas Schneller, Carol Greenwood, Leigh Seaver **Awards:** 2008, 2007 RAMW Rising Star nominee; 2006 StarChefs.com Rising Star Chef Washington DC; 2004 RAMW Best Neighborhood Gathering Place; Blue Ocean Institute award; Seafood Choices Alliance Seafood Champion **Affiliations:** HFAC, JB, SCA, OCA, Chefs Collaborative, Slow Food **Books Published:** Hook to Plate **Languages Spoken:** Spanish

NOTABLE DISH(ES): Toasted Almond and Garlic Soup with Grilled Radicchio; Jalapeño-Crusted Walu with Sweet Potato Purée and Orange-Parsley Salad

FAST FACTS
Restaurant Recs: Pupuseria San Miguel for pupusas reveultas. I have been eating these for 12 years now and they have been the same delicious product every time. **Kitchen Tool(s):** Aztec wood grill because of the flavor it imparts and the ease of cooking with it **Interview Question:** How do you spend your mornings? It gives a great sense of the focus and attention of the candidate. If they answer that they spend the morning recovering, well, you'll probably face that issue down the line somewhere. If they answer that they got up, went running, read the paper and made use of their time, it shows they're in balance (which is key to personal success and to a healthy work environment for others). Obviously not everyone is a morning person but I'm looking to see if they person is dedicated to themselves and subsequently to any job that they take on. **Flavor Combo(s):** Nutmeg and mint with fish; smoked paprika and cinnamon with meat; nut pestos with citrus **Fave Cookbook(s):** Sunday Suppers at Lucque's by Suzanne Goin is phenomenal. Jeremiah Tower Cooks by Jeremiah Towers is unbelievable! I enjoy all of Elizabeth David's books. She wrote about food, she lived food and had a great prose style. I like Paul Bertolli's Cooking by Hand. He includes a recipe for something that takes 2½ years! That takes courage! **Chef to Cook for You:** Suzanne Goin. I have a professional crush on her. She has such a unique and sensual way of coaxing the essential flavors out in a dish. The way she keeps thing simple yet creative is inspiring. **Culinary Travel:** I'd really love to go back to San Francisco; I really respect Incanto, Chez Panisse and Aziza and their chefs for what they are accomplishing. I also loved Zuni Café. The quality of food in San Francisco is so good, even at corner bistros. People really take pride in their food there.

Guenter Seeger
Chef

New York, NY

CHEF FACTS
Born: 1949 **Began Career:** 1963 **Culinary School:** The Hotel School
Montana, Lucerne, Switzerland **Grad Year:** 1970 **Stages:** Germany:
Dober Hotel **Work History:** Germany: Hoheneck; Washington, D.C.:
Regent Hotel; Atlanta, GA: The Dining Room at the Ritz-Carlton
Buckhead, Mumbo Jumbo Bar & Grill, Fusebox, Seeger's **Protégée(s):**
There have been many people who have passed through my kitchens
and gone on to great things. It would be difficult to name them all.
Awards: 1997-2006 Atlanta Journal-Constitution 5 stars; 1998-2006
Mobil Travel Guide 5 stars; 1998-2006 AAA Travel Guide 5 diamonds;
1998-2006 Gayot Top 40 Restaurants in the Nation; 1998-2006
Wine Spectator "Best of" Award of Excellence; 2000-2006 Relais
& Château, Relais Gourmand Member; 2005-2006 Traditions et
Qualité Member; 2002 Chef of Clever Ideas Cutting Edge Award;
2001 Nation's Restaurant News Fine Dining Hall of Fame Inductee;
1997 Esquire Magazine Restaurant of the Year; 1978-1984 Michelin 1 star; 1978-1984 Aral Guide
5 spoons; 1978-1984 Varta Guide 5 diamonds; Food & Wine Magazine Top 15 Restaurants in the
Nation; Atlanta Magazine Best Chef in Atlanta – 9 Years; Atlanta Magazine Best Restaurant in Atlanta
– 9 Years

FAST FACTS
Restaurant Recs: In Atlanta: I love Shaun's and Table 1280 **Kitchen Tool(s):** The steamer is very
important. Steaming is a technique that keeps nutrition, taste and color in your food. **Interview Question:** I don't put too much focus on where they came from. I look at their appearance, their hands,
and their background. I look for a certain sensitivity. Can they be precise? Do they have integrity?
Do they believe in what they do? **Flavor Combo(s):** That is really hard to say, as they are constantly
changing. I love fruit. The flavors are so fresh, you can almost visualize the colors as you eat them. I
like to use fruit in a lot of combinations like with fish. **Fave Cookbook(s):** I have lots of old books I like,
such as Escoffier. The classic type of cooking interests me. **Chef to Cook for You:** Cesare in the town
of Albareto de la Torre. I want him to cook for me like he cooked thirty years ago. **Culinary Travel:** I
love to visit Paris and other European cities with history. I also love regions like Northern Italy where
there is a depth of culture.

Mindy Segal
Chef/Owner | Hot Chocolate

1747 N Damen Ave. Chicago, IL 60647

Phone: (773) 489-1747

RESTAURANT FACTS
Seats: 65 **Tasting Menu:** No **Kitchen Staff:** 15

CHEF FACTS
Cuisine: American **Born:** 1967 **Began Career:** 1989 **Culinary School:** Kendall College, Chicago, IL **Grad Year:** 1989 **Stages:** Chicago, IL: St Tropez **Work History:** Chicago, IL: Charlie Trotters, Marche, Ambria, Spago, mk, Mia Francesca **Mentor(s):** Charlie Trotter, Michael Kornick **Protégée(s):** Kate Neuman, Mark Steuer **Awards:** 2008 James Beard Foundation Outstanding Pastry Chef Nominee; 2005 StarChefs.com Rising Star Pastry Chef Chicago **Affiliations:** Slow Food, Chefs Collaborative

NOTABLE DISH(ES): Honeycrisp Apple Tartlet with Smoky Apple and Cider Ice Cream; Blueberry Coffee Cake, Sweet Corn Ice Cream Napoleon, Corn Nut Tuile, Caramel Corn, Blueberry-Merlot Reduction

FAST FACTS
Restaurant Recs: Song Dong Tofu House for dol sop bi bim bop; La Islas Marias for langoustines **Kitchen Tool(s):** Spoon because if you ain't eatin' your food, who is? **Interview Question:** Where do you anticipate being, career-wise, in 5 years? **Flavor Combo(s):** Strawberry, rhubarb, vanilla and fresh licorice root; bananas, barley malt, hot fudge and butterscotch; fresh mint, white chocolate with a surprise of really bittersweet chocolate; milk chocolate, coffee and cocoa nibs; milk chocolate and ginger **Fave Cookbook(s):** Dessert by the Yard by Sherry Yard; Chocolate Obsessions by Michael Recchiuti; Pure Desserts by Alice Medrich **Chef to Cook for You:** Anthony Bourdain. He is so kooky and crazy and he has traveled so much and seen so many cuisines. I think it would just be blast! **Culinary Travel:** I am dying to go to Oaxaca, Mexico

Scott Serpas
Executive Chef | Serpas

Atlanta, GA

Restaurant E-mail: justeat@aol.com

RESTAURANT FACTS
Seats: 135-145 **Weeknight Covers:** 200 **Weekend Covers:** 200
Check Average (with Wine): $38-$42 **Kitchen Staff:** 5-6

CHEF FACTS
Born: 1967 **Began Career:** 1987 **Stages:** Dallas, TX: Laurels **Work History:** New Orleans, LA: Algiers Landing, La Meridien; Dallas, TX: Baby Routh; Atlanta, GA: Nava, Two Urban Licks **Mentor(s):** My mom and dad – they got me started **Affiliations:** The James Beard House, Share Our Strength, Southern FoodWays Alliance and the "Flavors of Atlanta" Liver Foundation Benefit

NOTABLE DISH(ES): Bronzed Scallops with Gouda Grits, Smoked Tomato Broth and Pico de Gallo; Lamb Lollipops with Grape Chile Jam

FAST FACTS
Restaurant Recs: Taqueria del Sol on Buford Highway – for the tacos de lengua **Kitchen Tool(s):** My vegetable peeler – I use it all the time **Interview Question:** What got you into the business? I'm looking for a light and a reference to where you have been. **Flavor Combo(s):** Salty and sweet, like feta and blood orange **Fave Cookbook(s):** On Food and Cooking by Harold McGee and The Food Lover's Companion **Chef to Cook for You:** My father - although he was not a professional chef, he was an amazing cook. Not only did he make delicious food, but he also was a big inspiration to me, and I learned a lot about cooking simply from watching him. **Culinary Travel:** I would love to go to Spain because my family lineage is from there. Spanish food is full of unique flavors and ingredients, and I want to expand my knowledge about not only the food, but also Spanish cooking techniques.

Mike Sheerin
Chef de Cuisine | Blackbird

619 W Randolph St Chicago, IL 60606

Restaurant E-mail: mike@blackbirdrestaurant.com

Phone: (312) 715-0708

RESTAURANT FACTS
Seats: 65 **Weeknight Covers:** 90 **Weekend Covers:** 120 **Check Average (with Wine):** $82 **Check Average (w/o Wine):** $55 **Tasting Menu:** Yes $100 **Kitchen Staff:** 7

CHEF FACTS
Cuisine: Modern American **Born:** 1976 **Began Career:** 1992 **Culinary School:** Grand Rapids Community College **Grad Year:** 1998 **Stages:** France: Le Manoir Aux Quat' Saisons **Work History:** New York, NY: wd~50, Jean-Georges, Atlas, Lutèce **Mentor(s):** Thierry Tritsch, my brother Pat, Wylie Dufresne **Awards:** 2008 StarChefs.com Rising Star Chef Chicago **Languages Spoken:** Some Spanish

NOTABLE DISH(ES): Wood Grilled Sturgeon, Mustard Consommé, Rye Gnocchi, Mustard Foam, English Peas, Oyster Mushrooms and Guanciale; Veal Ribeye with Cornbread Porridge

FAST FACTS
Restaurant Recs: Hot Doug's, Avec **Kitchen Tool(s):** Spoon, because that is what I cook and taste with **Interview Question:** I look at how many years of experience they have and then have them come in and put them to work, always on onions or carrots. **Flavor Combo(s):** I like Pernod, wasabi and chocolate. I also like tarragon and chocolate and nasturtiums with plantains and coffee. **Fave Cookbook(s):** The Whole Beast: Nose to Tail Eating by Fergus Henderson **Chef to Cook for You:** Pierre Gagnaire, because he is a master, a ninja **Culinary Travel:** Japan, because I love ramen!

Stephen Sherman
Chef de Cuisine | Union Bar and Grille

1357 Washington St. Boston, MA 02118

Restaurant E-mail: kitchen@unionrestaurant.com

Phone: (617) 423-0555

RESTAURANT FACTS
Seats: 104 **Weeknight Covers:** 140 **Weekend Covers:** 280+ **Check Average (with Wine):** $60 **Tasting Menu:** No **Kitchen Staff:** 5

CHEF FACTS
Cuisine: Contemporary American **Born:** 1968 **Began Career:** 1994 **Culinary School:** The Culinary Institute of America, Hyde Park, NY **Grad Year:** 1994 **Stages:** Spain: Arzak, Zuberoa; New York, NY: River Café, Union Square Café **Work History:** Spain: Arzak, Zuberoa; New York, NY: Union Square Café; Boston, MA: Aquitaine and Aquitaine Bis **Mentor(s):** Michael Romano **Protégée(s):** Rebecca Newell **Awards:** 2004 Durkee Spice Recipe Contest Grand Prize Winner **Languages Spoken:** Spanish

FAST FACTS
Restaurant Recs: El Oriental de Cuba for Cuban sandwiches **Kitchen Tool(s):** Chinois – because it is absolutely necessary for silky smooth purées and fine, glossy reductions **Interview Question:** What would you admit as being your one weakness in the kitchen? It reveals whether or not the cook has a good ability for introspection and self criticism. **Flavor Combo(s):** Garlic and parsley **Fave Cookbook(s):** Simple French Food by Richard Olney **Chef to Cook for You:** Gordon Ramsay – he has a great attitude and philosophy and his cooking is fresh, flavorful and honest **Culinary Travel:** Southeast Asia – I love the food and I've never been

Bruce Sherman
Chef | North Pond

2610 N Cannon Dr. Chicago, IL 60614

Restaurant E-mail: chef@northpondrestaurant.com

Phone: (773) 477-5845

RESTAURANT FACTS
Seats: 92 **Weeknight Covers:** 90 **Weekend Covers:** 150 **Check Average (with Wine):** $80 **Tasting Menu:** Yes $85 **Kitchen Staff:** 8

CHEF FACTS
Cuisine: Seasonal American **Born:** 1961 **Began Career:** 1985-ish **Culinary School:** L'École Superieure de Cuisine Française, France **Grad Year:** 1997 **Work History:** Chicago, IL: The Ritz-Carlton; France: La Verriere, Le Bamboche **Mentor(s):** Gabriel Bousquet, Sarah Stegner **Awards:** 2008 James Beard Foundation Best Chef Great Lakes Nominee; 2003 Food & Wine Best New Chef; 2003 Chicago Tribune Good Eating Award **Affiliations:** Chefs Collaborative, Slow Food, Chicago Green City Market **Languages Spoken:** French

NOTABLE DISH(ES): Poached Halibut; Farm Egg Eggplant

FAST FACTS
Restaurant Recs: Lengua or pastor tacos at Chorrito Tacos **Kitchen Tool(s):** Kuhn Rikon peeler, Microplane **Interview Question:** What are the last three books you read? **Flavor Combo(s):** Hazelnut, orange, chocolate and salt **Fave Cookbook(s):** Larousse Gastronomique by Prosper Montagne **Chef to Cook for You:** Bernard Loiseau. I never had a chance to taste his food and would be curious to do so, especially since he led such a tragic life. **Culinary Travel:** Vietnam for the exotic and intense food, culture and scenery

Kitchen Spanish, Japanese

Masato Shimizu
Executive Sushi Chef | 15 East

15 E 15th St. New York, NY 10003

Restaurant E-mail: kim@15eastrestaurant.com

Phone: (212) 647-0015

RESTAURANT FACTS
Seats: 59 **Weeknight Covers:** 80 **Weekend Covers:** 100 **Check Average (w/o Wine):** $100 **Tasting Menu:** Yes $95/$120 and up **Kitchen Staff:** 3

CHEF FACTS
Cuisine: Japanese/Sushi **Born:** 1973 **Began Career:** My uncle is a sushi chef – he cut a whole tuna in front of me when I was 5! **Stages:** 1993-2000 under Master Kuguo **Work History:** Japan: Sukeroku Sushi; New York, NY: Jewel Bako **Mentor(s):** Rikio Kuguo at Sukeroku in Tokyo, taught me to endure hardships **Awards:** 2007 StarChefs.com Rising Star Chef New York **Languages Spoken:**

NOTABLE DISH(ES): Poached Madako Octopus; Ikura (Salmon Roe) Marinated in Dashi and Soy

FAST FACTS
Restaurant Recs: Prune for the cow heart dish; Keens Steak House for 200 different kinds of single malt Scotch. My favorite is Japanese Nikka Single Cask Malt Whiskey. **Kitchen Tool(s):** Anago knife for butchering sea eel that was given to me by my master chef **Interview Question:** Where have you worked and for how long? This is valuable information to know. **Flavor Combo(s):** Ground ginger with yakumi (a Japanese seasoning). I also like jack mackerel or sardines paired with scallion. **Fave Cookbook(s):** Chez Panisse Menu Cookbook by Alice Waters **Chef to Cook for You:** I would like Joël Robuchon to make a meal for me **Culinary Travel:** I'd go to France – you can always see and taste quality cuisine there

Gregory Short
Executive Chef | Masa's Restaurant

648 Bush St. San Francisco, CA 94108

Restaurant E-mail: greg@executivehotels.net

Phone: (415) 989-7154

RESTAURANT FACTS
Seats: 65 **Weeknight Covers:** 50 **Weekend Covers:** 80 **Check Average (with Wine):** $175 **Check Average (w/o Wine):** $100 **Tasting Menu:** Yes $100/$150 **Kitchen Staff:** 9

CHEF FACTS
Cuisine: California French **Born:** 1968 **Began Career:** 1993 **Culinary School:** The Culinary Institute of America, Hyde Park NY **Grad Year:** 1993 **Stages:** France: Taillevent, Pierre Orsi, La Cote d'Or, Les Jardin des Sens **Work History:** Snoqualmie Falls, WA: The Salish Lodge; Yountville, CA: The French Laundry; Laguna Beach, CA: Montage Resort and Spa **Mentor(s):** Thomas Keller, Rolland Henin, Julia Child, Santi Santa Maria **Awards:** First Prize 2000 Bertoli Sous Chef Awards **Languages Spoken:** French (not fluent)

NOTABLE DISH(ES): "Bubble Tea" Green Tea, Shiso Ice, Pearl Tapioca; Chilled Maine Crab, Tomato Gazpacho, Cucumber Gelee, Cilantro Oil, Brioche Croutons

FAST FACTS
Restaurant Recs: Sushi Rika for the spider roll and aged dashi tofu **Kitchen Tool(s):** French palette knife for turning food in a sauté pan and picking up delicate food items to move them **Interview Question:** Why do you want to work for me? It tells me just how much the person knows or doesn't know about me and the restaurant. **Flavor Combo(s):** Fennel and mission figs **Fave Cookbook(s):** La Cocina de Santi Santa Maria by La Etica del Gusto **Chef to Cook for You:** Thomas Keller **Culinary Travel:** Spain

Michael Sichel
Chef | Cuvee Beach

36120 Emerald Coast Pkwy. Destin, FL 32541

Restaurant E-mail: msich@hotmail.com

Phone: (850) 650-8900

RESTAURANT FACTS
Seats: 240 **Check Average (with Wine):** $35–$40 **Tasting Menu:** No
Kitchen Staff: 5–6

CHEF FACTS
Cuisine: Italian-Californian with an emphasis on fresh produce **Born:** 1967 **Began Career:** 1995 **Culinary School:** The Culinary Institute of America, Hyde Park, NY **Grad Year:** 1998 **Stages:** France: L'Abbeye de St. Croix **Work History:** San Francisco, CA: Hawthorne Lane, Rubicon; Napa, CA: L'Auberge du Soleil; New Orleans, LA: 7 on Fulton, The Cellar, Indigo; New York, NY: Gotham Bar and Grill; France: The Ritz-Carlton **Mentor(s):** I can't choose one person as I have learned so much from all my former chefs **Affiliations:** The Louisiana Restaurant Association **Languages Spoken:** Kitchen French, kitchen Spanish

NOTABLE DISH(ES): Bacon-Wrapped Pork Tenderloin with Sunchokes, Bacon and Spinach and Sherry Vinegar Sauce

FAST FACTS
Restaurant Recs: Parkway Bakery for great Po' Boys **Kitchen Tool(s):** The blender - I love making baby food **Interview Question:** Tell me about your passion for food **Flavor Combo(s):** Earth, meat and seafood **Fave Cookbook(s):** The Encyclopedia of Louisiana Cuisine by John Folse **Chef to Cook for You:** Richard Reddington because he was always so generous and appreciative of his cooks. He taught me the importance of giving back to the people who worked for you. I would love to have him make me another meal. **Culinary Travel:** I hear Morocco is incredible and I know nothing about it; I would be curious to go.

Sergio Sigala
Executive Chef | Casa Tua Restaurant

1700 James Ave. Miami Beach, FL 33139

Restaurant E-mail: sergiosigala@hotmail.com

Phone: (305) 673-1010

RESTAURANT FACTS
Seats: 150 **Weeknight Covers:** 150 **Weekend Covers:** 200 **Check Average (w/o Wine):** $120 **Tasting Menu:** No **Kitchen Staff:** 9

CHEF FACTS
Cuisine: Italian **Born:** 1969 **Began Career:** 1987 **Culinary School:** Istituto Professionale Alberghiero di Stato Darfo Boario Terme, Italy **Grad Year:** 1989 **Stages:** France: Le Diamante Rose; Italy: La skeletal **Work History:** Italy: Villa Fiordaliso Gardone Riviera, Grand Hotel Villa, Il Bersagliere Goito; Switzerland: Hotel Steffany **Mentor(s):** Gualtiero Marchesi **Awards:** 2004 StarChefs.com Rising Star Chef Miami **Languages Spoken:** Italian, Spanish

NOTABLE DISH(ES): Sautéed Prosciutto Crudo-Wrapped Zucchini Blossoms Stuffed with Buffalo Mozzarella; Grilled Turbot with Fennel, Blood Oranges, Niçoise Olives Salad and Fresh Marjoram

FAST FACTS
Restaurant Recs: Azul at the Mandarin **Kitchen Tool(s):** My agenda – although it's not an actual tool, it is very important that I am organized **Interview Question:** Why do you want the job? I want to see if they are inspired and are passionate. **Flavor Combo(s):** Roasted fennel, black olives, and orange **Fave Cookbook(s):** Cookbooks by Alain Ducasse **Chef to Cook for You:** Alain Ducasse **Culinary Travel:** Milan and small restaurants in my home town of Boario Terme, Italy. I also like France and New York City.

Bryan Sikora
Chef/Owner | Talula's Table

102 W State St. Kennett Square, PA 19348

Restaurant E-mail: amieolexy@hotmail.com

Phone: (610) 444-8255

RESTAURANT FACTS
Seats: 8–12 **Weeknight Covers:** 8–12 **Weekend Covers:** 8–12
Check Average (w/o Wine): $90 **Tasting Menu:** Yes $90 **Kitchen Staff:** 2

CHEF FACTS
Cuisine: Regional European **Born:** 1970 **Began Career:** 1994
Culinary School: The Culinary Institute of America, Hyde Park, NY
Grad Year: 1994 **Stages:** Chatham, MA: Chatham Bars Inn **Work History:** Philadelphia, PA: Django, Tangerine; Washington, DC: Nora
Mentor(s): Joël Robuchon, Alain Ducasse, Michel Bras **Protégée(s):** Claire Shears, Sheri Waide **Awards:** 2004 StarChefs.com Rising Star Chef Philadelphia **Affiliations:** James Beard Foundation, Share our Strength, Alex's Lemonade, and we also work with a lot of local charities and the local nature and historic conservancies

NOTABLE DISH(ES): Venison Carpaccio with White Bean Purée, Chickpea Chips and Asparagus; Smoked Seafood Sausage with Whole Grain Mustard Glaze and Caraway Buns

FAST FACTS
Restaurant Recs: Veracruzana for tacos **Kitchen Tool(s):** Chinois – because it brings clarity and beauty to stocks and sauces **Interview Question:** Do you smoke? I am allergic to smoke, and I feel it can hurt the palate and senses. **Flavor Combo(s):** Cocoa with foie gras and honey **Fave Cookbook(s):** A Return to Cooking by Eric Ripert **Chef to Cook for You:** Any chef with an ethnic background. Someone who could teach me the true flavor combinations of a certain cuisine in an ethnic sense. **Culinary Travel:** Every city has such a different environment. They're more ingredient-driven on the west coast and on Cape Cod. I prefer the towns where there are actual working markets.

Dan Silverman
Executive Chef | Sunset Beach

35 Shore Rd. Shelter Island, NY 11965

Restaurant E-mail: dan.silverman@hotelsab.com

Phone: (631) 749-2001

RESTAURANT FACTS
Seats: 125–150 **Tasting Menu:** No

CHEF FACTS
Cuisine: Mediterranean **Born:** 1962 **Began Career:** 1988 **Culinary School:** The French Culinary Institute, New York, NY **Grad Year:** 1988 **Work History:** New York, NY: Bouley, Alison, Union Square Café, Lever House **Mentor(s):** David Bouley, Alain Ducasse, Richard Olney **Awards:** 2005 Michelin 1 star; 1997 Food & Wine Best New Chefs **Affiliations:** JBF **Books Published:** The Lever House Cookbook **Languages Spoken:** Kitchen Spanish, Italian, French

NOTABLE DISH(ES): Spring Risotto; Ricotta Gnocchi with Asparagus and Ramps

FAST FACTS
Restaurant Recs: Tia Pol – it's all great **Kitchen Tool(s):** Japanese mandolin **Interview Question:** What do you think your previous employer will say about you? Why do you cook? **Flavor Combo(s):** I love salty-tart flavors: capers, anchovies, lemon, sea salt, olives and preserved lemon **Fave Cookbook(s):** Honey From a Weed by Patience Gray; Simple French Food by Richard Olney **Chef to Cook for You:** Isidre Girones of Ca l'Isidre in Barcelona. I would go to the Boqueria market with him in the morning and then have him cook me a rustic four-hour lunch, and have him select wines from his wonderful cellar. **Culinary Travel:** Southern Spain, Sardinia, and Corsica for the ultra-fresh seafood, great cheeses, and great little wineries

Nancy Silverton
Chef/Co-Owner | Osteria Mozza

641 N Highland Ave. Los Angeles, CA 90036

Restaurant E-mail: kbrucker@labreabakery.com

Phone: (323) 297-0101

RESTAURANT FACTS
Seats: 140 **Weeknight Covers:** 250 **Weekend Covers:** 300 **Check Average (with Wine):** $75 **Tasting Menu:** Yes $69/$119 **Kitchen Staff:** 8

CHEF FACTS
Other Restaurants: La Brea Bakery, Pizzeria Mozza **Cuisine:** Local **Born:** 1954 **Began Career:** 1977 **Culinary School:** Cordon Bleu, England; École Lenôtre, France **Stages:** Larkspur, CA: 464 Magnolia **Work History:** Los Angeles, CA: Michael's Restaurant, Spago **Mentor(s):** Alice Waters, Judy Rodgers, Richard Olney, Paul Bertolli, Madeline Kamman, Mario Batali, Paula Wolfert, Wolfgang Puck

Protégée(s): Suzanne Goin, Suzanne Tract, Govind Armstrong, Dan Barber, Lissa Doumani **Awards:** 2006 LA Times The West 100: The Most Influential People in Southern California; 2005 WCR Golden Bowl Award; 2004 International Star Diamond Award for Outstanding Hospitality; 2003 RCA Pioneer Award; 2001 James Beard Foundation Outstanding Restaurant Award; 1999 Bon Appétit Best of Food & Entertaining; "Food Artisan"; 1999 Nation's Restaurant News "50 New Taste Makers"; 1997 Fine Dining Award; 1995 Chocolatier Magazine one of the 10 Best Pastry Chefs of the Year; 1990 James Beard "Who's Who in American Cooking"; 1990 James Beard Best Pastry Chef of the Year; 1990 Food & Wine Magazine Best New Chefs **Affiliations:** JBF **Books Published:** Desserts; Nancy Silverton's Breads from the La Brea Bakery; Nancy Silverton's Pastries from the La Brea Bakery; Nancy Silverton's Sandwich Book; Twist of the Wrist; Two Chefs Cook for Family and Friend; Mark Peel and Nancy Silverton at Home; The Food of Campanile

FAST FACTS
Restaurant Recs: Pollo a la Brasa for roast chicken **Kitchen Tool(s):** Wooden spatula, because whether I'm cooking or baking, ingredients need to be stirred together. I prefer the feel of a wooden spoon over a metal one. **Interview Question:** Have you ever eaten here (at the restaurant)? **Flavor Combo(s):** Spicy and salty **Fave Cookbook(s):** Mastering the Art of French Cooking by Julia Child **Chef to Cook for You:** Chef Fredy Girardet – I had the most memorable meal at a restaurant that he used to have in Switzerland. It was simply wonderful. **Culinary Travel:** Italy – I love to immerse myself in the love and passion that Italians have for food. Italy also inspires new ideas for my restaurant.

Erick Simmons
Executive Chef | MK

868 N. Franklin Chicago, IL 60610

Restaurant E-mail: etsimmons@aol.com

Phone: (312) 482-9179

RESTAURANT FACTS

Seats: 150 **Weeknight Covers:** 125 **Weekend Covers:** 250-260
Check Average (with Wine): $90 **Tasting Menu:** Yes $79 **Kitchen Staff:** 12

CHEF FACTS

Cuisine: American Contemporary **Born:** 1979 **Began Career:** 1996
Culinary School: California School of Culinary Arts, Pasadena, CA
Grad Year: 2004 **Work History:** Los Angeles, CA: Water Grill; Las Vegas, NV: Bradley Ogden at Caesar's Palace **Mentor(s):** Michael Kornick **Affiliations:** SOS, Green City Market, Greater Chicago Food Bank, Children's Oncology Service

NOTABLE DISH(ES): Hardwood Charcoal Grilled Breast of Squab with Creamy Polenta, Baby Broccoli, Basil and Squab Jus

FAST FACTS

Restaurant Recs: TAC Thai in North Chicago **Kitchen Tool(s):** The spoon – gotta love it. I have three spoons; they're sentimental. **Interview Question:** I ask them "what are you in it for?" I want to see if I get a good feel for somebody, if they have the same type of commitment, if they ask good questions. Right now we're taking in a lot of kids who are fresh from culinary school or still in it. That's huge for me – they're green as can be, and if we can give them their chops, then they can leave here and say that they learned a lot of great things in the year or two years they stayed – that's what we're looking for. **Flavor Combo(s):** They change with the seasons but currently I like fennel and orange, and horseradish and beets **Fave Cookbook(s):** The French Laundry Cookbook. Where I came from you didn't see anything like that. The recipes, the pictures, and the attention to detail when it came out showed a level of commitment that I didn't know even existed. **Chef to Cook for You:** Alice Waters because she is a California icon. She was at the start of everything we as chefs are trying to do as far as sourcing only the most local and seasonal ingredients. Her farm to table approach is what I model my cuisine after. A close second would be Marco Pierre White, just to see what all the hype is about. **Culinary Travel:** I would like to travel anywhere in the Mediterranean because I love seafood done simply. Olive oil, garlic, and that's it!

Jared Simons
Executive Chef | Violet

3221 Pico Blvd. Santa Monica, CA 90405

Restaurant E-mail: info@violetrestaurant.com

Phone: (310) 453-9113

RESTAURANT FACTS
Seats: 60 **Weeknight Covers:** 60 **Weekend Covers:** 90 **Check Average (with Wine):** $45 **Tasting Menu:** No **Kitchen Staff:** 3

CHEF FACTS
Cuisine: New American **Born:** 1978 **Began Career:** 1994 **Culinary School:** California Culinary Academy, San Francisco, CA **Grad Year:** 1998 **Stages:** Rancho Santa Fe, CA: Milles Fleurs **Work History:** Carlsbad, CA: Le Passage **Mentor(s):** Anthony Gangale **Awards:** 2006 Restaurant Hospitality Rising Star **Affiliations:** None specific, although we participate in events both locally and nationally

FAST FACTS
Restaurant Recs: Five Feet restaurant in Laguna Beach **Kitchen Tool(s):** A meat mallet. I love to pound a piece of pork paper thin and make a good saltimbocca. Plus it doubles as a handy household tool. **Interview Question:** I ask why they got into cooking. I'm looking for an answer with some enthusiasm and excitement. **Flavor Combo(s):** Salt and chocolate. I loved sweets when I was young but not as much as I've aged. Now I enjoy a bit of sweet and savory. **Fave Cookbook(s):** Essential Cuisine by Michel Bras and Simply French by Joël Robuchon **Chef to Cook for You:** Marco Pierre White – the first rock star chef **Culinary Travel:** Italy – I could eat pasta until I looked like the Goodyear blimp

Lee Skawinski
Chef/Owner | Cinque Terre

36 Wharf St. Portland, ME 04101

Restaurant E-mail: reservations@cinqueterremaine.com

Phone: (207) 347-6154

RESTAURANT FACTS
Seats: 90 **Weeknight Covers:** 45-55 **Weekend Covers:** 125 **Check Average (with Wine):** $55-$60 **Tasting Menu:** Yes $65

CHEF FACTS
Other Restaurants: Vignola, Habañeros Tequilaria and Barbeque **Cuisine:** Traditional Italian **Born:** 1967 **Began Career:** 1988 **Culinary School:** Newbury College, Brookline, MA **Work History:** Boston, MA: The Four Seasons; Freeport, ME: Harraseeket Inn **Mentor(s):** Jake Jacobus and Bob Davis **Affiliations:** JBF, Slow Food, GRI, MOFGA, SOS **Languages Spoken:** Some Italian

FAST FACTS
Restaurant Recs: Butcher Shop for the steak tartare and charcuterie plate **Kitchen Tool(s):** Cast iron pans for versatility – I can fry, bake, sear, and roast, and they last for ever **Interview Question:** What are your plans for the next couple years? **Flavor Combo(s):** Pork shoulder, sea salt, fennel pollen, and black pepper **Fave Cookbook(s):** Science in the Kitchen and the Art of Eating Well by Pellegrino Artusi **Chef to Cook for You:** Bernard Loiseau – I had the most memorable meals of my life with him and Daniel Boulud **Culinary Travel:** I would like to stage at the five 3-star Michelin restaurants in Italy

Kimberly Sklar
Pastry Chef | New Project in the works

Los Angeles, CA

Restaurant E-mail: kimsklar@roadrunner.com

CHEF FACTS
Cuisine: Eclectic desserts **Born:** 1968 **Began Career:** 1983 **Culinary School:** Tante Marie's, San Francisco, CA **Grad Year:** 1994 **Stages:** Los Angeles, CA: Campanile **Work History:** Los Angeles, CA: Campanile, La Brea Bakery, Lucques, AOC, Literatti II **Mentor(s):** Nancy Silverton and my husband, Chris Kidder **Protégée(s):** Ann Kirk **Affiliations:** JBF, Chefs Collaborative

NOTABLE DISH(ES): Kumquat Semi-Freddo; Sourdough Chocolate Cake

FAST FACTS
Restaurant Recs: Shibuya – for Spanish mackerel **Kitchen Tool(s):** Three-sided spatula – it's great for chocolate work **Interview Question:** Have you eaten here? They should be excited by the food. If they don't like or know exactly what you are doing, they're probably are not a good candidate. **Flavor Combo(s):** Rhubarb sorbet, whipped cream and toasted walnut meringue **Fave Cookbook(s):** Chez Panisse Desserts by Lindsey Shere **Chef to Cook for You:** Alice Waters – I love her tastes and simplicity of cooking (I'm sure I'd learn a lot, too) **Culinary Travel:** Spain – I haven't been there yet and would love to experience the culture

David Slater
Chef de Cuisine | Emeril's New Orleans

800 Tchoupitoulas St. New Orleans, LA 70130

Restaurant E-mail: dslater@emerils.com

Phone: (504) 528 9393

RESTAURANT FACTS
Seats: 180 **Weeknight Covers:** 200 **Weekend Covers:** 300-350
Check Average (with Wine): $65 **Tasting Menu:** Yes $65 **Kitchen Staff:** 15

CHEF FACTS
Cuisine: New New Orleans cuisine **Born:** 1974 **Began Career:** 1998
Culinary School: The Florida Culinary Institute, West Palm Beach,
FL **Grad Year:** 1998 **Work History:** New Orleans, LA: La Provence,
Cuvee; Orlando, FL: Emeril's; Atlanta, GA: Emeril's **Mentor(s):** Rene
Bajeux, Emeril Lagasse, Linton Hopkins, my parents

NOTABLE DISH(ES): Veal Two Ways: Scaloppini with Sweetbreads and Saltimbocca with Hash; Creole Tomato-Chile Glazed Colorado Lamb Spare Ribs

FAST FACTS
Kitchen Tool(s): Tasting spoon **Flavor Combo(s):** I like every sense to be represented – for the taste and texture to be playful in your mouth **Fave Cookbook(s):** Susur: A Culinary Life by Susur Lee **Chef to Cook for You:** Michel Bras

Holly Smith
Chef/Owner | Café Juanita

9702 NE 102nd Pl. Kirkland WA 98034

Restaurant E-mail: holly@cafejuanita.com

Phone: (425) 823-1505

RESTAURANT FACTS
Seats: 62–86 **Weeknight Covers:** 85 **Weekend Covers:** 110 **Check Average (with Wine):** $85–90 **Tasting Menu:** Yes $120 **Kitchen Staff:** 3–6

CHEF FACTS
Other Restaurants: Poco Carretto Gelato (serves organic local and sustainable gelato on a mobile cart in farmers markets) **Cuisine:** Northern Italian **Born:** 1966 **Began Career:** 1991 **Culinary School:** Baltimore International Culinary College, MD **Grad Year:** 1991 **Stages:** Park Hotel, County Caven, Ireland with Master Chef Peter Timmons **Work History:** Baltimore, MD: Milton Inn; Seattle, WA: Dahlia Lounge, Brasa **Mentor(s):** Tom Douglas, Tamara Murphy **Protégée(s):** Jason Stratton **Awards:** 2008 James Beard Foundation Best Chef Northwest; 2003 StarChefs.com Rising Star Chef Seattle **Affiliations:** WCR, Chefs Collaborative, Slow Food, Les Dames d'Escoffier

NOTABLE DISH(ES): Piemontese Plin of Rabbit; Crisp Veal Sweetbreads

FAST FACTS
Restaurant Recs: Oliver's Twist in the Greenwood neighborhood – it is all great and ever-changing **Kitchen Tool(s):** A hand forged knife; blow torch; Microplane **Interview Question:** What do you like to eat? Why are you here? **Flavor Combo(s):** Lamb and anchovy; English peas and bronze fennel; egg and white truffle **Fave Cookbook(s):** An oldie and goodie is Marco Pierre White's first book, White Heat; now it seems a bit dated but in 1990 it was amazing to me as a young wanna-be cook in Ireland. I love the Culinaria Italy book as well. **Chef to Cook for You:** Cesare from Da Cesare in the Alto Langhe. His food has surprising lightness. **Culinary Travel:** I would like to go to Sicily and back to Bologna

Adam Sobel
Consulting Chef | Culinary Solutions LLC

Las Vegas, NV

Restaurant E-mail: sobel.adam@yahoo.com

CHEF FACTS

Cuisine: Seasonal market-driven cuisine **Born:** 1980 **Began Career:** 2001 **Culinary School:** The Culinary Institute of America, Hyde Park, NY **Grad Year:** 2000 **Work History:** Las Vegas, NV: Bradley Ogden, Charlie Trotters, Guy Savoy, Pure, Company American Bistro; Atlanta, GA: Seeger's; France: Guy Savoy **Mentor(s):** John Murphy, John Johnston, Guenter Seeger, Matthias Merges, Bradley Ogden **Awards:** 2004 James Beard Foundation Best New Restaurant in America; 1998 New York State VICA Culinary Arts Champion **Affiliations:** ACF **Languages Spoken:** Some French

NOTABLE DISH(ES): Mosaique of Milk-Fed Poularde, Foie Gras, Celery Root and Black Truffle Vinaigrette; Blue Fin Toro Tartare, Cauliflower "Cru et Cuit" with Golden Oscetra Caviar

FAST FACTS

Restaurant Recs: Archie's Authentic Thai Cuisine for spicy eggplant with fried tofu and pork **Kitchen Tool(s):** Immersion circulator; my palate **Interview Question:** Is the restaurant business your true passion? I like to know how serious someone is about the craft. **Flavor Combo(s):** Salty and sweet **Fave Cookbook(s):** Cooking with the Seasons by Jean-Louis Palladin; Culinary Artistry by Andrew Dornenburg and Karen Page **Chef to Cook for You:** Grant Achatz because he is so creative. He is on another level when it comes to technique. **Culinary Travel:** China: Beijing, Shanghai, Hong Kong for the street food

Hiro Sone
Executive Chef/Owner | Terra

1345 Railroad Ave. Saint Helena, CA 94574

Restaurant E-mail: lissasan@terrarestaurant.com

Phone: (707) 963-8931

RESTAURANT FACTS
Seats: 92 **Weeknight Covers:** 80–100 **Weekend Covers:** 120–140
Tasting Menu: Yes **Kitchen Staff:** 7

CHEF FACTS
Other Restaurants: Ame **Cuisine:** Personal cuisine **Born:** 1959 **Began Career:** 1978 **Culinary School:** École Technique Hôtelière Tsuji, Osaka, Japan **Grad Year:** 1977 **Work History:** Japan: Sakae sushi; La Colomba; Italy: Dal Pescatore; Los Angeles, CA: Spago **Mentor(s):** Wolfgang Puck **Awards:** 2008 Michelin 1 star; 2008 James Beard Foundation Outstanding Service Nominee; 2007 Zagat Guide Book Best New Restaurant (Ame); 2007 James Beard Foundation Outstanding Service Nominee; 2006 San Francisco Chronicle Top Ten Restaurants of 2006 (Ame); 2006 Esquire Magazine Best New Restaurant in the USA; 2003 James Beard Foundation Best Chef of California; 2000 Robert Mondavi Culinary Excellence Award Recipient; 1991 Food & Wine Magazine America's Best New Chefs **Affiliations:** We are affiliated with many charities, MOW both in San Francisco and Los Angeles, Planned Parenthood, Project Open Hand, SOS to name a few. There are many others that we work with as we have time. **Books Published:** Terra, Cooking from the Heart of Napa Valley **Languages Spoken:** Japanese, English

NOTABLE DISH(ES): Lamb with Black Olive Anchovy Sauce; Soup Pistou with Goat Cheese Ravioli

FAST FACTS
Restaurant Recs: Miguel's for chilaquiles **Kitchen Tool(s):** Dining out – because without dining experiences, chefs cannot create great meals for customers **Interview Question:** What's a food memory from when you were young? You can tell something about their food background. **Flavor Combo(s):** Sea salt and lemon **Fave Cookbook(s):** The Great Chefs of France: The Masters of Haute Cuisine and their Secrets by Anthony Blake and Quentin Crewe **Chef to Cook for You:** Fernand Point, because he is my idol **Culinary Travel:** Lebanon, Greek and Morocco – I love the flavors of their cuisines

Ana Sortun
Chef | Oleana

134 Hampshire St. Cambridge, MA 02139

Restaurant E-mail: info@oleanarestaurant.com

Phone: (617) 661-0505

RESTAURANT FACTS
Seats: 80–130 **Weeknight Covers:** 120 **Weekend Covers:** 160
Check Average (with Wine): $65 **Tasting Menu:** Yes $42 **Kitchen Staff:** 7

CHEF FACTS
Cuisine: Mediterranean focusing on Arabic foods **Born:** 1967 **Began Career:** 1982 **Culinary School:** La Varenne, France **Grad Year:** 1987 **Stages:** Spain: Neichel **Work History:** Cambridge, MA: Casablanca, 8 Holyoke, Concord, MA: Aigo Bistro **Mentor(s):** Alice Waters **Awards:** 2005 James Beard Foundation Best Chef in the Northeast; 2003 StarChefs.com Rising Star Chef Boston **Affiliations:** Chefs Collaborative **Books Published:** Spice: Flavors of the Eastern Mediterranean **Languages Spoken:** French

NOTABLE DISH(ES): Ricotta and Bread Dumplings with Red Wine Porcini Broth; Egyptian Spiced Carrot Purée

FAST FACTS
Restaurant Recs: Oishi for spicy tuna in a cucumber wrap **Kitchen Tool(s):** Blender – because it makes really tight purees **Interview Question:** If you were a vegetable, what would you be? **Flavor Combo(s):** Sumac with aleppo peppers and dried mint **Fave Cookbook(s):** The New Book of Middle Eastern Food by Claudia Roden **Chef to Cook for You:** Morimoto – I love watching him cook **Culinary Travel:** I've always wanted to go to Beirut. I'm just waiting for it to calm down a little.

Angelo Sosa
Executive Chef | AS2 Consulting

63 Downing St. New York, NY 10014

Restaurant E-mail: sosaangelo@yahoo.com

CHEF FACTS
Cuisine: Modern Chinese **Born:** 1974 **Began Career:** 1993 **Culinary School:** The Culinary Institute of America, Hyde Park, NY **Grad Year:** 1997 **Stages:** Spain: Restaurant Arzak; Thailand: Peninsula Hotel; Vietnam: Sofitel Hotel Hanoi; China: Royal Garden Hotel **Work History:** New York, NY: Jean-Georges, Spice Market, Yumcha

NOTABLE DISH(ES): Chili-Marinated Jelly Fish; Crab Salad with Cardamom Custard

FAST FACTS
Restaurant Recs: Anzu Restaurant for sashimi of red snapper with young ginger slivers **Kitchen Tool(s):** Chopsticks **Interview Question:** What do I have to offer to you? **Flavor Combo(s):** Smokey, bitter and sweet **Fave Cookbook(s):** The Indian Spice Kitchen by Monisha Bharadwaj **Chef to Cook for You:** Escoffier – it would be so intriguing to see, and would give so much perspective on the evolution of food. **Culinary Travel:** Goa, India – it would be interesting to learn their traditional techniques and then find a way to modernize them

Jesse Souza
Executive Chef | La Playa Beach and Golf Club Resort

9891 Gulf Shore Dr. Naples, FL 34108

Restaurant E-mail: jsouza@laplayaresort.com

Phone: (800) 237-6883

RESTAURANT FACTS
Seats: 140 **Weeknight Covers:** 80 **Weekend Covers:** 140 **Check Average (with Wine):** $65 **Tasting Menu:** No **Kitchen Staff:** 5

CHEF FACTS
Cuisine: New American **Born:** 1975 **Began Career:** 1993 **Work History:** Berkeley, CA: Claremont Resort & Spa; Florida Keys, FL: Noble House Resort, Little Palm Island Hotel & Spa; Miami, FL: Chispa; Portland, ME: Havana Restaurant, Natasha's **Mentor(s):** Hans Wiegand, Adam Votaw

FAST FACTS
Restaurant Recs: Hiro's Yakko San in North Miami Beach. They're open late (3 am) for the chef crowd. They have Japanese small plates, an their noodles with salted fish roe and nori are the absolute best. **Kitchen Tool(s):** My chef's knife and a good spoon – very utilitarian **Interview Question:** "Why do you want to work in this industry? Why do you want to work here?"The truth could be anything from "I'm 19 and I love the kitchen" to "I need a second job and I'll work through season." **Flavor Combo(s):** Truffle, soy, lemon; butter, garlic; peanut butter and jelly **Fave Cookbook(s):** Lately, I like reference books. Peterson's Fish & Shellfish, the CIA Baking and Pastry book. I have never been big on using other people for my menus. **Chef to Cook for You:** Jean-Louis Palladin – he was a wild man who created his own rules of cuisine **Culinary Travel:** Portugal – to find my family. Italy, Thailand, China, Mexico, Japan – for obvious reasons.

Susan Spicer
Chef/Owner | Bayona

430 Dauphine St. New Orleans, LA 70112

Restaurant E-mail: bayona@bellsouth.net

Phone: (504) 522-0588

RESTAURANT FACTS
Seats: 130–160 **Weeknight Covers:** 160–180 **Weekend Covers:** 200 **Check Average (with Wine):** $55 **Tasting Menu:** Yes Upon request **Kitchen Staff:** 6–8

CHEF FACTS
Other Restaurants: Herbsaint, Spice Inc., Wild Flour Breads **Cuisine:** New American **Born:** 1952 **Began Career:** 1979 **Stages:** New Orleans, LA: Lous XVI; France: Hotel Sofitel **Work History:** New Orleans, LA: Savoir Faire at the St. Charles Hotel, Henri at the Meridien Hotel, Maison de Ville **Mentor(s):** Daniel Bonnot, Roland Durand **Protégée(s):** Donald Link, John Harris, Michele Nugent **Awards:** 1996 Times-Picayune 5 beans; 1996 Restaurants and Institutions Ivy Award Winner; 1995 Mondavi Award for Culinary Excellence; 1993 James Beard Foundation Best Chef Southeast **Affiliations:** WCR, Chefs Collaborative **Books Published:** Crescent City Cooking: Unforgettable Recipes from Susan Spicer's New Orleans **Languages Spoken:** French

NOTABLE DISH(ES): Duck Sandwich with Cashew and Pepper Jelly; Pork Medallions with Prosciutto, Marsala and Fontina

FAST FACTS
Restaurant Recs: Divina Corozon for pupusas **Kitchen Tool(s):** Two-inch beveled edge spatula; blender **Interview Question:** What would your last boss say about you? **Flavor Combo(s):** Pineapple and kaffir lime leaf **Fave Cookbook(s):** Italy in Small Bites by Carol Field; Paula Wolfert's books **Chef to Cook for You:** Jean-Georges Vongerichten, because he has such a wide range **Culinary Travel:** China, because I think it must be completely different from anything I know

Joachim Splichal
Chef/Founder | Patina Restaurant Group

141 Grand Ave. Los Angeles, CA 90012

Restaurant E-mail: jsplichal@patinagroup.com

Phone: (213) 972-3331

RESTAURANT FACTS
Seats: 120 **Weeknight Covers:** 80–140 **Weekend Covers:** 160
Check Average (with Wine): $160 **Tasting Menu:** Yes $120/$150
Kitchen Staff: 15

CHEF FACTS
Cuisine: French California **Born:** 1954 **Began Career:** 1973 **Stages:**
France: Hotel Negresco **Work History:** France: Hotel Negresco,
L'Oasis, La Napoule, La Bonne Auberge **Protégée(s):** Octavio Bec-
erra, Tracy Des Jardins, David Meyers, Josiah Citrin, Walter Manske
Awards: 2008 James Beard Foundation Outstanding Restauranteur
Nominee; 1997 California Restaurant Writers Association Restau-
rateur of the Year; 1996 Central City Association and Los Angles Mayor Richard Riordan Treasure of
Los Angeles; 1995 James Beard Foundation Who's Who of Food & Beverage in America; 1991 James
Beard Foundation Best California Chef **Affiliations:** JBF, ICP, Relais & Chateaux-Relais Gourmand,
Who's Who in America, SOS, MOW, Children's Hospital, Bogart Cancer Foundation, Heal the Bay and
many more **Books Published:** Patina Cookbook Spuds: Truffles & Wild Gnocchi; Feeding Baby **Languages Spoken:** French, German, Italian, Spanish

NOTABLE DISH(ES): Venison Medallions with Persimmons; Wienerschnitzel of Artichoke with Roast
Rabbit Loin and Chive Vinaigrette

FAST FACTS
Restaurant Recs: Pie Burger for the pie burger **Kitchen Tool(s):** Tongs – because they are so versatile
Interview Question: How do you know that you are a good cook? I want to learn how they gauge their
own professional skills. **Flavor Combo(s):** I prefer Asian spice combinations **Fave Cookbook(s):** My
favorite cookbook is one that I wrote, called Feeding Baby, because it focuses on healthy, innovative
dishes specifically for children that are easy for parents to prepare. The inspiration was the birth of
my twin sons. **Chef to Cook for You:** Jacques Maximin because it would remind me of my youth. I
worked for him when I was a young kid and he was widely recognized worldwide as an extraordinary
chef! **Culinary Travel:** If I ever get a break from my busy schedule opening restaurants for Patina
Restaurant Group, I would love to travel to Italy, Turkey, Greece, and throughout Asia. It has been too
many years since I've visited these countries. I'd like to go again to expand my culinary horizons and
experience more of the great ethnic cooking in these parts of the world.

Jonathan St. Hilaire
Corporate Pastry Chef | Concentrics Restaurants

566 Dutch Valley Rd. Atlanta, GA 30324

Restaurant E-mail: jsthilaire@ctrxhs.com

Phone: (404) 961-7370

CHEF FACTS

Other Restaurants: Atlanta, GA: One Midtown kitchen, Two Urban Licks, Trois, Piebar, Murphy's, Lobby at Twelve; Winter Park, FL: Luma on Park **Cuisine:** Modern French-inspired desserts **Born:** 1974 **Began Career:** 1988 **Culinary School:** The French Culinary Institute, New York, NY **Grad Year:** 1998 **Stages:** New York, NY: wd~50, Alain Ducasse, DB Bistro Moderne, Washington Park **Work History:** New York, NY: Picholine, Payard's Patisserie, Eleven Madison Park, Bouley Bakery **Mentor(s):** My father, who taught me that working hard was the only way to produce exceptional results. He told me to never cut corners. Also Pierre Hermé, David Bouley and Jacques Torres. **Awards:** 2006 Atlanta Journal-Constitution 50 Best Desserts in Atlanta; 2002 Bon Appetit Best New American Chef in Atlanta; 2000 Southern Pastry Classic Gold Medal **Affiliations:** USPA

NOTABLE DISH(ES): Toffee Pudding with Poached Pear and Dulce de Leche Ice Cream

FAST FACTS

Restaurant Recs: Sotto Sotto for the most incredible, fluffy risotto and for the sweet and flavorful 10 year aged balsamic vinegar; Surin for fresh, limey Thai beef salad with a kick of spice; Taqueria del Sol for fried chicken tacos that are so addictive it's hard to stop chowing down on them **Kitchen Tool(s):** Pacojet is one tool that I turn to constantly to help me create new, innovative desserts. It is a machine that mixes and purees frozen foods, like fruit, without thawing them, to create a fluffy, airy, perfectly textured mousse. **Interview Question:** Why do you want to get into this business of cooking? I want to hear something from them that comes from their heart and also shows that they realistically know what they are getting into. **Flavor Combo(s):** Vanilla and lemon verbena **Fave Cookbook(s):** Paco Torreblanca by Paco Torreblanca **Chef to Cook for You:** David Bouley **Culinary Travel:** Spain

Caryn Stabinsky
Pastry Chef

New York, NY

Restaurant E-mail: caryn@dellmail.com

Phone: (212) 767-0555

CHEF FACTS
Cuisine: Desserts **Born:** 1970 **Began Career:** 2002 **Culinary School:** Peter Kumps, New York, NY **Grad Year:** 2003 **Stages:** New York, NY: Oceana **Work History:** New York, NY: Oceana, wd~50, Jefferson, Ureña, Michael's **Mentor(s):** David Carmichael **Awards:** 2006 Time Out NY Critics Pick

FAST FACTS
Restaurant Recs: Little Frankie's – for prosciutto cotto with mozzarella, and the parmesan and four egg pizza **Kitchen Tool(s):** Vita-Prep **Interview Question:** What do you read in your free time? **Flavor Combo(s):** Bananas and fennel; poppy seed, raspberry and smoke **Fave Cookbook(s):** The Essential Cuisine by Michel Bras **Chef to Cook for You:** Michel Bras – his food interests me and is incredibly creative **Culinary Travel:** I would go back to Spain. I love Spanish food and everything that is going on over there.

Scott Staples
Chef/Owner | Restaurant Zoë

2137 2nd Ave. Seattle, WA 98121

Restaurant E-mail: restaurantzoe@msn.com

Phone: (206) 256-2060

RESTAURANT FACTS
Seats: 80–92 **Weeknight Covers:** 90 **Weekend Covers:** 160 **Check Average (with Wine):** $50 **Tasting Menu:** No **Kitchen Staff:** 12

CHEF FACTS
Other Restaurants: Quinn's **Cuisine:** Seasonal comfort food **Born:** 1963 **Began Career:** 1977 **Stages:** Milan, Italy: Ristorante Gualtiero Marchesi **Work History:** Steamboat Springs, CO: Mattie Silks; Telluride, CO: La Marmotte; Boston, MA: 29 Newbury, Rowes Wharf Restaurant; Seattle, WA: Palm Court **Mentor(s):** Dixon Staples, Gualtiero Marchesi **Awards:** 2003 StarChefs.com Rising Star Chef Seattle

NOTABLE DISH(ES): Tempura Squash Blossom; House-Smoked Hanger Steak

FAST FACTS

Restaurant Recs: La Medusa in Columbia City **Kitchen Tool(s):** My favorite peeler; Japanese mandolin **Interview Question:** Have you participated in anything highly competitive? How did you do? **Flavor Combo(s):** Chocolate and Armagnac **Fave Cookbook(s):** Thomas Keller's Bouchon **Chef to Cook for You:** Daddy Bruce from Denver's best BBQ place **Culinary Travel:** India for the seasonings, spices, bread and culture

Sarah Stegner
Chef | Prairie Grass Cafe

601 Skokie Blvd. Northbrook, IL 60062

Restaurant E-mail: sarah@prairiegrasscafe.com

Phone: (847) 205-4433 and (847) 205-4435

RESTAURANT FACTS
Seats: 150 **Weeknight Covers:** 150 **Weekend Covers:** 300 **Check Average (with Wine):** $36 **Kitchen Staff:** 4–6

CHEF FACTS
Cuisine: Contemporary French cuisine and American food **Began Career:** 1984 **Culinary School:** Dumas Pere, Glencoe, IL **Grad Year:** 1984 **Stages:** France: Pierre Orsi **Work History:** Chicago, IL: The Ritz-Carlton **Mentor(s):** Fernand Gutierrez **Awards:** 1998 James Beard Foundation Best Chef of the Midwest; 1994 James Beard Foundation Rising Star Chef of the Year **Affiliations:** Green City Market, LDE

NOTABLE DISH(ES): Ancho Marinated Skirt Steak over Mushroom Ragout with Caramelized Onion; Crispy Roasted Chicken with Broccoli Rapini and Roasted Glazed Squash

FAST FACTS

Restaurant Recs: Al's Deli for their tomato soup served on Saturday and their pork loin sandwich **Kitchen Tool(s):** Sausage stuffing machine. We sell so much homemade sausage, and the process is very intense – without the machine it would be impossible to do. **Interview Question:** Why did you leave your last job? **Flavor Combo(s):** Tomato and basil **Fave Cookbook(s):** The Naked Chef by Jamie Oliver **Chef to Cook for You:** Jamie Oliver. I want to be invited to one of his parties. The food looks so good and they always look like they are having fun. **Culinary Travel:** Ireland's Ballymaloe – I always wanted to experience it. Also, Kerala India. I would like to learn how to cook some of the foods from the south of India.

Todd Stein
Executive Chef | David Burke Las Vegas

3355 Las Vegas Blvd. South Las Vegas, NV 89101

Restaurant E-mail: davidburkelasvegas@ebrand.com

Phone: (702) 414-7111

RESTAURANT FACTS

Seats: 186 **Weeknight Covers:** 250+ **Weekend Covers:** 300+ **Check Average (with Wine):** $92 **Tasting Menu:** No **Kitchen Staff:** 10

CHEF FACTS

Cuisine: French and Italian with local ingredients **Born:** 1971 **Began Career:** 1996 **Culinary School:** Kendall College, Chicago, IL **Grad Year:** 1996 **Stages:** Chicago, IL: Gordon Restaurant; New York, NY: Le Bernardin **Work History:** France: Moulin de la Vierge; Chicago, IL: MK, Spruce, Hudson Club; Cleveland, OH: Piccolo Mondo, Sans Souci, Vivo; Minneapolis, MN: Bank **Mentor(s):** Michael Kornick, Keith Korn **Protégée(s):** David Connelly, Matt Sieger **Awards:** 2005 StarChefs.com Rising Star Chef Chicago; 2000 Restaurant Hospitality Rising Star **Affiliations:** Chefs Collaborative **Languages Spoken:** Some Spanish, some French

NOTABLE DISH(ES): Grilled Baby Octopus Frisée, Saffron Aïoli; Cannelloni of Brandade, Piquillo Pepper Purée, Black Olives

FAST FACTS

Restaurant Recs: Chicago, IL: Chicago Food Corp for really good and cheap food; Hot Doug's for the best Polish sausage **Kitchen Tool(s):** My knives, including a Glestain 11-inch Japanese knife **Interview Question:** Have you ever played team sports? It gives me an idea if the person knows what it is like to be a part of a team, and what it takes. **Flavor Combo(s):** Peanut butter and jelly; tomatoes and basil; lobster and beets; caramel and salt **Fave Cookbook(s):** The French Laundry Cookbook by Thomas Keller; East of Paris by David Bouley; White Heat by Marco Pierre White **Chef to Cook for You:** Alain Ducasse – he's the king. I think he is the reason why people from my generation cook. It would be an honor. **Culinary Travel:** Spain – what's going on in Spain right now is really amazing, even beyond Ferran. Also the Middle East – it's something interesting and completely different to see.

Adam Stevenson
Executive Chef | Earth & Ocean

1112 Fourth Ave. Seattle, WA 98101

Restaurant E-mail: adam.stevenson@whotels.com

Phone: (206) 264-6162

RESTAURANT FACTS
Seats: 96 **Weeknight Covers:** 40-60 **Weekend Covers:** 60-85 **Check Average (w/o Wine):** $42 **Tasting Menu:** Yes $70/$90 **Kitchen Staff:** 6-8

CHEF FACTS
Cuisine: Redefined American with an emphasis on artisan products **Born:** 1971 **Began Career:** 1989 **Culinary School:** Western Culinary Institute, Portland, OR **Grad Year:** 1991 **Stages:** New York, NY: Daniel, Public, Café Boulud **Work History:** Tacoma, WA: The Cliff House; Seattle, WA: Tullio's at The Vintage Park Hotel, The Hunt Club at the Sorrento Hotel, W Seattle **Mentor(s):** Walter Pisano **Affiliations:** Slow Food, Chefs Collaborative

FAST FACTS
Restaurant Recs: Malay Satay Hut for the noodle soups **Kitchen Tool(s):** The Vita-Prep – it makes things velvety and smooth **Interview Question:** Where do you like to eat? If I gave you $500 to eat in New York where would you go? **Flavor Combo(s):** Lavender and lamb **Fave Cookbook(s):** The Splendid Table: Recipes from Emilia-Romagna **Chef to Cook for You:** Thomas Keller – I think he is a great chef and I have heard that he is a very straightforward, approachable guy **Culinary Travel:** London, so that I could visit Fergus Henderson's restaurant (St. John)

Craig Stoll
Chef | Delfina

3621 18th St. San Francisco, CA 94110

Restaurant E-mail: craig@delfinasf.com

Phone: (415) 552-4055

RESTAURANT FACTS
Seats: 70 **Weeknight Covers:** 175 **Weekend Covers:** 220 **Check Average (with Wine):** $44 **Tasting Menu:** No **Kitchen Staff:** 6

CHEF FACTS
Other Restaurants: Pizzeria Delfina **Cuisine:** Italian **Born:** 1965 **Began Career:** 1980 **Culinary School:** The Culinary Institute of America, Hyde Park, NY **Grad Year:** 1985 **Stages:** Italy: Da'Delfina Enoteca **Work History:** San Francisco, CA: Timo's, Campton Place, Postrio **Mentor(s):** Carlo Ciono, Carlo Belle **Awards:** 2008 James Beard Foundation Best Chef Pacific; 2005 James Beard Foundation Best Chef California; 2004 Food & Wine Best New Chef; 2000 San Francisco Magazine Rising Star Chef; 2000 San Francisco Chronicle Rising Star Chef **Affiliations:** We work with tons of charities **Languages Spoken:** Italian

NOTABLE DISH(ES): Roasted Liberty Duck with House-Made Sauerkraut and Kumquats

FAST FACTS
Restaurant Recs: Taco trucks; Saigon Sandwich Shop for Vietnamese sandwiches **Kitchen Tool(s):** Mortar and pestle **Interview Question:** What's your favorite cookbook? What kitchen did you learn the most in? What do you like to eat? Tell me about your favorite dish. **Flavor Combo(s):** Olive oil and salt **Fave Cookbook(s):** The Food of Italy by Waverly Root **Chef to Cook for You:** Daniel Patterson (of Coi) – anytime. His food is so different from what we cook everyday but still grounded in the same principle. **Culinary Travel:** I love Spain. It is amazing and I would go back anytime, but I've never been to Southeast Asia, and that's always been on my list.

Ethan Stowell
Chef | Union

1400 First Ave. Seattle, WA 98101

Restaurant E-mail: ethan@unionseattle.com

Phone: (206) 838-8000

RESTAURANT FACTS
Seats: 60-80 **Weeknight Covers:** 80 **Weekend Covers:** 120 **Check Average (with Wine):** $55-$60 **Tasting Menu:** No **Kitchen Staff:** 5

CHEF FACTS
Other Restaurants: Tavolata, How to a Cook a Wolf **Cuisine:** New American **Born:** 1974 **Began Career:** 1996 **Work History:** Seattle, WA: The Ruins, Painted Table; Atlanta, GA: Seeger's **Mentor(s):** Philip Mihalski, Joe McDonnald **Awards:** 2005 Seattle P.I. 5 to Watch; 2005 Eat, Shop Seattle Sexiest Chef; 2005 James Beard Foundation Rising Star; 2005, 2006 Seattle Magazine The 10 Very Best Restaurants **Affiliations:** James Beard Foundation, we also do a lot of charity events

FAST FACTS
Restaurant Recs: Carniceria el Paisano - the pork tamales are amazing **Kitchen Tool(s):** All-Clad vegetable pans – they have a bowl shape and are outstanding for cooking vegetables and pasta **Interview Question:** Have you heard about the work load here? **Flavor Combo(s):** Olive oil and lemon juice **Fave Cookbook(s):** Books by Antonio Carluccio; The River Café Cookbook by Rose Gray and Ruth Rogers;Oliveto by Paul Bertolli **Chef to Cook for You:** Michael Roux Jr. from La Gavroche. His style of food is healthy with clean flavors. He's and awesome guy and an awesome chef. **Culinary Travel:** Any region of Northern Italy – I love the style of food

S

Alessandro Stratta
Executive Chef | Alex

3131 Las Vegas Blvd.Las Vegas, NV 89109

Restaurant E-mail: alex.stratta@wynnlasvegas.com

Phone: (702) 770-3301

RESTAURANT FACTS
Seats: 120 **Weeknight Covers:** 100–120 **Weekend Covers:** 120–150 **Check Average (with Wine):** $380 **Tasting Menu:** Yes $145/$195/$325 with wine

CHEF FACTS
Other Restaurants: Corsa Cucina & Bar **Cuisine:** Contemporary French **Born:** 1964 **Began Career:** 1985 **Culinary School:** California Culinary Academy, San Francisco, CA **Grad Year:** 1984 **Work History:** San Francisco, CA: Stanford Court Hotel; Beverly Hills, CA: Beverly Hills Hotel; France: Le Louis XV; New York, NY: Le Cirque; Scottsdale, AZ: Mary Elaine's; Las Vegas, NV: Renoir **Mentor(s):** Alain Ducasse, Daniel Boulud, Sotha Khun, Franck Cerrutti **Protégée(s):** Bradford Thompson, Dan Rossi, Jennifer Witte **Awards:** 2008 Michelin 2 stars; 2008, 2007, 2006 AAA Five Diamond Award; 2008, 2007, 2006 Mobil 5 atars; 2006 Taste of Vegas Best of the Best; 2006 Cigar Aficionado Best Fine Dining Experience in Las Vegas; 2006 Gayot Guide Top 40 Restaurants in the USA; 2005 Esquire Magazine Best New Restaurant in America; 1998 James Beard Foundation Best Chef Southwest; 1992 James Beard Foundation Best Hotel Chef **Languages Spoken:** French, Spanish, Italian

NOTABLE DISH(ES): Spiced Kanpachi Tartare with Chilled Cucumber, Cantaloupe Gelée and Osetra Caviar; Butter Braised Main Lobster with Sweet Corn Custard, Chanterelles and Tomato Confit

FAST FACTS
Restaurant Recs: TC Rib shack for the ribs and coleslaw; Pho Saigon 8 for the noodle dishes; Lotus of Siam for anything hot **Kitchen Tool(s):** Motivated and passionate cooks **Interview Question:** Why do you want to be a chef? **Flavor Combo(s):** Sweet and spicy **Fave Cookbook(s):** Anything by Coleman Andrews or Jeffery Steingarten **Chef to Cook for You:** Chef Masa of Masa in New York – I've eaten at his restaurant before and it was the best meal I ever had **Culinary Travel:** I would go to Japan to be introduced to a different culture and cuisine. I'm very interested in going there.

Alex Stupak
Pastry Chef | wd~50

50 Clinton St New York, NY 10002-2401

Restaurant E-mail: edufresne@earthlink.net

Phone: (212) 477-2900

RESTAURANT FACTS
Seats: 65–72 **Weeknight Covers:** 80 **Weekend Covers:** 120 **Check Average (with Wine):** $110 **Tasting Menu:** Yes $125/$200 with wine **Kitchen Staff:** 1–2

CHEF FACTS
Cuisine: Creative desserts **Born:** 1980 **Began Career:** 2000 **Culinary School:** The Culinary Institute of America, Hyde Park, NY **Grad Year:** 2000 **Work History:** Boston, MA: The Federalist, Clio; Chicago, IL: Alinea, Tru **Mentor(s):** Ken Oringer, Grant Achatz, Wylie Dufresne **Awards:** 2008 New York Times 3 stars; 2008 Iron Chef Victory for the Chocolate Challenge; 2005 StarChefs.com Rising Star Pastry Chef Chicago; 2003 Boston Magazine Best Pastry Chef

NOTABLE DISH(ES): Coconut Mousse with Cashew, Cucumber and Coriander; Fried Butterscotch Pudding, Mango, Taro and Smoked Macadamia

FAST FACTS
Restaurant Recs: I just moved to New York, so I'm still discovering places **Kitchen Tool(s):** The freezer – it has the widest range of application; laboratory-grade homogenizer - it's like a hand blender on steroids **Interview Question:** What do you ultimately want to do with your life and why will working with me help you get there? **Flavor Combo(s):** Juniper, quince, and lime **Fave Cookbook(s):** Los Postres de el Bulli by Albert Adriá **Chef to Cook for You:** Jacques Pépin - he's a great technician and everything he makes comes with a lesson or a story **Culinary Travel:** I'd like to return to Mexico. The cuisine and its anthropology fascinate me.

Kristine Subido
Executive Chef | Wave Restaurant

644 N Lakeshore Dr. Chicago, IL 60611

Restaurant E-mail: kristin.subido@whotels.com

Phone: (312) 255-4460

RESTAURANT FACTS
Seats: 110–160 **Weeknight Covers:** 80–100 **Weekend Covers:** 150
Check Average (with Wine): $42 **Check Average (w/o Wine):** $35
Tasting Menu: Yes $55, $65, $75 **Kitchen Staff:** 5

CHEF FACTS
Cuisine: Mediterranean **Born:** 1974 **Began Career:** 1992 **Culinary
School:** Kendall College, Evanston, Il **Grad Year:** 1994 **Stages:**
France: Le Sud Lyon, Paul Bocuse **Work History:** Chicago, IL: Mango
Restaurant, Spiaggia; France: Le Sud Lyon **Mentor(s):** Julia Child,
Alice Waters **Awards:** 2008 StarChefs.com Rising Star Hotel Chef
Award Chicago **Affiliations:** Step It Up, WCR **Languages Spoken:**
Tagalog, Spanish

NOTABLE DISH(ES): Ahi Tuna Crudo, Citrus and Pear Salad, Cracked Fennel Seed Vinaigrette;
Roasted American Lamb with Chickpea Puree and Merguez Cassoulet

FAST FACTS
Restaurant Recs: 777 Vietnamese Noodle House for really good pho **Kitchen Tool(s):** Vita-Prep – because it makes such silky soups and purees **Interview Question:** What is your favorite cuisine? What
is your favorite recipe to prepare? Their answers gives me an idea about their taste and what flavors
interest them. **Flavor Combo(s):** Fruit and fish, fruit and meat. I use spices but I'm not heavy handed.
Fave Cookbook(s): The French Laundry Cookbook by Thomas Keller **Chef to Cook for You:** Pierre
Gagnaire. I'm a really big fan, his food is absolutely beautiful and his flavor combinations are incredible. Watching him cook is like watching an artist paint. **Culinary Travel:** I would go to South Thailand
and Vietnam. I just came back from the Philippines where I got to visit the different regions and try
the food. Since I grew up here, I didn't get to taste that food except through my mom.

Chuck Subra
Executive Chef | La Côte Brasserie

700 Tchoupitoulas St. New Orleans, LA 70130

Restaurant E-mail: chuck.subra@marriot.com

Phone: (504) 613-2364

RESTAURANT FACTS
Seats: 120-160 **Weeknight Covers:** 50-60 **Weekend Covers:** 100-120 **Check Average (with Wine):** $50-$60 **Tasting Menu:** Yes $65/$90 **Kitchen Staff:** 4-6

CHEF FACTS
Cuisine: Southern Louisiana with French influence **Born:** 1971 **Began Career:** 1990 **Culinary School:** Delgado Community College, New Orleans, LA **Grad Year:** 1995 **Work History:** New Orleans, LA: Windsor Court Grill Room, René Bistrot **Mentor(s):** Grandmother, René Bajeux **Protégée(s):** Brian Landry, Shane McBride **Awards:** 2005 Louisiana Cooking Chefs to Watch; 2005 Marriott Corporation National Award of Culinary Excellence; 2004 Jamie Shannon Award **Affiliations:** March of Dimes, Childrens Hospital, Kidney Foundation, a lot of local charities

FAST FACTS
Restaurant Recs: Rio Mar for ceviche with a chilled bottle of wine **Kitchen Tool(s):** Microplane; sauce spoon **Interview Question:** What experience do you have? Are you willing to learn? **Flavor Combo(s):** I like sweet and tangy with a little heat and vinegar **Fave Cookbook(s):** Larousse Gastronomique by Prosper Montagne **Chef to Cook for You:** Gordon Ramsay – not only is he a great culinarian, but he is also a great businessman. He has everything down pat. **Culinary Travel:** France – I worked under a French master chef for eight years and I would just like to go over there and work and learn

Yosuke Suga
Executive Chef | L'Atelier de Joël Robuchon

57 East 57th St. New York, NY 10022

Restaurant E-mail: yosuke.suga@fourseasons.com

Phone: (212) 350-6658

RESTAURANT FACTS
Seats: 50 **Weeknight Covers:** 100 **Weekend Covers:** 110–120
Check Average (w/o Wine): $100 **Tasting Menu:** Yes $190 **Kitchen Staff:** 12

CHEF FACTS
Cuisine: Modern French **Born:** 1976 **Began Career:** 1994 **Work History:** Japan: Chex Kobe; every opening of L'Atelier de Joël Robuchon around the world (Vegas, Tokyo, and beyond) **Mentor(s):** Joël Robuchon **Awards:** 2007 StarChefs.com Rising Star Chef New York **Affiliations:** James Beard Foundation, Citymeals-on-Wheels, and various charity events. **Languages Spoken:** French, Japanese

NOTABLE DISH(ES): Maine Lobster, White Asparagus Cream and Truffle Dressing; Pan Sautéed Amadai with Lily Bulb and Yuzu-Citrus Broth

FAST FACTS
Restaurant Recs: I like Daniel, and I want to go to Blue Hill at Stone Barns. I also like Casa Mono – I want to have a restaurant like that one day – just a fun Spanish tapas place for my friends. **Kitchen Tool(s):** My own hands **Interview Question:** What is your favorite restaurant? Why do you want to work with me? **Flavor Combo(s):** I like light, bright things. Of course I use cream, and I like it, but for meat, for example, I don't use too much anymore. I like herb flavors like garlic, thyme and rosemary for meat. We prepare our Kobe in a simple jus – an essence with garlic, thyme and rosemary – nothing else. I like salads to have a very herbaceous flavor as well. **Fave Cookbook(s):** Zagat NYC Restaurant guide or L'Art de Joël Robuchon by Joël Robuchon **Chef to Cook for You:** Escoffier. I would like to watch him cook to see how he seasoned and prepared his food. **Culinary Travel:** I think France. I haven't been there for three or four years and I want to be reminded of everything that's great there. I forget about the products! The flavor of vegetables and meat are so wonderful, especially in the countryside.

Noriyuki Sugie
Executive Chef | Name TBA

1080 Haight Street San Francisco, CA 94117

Restaurant E-mail: info@chefnori.com

RESTAURANT FACTS
Seats: 40 **Kitchen Staff:** 1–2

CHEF FACTS
Cuisine: Contemporary French **Born:** 1971 **Began Career:** 1990 **Culinary School:** Tsuji Culinary School, Japan **Grad Year:** 1989 **Stages:** France: L'Aubergade, Le Moulin de Martorey, Hostellerie de Vieux **Work History:** Chicago, IL: Charlie Trotter's; Australia: Restaurant VII, Tetsuya; New York, NY: Asiate **Mentor(s):** Michele Trama, Charlie Trotter, Tetsuya Watuda **Protégée(s):** Joel Hough **Awards:** 2006 New York Magazine Top 101 Restaurants; 2005 StarChefs.com Rising Star Chef New York; 2005 Time Out Top 25 Dishes **Languages Spoken:** Japanese

NOTABLE DISH(ES): Scallop Tartare with Fennel Cream and Crushed Rice Cracker; Caesar Salad Soup with Bacon Foam

FAST FACTS
Restaurant Recs: Sushi Seki for omakase **Kitchen Tool(s):** Masanobu knife – because it holds its edge and has a good feel **Interview Question:** Why do you want to work here? **Flavor Combo(s):** I like raw fish with olive oil and salt **Fave Cookbook(s):** Food Fantasy of the Hotel de Mikuni by Mikuni Kiyomi **Chef to Cook for You:** Masa Takayama – he is a mentor and I really like to sit in front of him and watch him make his food **Culinary Travel:** Turkey – I heard it's beautiful. Great architecture, food and spices. Brazil has a growing Japanese community. Its mix of culture is interesting to me.

John Suley
Chef/Owner | Cafe Joley

187 SE Mizner Blvd. Boca Raton, FL 33432

Restaurant E-mail: john@grandcrew.us

Phone: (561) 361-4224

RESTAURANT FACTS
Seats: 75 **Weeknight Covers:** 70 **Weekend Covers:** 125 **Check Average (with Wine):** $65 **Check Average (w/o Wine):** $45 **Tasting Menu:** No **Kitchen Staff:** 2

CHEF FACTS
Other Restaurants: South Beach, FL: Joley **Cuisine:** American with European influences **Born:** 1974 **Began Career:** 1994 **Culinary School:** Culinary Institute of America, Hyde Park, New York **Grad Year:** 1995 **Stages:** France: Pierre Gagnaire; England: Gordon Ramsay **Work History:** New York, NY: Daniel, Peacock Alley, Lespinasse; France: Pierre Gagnaire; England: Gordon Ramsay; Miami, FL: The Palms Hotel **Mentor(s):** Daniel Boulud - he is very business-minded and very talented as well. He learned how to grow his corporation. Laurent Gras - he is very disciplined and technical in his processes of food and cooking **Affiliations:** March of Dimes

NOTABLE DISH(ES): Kataifi-Wrapped Shrimp with Sweet Potato Purée and Collard Greens with a Chorizo Butter Sauce

FAST FACTS
Restaurant Recs: Matsuri in South Miami. It's kind-of a sushi place, sort of freestyle. **Kitchen Tool(s):** A Gray Kunz spoon - it holds the perfect amount of sauce, and I can't work properly without it. **Interview Question:** I like to ask them what book they are currently reading - it doesn't' have to be a cookbook. It gives you an idea of their state of mind - though it makes people think I'm crazy when I ask this. **Flavor Combo(s):** Chorizo, shellfish, and cilantro **Fave Cookbook(s):** Jean-Louis Palladin's Cooking with the Seasons, and Elements of Taste by Gray Kunz **Chef to Cook for You:** Jean-Louis Palladin, because he was so creative and was one of the true culinary geniuses **Culinary Travel:** Japan – to understand their culture and cuisine

Jessica Sullivan
Pastry Chef | Boulevard

1 Mission St. San Francisco, CA 94105

Restaurant E-mail: info@boulevardrestaurant.com

Phone: (415) 543-6084

RESTAURANT FACTS
Seats: 175 **Weekend Covers:** 290+ **Check Average (with Wine):** $90 **Tasting Menu:** No **Kitchen Staff:** 2–3

CHEF FACTS
Cuisine: American-style pastry with French influence **Born:** 1975 **Began Career:** 2005 **Culinary School:** California Culinary Academy, San Francisco, CA **Grad Year:** 2005 **Stages:** San Francisco, CA: Boulevard **Work History:** Portland, OR: Fratelli **Mentor(s):** Nancy Oakes, Paul Klitsie **Affiliations:** We are co-hosts of Meals-on-Wheels of San Francisco. We support a number of charities throughout the year, including Project Open Hand of San Francisco and Girls Inc. of Oakland.

NOTABLE DISH(ES): Puff Pastry with Caramelized Banana, Bananas Foster, Chocolate, and Vanilla Ice Cream; Trifle with Lychee Foam, Dried Mango Powder, Lady Fingers, Mango Mousse, Greek Yogurt Panna Cotta, Kiwi Shaved Ice, Diced Kiwi

FAST FACTS
Restaurant Recs: La Taqueria for tacos; Scala's **Kitchen Tool(s):** Candy thermometer, Silpats **Interview Question:** Do you enjoy working with other people? Can you have fun? **Flavor Combo(s):** Plums with lavender; caramel and sea salt; chocolate and smoke; goat cheese with strawberries **Fave Cookbook(s):** Wild Sweets by Dominique and Cindy Duby **Chef to Cook for You:** Rose Gray and Ruth Rogers of River City Cafe **Culinary Travel:** Italy and Spain – because of the innovation taking place in both counties

John Sundstrom
Executive Chef

Johnathan Sundstrom
Executive Chef | Lark

926 12th Ave. Seattle, WA 98122

Restaurant E-mail: johnathan@larkseattle.com

Phone: (206) 323-5275

RESTAURANT FACTS
Seats: 50 **Weeknight Covers:** 90 **Weekend Covers:** 120 **Check Average (with Wine):** $60–$65 **Tasting Menu:** No **Kitchen Staff:** 6

CHEF FACTS
Other Restaurants: Licorous **Cuisine:** Adventurous Northwestern **Born:** 1967 **Began Career:** 1987 **Culinary School:** The New England Culinary Institute, Montpelier, VT **Grad Year:** 1989 **Stages:** New York: Jean-Georges, Aureole, Daniel, Cafe Boulud, Verbena; San Francisco, CA: Gary Danko, Jardiniere **Work History:** Laguna Niguel, CA: Ritz-Carlton Laguna Niguel, Club XIX at the Lodge at Pebble Beach; Deer Valley, UT: The Stein Ericksen Lodge; Seattle, WA: Earth & Ocean, Raison d'être Café, Café Sport, Campagne, Dahlia Lounge, Carmelita, Lark **Mentor(s):** Tom Douglas and Mark Benet **Awards:** 2007 James Beard Foundation Best Chef Northwest; 2003 StarChefs.com Rising Star Chef Seattle; 2001 Food & Wine Best New Chef **Affiliations:** Chefs Collaborative, James Beard Foundation, Slow Food

NOTABLE DISH(ES): Kauai Saifun Shrimp; Dungeness Crab and Corn Bisque

FAST FACTS
Restaurant Recs: La Carta de Oaxcaca for the braised lamb with guajillo chiles **Kitchen Tool(s):** Thermomix **Interview Question:** Tell me about the best meal you've had in the last year and what made it so special **Flavor Combo(s):** Lately I have been using this great Welsh salt that comes mixed with Tahitian vanilla bean. I like to use it on foie gras and with poached rhubarb. **Fave Cookbook(s):** Cooking by Hand by Paul Bertolli totally embodies our ideals at Lark; Shunju by Takashi Sugimoto – I really want to do a dinner in the woods like their bamboo feast but with porcinis or morels **Chef to Cook for You:** Adoni Luis Aduriz of Mugaritz. He combines the best of all approaches. I love that he is so innovative and can be so futuristic and scientific while at the same time maintaining a close relationship with the land and with local ingredients. **Culinary Travel:** Right now I'm thinking about South America, especially Chile, Peru and Argentina. These are places that are a little farther away and a little less spoiled.

Anthony Susi
Chef/Owner | Sage

69 Prince St. Boston, MA 02113

Restaurant E-mail: mail@sageboston.com

Phone: (617) 248-8814

RESTAURANT FACTS
Seats: 48 **Weeknight Covers:** 50 **Weekend Covers:** 100 **Check Average (with Wine):** $55 **Tasting Menu:** Yes $65/$90 **Kitchen Staff:** 6

CHEF FACTS
Cuisine: Modern Italian **Born:** 1969 **Began Career:** 1989–1990 **Stages:** Italy: Il Rigoletto **Work History:** Boston, MA: Olives, Restaurant Zinc, Davide; San Francisco, CA: Grande Café, Campton Place **Mentor(s):** Todd English **Awards:** 2003 StarChefs.com Rising Star Chef Boston; 2002 Gourmet Magazine Top 50 Chefs **Languages Spoken:** Italian

NOTABLE DISH(ES): Lobster Tortelloni with Braised Mushrooms and Ginger Crema; Potato Gnocchi in Horseradish Cream and Bolognese

FAST FACTS
Restaurant Recs: Lineage for striped bass **Kitchen Tool(s):** Global plating tongs **Interview Question:** What do you have to offer? **Fave Cookbook(s):** Jasper White's Cooking from New England: More Than 300 Traditional Contemporary Recipes by Jasper White **Chef to Cook for You:** The best meal I ever had was at Can Fabes outside of Barcelona. I would love to have the chef, Santi Santamaria, make me another meal. **Culinary Travel:** France or Italy – I've been before and I always enjoy myself

Allen Susser
Chef/Owner | Chef Allen's

19088 NE 29th Ave. Aventura, FL 33180

Restaurant E-mail: chef@chefallens.com

Phone: (305) 935-2900

RESTAURANT FACTS
Seats: 85–90 **Weeknight Covers:** 75–80 **Weekend Covers:** 150 **Check Average (with Wine):** $85 **Tasting Menu:** Yes $75/$125 with wine **Kitchen Staff:** 5–6

CHEF FACTS
Cuisine: New World cuisine **Born:** 1956 **Began Career:** 1976 **Culinary School:** New York City Technical College, Restaurant Management School, New York, NY; Florida International University, Miami, FL; Le Cordon Bleu, France **Grad Year:** 1976, 1978, 1980 **Stages:** New York, NY: Le Cirque **Work History:** France: Le Bristol Hotel; New York, NY: Le Cirque; Miami, FL: Turnberry Resort **Mentor(s):** Alain Sailhac **Protégée(s):** Tim Andriola, Tomas Rodriguez, Ryan d'Alessandro **Awards:** 2005 AAHS International Star Diamond Award; 1993-2002 DiRona Top 300 in American Award; 1989-2002 Wine Spectator Award of Excellence; 1992-2002 AAA 4-Diamond Award; 2001 FIU Torch Award for Distinguished Alumn; 2001 Consileur Culinaire Chaine des Rôtisseurs; 2000 Club de Sabeur Inductee; 1997 & 1999 Gourmet Magazine Top Table Award; 1996 South Florida Magazine Best Chef; 1994 Johnson & Wales University Honorary Doctorate Degree Recipient; 1994 James Beard Foundation Best Chef Southeast; 1993 Nation's Restaurant News Hall of Fame Inductee; 1992 New York City Technical College Alumnus of the Year; 1991 Food & Wine Magazine Best New Chef; 1989 James Beard Foundation Rising Star in American Cuisine **Affiliations:** JBF, AIWF, IACP, RCA, SOS **Books Published:** New World Cuisine and Cookery; The Great Citrus Book ; The Great Mango Book **Languages Spoken:** French, some Spanish

NOTABLE DISH(ES): Watermelon and Lychee Salad; Adobo Filet Mignon

FAST FACTS
Restaurant Recs: LC's Roti for curry conk roti, ginger beer and hot mango chutney **Kitchen Tool(s):** Mango splitter **Interview Question:** Why do you want to cook? When did you start cooking? I'm looking for passion, not technical answers. **Flavor Combo(s):** Mangos and seafood, like a shrimp and mango curry; coconut milk and fish; chilies in ceviche **Fave Cookbook(s):** Complete Book of Caribbean Cooking by Elizabeth Lambert Ortiz; Jeremiah Tower's New American Classics by Jeremiah Tower; The Way to Cook by Julia Child **Chef to Cook for You:** Julia Child – her food was tremendous. She had a great palate and was a lot of fun. It would be a pleasure to eat with her. **Culinary Travel:** India – I'm a big spice guy and I love the variety and depth of the spices used in Indian cooking

Johan Svensson
Executive Chef | Aquavit

65 East 55th St. New York, NY 10022

Restaurant E-mail: info@aquavit.org

Phone: (212) 867-1700

RESTAURANT FACTS
Seats: 55–137 **Weeknight Covers:** 100 **Weekend Covers:** 150
Check Average (w/o Wine): $95 **Tasting Menu:** Yes $115/$195
Kitchen Staff: 25

CHEF FACTS
Cuisine: Scandinavian **Born:** 1971 **Began Career:** 1990 **Culinary School:** Culinary Institute of Gothenburg, Sweden **Grad Year:** 1990 **Stages:** Sweden: Leijontornet; New York, NY: Aquavit **Work History:** New York, NY: Aquavit, Bond St., Thom, Town, Riingo; England: Nobu **Mentor(s):** Erlinda Rodriguez **Protégée(s):** Michael Garret **Affiliations:** James Beard Foundation, lots of charity events **Languages Spoken:** Swedish

NOTABLE DISH(ES): Cucumber and Melon Soup; Caesar Salad with Yuzu and Asian Greens

FAST FACTS
Restaurant Recs: Momofuku – for pork ramen **Kitchen Tool(s):** Skimmer; spider **Interview Question:** Do you know how to make an omelette? **Flavor Combo(s):** Asian flavors: sweet, sour and salty **Fave Cookbook(s):** Tetsuya by Tetsuya Wakuda **Chef to Cook for You:** James Beard – it would be interesting to go back and compare the styles and techniques he used to what we are doing today **Culinary Travel:** Japan – I am really interested in Asian cuisine because it is not just about the cooking, it has a deep culture and soul behind it

Shannon Swindle
Pastry Chef | Craft, Dallas

2440 Victory Park Ln. Dallas, TX 75219

Restaurant E-mail: sswindle@craftdallas.com

Phone: (214) 397-4111

RESTAURANT FACTS
Seats: 130 **Weeknight Covers:** 100 **Weekend Covers:** 200 **Check Average (with Wine):** $85 **Tasting Menu:** No **Kitchen Staff:** 2–3

CHEF FACTS
Cuisine: Ingredient-focused new American pastry **Born:** 1968 **Began Career:** 1994 **Stages:** New York, NY: Craft **Work History:** Dallas, TX: Abacus, Star Canyon, Mansion on Turtle Creek **Mentor(s):** Lisa Fox, Emmett Fox, Stephan Pyles, Kent Rathbun **Protégée(s):** Jill Bates **Awards:** 2007 StarChefs.com Rising Star Pastry Chef Dallas **Affiliations:** Toast of Life, Taste of the Nation

NOTABLE DISH(ES): Ellis Country Pecan Chocolate Tart with Cinnamon Ice Cream; Croissant with House-Churned Goat Butter and Apple Compote

FAST FACTS
Restaurant Recs: Thai Noodle+Rice for great duck soup; Dodies for the best gumbo ever **Kitchen Tool(s):** A sharp knife. We are not a particularly gadgety kitchen so a sharp knife has to come into play when other more high-tech tools might have been utilized. **Interview Question:** I ask a series of questions: How do you make ice cream? When following a recipe for a 10 inch-cake where there is no cooking time, when and how do you check the cake? Or, if a recipe calls for pecan pieces and we are out of them, what do you do? I want to see how they think and how flexible they are. **Flavor Combo(s):** I like caramel and salt. Chocolate, bananas and cinnamon also combine well. **Fave Cookbook(s):** Chez Panisse Menu Cookbook by Alice Waters **Chef to Cook for You:** Sharon Hage at York Street. She cooks my birthday dinner each year. Her focus on seasonal, local food, cared for simply, is my idea of perfection. **Culinary Travel:** Italy – because they produce such ingredient-focused dishes

James Syhabout
Chef de Cuisine | Manresa

320 Village Ln. Los Gatos, CA 95030

Restaurant E-mail: james@manresarestaurant.com

Phone: (408) 354-4330

RESTAURANT FACTS
Seats: 65 **Weeknight Covers:** 50 **Weekend Covers:** 70 **Tasting Menu:** Yes $145 **Kitchen Staff:** 8

CHEF FACTS
Cuisine: Modern American **Born:** 1979 **Began Career:** 1995 **Grad Year:** 1999 **Stages:** England: The Fat Duck; Spain: Mugaritz, el Bulli **Work History:** Los Gatos, CA: Manresa; Spain: el Bulli, Alkimia; San Francisco, CA: Coi, PlumpJack Café **Mentor(s):** My mother, David Kinch **Awards:** 2008 James Beard Foundation Rising Star Nominee; 2007 StarChefs.com Rising Star Chef San Francisco; 2007 San Francisco Chronicle Rising Star Chef; 2007 San Francisco Magazine Rising Star Chef

NOTABLE DISH(ES): Roasted Sweetbread with Mustard Chlorophyll; Tempered Foie with Dates, Sweet Vermouth and Hazelnuts

FAST FACTS
Restaurant Recs: The Taco Truck on 23rd Ave; Jai Yun in Chinatown; Jojo in the East Bay **Kitchen Tool(s):** Spoons – they are like an appendage of my hand **Interview Question:** We ask a prospective employee what cuisine they would focus on if they had their own restaurant. We also ask what their favorite restaurant is and what's the best dish they've ever had in their life. **Flavor Combo(s):** I love anise and licorice flavors mixed with acidic ingredients. And butter offsets spice well. **Fave Cookbook(s):** On Food and Cooking by Harold McGee; In Search of Perfection by Heston Blumenthal **Chef to Cook for You:** If it was my final meal it would have to be my mom **Culinary Travel:** I like to go to Japan because they have such a love for food. It's all so pure. They're obsessive about the quality of ingredients, they pay incredibly close attention to detail, and they're really delicate in their approach.

T

{ Tees - Tustin }

Jared Tees
Partnering Chef | Lüke

333 St. Charles Ave. New Orleans, LA 70130

Restaurant E-mail: jtees@lukeneworleans.com

Phone: (504) 378-2840

RESTAURANT FACTS
Seats: 114 **Weeknight Covers:** 170 **Weekend Covers:** 220 **Check Average (with Wine):** $40 **Check Average (w/o Wine):** $30 **Tasting Menu:** No **Kitchen Staff:** 12

CHEF FACTS
Other Restaurants: August, La Provence **Cuisine:** German, French Creole **Born:** 1971 **Began Career:** 1992 **Culinary School:** Delgado Culinary Institute, New Orleans, LA **Stages:** New Orleans, LA: Commander's Palace, Mr. B's Bistro, Bacco **Work History:** New Orleans, LA: Commander's Palace, Mr. B's Bistro, Bacco, Bourbon House **Mentor(s):** Jamie Shannon, Eman Loubier, Dickie Brennan **Protégée(s):** Matt Murphy **Awards:** 2003 Esquire Best New Restaurant **Affiliations:** LRA

FAST FACTS
Restaurant Recs: Clancy's for veal and sweetbreads **Kitchen Tool(s):** French meat fork, as I use it for everything **Interview Question:** What do you know about Louisiana cuisine? A potential employee needs to exhibit a desire and knowledge of the local cuisine. I see it as a building block. **Flavor Combo(s):** Things that are sweet and tart, like honey and cane vinegar **Fave Cookbook(s):** Mme. Begue and Her Recipes; The Picayune's Creole Cookbook by Antique American Books **Chef to Cook for You:** Alton Brown **Culinary Travel:** Germany

Maximo Tejada
Executive Chef | Rayuela

165 Allen St. New York, NY 10002

Restaurant E-mail: mtejada@rayuela.com

Phone: (212) 253-8840

RESTAURANT FACTS
Seats: 120-180 **Weeknight Covers:** 120 **Weekend Covers:** up to 300 **Check Average (with Wine):** $65-$100 **Tasting Menu:** Yes On Mondays **Kitchen Staff:** 5

CHEF FACTS
Other Restaurants: Macondo **Cuisine:** Freestyle Latino **Born:** 1962 **Began Career:** 1997 **Culinary School:** The French Culinary Institute, New York, NY **Grad Year:** 1996 **Work History:** New York, NY: Patria, Chicama, Pipa, Ola, Lucy's Latin Kitchen **Mentor(s):** Douglas Rodriguez **Languages Spoken:** Spanish

FAST FACTS
Restaurant Recs: La Tabla for anything spicy – it never fails **Kitchen Tool(s):** Peeler **Interview Question:** I ask a person what they have inside – what gets them upset, how they may behave around people they do not like, what makes them angry, etc. **Flavor Combo(s):** Mushrooms, truffles and rosemary **Fave Cookbook(s):** The French Laundry Cookbook by Thomas Keller **Chef to Cook for You:** José Andrés – I love his personality and his food, which I find light and to the point. He also has that new European energy that I love. **Culinary Travel:** Spain – in terms of cuisine, they are always moving forward and experimenting with new ideas and ways to impress their guests.

Bill Telepan
Chef/Owner | Telepan

72 W 69th St. New York, NY 10023

Restaurant E-mail: bill@telepan-ny.com

Phone: (212) 580-4300

RESTAURANT FACTS
Seats: 115 **Weeknight Covers:** 150 **Weekend Covers:** 250 **Check Average (with Wine):** $80 **Tasting Menu:** Yes $64/$74 **Kitchen Staff:** 7–9

CHEF FACTS
Cuisine: Seasonal new American **Born:** 1966 **Began Career:** 1983 **Culinary School:** The Culinary Institute of America, Hyde Park, NY **Grad Year:** 1987 **Stages:** France: Alain Chapel-Mionnay **Work History:** New York, NY: Le Bernardin, Le Cirque, Gotham Bar and Grill, Judson Grill; France: Alain Chapel-Mionnay **Mentor(s):** Alfred Portale, Alain Chapel **Protégée(s):** Mitch Sudock, Mark Slutzky-Hickory **Awards:** 2006 New York Times 2 stars **Affiliations:** City Harvest, City-Meals-on Wheels, Slow Food, James Beard House, Days of Taste, C-Cap, Wellness-in-the-Schools **Books Published:** Inspired by Ingredients **Languages Spoken:** Some Spanish, French

NOTABLE DISH(ES): Braised Wild Striped Bass with Leek Fondue and Vermouth

FAST FACTS
Restaurant Recs: Celeste, Daisy May's BBQ, Momofuku **Kitchen Tool(s):** Smoker **Interview Question:** Do you love doing this? It becomes a lifestyle, not just a job. **Flavor Combo(s):** I love the combination of salt, garlic and herbs like oregano, rosemary or thyme. They can make any meat, with time, taste great. **Fave Cookbook(s):** Chez Panisse Cookbook by Alice Waters; White Heat by Marco Pierre White **Chef to Cook for You:** Dead – Alain Chapel – I loved my time working with him but never got the chance to eat at the restaurant. Alive – Andrew Carmellini – one of my best meals ever was in his final week at Café Boulud. **Culinary Travel:** I haven't been to Spain yet, and would also love to travel to Hungary and the Czech Republic

Giuseppe Tentori
Executive Chef | Boka

1729 N. Halsted St. Chicago, IL 60614

Restaurant E-mail: kevin@bokagrp.com

Phone: (312) 337-6070

RESTAURANT FACTS
Seats: 90–130 **Weeknight Covers:** 120 **Weekend Covers:** 190–220
Check Average (with Wine): $80 **Tasting Menu:** Yes **Kitchen Staff:**
13

CHEF FACTS
Other Restaurants: Perennial **Cuisine:** Progressive American **Born:**
1972 **Began Career:** 1986 **Culinary School:** Antica Osteria la Rampi-
na in Milan, Italy **Grad Year:** 1986 **Work History:** Highland Park, IL:
Gabriel's; Salt Lake City, UT: Metropolitan; Chicago, IL: Charlie Trot-
ter's **Mentor(s):** Charlie Trotter **Awards:** 2008 StarChefs.com Rising
Star Chef Chicago; 2008 Food & Wine Best New Chefs **Affiliations:**
Common Thread, Make a Wish Foundation **Languages Spoken:** Italian, English and a little Spanish

NOTABLE DISH(ES): Japanese Hamachi with Grapefruit and Curry Sauce; Pork Belly with Tamarind
Sauce and Soba Cake

FAST FACTS
Restaurant Recs: Kuma Corner for the Metallica Burger **Kitchen Tool(s):** I like the Vita-Prep because
it blends so smoothly. I also want a Turbo Chef oven to cook things faster. **Flavor Combo(s):** I love
tuna with jalapeño jelly, apple, jicama and togarashi. I also love octopus with flageolet beans, barbecued eel, tomatillo sauce and pickled red onion. **Fave Cookbook(s):** I like Gourmet for Dummies –
Charlie Trotter put it together and it's fun and simple. I also like el Bulli 2003-2004. **Chef to Cook for
You:** Matthias Merges (of Charlie Trotter's) – we have been cooking together for 15 years, and he is
an amazing chef **Culinary Travel:** Japan, because of the respect that they have for the product. Here
in the US we're so spoiled that we have lost respect for ingredients. We've become disconnected from
the land. In Japan the way the food is given to you and the way you are welcomed is very unique and
respectful.

Executive Chef
Koji Terano

Koji Terano
Executive Chef | Sushi-Ko

2309 Wisconsin Ave. NW Washington, DC 20007

Restaurant E-mail: sushikoinc@aol.com

Phone: (202) 333-4187

RESTAURANT FACTS
Seats: 100 **Weeknight Covers:** 150 **Weekend Covers:** 220 **Check Average (w/o Wine):** $35 **Tasting Menu:** No **Kitchen Staff:** 7–9

CHEF FACTS
Cuisine: Japanese **Born:** 1975 **Began Career:** 1993 **Work History:** Kyoto, Japan: Gorohachi **Mentor(s):** Hideo Okuda **Awards:** 2003 StarChefs.com Rising Star Chef Washington, DC **Languages Spoken:** Japanese

NOTABLE DISH(ES): Salmon Confit; Flounder Carpaccio

FAST FACTS
Restaurant Recs: Komi for lobster stock risotto with sea urchin **Kitchen Tool(s):** Knife **Interview Question:** What do you want to be and what are you doing to get there now? Because I would like to work with a person who has goals. **Flavor Combo(s):** In Japanese cuisine, we have five elements of flavor (taste) that are saltiness, sweetness, sourness, bitterness and spiciness. I especially like the combination of saltiness and natural sweetness from food material plus optional acidity and herbs. **Fave Cookbook(s):** Senmon Ryori – a monthly Japanese professional cooking magazine **Chef to Cook for You:** I can't pick one chef. I just dream about having specialty dishes from grand chefs who passed away. It's impossible now. **Culinary Travel:** New York – because I have not eaten out there yet. I'd like to see a variety of restaurants and foods in the top restaurant city in America.

John Tesar
Executive Chef | The Tasting Room

2821 Turtle Creek Blvd. Dallas, TX 75219

Restaurant E-mail: john.tesar@rosewoodhotels.com

Phone: (214) 559-2100

RESTAURANT FACTS
Seats: 20 **Weeknight Covers:** 15–20 **Weekend Covers:** 30–40 **Check Average (with Wine):** $250 **Tasting Menu:** Yes $140/$150/$200 **Kitchen Staff:** 2–4

CHEF FACTS
Other Restaurants: The Mansion at Turtle Creek **Cuisine:** Contemporary American with regional overtones **Born:** 1957 **Began Career:** 1980 **Culinary School:** La Varenne Ecole de Cuisine, France **Grad Year:** 1982 **Work History:** New York, NY: RM Seafood, 44 & X Hell's Kitchen, 13 Barrow Street; Las Vegas, NV: RM **Mentor(s):** David Bouley, Gray Kunz **Affiliations:** James Beard Foundation, we also work with tons of charities

NOTABLE DISH(ES): Mussels in a Green Curry Souffle; Lobster Bisque

FAST FACTS
Restaurant Recs: York Street in Dallas. I love that dinner begins with dry sherry and warm, salted almonds. **Kitchen Tool(s):** My Vita-Prep – it's indispensable. From soups to sauces, it is a powerful tool and saves time. **Interview Question:** Do you plan on making this your career? I also ask them to describe their passion for food. Both of these questions allow me to gauge the dedication level of a potential line cook. **Flavor Combo(s):** I just love the flavor of the sea. **Fave Cookbook(s):** The Zuni Cafe Cookbook by Judy Rodgers **Chef to Cook for You:** Eric Ripert – I love his simplicity and his approach. And he's a heck of a nice guy. **Culinary Travel:** Basque Country, because it has amazing wine, cheese, fish and shellfish. It's on the ocean, and has such an interesting cultural mix of people.

Dan Thiessen
Chef/Owner | 0/8 Seafood Grill

900 Bellevue Way, Suite 100 Bellevue, WA 98004

Restaurant E-mail: dan@08seafoodgrill.com

Phone: (425) 637-0808

RESTAURANT FACTS
Seats: 200–345 **Weeknight Covers:** 200 **Weekend Covers:** 325
Check Average (with Wine): $55 **Check Average (w/o Wine):** $95
Tasting Menu: No **Kitchen Staff:** 6–8

CHEF FACTS
Cuisine: Northwest **Born:** 1972 **Began Career:** 1927 **Culinary School:** The Culinary Institute of America, Hyde Park, NY **Grad Year:** 1992 **Stages:** Switzerland: Hotel Alpenblick **Work History:** Aspen, CO: Hotel Jerome; Switzerland: Hotel Erlibacherhof, Hotel Alpenblick, Beverly's Restaurant; Seattle, WA: SkyCity at the Needle, Chandler's Crabhouse **Mentor(s):** My father, a very successful cattle rancher in Eastern Washington; Roland Henin CMC **Protégée(s):** Three of my prior sous chefs have become executive chefs in Seattle **Awards:** 2005 Puget Sound Business Journal, Top 40 under 40 Business Professionals; 2005 South Seattle Community College Outstanding Community Leader; 2000 & 2001 Best Grilled Seafood Dish in the Gills and Grills Competition, Seattle; ACF for Culinary Competition Gold, Silver and Bronze Medals **Affiliations:** I am involved in over 20 events a year, either as a participating Chef or Emcee. Most of those events are for charities. Our focus on charity events is first FareStart, and also organizations that support women's and children organization. **Languages Spoken:** Spanish, German, some French

NOTABLE DISH(ES): Black Bean-Roasted Dungeness Crab

FAST FACTS
Restaurant Recs: Bis on Main in Bellevue for gnocchi **Kitchen Tool(s):** Personality! You must be able to be flexible and engaging under any situation. **Interview Question:** Why do you want to work here? It allows me to see what sort of research they have done about the restaurant, myself, etc. I'm not looking for a team member who just wants a job. I look for people who have a passion for the business and want to work in an environment in which they'll have a chance to grow and blossom. **Flavor Combo(s):** Our focus is always on the best ingredients available, and showcasing them with the right variety of layered combinations in flavor, texture and temperature. My favorite example of that is our Dungeness crab cakes served on a cold Fuji apple slaw and curry aïoli. **Fave Cookbook(s):** All those with lots of pictures. I never read the recipes. **Chef to Cook for You:** Nobu Matsuhisa. He takes the quality of his ingredients and combinations to the next level. He focuses on traditional techniques in his contemporary presentations. **Culinary Travel:** Japan – here in the Northwest we have a lot of Pacific Rim influences in our food based on the demographics. They have a very sophisticated palate and use incredible flavor combinations in some of their contemporary dishes.

T

Bradford Thompson
Chef | Lever House

390 Park Avenue New York, NY 10022

Restaurant E-mail: bradford@leverhouse.com

Phone: (212) 888-2700

RESTAURANT FACTS
Seats: 120 **Weeknight Covers:** 100 **Weekend Covers:** 120 **Tasting Menu:** Yes **Kitchen Staff:** 5–6

CHEF FACTS
Cuisine: Modern French, contemporary American **Born:** 1969 **Began Career:** 1992 **Stages:** France: Louis XV Monaco, Le Moulins de Mougins, Guy Savoy **Work History:** Hartford, CT: Max on Main; Phoenix, AZ: Vincent on Camelback, Mary Elaine's at the Phoenician; New York, NY: Restaurant Daniel, Café Boulud, DB Bistro Moderne, Mary Elaine's **Mentor(s):** Alex Stratta, Daniel Boulud, Billy Grant **Awards:** 2006 Scottsdale Culinary Hall of Fame Inductee; 2006 James Beard Foundation Best Chef Southwest; 2005 Share our Strength Outstanding Chef; 2004 Food & Wine Best New Chefs **Languages Spoken:** Kitchen French

NOTABLE DISH(ES): Chickpea Crèpes; Watermelon and Ginger Lemonade

FAST FACTS
Restaurant Recs: Phoenix, AZ: Pho Bang for the pho and catfish cooked in a clay pot; New York, NY: Sandy's for the Cuban sandwiches **Kitchen Tool(s):** Plating spoon for saucing plates, stirring and checking doneness of braises **Interview Question:** Why should I hire you? **Flavor Combo(s):** There are too many to name, but I like fennel with anything and I love what acid (especially citrus) can do for most dishes **Fave Cookbook(s):** Sauces by James Peterson **Chef to Cook for You:** My great grandmother was a chef and ran two restaurants in Leominster, Massachusetts in the 40's. I vaguely remember her and would love to taste her food and see where my passion for food may have come from. **Culinary Travel:** I went to Asia for the first time last year and am going to go back to visit Vietnam, Cambodia and Malaysia next year. These flavors were all so vibrant and new to me. It was very stimulating. I also look forward to going to Africa because of their use of spices and cooking techniques.

Troy Thompson
Executive Chef | The "Kress" Hollywood

6608 Hollywood Blvd. Hollywood, CA 90028

Restaurant E-mail: troy@thekress.net

Phone: (323) 785-5015

CHEF FACTS
Cuisine: Inspirational cuisine **Born:** 1963 **Began Career:** 1978 **Work History:** Atlanta, GA: Fusebox; Marina del Rey, CA: JER-NE; Las Vegas, NV: David Burke at the Mandarin Oriental **Mentor(s):** Guenter Seeger, Lee Hefner, Matt Lyman **Awards:** 2005, 2002 AAA of America "Four Diamond Award"; 2004 StarChefs.com Rising Star Chef Los Angeles; 2003 Los Angeles Magazine Best Fusion Cuisine, Best of LA; 2003 Wine Spectator Magazine Award of Excellence; 2003 Los Angeles Magazine Great Restaurants on the Coast; 2003 Southern California Restaurant Writers Gold Award; 2003 Southern California Writers 2003 Golden Bacchus Award; 2002 James Beard House Best Hotel Chefs of America Series; 2002 California Homes Top Ten Most Beautiful Restaurants;Atlanta Magazine Best New Restaurant; 2000 Food & Wine Best New Restaurant of the Year; 1998 Esquire Magazine Best New Restaurant of the Year **Affiliations:** Soritos College; The Kidney Foundation; SOS; JBF; March of Dimes; Meals-on-Wheels

NOTABLE DISH(ES): Baby Cuttlefish with Lemon and Herbs; Kobe Beef Carpaccio with Pickled Onions

FAST FACTS
Restaurant Recs: There are so many incredible little places in Korea Town. One whose name I can remember is Wako on Olympic. They serve tonkatsu, an incredible panko-coated fried pork with cheese, but you can have chicken or shrimp as well. The whole meal will cost you $9. **Kitchen Tool(s):** A Japanese knife. I have a Japanese knife collection from Kyoto. I also couldn't live without chopsticks. **Interview Question:** Why did you come here? Why did you pick me? You should always be open and respond with "yes sir, and no sir." **Flavor Combo(s):** Nori and cheese. Any cheese works – the fat mixed with the roast-y and lean nori is delicious. **Fave Cookbook(s):** The Joy of Cooking. Mine is from 1975, it's completely falling apart from use. It has all the basics. **Chef to Cook for You:** Guenter Seeger – I miss his cooking, especially his corn soup with the crab cake. He's one of the best chefs in America; his style is intelligent and makes you think. **Culinary Travel:** I'm an Asia guy. One fascinating place I haven't been to yet is Vietnam. I would love to go and try all of the street food.

Casey Thompson
Chef | Shinsei

7713 Inwood Road Dallas, TX 75209

Restaurant E-mail: cthompson@shinseirestaurant.com

Phone: (214) 352-0005

RESTAURANT FACTS
Seats: 125 **Weeknight Covers:** 150–200 **Weekend Covers:** 300+
Check Average (with Wine): $100 **Check Average (w/o Wine):** $60
Tasting Menu: No **Kitchen Staff:** 5

CHEF FACTS
Cuisine: Pan-Asian **Born:** 1978 **Began Career:** 2001 **Work History:**
Dallas, TX: The Rosewood Mansion on Turtle Creek **Mentor(s):** Dean
Fearing, Kent Rathbun, Soda Takashi-Richardson **Affiliations:** March
of Dimes, Local Farmer's Markets and we participate in several other
charities annually

NOTABLE DISH(ES): Spanish Mackerel with Yuzu Dressing, Paper-Thin Radish, Cucumber and Julienne of Radish

FAST FACTS
Restaurant Recs: Pomodoro; Tei Tei for whole grilled fish **Kitchen Tool(s):** Antigriddles – aren't they
fun? **Interview Question:** How much do you know about Japanese fish? How long were you at your
first job? **Flavor Combo(s):** Soy and sesame oil **Fave Cookbook(s):** The French Laundry Cookbook and
Bouchon by Thomas Keller; Molto Mario by Mario Batali **Chef to Cook for You:** I would keep it simple
(not that his food is) and have Mario Batali cook for me. I adore Italian and he absolutely intrigues
me. **Culinary Travel:** Spain – for the traditional and regional cuisine and the fresh fish

Matt Tinder
Pastry Chef | Campton Place

240 Stockton Street San Francisco, CA 94108

Restaurant E-mail: matthew.tinder@tajhotels.com

Phone: (415) 955-5555

RESTAURANT FACTS
Seats: 55 **Weeknight Covers:** 40–50 **Weekend Covers:** 80 **Check Average (with Wine):** $100 **Tasting Menu:** Yes $110 **Kitchen Staff:** 2

CHEF FACTS
Cuisine: Californian Mediterranean **Born:** 1979 **Began Career:** 1997 **Stages:** Chicago, IL: Blackbird, Everest; New York, NY: Daniel; San Francisco, CA: Michael Mina **Work History:** Hawaii: The Tri-Star Restaurant Group; Las Vegas, NV: Nobhill; New Orleans, LA: Commander's Palace; Sweden: Berns; San Francisco, CA: Brick, Michael Mina **Mentor(s):** George Gomes Jr., Paul Kahan, Sam Mason **Languages Spoken:** A little Swedish

NOTABLE DISH(ES): Passion Fruit Chèvre Cake with Hibiscus-Tamarind Molasses, Pistachio and Torn Basil; Vanilla Bean Grits with Horseradish Caramel, Pickled Quince and Bleu Shortbread

FAST FACTS
Restaurant Recs: Tulin for Vietnamese; Brother's Korean on Geary for the pickled vegetables **Kitchen Tool(s):** Plastic bench scraper **Interview Question:** What's on your IPod? **Flavor Combo(s):** Radish and salt; licorice and caraway **Fave Cookbook(s):** The Art of Modern Cooking **Chef to Cook for You:** Jean-Louis Palladin – I never got to try his food and he is someone I admired a lot. I would definitely pick a time near the end of his career when he cared so little about food cost that he went crazy with ingredients. **Culinary Travel:** Morocco to see all the old towns and old cooking techniques

Michael Tong
Chef | Shun Lee Palace

155 E 55th St. New York, NY 10020

Restaurant E-mail: michaeltong@shunlee.com

Phone: (212) 371-8844

RESTAURANT FACTS
Seats: 120 **Weeknight Covers:** 300 a day + 300 deliveries **Weekend Covers:** 300 a day + 300 deliveries **Tasting Menu:** No **Kitchen Staff:** 10–20

CHEF FACTS
Other Restaurants: Shun Lee West, Shun Lee Café **Cuisine:** Chinese **Born:** 1944 **Began Career:** 1963 **Work History:** New York, NY: Shun Lee Palace, Shun Lee West; Shun Lee Café **Awards:** 2006 Ellis Island Metal of Honor **Books Published:** Shun Lee Cookbook **Languages Spoken:** Chinese

NOTABLE DISH(ES): Chicken Soong; Crispy Orange Beef

FAST FACTS
Restaurant Recs: Daniel for the best French food **Kitchen Tool(s):** Wok; bamboo steamer **Interview Question:** What is your philosophy on Chinese cooking? **Flavor Combo(s):** For Szechuan cuisine, the most important elements are sugar, vinegar and spicy peppers and chilies **Fave Cookbook(s):** The New York Times Cookbook by Craig Claiborne **Chef to Cook for You:** In 1979 or 1980 I went to an incredible dinner in Monte Carlo to honor Craig Claiborne. There were over 32 two- and three-star Michelin chefs cooking that night; I don't think anything can top that! **Culinary Travel:** China – I go every year to see the developments in regional Chinese cuisine. It is always improving with increasing variety and there is always something new to learn; France – their cuisine is the root of all European and American cooking. If you look back twenty years ago, Americans were still eating steak and potatoes. Now, so many great American chefs have trained in France and we have an amazing American nouvelle cuisine.

Sue Torres
Chef/Owner | Sueños

311 W 17th St. New York, NY 10011

Restaurant E-mail: info@suenosnyc.com

Phone: (212) 243-1333

RESTAURANT FACTS
Seats: 73 **Weeknight Covers:** 70–100 **Weekend Covers:** 130–160
Check Average (with Wine): $55–$58 **Tasting Menu:** No **Kitchen Staff:** 2–3

CHEF FACTS
Other Restaurants: Los Dados **Cuisine:** Mexican **Born:** 1973 **Began Career:** 1993 **Culinary School:** The Culinary Institute of America, Hyde Park, NY **Grad Year:** 1993 **Work History:** New York, NY: 21 Club, La Grenouille, Arizona 206 **Mentor(s):** Miles Angelo **Awards:** 2004 Bon Appétit January Best Cocktail List; 2003 Vogue Taster's Choice The Lasting Moments; 2000 Working Woman Magazine Featured Chef **Affiliations:** JBF, WCR, Cystic Fibrosis, A Slice of Latin America, Autism Speaks, Share, Women's Breast and Ovarian Cancer **Languages Spoken:** Spanish

NOTABLE DISH(ES): Guava Suave Margarita; Tres Leches with Dulce de Leche

FAST FACTS
Restaurant Recs: Taza de Oro for pasteles, a Puerto Rican tamale **Kitchen Tool(s):** Tortilla press is a priceless tool for making quick, uniform tortillas **Interview Question:** Where do you see yourself in 5 years? It reveals their ambitions. **Flavor Combo(s):** Definitely things salty and sweet. As far back as I can remember, my Puerto Rican grandmother would spoil me with guava and cheese or sweet plantains with salt. **Fave Cookbook(s):** The Cuisines of Mexico by Diana Kennedy **Chef to Cook for You:** Marta Ortiz Chapa of Aguila y Sol in Mexico City. I crave her food like no other chef's in the world. She has reinvented Mexican street food and typical Mexican dishes. Her food is the real deal! Her dishes have an incredible balance for such bold flavors and her plates are so appealing that you just stare at it for a minute before digging in. Her mother is a famous painter so its no surprise her food looks as good as it does. **Culinary Travel:** Mexico. Home is where the heart is. I'm half Italian, half Puerto Rican, but my heart is Mexican!

John Toulze
Executive Chef | The Girl & The Fig

110 W Spain St. Sonoma, CA 95476

Restaurant E-mail: john@thegirlandthefig.com

Phone: (707) 938-3634/(707) 933-3000 ext.11

RESTAURANT FACTS
Seats: 130 **Weeknight Covers:** 150–180 **Weekend Covers:** 180–250 **Check Average (with Wine):** $45 **Tasting Menu:** No **Kitchen Staff:** 7

CHEF FACTS
Other Restaurants: The Fig Pantry, Les Petites Maisons **Cuisine:** French-inspired Wine Country food **Born:** 1974 **Began Career:** 1995 **Work History:** Sonoma, CA: Viansa Winery **Mentor(s):** Sandra Bernstein **Affiliations:** I give culinary classes up and down the coast at any food-related establishment you can think of **Books Published:** The Girl & the Fig **Languages Spoken:** Very rough Spanish

NOTABLE DISH(ES): Sonoma Rabbit Pasta: Pappardelle, Fava Beans, Baby Carrots, English Peas, Garlic, Pancetta and Arugula Pesto

FAST FACTS
Restaurant Recs: Underwood in Graton, CA – they have great specials; Juanita Juanita – they have the greatest carne asada and enchiladas **Kitchen Tool(s):** Spoon – you do everything with it **Interview Question:** Tell me what you know. How presumptive they are tells me what they are willing to learn. **Flavor Combo(s):** Sweet and salty; apricot and sea salt; bitter and smoky **Fave Cookbook(s):** Books by Louis Diat **Chef to Cook for You:** I love food history, so would have to pick Escoffier. He was such a pioneer - he changed how food was viewed and applied. It would be interesting to go back to that tipping point in history and see what the inspiration was. **Culinary Travel:** Thailand – I'm not very familiar with Far Eastern food, but I'm fascinated by it

Cedric Tovar
Executive Chef | Peacock Alley

301 Park Ave. New York, NY 10022

Restaurant E-mail: cedric@tovar.com

Phone: (212) 872-4895

RESTAURANT FACTS
Seats: 45–145 **Weeknight Covers:** 70 **Weekend Covers:** 80–90
Tasting Menu: No **Kitchen Staff:** 5–6

CHEF FACTS
Cuisine: Global Cuisine; modern American **Born:** 1969 **Began Career:** 1988 **Culinary School:** Mederic Culinary School, France **Grad Year:** 1988 **Stages:** France: Duquesnoy **Work History:** France: Duquesnoy, Tour d'Argent, Jamin, Plaza Athenée Hotel **Mentor(s):** Joël Antunes, Eric Brifard, Joël Robuchon **Protégée(s):** Vincent Nargi, Hideya Nagai **Awards:** 2005 AAA Five Diamonds **Languages Spoken:** French, Spanish

NOTABLE DISH(ES): Grilled Foie Gras and Spring Vegetable Napoleon

FAST FACTS
Restaurant Recs: Alto for the Vermont suckling pig **Kitchen Tool(s):** Jade Plancha because it's fast, reliable, and it doesn't alter the product **Interview Question:** Where do you see yourself 5 years from now? **Flavor Combo(s):** Savory with fruits and spices **Fave Cookbook(s):** Essential Cuisine by Michel Bras **Chef to Cook for You:** Chef Jacques Thorel from L'Auberge Bretonne in France – it is the best food I have had in the last 15 years **Culinary Travel:** Southern India

T

Fabio Trabocchi
Chef | Fiamma

206 Spring St. New York, NY 10012

Restaurant E-mail: ftrabocchi@brguestinc.com

Phone: (212) 653-0100

RESTAURANT FACTS
Seats: 128 **Weeknight Covers:** 80 **Weekend Covers:** 120–200 **Check Average (with Wine):** $135 **Check Average (w/o Wine):** $85 **Tasting Menu:** Yes $105/$194 **Kitchen Staff:** 7–9

CHEF FACTS
Cuisine: Italian **Born:** 1974 **Began Career:** 1988 **Culinary School:** Instituto Alberghiero Panzine, Italy **Grad Year:** 1991 **Stages:** Italy: Ristorante Gualtiero Marchesi **Work History:** Italy: Ristorante Gualtiero Marchesi, Ja Navalge Restaurant; Tyson's Corner, VA: Maestro **Mentor(s):** Every chef I have worked for **Protégée(s):** Sean McDonald, Cliff Denny, Stefano Frigerio, Nick Stefanelli **Awards:** 2008 New York Times 3 stars; 2003 StarChefs.com Rising Star Chef Washington DC **Affiliations:** Fiamma is affiliated with culinary organizations and charities such as City Harvest **Books Published:** Cucina of Le Marche **Languages Spoken:** Italian, French, Spanish

NOTABLE DISH(ES): Lobster Ravioli with Lobster Bisque Sauce; Rolled Dry-Aged Beef Carpaccio Maestro Style; Hay-Smoked Turbot with Smoked Potatoes

FAST FACTS
Restaurant Recs: In Washington DC: Palena – because everything Frank Ruta does is great **Kitchen Tool(s):** Spoon; surgical tweezers **Interview Question:** Why do you want to be a cook? It shows the true colors of a person. **Flavor Combo(s):** It really depends on the season. From fall to spring I rely on more hearty combinations of meats and root vegetables, whereas in the summer I lighten my dishes by using a lot of fresh vegetables, fruit, and seafood. **Fave Cookbook(s):** La Cuisine Paysanne by Marc Veyrat and Gerard Gilbert **Chef to Cook for You:** Cesare Casella – his cooking makes me feel right at home, and reminds me of my childhood in Italy **Culinary Travel:** Italy – I always wish I could go more often than I do

Suzanne Tracht
Chef/Owner | JAR

8225 Beverly Blvd. Los Angeles, CA 90048

Restaurant E-mail: info@thejar.com

Phone: (323) 655-6566

RESTAURANT FACTS
Seats: 110 **Weeknight Covers:** 90 **Weekend Covers:** 200 **Check Average (with Wine):** $70 **Tasting Menu:** No **Kitchen Staff:** 5

CHEF FACTS
Other Restaurants: Long Beach, CA: Tracht's; Los Angeles, CA: Suzpree (to open 2009) **Cuisine:** American comfort food **Born:** 1963 **Began Career:** 1982 **Stages:** Phoenix, AZ: Arizona Biltmore Resort and Spa **Work History:** Los Angeles, CA: Westin Century Plaza Hotel, Noa Noa, Hotel Bel Air, Campanile, Jozu **Mentor(s):** Siegbert Wendler **Awards:** 2007 Nation's Restaurant News Fine Dining Hall of Fame Inductee; 2005 Los Angeles Times Top 25 Restaurants; 2002 Food & Wine Best New Chef **Affiliations:** Cooking for a Cause, Planned Parenthood, Culinary Winemasters for Cystic Fibrosis, Environmental Media Awards, Taste of the Nation, Share our Strength, JBF, ACF

NOTABLE DISH(ES): Veal Chops with Tomato and Green Mango; Potato Parsnip Latkes with Savory Apple Sauce

FAST FACTS
Restaurant Recs: Yu Chun in Korea Town for Neng Myun and Kim Chi Wang Man Doo **Kitchen Tool(s):** Microplane for grating cheese, orange zest and vegetables **Interview Question:** When did you first start cooking? Nothing is more valuable than time spent in the kitchen. **Flavor Combo(s):** Olive oil, lemon and Italian parsley **Fave Cookbook(s):** The Way to Cook by Julia Child **Chef to Cook for You:** Spooney from Spooney's in Greenwood, Mississippi – because he just makes the best BBQ I've ever had **Culinary Travel:** Japan – to explore the fish markets and noodle bars. I'm drawn to the simplicity and clean flavors of Japanese cooking.

T

Rick Tran

Rick Tramonto
Executive Chef | Tru

676 St. Clair St. Chicago, IL 60611

Restaurant E-mail: cheftramonto@aol.com

Phone: (312) 202-0001

RESTAURANT FACTS
Seats: 60–100 **Weeknight Covers:** 50–80 **Weekend Covers:** 130–180 **Check Average (with Wine):** $150 **Tasting Menu:** Yes $145 **Kitchen Staff:** 14

CHEF FACTS
Other Restaurants: Gale's Coffee Bar, Osteria Di Tramonto, Tramonto's Steak & Seafood, Osteria Via Stato **Cuisine:** Progressive American with Italian and French **Born:** 1963 **Began Career:** 1997 **Work History:** New York, NY: Tavern on the Green, Gotham Bar & Grill; England: Stapleford Park, The Criterion Brasserie; Evanston, IL: Trio; Northfield, IL: Brasserie T; Chicago, IL: Osteria Di Tramonto, Tramonto's Steak & Seafood; Wheeling, IL: RT Lounge **Mentor(s):** Pierre Gagnaire, Michel Guerard, Ferran Adriá **Protégée(s):** Shawn McClain **Awards:** 2004, 2002 Chicago Magazine Best Restaurant; 2002 James Beard Foundation Best Chef Midwest; 2004 Fine Dining Hall of Fame Inductee; 2002 Relais & Chateaux Relais-Gourmand Property; 1994 Food & Wine Best New Chefs; 1994 Food & Wine Best New Chefs; Mobil 4-Stars; AAA Five Diamonds; Chicago Tribune 4 stars **Affiliations:** IACP; JBF; Relais & Chateaux; National Restaurant Association, we help raise money for Make a Wish Foundation, and also I'm personally involved with Angel Tree Ministries. **Books Published:** American Brasserie; Butter Sugar Flour Eggs; Amuse-Bouche; Tru: A Cookbook From the Legendary Chicago Restaurant; Fantastico!

NOTABLE DISH(ES): Frog Legs Risotto; Carrot Ginger Soup

FAST FACTS
Restaurant Recs: Sushi Masa in Vernon Hills for the tempura dragon rolls **Kitchen Tool(s):** A sharp knife – you can do anything with it **Interview Question:** What meal have you eaten that sticks in your head, and why? **Flavor Combo(s):** Definitely nothing with cinnamon, I don't like cinnamon. I love orange and almond together. Also, who can resist chocolate and banana? **Fave Cookbook(s):** A Culinary Life by Susur Lee **Chef to Cook for You:** Pierre Gagnaire – he's my all-time mentor and inspiration **Culinary Travel:** I'd love to go to Thailand. It's one of the few places I haven't been and I'm fascinated with the flavors in Thai and Asian food in general.

Miho Travi
Pastry Chef | Fraîche

9411 Culver Blvd. Culver City, CA 90232

Restaurant E-mail: thierry@fraicherestaurantsla.com

Phone: (310) 839-6800

RESTAURANT FACTS
Seats: 90–122 **Weeknight Covers:** 170 **Weekend Covers:** 200
Check Average (w/o Wine): $45 **Tasting Menu:** No **Kitchen Staff:** 2

CHEF FACTS
Cuisine: Modern European comfort food **Born:** 1976 **Began Career:** 2001 **Culinary School:** The California School of Culinary Arts, Pasadena, CA **Grad Year:** 2001 **Stages:** Los Angeles, CA: Spago **Work History:** Los Angeles, CA: Spago, Sona, La Terza, Tower Bar **Mentor(s):** Sherry Yard, Michelle Myers **Languages Spoken:** Japanese, kitchen Spanish

NOTABLE DISH(ES): Chocolate Beignets; Goat Ricotta Tart with Citrus Granita

FAST FACTS
Restaurant Recs: La Super Rica in Santa Barbara for great tacos and pozole **Kitchen Tool(s):** Matfer bench scraper **Interview Question:** What restaurant is your favorite and why? **Flavor Combo(s):** Vanilla with anything **Fave Cookbook(s):** The Last Course by Claudia Fleming **Chef to Cook for You:** Alice Waters – the food would be fantastic, and the conversation fascinating **Culinary Travel:** Japan – I would get to be with my family and I would never get bored of eating noodles and rice

Jason Travi
Chef | Fraîche

9411 Culver Blvd. Culver City, CA 90232

Restaurant E-mail: thierry@fraicherestaurantla.com

Phone: (310) 839-6800

RESTAURANT FACTS
Seats: 90-122 **Weeknight Covers:** 170 **Weekend Covers:** 200
Check Average (w/o Wine): $45 **Tasting Menu:** No **Kitchen Staff:** 9

CHEF FACTS
Cuisine: Modern European comfort food **Born:** 1975 **Began Career:**
1997 **Culinary School:** Culinary Institute of America, Hyde Park, NY
Grad Year: 1997 **Stages:** Italy: Al Cavalino Bianco **Work History:** Los
Angeles, CA: Spago, La Terza, Opaline **Mentor(s):** Lee Hefter, Gino
Angelini **Awards:** 2006 StarChefs.com Rising Star Chef Los Angeles

NOTABLE DISH(ES): Chestnut Ravioli with Sage Brown Butter; Veal
Osso Bucco Agnolotti

FAST FACTS
Restaurant Recs: Sunnin for kibbeh, a Lebanese fried meat patty **Kitchen Tool(s):** Spoon – because,
unlike tongs, a spoon preserves the integrity of the food that you are serving to your guests **Interview Question:** What food do you like to eat? **Flavor Combo(s):** Mint with just about anything **Fave
Cookbook(s):** Cooking the Roman Way by David Downie **Chef to Cook for You:** Daniel Boulud – the
fried tripe that he made has made me a convert for life **Culinary Travel:** New York. It seems that the
whole dining population there is interested in the dining experience. Also, Tokyo has amazing food
and culture and it re-works other countries' food.

Charlie Trotter
Executive Chef | Charlie Trotter's

816 W. Armitage Chicago, Il 60614

Restaurant E-mail: katy@charlietrotters.com

Phone: (773) 248-6228

RESTAURANT FACTS
Seats: 90 **Weeknight Covers:** 140–180 **Weekend Covers:** 140–180
Tasting Menu: Yes $165/$225 **Kitchen Staff:** 16–20

CHEF FACTS
Other Restaurants: Las Vegas, NV: Restaurant Charlie & Bar Charlie at the Palazzo; Los Cabos, Mexico: Trotter's to Go, "C" **Cuisine:** Spontaneous **Born:** 1959 **Began Career:** 1982 **Work History:** Norfolk, VA: The Monastery; Lake Forest, IL: Sinclair's; San Francisco, CA: Campton Place; Jupiter Beach, FL: Sinclair's American Grill **Mentor(s):** Fredy Girardet, Fernand Point, Miles Davis – though I did not work for any of these people **Awards:** 2005 International Association of Culinary Professionals Humanitarian of the Year Award; 2000 Wine Spectator America's Best Restaurant; 2000 James Beard Foundation Outstanding Restaurant; 1999 James Beard Foundation Outstanding Chef; 1998 Wine Spectator Best Restaurant in the World for Wine and Food; 1998 AAA Five Diamond Award; 1998 Mobil Travel Guide 5 stars; 1995 inducted into Relais & Châteaux **Affiliations:** Relais & Châteaux, The Charlie Trotter Culinary Education Foundation

FAST FACTS
Flavor Combo(s): Artichokes, fennel, corn **Fave Cookbook(s):** Norman Van Aken's Feast of Sunlight, Ken Hom's East Meets West Cuisine **Culinary Travel:** Spain, Japan, Singapore

T

Joseph Truex
Co-Chef/Pastry Chef/Owner | Repast

620 N Glen Iris Dr. Atlanta, GA 30308

Restaurant E-mail: info@repastrestaurant.com

Phone: (404) 870-8707

RESTAURANT FACTS
Seats: 60/35–40/20 **Weeknight Covers:** 50-80 **Weekend Covers:** 150+ **Check Average (with Wine):** $50–$60 **Tasting Menu:** No

CHEF FACTS
Cuisine: Contemporary American **Born:** 1965 **Began Career:** 1989 **Culinary School:** The Culinary Institute of America, Hyde Park, NY **Stages:** New York, NY: Le Cirque (CIA externship) **Work History:** Switzerland: Plaza Hotel; New York, NY: The Peninsula, The Fireman Group; Cambridge, NY: The Cambridge Hotel **Mentor(s):** Daniel Boulud **Awards:** 2007 StarChefs.com Rising Star Pastry Chef Atlanta; 2006 Esquire Best New American Restaurant; 1991 American Culinary Federation Hot Food Competition Gold Medal **Affiliations:** Slow Food, ACF **Languages Spoken:** Spanish, Japanese, some French, German

NOTABLE DISH(ES): Banana Pecan Bread Pudding with House-Made Banana Ice Cream, Dark Jamaican Rum Sauce; Japanese-Style Soufflé Cheesecake Citrus Zest, Tropical Purées

FAST FACTS
Restaurant Recs: Buford Highway – because it's real deal stuff; Pho 96 – for pho; China Delight – for dim sum **Kitchen Tool(s):** Rational cooking system **Interview Question:** Where was the last place that you had a great dining experience and why? **Flavor Combo(s):** Smokey, sweet and salty – like smoked paprika, chocolate and salt **Fave Cookbook(s):** Bouchon by Thomas Keller **Chef to Cook for You:** I would like to experience Ferran Adriá's cooking **Culinary Travel:** Japan

Ming Tsai
Chef/Owner | Blue Ginger

583 Washington St. Wellesley, MA 02482

Restaurant E-mail: ming@ming.com

Phone: (781) 283-5790

RESTAURANT FACTS
Seats: 170–258 **Weeknight Covers:** 240 **Weekend Covers:** 300+
Check Average (with Wine): $73 **Tasting Menu:** Yes Varies **Kitchen Staff:** 7–9

CHEF FACTS
Cuisine: East-West **Born:** 1964 **Began Career:** 1977 **Culinary School:** Le Cordon Bleu, France; Cornell School of Hotel Administration, Ithaca, NY **Grad Year:** 1985/1989 **Work History:** New York, NY: Fauchon; France: Natacha; San Francisco, CA: Silks **Mentor(s):** Ken Hom, who urged me to keep doing East-West cuisine **Awards:** 2007 Restaurants and Institutions Magazine Ivy Award; 2005 MRA Restaurateur of the Year; 2002 James Beard Foundation Best Chef Northeast; 1998 Emmy Award for Outstanding Service Show Host; 1998 Esquire Chef of the Year; 1998 Boston Magazine Best New Restaurant; 1998 James Beard Nomination for Best New Restaurant **Affiliations:** Food Allergy and Anaphylaxis Network, Chefs for Humanity, Target, Food Network **Books Published:** Blue Ginger: East Meets West Cooking with Ming Tsai; Simply Ming; Ming's Master Recipes **Languages Spoken:** French, Mandarin

NOTABLE DISH(ES): Chipotle Sweet Potato Soup With Bell Pepper-Bacon Salsa

FAST FACTS
Restaurant Recs: Sapporo Ramen in Porter Square for miso butter noodles **Kitchen Tool(s):** All-Clad Stir-fry pan, which I use like a wok – it conducts heat really well, which is key with stir-frying **Flavor Combo(s):** Sweet and sour; spicy and sweet (like chile and fruit); fish sauce and lime juice; soy sauce, garlic and ginger **Fave Cookbook(s):** On Food and Cooking by Harold McGee which makes a fascinating subject even more interesting; Molecular Gastronomy by Hervé This **Chef to Cook for You:** Alive: Fredy Girardet because he is reputed to be the best chef alive, and I've never had his food, and also Ferran Adriá of el Bulli. Dead: Escoffier. He's the basis of French cuisine, what more is there to say? **Culinary Travel:** I would travel to Asia, solo, so I could truly immerse myself in the cuisine and culture. I'd eat my way from one end to the other and seek out every dive, every street food stand, every little hole in the wall serving fantastic, authentic cuisine, and really, truly experience Asia and all that it has to offer.

Amalea Tshilds
Chef/Owner | Lula Café

2537 N Kedzie Blvd. Chicago, IL 60647

Restaurant E-mail: lea@lulacafe.com

Phone: (773) 489-9554

RESTAURANT FACTS
Seats: 65/130 **Weeknight Covers:** 150 **Weekend Covers:** 150/175
Tasting Menu: No **Kitchen Staff:** 14

CHEF FACTS
Cuisine: Seasonal, Rustic American **Born:** 1968 **Began Career:** 1999
Work History: Chicago, IL: Lula Café **Mentor(s):** Alice Waters, Judy
Rodgers **Protégée(s):** Kazu Yoshi Yamada **Awards:** 2005 StarChefs.
com Rising Star Chef Chicago **Affiliations:** Lula supports many local
farms and organizations. We donate food and time for fundraising
events. A few examples would be Common Threads and The Green
City Market in Chicago.

NOTABLE DISH(ES): Parmesan Panna Cotta with Guanciale Croutons; Rainbow Trout with Sunchoke
and Winter Radishes

FAST FACTS
Restaurant Recs: Tre Kronor for Swedish home-style food; Dang Than for pho ga **Kitchen Tool(s):**
Cast iron skillet for seared proteins, home-style greens, corn breads and tarte tatin **Interview Question:** What have been your best work experiences and why? **Flavor Combo(s):** Cinnamon and olive oil
Fave Cookbook(s): French Laundry – it's impeccable, it sets a standard of care for how all kitchens
should be run. Zuni Café – it's deep and passionate. Soul of a Chef by Michael Ruhlman – for how
it connects with the French Laundry Cookbook and creates a culture. **Chef to Cook for You:** It would
be fascinating to experience el Bulli and the magic of Ferran Adriá. It would be equally interesting to
experience the Arzak family. I've also been itching to go to Masa in New York. **Culinary Travel:** I would
travel in the Mediterranean, preferably in villages, to pick up techniques and tricks from the older
generation

Jeff Tunks
Chef/Owner | DC Coast

1401 K St. NW Washington, DC 20005

Restaurant E-mail: info@dccoast.com

Phone: (202) 216-5988

RESTAURANT FACTS
Seats: 186 **Weeknight Covers:** 220 **Weekend Covers:** 280 **Check Average (with Wine):** $60 **Tasting Menu:** No **Kitchen Staff:** 7

CHEF FACTS
Other Restaurants: Acadiana, Ceiba, Tenpenh **Cuisine:** Regional American **Born:** 1961 **Began Career:** 1983 **Culinary School:** The Culinary Institute of America, Hyde Park, NY **Grad Year:** 1983 **Stages:** Atlanta, GA: Nicolas Roof **Work History:** Dallas, TX: Loews Anatole Hotel, Crescent Court Hotel, River Club, Notte Luna, Loews Coronado Bay Resort; New Orleans, LA: Windsor Court Hotel **Mentor(s):** Dean Fearing, Takashi Shiramizu, John Coletta, Jean Marie Josselin **Protégée(s):** Linton Hopkins, Anthony Lamas **Awards:** 2006 Esquire Best New Restaurant; 1999, 1996 Gourmet Number One Restaurant New Orleans, DC; 1988 Bocuse D'or Finalist; 1997 Mobil 5 stars; 1997 AAA Five Diamond Award **Affiliations:** Southern Food and Beverage Museum, Children's Hospital **Languages Spoken:** Kitchen Spanish

FAST FACTS
Restaurant Recs: Bombay Curry Company for chicken wings **Kitchen Tool(s):** Vita-Prep blender – because it eliminates the need to strain many purées and gives everything a great texture **Interview Question:** Why did you choose this business? **Flavor Combo(s):** Citrus, chile, and soy **Fave Cookbook(s):** The Encyclopedia of Cajun & Creole Cuisine by John Folse **Chef to Cook for You:** Fredy Girardet – I never got the opportunity to have him cook for me **Culinary Travel:** Japan – I love the style and commitment to ingredients and quality

Michael Tuohy
Executive Chef | Grange

The Citizen Hotel

926 J St. Sacramento, CA 95814

Restaurant E-mail: michaeltuohyl@mac.com

CHEF FACTS

Cuisine: Local, seasonal **Born:** 1961 **Began Career:** 1982 **Culinary School:** City College, San Francisco, CA **Grad Year:** 1982 **Stages:** San Francisco, CA: Four Seasons, Clift Hotel, Square One; Sante Fe, NM: Coyote Café **Work History:** San Francisco, CA: Square One, Caffe Quadro; Atlanta, GA: Chef's Cafe, Woodfire Grill **Mentor(s):** Joyce Goldstein, Mark Miller**Affiliations:** Chefs Collaborative, Slow Food, and I'm on the board at Georgia Organics **Languages Spoken:** A little French

NOTABLE DISH(ES): Whole-Roasted Pompano with Spring Vegetable Ragout; Soft Shell Crab with Aïoli, Arugula and Sun-Dried Tomatoes

FAST FACTS

Restaurant Recs: In Atlanta: Pung Mie for steamed dumplings and pork with nida **Kitchen Tool(s):** Cast iron grill pan as a good substitute for grilling while indoors **Interview Question:** Why did you apply here? **Flavor Combo(s):** I like the perfect balance of salt, acidity, sweet and hot **Fave Cookbook(s):** Jeremiah Towers' New American Classics by Jeremiah Towers **Chef to Cook for You:** Marco Pierre White – I think he's a badass and I know I'd love his food **Culinary Travel:** Morocco – I've never been and I really like those flavors. It would be intriguing.

Angela Tustin
Pastry Chef | Plate

105 Coulter Ave., Suburban Sq. Ardmore, PA 19003

Restaurant E-mail: platepastrychef@aol.com

Phone: (610) 642-5900

RESTAURANT FACTS
Seats: 130 **Weeknight Covers:** 130 **Weekend Covers:** 210 **Check Average (w/o Wine):** $35 **Tasting Menu:** No **Kitchen Staff:** 1

CHEF FACTS
Cuisine: American eclectic modern comfort food **Born:** 1979 **Culinary School:** The Restaurant School, Philadelphia, PA **Grad Year:** 1998 **Stages:** Philadelphia, PA: Le Bec-Fin **Work History:** Philadelphia, PA: Fountain Restaurant and Swann Lounge at The Four Seasons Hotel, Circa **Mentor(s):** En-Ming Hsu from the Ritz-Carlton, Chicago. I also admire Eddie Hales at the Four Seasons. **Awards:** 2004 StarChefs. com Rising Star Pastry Chef Philadelphia **Affiliations:** Zoobilie, Chocolate Symphony, Alzheimer's Association

NOTABLE DISH(ES): Blackberry Marsala Cobbler with Buttermilk Ice Cream and Candied Fennel

FAST FACTS
Restaurant Recs: My favorite places to grab a bite are Pho Hoa, for pho, of course, and El Jarocho for Mexican. Both because they are authentic regional cuisines that are delicious and quick! **Kitchen Tool(s):** Long spatula; 10 inch cake icing spatula. I practically use it as a third, super-flexible hand. **Interview Question:** I like to ask cooks what their favorite thing to make is, and what they are excited about in cooking. What they choose is not important, you can teach them your dishes, but you cannot make them feel for it, or love it. They have to already have that. **Flavor Combo(s):** I'm pretty traditional when it comes to baking, with the addition of a surprise element like fennel with blackberries, or thyme in a pound cake **Fave Cookbook(s):** My favorite cook books are Dinosaur BBQ and The Last Course by Claudia Fleming **Chef to Cook for You:** I'd love to work with Claudia Fleming, she's got a great simplistic style, and she practices restraint, which I could definitely learn from **Culinary Travel:** I'd like to go to Italy, mostly because I love to eat the food. But I'd love to learn traditional Italian bread baking.

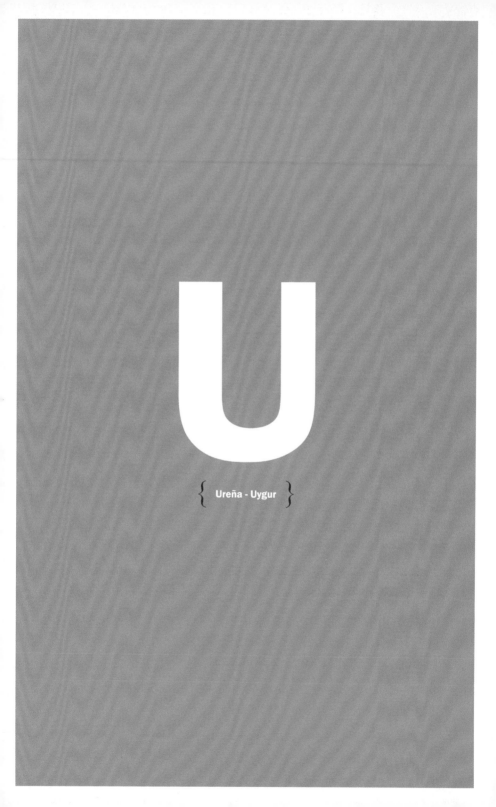

U

{ Ureña - Uygur }

Alex Ureña
Chef/Owner | Pamplona

37 E 28th St. New York, NY 10016

Restaurant E-mail: chefau@aol.com

Phone: (212) 213-2328

RESTAURANT FACTS
Seats: 55–70 **Weeknight Covers:** 60–70 **Weekend Covers:** 120-140 **Check Average (with Wine):** $45–$65 **Tasting Menu:** Yes $65 **Kitchen Staff:** 5

CHEF FACTS
Cuisine: Spanish; French **Born:** 1971 **Began Career:** 1988 **Stages:** Spain: el Bulli **Work History:** Spain: Martin Berasategui, el Bulli; New York, NY: Bouley, Ureña **Mentor(s):** David Bouley **Protégée(s):** Luke Young; Bruce Dillon **Awards:** 2006 StarChefs.com Rising Star Chef New York **Languages Spoken:** Spanish

NOTABLE DISH(ES): Salt-Cured Tuna with Caviar and Chorizo Aïoli; Marinated Grouper with Paprika and Jalapeño Oil

FAST FACTS
Restaurant Recs: Bar Veloce **Kitchen Tool(s):** Thermomix **Interview Question:** What's your goal? **Flavor Combo(s):** I like to combine meaty with sweet. A popular dish we are doing is suckling pig with a granny smith apple purée. Another combo I like is salt cured tuna with chorizo aioli - it is sort of creamy but meaty. **Fave Cookbook(s):** Paco Torreblanca's self titled pastry book – he's the best pastry chef in Spain. And Oriol Balaguer's book Dessert Cuisine, I worked for him for three weeks – his whole family is into pastry! I like Michel Bras and Pierre Gagnaire as well. **Chef to Cook for You:** I would like to go back and eat at Bouley. I miss some of the things I learned over there as well as the personal touch on the food. It would be good to refresh my memory. **Culinary Travel:** London, Barcelona, San Sebastián. I want to go to Rome, Bangkok, and Japan too.

David Uygur
Chef | Lola

2917 Fairmount St. Dallas, TX 75201

Restaurant E-mail: lola4dinner@sbcglobal.net

Phone: (214) 855-0700

RESTAURANT FACTS
Seats: 80 **Weeknight Covers:** 30–50 **Weekend Covers:** 50–80
Check Average (w/o Wine): $36-$45 **Tasting Menu:** Yes $69
Kitchen Staff: 5

CHEF FACTS
Other Restaurants: The Tasting Room **Cuisine:** Italian and French-influenced with a focus on local ingredients **Born:** 1973 **Began Career:** 1988 **Culinary School:** Texas Culinary Academy, Austin, TX **Grad Year:** 1994 **Work History:** Austin, TX: Basil; Atlanta, GA: Terra Cotta; Portland, OR: Castagna **Mentor(s):** Scott Annard **Affiliations:** Slow Food **Languages Spoken:** Spanish, kitchen Italian

NOTABLE DISH(ES): Venison with Butternut Squash, Chestnuts, Brussels Sprouts and Dried Cherry Purée; Cured Scottish Smoked Salmon, Ctirus, Mint and Sea Beans

FAST FACTS
Restaurant Recs: Angry Dog for dogs, hamburgers and bar food; Dumpling House **Kitchen Tool(s):** Cake tester **Interview Question:** Why did you start cooking? What are your goals? Ideally they want to learn all aspects of the business and open their own place. **Flavor Combo(s):** Cured pork with shellfish; garlic, parsley and olive oil **Fave Cookbook(s):** Time Life 'The Good Cook' Series by Richard Olney **Chef to Cook for You:** David Chang from Momofuku. His style is definitely his own. His food is kind of a subtle mix of Korean and American South. He also uses a lot of pork, which I like. **Culinary Travel:** I was in Alba, Italy during truffle season, which is hard to beat! I guess I would have to go to Southern Italy for my next trip, because I haven't been there.

V

{ Valles - Vongerichten }

Jordi Valles
Executive Sous Chef | Ritz-Carlton Key Biscayne

465 Grand Bay Dr. Key Biscayne, FL 33149

Restaurant E-mail: jordi.valles@ritzcarlton.com

Phone: 904 277 1100

RESTAURANT FACTS
Seats: 60 **Weeknight Covers:** 90 **Weekend Covers:** 180 **Check Average (with Wine):** $60 **Tasting Menu:** Yes $90 **Kitchen Staff:** 45

CHEF FACTS
Other Restaurants: Cioppino, Cantina Beach, RUMBAR, Dune Oceanfront Burger Lounge, The Lobby Lounge **Cuisine:** It can be classic or avant-garde cuisine, but always using the freshest ingredients **Born:** 1973 **Began Career:** 1991 **Culinary School:** Escola Universitària d' Hostelaria Sant Ignasi in Barcelona **Grad Year:** 1994 **Work History:** Spain: Akelarre Restaurant, Arzak, El bulli; Newport Room in the Hotel Arts; Mexico: The Ritz-Carlton; Miami, FL: Mosaico, Salero **Mentor(s):** Pedro Subijana, Juan Mark Arzak, Ferran Adria **Awards:** 2004 StarChefs.com Rising Star Chef Miami **Affiliations:** We do a lot of social events as a part of our contribution to many charity associations **Languages Spoken:** Spanish, Catalan, French and English

NOTABLE DISH(ES): Lobster Esqueixada with Tomato Consomé and Olive Powder

FAST FACTS
Restaurant Recs: Yakkosan in Miami for the Fried Baby Bok Choi and Sweetbreads **Kitchen Tool(s):** Aside from my staff, the Thermomix blender which mixes and heats at the same time. So, for example, for Hollandaise sauce, you program the weight, temperature, and level of blend; it's an amazing tool. **Interview Question:** What will you offer to our cuisine with your experience? It's a way to see if a person will be involved and whether they're passionate or not. **Flavor Combo(s):** A good combination first evolves in my mental palate. A few times you can get surprises but basically, you need to be able to do the mix of ingredients in your mind and then proceed to combine. **Fave Cookbook(s):** Ferrán Adriá's first cookbook - not el Bulli. Also Escoffier's Ma Cuisine, Reflections of Culinary Artistry by Pierre Gagniere, and all of the books by Michel Bras. **Chef to Cook for You:** Pierre Gagnaire **Culinary Travel:** London, New York, Las Vegas, Paris. A lot of good restaurants are outside of the major cities in the country, besides Spain.

Norman Van Aken
Chef/Owner | Norman's

12328 SW 117th CT Miami, FL 33185

Phone: (407) 206-2400

RESTAURANT FACTS
Seats: 120–150 **Weeknight Covers:** 100 **Weekend Covers:** 150 **Check Average (with Wine):** $110 **Tasting Menu:** No **Kitchen Staff:** 10–12

CHEF FACTS
Cuisine: New World cuisine **Born:** 1951 **Began Career:** Washing dishes in high school **Stages:** Key West, FL: The Port of Call **Work History:** Key West, FL: Louie's Backyard; Lake Forest, IL: Sinclair's **Mentor(s):** Tokio Suyehara and my mother **Protégée(s):** Charlie Trotter, Scott Howard, Randy Zweiban **Awards:** 2008 StarChefs.com Rising Star Mentor Award South Florida; 2006 Madrid Fusion "Founders of American Gastronomy;" 2003 James Beard Who's Who of Food and Beverage Inductee; 1997 James Beard Foundation Best Chef Southeast **Affiliations:** JBF Trustee, IACP, JLP Foundation, The Chef's Garden, StarChefs.com Advisory Board **Books Published:** Feast of Sunlight; The Exotic Fruit Book; Norman's New World Cuisine; New World Kitchen **Languages Spoken:** Kitchen Spanish

NOTABLE DISH(ES): Rhum and Pepper-Painted Fish with a Mango-Habañero Mojo; "Down Island" French Toast with Curaçao-Scented Foie Gras and a Savory Passion Fruit Caramel

FAST FACTS
Restaurant Recs: Hogfish Bar and Grill for Hogfish fingers **Kitchen Tool(s):** My library **Interview Question:** Do you want to kick some king-sized ass with this life? **Flavor Combo(s):** Fat, acid, meat, starch and sweet **Fave Cookbook(s):** The Auberge of the Flowering Hearth by Roy Andries De Groot **Chef to Cook for You:** Tetsuya Wakuda – he's an angelic man who cooks like a shaman **Culinary Travel:** Vietnam. My friend Tony Bourdain won't let up on how much I'm missing by not having gone there yet.

V

Drew Van Leuvan
Pasty Chef | Trois

1180 Peachtree St. Atlanta, GA 30309

Restaurant E-mail: dvanleuvan@trois3.com

Phone: (404) 815-3337

RESTAURANT FACTS
Seats: 140–340 **Weeknight Covers:** 150–250 **Weekend Covers:** 250–300 + private dinning **Check Average (with Wine):** $75 **Check Average (w/o Wine):** $50 **Tasting Menu:** No **Kitchen Staff:** 4

CHEF FACTS
Cuisine: Modern Italian; French **Born:** 1975 **Culinary School:** The Culinary Institute of America, Hyde Park, NY **Stages:** New York, NY: Bouley Bakery, Daniel **Work History:** Washington, DC: Palladin; Atlanta, GA: Saga, Woodfire Grill, Seeger's, Toast, Asher, Spice **Mentor(s):** Jean-Louis Palladin, Guenter Seeger **Protégée(s):** Ryan Smith, Brad Jenkins **Awards:** 2007 StarChefs.com Rising Star Chef Atlanta; 2005 Bon Appétit Hot 50 **Affiliations:** Slow Food, ACF **Languages Spoken:** Spanish, some German

NOTABLE DISH(ES): Involtini of Peekytoe Crab with Gazpacho and Avocado Sorbet; English Pea and Brown Butter Cappeletti with Curried Hazelnuts

FAST FACTS
Restaurant Recs: Joël – for the gnocchi romaine with sweetbreads **Kitchen Tool(s):** Pacojet; Imperial pasta machine **Interview Question:** Where do you see yourself in five years? **Flavor Combo(s):** Right now I am doing a dessert with peanut butter, banana, concord grape and chocolate **Fave Cookbook(s):** The French Laundry Cookbook by Thomas Keller **Chef to Cook for You:** Joël Antunes – he is a mentor, and one of the best chefs ever **Culinary Travel:** New York – everything is there

Jacques Van Staden
Vice President of Food and Beverage | Celebrity and Azamara Cruises

1050 Caribbean Way Miami, FL 33132

Restaurant E-mail: jvanstaden@rccl.com

Phone: (954) 682-2363

CHEF FACTS

Cuisine: French **Born:** 1970 **Began Career:** 1981 **Culinary School:** L'Academie de Cuisine, France **Grad Year:** 1993 **Stages:** Switzerland: Hotel Dusseldorf; New York, NY: Daniel; England: Fifty St. James **Work History:** Washington, DC: Palladin, Citronelle; New York, NY: Lespinasse; England: Fifty St. James; Las Vegas. NV: Alize at the Palm Springs Casino **Mentor(s):** Jean-Louis Palladin, Francois Dionot, Michel Richard, Gray Kunz **Protégée(s):** Josh Smith, John Suley **Awards:** 2004 StarChefs.com Rising Star Chef Las Vegas **Languages Spoken:** Afrikaans, Spanish

NOTABLE DISH(ES): Roasted Muscovy Duck Breast with Almond Toast; Creamy Risotto Croquette with Sweetbreads and Black Truffle Coulis

FAST FACTS

Restaurant Recs: Marché Bacchus, Nora's **Kitchen Tool(s):** A tilting skillet or brazier – it's so much easier to sauté or reduce things in. They keep the heat so whatever you make, you can do a bunch of stuff at one time. **Interview Question:** Are you sure you want to do this? Why do you want to get into this business? From the answer I can tell immediately whether this guy is going to make it. If they say cooking is fun, I know they are not going to make it. It's fun to cook for your friends. Cooking is hell. If you can survive hell, then it becomes fun again. **Flavor Combo(s):** Sweet, sour and spicy **Fave Cookbook(s):** Elements by Gray Kunz. Thomas Keller's French Laundry cookbook for the techniques. Daniel Boulud's cookbooks. Alain Ducasse with Frederick Labon's pastry cookbook. el Bulli is phenomenal. Jean-Georges Vongerichten's books –there's simplicity but they're also very intricate. Marco Pierre White's White Heat – growing up in South Africa, it was the first cookbook I ever got. I wanted to work for him so bad! **Chef to Cook for You:** Michel Richard – because of his passion for food, superb creativity displayed in striking simplicity, which surpass your expectation with the first bite. He understands food! **Culinary Travel:** Middle East – I've always been fascinated by the cuisine, the little effort to prepare, yet bold taste and textures is so apparent

Bart Vandaele
Chef/Owner | Belga Café

514 8th St. SE Washington, DC 20003

Restaurant E-mail: eurochef1@aol.com

Phone: (202) 544-0100

RESTAURANT FACTS
Seats: 65–100 **Weeknight Covers:** 250 a day **Weekend Covers:** 250 a day **Check Average (w/o Wine):** $45-$50 **Tasting Menu:** Yes $49 **Kitchen Staff:** 6

CHEF FACTS
Cuisine: Modern Belgian **Born:** 1970 **Began Career:** 1988 **Culinary School:** The Culinary Institute for Restaurant and Hotel Management, Bruges, Belgium **Grad Year:** 1988 **Stages:** Belgium: Restaurant Christoffel, Restaurant Au Vigneron, Aloyse Kloos **Work History:** Belgium: Restaurant Scholteshof, Restaurant Piet Huysentruyt, Restaurant Au Vigneron **Mentor(s):** Piet Huysentruyt, Roger Souvereyns, my dad **Awards:** 2006 StarChefs.com Rising Star Chef Washington DC **Affiliations:** I will do charity work with any organizations focused on kids or on cancer **Languages Spoken:** Dutch, French, German

NOTABLE DISH(ES): Cervena Venison Cous Cous Waffle with Fresh Herbs and Mushrooms; Belgian Endive Salad with Prosciutto, Arugula Salad, Orange-Cardamom Gelée

FAST FACTS
Restaurant Recs: Zaytinya because Mediterranean is something I don't know how to cook; Citronelle **Kitchen Tool(s):** Spoon; rubber spatula, knife, a good cutting board **Interview Question:** Why do you want to come and cook for me? **Flavor Combo(s):** I like the classic combinations. Everyone always seems to go back to them. In my mind stick to it, don't go over the edge. **Fave Cookbook(s):** Essential Cuisine by Michel Bras; Everybody Eats Well in Belgium Cookbook by Ruth Van Waerebeek; Nobu the Cookbook by Nobu Matsuhisa **Chef to Cook for You:** Chef Peter Goosens. He is a good friend of mine, and I haven't tried his food since he received his three Michelin stars. **Culinary Travel:** Asia

Adrian Vasquez
Pastry Chef | Providence

5955 Melrose Ave. Los Angeles, CA 90038

Restaurant E-mail: info@providencela.com

Phone: (323) 460-4170

RESTAURANT FACTS
Seats: 90 **Weeknight Covers:** 65-70 **Weekend Covers:** 120 **Check Average (with Wine):** $120 **Tasting Menu:** No

CHEF FACTS
Cuisine: Pastry **Born:** 1969 **Stages:** England: Pied á Terre; Boston: Clio; San Francisco: Aqua; Yountville, CA: The French Laundry **Work History:** San Francisco, CA: Aqua; Chicago, IL: Bin36; Los Angeles, CA: Providence **Protégée(s):** Rosio Sanchez **Languages Spoken:** Spanish

NOTABLE DISH(ES): White Chocolate Mousse with Black Olive Nougatine and White Chocolate Powder

FAST FACTS
Restaurant Recs: Truly Mediterranean, in San Francisco, for it's amazing lamb shwarma. It's always my first and last meal when I go back home. **Kitchen Tool(s):** Handheld blender because I use it all the time. **Interview Question:** Tell me about your last memorable meal; I like to see how excited someone gets about food. **Fave Cookbook(s):** Dessert Cuisine by Oriol Balaguer

Ray Villalobos
Chef | Table 52

52 West Elm St. Chicago, IL 60610

Restaurant E-mail: detoroner@msn.com

Phone: (312) 573-4000

RESTAURANT FACTS
Seats: 71 **Weeknight Covers:** 150 **Weekend Covers:** 205 **Check Average (with Wine):** $40 **Tasting Menu:** No **Kitchen Staff:** 7

CHEF FACTS
Cuisine: Modern American **Born:** 1982 **Began Career:** 2001 **Culinary School:** Washburn, Topeka, KS **Grad Year:** 2002 **Stages:** Chicago, IL: Le Lan, MK **Work History:** Chicago, IL: Bon Appétit Catering; The Art Institute; The Chicago Tribune Test Kitchen **Mentor(s):** My mother, Art Smith **Affiliations:** Common Threads

NOTABLE DISH(ES): Neuske's Smoked Duck-Caramelized Onion-Gouda Pizza with Velouté; Wood-Fired Mac n' Cheese

FAST FACTS
Restaurant Recs: I'd rather go home and eat my mother's cooking! But there's a Chinese/Thai/Japanese place on 95th and Kensey called Shai Tun - great orange chicken, Mongolian beef, pad see yu and shrimp. **Kitchen Tool(s):** My peeler. It can do everything – and you need it! You shouldn't walk into a kitchen without one in your knife bag. And, when you're first starting in a kitchen, you're going to be peeling. **Interview Question:** The first thing I do is have them stage. I ask how long they've been cooking and if they have they ever cooked on a line. I'm looking for energy and a great attitude. **Flavor Combo(s):** Leeks and pork; leeks and fish; great stocks **Fave Cookbook(s):** Culinary Artistry by Andrew Dornenburg and Karen Page; books by Escoffier **Chef to Cook for You:** My mother – she is the reason why I cook. She inspired me to do this. **Culinary Travel:** I'd go to Italy – it's the one place I haven't been. I hear the food is amazing.

Alison Vines-Rushing
Executive Chef | Mila

817 Common Street New Orleans, LA 70112
Restaurant E-mail: alison.vinerushing@renaissancehotels.com
Phone: (504) 412-2580

RESTAURANT FACTS
Seats: 80 **Weeknight Covers:** 50 **Weekend Covers:** 70 **Check Average (with Wine):** $150 **Check Average (w/o Wine):** $100 **Tasting Menu:** Yes $65 **Kitchen Staff:** 4-6

CHEF FACTS
Cuisine: Nouvelle southern cuisine **Born:** 1975 **Began Career:** 1991 **Culinary School:** The Institute of Culinary Education, New York, NY **Grad Year:** 2001 **Work History:** Abita Springs, LA: Longbranch, New York, NY: Jack's Luxury Oyster Bar **Mentor(s):** Gerard Maras and Alain Ducasse **Awards:** James Beard Foundation Rising Star Chef of the Year 2004 **Affiliations:** WCR head chef **Languages Spoken:** French

NOTABLE DISH(ES): Porcini-Dusted Monkfish on Asparagus Purée, Braised with Coffee Glaze, Confit Shallot, and Aspargus

FAST FACTS
Restaurant Recs: We don't eat out much – we're into late night cooking at home (I do curried tofu) **Kitchen Tool(s):** A tournet knife **Interview Question:** What's your sign? **Flavor Combo(s):** Eggs and hot sauce **Fave Cookbook(s):** Ducasse's Grand Livre de Cuisine **Chef to Cook for You:** Julia Child, she would be a riot, and there would be plenty of wine. I'd have her pull out the cleaver. **Culinary Travel:** I'm a huge Francophile. It's my dream place, but there are so many others places to see as well. I've always been fascinated by Africa, and drawn to a lot more than the food. I'm a Southerner, and a lot of the food I grew up on originated in Africa.

V

Paul Virant
Chef/Owner | Vie Restaurant

4471 Lawn Ave. Western Springs, IL 60558
Restaurant E-mail: celebratingvie@yahoo.com
Phone: (708) 246-2082

RESTAURANT FACTS
Seats: 85 **Weeknight Covers:** 50 **Weekend Covers:** 150 **Check Average (with Wine):** $75 **Tasting Menu:** No **Kitchen Staff:** 11

CHEF FACTS
Cuisine: Seasonal American **Began Career:** 1988 **Culinary School:** The Culinary Institute of America, Hyde Park, NY **Grad Year:** 1994 **Stages:** New York, NY: Lutèce, Bouley, Gotham Bar and Grill, Hudson River Club, River Cafe **Work History:** New York, NY: March; Chicago, IL: Everest, Ambria, Blackbird **Mentor(s):** My parents, my father-in-law (Al Tangora), Paul Kahan, Alice Waters, Rachael Carson **Protégée(s):** Mike Sheerin **Awards:** 2008 James Beard Foundation Best Chef Great Lakes Nominee; 2006 Jean Banchet Rising Chef; 2005 StarChefs.com Rising Star Chef Chicago; 2005 Chicago Magazine Best New Chef; 2005 Restaurant Hospitality Magazine Rising Star **Affiliations:** Green City Market **Languages Spoken:** Some Spanish

NOTABLE DISH(ES): Sweet Potato Gnocchi with Chestnuts, Fresh Thyme, Honey, Brown Butter; Crispy Grits with Sweet and Sour Beets

FAST FACTS
Restaurant Recs: Avec for braised octopus with spicy piquillo pepper; Page's Restaurant in Hinsdale for the most delicious patty melt **Kitchen Tool(s):** Custom wood fire grill because it's very versatile and contributes a sweet, smoky element to the food **Interview Question:** What's your favorite cookbook? **Flavor Combo(s):** I like richness combined with acidity, like using protein with a vinaigrette or with something pickled **Fave Cookbook(s):** The Lutèce Cookbook by Andre Soltner; French Regional Cooking by Anne Willan; Cookbooks from Chez Panisse **Chef to Cook for You:** Gordon Ramsay – I like his style of food, and we get a lot of inspiration from the things that he does. I can relate to his style. **Culinary Travel:** Italy – I've always wanted to go to Italy

Bryan Voltaggio
Executive Chef/Owner | VOLT

228 North Market St. Frederick, MD

Restaurant E-mail: bryan@voltrestaurant.com

RESTAURANT FACTS
Seats: 64 **Tasting Menu:** Yes **Kitchen Staff:** 11–12

CHEF FACTS
Cuisine: Modern American **Born:** 1976 **Began Career:** 1990 **Culinary School:** The Culinary Institute of America, Hyde Park, NY **Grad Year:** 1999 **Stages:** France: Pic á Valence; New York, NY: Gramercy Tavern; Washington, DC: Charlie Palmer Steak **Work History:** New York, NY: Aureole **Mentor(s):** Charlie Palmer, my grandfather Thomas Dimond **Protégée(s):** Mike Voltaggio, my brother **Awards:** 2005 Washington Post 3 stars **Affiliations:** The DC Chef's Club, JBF, Chefs Collaborative **Languages Spoken:** Kitchen Spanish

NOTABLE DISH(ES): Fennel and Lemon Verbena Snow Cone; Crisp Lobster Corn Dog with Warm Black Truffle Aïoli

FAST FACTS
Restaurant Recs: The Tasting Room in Frederick, MD, is the first great white table cloth venture in my hometown **Kitchen Tool(s):** Cryovac machine for marinating, storage and cooking **Interview Question:** Why did you get into cooking? Who or what was your inspiration? Why do you enjoy the career you have chosen? **Flavor Combo(s):** For the spring: fennel and citrus. For the summer: tomatoes with fruity olive oil and salt; tree ripened fruits and caramel; sweet corn and spicy greens like rocket and pepper cress. Fall: spices with squash and root vegetables. Winter: roasted game and cranberries or chestnuts and braised pork. **Fave Cookbook(s):** The Last Course by Claudia Fleming; the el Bulli books by Ferran Adriá **Chef to Cook for You:** Bringing Escoffier back for one last dinner would be my first choice. But it would take me weeks to decide which combinations from his book I would request on the menu. There are so many dishes that I would love to have the opportunity to see how he intended them to be executed. **Culinary Travel:** I've never had the opportunity to travel in Asia. I have a friend who travels there regularly and always has a great story about a new find a new understanding of the regional cuisine.

Jean-Georges Vongerichten
Chef/Restaurateur | Jean-Georges

1 Central Park West New York, NY 10023

Restaurant E-mail: twood@jean-georges.com

Phone: (212) 299-3900

RESTAURANT FACTS
Seats: 64 **Weeknight Covers:** 110 **Weekend Covers:** 140 **Tasting Menu:** Yes $148

CHEF FACTS
Other Restaurants: New York, NY: Spice Market, Perry Street, Nougatine, JoJo, Mercer Kitchen, Vong, Matsugen, Café Martinique; Paris, France: Market; Las Vegas, NV: Prime Steakhouse; Minneapolis, MI: Chambers Kitchen; Bora Bora, French Polynesia: Lagoon; Shanghai, China: Jean-Georges Shanghai; Chicago, IL: Vong's Thai Kitchen;London, England: Rama, V **Cuisine:** French Heritage with Asian flavors **Born:** 1957 **Began Career:** 1976 **Culinary School:** École Hoteliere, France; Apprenticeship with Chef Paul Haeberlin **Stages:** France: Auberge de l'Ill **Work History:** France: L'Oasis; Auberge de l'Ill, Paul Bocuse; Germany: Tantris; Switzerland: Beau Rivage; England: Grosvenor House; Thailand: Oriental Hotel; China: Mandarin Hotel, Oriental Hotel; New York, NY: Lafayette in the Drake Swissotel **Mentor(s):** Paul Haeberlin, Paul Bocuse, Louis Outhier **Protégée(s):** Wylie Dufresne, Kerry Simon, Quinn and Karen Hatfield **Awards:** 2008 James Beard Foundation Outstanding Restauranteur Nominee; 1998 James Beard Foundation Best New Restaurant; Outstanding Chef, Who's Who of Food & Beverage; 1998 New York Times 3 stars; 1996 The London Evening Standard Newcomer of the Year; 1991 Esquire Best New Restaurant of the Year **Books Published:** Asian Flavors; Simple Cuisine: The Easy, New Approach to Four-Star Cooking; Jean-Georges: Cooking at Home with a Four-Star Chef; Co-author: Simple to Spectacular **Languages Spoken:** French, German, Alsatian, Asian slang

NOTABLE DISH(ES): Poached Maine Lobster with Tangerine Saffron Broth, Shiitake Mushrooms, Celery Root, and Chervil; Bluefin Tuna Ribbons with Avocado, Spicy Radish and Ginger Marinade

FAST FACTS
Restaurant Recs: Sushi Seki – for the 12 piece; Aqua Grill – for the great oysters **Kitchen Tool(s):** Champion juicer; Vita-Prep; C-Vap Cook and Hold oven **Interview Question:** What is your favorite food? This tells me if the cook's in the wrong place. **Fave Cookbook(s):** The Encyclopedia of Practical Gastronomy by Ali-Bab; The Breakfast Book by Marion Cunningham; el Bulli collection by Ferran Adriá

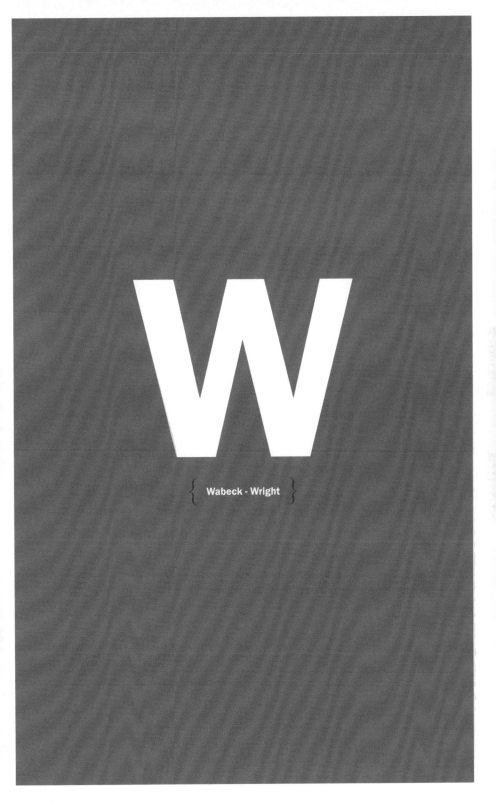

W

{ Wabeck - Wright }

John Wabeck
Chef | New Heights

2317 Calvert St. NW Washington, DC 20008

Restaurant E-mail: newheightsrestaurant@comcast.net

Phone: (202) 234-4110

RESTAURANT FACTS
Seats: 90ish **Weeknight Covers:** 70 **Weekend Covers:** 120 **Check Average (with Wine):** $70 **Tasting Menu:** No **Kitchen Staff:** 2–4

CHEF FACTS
Cuisine: French Asian **Born:** 1968 **Began Career:** 1992 **Culinary School:** The Culinary Institute of America, Hyde Park, NY **Grad Year:** 1992 **Work History:** Washington, DC: Red Sage, 1789, Restaurant Nora, Asia Nora, New Heights **Mentor(s):** Bill Phillips, Ris Lacoste, Nora Pouillon **Awards:** 2003 Restaurant Association of Metropolitan Washington Rising Culinary Star; 2003 StarChefs.com Rising Star Chef Washington, DC **Affiliations:** I help a lot of local charities **Languages Spoken:** Spanish

NOTABLE DISH(ES): Gnocchi with Smoked Trout and Sage Butter; Roasted Atlantic Salmon with Basmati Rice Salad, Pea Shoots and Curry; Stir Fry of Scallops and Shiitake Mushrooms with Gingered Grits and Bacon Vinagrette

FAST FACTS
Restaurant Recs: Bistrot Du Coin for poulet roti **Kitchen Tool(s):** Wooden spoon – you can caramelize onions like a champ **Interview Question:** How much coffee do you drink? **Flavor Combo(s):** Pork and salt **Fave Cookbook(s):** The French Laundry Cookbook by Thomas Keller **Chef to Cook for You:** Fernand Point – what I read about his cooking I think I'd like. Plus he started a whole lot of this. **Culinary Travel:** I can go back to Burgundy any time. It is familiar enough to be relaxing but at the same time there's plenty to see and learn.

Julien Wagner
Baker | Feel Good Bakery

1650 Park St. Alameda, CA 94501

Phone: (415) 552-4055

RESTAURANT FACTS
Kitchen Staff: 3–6

CHEF FACTS
Cuisine: Pastry **Born:** 1977 **Began Career:** 1991 **Culinary School:** I'm self-taught. I have always worked with great talent and I believe that the best education is experience. **Stages:** France: The Town Bakery **Work History:** Boston, MA: Pignoli, Radius, Clear Flour Bakery; Los Angeles, CA: Opaline; San Francisco, CA: Delfina **Mentor(s):** Craig Stoll, Paul Connors – I worked with him for three years at Radius and he helped me think with a pastry chef's mind **Protégée(s):** PJ Waters at Radius **Awards:** 2005 StarChefs.com Rising Star Pastry Chef Los Angeles **Affiliations:** Bread Bakers Guild of America **Languages Spoken:** French, Spanish

NOTABLE DISH(ES): Valrhona Chocolate Torte with Pistachio Ricotta Purses

FAST FACTS
Restaurant Recs: La Quinta – for the Birria (goat stew) **Kitchen Tool(s):** Experience; sharp knives – pastry knives are notoriously dull **Interview Question:** "Can you do my job?" – because I need to know that when I'm not there, things will be up to my standards **Flavor Combo(s):** Basil and watermelon – I made a watermelon and Thai basil lemonade that was so refreshing **Fave Cookbook(s):** Bread by Jeffrey Hamelman; The Making of a Pastry Chef by Andrew MacLauchlan for inspiration **Chef to Cook for You:** Daniele Baliani, the first chef I worked for. I wasn't that easy to manage back then and he dealt with me well. He put me on the right track and really pushed me. I would love to have him cook for me now that I'm at a point when I can really appreciate what he was teaching me back then. **Culinary Travel:** I would like to go to Italy, especially Northern Italy for the pastries. I've never been. Working at Delfina under Craig showed me how crucial it is for an aspiring chef to learn to cook in an Italian way, not just for the food but for the philosophy behind it.

W

Mike Wagner
Executive Chef | Lola's on Harrison

2032 Harrison Street Hollywood, FL 33020

Restaurant E-mail: chefmike@lolasonharrison.com

Phone: (954) 927-9851

RESTAURANT FACTS
Seats: 80 **Weeknight Covers:** 80–100 **Weekend Covers:** 150+ **Check Average (with Wine):** $40–$50 **Tasting Menu:** No **Kitchen Staff:** 3

CHEF FACTS
Born: 1973 **Began Career:** 1995 **Culinary School:** The Culinary Institute of America, Hyde Park, NY **Grad Year:** 1995 **Work History:** Miami, FL: Marks Place, Astor Place, Timo, Chef Allen's, Tuscan Steak, Perricone's Marketplace and Café, Abe and Louie's, Johnny V's **Mentor(s):** My family has really inspired me **Affiliations:** We support the local high school, police and charities **Languages Spoken:** Kitchen Spanish, a little French

NOTABLE DISH(ES): Coca Cola Beef Barbecued Ribs with Buttermilk Onion Rings and Creamed Yellow Corn

FAST FACTS
Restaurant Recs: Joe Allen's; Michael Schwartz's place **Kitchen Tool(s):** Immersion blender – for pureés, sauces, soups and cocktails **Interview Question:** I look for the right personality. I also ask: if I speak to your last employer, what would he say about you? **Flavor Combo(s):** Sweet and spicy; smoky and sweet **Fave Cookbook(s):** Bold American Flavor by Bobby Flay **Chef to Cook for You:** Rick Bayless – I love Mexican food and cook it quite a bit at home **Culinary Travel:** France and Italy – to see the comparisons across the board, from cooking to sourcing

Seiji Wakabayashi
Chef | Bushi-Tei

1638 Post St. San Francisco, CA 94115

Restaurant E-mail: info@bushi-tei.com

Phone: (415) 440-4959

RESTAURANT FACTS
Seats: 40 **Weeknight Covers:** 37–40 **Weekend Covers:** 50 **Check Average (with Wine):** $70 **Tasting Menu:** Yes $95 **Kitchen Staff:** 4

CHEF FACTS
Cuisine: French-Japanese **Born:** 1961 **Began Career:** 1976 **Stages:** Japan: Kihachi **Work History:** Marina Del Rey, CA: Café Del Rey; Los Angeles, CA: Spago; Tokyo: Kihachi **Mentor(s):** Wolfgang Puck **Awards:** 2007 StarChefs.com Rising Star Chef San Francisco **Languages Spoken:** Japanese, Spanish

NOTABLE DISH(ES): Sautéed Sea Robin, Squid Risotto, Tomato Fondue and Saffron Vermouth Sauce; Quail Confit with Shimeiji Mushrooms

FAST FACTS
Restaurant Recs: Nova for flat bread, butternut squash and goat cheese **Kitchen Tool(s):** Metal chopsticks for placing things with accuracy **Interview Question:** How do you make a simple vinaigrette? How do you make a beurre blanc sauce? How do you make a veal stock? I also like to see if a candidate can julienne vegetables. **Flavor Combo(s):** Vanilla bean and olive oil **Fave Cookbook(s):** Terra: Cooking from the Heart of Napa Valley by Hiro Sone and Lissa Doumani; The French Laundry Cookbook by Thomas Keller **Chef to Cook for You:** Thomas Keller **Culinary Travel:** Spain – because Spanish chefs are at the top of the world and I want very much to try their food

Gregg Wangard
Chef de Cuisine | Marisol Restaurant

2757 Shell Beach Rd. Shell Beach, CA 93449

Restaurant E-mail: gregg@cliffsresort.com

Phone: (800) 826-7827

RESTAURANT FACTS
Seats: 85 **Weeknight Covers:** 50 **Weekend Covers:** 80–130 **Check Average (w/o Wine):** $35 **Tasting Menu:** Yes **Kitchen Staff:** 20

CHEF FACTS
Cuisine: Modern Latin **Born:** 1977 **Began Career:** 1992–1993 **Culinary School:** Waukesha County Technical College, Pewaukee, Wisconsin American Culinary Federation Apprenticeship **Grad Year:** 2000 **Stages:** St. John, US Virgin Islands: Rosewood Caneel Bay Resort **Work History:** Kohler, WI: Cucina Restaurant; The Immigrant Room & Winery Bar at The American Club; St. John, US Virgin Islands: Turtle Bay Restaurant and The Equator Restaurant at Caneel Bay Resort; Santa Monica, CA: Ocean and Vine **Mentor(s):** Rhys Lewis, Hans Schadler **Protégée(s):** Robert Trester**Affiliations:** ACF, Wisconsin Milk Marketing Board

NOTABLE DISH(ES): Salad Lyonnaise; Prime Short Rib Osso Bucco with Beets and Salsify

FAST FACTS
Restaurant Recs: Lares for great Mexican food; Neptune's Net for fish and chips and microbrew **Kitchen Tool(s):** Fish spatula for its ability to get along well with others **Interview Question:** Why should I hire you? **Flavor Combo(s):** I love salty and sweet. I also really like things to taste natural, where you can taste what you see, the ingredient is unmasked. **Fave Cookbook(s):** Cookbooks by Charlie Trotter **Chef to Cook for You:** My grandmother, then Charlie Trotter, Grant Achatz, and Hubert Keller **Culinary Travel:** Chicago since I know a few Chefs and it's always fun to see what they're doing and taste their food. Las Vegas because I love to gamble and I love night life, as far as the food goes you really get a feel for what's going on. And New York for all the different pockets of culture.

Alice Waters
Chef | Chez Panisse

1517 Shattuck Ave. Berkeley, CA 94709

Restaurant E-mail: office@chezpanisse.com

Phone: (510) 548-5525

RESTAURANT FACTS
Seats: 50 **Weeknight Covers:** 100 **Weekend Covers:** 100 **Check Average (w/o Wine):** $80 **Tasting Menu:** Yes Varies **Kitchen Staff:** 8-9

CHEF FACTS
Cuisine: Seasonal Californian **Born:** 1944 **Began Career:** 1971 **Mentor(s):** Lulu Peyraud, Cecilia Chiang, Marion Cunningham, Richard Olney **Awards:** 2004 James Beard Foundation Lifetime Achievement Award; 2004 Natural Resources Defense Council Force For Nature Award; 2004, 2002 Audubon Society Women in Conservation Award, 2002 Rachel Carson Environmental Award; 2001 Gourmet Magazine Best Restaurant; 2000 Bon Appétit Lifetime Achievement Award; 1999 University of California at Berkeley Alumna of the Year; 1998 Senator Barbara Boxer Excellence in Education Award; 1997 James Beard Foundation Humanitarian of the Year; 1994 James Beard Foundation Best Chef in America; 1994 James Beard Foundation Best Restaurant in America **Affiliations:** Chez Panisse Foundation, Founder and President; Ferry Plaza Farmer's Market; Edible Schoolyard, Founder and Board of Directors; Martin Luther King, Jr., Middle School Board of Advisors; Slow Food **Books Published:** Chez Panisse Fruit; Chez Panisse Café Cookbook; Chez Panisse Vegetables; Fanny at Chez Panisse; Chez Panisse Cooking; Chez Panisse Desserts; Chez Panisse Pasta, Pizza, and Calzone; Chez Panisse Menu Cookbook **Languages Spoken:** French

FAST FACTS
Kitchen Tool(s): Mortar and pestle **Interview Question:** Please cook me lunch **Fave Cookbook(s):** Simple French Food by Richard Olney

Jonathan Waxman
Chef/Owner | Barbuto

775 Washington St. New York, NY 10014

Restaurant E-mail: jmwaxman@gmail.com

Phone: (212) 924-9700

RESTAURANT FACTS
Seats: 75–101 **Weeknight Covers:** 125–220 **Weekend Covers:** 200–300 **Check Average (w/o Wine):** $45 **Tasting Menu:** No **Kitchen Staff:** 4

CHEF FACTS
Other Restaurants: Sebastopol, CA: West County Grill; Guadeloupe: Barbuto **Cuisine:** Italian-inspired **Born:** 1950 **Began Career:** 1977 **Culinary School:** La Varenne, France **Grad Year:** 1977 **Stages:** France: Claire Fontaine **Work History:** Napa Valley, CA: Domaine Chandon; Berkeley, CA: Chez Panisse; Los Angeles, CA: Michael's Los Angeles; New York, NY: Jams **Mentor(s):** Alice Waters, Traci Des Jardins, Phillipe Jeanty **Awards:** 1984 James Beard Foundation Who's Who Award **Affiliations:** City Meals-on-Wheels, March of Dimes, and the American Cancer Society **Books Published:** A Great American Cook **Languages Spoken:** French

NOTABLE DISH(ES): Guanciale di Maiale: Wood Oven Roasted Braised Pork Cheek and Savoy Cabbage; Manzo ai Ferre con Salsa: Piccante-Grilled Skirt Steak and Fresno Chili Salsa

FAST FACTS
Restaurant Recs: Gabriella's for chile rellenos and margaritas **Kitchen Tool(s):** Ten-inch copper skillet made in Belgium **Interview Question:** What do you like to eat? Can you multitask? Can you handle four sauté pans and twenty tickets at 8pm and still smile? **Fave Cookbook(s):** Simple French Food by Richard Olney; La Cuisine: Secrets of Modern French Cooking by Raymond Oliver; Cookbooks by Marcella Hazan **Chef to Cook for You:** Alice Waters for obvious reasons **Culinary Travel:** Anywhere! The world of food constantly amazes me.

Jason Weaver
Executive Chef | French Room

1321 Commerce St. Dallas, TX 75202

Restaurant E-mail: chefweaver@sbcglobal.net

Phone: (214) 742-8200

RESTAURANT FACTS
Seats: 72 **Weeknight Covers:** 30–40 **Weekend Covers:** 110 **Check Average (w/o Wine):** $90 **Tasting Menu:** Yes $60/$95/$160 **Kitchen Staff:** 8

CHEF FACTS
Cuisine: Modern French **Born:** 1973 **Began Career:** 1997 **Culinary School:** School Craft College, Levonia, MI **Grad Year:** 1997 **Work History:** Dearborn, MI: Ritz-Carlton; Miami, FL: Café Sambal at the Mandarin Oriental; New York, NY: The Mandarin Oriental **Mentor(s):** Christian Schmidt **Affiliations:** March of Dimes, Cotes du Coeurs, Love for Children, Save our Dallas

NOTABLE DISH(ES): Fluke and Foie Gras Terrine with Rhubarb Sauce and Wasabi Sprouts; House-Smoked Hickory Salmon with Hackleback Caviar, Horseradish Cream, Crispy Tarot Root and Thai Basil

FAST FACTS
Restaurant Recs: Thai Pan for Pad Thai **Kitchen Tool(s):** Cutlery **Interview Question:** What is your favorite thing to cook? I ask candidates to cut chives. I want them sliced perfectly. **Flavor Combo(s):** Foie gras and truffles; fresh fruit and lavender; basil, lime, cilantro, and peanuts **Fave Cookbook(s):** Japanese Cooking: A Simple Art by Shizuo Tsuji; Sous Vide Cuisine by Joan Roca; The French Laundry Cookbook by Thomas Keller, el Bulli by Ferran Adriá; Culinary Artistry by Andrew Dornenburg and Karen Page; and Charcuterie by Brian Polcyn **Chef to Cook for You:** Ferran Adriá – just out of curiosity **Culinary Travel:** Back to Southeast Asia because I love the flavor combinations and food

W

Tom Wellings
Pastry Chef | Fiamma

206 Spring St. New York, NY 10012

Restaurant E-mail: twellings@brguestinc.com

Phone: (703) 506-4300

RESTAURANT FACTS
Seats: 128 **Weeknight Covers:** 80 **Weekend Covers:** 120–200
Check Average (with Wine): $135 **Check Average (w/o Wine):** $85
Tasting Menu: Yes $105/$194 **Kitchen Staff:** 3

CHEF FACTS
Cuisine: Modern Italian pastry **Born:** 1978 **Began Career:** 2004
Culinary School: French Culinary Institute, New York, NY **Grad Year:**
2004 **Stages:** New York, NY: Ilo, wd~50 **Work History:** Portland, ME:
Hugo's; Alexandria, VA: Restaurant Eve; McLean, VA: Maestro at the
Ritz-Carlton **Mentor(s):** Sam Mason, Fabio Trabocchi **Awards:** 2006
StarChefs.com Rising Star Pastry Chef Washington, DC

NOTABLE DISH(ES): Tiramisu; Milk Chocolate Crema with Chicory Powder

FAST FACTS
Restaurant Recs: Fatty Crab **Kitchen Tool(s):** Immersion blender - for puréeing small quantities and frothing liquids. My offset spatula is indispensable for picking things up and smoothing them over - I've gone through lots of them. **Interview Question:** What cookbooks are you reading? What chefs do you admire? The answers give me insight into how they think and what their aspirations are. **Flavor Combo(s):** I really like using different nuts and cheeses in my desserts. Overall, I like simplicity in my dishes. **Fave Cookbook(s):** el Bulli, 1998-2002 by Ferran Adriá **Chef to Cook for You:** Pierre Hermé **Culinary Travel:** France for the tradition and the amount of restaurants

Vicki Wells
Pastry Chef | Mesa Grill

102 Fifth Ave. New York, NY 10011

Restaurant E-mail: wells.v@gmail.com

Phone: (212) 807-7400

RESTAURANT FACTS
Seats: 125 **Weeknight Covers:** 150–300 **Weekend Covers:** 400–450 **Tasting Menu:** No **Kitchen Staff:** 2

CHEF FACTS
Other Restaurants: Las Vegas, NV: Bar American, Mesa **Cuisine:** American **Born:** 1958 **Began Career:** 1984 **Culinary School:** Madeleine Kamman and Creative Cuisine, Cambridge, MA **Grad Year:** 1983 **Stages:** France: Hotel de Paris; Rostang **Work History:** New York, NY: Montrachet, Rakel, La Plaza Athenée, Le Bernadin, Sara Beth's Kitchen, Trattoria del Aire **Mentor(s):** Madeline Kaman, Peter Schoner **Affiliations:** We do a lot of charity events, mostly for food-related charities like Meals-on-Wheels, Share our Strength, etc. **Books Published:** Hollywood Hotplates **Languages Spoken:** French

NOTABLE DISH(ES): Muscat Grape Shortcake with Rioja Reduction and Grape Sorbet; Chocolate Cake with Coconut and White Chocolate

FAST FACTS
Restaurant Recs: Dressler for smoked sturgeon with crispy potato cakes; Tempo for porchetta with friseé salad **Kitchen Tool(s):** Offset spatula **Interview Question:** What is your ultimate goal? **Flavor Combo(s):** Chocolate, brown sugar and pecan; Seville orange, vanilla, creme fraîche, and sage; bitter chocolate, ancho chile, chile de arbol, cinnamon, vanilla and kahlua **Fave Cookbook(s):** La Maison du Chocolat: Transcendent Desserts by the Legendary Chocolatier by Robert Linxe; any cookbooks by the Roux Brothers and Pierre Hermé **Chef to Cook for You:** Whoever the chef is at the Sukkhotai in Bangkok. I love the food there. **Culinary Travel:** I've traveled to lots of places, but would love to go to Brazil, see the rain forest and try some of the exotic fruits and vegetables there

Ryan Wells
Pastry Chef | XYZ at the W Hotel

181 Third St. San Francisco, CA 94103

Restaurant E-mail: ryan.wells@whotels.com

Phone: (415) 817-7836

RESTAURANT FACTS
Seats: 90 **Weeknight Covers:** 150–250 **Weekend Covers:** 150–250 **Check Average (w/o Wine):** $40 **Tasting Menu:** Yes $48/$72 with wine **Kitchen Staff:** 2

CHEF FACTS
Cuisine: Californian with French and Italian influences **Born:** 1974 **Began Career:** 1993 **Culinary School:** Diablo Valley College, Pleasant Hill, CA; Continuing education course at the Culinary Institute of America;The French Culinary Institute in Chicago **Stages:** San Francisco, CA: Aqua **Work History:** Burlingame, CA: Butterfly Bakery; Larkspur, CA: Bradley Ogden at the Lark Creek Inn; San Francisco, CA: Azie **Mentor(s):** Katrina Topp **Affiliations:** Meals-on-Wheels, My Tree, and many other charities

NOTABLE DISH(ES): Cara Cara Push Up Pop with Black Olive Caramel, Shaved Fennel and Orange Salad, Orange Soda, Black Olive Gelée and Fennel Vanilla Foam

FAST FACTS
Restaurant Recs: Tommy's Joynt on Van Ness for the roast beef **Kitchen Tool(s):** My metal ruler – I've had it for 18 years. It's been through everything. **Interview Question:** Why pastry? What about pastry interests you? I'm looking for passion, someone who can get excited about pastry. **Flavor Combo(s):** Strawberries and black olives; peaches and black truffles **Fave Cookbook(s):** The Last Course by Claudia Fleming **Chef to Cook for You:** Fergus Henderson because of his commitment to utilizing the entire product. I love slow braised meats and his overall style of cooking. **Culinary Travel:** Spain – I want to tap into the soul of Spain by visiting all of the little tapas places

Kris Wessel
Chef/Owner | Red-Light Diner

7700 Biscayne Blvd. Miami, FL 33138

Restaurant E-mail: redlightmiami@gomiami.com

Phone: (305) 322-2490

RESTAURANT FACTS
Seats: 107 **Weeknight Covers:** 100–130 **Weekend Covers:** 200–240 **Check Average (with Wine):** $41 **Tasting Menu:** No **Kitchen Staff:** 4

CHEF FACTS
Other Restaurants: M Patio **Cuisine:** Regional Southeast **Born:** 1970 **Began Career:** 1985 **Stages:** Austria: Post Hotel **Work History:** Miami, FL: Marks Place, Liaison, Elia **Mentor(s):** Mark Militello **Protégée(s):** Michelle Bernstein, Scott Fredel, Timon Baloo **Awards:** AAA Four Diamond Award; James Beard Rising Star; Zagat (25); Liaison-Best New American; South Florida- East Regional **Affiliations:** A.I.W.F, S.O.S , R.C.A., Florida Restaurant Association, Side Chef Intervention **Languages Spoken:** French

NOTABLE DISH(ES): Tunisian Lamb Spare Ribs; Pomegranate and Lemon Shrimp

FAST FACTS
Restaurant Recs: S&S Diner for the pork chop **Kitchen Tool(s):** Hold-O-Mat – it's slow quality creates a soul for whatever is being cooked inside **Interview Question:** Where are you from? I want to know everyone's background and the culture they might bring to my own food. **Flavor Combo(s):** Habañero and watermelon **Fave Cookbook(s):** Talk About Good by the Junior League **Chef to Cook for You:** Heston Blumenthal, because he is brilliant and crazy at the same time **Culinary Travel:** Australia or New Zealand. I've never been and would love to taste the fare.

W

Phil West
Chef/Owner | Range

842 Valencia St. San Francisco, CA 94110

Restaurant E-mail: phil@rangesf.com

Phone: (415) 282-8283

RESTAURANT FACTS
Seats: 70 **Weeknight Covers:** 120 **Weekend Covers:** 160 **Check Average (w/o Wine):** $46 **Tasting Menu:** No

CHEF FACTS
Cuisine: Seasonal American **Born:** 1970 **Culinary School:** Kendall College, Chicago, IL **Grad Year:** 1994 **Stages:** San Francisco, CA: Delfina, Gary Danko **Work History:** San Francisco, CA: EOS, Bacar **Mentor(s):** Arnold Wong, Dan Barber **Affiliations:** I work with the local farmer's markets, Eco Farm Conference, Slow Food **Languages Spoken:** Kitchen Spanish, I understand French and Italian

NOTABLE DISH(ES): Wild Nettle stuffed Pasta with Goat Cheese and Olive Oil; Coffee-Rubbed Pork Shoulder with Creamy Hominy and Braised Greens

FAST FACTS
Kitchen Tool(s): My chef's knife **Flavor Combo(s):** I like combinations with balance. Dishes need acidity and sweetness. **Fave Cookbook(s):** Larousse Gastronomique **Culinary Travel:** Asia, especially Japan. The intense precision and technique over there is intriguing to me.

Cliff Wharton
Chef | TenPenh

1001 Pennsylvania Ave. NW Washington, DC 20004

Restaurant E-mail: chefs@tenpenh.com

Phone: (202) 393-4500

RESTAURANT FACTS
Seats: 168–200 **Weeknight Covers:** 180–220 **Weekend Covers:** 280–350 **Check Average (w/o Wine):** $50 **Tasting Menu:** No **Kitchen Staff:** 8

CHEF FACTS
Cuisine: American/Asian **Born:** 1962 **Began Career:** 1988 **Stages:** New Orleans, LA: Windsor Court Hotel **Work History:** San Diego, CA: Loews Coronado Bay; New Orleans, LA: The Grill Room at The Windsor Court Hotel; Washington, DC: DC Coast **Mentor(s):** Jeff Tunks, Gilbert Javier **Protégée(s):** Chris Clime, Travis Timberlake **Awards:** 2003 StarChefs.com Rising Star Chef Washington, DC **Affiliations:** Chefs on Bikes **Languages Spoken:** French

NOTABLE DISH(ES): Pan Seared Ahi Tuna Burger with Wasabi Aïoli, Pickled Ginger, and Asian Slaw; Grilled Thai Beef Salad with Vine-Ripened Tomatoes, Vidalia Onions and Spicy Thai Vinaigrette

FAST FACTS
Restaurant Recs: Pho 75 for pho; Full Key for shrimp dumpling wonton soup **Kitchen Tool(s):** Vita-Prep; immersion blender; tongs **Interview Question:** What is your passion? **Flavor Combo(s):** Hot, sour, salty, sweet **Fave Cookbook(s):** Blue Ginger by Ming Tsai; A Culinary Life by Susur Lee; Cookbooks by Nobu Matsuhisa **Chef to Cook for You:** Nobu or Ming Tsai as they cook the cuisine I'm interested in **Culinary Travel:** Asia – because it is related to what I do

Michael White
Chef/Owner | Alto

11 East 53rd St. New York, NY 10022

Restaurant E-mail: altorestaurant@gmail.com

Phone: (212) 308-1099

RESTAURANT FACTS

Seats: 110 **Weeknight Covers:** 100-120 **Weekend Covers:** 175 **Check Average (with Wine):** $130 **Tasting Menu:** Yes $136 **Kitchen Staff:** 8

CHEF FACTS

Other Restaurants: Convivio (formerly L'Impero) **Cuisine:** Italian **Born:** 1971 **Began Career:** 1990 **Culinary School:** Kendall College, Evanston, IL **Grad Year:** 1991 **Stages:** France: La Terrasse in Hotel Juana **Work History:** Italy: Oasis; France: Moulin de Mougins Verge; New York, NY: Fiamma **Mentor(s):** Valentino Marcatili, Paul Bartolotta, Alain Ducasse **Awards:** 2003 Top 50 Nation's Restaurant News Best Research and Development Culinarians; 2002 Nation's Restaurant News Hall of Fame Inductee; 2001 Top 100 Saveur Magazine; 2001 James Beard Foundation Best New Restaurant in America Nominee; 1998 Best Children's Menu Masters Award; 1998 Food Arts Silver Spoon Award; 1996 The Culinary Institute of America "Augie" Trendsetter Award; 1994 James Beard Foundation Outstanding Chef Nominee; 1994 Johnson & Wales University Distinguished Visiting Chef; 1993-1995 DIRoNA; 1992-1995 AAA Four Diamonds; 1990 James Beard Best Chef Northeast Award; 1984-1995 Boston Magazine Best of Boston Magazine; 1988 Nations Restaurant News Fine Dining Hall of Fame; 1984 Cook's Magazine Who's Who; 1983 Food & Wine Honor Roll of American Chefs **Affiliations:** Absolutely – I am a big supporter of City Harvest, The James Beard Foundation and Share our Strength **Books Published:** Fiamma: The Essence of Contemporary Italian Cooking **Languages Spoken:** Italian, Spanish, kitchen French

NOTABLE DISH(ES): Octopus and White Bean Salad; Seared Sea Scallops with Porcini Mushrooms and Mâche

FAST FACTS

Restaurant Recs: Sripraphai Thai in Woodside, Queens **Kitchen Tool(s):** Truffle Slicer for cutting truffles, mushrooms and bottarga **Interview Question:** Do you really want to be a cook? A lot of kids don't really know what they want to be. **Flavor Combo(s):** Ah – anything Italian, of course! Rosemary and garlic with meat or pork. To me, these are the flavors of the Italian kitchen. Garlic with anything, really, and as a flavoring agent. In addition to using it in dishes, we will bruise it gently and add to a sauce or roast so the essence of the garlic adds a new element to the dish. **Fave Cookbook(s):** Anything by Alain Ducasse **Chef to Cook for You:** Alain Ducasse – I respect his command of Mediterranean flavors immensely **Culinary Travel:** I would love to go to Bangkok. I actually had a trip scheduled but I couldn't make it. The flavors there are so different that what I use in my roster day to day, and I would love to experience them.

Jasper White
Chef/Partner | The Summer Shack

1 Mohegan Sun Blvd. Uncasville, CT 06382

Restaurant E-mail: jwhite@shackfoods.com

Phone: (617) 520-9501

RESTAURANT FACTS
Seats: 350 **Weeknight Covers:** 500–1000 **Weekend Covers:** 2000 **Check Average (with Wine):** $34 **Tasting Menu:** No **Kitchen Staff:** 35

CHEF FACTS
Other Restaurants: Boston, MA: The Summer Shack; Logan Airport, MA: The Summer Shack; Cambridge, MA: Shack Sports Bar **Cuisine:** Rustic shorefood **Born:** 1954 **Began Career:** 1976 **Culinary School:** The Culinary Institute of America, Hyde Park, NY **Grad Year:** 1976 **Work History:** San Francisco, CA: Marenzi's, Carnelian Room; Seattle, WA: Anniques; West Yellowstone, Montana: Parade Rest Ranch; New York, NY: Berkshire Place; Boston, MA: The Copley Plaza Hotel, The Parker House, The Bostonian Hotel, Jaspers, The Summer Shack **Mentor(s):** Luigi Marenzi, Yves Lansac, Alfonse Tomas, Julia Child **Awards:** 2005 Michelin 1-star; 2002 Esquire Chef of the Year; New York Times 3-stars **Affiliations:** Many Charities – our largest are the Make-A-Wish Foundation, Boston Food Bank, Artist for the Humanities, Meals-on-WheelS, etc. See our website for a complete list. **Books Published:** Jasper White's Cooking From New England; Lobster at Home; Fifty Chowders; The Summer Shack Cookbook

NOTABLE DISH(ES): Creamy Clam Chowder; Oysters in Cornbread Crumbs

FAST FACTS
Restaurant Recs: The Peach Farm in Chinatown for their spicy crab **Kitchen Tool(s):** Big steam kettle **Interview Question:** Where do you want to be in five years? I like to see a person's resume to see where they've been, then I like to see where they want to be going and if we fit in that journey. If we are good fit for that person, then I hire them. **Flavor Combo(s):** Here are a few – in no particular order: Champagne and caviar; shellfish and butter; seafood with saffron, fennel and tomatoes; grilled beef with garlic and fresh wasabi; lamb with garlic and herbs; truffles and pasta; truffles and eggs; pork with fennel; fish with brown butter; capers and lemon; crabs and Old Bay; crab with coconut and curry; chocolate and nuts; maple and butter; strawberries and cream. I really could go on for hours here... **Fave Cookbook(s):** American Food by Evan Jones **Chef to Cook for You:** Jocelyn Goldsmith, who is a very talented professional chef. She is my girlfriend and I like to eat great food at home. **Culinary Travel:** I would like to spend time in Africa, Austalia, South America, and when the time is right, the Middle East.

W

Tre Wilcox
Consulting Chef

Dallas, TX

Restaurant E-mail: tre4food@gmail.com

CHEF FACTS

Cuisine: Contemporary European **Born:** 1976 **Began Career:** 1991
Work History: Dallas, TX: Toscana, Mediterranea, Eatzi's, Abacus
Mentor(s): Kent Rathbun, Thomas Keller **Awards:** 2007 StarChefs.
com Rising Star Chef Dallas **Languages Spoken:** Spanish

NOTABLE DISH(ES): Duck Three Ways: Hudson Valley Foie Gras,
Crispy Breast, Confit Crêpe with Huckleberry Maple; Grilled Lamb
Rack with Wisconsin Blue Cheese-Crusted Potatoes and Rosemary
Sauce

FAST FACTS

Restaurant Recs: York Street for the scrambled maple leaf duck
eggs with shaved truffles and ciabatta croutons **Kitchen Tool(s):** My Gray Kunz spoons - I use five
spoons when I am cooking, they are like extensions of my fingers. The spoons are my paintbrushes
and the plate is my canvas. **Interview Question:** Do you love to cook? **Flavor Combo(s):** I focus on
stimulating the five senses of taste with the perfect balance of sweet, salty, bitter, sour and umame
Fave Cookbook(s): Art Culinaire **Chef to Cook for You:** Michel Richard – he has a great character. His
pursuit of food as art due to his pastry influence is really amazing. Thomas Keller would be a close
second. **Culinary Travel:** Back to Paris – I trained there and just think it is an absolutely phenomenal
city

Janos Wilder
Chef/Owner | Janos

3770 E Sunrise Dr. Tucson, AZ 85718

Restaurant E-mail: janosrest@aol.com

Phone: (520) 615-6100

RESTAURANT FACTS
Seats: 120 **Weeknight Covers:** 90 **Weekend Covers:** 160 **Check Average (with Wine):** $80 **Tasting Menu:** Yes $85/$125 with wine **Kitchen Staff:** 6

CHEF FACTS
Other Restaurants: J Bar **Cuisine:** French-inspired Southwestern cooking **Born:** 1954 **Began Career:** 1970 **Stages:** La Reserve and Le Duberne, France **Work History:** Gold Hill, CO: The Gold Hill; Phoenix, AZ: Kai Restaurant **Mentor(s):** Joe Boches **Protégée(s):** Neal Swidler, Mark Dow, David LaForce, Elizabeth Wools, Ellen Burke, Van Slyke **Awards:** 1994-2005 Distinguished Restaurants of North America Award of Excellence; 1993–2005 AAA Four Diamond Award; 2000-2004 Wine Spectator Award of Excellence; 2004 Phoenix Magazine Master of the Southwest; 1988-2002 Mobil Travel Guide 4 stars; 2000 James Beard Foundation Best Chef Southwest; 1992-1999 James Beard Foundation Best Chef Southwest Nominee; 1995 Condé Nast Traveler Top 3 Restaurants in Southwest **Affiliations:** Council of Independent Restaurants of America Executive Board, Native Seeds Research Executive Board, JBF **Books Published:** Janos: Recipes and Tales from a Southwest Restaurant

NOTABLE DISH(ES): Smoke Cured Grilled Rib Eye Steak with Calabacitos Con Queso, Frijoles de la Olla and Salsa Fresca

FAST FACTS
Restaurant Recs: El Guero Canelo on South 12th St. for chicken tortas and Sonoran hot dogs; Pico de Gallo for tacos **Kitchen Tool(s):** My palate **Interview Question:** What are your strengths and weaknesses? What cookbooks and magazines do you own and read? **Flavor Combo(s):** Coconut milk, lime, jalapeño syrup and candied kumquats **Fave Cookbook(s):** Jacques Pépin's Complete Techniques by Jacques Pépin; Larousse Gastronomique by Prosper Montagne; Le Guide Culinaire by Auguste Escoffier **Chef to Cook for You:** Jacques Pépin because he cooks with such passion, feeling, sensitivity and love. And his technique is impeccable. **Culinary Travel:** China because it has an extremely diverse culinary heritage

W

Johnny Miller

Jody Williams
Executive Chef | Gottino Enoteca e Salumeria

52 Greenwich Ave. New York, NY 10011

Restaurant E-mail: Ilovegottino@gmail.com

Phone: (212) 633-2590

RESTAURANT FACTS
Seats: 35 **Weeknight Covers:** 100 **Weekend Covers:** 150 **Check Average (with Wine):** $45 **Tasting Menu:** No **Kitchen Staff:** 2

CHEF FACTS
Cuisine: Italian/American heirloom **Born:** 1962 **Began Career:** 1984 **Work History:** New York, NY: Il Buco, Morandi **Mentor(s):** Mario Batali, Alice Waters, Judy Rodgers, Thomas Keller, Mimi Sheraton, Mona Talbot **Awards:** 2008 New York Magazine Best Wine Bar **Affiliations:** Slow Food **Languages Spoken:** Italian, Spanish

NOTABLE DISH(ES): Fave e Pecorino: Escarole, Fava Beans, Pecorino and Mint

FAST FACTS
Restaurant Recs: Pearl Oyster Bar for the lobster rolls; Shake Shack **Kitchen Tool(s):** Vintage Berkel hand crank slicer **Interview Question:** I put them in the kitchen and see how they interact. I look for willingness and a desire to be there. I notice little things, like if they shake hands when they leave. You should make yourself a good guest. **Flavor Combo(s):** Mint and basil; fennel seed and pollen with fish or white meat **Fave Cookbook(s):** Italian Cooking by Elizabeth David; Basic Italian by Tony May; Zuni Cafe Cookbook by Judy Rodgers **Culinary Travel:** Hong Kong – because it is exotic, vibrant and colorful

Brooke Williamson
Chef | Beechwood

822 Washington Blvd. Venice, CA 90292

Restaurant E-mail: brooke@beechwoodrestaurant.com

Phone: (310) 448-8884

RESTAURANT FACTS
Seats: 70-220 **Weeknight Covers:** 120 **Weekend Covers:** 350 **Check Average (with Wine):** $30 **Tasting Menu:** No **Kitchen Staff:** 3-5

CHEF FACTS
Cuisine: Rustic comfort **Born:** 1978 **Began Career:** 1994 **Stages:** Los Angeles, CA: Fenix at The Argyle; New York, NY: Daniel **Work History:** Los Angeles, CA: Fenix at the Argyle, Michael's, Luques, Boxer, Zax; Venice, CA: Amuse Café, Beechwood; New York, NY: Daniel **Mentor(s):** Ken Frank and the whole team at the Argyle; Michael McCarty and the Michael's team **Awards:** 2004 StarChefs.com Rising Star Chef Los Angeles **Affiliations:** A group of women chefs that get together for dinner once in a while **Languages Spoken:** Some Spanish

NOTABLE DISH(ES): Fig, Prosciutto di Parma and Cabrales Tart; Duck Leg Confit with Fingerling Potatoes and Bacon; Baked Rigatoni

FAST FACTS
Restaurant Recs: Soot Bul Jeep for cold spicy noodles. I like Korean and Japanese cuisine. **Kitchen Tool(s):** Spoons of all shapes and sizes – in my opinion, there's no better extension of the hand **Interview Question:** I like to know what they read in their off time and where they eat. Nothing says passion about the business more to me than a person who enjoys learning about food. **Fave Cookbook(s):** That's a tough one. As I like to read about so many different styles and areas of cuisine, it would be almost impossible for me to narrow it down! **Culinary Travel:** South of France – where there is simplicity and attention to good quality ingredients

W

Micah Willix
Executive Chef | Ecco

40 7th St. NE Atlanta, GA 30308

Restaurant E-mail: mwillix@fifthgroup.com

Phone: (404) 347-9555

RESTAURANT FACTS
Seats: 280 **Weeknight Covers:** 200 **Weekend Covers:** 350 **Check Average (with Wine):** $45 **Tasting Menu:** No **Kitchen Staff:** 4-6

CHEF FACTS
Cuisine: French/Italian **Born:** 1977 **Began Career:** 1998 **Culinary School:** Johnson & Wales University, North Miami, FL **Grad Year:** 1999 **Work History:** Ft. Lauderdale, FL: Seasons 52, Mark's Las Olas **Mentor(s):** Everyone that I work with I look up to and I learn from **Awards:** 2006 Esquire Top 20 Best New Restaurants; 2006 Atlanta Magazine Best New Restaurant **Affiliations:** Yes **Languages Spoken:** Kitchen Spanish

NOTABLE DISH(ES): Grilled Wild Boar, Brussels Sprouts, Roasted Crab Apples; Fig-Glazed Lamb Loin, Grilled Frisée, Goat Cheese, Roasted Potato

FAST FACTS
Restaurant Recs: Floataway Café for rustic, elegant, light food; Woodfire Grill **Kitchen Tool(s):** Pasta roller, hand cranked – I couldn't go a day without it **Interview Question:** What do you hope to achieve by working with me? **Fave Cookbook(s):** It depends on what I am into at the time, like right now I am into just veggies and eating vegetarian. I love it when I cook for my family and the most popular item is the vegetable. **Chef to Cook for You:** Alice Waters because she is real. She seems to love what she does and it shows in her restaurant and her food. **Culinary Travel:** India because I know nothing about the culture or the cuisine

Morgan Wilson
Executive Pastry Chef | The Ritz-Carlton Dallas

2121 McKinney Ave. Dallas, TX 75201

Restaurant E-mail: morgan.wilson@ritzcarlton.com

Phone: (214) 350-6100

RESTAURANT FACTS
Kitchen Staff: 12

CHEF FACTS
Cuisine: Modern American pastry **Born:** 1973 **Began Career:** 1997
Culinary School: California Culinary Academy, San Francisco, CA; Le
Cordon Bleu, France **Grad Year:** 1997 **Work History:** San Francisco,
CA: One Market; Brazil: Cannelle; New Port Beach, CA: Aubergine;
Sao Paolo, Brazil: Cannelle; Supra; Payard Patisserie & Bistro; Dallas,
TX: Bijoux **Mentor(s):** Nicholas Snell, François Payard, Scott Gottlich
Awards: 2007 StarChefs.com Rising Star Pastry Chef Dallas **Affiliations:** North Texas Food Bank, Give Back Getaways **Languages
Spoken:** French, Portuguese

NOTABLE DISH(ES): Espresso and Wisconsin Mascarpone Trifle; Carrot Baby Cake

FAST FACTS
Restaurant Recs: Blue Goose for Mexican Tortillas **Kitchen Tool(s):** Scale – everything starts with
a scale in my kitchen **Interview Question:** Tell me how to make pastry cream. If they can't do that, I
don't want them! **Flavor Combo(s):** It sounds strange, but the earthiness of mushrooms goes so well
with chocolate. I also love salt and chocolate. **Fave Cookbook(s):** The Last Course: The Desserts of
Gramercy Tavern by Claudia Fleming; Anything by Jacques Torres, Norman Love, Richard Leech and
Emily Luchetti **Chef to Cook for You:** Jean-Louis Palladin, Escoffier, or Fernand Point. I never got to
experience their food. For those who are still living, I still have that chance. **Culinary Travel:** Spain
because it is so hip right now. It seems to be the current culinary center.

Damon Wise
Executive Chef | Craft

43 E 19th St. New York, NY 10003

Restaurant E-mail: dwise@craftrestaurant.com

RESTAURANT FACTS
Seats: 103 **Weeknight Covers:** 120–160 **Weekend Covers:** 200+
Check Average (with Wine): $100 **Tasting Menu:** Yes $110/$185
with wine **Kitchen Staff:** 10

CHEF FACTS
Cuisine: Modern American **Born:** 1971 **Began Career:** 1992 **Culinary
School:** 1.5 years at Baltimore International College for Culinary Arts
Work History: New York, NY: Gramercy Tavern, Lespinasse, Cello; Phil-
adelphia, PA: Le Bec-Fin; White Sulphur Springs, WA: The Greenbrier
Mentor(s): Tom Colicchio, Laurent Tourondel, Christian Delouvrier
Awards: 2007 StarChefs.com Rising Star Chef New York **Affiliations:**
SOS, Children of Bellevue

NOTABLE DISH(ES): Braised Snails with Quail Egg; Wagyu Sirloin with Chickpeas and Rhubarb

FAST FACTS
Restaurant Recs: My own home; PJ Clarke's; Casa Mono **Kitchen Tool(s):** Cake tester, Vita-Prep
Interview Question: I ask for a one-year commitment **Flavor Combo(s):** Salty and sweet **Fave
Cookbook(s):** All of Julia Child's books **Chef to Cook for You:** Any three-star Michelin chef, as they
have committed their lives to perfection **Culinary Travel:** Spain for tapas – I learned a lot about how
standard dishes can range in quality there. I'd like to go to Japan to learn about raw fish.

Thomas Wolfe
Chef/Owner | Peristyle

1041 Rue Dumaine New Orleans, LA 70116

Restaurant E-mail: peristyle@earthlink.net

Phone: (504) 593-9535

RESTAURANT FACTS
Seats: 68 **Weeknight Covers:** 90 **Weekend Covers:** 90–100 **Check Average (with Wine):** $65–$70 **Tasting Menu:** Yes **Kitchen Staff:** 4

CHEF FACTS
Cuisine: Contemporary Southern French **Born:** 1968 **Began Career:** 1990 **Culinary School:** Delgado Community College, New Orleans, LA **Work History:** New Orleans, LA: Mr. B's Bistro, Emeril's, Wolfe's **Mentor(s):** Emeril Lagasse, Gerard Maras, Thomas Keller, Patrick Clark **Awards:** 2003-2005 New Orleans Food and Wine Experience Grand Tasting Gold Medal; 2003 StarChefs.com Rising Star Chef New Orleans; 2001 Bon Appétit Best New Formal Dining Restaurant; 2001 Esquire Chefs to Watch **Affiliations:** I am Chef-Chair of March of Dimes, and we are very supportive of charities that work with muscular dystrophy and cystic fibrosis. I also am a member of the Louisiana Restaurant Association. **Languages Spoken:** Kitchen French

NOTABLE DISH(ES): Louisiana Blue Crab with Pickled Red Onion, Roasted Beets and Beet Vinaigrette; Foie Gras with Brioche Toast, Blackberries and Black Pepper Balsamic Reduction

FAST FACTS
Restaurant Recs: Taqueria Corona for tongue tacos with salsa verde **Kitchen Tool(s):** Chinois for perfect, silky smooth sauces **Interview Question:** How does pressure affect your ability to perform? Can you work well in a team? It's all about good chemistry in a kitchen. **Flavor Combo(s):** Hard-seared scallops with mushrooms braised in veal demi-glacé and shaved truffles; steamed cane syrup with slow-roasted duck, mustard and collard greens braised with bacon, caramelized onions, seasoned Rice vinegar and brown sugar **Fave Cookbook(s):** On Food and Cooking by Harold McGee **Chef to Cook for You:** Grant Achatz, because of his molecular gastronomy. I haven't experienced much of that food and it would be very, very interesting. **Culinary Travel:** Either to Japan or France

W

Alan Wong
Chef/Owner | Alan Wong's

1857 King St., 3rd Floor Honolulu, HI 96826

Restaurant E-mail: ntajima@alanwongs.com

Phone: (808) 949-2526

RESTAURANT FACTS
Seats: 90 **Weeknight Covers:** 150+ **Weekend Covers:** 200+ **Check Average (with Wine):** $70 **Tasting Menu:** Yes $75/$95 **Kitchen Staff:** 10–12

CHEF FACTS
Other Restaurants: Japan: The Pineapple Room; Big Island, HI: The Hualalai Grille by Alan Wong, Alan Wong's Hawaii **Cuisine:** Hawaii regional cuisine **Born:** 1956 **Began Career:** 1979 **Culinary School:** Kapiolani Community College, Honolulu, Hawaii **Grad Year:** 1979 **Stages:** White Sulphur Springs, WV: Greenbrier Hotel **Work History:** New York, NY: Lutece; South Kohala, Hawaii: The Canoe House, Mauna Lani Bay Hotel & Bungalows **Mentor(s):** Andre Soltner, Christian Bertrand, Mark Erickson, Rod Stoner **Protégée(s):** Randall Ishizu, Mark Oyama, Elmer Guzman, Jon Matsubara **Awards:** 2007 Honolulu Magazine Hale Aina Awards Restaurant of the Year, Top Oahu Restaurant, Best New Restaurant, Best Service, Gold Award, Best Wine Program Bronze Award, Best Big Island Restaurant Silver Award; Industry Leadership Award; Best Special Occasion Restaurant; 2006-2007 AAA Four Diamonds; 2006 Food & Wine Magazine The GO List 376 Hottest Restaurants in the World; 2006 Gourmet Magazine America's Best 50 Restaurants Number 8; 2003 Bon Appétit "The Legends: Master of Hawaii Regional Cuisine"; 2002 Nation's Restaurant News Fine Dining Hall of Fame Inductee **Affiliations:** Maitre Grillardin, La Chaîne des Rôtisseurs; Culinary Institute of the Pacific; Culinary Arts Advisory Committee; Hale 'Aina Ohana Board of Directors; HRA; Hawaii Seafood Promotion Committee Board of Directors; Leeward Community College Advisory Committee; Les Amis d'Escoffier Society; Easter Seals of Hawaii Board of Directors; University of Hawaii Alumni Association Board of Directors **Books Published:** Alan Wong's New Wave Luau

NOTABLE DISH(ES): Chilled Vine Ripened Tomato Soup; Poached Pear Salad with Cambozola Cheese Lumpia with Candied Macadamia Nuts and a Jordan Blackberry Vinaigrette

FAST FACTS
Restaurant Recs: Side Street Inn in Honolulu for pork chops **Kitchen Tool(s):** Cuisinart blender and hand mixer – they are handy for sauces, purées, liquids and vinaigrettes **Interview Question:** What is most important to you? Attitude is more important than skill or knowledge. **Flavor Combo(s):** Fats and acids; sweet and sour; hot and sweet; bitter and sour; miso and acid; ginger, garlic, cilantro, basil and chili pepper; lemongrass, kaffir lime leaves; soy combinations **Fave Cookbook(s):** The Food of Paradise: Exploring Hawaii's Culinary Heritage by Rachel Laudan **Chef to Cook for You:** My Chinese grandfather. I enjoyed his cooking, however, when I got into cooking, he had already long passed away. I know he could have taught me many things Chinese. **Culinary Travel:** Vietnam, India, Spain, Portugal, France, Hong Kong. These are countries I have not been to yet, and I love their food. I want to see and experience the real deal and see the culture.

Jonathan Wright
Executive Chef | The Setai

2001 Collins Ave. Miami, FL 33139

Restaurant E-mail: jonathan.wright@ghmamericas.com

Phone: (305) 520-6000

RESTAURANT FACTS
Seats: 150 **Tasting Menu:** No

CHEF FACTS
Other Restaurants: The Restaurant at the Setai, The Grill, The Bar and Courtyard, The Pool and Beach Bar **Cuisine:** Modern European **Born:** 1966 **Began Career:** 1987 **Work History:** England: Le Manoir Aux Quat Saisons, La Gousse D'ail; New Orleans, LA: The Grill Room at the Windsor Court Hotel; Larkspur, CA: The Lark Creek Inn **Mentor(s):** Raymond Blanc **Awards:** 2003 StarChefs.com Rising Star Chef New Orleans **Affiliations:** Share our Strength, and many events with various charities, such as the Heart Foundation and the National Breast Cancer Foundation

NOTABLE DISH(ES): Seared Filets of Mediterranean Rouget, Creole Tomato and Smoked Andouille Risotto; Shellfish Escabeche and Bouillabaise

FAST FACTS
Restaurant Recs: London: It's not such small place anymore, but Tom Aikens does a fabulous job **Kitchen Tool(s):** Thermomix – It is just so efficient and so well designed. For me, it is the best blender on the market. **Interview Question:** Why do you want to work here? **Flavor Combo(s):** Hot, cold and crispy textures. Sweet, sour and salty. We use tamarind or palm sugar. **Fave Cookbook(s):** Pork and Sons by Stephane Reynaud. It reminds me of the old English butcher shops. And Recipes from Le Manoir Aux Quat' Saisons by Raymond Blanc. I have had my copy since 1988! **Chef to Cook for You:** Pierre Gagnaire. He just exudes passion and creativity. His combinations are thrilling and sometimes off the wall, yet he is someone who never loses sight of the fact that it is food. **Culinary Travel:** I'd love to go back to Paris as well as to Tuscany. I love the rustic richness and heaviness of it all. The best time for this would be the autumn and the winter. I also like the Basque region as there are so many exciting and wonderful ingredients.

Yagihashi - Youkilis

Takashi Yagihashi
Chef | Takashi

1952 N. Damen Ave. Chicago, IL 60647

Restaurant E-mail: takayagi@aol.com

Phone: (773) 772-6170

RESTAURANT FACTS
Seats: 55 **Weeknight Covers:** 60–75 **Weekend Covers:** 100–120
Check Average (with Wine): $60–$80 **Check Average (w/o Wine):**
$40–$50 **Tasting Menu:** No

CHEF FACTS
Cuisine: French American with Japanese influences **Began Career:**
1981 **Work History:** Farmington Hills, MI: Tribute Restaurant; Las Vegas: Okada at the Wynn Las Vegas; Chicago, IL: Les Plumes, Yoshi's Café, Ambria, Noodles; Detroit, MI: Tribute **Mentor(s):** Rokura Hirano **Awards:** 2004 Wine Spectator Best of Award of Excellence; 2003 James Beard Foundation Best Chef Midwest; Food & Wine Magazine Best New Chef; 2000 Detroit Free Press Restaurant of the Year **Affiliations:** Macy's Culinary Council

NOTABLE DISH(ES): Duck Fat Fried Chicken, Ginger, Lemon Grass, Spicy Napa Cabbage Slaw; Sauteed Maine Scallops and Soba Gnocchi, Trumpet Royale Mushroom, Celery Root-Parmesan Foam

FAST FACTS
Restaurant Recs: Chicago Kalbi – for BBQ short ribs **Kitchen Tool(s):** My Benriner Japanese mandolin **Interview Question:** Are you ready to die with me? **Chef to Cook for You:** Rokuro Hirano, my mentor

Y

Sherry Yard
Pastry Chef | Spago

176 N Canon Dr. Beverly Hills, CA 90210

Phone: (310) 385-0880

RESTAURANT FACTS
Seats: 140 **Weeknight Covers:** 220–250 **Weekend Covers:** 250–325 **Check Average (with Wine):** $96 **Tasting Menu:** No

CHEF FACTS
Other Restaurants: Puck Worldwide **Cuisine:** Farm-Inspired Californian **Began Career:** 1986 **Culinary School:** The Culinary Institute of America, Hyde Park, New York **Stages:** Austria: Hotel Sacher **Work History:** New York, NY: McDonald's, Rainbow Room, Montrachet, Tribeca Grill; San Francisco, CA: Campton Place **Mentor(s):** Eckart Witzigmann, Jacques Pépin **Protégée(s):** Sixto Poscasangre, Suzanne Griswold, Annie Miller **Awards:** 2007 Food Arts Silver Spoon Award for Lifetime Achievement; 2005, 2006 Pastry Art and Design "Top Ten" Pastry Chef; 2004 Women Chefs and Restaurateurs Golden Bowl; 2002 James Beard Foundation Outstanding Pastry Chef of the Year; 2002 James Beard Foundation Best Cookbook Baking; 2000 Bon Appétit American Food and Entertaining Awards Pastry Chef of the Year **Affiliations:** JBF, WCR, CCAP **Books Published:** Secrets of Baking; Desserts by the Yard

FAST FACTS
Restaurant Recs: Take Sushi – I let Nobu work his magic **Kitchen Tool(s):** Tongue; taste; tool box **Interview Question:** Do you want my job? My crew consists of passionate people with a hunger to learn, grow, and set goals! **Flavor Combo(s):** I focus on staying true to the ingredient. It's as simple as that. **Fave Cookbook(s):** Cookbooks by Christopher Kimball **Culinary Travel:** Argentina – just for an ice cream run

Noriaki Yasutake
Sushi Chef | SEI

444 7th St. NW Washington, DC 20004

Phone: (202) 783-7007

RESTAURANT FACTS
Seats: 50-62 **Check Average (w/o Wine):** $35-$40 **Kitchen Staff:** 6

CHEF FACTS
Cuisine: Modern Japanese **Born:** 1975 **Began Career:** 1993 **Work History:** Bethesda, MD: Matsuba; Washington, DC: Perry's; New York, NY: Bond Street Sushi, Inagiku Restaurant **Mentor(s):** My father, Morou Outtara, Haruo Ohbu, Hiroshi Nakahara **Awards:** 2006 World Sushi Olympics Second Place; 2006 StarChefs.com Rising Star Chef Washington DC; 2006, 2002 National Sushi Society of Washington Creative Sushi; 2003 National Sushi Society of New York First Place **Affiliations:** March of Dimes, The National Zoo **Languages Spoken:** Japanese

NOTABLE DISH(ES): Fish and Chips Roll; Smoked Toro with Wasabi Jelly and Watermelon

FAST FACTS
Restaurant Recs: Café Atlantico; Makoto Restaurant for a great lunchbox special with grilled fish and mackerel; Sushi Taro has very good quality sushi; Anangol Korean for late-night Korean barbeque with my kitchen crew **Kitchen Tool(s):** Long metal chopsticks for plating and manipulating delicate elements **Interview Question:** Do you like cooking? Do you cook from your heart? **Flavor Combo(s):** I like tuna and garlic chips. I'm also experimenting with white fish and ponzu sauce. **Fave Cookbook(s):** Nobu: The Cookbook **Chef to Cook for You:** Nobu Matsuhisa – because he was one of the first to modernize Japanese cuisine. I love the way he uses different tastes and texture to stimulate the palate. **Culinary Travel:** Everywhere in Spain and Europe!

Y

Patricia Yeo
Consulting Chef
New York, NY

CHEF FACTS
Cuisine: Asian fusion **Born:** 1962 **Began Career:** 1989 **Culinary School:** New York Restaurant School, New York, NY **Grad Year:** 1988/89 **Work History:** San Francisco, CA: China Moon, Hawthorne Lane; New York, NY: Miracle Grill, Mesa Grill, Bolo, AZ, Pazo, Sapa, Monkey Bar **Mentor(s):** Bobby Flay, Barbara Tropp **Protégée(s):** Pino Maffeo **Awards:** 2002 StarChefs.com Rising Star Chef New York **Affiliations:** WCR **Books Published:** Patricia Yeo: Cooking from A to Z; Everyday Asian **Languages Spoken:** Some Spanish, some Italian, truly bad Chinese

NOTABLE DISH(ES): Ginger Lacquered Quail; Vanilla Roasted Pineapple; Soy-Ginger Steamed Dorade wtih Silken Tofu and Dried Cherry Tomatoes

FAST FACTS
Restaurant Recs: Otto for simple, consistent Italian; Ici is a great neighborhood café in Fort Greene, Brooklyn **Kitchen Tool(s):** Mortar and pestle **Interview Question:** I usually start prepping next to someone when they trail and generally chat about work, their past experience, that sort of thing. There are cooks who cook because it is a job, those who do it because they have visions of becoming the next celebrity chef, and a few cooks who do it because they truly enjoy it – I find I can tell which type of cook someone is pretty quickly. That said, there is room for all types of cooks in a kitchen, you just can't have too many of one type because it throws off the balance. **Flavor Combo(s):** Spice and acid **Fave Cookbook(s):** Thai Food by David Thompson **Chef to Cook for You:** I would pick one of those great yet obscure sushi masters. The flavors in Japanese food are so clean and fresh; it is also very different from my own cooking. **Culinary Travel:** Spain – I have always loved the culture. You can find robust and hearty food or you can go the ultra-sophisticated track. They have the whole spectrum.

Jack Yoss
Executive Chef | 10 01

1001 NW Couch St. Portland, OR 97209

Restaurant E-mail: info@ten-01.com

Phone: (310) 208-8765

RESTAURANT FACTS
Seats: 184 **Weeknight Covers:** 180 **Weekend Covers:** 250 **Check Average (with Wine):** $67 **Check Average (w/o Wine):** $53 **Tasting Menu:** Yes $75 **Kitchen Staff:** 6

CHEF FACTS
Cuisine: Modern American **Born:** 1975 **Began Career:** 1991 **Work History:** San Francisco, CA: Postrio; Las Vegas, NV: Neros, Chinois; Los Angeles, CA: Nine Thirty at the W **Mentor(s):** Mitch Rosenthal, Jacques Pépin **Protégée(s):** Chad Newton, Jeff McCarthy **Affiliations:** MOD, SOS, Morisson Child Service Centers, Seasonal Wine Workers and lots of charity events

NOTABLE DISH(ES): Thai Curry Soup with Marinated Shellfish; Seared Scallops and Kuri Squash Soup with Roasted Chestnuts

FAST FACTS
Restaurant Recs: Thai House and Thai Emporium for spicy fried rice and southern green curry **Kitchen Tool(s):** Shun 8-inch chef's knife **Interview Question:** Why are you cooking? Do you love what you do? **Flavor Combo(s):** Anything Thai: curry, lemongrass and ginger; sweet, spicy and sour **Fave Cookbook(s):** The Elements of Taste by Gray Kunz; A Chef for All Seasons by Gordon Ramsay **Chef to Cook for You:** Eric Ripert because he's a badass. He's the youngest guy to receive four stars from the New York Times. **Culinary Travel:** Thailand for sure, for my favorite flavors

Scott Youkilis
Executive Chef/Owner | Maverick

3316 17th St. San Francisco, CA 94110

Restaurant E-mail: scott@sfmaverick.com

Phone: (415) 863-3061

RESTAURANT FACTS
Seats: 40 **Weeknight Covers:** 50 **Weekend Covers:** 85-199 **Check Average (with Wine):** $50 **Tasting Menu:** No **Kitchen Staff:** 2-3

CHEF FACTS
Born: 1976 **Began Career:** 1992 **Culinary School:** Johnson & Wales, Providence, RI **Grad Year:** 1999 **Stages:** San Francisco, CA: 42 Degrees; Boulder, CO: Black Cat **Work History:** New York, NY: Odeon, Bar Odeon; San Francisco, CA: North Star, Sociale; Tahoe City, CA: Resort at Squaw Creek **Affiliations:** Slow Food, CUESA, GGRA

NOTABLE DISH(ES): Crispy Pork Belly with Black Eyed Peas, Sugar Snap Pea Salad, Roasted Garlic Purée and Pork Jus

FAST FACTS
Restaurant Recs: Eliza's for the potstickers and the Shanghai Chicken; Tommaso's for the pizza **Kitchen Tool(s):** The Vita-Prep – because it's badass. I use it for all my soups and sauces. **Interview Question:** Where do you see yourself in five years? I want to make sure they have a career path - that they don't just want a job. **Flavor Combo(s):** I like a spicy-sweet balance **Fave Cookbook(s):** The French Laundry Cookbook by Thomas Keller; The Dessert Bible by Christopher Kimball **Chef to Cook for You:** Iron Chef Rokusaburo Michiba. I loved the original show and since I am an American chef, I would want a meal prepared that I could never do using ingredients I never use. **Culinary Travel:** Italy, particularly Central and Northern, including cities like Rome, Bologna, Firenze, Milano and Terni

Z

{ Zakarian - Zweiban }

Geoffrey Zakarian
Executive Chef/Owner | Country

90 Madison Ave. New York, NY 10016

Restaurant E-mail: geoffreyz@countryinnewyork.com

Phone: (212) 889-7100

RESTAURANT FACTS
Seats: 70 **Weeknight Covers:** 50–60 **Weekend Covers:** 80–110 **Check Average (with Wine):** $125 **Tasting Menu:** Yes $75/$89/$135 **Kitchen Staff:** 6

CHEF FACTS
Other Restaurants: Town **Cuisine:** European American **Born:** 1959 **Began Career:** 1981 **Culinary School:** The Culinary Institute of America, Hyde Park, NY **Grad Year:** 1981 **Stages:** France: l'Arpege, Au Quai des Ormes, Auberge de l'Ile, Le Chantecler, Pierre Orsay; England: The Dorchester **Work History:** New York, NY: Le Cirque, 21 Club, 44 at the Royalton, Patroon; Miami, FL: Blue Door at the Delano Hotel **Mentor(s):** Alain Saihac, Daniel Boulud, Sirio Macioni **Awards:** Food & Wine 50 Best Hotel Restaurants (Town); Travel & Leisure Best New Hotel Restaurant (Country); Forbes Magazine 4 stars (Town, Country); Esquire Magazine Best New Restaurant; New York Times 3 stars (Town, Country); Michelin Macaroon (Country) **Affiliations:** Elizabeth Glasier Pediatric Aids Foundation, City Harvest, Food Bank, Tap Project **Books Published:** Geoffrey Zakarian's Town/Country

FAST FACTS
Restaurant Recs: The Neopolitan pizza at Una Pizza Neopolitana **Kitchen Tool(s):** Bonnet Oven **Interview Question:** "What are your weaknesses?" **Flavor Combo(s):** Lemon and olives; pork and shallots; lamb and rosemary; chocolate and salt **Fave Cookbook(s):** La Raison Gourmande: Philosophie du Goût by Michel Onfray **Chef to Cook for You:** My mother, who passed away. She formulated my tastes and taught me the craft of cooking. **Culinary Travel:** Italy – I'm intrigued by the philosophy of the culture and the food

Galen Zamarra
Chef/Owner | Mas (farmhouse)

39 Downing St. New York, NY 10014

Restaurant E-mail: gzamarra@verizon.net

Phone: (212) 255-1790

RESTAURANT FACTS
Seats: 60 **Weeknight Covers:** 80 **Weekend Covers:** 110 **Check Average (with Wine):** $120 **Check Average (w/o Wine):** $75 **Tasting Menu:** Yes $68/$95 **Kitchen Staff:** 5

CHEF FACTS
Cuisine: New French-American **Born:** 1975 **Began Career:** 1990 **Culinary School:** The Culinary Institute of America, Hyde Park, NY **Grad Year:** 1995 **Stages:** New York, NY: Union Pacific; France: L'Arpege, Michel Bras et Languiole **Work History:** New York, NY: Bouley, Union Pacific; France: Michel Bras et Laguiole, Georges Blanc, L'Arpege **Mentor(s):** David Bouley, Michel Bras, Alain Passard **Awards:** 2006 StarChefs.com Rising Star Chef New York; 2001 James Beard Foundation Rising Star Chef **Affiliations:** JBF, Slow Food, Chefs Collaborative **Languages Spoken:** Spanish, French

NOTABLE DISH(ES): Pork Belly Sandwich with Red Eye Gravy and Onion Marmalade; Fig Tart with Black Olive Ice Cream

FAST FACTS
Restaurant Recs: Blaue Gans **Kitchen Tool(s):** Champion Juicer, because vegetable juice is the best way to get pure vegetable flavor, and it can then be used in any number of applications **Interview Question:** I like to ask people what their ultimate goals are. Not all cooks want to be a "4-star chef," so it is interesting to see where they are headed. **Flavor Combo(s):** Orange and truffles **Fave Cookbook(s):** Le Guide Culinaire by Escoffier. It's boring, I know, but I still use it for inspiration, and I love reading the old menus in the back **Chef to Cook for You:** Joël Robuchon twenty years ago. I love his current restaurants, but it would be really cool to eat the food he made as a working chef. He was such an influence on a lot of the chefs that I grew up cooking under and wish I could have seen his dishes and how he executed them first hand. **Culinary Travel:** Japan – I had a great time the last time I went and the food was amazing. That trip was so structured though that I'd like to return with a little more freedom.

Z

Mark Zeitouni
Chef | The Lido Restaurant & Bayside Grill

40 Island Avenue Miami Beach, FL 33139

Restaurant E-mail: mzeitouni@standardhotel.com

Phone: (305) 673-1717

RESTAURANT FACTS
Seats: 65–185 **Weeknight Covers:** lunch 100–150/dinner 100–120 **Weekend Covers:** lunch 400–600/dinner 200 **Check Average (with Wine):** lunch $35/dinner $50 **Kitchen Staff:** 4–5

CHEF FACTS
Cuisine: Modern spa cuisine **Born:** 1970 **Began Career:** 1988 **Culinary School:** Johnson & Wales, North Miami, Florida **Grad Year:** 2005 **Work History:** Miami, FL: Colony Bistro, Mark's Place, The Century Hotel, The Delano Hotel, The Astor Hotel, Azul at the Mandarin Oriental, The Premier Financial Private Club; San Francisco, CA: One Market, Black Cat, The Fifth Floor; Berkeley, CA: Bistro Viola **Mentor(s):** George Morrone, Hans Hoffman **Awards:** 2000 San Francisco Chronicle Rising Star **Affiliations:** Dinner in Paradise, South Beach Food & Wine Festival, Slow Food Miami

NOTABLE DISH(ES): Charred Spanish Octopus with Giant White Bean and Artichoke Salad with Oregano Vinaigrette

FAST FACTS
Restaurant Recs: Zuper Pollo – an Uruguayan steak house **Kitchen Tool(s):** Extraction juicer (Nutrifaster) for veggies and fruits **Interview Question:** Do you really live the life of the guests we're feeding? I'm looking for people with a clean, healthy lifestyle. **Flavor Combo(s):** Sea salt and meat **Fave Cookbook(s):** Cooking With the Seasons by Jean-Louis Palladin **Chef to Cook for You:** Joël Robuchon – as I was starting out this career, I would constantly reference his books and became very attached to his philosophy on cooking **Culinary Travel:** Burgundy and Champagne

Eric Ziebold
Chef | CityZen

1330 Maryland Ave. SW Washington, DC 20024

Restaurant E-mail: eziebold@mohg.com

Phone: (202) 554-8588

RESTAURANT FACTS

Seats: 67 **Weeknight Covers:** 75 **Weekend Covers:** 100 **Check Average (with Wine):** $140 **Tasting Menu:** Yes $110 **Kitchen Staff:** 6–8

CHEF FACTS

Cuisine: American **Born:** 1972 **Began Career:** Early teens **Culinary School:** The Culinary Institute of America, Hyde Park, NY **Grad Year:** 1994 **Stages:** France: Taillevent **Work History:** Washington, DC: Vidalia; Yountville, CA: The French Laundry; Beverly Hills, CA: Spago **Mentor(s):** Thomas Keller **Awards:** 2008 James Beard Foundation Best Chef Mid-Atlantic; 2007 AAA 5 Diamond Award; 2006 StarChefs.com Rising Star Chef Washington, DC; 2005 Food & Wine Best New Chefs; 2005 Esquire Best New Restaurant 2005 RAMMY Best New Restaurant; 2005 Robb Report Best of the Best; 2006 Washington Post 4 stars

NOTABLE DISH(ES): Tartiflette: Yukon Gold Potato Millefeuille With Frisée Lettuce, Crispy Shoat Confit, and Warm Brillat-Savarin; Hudson Valley Foie Gras Shabu Shabu

FAST FACTS

Restaurant Recs: Pollo Rico – it's just really good Peruvian pollo a la brasa **Kitchen Tool(s):** Palette knife – I use it instead of tongs for flipping things or molding butters **Interview Question:** What is the difference between pressure and stress? The correct answer is preparation. **Flavor Combo(s):** Herbaceous and sour **Fave Cookbook(s):** Ma Gastronomie by Fernand Point. It's a recipe book, a storybook, and a glimpse into the author's philosophy. **Chef to Cook for You:** Thomas Keller – it would be nice to have dinner with the guy! **Culinary Travel:** I like Bangkok for its fruit and ingredients

Z

Josh Ziskin
Chef | La Morra

48 Boylston St. Brookline, MA 02445

Restaurant E-mail: josh@lamorra.com

Phone: (617) 739-0007

RESTAURANT FACTS
Seats: 72 **Weeknight Covers:** 75 **Weekend Covers:** 150 **Check Average (with Wine):** $45 **Tasting Menu:** Yes **Kitchen Staff:** 3–5

CHEF FACTS
Cuisine: Northern Italian **Born:** 1970 **Began Career:** 1997 **Culinary School:** Cambridge School of Culinary Arts, Cambridge, MA **Grad Year:** 1996 **Stages:** Italy: Belvedere Villa **Work History:** Italy: Belvedere Villa; Waltham, MA: Tuscan Grill; Cambridge, MA: Chez Henri **Mentor(s):** Paul O'Connell, Rene Michelena **Affiliations:** SOS **Languages Spoken:** Some Spanish and Italian

FAST FACTS
Restaurant Recs: Marcos in the North End for the stuffed shells with crab **Kitchen Tool(s):** Pasta machine **Interview Question:** What cook books do you read? Where have you eaten? **Flavor Combo(s):** Lobster and butter **Fave Cookbook(s):** The Splendid Table: Recipes from Emilia-Romagna, The Heartland of Northern Italian Food by Lynne Rossetto Kasper **Chef to Cook for You:** The Chef at La Libera in Alba – I always had the best meals there, and they make great pasta **Culinary Travel:** Italy – I have an Italian restaurant and I love Italian food

Randy Zweiban
Executive Chef | Province

161 North Jefferson Chicago, IL 60661

Restaurant E-mail: randyz@leye.com

RESTAURANT FACTS
Seats: 135 **Weeknight Covers:** 100+ **Weekend Covers:** 200 **Tasting Menu:** Yes $45 **Kitchen Staff:** 5–7

CHEF FACTS
Other Restaurants: Brasserie Jo **Cuisine:** Modern Latin cuisine **Born:** 1958 **Culinary School:** Peter Kumps Cooking School, New York, NY **Grad Year:** 1987–1989 **Stages:** New York, NY: Daniel; Chicago, IL: Charlie Trotter's **Work History:** Miami Beach, FL: Mano a Mano; Coral Gables, FL: Norman's; Los Angeles, CA: The Gate; Chicago, IL: Nacional 27 **Mentor(s):** Richard Melman, Norman Van Aken **Awards:** 2004 Nations Restaurant News Best Independent Operator Menu; Institute of Culinary Education Hall of Achievement Inductee

NOTABLE DISH(ES): Shrimp and Scallop Ceviche; Ahi and Watermelon Ceviche

FAST FACTS
Restaurant Recs: Bob San Sushi for hamachi and jalapeño sashimi **Kitchen Tool(s):** High speed blender for sauces, purées and soups **Interview Question:** Why do you want to work here? **Flavor Combo(s):** Big, bold flavors with the ingredients inspired by the southern hemisphere and Spain. Things like citrus and chilies, chocolate and salt, spices and sweetness. **Fave Cookbook(s):** Cookbooks by Alice Waters **Chef to Cook for You:** Nobu – his simplicity and complexity are amazing and his food is a work of art **Culinary Travel:** Brazil – for the many different regions and very different cuisines in those regions

International Chefs

We would be remiss if we did not recognize some of the bright culinary lights we've been fortunate enough to meet in our journeys outside the United States. This list of international chefs is by no means an exhaustive one; rather it's meant to be a guide to some of the compelling minds and restaurants across the world, some well-known outside their countries, and others not.

Tip/Advice: a tip for young cooks just starting in the industry

Underappreciated Ingredient: your favorite underappreciated or underutilized ingredient

Carles Abellan
Executive Chef | COMERÇ 24

Carrer del Comerç, 24

Barcelona, 08003 Spain

Phone: +34 933 192 102

Chef You Most Admire: Ferran Adría **Underappreciated Ingredient:** Saffron **Culinary Travel:** Japan

Albert Adriá
Executive Pastry Chef | El bulli

Cala Montjoi. Ap. 30

Roses, Girona, 17480 Spain

Restaurant E-mail: bulli@elbulli.com

Phone: +34 972 150 717

Cuisine: We aim to create enjoyment through creativity **Culinary Travel:** Peru - and luckily I get to go in September!

Ferran Adriá
Executive Chef | El bulli

Cala Montjoi. Ap. 30

Roses, Girona, 17480 Spain

Restaurant E-mail: bulli@elbulli.com

Phone: +34 972 150 717

Favorite Tool: Meat slicer **Interview Question:** Are you passionate about food and cooking? **Chef You Most Admire:** I admire all those that work kitchen hours for the only reward of a job well done **Underappreciated Ingredient:** Young pine nuts **Culinary Travel:** The Amazon – I hope to go this November

Adoni Luis Aduriz
Executive Chef | Mugaritz

Otzazulueta Baserria. Aldura Aldea 20 zk.

Errenteria, Gipuzkoa, 20100 Spain

Phone: +34 943 522 455

Favorite Tool: Hands are the first tools that you use to cook. They are good for feeling the texture of the product, and they are also the point between technology and your ideas. **Chef You Most Admire:** There are many chefs that I admire. I couldn't name just one. **Underappreciated Ingredient:** The best ingredients are attention to detail and common sense.

Sergi Arola
Executive Chef | La Broche

Miguek Angel 29, Chamberi

Madrid, 28010 Spain

Restaurant E-mail: sergiarola@labroche.com

Phone: +34 913 993 437

Favorite Tool: A Thermomix is my most important tool. It can chop and give heat at the same time. **Tip/Advice:** Learn to respect the guest. You can never think you are more important than the guest. Behind Ferran, there is a long road to travel. You must learn the job, and you must learn respect. **Interview Question:** Are you ready to sacrifice? That is all I want to know. I don't believe in CV's. **Chef You Most Admire:** Pierre Gagnaire. I met him in 1991 and he changed my vision of food. Usually when you are creative, you don't make money. After meeting Pierre, I felt I was going in the right direction.

Martin Arrieta
Executive Chef | Gran Bar Danzón

Libertad 1161

Capital Federal Buenos Aires, Argentina

Phone: +54 11 4811 1108

Mentors: Francis Mallmann (one of the most famous chefs in Argentina) – I used to watch him on TV and that is why I wanted to become a chef. When I came out of school I worked for Pablo Massey who worked for Francis Mallmann at Patagonia. He later introduced me to Francis whom I consider to be my mentor. **Tip/Advice:** Choose carefully who you work for and sacrifice to learn. Whom you work for is most important to providing you with the tools to learn your whole career. **Interview Question:** Are you willing to sacrifice and work 14 hour days? **Underappreciated Ingredient:** Vanilla. I like its flavor, aroma, and texture when it's very young. I also like to cook with fruits. **Culinary Travel:** I have always wanted to go and still have never been to Australia. I want to see fusion there and Tetsuya.

Elena Arzak
Executive Chef | Restaurante Arzak

Alcalde José Elósegui, 273

San Sebastian, Spain

Phone: +34 943 278 465

Favorite Tool: A spoon and a lyophilizer. **Interview Question:** I ask if cooking is their life. I like cooks that have passion! **Chef You Most Admire:** Ferran Adriá – I think he is the most imaginative chef in history.

Alex Atala
Executive Chef | D.O.M

Rua Barao de Capanem, 549 Jardins

Sao Paolo, 01411-01 Brazil

Phone: +55 30 88 07 61

Favorite Tool: Sauté pan – because it has so many uses in the kitchen. **Interview Question:** What is the best-selling plate in your restaurant? What sort of cuisine are you used to cooking? What sort of cuisine do you like and want to cook? **Chef You Most Admire:** Ferran Adriá – because he is the chef who most touches me. He has a very investigative cuisine. **Underappreciated Ingredient:** Tucupi, because it has a very Brazilian flavor.

Sat Bains
Executive Chef | Restaurant Sat Bains

Lenton Lane

Nottingham, NG7 2SA UK

Restaurant E-mail: info@restaurantsatbains.net

Phone: +44 01 15 986 6566

Mentors: I haven't got a mentor. I don't have any heritage of culinary style. So I look at each ingredient without any history. **Tip/Advice:** Be realistic and get a career plan. Be prepared to work very hard, anti-social hours and you will be rewarded. Have a 5 year plan. **Interview Question:** We make them cook. Trial. We don't tell them either. They come to the kitchen to do a trial and we surprise them with a box of ingredients. They have one hour to prepare something delicious. **Underappreciated Ingredient:** Wild ingredients. Hare. It represents a real feel for the land. It demands respect from the chef not to overdo it. It has a secret of life. **Culinary Travel:** Japan, because I think the Japanese have a view on their heritage. Clean flavors. You never feel full or bloated after eating. It is textural.

Stefano Baiocco
Executive Chef | Villa Feltrinelli a Gargnano

Via Rimembranza 38-40

Gargagno, Brescia 25084 Italy

Restaurant E-mail: booking@villafeltrinelli.com

Phone: +39 03 65 79 80 00

Mentors: Chef Annie Feolde of Enoteca Pinchiorri in Florence – this was the first important restaurant that I worked at. He taught me the importance of the quality product. Alain Ducasse taught me the profession – how things are done the right way. **Tip/Advice:** This job is hard work. If you have a lot of passion do it - otherwise, forget it. **Underappreciated Ingredient:** Herbs and aromatic and edible flowers

Oriol Balaguer
Executive Pastry Chef | Oriol Balaguer

Pl. Sant Gregori Taumaturg, 2

Barcelona, 08021 Spain

Phone: +34 932 011 846

Favorite Tool: Frying pan **Chef You Most Admire:** Ferran Adriá sets a great, high standard **Underappreciated Ingredient:** Spanish olive oil

Pascal Barbot
Executive Chef | L'Astrance

4 Rue Beethoven

Paris, 75016 France

Phone: +33 1 40 50 84 40

Favorite Tool: Mortar and pestle – I brought it back from Thailand and I love to make my curry paste with it. **Interview Question:** Are you open-minded? I'm looking for the cook who is ready to jump into a new environment with both feet, who isn't afraid to find him/herself in front of a completely new ingredient, using a new technique. I may ask: Do you like to take risks in the kitchen? The ideal response: "Yes, I like to experiment – I'll test new ideas on staff meal." Of course, an interview is never enough for me to decide if someone will be successful in the kitchen - they have to step behind the line to prove that! **Chef You Most Admire:** In Australia, Tetsuya Wakuda and Cheong Liew. In France, Alain Passard, Pierre Gagnaire, Michel Bras, and Marc Veyrat.

Frederic Bau
Executive Pastry Chef | Valrhona

Quai Général de Gaulle

Tain L'Hermitage, 26601 France

Restaurant E-mail: info-egc@valrhona.fr

Phone: +33 4 75 07 90 90

Favorite Tool: The mixer, to make magical emulsions, to create great tasting things, and for smoothness. I can't imagine cooking without it in my kitchen. **Interview Question:** Tell me four words that characterize your style as a pastry cook. What cake do you like to eat? Do you consider yourself an innovator or creator? **Chef You Most Admire:** Pierre Hermé and Pierre Gagnaire are two that I admire for what they do and how they do it. Their actions and their way of being are remarkable and influential on our trade. They are watched, followed, sometimes judged. They surpass themselves, they inspire, and consequently they motivate me to surpass myself, too.

Heinz Beck
Executive Chef | La Pergola

Via A. Cadlolo, 101

Cavalieri Hilton Hotel Rome, 00136 Italy

Restaurant E-mail: fb@cavalieri-hilton.it

Phone: +39 06 35 09 20 55

Shannon Bennett
Executive Chef | Vue de Monde

430 Little Collins Street

Melbourne, 3000 Australia

Phone: +61 3 9691 3888

Favorite Tool: The Pacojet for ice creams. It makes every dessert 100% consistent. **Interview Question:** Why did you become a chef? **Chef You Most Admire:** There are too many to name just one!

Martin Berasategui
Executive Chef | Martin Berasategui

Loidi Kalea n° 4

Lasarte-Oria, 20160 Gipuzkoa, Spain

Phone: +34 943 366 471

Heston Blumenthal
Executive Chef | The Fat Duck

High Street

Bray, Berkshire UK

Phone: +44 0 1628 580 333

Cuisine: A multi-sensory journey inspired by memory and emotion but above all if I had to pick one word, fun **Favorite Tool:** My knives! I recently discovered Tojiro Senkou knifes and now use them for everything. Fantastic balance and the way the steel is layered make the knife unbelievably sharp. **Interview Question:** I love talking about whatever is most recent in development, our latest multi-sensory discoveries and most recent dishes. At the moment it would be anything to do with historic British dishes that we are researching for the Fat Duck menu and of course the book. **Chef You Most Admire:** This is an impossible question for me as there are too many to mention in one answer. I think, however, I would have to say I most admire what is happening restaurant wise in the UK at the moment. Gourmet Magazine voted London the gastronomic capital of the world for its amazing diversity and exciting restaurant scene. **Underappreciated Ingredient:** Enthusiasm. For a chef, all the knowledge in the world is worthless without it. **Culinary Travel:** At the moment I am working with food historians researching historic British dishes that I am reinterpreting for the Fat Duck menu. I would love to travel back to the 16th and 17th century and see those kitchens in operation first hand.

Graham Brown
Executive Chef | The Cookhouse

110 Rossiters Rd.

Rangiora, RD 2 New Zealand

Restaurant E-mail: graham@thecookhouse.co.nz

Phone: +64 3 312 8559

Cuisine: I am rooted to classic techniques, and continue to be influenced by the new culinary experiences I have enjoyed through traveling. **Chef You Most Admire:** Michel Guèrard and Tetsuya Wakuda. About the time I finished my culinary training, and was so full of ideas for my own future, Michel Guèrard was credited with creating the original concept of nouvelle cuisine, the light and modern approach to food that originated in the 80's. He turned classic French food up on its ear. Tetsuya Wakuda is very innovative and has intense flavors. His dishes are simple, stripped of excess gestures, but still elegant and quite delectable. **Underappreciated Ingredient:** Parsnips – they can be prepared and appreciated in so many different ways **Culinary Travel:** Strangely enough I have not had the chance to get to Spain and Portugal; I was always interested in the traditional simplicity of their food techniques and clarity of their flavors.

Jordi Butrón
Executive Pastry Chef | Espai Sucre

c. princesa 53

Barcelona 08003 Spain

Phone: +34 932 681 630

Favorite Tool: The brain – in pastry accuracy, order and precision are indispensable **Tip/Advice:** The restaurant's logo is an ant. The ant is organized, precise, and diligent. This is what we teach here. **Chef You Most Admire:** Pierre Gagnaire – after I met him, my vision of cooking changed radically. He was my teacher and is my inspiration. I envy his talent and energy. **Underappreciated Ingredient:** Salt, because it seems that it's not a traditional ingredient in pastry **Culinary Travel:** Thailand - a lot of creative cuisine is influenced by Thai flavor pairings

Ada and Ebe Concaro
Executive Chefs | Tomo I

Hotel Panamericano Buenos Aires

Carlos Pellegrini 521 Buenos Aires, C1009 Argentina

Phone: +54 11 4326 6695

Mentors: Our family – who taught us to cook **Tip/Advice:** Cuisine is made to flatter your palate. Of course presentation is important, but the main thing is taste. You have to have textures, perfumes. Balance is absolutely important. **Interview Question:** It is very important to us that they eat and feel pleasure – that they enjoy food and have a sensibility about food and taste. You can teach about taste, but you cant teach about pleasure. **Underappreciated Ingredient:** Dill – in very little quantities. It should be a nuance, not taste of dill. **Culinary Travel:** Paris but really France. We love the cuisine of Provence. It is the cuisine that is closest to North Italian cuisine. If you want to learn the essence of North Italian cuisine you will find it in the South of France. It is very sophisticated. Even when we went to NY or Washington DC, our best meals were at French restaurants.

Richard Corrigan
Executive Chef | Lindsay House

21 Romilly Street

London, W1D 5AF UK

Restaurant E-mail: richardcorrigan@lindsayhouse.co.uk

Phone: +44 020 7439 0450

Mentors: Albert Rouix, Michel Nichand **Favorite Tool:** A big stone mortal and pestle **Tip/Advice:** Keep you ears wide open, and your mouth wide shut **Interview Question:** I'm looking for someone who is intelligent with their own sense of humor, I can't stand stupidity. I don't care about formal training – I care more about intelligence. They have to feel this is where they want to be, and that they can play on the same playing field. **Culinary Travel:** To China – they have been cooking for thousands of years and there is lots to learn. Also to Spain – I love the flavors of Spain.

Carlo Cracco
Executive Chef | Ristorante Cracco

Via Hugo Victor, 4

Milan, 20123 Italy

Phone: +39 02 87 67 74

Mentors: Gualtiero Marchesi – he is a philosopher **Favorite Tool:** Knife **Interview Question:** When you're interviewing a cook for a position in your kitchen, I want a person that wants to work. I don't want someone who will be bouncing around, I want someone who wants to be here for at least a year. There are lots of kids that can work, can plate things, but don't understand with their heads and mouths. I want someone who can understand what I want and what I need to do – someone who is eager to learn. **Chef You Most Admire:** My mentor, Marchesi, because he taught people how to eat, how to plate a dish **Underappreciated Ingredient:** Carte Vegetale – vegetable paper and potato paper. It is useful for many things. It is very diverse – you can layer it, you can use it sweet and savory and also rolled by hand into risotto. **Culinary Travel:** I like to go where I can find tradition. I would like to go to China. Also Madagascar.

Paul Cunningham
Executive Chef | The Paul

Vesterbrogade 3

København V, 1630 Denmark

Restaurant E-mail: info@thepaul.dk

Phone: +45 3375 0775

Mentors: Monsieur Serge Bossen, Clive Dixon **Chef You Most Admire:** I will never forget a very short stage in kitchen of Marco Pierre White at Harvey's in Wandsworth. Inspirational – Mr. White is undoubtedly the most influential figure to my generation of British cooks – there are a lot of people out there that owe more to him than they would initially own up to.

Hélène Darroze
Executive Chef/Owner | Hélène Darroze

4, rue d'Assas

Paris, 75006 France

Restaurant E-mail: darroze@relaischateaux.com

Phone: +33 1 42 22 00 11

Cuisine: Southwestern French cuisine, with roots from Bordeaux to the Basque region all the way through Périgord. **Mentors:** Alain Ducasse **Tip/Advice:** The way you cook reveals what you are. Cook to please your clients and yourselves. It all works in unison.

Carmen Titita Degollado
Executive Chef | El Bajio

Colonia Obrero Popular

Mexico, DF 02840 Mexico

Phone: +52 555 234 3763

Favorite Tool: The molcajete, because I learned how to cook with it **Interview Question:** Where did you learn to love Mexican cuisine? **Chef You Most Admire:** Diana Kennedy, because of her dedication to the investigation of traditional Mexican cuisine and ingredients **Underappreciated Ingredient:** Epazote and chipotle peppers because I grew up with them

Patrice Demers
Executive Pastry Chef | Laloux

250 Avenue des Pins Est

Montreal, QC H2W 1P3 Canada

Phone: (514) 287-9127

Favorite Tool: Pacojet **Tip/Advice:** Be patient. To try to learn everything ask questions. Don't be too shy and don't try to do everything by yourself. **Interview Question:** Do you really love pastry that much? I like to ask him/her what their favorite things are. He/she need to have passion.

Alejandro Digilio
Executive Chef | La Vineria de Gualtiero Bolivar

Bolivar 865, San Telmo

Buenos Aires, Argentina

Restaurant E-mail: lavineriadebolivar@gmail.com

Phone: +54 11 4360 4709

Juan Pablo Felipe
Executive Chef | El Chaflan

Avda. de Pio XII 34

Madrid, 28016 Spain

Restaurant E-mail: restaurante@elcheflan.com

Phone: +34 913 506 193

Ramon Freixa
Executive Chef | El Raco d'en Freixa

Carrer de Sant Elies, 22

Barcelona, 08006 Spain

Phone: +34 932 097 559

Dani Garcia
Executive Chef | Calima

c/ José Meliá S/N

Marbella, 29602 Spain

Phone: +34 952 764 252

Cuisine: Modern, experimental Andalusian **Favorite Tool:** Thermomix – which makes all our soups have a very smooth texture **Chef You Most Admire:** Ferran Adriá – because thanks to him I enjoy each day in my kitchen more than the one before

Laurent Godbout
Executive Chef | Chez L'Epicier

311 rue Saint-Paul Est

Montreal, QC H2Y 1H3 Canada

Restaurant E-mail: info@chezlepicier.com

Phone: (514) 878-2232

Favorite Tool: iSi siphon **Tip/Advice:** Be patient. Work hard. You have to be prepared to sacrifice. **Interview Question:** Can you work under pressure? What restaurants do you know? What restaurants have you been to? **Chef You Most Admire:** Alain Ducasse – I've never worked for him but have learned so much from him

Angela Hartnett
Executive Chef | York & Albany

127–129 Parkway

Camden, NW1 7PS UK

Restaurant E-mail: y&a@gordonramsay.com.

Mentors: Gordon Ramsay and Marcus Warering **Favorite Tool:** Robo-Coupe; Thermomix **Tip/Advice:** Dedication is very important. Never feel embarrassed about what you don't know – ask questions **Interview Question:** First I look for enthusiasm. If they ask what's the money, what are the hours, you know that is not the right person. And, if a cook can't pick up a knife you can say goodbye at the door. **Culinary Travel:** San Sebastian, Southern France, Northern Italy. I have a great travel book for these places that has out of the way restaurants.

Fergus Henderson
Executive Chef | St. JOHN Bar & Restaurant

26 St John Street

London, EC1M 4AY UK

Restaurant E-mail: kirsty@stjohnrestaurant.com

Phone: +44 020 7251 4090

Favorite Tool: A cork screw – for obvious reasons **Interview Question:** There's not a specific question – it's more if they say the menu looks easy, I know they're not right (for the position) **Chef You Most Admire:** Many chefs, almost all of them, but if you want me to be specific, to watch Giorgio Locatelli make ravioli is a joy to behold. Jonathon Jones of the Anchor & Hope cooks like a dream, and of course Jeremy Lee of Blueprint Café.

Pierre Hermé
Pastry Chef | Pierre Hermé

72, rue Bonaparte

Paris, 75006 France

Phone: +33 1 43 54 47 77

Favorite Tool: Scale – I create with the head, but I always need a scale to be exact. **Interview Question:** No key question, per se. I want to highlight motivation in an interview. **Chef You Most Admire:** Gaston Lenôtre, because he handed down the technique and the passion of the job **Underappreciated Ingredient:** Salt, as it is the most important thing in sweet food

Jordi Herrera
Executive Chef | Manairo Restaurant

c. Diputació, 424

Barcelona, 08013 Spain

Restaurant E-mail: info@manairo.com

Phone: +34 932 31 00 57

Marc Andre Jette
Executive Chef and Owner | Laloux

250 avenue des Pins Est

Montreal,QC H2W 1P3 Canada

Restaurant E-mail: matraiteur@videtron.ca

Phone: (514) 287-9127

Favorite Tool: Vita-Prep – because of the consistency **Tip/Advice:** Work hard. One day it is going to pay off, not necessarily in money. **Interview Question:** What is the craziest thing you will do to work at one place? They need to have passion. They need to know a lot about food and what's happening in the restaurants in NY, all around the world and love what they are doing. Crazy about their job. **Chef You Most Admire:** Daren from Decca 77 – I learned managing, respect, and how to treat the food. Simple food, but very well organized.

Atul Kochhar
Executive Chef | Benares

12 Berkeley Sq.

Berkeley Square House London, W1J 6BS UK

Phone: +44 020 7629 8886

Cuisine: Contemporary Indian food based on classical and modern presentation **Mentors:** My father, Bernard Kunig (a German chef) who worked in India; George Locatili, Marcus Wearing, Michael Caine **Favorite Tool:** Wooden spatula **Tip/Advice:** One must have a passion for food. You have to be dedicated and you must understand that you have to put in the hours necessary to master the skill. **Interview Question:** I look for basic skills: sautéeing, braising, and an understanding of ingredients. Then I put them on the line for a week and watch their skills and technique. **Mentor:** Arun Agarwal **Favorite Tool:** Knife **Chef You Most Admire:** Gordon Ramsay **Culinary Travel:** I want to explore South America and China

Susur Lee
Executive Chef | Susur

601 King Street West

Toronto, M5V 1M5 Canada

Phone: (416) 603-2205

Favorite Tool: An apron, because it is a chef's kitchen "costume" of sorts, symbolizing a certain security and signaling that it is time to get to work **Interview Question:** Do you do drugs? And are you in a serious relationship? I don't hire drug users. And I don't hire people who are in serious relationships (just kidding!) **Chef You Most Admire:** Jean-Georges Vongerichten

Candido Lopez
Chef | Mesón de Cándido

Azoguejo, 5

Segovia, 40001 Spain

Restaurant E-mail: candido@mesondecandido.es

Phone: +34 921 425 911

Cuisine: Traditional Castilian cuisine **Favorite Tool:** The wood oven. It is an essential tool because our cuisine is based on roasted meat (pork and lamb). **Interview Question:** Why is it a tradition to cut the suckling pig with a dish? **Chef You Most Admire:** Ferran Adrià. I believe Ferran has set the guidelines in culinary art and technique at a worldwide level. **Underappreciated Ingredient:** Bread. It is increasingly under-appreciated in modern cuisine. I think it is the ideal companion for all meals. **Culinary Travel:** I love New York as a city and also as a place to learn new culinary trends

Gualtiero Marchesi
Executive Chef | Ristorante Gualtiero Marchesi

Via Vittorio Emanuele, 23

Ercbusco-Brescia, 25030 Italy

Restaurant E-mail: ristorante@marchesi.it

Phone: +39 03 07 76 05 62

Mentors: The cousin of my father – he taught me intelligence, passion, and gusto **Favorite Tool:** My knife – I can't cook without it **Tip/Advice:** Learn the materials, learn the technical parts, then the creative side can come out – the "music inside." You need the deep knowledge first. **Interview Question:** Any intelligent, thoughtful question **Chef You Most Admire:** Bergamaschi Domenico, my father's cousin **Underappreciated Ingredient:** Rice **Culinary Travel:** I believe in being a "traveler of taste." I want to visit each culture – to know and to create something new.

Guy Martin
Executive Chef | Le Grand Véfour

17, rue de Beaujolais

Paris, 75001 France

Restaurant E-mail: grand.vefour@wanadoo.fr

Phone: +33 1 42 96 56 27

Cuisine: Modern and lively **Mentors:** I was never trained by the great chefs. My inspiration comes from other places. I am lucky to work near the Louvre. I go there often in the afternoons after lunch. Paintings really inspire me. **Tip/Advice:** Cooking is a job of sharing. Preparing food for someone is a loving act. If you do not understand the other person, you cannot serve him or her well.

Joe Mercuri
Chef | Brontë

1800 Sherbrooke West

Montreal, H3H 1E4 Canada

Restaurant E-mail: bronte1800@yahoo.ca

Phone: (514) 934-1801

Mentors: My mother, my wife, my staff. No chef guided my way. **Favorite Tool:** PolyScience immersion circulator **Tip/Advice:** Work hard, absorb knowledge and read a lot **Interview Question:** I don't look to interview. I look for passion, the way they talk about food. What do you like to eat; what do you do on your days off; what are their last jobs in the business.

Enrique Olvera
Executive Chef | Pujol

F. Petrarca 254 Chapoltepec

Mexico D.F. 11570 Mexico

Phone: +52 555 545 4111

Favorite Tool: A great knife. It makes your work easier and makes the food look sharp. **Interview Question:** Chaos or perfection? **Chef You Most Admire:** Chef Thomas Keller. His work is timeless and his philosophy inspires me to strive for perfection.

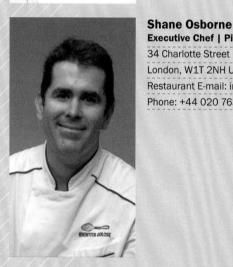

Shane Osborne
Executive Chef | Pied-á-Terre

34 Charlotte Street

London, W1T 2NH UK

Restaurant E-mail: info@pied-a-terre.co.uk

Phone: +44 020 7636 1178

Xavier Pellicer
Executive Chef | Abac Restaurant

Av. Tibidado 1

Barcelona, 08022 Spain

Restaurant E-mail: abac12@telefonica.net

Phone: +34 932 542 299

Patricia Quintana
Executive Chef | Izote

Presidente Mazarik 513 Local 3

Col. Polanco Mexico D.F. 11560 Mexico

Restaurant E-mail: pquintan@data.net.mx

Phone: +52 555 280 1671

Favorite Tool: The molcajete in Mexican cuisine is a special grinding tool that keeps the flavor in salsas **Interview Question:** Do you love what you do? I am looking for them to respond that they have the heart and the passion. **Chef You Most Admire:** For years since the Nouvelle Cuisine started in the '70's I have admired Michel Guérard. I think he started all the new ways of cooking with Bocuse, Troisgros, and Alain Chapel. Nowadays Ferran Adriá is the person who is many ways is changing cooking, introducing new forms and presenting ingredients - he has an ingenious way of doing food. I admire Daniel Boulud for his combination of classical and modern interpretations in his culinary efforts.

René Redzepi
Executive Chef /Partner | Noma

Strandgade 93 Copenhagen 1401 Denmark

rr@noma.dk

+45 3296 3287

Cuisine: Modern Nordic cuisine with a focus on local products and techniques **Favorite Tool:** My hands. Without them nothing would be possible! **Interview Question:** What is your favorite ingredient? **Under-Appreciated Ingredient:** Vinegar – it is essential and a big part of Nordic cuisine. Having the right balance of acidity is really important. **Culinary Travel:** Holland and Belgium. They are two of the last stops on the European subway.

Joan Roca
Executive Chef | El Cellar de Can Roca

Can Sunyer, 46

Girona, 17007 Spain

Favorite Tool: Good knives. I need to work with knives that are in perfect condition, fit for their purpose. **Interview Question:** How has you parents' work influenced your way of understanding cuisine? **Chef You Most Admire:** Ferran Adrià, for being so generous to the chef community **Underappreciated Ingredient:** Sea urchins – I love their peculiar taste and the memories they evoke **Culinary Travel:** Now that the East has become a part of our cooking tradition, I'd like to visit and get to know South America (Peru).

Gonzalo Sacot
Executive Chef | Sucre

Sucre 676

Buenos Aires, Argentina

Phone: +54 11 4782 9082

Mentors: Francis Mallman. He taught me to take very good care in handling product. **Favorite Tool:** Japanese Chef's knife – Misono **Tip/ Advice:** Have a lot of patience, a will to learn and strength to work long hours **Interview Question:** Are you willing to learn? **Culinary Travel:** Europe – I haven't been to Italy

Davide Scabin
Executive Chef | Combal Zero

Piazza Mafalda di Savoia

Rivoli, Torino 10098 Italy

Restaurant E-mail: combal.zero@combal.org

Phone: +39 011 95 65 225

Favorite Tool: Paper and pen – to never miss a single thought, idea, aroma and flavor **Interview Question:** Do you want to become a soloist or an orchestra conductor? There is not a right answer. I realize which one the candidate really is when he or she is "left alone" in the kitchen. **Chef You Most Admire:** Michel Bras

Claude Troisgros
Execuitve Chef | Olympe

Rua Custódio Serrão 62

Rio de Janeiro, Brazil

Phone: +55 21 22 66 08 38

Mentors: Paul Bocuse, Eckart Witzigmann **Favorite Tool:** Whisk **Interview Question:** When do you want to come and how long do you want to stay? We have a program for stages. We receive new students every month for a rotation. They need to be humble and interested in what we are doing. **Culinary Travel:** Thailand – I've never been

Hans Valimaki
Chef | Chez Dominique

Rikhardinkatu 4

Helsinki, 00130 Finland

Restaurant E-mail: info@chezdominique.fi

Phone: +358 9612 7393

Mentors: I had mentor at the pastry school – Pentti Painivaara. He taught me discipline – anger – he yelled a lot. He really liked what he did. He also taught me attitude. **Tip/Advice:** First of all – learn some languages. Start at the bottom and take in everything you can. Don't be in a hurry if you want to be a really good chef. This profession is made by hand and you need to learn it by doing it. Be prepared to work long days. **Interview Question:** Usually we don't interview. People send us their resume. We ask about their girlfriend, what they did last weekend, some basic things – we look for their passion and if there are any attitude problems. **Underappreciated Ingredient:** Cloudberries – very expensive in Finland but used a lot by top chefs. In Finland we don't respect our own products as much as we could. Like white fish like perch. It's local, fresh. **Culinary Travel:** Definitely France – I love France. It's about feeling, the atmosphere, and they have good bread.

Tetsuya Wakuda
Executive Chef/Owner | Tetsuya's

529 Kent St.

Sydney, NSW 2000 Australia

Phone: +61 2 9267 2900

Favorite Tool: The latest convection steam oven **Tip/Advice:** Make sure that you love eating, not just cooking. If not, you should look for another profession. **Interview Question:** Are you willing to marry me? You will spend more time with me than your spouse. In fact, you will spend half your life with me. Are you willing to do that? **Chef You Most Admire:** Alfonso Laccarino, whom I admire for his purity of food and cooking. Also Charlie Trotter, because he started out washing dishes and taught me about the business.

Marcus Wareing
Executive Chef | Pétrus

Wilton Place

The Berkeley Knightsbridge, London SW1X 7RL UK

Phone: +44 020 7592 1609

Tip/Advice: Never forget what you have learned in school, but when you begin working, you need to open your mind, set aside what you have learned, and absorb new information. **Interview Question:** I am aware of how they present themselves and of the questions they ask. If they ask about hours and pay, forget them. **Culinary Travel:** Italy – I've been once and want to go again. Italians put together great flavors.

Seiji Yamamoto
RyuGin

7-1 7-24. Roppomgi

Minato-ku Tokyo, 106-0032 Japan

Phone: +81 03 3423 8006

Favorite Tool: Sashimi knife **Interview Question:** What do you do to promote Japanese food throughout the world? **Chef You Most Admire:** Andoni Luis Aduriz

Mixologists

Abou-Ganim - Wondrich

KEY

Cocktail Book: favorite cocktail resource

Mixologists

Tony Abou-Ganim
Mixologist | The Modern Mixologist

Suite 104-266

6935 Aliante Pkwy Las Vegas, NV 89084

Restaurant E-mail: tony@themodernmixologist.com

Phone: (702) 228-7207

Cocktail Style: Contemporary approach that is founded in the classics **Work History:** Port Huron, MI: The Brass Rail Bar; San Francisco, CA: Balboa Cafe, Harry Denton's Starlight Room; New York, NY: Po, Bar Milano; Las Vegas, NV: The Bellagio **Cocktail Book:** The Fine Art of Mixing Drinks by David Embury **Fave Tool:** Hand-held lime juicer **Cocktail to Drink:** Negroni **Cocktail to Make:** A fresh-fruit seasonal variation on the mojito **Underappreciated Ingredient:** Bitters and Campari

Anthony Alba
Mixologist | Liquidity Global LLC

Las Vegas, LV

Cocktail Style: Cutting edge and very influenced by culinary traditions **Work History:** Las Vegas, NV: The Rio Hotel, The Paris Hotel, Bally's Hotel, Caesar's Palace, The Venetian, Mandalay Bay **Cocktail Book:** I have all these old books form the 1700s, and I use them in conjunction with the internet **Fave Tool:** Torch **Cocktail to Drink:** I drink the whole gambit. It depends on where I am and what I'm doing. I wouldn't have a margarita after dinner, but I'd have it at a pool. There's always a time and a place. **Cocktail to Make:** Anything custom-made **Underappreciated Ingredient:** Bourbon – it's America's spirit and most Americans don't know much about it. Ask any Frenchman about Cognac or a Mexican about Tequila – we need to put Bourbon on the map!

Scott Baird
Bartender | 15 Romolo

15 Romolo St. San Francisco, CA 94133

Restaurant E-mail: scott@basquesf.com

Phone: (415) 398-1359

Cocktail Style: Delicious and not precious (kitchen-inspired, classics) **Work History:** San Francisco, CA: Cesar, Coco500, Rye **Cocktail Book:** The Savoy Cocktail Book by Harry Craddock **Fave Tool:** Chefs knife **Cocktail to Drink:** Silver Tequila **Cocktail to Make:** Sazerac **Underappreciated Ingredient:** Pastis

Justin Beam
Mixologist | Fearing's at the Ritz-Carlton Dallas

2121 McKinney Ave. Dallas, TX 75201

Restaurant E-mail: justin.beam@ritzcarlton.com

Phone: (214) 922-4848

Cocktail Style: Seasonal, fresh, fun **Work History:** Dallas, TX: Craft, M Crowd Restaurant Group **Cocktail Book:** The Craft of the Cocktail by Dale DeGroff **Fave Tool:** Vita-Mix Bar Boss **Cocktail to Drink:** Single-malt Scotch, neat **Cocktail to Make:** Dean's Margarita with damiana (herbal liqueur from mexico), lime juice, organic blue agave, Cabo-Wabo tequila **Underappreciated Ingredient:** Cachaça – although it caught on in the big markets, it hasn't caught up in smaller markets yet. I like the Leblon brand.

Mixologists

Greg Best
Mixologist | Holeman and Finch

2277 Peachtree Road Suite B Atlanta, GA 30309

Restaurant E-mail: greg@holeman-finch.com

Phone: (404) 948-1175

Cocktail Style: Classic-minded, minimal ingredients **Work History:** Las Vegas, NV: Delmonico Steakhouse; Atlanta, GA: Emeril's Atlanta, Restaurant Eugene **Cocktail Book:** The Joy of Mixology by Gary Regan, The Craft of the Cocktail by Dale DeGroff **Fave Tool:** My bar spoon – I have a sick infatutation with my bar spoon (in all the right ways) **Cocktail to Drink:** Sazerac **Cocktail to Make:** Aviation **Under-appreciated Ingredient:** Bitters

Neil Bodenheimer
Mixologist | The Delachaise

3442 Saint Charles Ave. New Orleans, LA 70115

Restaurant E-mail: neil@curenola.com

Cocktail Style: Classicly inspired with updated flavors **Work History:** New York, NY: The Modern **Cocktail Book:** The Savoy Cocktail Book by Harry Craddock **Fave Tool:** Fruit peeler, because it gives you great twists; the barstomp – you can do so many things with it **Cocktail to Drink:** If I'm going out, I like the perfect Manhattan **Cocktail to Make:** Really good tequila with a bit of lime **Underappreciated Ingredient:** Homemade vermouth. Why not make your own?

Ame Brewster
Bar Director | Café Boulud

The Brazilian Court Hotel

301 Australian Ave. Palm Beach, FL 33480

Phone: (561) 655-6060

Cocktail Style: Seasonal with artisanal and unusual spirits, wine-influenced **Work History:** New York, NY: Otto Enoteca, Alto **Cocktail Book:** Anything by Dave Wondrich. His work on classic cocktails has been my main resource. **Fave Tool:** I have a simple bar and I like to keep it that way. I like my long handled spoon, my muddler, and my food processor. **Cocktail to Drink:** I like the old-school Presbyterian – ginger beer and whiskey **Cocktail to Make:** I like things that I get to muddle, like Mojitos and Caipirinhas

Dale DeGroff
Mixologist

New York, NY

Restaurant E-mail: kingcocktl@aol.com

Cocktail Style: Classic, culinary cocktails **Work History:** Los Angeles, CA: Charlie O's, Hotel Bel-Air; New York, NY: Aurora, The Rainbow Room; consulting projects for: Pastis, Zoe, Pravda, Balthazar, Beacon, Bemelmen's Bar **Cocktail Book:** I use modern ones to check on how recipes have changed. I like The Savoy Cocktail Book by Harry Craddock, How to Mix Drinks by Jerry Thomas, The Artistry of Mixing Drinks by Charles Schumann and The Joy of Mixology by Gary Regan. **Fave Tool:** Muddler – I was using one in the 80's when no one else was. Other than that, the Boston shaker, which is the chef knife of the bartending trade. **Cocktail to Drink:** Gin Martini or a Sazerac **Cocktail to Make:** A stirred drink – I love stirring and the calmness and relaxation of when you stir a drink. You stop what you're doing, stir, and have a chat. **Underappreciated Ingredient:** Velvet Falernum, Pimento, Amer Picon, Orange Curaçao

Mixologists

Joel Finsel
Mixologist | Caffe Phoenix

9 South Front St. Wilmington, NC 28401

Restaurant E-mail: joelfinsel@gmail.com

Phone: (910) 797-3501

Cocktail Style: Classic, clean, simple **Work History:** Philadelphia, PA: Astral Plane; I also cover spirits for travelbeat.com **Cocktail Book:** The Art of the Bar by Jeff Hollinger and Rob Schwartz **Fave Tool:** Ice scoop **Cocktail to Drink:** Hendrick's & tonic with a splash of Campari **Cocktail to Make:** Negroni – according to mixologist Toby Cecchini, the Negroni should taste "like a cool brook perambulating through a spice bazaar" **Underappreciated Ingredient:** Limoncello and indigenous liquors

Eben Freeman
Bar Manager | Tailor

525 Broome St. New York, NY 10013

Restaurant E-mail: eben_freeman@tailornyc.com

Phone: (212) 334-5182

Cocktail Style: Progressive
Work History: New York, NY: wd~50, Wallse, Red Cat, Fanelli's, Eleven Madison Park, Palladin, Mad 61 **Cocktail Book:** Cosby Gaige's "Ladies Companion" **Fave Tool:** My Japanese bar spoon
Cocktail to Drink: The first one **Cocktail to Make:** The next one
Underappreciated Ingredient: Imagination

Amanda Gager
Mixologist | Stripsteak

3950 Las Vegas Blvd. Las Vegas, LV 89119

Phone: (702) 632-7414

Cocktail Style: New take on classics **Cocktail Book:** The Craft of the Cocktail by Dale DeGroff **Fave Tool:** Hand-held torch **Cocktail to Drink:** I've been drinking lots of Champagne lately **Cocktail to Make:** Old Fashioned – when someone orders one I always get a little excited

John Gertsen
Mixologist | No. 9 Park

9 Park St. Boston, MA 02108

Phone: (617) 742-9991

Cocktail Style: Classic and seasonal **Work History:** Boston, MA: Salamander **Cocktail to Drink:** A Manhattan **Cocktail to Make:** I love making a Ramos Gin Fizz. People look at you like you're insane when you make it.

Mixologists

Ken Hall
Mixologist | Noir Bar

Luxor Hotel

3900 Las Vegas Blvd S Las Vegas, LV 89136

Cocktail Style: Culinary (dessert-based) cocktails **Work History:** Orlando, FL: Pleasure Island at Walt Disney World; Ft. Lauderdale, FL: Voodoo Lounge; Las Vegas, NV: Pure **Cocktail Book:** The Art of the Bar by Jeff Hollinger and Rob Schwartz; The Craft of the Cocktail by Dale DeGroff **Fave Tool:** Lemon/lime squeezer **Cocktail to Drink:** It really depends on the day – a nicely made Margarita is a good one **Cocktail to Make:** It's really just the one that my guest wants. It's the best one when someone says that is the best drink they've ever had. **Underappreciated Ingredient:** Sherry and bitters

John Kinder
Mixologist

Chicago, IL

Restaurant E-mail: moonshots@hotmail.com

Cocktail Style: My mixology style is grounded in blending classic and contemporary approaches to both taste and technique while utilizing fresh, seasonal ingredients **Work History:** Chicago, IL: Moxie, The Pump Room, mk **Cocktail Book:** The Savoy Cocktail Book by Harry Craddock. It's inspiring every time I pick it up. **Fave Tool:** My cryovac machine – I can infuse in hours what it takes others weeks to macerate **Cocktail to Drink:** Manhattan – I like a dry Manhattan with orange bitters, but I mostly drink French farmhouse ale when I go out **Cocktail to Make:** The Pear Fumé – it has a tincture thing at the end that a lot of people aren't used to. I like it when people give me questionable looks when I'm making a drink. **Underappreciated Ingredient:** Cognac – it's fallen victim to its own marketing as an after-dinner drink. People should try it more as an aperitif (straight or in cocktails).

Eben Klemm
Mixologist | BR Guest Corporate Mixologist

206 Spring St. New York, NY 10012

Restaurant E-mail: eklemm@brguestinc.com

Phone: (212) 529-0900

Cocktail Style: I like to think of what I do as "cognitive mixology." The best drinks occur when the ingredients relate to each other not just because they taste right, but in that they also make the imbiber think about why or how they are combined. **Work History:** Massachusettes Institute of Technology, MASS: Molecular Biology Lab Manager (pre-mixology days); New York, NY: The Campbell Apartment, Pico; consulting projects, including Fiamma (Las Vegas), The James Hotel (Chicago) **Cocktail Book:** Any novel by Dawn Powell **Fave Tool:** An ice cube tray **Cocktail to Drink:** A 3 to 1 Plymouth Martini that I spend 5 minutes putting together **Cocktail to Make:** The last thing I've invented – it teaches me the most **Underappreciated Ingredient:** Salt

Jason Kosmas
Mixologist | Employees Only

510 Hudson St. New York, NY 10014

Restaurant E-mail: jkosmas@employeesonly.com

Phone: (212) 242 3021

Cocktail Style: Culinary approach to classic mixology **Work History:** New York, NY: Pravda, Cocktail Conceptions (consulting) **Cocktail Book:** The Craft of the Cocktail by Dale DeGroff **Fave Tool:** Boston shaker **Cocktail to Drink:** Negroni **Cocktail to Make:** Hemingway Daiquiri or La Floradita **Underappreciated Ingredient:** The whole range of bitters

Mixologists

Tim Lacey
Bar Manager | Custom House and Spring

500 S Dearborn St. Chicago, IL 60605

Restaurant E-mail: tim@srgchicago.com

Phone: (773) 395-7100

Cocktail Style: Creative, classically inspired **Work History:** Largely self-taught **Cocktail Book:** The Savoy Cocktail Book **Fave Tool:** Microplane grater **Cocktail to Make:** #4: Coffee infused Ron Zacapa, housemade cherry liqueur, Navan rinse served up

Toby Maloney
Mixologist | Alchemy Consulting & The Violet Hour

New York, NY

Restaurant E-mail: alchemyconsulting@gmail.com

Phone: (917) 796-8618

Cocktail Style: A culinary approach to classic cocktails, with a tweak **Work History:** New York, NY: The Grange Hall, Milk and Honey, Flat-iron Lounge, Pegu, Freemans; Chicago, IL: The Violet Hour **Cocktail Book:** Around the World with Jigger, Beaker and Flask by Charles Baker; The Joy of Mixology by Gary Regan **Fave Tool:** The Wusthof channel knife **Cocktail to Drink:** Havana Club Seven Daiquiri **Cocktail to Make:** Neptune's Wrath – gin, lemon, egg white, absinthe, flaming green chartreuse **Underappreciated Ingredient:** Bitters, Amaros

Vincenzo Marianella
Mixologist | The Doheny

714 W Olympic Blvd. Los Angeles, CA 90015

Cocktail Style: A culinary approach influenced by classic cocktails
Work History: Los Angeles, CA: Valentino, Providence, Smollensky's,
MyMixology **Cocktail to Drink:** Margarita **Cocktail to Make:** Blazer

Gaston Martinez
Mixologist | Nora's

6020 W Flamingo Rd., #10 Las Vegas, LV, 89103

Phone: (702) 365-6713

Cocktail Style: Classics **Work History:** Las Vegas, NV: Nora's (for
13 years – developed the bar program) **Fave Tool:** Muddler **Cocktail to Drink:** Pisco Sour **Cocktail to Make:** I just like to make good
cocktails, I don't think about it when I'm making it. The reward is in
the person's face. Making it is just part of the work, the reward is
afterward. **Underappreciated Ingredient:** Blood orange – I think a
lot of the in-the-know people use it and know what to do with it, but
others don't. It's such a beautiful fruit.

Mixologists

Duggan McDonnell
Mixologist | Cantina

580 Sutter St. San Francisco, CA

Restaurant E-mail: life@cantinasf.com

Phone: (415) 398-0195

Cocktail Style: Wild, rustic local, marrying of fresh ingredients, wine-influenced, boutique esoteric spirits **Work History:** San Francisco, CA: Absinthe Brasserie, Frisson, Wild Ginger **Cocktail Book:** Old Mr. Boston Bartender's Guide **Fave Tool:** Tasting straw **Cocktail to Drink:** Sidecar **Cocktail to Make:** Caipirinha **Underappreciated Ingredient:** All forms of wine, from Madeiras to Malbecs

Jim Meehan
Mixologist | PDT

113 St Marks Pl. New York, NY 10009

Restaurant E-mail: jim@pdtnyc.com

Phone: (212) 614-0386

Cocktail Style: Classic, using artisanal ingredients **Work History:** New York, NY: Five Points, Pace, Gramercy Tavern **Cocktail Book:** Killer Cocktails by Dave Wondrich, Difford's Guide by Simon Difford, and Vintage Spirits and Forgotten Cocktails by Ted Haigh are my current favorites **Fave Tool:** I love Chris Gallagher's Pug Muddler, Alessi Boston shakers, Bonzer Hawthorne strainers, and Bar Store's mixing glasses **Cocktail to Drink:** Sazerac – it's classic, balanced, sophisticated, strong, and simple **Cocktail to Make:** A Jimmie Roosevelt

Junior Merino
Mixologist | The Liquid Chef, Inc.

New York, NY

Restaurant E-mail: junior@theliquidchefinc.com

Phone: (646) 342-8302

Cocktail Style: A little bit of everything: classics, modern, molecular, healthy – it's more about the art of cocktails on the kitchen side **Work History:** New York, NY: Boulevard Café, Roth's Westside Steakhouse, The Modern, Rayuela **Cocktail Book:** I don't really have one, just because there are a lot of really good ones that give knowledge in different areas **Fave Tool:** Boston shaker, muddler and a knife. You can make anything with these tools. **Cocktail to Drink:** Depends on the mood. For summer I like something refreshing and hydrating, and for winter I like something spicy. **Cocktail to Make:** I enjoy mixing all sorts of drinks, because even the simplest drinks need to be made with care **Underappreciated Ingredient:** We're definitely starting to get all sorts of new ingredients. I think there is an evolution to it all and this is just the beginning. I like to incorporate Latin ingredients: Cachaça, hibiscus, chilies.

Jeremy Merritt
Mixologist | Restaurant Charlie

Space 1560

3325 South Las Vegas Blvd. Las Vegas, LV 89109

Restaurant E-mail: jeremy@charlietrotters.com

Phone: (702) 607-6336

Cocktail Style: Focus on organic, pure ingredients and seasonality of products. An ever-changing style depending on the mood of the day. **Work History:** Las Vegas, NV: Imperial Palace, Planet Hollywood, Platinum Hotel and Spa **Cocktail Book:** The Craft of the Cocktail by Dale DeGroff **Fave Tool:** My hands; kitchen staff **Cocktail to Drink:** It all depends on my mood **Cocktail to Make:** Depends on the season **Underappreciated Ingredient:** Herbs like sage and tarragon

Mixologists

Andy Minchow
Mixologist | Holeman and Finch

2277 Peachtree Road, Suite B Atlanta, GA 30309

Restaurant E-mail: minchowdrew@hotmail.com

Phone: (404) 948-1175

Cocktail Style: Fresh **Work History:** Las Vegas, NV: Delmonico Steakhouse; Atlanta, GA: Emeril's Atlanta, Repast, Posh **Cocktail Book:** Imbibe! By Dave Wondrich; The Bon Vivant's Companion by Jerry Thomas **Fave Tool:** Hand juicer **Cocktail to Drink:** Manhattan **Cocktail to Make:** Manhattan **Underappreciated Ingredient:** Grapefruit

Somer Perez
Beverage Director | The Royalton

44 West 44th St. New York, NY 10036

Restaurant E-mail: somer.perez@morganshotelgroup.com

Phone: (212) 869-4400

Cocktail Style: Classic meets new, farm to table, seasonal, straight from the crate **Work History:** New York, NY: Beacon, The Hotel on Rivington **Cocktail Book:** The Art and Science of the Cocktail by James Waller **Fave Tool:** I use very few tools, but I do enjoy a fun muddler **Cocktail to Drink:** A well-made Margarita **Cocktail to Make:** I really don't think there's anything better then turning out a perfect stirred martini. It's not as easy to make as people think, as you have to find that perfect balance between the ice, vermouth, and gin – and then a perfect pour in a cold martini glass.... what's better than that? **Underappreciated Ingredient:** Lillet Blanc – such a classic. It's a classy, smooth and sophisticated spirit that is so versatile! Not nearly as many bars use it as probably should.

Jonny Raglin
Mixologist | Absinthe

398 Hayes St. San Francisco, CA 94110

Restaurant E-mail: jonny@properpotion.com

Phone: (415) 551-5127

Cocktail Style: Old soul revival **Work History:** Oklahoma City, OK: Pearl Oyster Bar; San Francisco, CA: Incanto, Stars Bar and Dining **Cocktail Book:** The Savoy Cocktail Book by Harry Craddock is a classic book with great pre-prohibition cocktails. I also like On Food and Cooking by Harold McGee. **Fave Tool:** My metal on metal shaker set **Cocktail to Drink:** The Sazerac is one of my favorites. It's a really simple drink – all that's in it is whiskey, bitters and sugar. However, it has to be well-executed to be good. **Cocktail to Make:** Pisco Sour **Underappreciated Ingredient:** Gin – it is the ultimate anchor of a cocktail

Julie Reiner
Mixologist | Flatiron Lounge, Clover Club

37 W 19th St. New York, NY 10011

Phone: (212) 727-7741

Cocktail Style: Classic cocktails, and a culinary approach to cocktails using fresh ingredients **Work History:** San Francisco: Red Room; New York, NY: C3, Aleutia, Pegu Club **Cocktail Book:** There are books I like for different reasons: Trader Vic's Book of Food and Drink by Victor Sperandeo, Imbibe! By Dave Wondrich, The Fine Art of Mixing Drinks by David Embury **Fave Tool:** An extra-long bar spoon that I found in an antique store in Florida **Cocktail to Drink:** Manhattan or Old Fashioned **Cocktail to Make:** Old Fashioned **Underappreciated Ingredient:** It would be nice to see bitters and amaros in other parts of the country

Mixologists

Sam Ross
Mixologist | Milk & Honey

134 Eldridge St. New York, NY 10002

Cocktail Style: Updates on classic-influenced cocktails using fresh ingredients **Work History:** Australia: Ginger; Los Angeles: Comme Ca; New York, NY: Pegu Club, Little Branch **Cocktail Book:** Imbibe! by Dave Wondrich **Fave Tool:** A good Hawthorne strainer – it's so important to have a really tight coil and a nice gap between the rim and the coil **Cocktail to Drink:** American Whiskey on the rocks **Cocktail to Make:** People put their trust in us – they give full creative control, and just say what type of cocktail they feel like, and let us do our thing. Or maybe they'll give one adjective – an emotion, description, word, or flavor. They come here to branch out. One table gave us a list of movies, and asked us to come up with a drink inspired by each. **Underappreciated Ingredient:** Amaros and Campari in drinks other than a negroni

Mike Ryan
Mixologist | MOTO

945 W Fulton Market Chicago, IL 60607

Phone: (312) 491-0058

Cocktail Style: Classical, modern, idiosyncratic **Work History:** Chicago, IL: Acqualina, Leonardo's, Tizi Melloul, D. Kelly, Blue Bayou **Cocktail Book:** The Savoy Cocktail Book by Harry Craddock and Imbibe! by Dave Wondrich. The latter, although principally about the state of mixology a half century prior to the former, provides an excellent background and some much-needed translation. **Fave Tool:** Right now I love high-proof grain alcohol, which I use for flavor extraction, tinctures, bitters, chlorophyll extraction, etc. It is delightfully flammable. **Cocktail to Drink:** Stressful days and bowling days call for a White Russian, after-work relaxation (or slower nights) calls for either a beer or a well-made Manhattan, and lazy Sundays beg for Caipirinhas or Dark 'n Stormies **Cocktail to Make:** Usually whatever I've just put on the menu is my current favorite to make, since it's the new baby **Underappreciated Ingredient:** Bitter, vegetal ingredients, like Cynar, Chartreuse, Becherovka, etc. Used with discretion, they add a wonderful complexity to a cocktail. As a counterbalance, bright, fresh herbs like summer savory and lemon balm can really lift and stimulate the aroma of a drink.

Audrey Saunders
Restaurant: Pegu Club

77 W Houston St. New York, NY 10014

Restaurant E-mail: peguclubsoho@aol.com

Phone: (212) 473-7348

Cocktail Style: New Classic **Work History:** New York, NY: Waterfront Ale House, Blackbird, Beacon Restaurant, The Tonic Restaurant, The Carlyle Hotel **Fave Tool:** Two sided jigger with 1/2 ounce and 3/4 ounce measurements **Cocktail to Drink/Make:** I don't have any favorites, there are too many variables involved. What time of day is it? Is it cocktail, postprandial, out causing trouble, or brunch? **Underappreciated Ingredient:** Madeira

Adam Seger
Mixologist | Nacional 27

325 W Huron St. Chicago, IL 60610

Phone: (312) 664-2727

Cocktail Style: Seasonal and culinary-driven **Work History:** Louisville, KY: Seelbach Hotel; Chicago, IL: Tru; Yountville, CA: The French Laundry; France: Chez Julien **Cocktail Book:** The Elements of Taste by Grey Kunz and Peter Kaminsky **Fave Tool:** Vita-Prep (you can grind spices) **Cocktail to Drink:** Champagne cocktails **Cocktail to Make:** Manhattan **Underappreciated Ingredient:** Cardamom

Mixologists

Eric Simpkins
Mixologist | Trois

1180 Peachtree St. NE Atlanta, GA 30309

Restaurant E-mail: eric@trois3.com

Phone: (404) 641-4069

Cocktail Style: Very classic bartending style with modern innovations **Work History:** Atlanta, GA: Woodfire Grill, Joel, Big City Cuisine,The River Room; New York, NY: Pegu Club **Cocktail Book:** That would definitely have to be The Gentleman's Companion: Around The World With Jigger, Beaker, and Flask, by Charles Baker **Fave Tool:** I always feel naked without my 1/2-ounce/ 3/4-ounce jigger **Cocktail to Drink:** An Old Fashioned whiskey cocktail – no fruit salad, no soda, and four dashes of Angostura bitters, with lemon and lime zest **Cocktail to Make:** An Old Fashioned **Underappreciated Ingredient:** Amer Picon, Suze

Regan Smith
Mixologist | Holeman and Finch

2277 Peachtree Road Suite B Atlanta, GA 30309

Phone: (404) 948-1175

Cocktail Style: Fresh and lighter style, easy to drink **Work History:** Las Vegas, NV: Delmonico Steakhouse; Atlanta, GA: Emeril's Atlanta, Posh **Cocktail Book:** Vintage Spirits and Forgotten Cocktails by Ted Haigh **Fave Tool:** Julep strainer; Rosle bar spoon **Cocktail to Drink:** Campari and soda with an orange slice, Fernet Branca with no ice or Coke with a lime wedge **Cocktail to Make:** The Monkey Gland – I like making it because it has fresh orange juice, gin and grenadine, and people love it and are surprised

Todd Thrasher
Mixologist | Restaurant Eve, The PX

110 S Pitt St. Alexandria, VA 22314

Restaurant E-mail: toddthrasher@restauranteve.com

Phone: (703) 706-0450

Cocktail Style: I try to make cocktails that taste good using the freshest ingredients **Work History:** Washington, DC: Carlyle Grand Café, Gabriel, Café Atlantico, Signatures; Alexandria, VA: Eamonn's, The Majestic Café **Cocktail Book:** I have an old Cuban drink book from the 50's, but I love to apply ideas from The French Laundry Cookbook **Fave Tool:** I like to use fresh herbs, fruits, and other seasonal produce **Cocktail to Drink:** Captain Morgan's rum with half soda water, half Sprite **Cocktail to Make:** My Wife's Manhattan **Underappreciated Ingredient:** Pisco

Peter Vestinos
Head Bartender/Bar Manager | Sepia

123 N Jefferson St. Chicago, IL 60661

Phone: (312) 441-1920

Cocktail Style: Back to basic, true to cocktail technique, straightforward, using fresh ingredients **Work History:** Chicago, IL: The Tasting Room **Cocktail Book:** The Savoy Cocktail Book by Harry Craddock; The Craft of the Cocktail by Dale DeGroff **Fave Tool:** Juicer **Cocktail to Drink:** Manhattan **Cocktail to Make:** Whiskey Smash **Underappreciated Ingredient:** Herbs (besides mint) are largely underutilized

Mixologists

Dave Wondrich
Mixologist

New York, NY

Restaurant E-mail: www.beveragealcoholresource.com

Cocktail Style: As classic as my somewhat limited dexterity allows
Cocktail Book: The World's Drinks and How to Mix Them by Bill
Boothby **Fave Tool:** The old mixing glass/mixing tin combo, because
it's still the easiest and most reliable thing to shake a drink in
Cocktail to Drink: Old-Fashioned, either with Cognac, Rye or Holland
gin (they're all good) **Cocktail to Make:** These days, it's a Mint Julep
made with old cognac and a splash of rye **Underappreciated Ingredient:** Sherry – it's a wonderful mixer

Sommeliers

{ Alexander - Zawieja }

KEY

Wine Book: favorite wine resource

Pairing: a great pairing you've come across

Region: favorite wine region (of the moment)

Sommeliers

Jason Alexander
Vice President of Wine Acquisitions | VinTrust

38 Keyes Ave., Suite 200

P.O. Box 29628 San Francisco, CA 94129

Restaurant E-mail: jason@vintrust.com

Phone: (877) 846-8787

Work History: Healdsburg, CA: Cyrus Restaurant; San Francisco, CA: Gary Danko **Affiliations:** The Court of Master Sommeliers **Wine Book:** The World Atlas of Wine – wine is so tied to geography and this book has great maps of every region that help to understand why certain wines show as they do **Pairing:** Mussel soup with saffron and Junmai Daiginjo sake. With intensely oceanic and sea flavors it is hard to match a suitable grape-based wine. The umami effect of the sake bridges that gap. **Wine Region:** Burgundy for all the new energy there – the young generations taking over have a whole new vigor and dedication to the history of the area

Darius Allyn, M.S.
Owner/Operator | WineWorks

Las Vegas, NV

Restaurant E-mail: dariusallyn@mac.com

Phone: (702) 528-9497

Work History: Seattle, WA: The Salish Lodge and Spa; Las Vegas, NV: Aureole, UNLV, Deluca Wine Distributors **Affiliations:** The Court of Master Sommeliers **Wine Book:** It depends on what I am researching, although I like Stevenson's yearly wine reports. They are updated each year and are very easy to use. **Pairing:** I'm really fond of Madeira with hard, salty cheeses. It is just like a sweet, dried, candied fruit, and balances well with the richness and texture of the cheese. **Wine Region:** The Saar region in Germany – the wines are light, low acid and terroir-driven. They are perfect and refreshing, especially when you live in a hot climate like Las Vegas.

David Alphonse
Vice President of Beverages | Back Bay Restaurant Group

284 Newbury St. Boston, MA 01125

Restaurant E-mail: davida@bbrginc.com

Phone: (617) 536-2800

Work History: Boston, MA: Legal Sea Foods **Affiliations:** The advisory board for Cheers magazine **Wine Book:** The Professional Wine Reference Guide – it has everything in it: regions, grapes, maps etc... and it's pocket size **Pairing:** Alsatian Riesling and lobster – the sweetness of the lobster is perfect with the fresh, vibrant acidity of the Alsatian wine **Wine Region:** It's a mood thing – I care more for French and Italian wines, my personal favorite being Barolo

Stephen Beckta
Sommelier/Owner | Beckta Fine Dining and Wine

226 Nepean St. Ottowa, ONT K2P 0B8

Restaurant E-mail: sbeckta@beckta.com

Phone: (613) 238-7063

List Size: 250 **Cellar Size:** 4-5,000

Work History: New York, NY: Café Boulud, Eleven Madison Park **Affiliations:** Governor of the National Capital Sommelier Guild **Wine Book:** The Oxford Companion to Wine – it is incredibly thorough and gives a balanced, un-biased perspective to new and old world wines **Pairing:** Homemade Linguini with Shaved Bottarga, Lemon Confit and Ligurian Olive Oil (prepared by Andrew Carmellini) with a Heidi Schröck Grauburgunder. Both the food and the wine were intensely briny and almost too much on their own, but together they became magic and ethereal. **Wine Region:** Niagra – it is local and it is exploding with new discoveries and possibilities. It is finding its stride.

Sommeliers

Jenny Benzie
Sommelier | Café Boulud Palm Beach

The Brazilian Court

301 Australian Ave. Palm Beach, FL 33480

Restaurant E-mail: jbenzie@danielnyc.com

Phone: (561) 655-5060

List Size: 600 **Cellar Size:** 5,000

Affiliations: The Society of Wine Educators **Wine Book:** The World Atlas of Wine by Hugh Johnson **Pairing:** We just had a wine dinner where we featured Chilean wines – I paired a Concha y Toro late harvest Sauvignon Blanc with a dessert of roasted fresh peaches, crème fraîche, almond sablé and white peach sorbet, and it worked really well **Wine Region:** Burgundy – the wines from there pair nicely with our menu so I have been more focused on that region recently

Cynthia Betancourt
Wine Director | Azul

Mandarin Oriental

500 Brickell Key Dr. Miami, FL 33131

Restaurant E-mail: cbetancourt@mohg.com

Phone: (305) 913-8254

List Size: 744 **Cellar Size:** 6,000

Work History: Coral Gables, FL: The Biltmore; Ft. Lauderdale, FL: Johnny V's **Affiliations:** International Sommelier Guild, The International Wine Fair judge, Miami, FL **Wine Book:** The Wine Bible by Karen MacNeil. It is such a great resource – it's not geeky at all – just straight information that you can use while talking at the table. It has great wine pairings and great notes on the side that are very helpful. It's older now – she needs to come out with a new edition. **Pairing:** We did an amazing pairing with a Catena Alta Malbec and a foie gras and chestnut soup with a cranberry gastrique and pecans **Wine Region:** Italy – there are over 2000 grape varietals in Italy. It has a wide range to choose from, and every region has a lot to offer.

Fernando Beteta
Sommelier and Manager | Nomi at the Park Hyatt Hotel

800 N Michigan Ave. Chicago, IL 60611

Restaurant E-mail: fbeteta@hyatt.com

Phone: (312) 239-4030

List Size: 1,500 **Cellar Size:** 10,000

Work History: Chicago, IL: The Dining Room at the Ritz-Carlton **Wine Book:** Every sommelier most likely has Sotheby's Wine Encyclopedia by Tom Stevenson. It is a go-to with maps, appellations and laws. **Pairing:** One of my latest is bananas and Gewürztraminer **Wine Region:** Greece – I am really impressed with the different styles and the new producers

Sandy Block, M.S.
Vice President of Beverage Operations | Legal Sea Foods

One Seafood Way Boston, MA 02210

Restaurant E-mail: sblock@legalseafoods.com

Phone: (617) 530-9000

Work History: Boston, MA: Horizon Beverage Company, Whitehall Imports, Whitehall Companies **Affiliations:** The Institute of Masters of Wine, Le Chaine des Rotisseurs, the editorial boards of Santè and Cheers magazines, the board of the Boston University Wine Program, Confraria do Vinho do Porto, Vigneron de Champagne **Wine Book:** The Oxford Companion to Wine by Jancis Robinson. It is comprehensive, encyclopedic, and has the best information. It is also very heavy so I get a good workout carrying it around. **Pairing:** Grilled salmon with a honey mustard sauce and Savennières. The really dry intense minerality and the high acid fruit flavor of the wine cuts the richness of the salmon, while also providing a balance for the slight sweetness of the honey. **Wine Region:** Overall, the Loire Valley for the diversity. I love the structure and minerality in these wines.

Sommeliers

JB Bolduc
Lead Sommelier | T-Bones Steakhouse and Lounge

Red Rock Casino Resort and Spa

11011 W Charleston Blvd. Las Vegas, NV 89135

Restaurant E-mail: john.bolduc@stationcasinos.com

Phone: (702) 797-7777

List Size: 400 **Cellar Size:** 7,500

Affiliations: Candidate for the Advanced diploma from the Court of Master Sommeliers **Wine Book:** Sotheby's Wine Atlas and The Oxford Companion to Wine keep you up to date on the regions and laws. **Pairing:** Duck ravioli with a morel sauce (a douxel) with a J.J. Prüm Wehlener Sonnenuhr Spätlese Riesling. The dish is so rich, yet the residual sugar in the wine helps to cleanse the palate between bites. The pairing is very synergenic. **Wine Region:** I'm less interested in regions these days and more focused on what is going on with wine-makers and wine-making specifically

Nadine Brown
Sommelier | Charlie Palmer Steak House

101 Constitution Ave. Washington, DC 20001

Restaurant E-mail: nbrown@charliepalmer.com

Phone: (202) 547-8100

List Size: 600 **Cellar Size:** 7,200

Work History: Washington, DC: Bistro Bis, Signatures, Butterfield 9, 701, Ten Penh **Affiliations:** Wine Spirit and Education Trust **Wine Book:** The Sotheby's Wine Encyclopedia by Tom Stevenson, or anything else by him – he does a really in-depth job **Pairing:** Pinot Noir-based sparkling wine and foie gras is great. I like Soter Estate, from Oregon. The acid and earthiness in the Pinot cuts through the fat in the foie gras. **Wine Region:** The Sonoma coast and the Sonoma mountains. We only have domestic wines on our list and I find that these cooler weather fruits have a lot of character and are very balanced.

Thomas Carter
Wine Director | Blue Hill at Stone Barns

630 Bedford Rd. Pocantico Hills, NY 10591

Restaurant E-mail: thomas@bluehillfarm.com

Phone: (914) 366-9600 x225

List Size: 900 **Cellar Size:** 15,000

Work History: New York, NY: Alain Ducasse, Le Bernardin **Affiliations:** Court of Master Sommeliers **Wine Book:** Wines and Domains of France by Clive Coates **Pairing:** Soft egg, guanciale, corn and chanterelle with François Cazin Cour- Cheverny 1996, Loire Valley France **Wine Region:** Loire Valley, France

Belinda Chang
Wine Director | The Modern

The MoMA

9 W 53rd St. New York, NY 10019

Restaurant E-mail: bchang@themodernnyc.com

Phone: (212) 333-1220

List Size: 1,600 **Cellar Size:** 15,000

Work History: Houston, TX: Café Annie; Chicago, IL: Charlie Trotter's; San Francisco, CA: The Fifth Floor **Wine Book:** The Sotheby's Wine Encyclopedia – it is the gold standard. It has the largest and most accurate amount of information. Google is great too, although it can be tricky with spellings, and there is a lot of information to sort through. **Pairing:** Rosé Champagne and anything! **Wine Region:** I just got back from Austria – the Wachau was really impressive. They have great quality wines across all levels, with amazing consistency.

Sommeliers

Ken Collura
Wine Director/Sommelier | Andina

1314 NW Glisan St. Portland, OR 97209

Restaurant E-mail: ken@andinarestaurant.com

Phone: (503) 228-9535

List Size: 175-200 **Cellar Size:** 1,000-2,500

Work History: Vero Beach, FL: Chez Yannick; Tampa, FL: Bern's Steakhouse; Taos, NM: Monte Sagrado **Wine Book:** Wines, Grapes and Vines by Jancis Robinson. It is more trade-oriented. It lists every grape that is available for wine around the world. **Pairing:** A salty cheese like Roquefort or Fourme d'Ambert with a Demi-Sec Vouvray. There is an amazing dichotomy between the salt and the sugar. **Wine Region:** Burgundy, Loire – I am a Francophile, always have been

Roberto Colombi
Head Sommelier | Cielo

Boca Raton Resort and Club

501 E Camino Real Boca Raton, FL 33432

Restaurant E-mail: robertocolombi@gordonramsay.com

Phone: (561) 447-3222

List Size: 500-600

Work History: Italy: Ristorante Gualtiero Marchesi; England: Angela Hartnett, Gordon Ramsay, Petrus **Affiliations:** The Association of Italian Sommeliers **Wine Book:** I prefer a wine atlas – it teaches me not only about the wine, but the terroir and the type of soil. It gives more of an idea of what the wine can be. **Pairing:** Scallops and Chardonnay. The scallop is a delicate kind of fish, with lots of character. Chardonnay has a creamy and buttery taste. **Wine Region:** Bordeaux – old vintages. I have a lot of respect for French wines. They started classifications all the way back in 1855!

Thomas Combescot-Lepère
Wine Director | Adour at the St. Regis

2 E 55th St. New York, NY 10022

Restaurant E-mail: thomas.combescot@stregis.com

Phone: (212) 710-2277

List Size: 600 or 1,800 – we have two books **Cellar Size:** 12,000

Work History: France: L'Escalier Restaurant, Hotel de Matignon; Bryn Mawr, PA: Savona, Bianca Restaurant; StarWine **Wine Book:** Le Monde du Vin: Art ou Bluff by Guy Renvoisé **Pairing:** One of the most surprising pairings we have is Lobster Thermidor with a red Bourdeaux from Medoc. It is very outside the of the box when you think about it but it is actually a traditional pairing for that region. The lobster has a refined quality but it also able to stand in front of a strong tannic wine, especially when cooked this way with Cognac and spices. **Wine Region:** I like Burgundy, Provence, Pasa Robles – I also like to promote local wine production so have been interested in a lot of wines from Long Island

Luis de Santos, M.S.
Asian Portfolio Manager | Southern Wines and Spirits

8400 South Jones Las Vegas, NV 89139

Restaurant E-mail: ldesantos@southernwine.com

Phone: (702) 876-4500

Work History: Healdsburg, CA: Charlie Palmer's Dry Creek Kitchen; Las Vegas, NC: Charlie Palmer Steak at the Four Seasons, Pinot Brasserie at the Venetian **Affiliations:** Sake Professional Course - Level 2, The Court of Master Sommeliers, Chaine des Rotisseurs-Vegas Chapter **Wine Book:** The Oxford Companion to Wine by Jancis Robinson is an encyclopedic go-to, and has been one of our bibles **Pairing:** I remember this to the day – it was at Gatsby's (at MGM Grand) – Seared Foie Gras with Sweetbreads, Mango Chutney and Reduction of Sauternes with Poached Mango. It was paired with a TBA (Trockenbeerenauslese) #7 Grüner Veltliner. The richness and acidity made it by far the best pairing. **Wine Region:** These days it is Japan for the sake – I am intrigued by the complexity of the flavor profiles that I continue to learn about

Sommeliers

Jerome Delpuch
Wine Manager/Sommelier | DB Brasserie

The Wynn Las Vegas

Las Vegas, NV 89109

Restaurant E-mail: jerome.delpuch@wynnlasvegas.com

Phone: (702) 770-3310

List Size: 600 **Cellar Size:** 35,000

Work History: New York, NY: Le Bernardin, Daniel Restuarant, DB Bistro, Café Boulud **Affiliations:** Mention Complémentaire de Sommelerie, France, The Court of Master Sommeliers, American Sommelier Association **Wine Book:** The Sotheby's Wine Encyclopedia Tom Stevenson **Pairing:** Rack of lamb and Châteauneuf-du-Pape, Rayas 2001 **Wine Region:** Priorat – Spanish wine for me is definitely a different thing. The price range and quality of wine is incredible. Priorat is a different kind of blend – it's very international and an interesting mix.

Reno DeRanieri
Sommelier and Restaurant Manager | Cuvee

322 Magazine St. New Orleans, LA 70130

Restaurant E-mail: reno@restaurantcuvee.com

Phone: (504) 587-9001

List Size: 500-600 **Cellar Size:** Several Thousand

Affiliations: The Court of Master Sommeliers **Wine Book:** Alan Meadows' burghound.com is an incredible reference **Pairing:** Bob Iacovone's Trio of Duck with a 1999 Jean Raphet et Fils Clos Vougeot. I love how the dusty, full nose compliments the full flavor of the duck. The dish has a blue cheese element as well, which is accentuated by the hints of menthol in the wine. **Wine Region:** It is always changing. I really like the Ribera del Duero and the Viratto in Spain for blending the new and the old. I also like the cool white varieties coming out of Northern Italy.

Arnaud Devulder
Beverage Director | Lever House

390 Park Ave. New York, NY 10022

Restaurant E-mail: arnaud@leverhouse.com

Phone: (212) 888 2700

List Size: 500 **Cellar Size:** 4,500-6,000

Work History: Scotch Plains, NJ: Stage House; New York, NY: Restaurant Daniel, DB Bistro Moderne **Affiliations:** The American Sommelier Association **Wine Book:** The World Atlas of Wine – for the geography **Pairing:** Soft shell crabs are in season now, and I like them pan-roasted with a light brown butter sauce and a little lemon, diced tomatoes, and old-fashioned pommes purees with some tiny capers. Pair this with a Crozes Hermitage Blanc Les Meysonniers 100% Marsanne. It's between a Chardonnay and a Sauvignon Blanc – a really perfect match for that dish. Right now that's what I like to do, but I move my wine list a lot to work with the menu. **Wine Region:** Besides Burgundy – Alsace, Austria and Germany

Alex DeWinter
Wine Director | Grill 23 & Bar

79 Park Plaza Boston, MA 02116

Restaurant E-mail: adewinter@grill23.com

Phone: (617) 542-2255

List Size: 1,500 **Cellar Size:** 16,000

Work History: Washington, DC: Calvert Woodly Wines **Wine Book:** The World Atlas of Wine by Hugh Johnson and Jancis Robinson **Pairing:** Our chef does a short rib wellington with a tamale and I serve it with a Grenache. The food is super, super rich and that wine is super rich, but it also has a lot of heat and alcohol. It's served with a heavy reduction sauce which you could have used a Barolo to cut through, but I was really into the richness of the Grenache. **Wine Region:** Spain – I have been reading and learning more about this region lately. There are a lot more wines coming from the region than before.

Sommeliers

Frederick Dexheimer, M.S.
Wine Director | BLT Steak and BLT Fish

106 W 17th St. New York, NY 10022

Restaurant E-mail: fred@bltsteak.com

Phone: (212) 752-7470

List Size: BLT Steak: 800 **Cellar Size:** BLT Steak: 5,000-6,000

Work History: New York, NY: Jean-Georges Management Group, L'Impero, Cello, Gramercy Tavern, Daniel, T. Edwards Wines **Affiliations:** The Court of Master Sommeliers **Wine Book:** The Sotheby's Wine Encyclopedia by Tom Stevenson **Pairing:** A dry-aged Kobe A5 rib-eye with a grand cru red Burgundy like a Chambertin or Bonne Mares. The Kobe is so rich and buttery, while the texture of the Burgundy has enough weight and acidity to provide a good backbone that will cleanse your palate for the next bite. **Wine Region:** Right now I like the Wachau for the power, balance and elegance in the wines, and the transparent flavors that come from the soil and climate

Richard DiGiacomo
Wine Steward | Escopazzo

1311 Washington Ave. Miami Beach, FL 33139

Restaurant E-mail: chefrichny@aol.com

Phone: (305) 674-9450

List Size: 250-300 **Cellar Size:** 2,500

Work History: Miami, FL: Cacao **Wine Book:** The Wine Bible by Karen MacNeil – it is easy to read and the subjects are broken down well **Pairing:** Albariño with ceviche – I like the way the crisp acidity pairs with the lime juice. It is refreshing on the palate. **Wine Region:** Probably the Priorato in Spain for the big bold wines with a lot of flavor – they have great meat wines

Christie Dufault
Wine Director | Quince

1701 Octavia St. San Francisco, CA 94109

Restaurant E-mail: cdufault@quincerestaurant.com

Phone: (415) 775-8800

List Size: 550 **Cellar Size:** 3,500

Work History: Phoenix, AZ: Restaurant Vincent Guerithault; San Francisco, CA: Bacar restaurant, Gary Danko **Affiliations:** Candidate for the Master Sommelier with the Court of Master Sommeliers, adjunct faculty member at CIA St. Helena, founding Sommelier at Vintrust **Wine Book:** Jancis Robinson's Oxford Companion to Wine because it is the most comprehensive **Pairing:** Rosé Champagne with lobster bisque – the flavors are so complimentary yet the textures so contrasting that it makes for a great pairing **Wine Region:** Right now I am enchanted by the Loire Valley. They have delicious wines that are well-balanced. The wines are classic and speak of where they are from.

Desmond Echavarrie
Sommelier | Restaurant Charlie

3325 South Las Vegas Blvd., Space 1560

Las Vegas, NV 89109

Restaurant E-mail: desmond@charlietrotters.com

Phone: (702) 607-6336

List Size: 447 **Cellar Size:** 2,901

Work History: Las Vegas, NV: Picasso; Scottsdale, AZ: Mary Elaine's at the Phoenician **Affiliations:** The Society of Wine Educators, I am a candidate for the Court of Master Sommeliers, Chaine des Rotisseurs **Wine Book:** I have two favorite wine resource books, one in English, one in French **Pairing:** A perfect wine and food match that I recently discovered was Chef Trotter's Spiced Globe Artichokes with Honeycomb, Pine Nuts and Mint together with the 2001 Albert Boxler Sylvaner from Alsace, France **Wine Region:** My current favorite wine region is the Loire Valley, although it might have something to do with the triple-digit temperatures in Vegas

Sommeliers

Jeff Eichelberger
Sommelier | RM Seafood

3930 Las Vegas Blvd. S Las Vegas, NV 89199

Restaurant E-mail: jeff@rmseafood.com

Phone: (702) 632-9300

List Size: 715 **Cellar Size:** 5,700

Work History: Las Vegas, NV: Bouchon, RM Seafood, Rao's, Guy Savoy; New York, NY: Per Se **Affiliations:** The Court of Master Sommeliers, various charity events for causes like breast cancer awareness and AIDS **Wine Book:** Sotheby's Encyclopedia of Wine; Clive Cotes' wine books; Michael Broadbent's writing in Decanter Magazine **Pairing:** Itsas Mendi Txakoli with fishy flavors like anchovies and caviar. The wine is crisp and clean with a beautiful combination of fruit and minerality. It matches well with these pungent and oily flavors as there is a breath of the sea about it. **Wine Region:** Greece – I am learning so much about these wines right now. Spain is my all-time favorite, and I like Austrian wines with seafood.

Chad Ellegood
Wine Director | Tru

676 N. Saint Clair St. #1 Chicago, IL 60611

Restaurant E-mail: cellegood@leye.com

Phone: (312) 202-0001

List Size: 1,800-1,900 **Cellar Size:** 14,000-18,000

Work History: Chicago, IL: Printers Row, Spiaggia **Affiliations:** Candidate for the Master Sommelier with The Court of Master Sommeliers **Wine Book:** I like The Oxford Companion to Wine by Jancis Robinson for sound bites and The World Atlas of Wine by Hugh Johnson and Jancis Robinson for geographical references **Pairing:** We have a dish here that is pork belly with roasted sweet corn and planks of granny smith apple. I pair it with a 2002 Premier Cru Meursault or a well-aged white Burgundy, which really elevates the flavor. I also really like caviar with wines that have residual sugar, like Riesling, Muscat or Gewürztztraminer. **Wine Region:** I really love New Zealand (I just returned from there) – I especially like the Pinot Noir. South Africa has great budget wines, and I will always love Austrian and German wines, especially something with age on it.

Emmanuel Faure
Wine Director | The Hotel Bel-Air

701 Stone Canyon Rd. Los Angeles, CA 90007

Restaurant E-mail: efaure@hotelbelair.com

Phone: (310) 472-5234

List Size: 1,600 **Cellar Size:** 45,000

Work History: Los Angeles, CA: L'Orangerie **Wine Book:** I don't have any – I try to stay away from books and rely solely on my palate, history and experience. If I need more information I go straight to the producer. **Wine Region:** Santa Barbara at the moment – the potential in this area is great, especially with new modern techniques. There is some outstanding wine.

Jason Ferris
Wine & Spirits Director | Gilt

The New York Palace Hotel

455 Madison Ave. New York, NY 10022

Restaurant E-mail: jferris@nypalace.com

Phone: (212) 891-8100

List Size: 1,600 **Cellar Size:** 9,500

Work History: New York, NY: Aureole; San Francisco, CA: Charles Nob Hill; Philadelphia, PA: Tangerine, Striped Bass **Affiliations:** Chaine des Rotisseurs **Wine Book:** Hugh Johnson's Wine Atlas **Pairing:** Chef Lee's Crispy Black Sea Bass Piperade with Chorizo paired with Sighardt Donnabaum "Brandstadt" Single-Vineyard Riesling from the Wachau in Austria **Wine Region:** The Wachau – the wines there represent a display of summer ripe fruit, so they are great summer wines seeing as all these flavors are appearing on the plate as well

Sommeliers

Michael Flynn
Wine and Beverage Director | The Mansion at Turtle Creek

2821 Turtle Creek Blvd. Dallas, TX 75219

Restaurant E-mail: michael.flynn@rosewood.com

Phone: (214) 559-2100

List Size: 11,000 **Cellar Size:** 11,000

Work History: Washington, DC: New Heights, Le Pavillon, Kinkead's **Affiliations:** The American Institute of Wine and Food, consultant for VinTrust **Wine Book:** The New Sotheby's Wine Encyclopedia by Tom Stevenson **Pairing:** Gewürtztraminer and foie gras – the wine matches the richness of the foie gras and adds exotic elements based on its beautiful perfume **Wine Region:** The Wachau valley in Austria because of the clarity and purity of the wine being produced there

Andy Fortgang
Sommelier and General Manager | Le Pigeon

738 E Burnside St. Portland, OR 97214

Restaurant E-mail: afortgang@gmail.com

Phone: (503) 546-8796

List Size: 150 **Cellar Size:** 1,000

Work History: New York, NY: Gramercy Tavern, Craft, CraftBar, CraftSteak **Wine Book:** I like The World Atlas of Wine because it has great maps and descriptions, and is very comprehensive **Pairing:** Beef tongue salad with a Grüner Veltliner – the dish and the wine have vibrant flavors that play well off each other **Wine Region:** Northern Rhône – I'm just really enjoying the spicy-earthy Syrahs

Doug Frost, M.S.
Master Sommelier

www.dougfrost.com

Kansas City, MO

Restaurant E-mail: winedog@att.net

Work History: United Airlines, Wine and Spirits Magazine, Santé Magazine, Monterey Wine Festival **Affiliations:** The Institute of Masters of Wine, American Board of Directors, Vice Chairman of the American Court of Master Sommeliers, Board of Directors for the Owen/Cox Dance Company, American Civil Liberties Union, National Organization for Women **Wine Book:** I use Sotheby's World Wine Encyclopedia and the Oxford Companion to Wine equally. Both are irreplaceable. **Pairing:** While there are many specific affinities, I would rather speak to a very strong issue that I have with most culinary training with regards to wine: "flavor bridging" is a terrible way to match food and wine. The flavor bridging concept derives from the idea that if the chef matches the flavor in the wine with a flavor in the food, then all will be well. Nonsense. Foods and wines should compliment each other, not mimic each other. In most cases, contrast is far more interesting than pulling the same flavors from the glass as are found on the plate. Even more importantly, the food should not overwhelm the flavors of the wine, nor should the wine obliterate the food. And all too often, I've seen chefs do just that simply because they thought the flavors simply needed to match. **Wine Region:** Priorat, Montsant, Bierzo, Calatayud, Jerez, Ribera del Duero, Toro, Rueda, Rias Baixas and other places in Spain; many, many regions in Victoria and Western Australia; anywhere in New Zealand; the Aconcagua and the Maipo in Chile; Mendoza and Cafayete in Argentina; Michigan, New York, Western Oregon, Eastern Washington and the more coastal areas of California; Sicily and (let's face it) anywhere in Italy; the Rhine and the Mosel (and its tributaries) in Germany; Hungary's Tokaji region; a million places in France; the multiple splendors of South Africa's Western Cape.

Sommeliers

Michael Garcia
Sommelier | XYZ

181 3rd St. San Francisco, CA 94103

Restaurant E-mail: michael.garcia@starwoodhotels.com

Phone: (415) 777-5300

List Size: 650 **Cellar Size:** 6,500-7,500

Work History: San Francisco, CA: Campton Place **Affiliations:** The Court of Master Sommeliers **Wine Book:** The New Sotheby's Wine Encyclopedia from Tom Stevenson and The World Atlas of Wine by Hugh Johnson **Pairing:** One of my favorites is 1999 Cappezzana "Riserva" Vin Santo di Carmignano with Pastry Chef Ryan Wells' Chocolate Caramel Bar with Salted Marcona Almonds and Coffee Sabayon **Wine Region:** I wouldn't say that I have a current favorite wine region but I have been enjoying exploring some of the interesting wines that are coming out of some of the lesser explored regions in Italy, like the Vallée d'Aoste, Oltrepo Pavese, and Sicily

Ben Giacchino
Sommelier | Five and Ten, Gosford Wine

1653 S. Lumpkin St. Athens, GA 30606

Restaurant E-mail: ben@gosfordwine.com

Phone: (706) 546-7300

List Size: About 250-300 **Cellar Size:** Around 1,000+

Work History: Atlanta, GA: I've worked in my own wine shop and various others **Wine Book:** I like Kermit Lynch's books and Terry Thiese's wine book **Pairing:** Corn soup and Pinot Blanc from Burgundy **Wine Region:** Languedoc – I just love the wine from there

David Gordon
Wine Director | Tribeca Grill

375 Greenwich St. New York, NY 10013

Restaurant E-mail: david@tribecagrill.com

Phone: (212) 941-3900

List Size: 1,800 **Cellar Size:** 20,000

Work History: I've been at Tribeca Grill 18 years **Wine Book:** The Wine Bible by Karen MacNeil. It is great for staff trainings, easy to read, and covers important information in a lively manner. **Pairing:** Chatêauneuf de Pape and beef short ribs – it is a powerful wine that stands up to the intensity and gaminess of the ribs **Wine Region:** Châteauneuf-du-Pape in the Rhône Valley. You get great value for the quality of wine.

Jill Gubesch
Wine Director | Frontera Grill and Topolobampo

445 N Clark St. Chicago, IL 60610

Restaurant E-mail: jgubesch@fronteragrill.net

Phone: (312) 661-1434

List Size: 200 **Cellar Size:** 3,000

Work History: Chicago, IL: Italian, French and Spanish restaurants throughout Chicago **Affiliations:** I am a member of WCR **Wine Book:** The Sotheby's Wine Encyclopedia by Tom Stevenson **Pairing:** Mole de Xico with Amarone De Valpolicella – this mole comes from the mountainous area of Veracruz. It is made with a variety of dried fruits, sweet spices, and dark, earthy chilies. Amarone is made from grapes which have been dried for several months before making the wine which gives it a rich, Port-like fruit character, matching the dried fruit flavors and rich, velvety texture of the mole. **Wine Region:** It's hard to pick a favorite. Usually my favorite is the place I've just visited, so I would have to say Austria, since I was there last summer with Terry Theise.

Sommeliers

Matt Gundlach
Sommelier/Wine Director | Moto, Otom

945 W Fulton Mkt. Chicago, IL 60607

Phone: (312) 491-0058

List Size: Moto and Otom each have approximately 50 bottles offered
Cellar Size: Each of these restaurants has approximately 300 bottles

Work History: Chicago, IL: Charlie Trotter's, The Tasting Room **Affiliations:** The Court of Master Sommeliers **Wine Book:** Oxford's Companion to Wine **Pairing:** Snickers candy bar and Tawny Port **Wine Region:** Mosel

Ira Harmon, M.S.
Sales Manager for J and P Wines | Southern Wines and Spirits

8400 S Jones Las Vegas, NV 89139

Restaurant E-mail: iharmon@southernwine.com

Phone: (702) 876-4500

Cellar Size: Personal: 1,200

Work History: Steamboat Springs, CO: Western Distributing, L'Apogee **Affiliations:** The Court of Master Sommeliers, Slow Food **Wine Book:** It's a toss up between Tom Stevenson's New Sotheby's Wine Encyclopedia and Jancis Robinson's Oxford Companion to Wine. These books have the fewest errors, but it's good to have them both to check one against the other. **Pairing:** Stilton and Port – it has synergy **Wine Region:** It is and will always be Burgundy. Old Burgundys are simply remarkable.

Greg Harrington, M.S.
Owner/Winemaker | Gramercy Cellars

1825 JB George Rd. Walla Walla, WA 99362

Restaurant E-mail: greg@gramercycellars.com

Phone: (646) 642-3138

Work History: San Francisco, CA: Square One; Emeril Lagasse Restaurants; Wolfgang Puck Fine Dining Group; BR Guest Restaurants **Affiliations:** The Court of Master Sommeliers **Wine Book:** Italian Wine by Joe Bastianich **Pairing:** Truffles and Condrieu at Emeril's – it was an absolute mistake at Daniel Boloud's table. I miscommunicated, and put down the wrong wine. He loved it! **Wine Region:** It has to be Walla Walla, Washington – why else would I sell everything and move here from NYC? I can't say that I'd kick Nebbiolo from Piemonte out of bed for eating crackers either.

Drew Hendricks, M.S.
Director of Beverage Education | Pappas Bros. Steakhouse

10477 Lombardy Ln. Dallas, TX 75220

Restaurant E-mail: dhendricks@pappas.com

Phone: (214) 366-2000

List Size: 2,700-2,900 **Cellar Size:** 30,000

Work History: Dallas, TX: Charlie Palmer Steakhouse **Affiliations:** The Court of Master Sommeliers **Wine Book:** Sotheby's Wine Encyclopedia by Tom Stevenson. It is accurate, comprehensive and updated. **Pairing:** An Eric Bordelet Poire Granite with foie gras – the sweetness of the pears in the wine coupled with the acidity match the richness of the dish **Wine Region:** Santorini in Greece – the region produces delicious, long-lived whites

Sommeliers

Erik Johnson
Wine Director | L'Espalier

30 Gloucester St. Boston, MA 01125

Restaurant E-mail: erikjohnson@lespalier.com

Phone: (617) 262-3023

List Size: 500 **Cellar Size:** 6,000

Work History: I've been at L'Espalier for 11 years **Wine Book:** The one I go to the most is Stevenson's Sotheby's Wine Encyclopedia. It provides a good overview and I keep going back to it. **Pairing:** Krug Champagne with bacon – the match is spot-on perfect and both are very decadent **Wine Region:** Burgundy, hands down. It is a region where there are only two grapes, but the resulting wines are vastly different. There are infinite nuances of flavor.

Josh Kaplan
Beverage Manager/Sommelier | mk

868 N Franklin St. Chicago, IL 60610

Restaurant E-mail: jkaplan@mkchicago.com

Phone: (312) 482-9179

List Size: 700 **Cellar Size:** 7,000

Work History: Cleveland, OH: Varietals, Lola's; Chicago, IL: Mantuano Mediterranean Table **Wine Book:** Tom Stevenson's The New Sotheby's Wine Book or Vino Italiano by Joe Bastianich. I have an old book by Victor Hazan called Italian Wine that is from the 80s, but is still really interesting. **Pairing:** I was a guest at a wedding here at MK and I had picked a Grüner Veltliner to go with seafood, but I still had some in my glass by the time we got to the bison course. It was an '03 with a lot of viscosity and ripeness, and I drank it with the steak – it was great! **Wine Region:** For the summer I am drinking a lot of Austrian Rieslings, so the Wachau region in Austria

Karen King
Sommelier | Winebow Inc.

236 W 26th St. New York, NY 10001

Restaurant E-mail: k_king@winebow.com

Phone: (212) 255-9414

Work History: New York, NY: The Union Square Café, The Modern **Wine Book:** My all-time favorite is Jancis Robinson's Oxford Companion to Wine. It is concise, well-coreographed, and easy to read. **Pairing:** A chocolate peanut butter tart with a Recioto Bella Valpolicella – the dark, sweet berry really worked with the saltiness in the peanut butter and chocolate. It was a surprise. **Wine Region:** It will always be Piemonte – I love the old Barolos and Barberescos done in the classic traditioinal way. They are beautiful, layered and complex wines.

Jennifer Knowles
Sommelier | Waterbar

399 The Embarcadero San Francisco, CA 94111

Restaurant E-mail: jennifer@waterbarsf.com

Phone: (415) 284-9922

List Size: 475 **Cellar Size:** 20,000

Work History: San Francisco, CA: Rubicon **Affiliations:** I am testing with the Court of Master Sommeliers **Wine Book:** I like The Wine Encyclopedia by Jancis Robinson because it is in dictionary form and I can look things up by name, not just by region. I also like The World Atlas of Wine for the great maps and regional information. **Pairing:** Alsatian Riesling and pork – either bacon or braised pork **Wine Region:** The Loire Valley – I love Chenin Blanc for the minerality and richness. They can be so different.

Sommeliers

Troy Kumalaa
Beverage Director | Vintner Grill

10100 Charleston Blvd. #150 Las Vegas, NV 89135

Restaurant E-mail: troy.kumalaa@cox.net

Phone: (702) 214-5590

List Size: 300 **Cellar Size:** 2,000

Work History: Las Vegas, NY: Charlie Palmer's at the Four Seasons, Wolfgang Puck **Wine Book:** Sotheby's Wine Encyclopedia – I find it to be the most accurate and the least opinionated. It provides a good base. **Pairing:** The last pairing I did was Bolognese and Barbera d'Alba with beets and boar

Jean Luc Le Dû
Owner/Sommelier | Le Dû's Wines

600 Washington St. New York, NY 10014

Restaurant E-mail: jeanluc@leduwines.com

Phone: (212) 924-6999

Work History: New York, NY: Daniel, Café Boulud, DB Bistro, Bouley **Affiliations:** Les Chevaliers du Tastevin, Les Confreries des Côste du Rhône **Wine Book:** Jancis Robinson's Oxford Companion to Wine – it has the most information **Pairing:** Prawns or langoustines and a good Muscadet such as a 2007 Domaine de la Pepiere – the sweetness in the prawns matches well with the acidity. Muscadet is a very lively wine. **Wine Region:** Northern Rhône – I love Côte Rotie and Cornas especially for their meaty, floral and pepper aromas

Steven Lee
Lounge and Garden Manager | The Park Hyatt Chicago

800 N Michigan Ave. Chicago, IL 60611

Restaurant E-mail: swlee@hyatt.com

Phone: (312) 335-1234

Work History: Chicago, IL: The Ritz-Carlton; Boston, MA: The Four Seasons **Affiliations:** The Court of Master Sommeliers **Wine Book:** Sales and Service of the Wine Professional by Brian Julyan, because it gives an overall perspective of wine regions and theory **Pairing:** A 1978 Diamond Creek with morels and lamb brains – the wine's age gives it an earthy complexity that pairs well with the earthiness of the mushroom and the soft texture of the lamb brains **Wine Region:** Alsace for the versatility. It pairs well with most food.

Erik Liedholm
Director of Wine/Sommelier | Seastar Restaurant and Raw Bar

205 108th Ave. #100 Bellevue, WA 98004

Restaurant E-mail: eliedholm@seastarrestaurant.com

Phone: (425) 456-0010

List Size: 600 **Cellar Size:** 4,500

Work History: Seattle, WA: The Elliot Grand Hyatt; Carmel, CA: Pacific's Edge Restaurant at the Highlands Inn Park Hyatt **Affiliations:** The Guild of Sommeliers through the Court of Master Sommeliers, The International Association of Culinary Professionals **Wine Book:** The Joy of Cooking – a sommelier needs to know just as much about cuisine as they do wine; Sotheby's Wine Encyclopedia and Windows on the World Complete Wine Course by Kevin Zraly **Pairing:** We have a hot and sour soup here that I serve with a wine from South Eastern France called Cerdon de Bugey. It is a pétillant and the sweetness of it works as a fire extinguisher on the hot soup, really highlighting the nuances of both. **Wine Region:** It will always be Champagne

Sommeliers

Shelley Lindgren
Wine Director | A16

2355 Chestnut St. San Francisco, CA 94123

Restaurant E-mail: shelley@a16sf.com

Phone: (415) 771-2216

List Size: 500 **Cellar Size:** 3,200

Work History: San Francisco, CA: Fleur De Lys, Bacar, Boulevard, Masa's **Affiliations:** Les Dames International, Women Chefs and Restaurateurs, Court of Master Sommeliers, Slow Food International **Wine Book:** The Oxford Companion to Wine **Pairing:** Nero d'Avola and pizza margherita **Wine Region:** Italy

Jennifer Lordan
Beverage Director | Dovetail

103 W 77th St. New York, NY 10024

Restaurant E-mail: jlordan@dovetailnyc.com

Phone: (212) 362-3800

List Size: 250 **Cellar Size:** 3,000

Work History: New York, NY: The Main Street Restaurant Company, BLT Fish; Washington, DC: BLT Steak, Citronelle, Central **Affiliations:** The Court of Master Sommeliers **Wine Book:** Sotheby's Wine Encyclopedia by Tom Stevenson. It has so much information and is a catch all reference that is very solid. **Pairing:** Really good fries with Côte du Rhône: salt and spice (black pepper) **Wine Region:** Right now I'm really into the German regions. In the southern Austrian region of Therman they're producing some really cool wines that are in a cool climate but typically dry, acid-driven and really delicious. They haven't gotten a lot of attention.

Kris Margerum
Wine Director of Auberge Resorts | Auberge du Soleil

180 Rutherford Hill Rd. Rutherford, CA 94573

Restaurant E-mail: kris@aubergedusoleil.com

Phone: (707) 963-1211

List Size: 1,700 **Cellar Size:** 17,000

Work History: 20 years with Auberge du Soleil **Affiliations:** I have finished the advanced level test at the Court of Master Sommeliers **Wine Book:** My own notebook, and Stevenson's Sotheby's Encyclopedia of Wine – it really breaks down apellations and is up to date on producers **Pairing:** One the first things I loved is still a favorite: Oysters Mignonette with a dry, crisp Sancerre, like a 2007 Vacheron **Wine Region:** I'm prettty happy with them all – I like German Rieslings quite a bit. Mosel has great wines from 2005, decent ones from 2006, and 2007 looks to be spectacular.

Lisa Minucci
Vice President of SOMMsource and Content | Vintrust

38 Keyes Ave, Ste. 200 San Francisco, CA 94129

Restaurant E-mail: lisa@vintrust.com

Phone: (877) 846-8787

Work History: Pebble Beach, CA: XIX at the Lodge; Rutherford, CA: Auberge du Soleil; San Francisco, CA: Cypress Club; New York, NY: Sherry Lehmann Wine and Spirits; Napa Valley, CA: Martini House, Wine Cellar Bar **Affiliations:** The Sommelier Society of America, Association de la Sommelier International **Wine Book:** The Oxford Companion to Wine by Jancis Robinson is so absolutely thorough **Pairing:** Roasted porcini pasta with an older Barolo – they both share the same earthy quality **Wine Region:** Piemonte – the wines are harmonious and balanced, with beautiful acidity. They are very age-worthy.

Sommeliers

David Mokha
Wine Director | Fontainebleau Resort

441 Collins Ave. Miami Beach, FL 33140

Restaurant E-mail: dmokha@fontainebleau.com

Phone: (305) 538-2000

Cellar Size: 50,000

Work History: Miami Beach, FL: Casa Tua, Emeril's South Beach, Field Development Group **Wine Book:** Sotheby's Wine Encyclopedia by Tom Stevenson **Pairing:** Zinfandel goes well with Indian cuisine. It has nice spice and fruit characteristics that match well. **Wine Region:** New Spanish regions like Priorat, where you can find extremely high quality wines at a fair price

Steve Morey, M.S.
General Manager | Vin Sauvage

4050 W Sunset Rd. Las Vegas, NV 89118

Restaurant E-mail: vinsauvage@cox.net

Phone: (702) 212-5600

Work History: San Francisco, CA: Ernie's Restaurant; Las Vegas, NV: Southern Wine & Spirits; Wine Spectator Magazine; Seagram Château & Estate Wines Company **Wine Book:** Decanter Magazine; The Wine Bible for background information **Pairing:** I adore an Alsatian Grand Cru Riesling with cold smoked trout. The combination of the smokiness of the trout and the floral quality of the wine provide a remarkable contrast. **Wine Region:** Burgundy for the quality of the wine. The Pinot Noirs have exceptional variety due to the fact that it is the ancestral and indigenous home of the grape.

Jorge Morgado
Sommelier | Oceanaire

900 S Miami Ave. Suite 111 Miami, FL 33130

Restaurant E-mail: jmorgado@theoceanaire.com

Phone: (305) 372-8862

List Size: 285 **Cellar Size:** 1,000-1,200

Work History: Florida: Noble House Hotels and Resorts **Wine Book:** The Wine Bible, StarChefs.com, and wine publications like Wine Advocate, Wine Spectator and Wine Enthusiast **Pairing:** We just did a wine dinner highlighting Chablis and one pairing that was great was a La Roche AOC Chablis with Squid Ink Tamale Stuffed with Calamari and Salsa Quemado. I also love foie gras with Chenin Blanc; it is incredible. **Wine Region:** Right now I love Chile, Argentina and Spain. Our list is certainly Spanish-influenced, considering we are catering to the residents of Miami.

Claire Paparazzo
Wine Director | Blue Hill

75 Washington Pl. New York, NY 10011

Restaurant E-mail: claire@bluehillfarm.com

Phone: (212) 539-1776

List Size: 115-120 **Cellar Size:** 40,000

Work History: New York, NY: An American Place, Vong, 'Cesca **Affiliations:** The American Sommelier Association **Wine Book:** The Wine Bible by Karen MacNeil **Pairing:** Fresh tomatoes in season with Kerner (a hybrid grape from Northern Italy) – the racy acidity and floral quality of the wine matches the sweetness and acidity of the tomato **Wine Region:** Piemonte – the wine is very classic

Sommeliers

Rajat Parr
Wine Director | Mina Group

335 Powell St. San Francisco CA 94102

Restaurant E-mail: rparr@minagroup.net

Phone: (415) 359-0791

List Size: 3,000 **Cellar Size:** 2,500

Work History: San Francisco, CA: The Fifth Floor, Rubicon **Wine Book:** The Great Vintage Wine Book by Michael Broadband **Pairing:** Root beer float with Boal Madeira **Wine Region:** Burgundy

Virginia Philip
The Breakers Palm Beach

1 South Country Rd. Palm Beach, FL 33480

Restaurant E-mail: virginia.philip@thebreakers.com

Phone: (561) 659-8466

Lists Size: varies by restaurant **Cellar Size:** 28,000

Work History: Aspen, CO: The Little Nell; San Antonio, TX: Ruth's Chris Steakhouse, A&S Holdings **Wine Book:** The Wine Lover's Companion by Ron and Sharon Herbst **Pairing:** Roasted almonds, Manchego cheese and Manzanilla Sherry **Organizations:** The Court of Master Sommeliers, American Sommelier Society

Joseph Phillips, M.S.
Head Sommelier | Sensi

The Bellagio

3600 Las Vegas Blvd. S Las Vegas, LV 89109

Restaurant E-mail: tedsvino@yahoo.com

Phone: (702) 693-8800

List Size: 840 **Cellar Size:** 4,200

Work History: Las Vegas, NV: Circo at the Bellagio, Aqua, Michael Mina **Affiliations:** The Court of Master Sommeliers **Wine Book:** The Oxford Companion to Wine, just because it is always a good resource and a good starting point **Pairing:** Sparkling Shiraz with the braised beef shortribs – it's not a gimmick. It's quite a rebel. **Wine Region:** Greece, New Zealand and Australia

Jason Quinn
Sommelier | Prime Steakhouse

The Bellagio

3600 Las Vegas Blvd.S Las Vegas, NV 89109

Restaurant E-mail: jquinn@bellagio.com

Phone: (702) 693-8484

List Size: 700-800 **Cellar Size:** 5,000

Work History: Las Vegas, NV: Olives, Aqua **Affiliations:** The Court of Master Sommeliers **Wine Book:** My colleagues at the Bellagio – everyone here feeds off one another in their learning **Pairing:** Champagne and caviar with fresh cream and egg – I've not come across two things that are more perfect with one another **Wine Region:** Argentina, Chile, South America, Australia, California – it is always changing. Being a steak house, we focus on that and definitely keep up with the new wines.

Sommeliers

John Ragan
Wine Director | 11 Madison Park

11 Madison Ave. New York, NY 10010

Restaurant E-mail: jragan@elevenmadisonpark.com

Phone: (212) 889-0905

List Size: 2,000

Work History: St. Helena, CA: Martini House; San Francisco, CA: Campton Place **Affiliations:** I am testing with the Court of Master Sommeliers **Wine Book:** The new edition of Sales and Service for the Wine Professional by Brian Julyan. It is thorough and concise with a lot of definitive answers. **Pairing:** Vin Santo paired with vanilla gelato and espresso; Champagne with cheese; young goat cheese from Andante Dairy with a dry Spanish sherry **Wine Region:** Lately I have been fascinated with the Savoie because it is fairly unknown. The grape, Roussane, has a lower alcohol content and is very interesting. It is floral, fragrant and expressive.

Julee Resendez
Sommelier | Monsieur Touton

129 W 27th Street New York, NY 10001

Restaurant E-mail: wineslave@gmail.com

Phone: (212)255-0786

Work History: New York, NY: Colors, Aquavit **Affiliations:** Diploma student at WSET, Vino Vixens, Women Chefs and Sommelier's event **Wine Book:** The Oxford Companion to Wine by Jancis Robinson – it has everything you need to know **Pairing:** I'm really into barbecue right now and I find that Rhône wines as well as Albariños go really beautifully with the spiciness of the meat **Wine Region:** I've been studying Champagne doing a lot of tastings, so Champagne is one favorite. I also love the Northwest American wines from Oregon and Washington. I know the area well and feel that it is one of the most prized regions in the United States.

Clay Reynolds
General Manager/Sommelier | COCO 500

500 Brannan St. San Francisco, CA 94107

Restaurant E-mail: clay@coco500.com

Phone: (415) 543-2222

List Size: 175 **Cellar Size:** 2,500

Wine Book: The Oxford Companion to Wine – it is the most comprehensive and seems to be the one indispensable guide **Pairing:** A dry Loire Valley Chenin Blanc with shaved asparagus and local goat cheese salad. Asparagus is the kryptonite for wine directors, however the minerality of the Chenin Blanc works beautifully with it. **Wine Region:** The Jura in France has an oxidized style of wine that is really delicious and underappreciated. The reds are light and beautiful.

Jim Rollston
Sommelier | Cyrus

29 N St. Healdsburg, CA 95448

Restaurant E-mail: jimrollston@cyrusrestaurant.com

Phone: (707) 433-3311

List Size: 1,000 **Cellar Size:** 4,500

Work History: Sonoma County, CA: Joseph Swan Vineyards, Roshambo; Berkeley, CA: Rivoli; Forestville, CA: The Farmhouse Inn **Wine Book:** The World Atlas of Wine and and Vintage Wine by Michael Broadbent **Pairing:** Thai Marinated Lobster with Alsatian Riesling. I really like Domaine Weinbach Cuvee Theo. The lobster is marinated in lime juice and the Riesling has a beautiful lime flavor – together you get an electric pop in your mouth. **Wine Region:** Mosel in Germany – wines are mapped to specific pieces of ground, and each plot has a name. One plot is so distinct from the next.

Sommeliers

Michael Shearin
Sommelier

Las Vegas, NV

Work History: Las Vegas, NV: Bouchon, Craft Steak, Guy Savoy, Bradley Ogden, DJT at Trump International Hotel **Affiliations:** The Court of Master Sommeliers **Wine Book:** Tom Stevenson's Sotheby's Wine Encyclopedia and Kevin Zraly's Wines Around the World for good basis for information. I also always carry around Michael Broadbent's pocket vintage book. **Pairing:** Something we did at DJT – sea trout with pink grapefruit and yuzu foam and a 1999 Riesling Cuvee. '99 Gewurtztraminer ages well, and lychee tropical flavors come through and pink grapefruit character comes through. **Wine Region:** Always Spain because it's so fascinating. Regions like Jumilla, Monastrell, and some of the whites – not just Albariño. I got to meet the people at Muga in the past – it means a lot to me when I get to meet the people who make the wines.

William Sherer M.S.
Wine Director | Aureole

3950 Las Vegas Blvd. S Las Vegas, NV 89119

Restaurant E-mail: wsherer@mandalay.com

Phone: (702) 632-7777

List Size: 3,000 **Cellar Size:** 20,000

Work History: New York, NY: The Ritz-Carlton Central Park; San Francisco, CA: Aqua **Affiliations:** The Court of Master Sommeliers **Wine Book:** Stevenson's Sotheby's Wine Encyclopedia for general information on apellations and grape varieties **Pairing:** A top notch Mosel Spätlese with green apple dipped in meyer lemon crème fraîche. It is a great match with the mixtures of sweet and acidity. **Wine Region:** Mendoza, Argentina for the great potential of the Malbec

Cat Silirie
Executive Wine Director | The No. 9 Group

9 Park St. Boston, MA 02108

Restaurant E-mail: catsilirie@aol.com

Phone: (617) 742-9991

List Size: No. 9 Park: 500 **Cellar Size:** No. 9 Park: 8,000

Work History: Boston, MA: Grill 23 & Bar, Harvest, Les Zygomates, Galleria Italiana **Wine Book:** The New France by Andrew Jeffords. The writing is excellent and I love the maps, the photos and the perspective. **Pairing:** I'm a classicist and one of my favorites is oysters and Chablis – it is a perfect statement of terroir, as the Chablis is grown in a soil of fossilized ancient shells **Wine Region:** My new favorites are the wines of Jerez

David Singer
Beverage Director/Sommelier | The Mandarin Oriental Boston

PO Box 990007 Boston, MA 02199

Restaurant E-mail: dsinger@mogh.com

Phone: (617) 531 0888

Work History: Boston, MA: Libation Education **Affiliations:** I have passed the Quartermaster Sommelier, The Society of Wine Education **Wine Book:** It's a toss up between The Oxford Companion to Wine and Sotheby's Wine Encyclopedia. I like Sotheby's for a quick reference and the Oxford for more detailed information. **Pairing:** Truffled risotto with a mature Barolo – there are similar earthy notes in the wine so the two accentuate each other **Wine Region:** Lately it has been the Wachau – the region is amazing for Rieslings and Gewürztraminers. There is a lot of intensity and depth of flavor in these wines.

Sommeliers

Alpana Singh, M.S.
Director of Wine and Spirits | Lettuce Entertain You Enterprises Inc.

5419 N Sheridan Rd. Chicago, IL 60640

Restaurant E-mail: asingh@leye.com

Work History: Chicago, IL: Everest **Affiliations:** The Court of Master Sommeliers **Wine Book:** The Oxford Companion to Wine **Pairing:** Slightly oxidized whites and Indian food **Wine Region:** Greece

Jason Smith, M.S.
Head Sommelier | Micheal Mina LV

The Bellagio Las Vegas

3600 Las Vegas Blvd. S Las Vegas, NV 89109

Restaurant E-mail: jasmith@bellagioresort.com

Phone: (702) 693-8199

List Size: 775 **Cellar Size:** 5,000

Work History: New York, NY: 21 Club; Chicago, IL: Charlie Trotter's; Aspen, CO: Little Nell **Affiliations:** The Court of Master Sommeliers **Wine Book:** Sotheby's Wine Encyclopedia by Tom Stevenson **Pairing:** Roquefort and Sauternes was my epiphany moment! I also like squab and red Burgundies, and tuna tartare with German Rieslings. **Wine Region:** Burgundy and then Spain – Rioja, Ribera del Duero, Rueda

Robert Smith, M.S.
Head Sommelier | Picasso

The Bellagio Las Vegas

3600 Las Vegas Blvd. S Las Vegas, NV 89109

Restaurant E-mail: robesmith@bellagioresort.com

Phone: (702) 693-7223

List Size: 1,800 **Cellar Size:** 26,000

Work History: I've been at Picasso since 1998! **Affiliations:** The Court of Master Sommeliers, Ambassador to the wines of Jerez (in the works) **Wine Book:** Auction books are great for purchasing. I also like any book that deals with a specific region. Generally though, there are two wine bibles: The Oxford Companion to Wine by Jancis Robinson and Stevensons' Sotheby's Wine Encyclopedia **Pairing:** The best pairing is the company that you are with **Wine Region:** I like any region that produces cool climate whites and Spanish reds. Actually, anything Spanish!

Vajra Stratigos
Director of Beverage Services | Fifth Group Restaurants

King Plow Arts Center, Ste. K102

887 W Marietta St. NW Atlanta, GA 30318

Restaurant E-mail: vajra@fifthgroup.com

Phone: (404) 815-4700

Work History: Florida: Consultant to Whole Foods; Vail, CO: Nobu, Real Restaurants; Boulder, CO: 15 Degrees **Affiliations:** The Society of Wine Educators **Wine Book:** James E. Wilson's Terroir; Oz Clark's Wine Atlas **Pairing:** Stilton and tepid roast beef with Sauternes. They are polar opposites, one having lots of power in salt and the other sugar. It is a tête à tête. **Wine Region:** Alsace – the wines have incredible finesse and deceptive intensity

Sommeliers

Matthew Strauss
Wine Director | Wilshire Restaurant

2454 Wilshire Blvd. Santa Monica, CA 90403

Restaurant E-mail: matt@wilshirerestaurant.com

Phone: (310) 586-1707

List Size: 400 **Cellar Size:** 3,500

Work History: Boston, MA: Tuscan Grill, Harvest, Federalist; Los Angeles, CA: Campanile, L'Orangerie, Sona, Grace **Wine Book:** The Wine Bible is comprehensive and easy to read **Pairing:** Epoisses cheese and a white wine grape called Savagnin from the Jura. Perhaps the two greatest savage, animalistic edibles ever bestowed on humans. Wait for the kids to go to sleep, though. Things could get racy. **Wine Region:** The Jura for the diverse flavors

Warner Strejan
NY Area Manager | Vignaioli Selections

18 West 27th St., 7th Floor New York, NY 10001

Phone: (212) 686-3095

Work History: New York, NY: The Cub Room, Babbo, AZ Restaurant, RM, The Harrison **Wine Book:** The Oxford Companion to Wine by Jancis Robinson for the detail. I like that she lists her resources so I can continue to self educate. **Pairing:** Filet Mignon with a Sighardt Donabaum Grüner Veltliner – this grower lets the grapes ferment naturally, which leads to a higher sugar content. He balances this by leaving the grapes on the vine to ripen longer than usual. You end up with a white wine that has the power of a red. The sweetness balances the salt in the meat, while the acids blow the fat away. **Wine Region:** Montalcino – the Sangiovese grape has over 3,000 years of vinification history. It has a taste that reaches back centuries.

Bobby Stuckey, M.S.
Owner and Wine Director | Frasca Food and Wine

1738 Pearl St. Boulder, CO 80302

Restaurant E-mail: bobby@frascafoodandwine.com

Phone: (303) 442-6966

List Size: 350 **Cellar Size:** 5,000

Work History: Aspen, CO: Little Nell; Yountville, CA: The French Laundry **Affiliations:** The Court of Master Sommeliers **Wine Book:** Vino Italiano by Joe Bastianich **Pairing:** Tocai Friulano with prosciutto di Sandrelli **Wine Region:** Friuli Venezia Giulia for whites and Piemonte for reds

Caroline Styne
Owner and Wine Director | Lucques/AOC Winebar

8474 Melrose Ave. Los Angeles, CA 90069

Restaurant E-mail: caroline@lucques.com

Phone: (323) 655-6277

List Size: 300 **Cellar Size:** 4,000

Work History: Los Angeles, CA: small catering company owner, Los Angeles restaurant group catering director, Jones Hollywood **Wine Book:** Wine Lover's Companion, Alexis Lichine's New Encyclopedia of Wines & Spirits **Pairing:** I recently paired the Le Macchiole Paleo Bianco – which is a blend of Sauvignon Blanc and Chardonnay from Bolgheri – with Chilled Lobster Salad with Roasted Apricots and Pistachio Aillade **Wine Region:** I always love Burgundy for the elegance of the Pinot Noir, but I'm starting to love Argentina for the value, especially in today's economic climate

Sommeliers

Becky Swanson
Sommelier | Delfina

3621 18th St. San Francisco, CA 94110

Restaurant E-mail: beckysf@gmail.com

Phone: (415) 552-4055

List Size: 150

Work History: Washington, DC: The Oval Room; San Francisco, CA: Armani Café, The Grand Café at the Hotel Monaco **Wine Book:** Vino Italiano by Joe Bastianich **Pairing:** Pigato – a Ligurian white wine – with green ravioli, and Tocai Friuliano with prosciutto and melon **Wine Region:** Marquez, because the indigenous grapes there are really unique – each producer can get something fantastic

James Tidwell
Sommelier | Café on the Green

Four Seasons Resort and Club

4150 N MacArthur Blvd. Irving, TX 75038

Restaurant E-mail: james.tidwell@fourseasons.com

Phone: (972) 717-2420

List Size: 425 **Cellar Size:** 3,700

Work History: Chatham, NJ: Restaurant Serenäde; Oakhurst, CA: Erna's Elderberry House **Affiliations:** Co-founder of the Texas Sommelier Conference and the Texas Sommelier Association, The Society of Wine Educator's board **Wine Book:** Hugh Johnson is a great wine writer. The New Sotheby's Wine Encyclopedia by Tom Sevenson is an essential reference book. I always try to read Decanter Magazine as well. **Pairing:** Grouper with a soy reduction and an older Burgundy – the soy flavor picks up the caramelized flavors and savory qualities in the Burgundy **Wine Region:** There is much potential in Greece. The wines have come a long way and can come a lot further still.

Madeleine Triffon, M.S.
Wine and Beverage Director | The Matt Prentice Restaurant Group

30100 Telegraph Rd., Ste. 251 Bingham Farms, MI 48025

Restaurant E-mail: madeline@mattprenticerg.com

Phone: (248) 646 0370

Work History: Detroit, MI: London Chop House, Westin Corporation **Affiliations:** The Court of Master Sommeliers **Wine Book:** The Sotheby's Wine Encyclopedia by Tom Stevenson **Pairing:** Oaky Chardonnay with a great mac and cheese **Wine Region:** Greece

Scott Tyree
Buyer | Hart Davis Hart Wine Co.

363 W Erie St. Chicago, IL 60610

Restaurant E-mail: styree@hdhwine.com

Phone: (312) 482-9996

Cellar Size: 1.2-1.5 Million

Work History: Chicago, IL: Tru **Affiliations:** Board of the Lyric Opera of Chicago, volunteer sommelier for the Rehabilitation Institute of Chicago at Northwestern University. **Wine Book:** Jancis Robinson's Oxford Companion to Wine. I find it comprehensive and a pleasure to read. She make technical things more understandable. **Pairing:** I love sparkling wines and/or Champagne with sushi. The acidity and minerality are great to cut through the oily fish. **Wine Region:** The Rhône – I find the combinations of savory, fruity and earthy to be delicious and compelling for both whites and reds

Sommeliers

Christian Vassilev
Sommelier | Meritage

70 Rowes Wharf Boston, MA 02110

Restaurant E-mail: kvassilev@bhh.com

Phone: (617) 439-3995

List Size: 950 **Cellar Size:** 8,000-10,000

Work History: Relais & Chateau; Cardoza **Wine Book:** The Oxford Companion to Wine by Jancis Robinson **Pairing:** A mild blue cheese with non-vintage Champagne **Wine Region:** Spain, for the quality and value of the wine

Kevin M. Vogt, M.S.
Wine Director | Emeril's Restaurants – Las Vegas (Based out of Delmonico Steakhouse)

3355 Las Vegas Blvd. S Las Vegas, NV 89109

Restaurant E-mail: kevinvogt2@cox.net

Phone: (702) 414-3737

List Size: 2,150 **Cellar Size:** 18,000

Work History: Santa Fe, NM: Coyote Café **Affiliations:** The Court of Master Sommeliers **Wine Book:** The New Sotheby's Wine Encyclopedia **Pairing:** Seared scallops and Pinot Gris from Alsace **Wine Region:** Since I am a California Cabernet producer... what do you think?

Aaron Von Rock
Wine Director | Telepan

72 W 69th St. New York, NY 10023
Restaurant E-mail: avonrock@aol.com
Phone: (212) 580-4300

List Size: 775 **Cellar Size:** 6,500

Work History: New York, NY: The Tribeca Grill, Verbena Grill, Bar Derni **Affiliations:** The Sommelier Society of America, The American Sommelier's Association **Wine Book:** Sotheby's Wine Encyclopedia provides good background and interesting opinions – qualitative judgments and quantitative information **Pairing:** Madeira and chocolate – Madeira is one of the few dessert wines that helps push the acidity of the chocolate forward, bringing a brightness of flavor **Wine Region:** It is always changing, but lately we have been seeing a lot of value and range in Châteauneuf-du-Pape

Ania Zawieja
Sommelier | Fiamma

206 Spring St. New York, NY 10012
Restaurant E-mail: azawieja@brguestinc.com
Phone: (212) 653-0100

List Size: 600 **Cellar Size:** 7,000

Work History: Philadelphia, PA: Panorama; New York, NY: Café Gray, The Modern, L'Atelier **Wine Book:** The Wine Bible – it's one of the first books that I've read that I actually still use. It's great for teaching, and it's about keeping things really basic. I recommend it for my students (in the past I've done wine class for the food and beverage managers for the Four Seasons and for the staff at L'Atelier). **Pairing:** Cod poached in olive oil and basil paired with Baigorri Tempranillo – it's like the Pinot Noir of Spain. Very delicate and perfect with the fish. **Wine Region:** Definitely Piemonte – the wines are very parallel to the wines of Burgundy. I think we are just hitting the tip of the iceberg.

Heather Sperling

Recipes

Recipes

Tempura Shrimp, Lemon, Black Plum, Vanilla Fragrance

Chef Grant Achatz of Alinea – Chicago, IL
Adapted by StarChefs.com

Yield: 8 Servings

Ingredients

Lemon Rind:
1 lemon
250 milliliters water
100 grams sugar

Black Plum Purée:
24 ounces black plums
100 milliliters water
200 grams sugar
4 sheets gelatin
16 grams agar agar

Shrimp:
4 large shrimp, peeled and deveined

Tempura Flour:
600 grams unbleached all-purpose flour
70 grams baking powder
90 grams cornstarch

Black Plum Salt:
100 grams kosher salt
100 grams dried black plum powder

To Assemble and Serve:
45 grams tempura flour
25 milliliters cold sparkling water, preferably Gerolsteiner
1 liter canola oil
8 whole vanilla beans

Method

For the Lemon Rind:
Using a vegetable peeler, remove lemon rind in large strips. Bring water and sugar to a boil over medium-high heat in a medium saucepan. Whisk to dissolve sugar and reduce heat to medium. Add rind and poach for 1 minute. Remove rind from poaching liquid and drain. Cut lemon rind into ½-inch squares. With the tip of a paring knife, make a slit in the center of each square.

For the Black Plum Puree:
Line a 9-inch x 12-inch pan with plastic. Bring plums, water, and sugar to a boil in a large saucepan over medium heat. Simmer plums for 30 minutes, stirring occasionally. Transfer mixture to blender and purée until smooth. Soak gelatin sheets in cold water for 5 minutes, or until flexible. Gather sheets and squeeze out excess water. Return black plum purée to clean saucepan and add agar agar. Bring mixture to a simmer and blend with immersion blender. Add gelatin and stir until combined. Strain mixture through a chinois into clean saucepan. Bring mixture to a simmer, remove from heat, and strain through chinois into the plastic-lined pan. Refrigerate purée until firm and cut into ½-inch cubes.

For the Shrimp:
Cut shrimp into 1-inch-long pieces.

For the Tempura Flour:
Thoroughly combine ingredients in a medium bowl.

For the Black Plum Salt:
Combine salt and black plum powder in a medium bowl and set aside.

To Assemble and Serve

Combine tempura flour and water in a large bowl, taking care not to over-mix. Heat oil to 375˚F in a large, heavy pot. Impale ingredients on a vanilla bean in the following order, with no space between them: one lemon rind square, one black plum cube, and one piece of shrimp. Position ingredients so that the lemon rind sits about 3" from the end of the skewer and the piece of shrimp sits flush with the tip of the bean. Dip the top 3 inches of the skewer in tempura batter. Holding the opposite end firmly, immerse the battered end in oil. Fry for 2 minutes, drain on paper towels, and sprinkle with black plum salt. Serve hot.

Sautéed Soft Shell Crab with Roasted Shiitake Vinaigrette

Chef Mark Andelbradt of Tao – Las Vegas, NV
Adapted by StarChefs.com

Yield: 4 Servings

Ingredients

Pickled Ramps:
4 ounces red wine vinegar
4 ounces water
1 clove garlic
1 sprig fresh thyme
1 bay leaf
1 teaspoon white peppercorns
1 bunch ramps, cleaned

Shiitake Vinaigrette:
8 ounces large shiitake mushrooms, stems removed
4 ounces sesame oil, plus 1 tablespoon for drizzling
2 large shallots
2 ounces rice wine vinegar
2 ounces mirin
4 ounces soy sauce

Crabs:
4 jumbo soft shell crabs, cleaned
Salt and white pepper
Grapeseed oil

To Assemble and Serve:
Chopped chives
Chive blossoms

Method

For the Pickled Ramps:
Place the red wine vinegar, water, garlic, herbs, and spices in a sauce pot and bring to a simmer. Add ramps and allow to cool at room temperature. Transfer to a separate container for storage in the refrigerator.

For the Shiitake Vinaigrette:
Preheat the oven to 400°F. Place the shiitake mushrooms and shallots in a shallow pan and drizzle with 1 tablespoon of sesame oil. Cover with aluminum foil and roast for 40 minutes. Remove and allow to cool before cutting both into a small dice. Mix the mushrooms and shallots with the rice wine vinegar, mirin, soy sauce, and remaining 4 ounces of sesame oil. Vinaigrette should be very chunky.

For the Soft Shell Crabs:
Cut each crab in half and season with salt and white pepper. Add grapeseed oil to a sauté pan over medium-high heat and cook crabs until crisp, about 2 minutes per side.

To Assemble and Serve

Arrange two crab halves on a plate and dress with the shiitake vinaigrette and few pieces of pickled ramp. Finish with chopped chive and chive blossoms.

Recipes

Averna Pork with Cucumber-Ginger Salad

Chef Zach Allen of B&B Ristorante, Carnevino, and Enoteca San Marco – Las Vegas, NV
Adapted by StarChefs.com

Yield: 8 Servings

Ingredients

Averna Pork:
1 5-pound pork butt
8 ounces salt
2½ ounces dark brown sugar
1½ ounces ground black pepper
2 tablespoons chili flakes
4 tablespoons ground ginger
4 cloves garlic
2 large white onions, sliced
2 medium pieces fresh ginger, sliced
1 pint white wine
4 fresh bay leaves
2½ pints chicken stock

Averna Glaze:
1 quart apple juice
1 quart Averna liqueur

Cucumber-Ginger Salad:
½ cup extra virgin olive oil
2 tablespoons red wine vinegar
Salt and pepper to taste
2 cucumbers, seeds removed and thinly sliced
1 red holland chile, slivered
⅛ teaspoon fresh ginger, peeled and grated

Method

For the Averna Pork:
Cut pork into 10 to 12 ounce cubes (you want at least 8 portions). Combine the remaining ingredients thoroughly and then rub into pork pieces. Preheat oven to 325°F. Heat a braising pan to smoking and sear pork pieces on all sides. Saute garlic, onion, and ginger until onion is translucent. Deglaze with wine and reduce liquid by three-fourths. Add bay leaves and stock; then transfer to a baking pan along with pork. Add water to cover, cover top with plastic and then foil, and seal edges. Put in oven and bake for 2 to 3 hours, until pork is very tender.

For the Averna Glaze:
Combine ingredients in a pot and reduce by half.

For the Cucumber-Ginger Salad:
Make a vinaigrette by whisking oil into vinegar and seasoning with salt and pepper. Toss cucumbers, chili, and ginger with vinaigrette. Set aside.

To Assemble and Serve

Remove pork pieces from braising liquid and flash fry in 50/50 peanut oil and olive oil until outside starts to crisp. In a saute pan, heat Averna glaze and add pork pieces. Coat each piece with glaze all over. Put pork in center of plate and drizzle with Averna glaze. Top with cucumber-ginger salad and serve immediately.

Zach Allen's Averna Pork with Cucumber-Ginger Salad

Recipes

Deconstructed White Wine
Chef José Andrés of Minibar – Washington, DC
Adapted by StarChefs

Yield: 4 Servings

Ingredients
White Wine Gelatin:
2 pounds white grapes
¾ cup water
½ teaspoon fresh lemon juice
3 sheets gelatin

Flavor Components:
3 grapes, halved
Seeds of 1 vanilla bean
Seeds of 1 pomegranate
Zest of 1 lemon
Zest of 1 orange
1 apple, peeled, cored, and finely diced
1 pineapple, peeled, cored and finely diced
4 fresh figs, finely diced
4 fresh mint leaves
Passionfruit reduction
1 grapefruit, cut into segments and finely sliced
1 cup whole milk, reduced by half

Method
For the White Wine Gelatin:
Rinse grapes and remove stems. Place grapes in freezer until completely frozen. In a blender, puree frozen grapes with water and lemon juice. Strain through fine mesh sieve and refrigerate juice overnight.

Place gelatin sheets in cold water to soften. While gelatin is softening, bring 1/3 cup of grape juice to a slight boil in a small saucepan. Gently wring out water from gelatin sheets, place in hot grape juice, and stir until melted. Add remaining grape juice and transfer to a chilled bowl. Refrigerate for 5 minutes. Lay out 4 plates on flat surface and pour approximately 1 ounce of liquid onto each plate. Place plates on to level shelf in refrigerator. Allow 2 hours to set.

To Assemble and Serve
As if looking at the face of a clock, mentally divide the surface of the gelatin-coated plate into 12 equal parts. Place each flavor component in its own section, like numbers on a clock. Finish with a drizzle of reduced milk. Serve immediately.

Warm Vegetable Salad

Chef Michael Anthony of Gramercy Tavern – New York, NY
Adapted by StarChefs.com

Yield: 8 Servings

Ingredients

Black Radish:
1 black radish
½ cup beet juice
1 cup raspberry vinegar
2 cups vegetable stock
1 tablespoon sumac
3 sprigs thyme
3 cloves garlic, peeled
1½ tablespoon unsalted butter
Salt and pepper

Sweet Potato:
1 sweet potato
Olive oil
Salt

Carrots:
12 Thumbelina carrots, peeled and halved
2 cups vegetable stock
1 tablespoon butter
1 tablespoon yellow clover honey
1 tablespoon garlic oil
3 tablespoons ginger juice
Salt and pepper

Sunchokes:
2 sunchokes, peeled and cubed
2 cups vegetable stock
1 tablespoon butter
1 tablespoon yellow clover honey
1 tablespoon garlic oil
3 tablespoons ginger juice
Salt and pepper

Salsify:
2 salsify, peeled
2 cups vegetable stock
1 tablespoon butter
1 tablespoon yellow clover honey
1 tablespoon garlic oil
3 tablespoons ginger juice
Salt and pepper

Baby Turnips:
20 baby turnips, scrubbed and trimmed
2 cups vegetable stock
1 tablespoon butter
1 tablespoon yellow clover honey
1 tablespoon garlic oil
3 tablespoons ginger juice
Salt and pepper

Asparagus Tips:
1 bunch asparagus tips
2 cups vegetable stock
1 tablespoon butter
1 tablespoon yellow clover honey
3 tablespoons ginger juice
Salt and pepper

Beets:
Olive oil
Salt and pepper
1 bunch red baby beets
1 bunch yellow baby beets
1 bunch candy cane baby beets
3 Tablespoons unsalted butter
1 cup water

Pickled Chard Stems:
4 cups batonnets of swiss chard stems
2 cups sugar
2 cups water
6 cups rice wine vinegar
2 cups salt
½ teaspoon mustard seed
½ teaspoon black peppercorns
½ teaspoons fennel seed
½ teaspoon coriander seed
1 red beet, peeled

Pickled Turnips:
½ teaspoon saffron
6 cups rice vinegar
2 cups water
½ quart sugar
½ quart salt
½ teaspoon coriander seed
½ teaspoon mustard seed
1 piece star anise
½ teaspoon black peppercorn
½ teaspoon fennel seed
4 cups batonnets of turnips

Candied Lemon Zest:
1 lemon, rinds only
Water
Simple syrup

Lemon-Fennel Puree:
Olive oil
1 ounce julienned garlic cloves
1 ounce julienned shallots
½ pounds julienned fennel
1 pinch saffron
1 lemon, juiced
6 pieces Candied Lemon Zest
Simple syrup
Salt and pepper

Lemon Vinaigrette:
2 cups lemon juice
3 tablespoons wild flower honey
3 tablespoons white wine vinegar
2 cups lemon oil
2 tablespoons olive oil
3 tablespoons onion puree
1 cup Lemon Fennel Puree
Salt and pepper

Beurre Blanc:
1 cup champagne vinegar
1 cup white wine vinegar
½ cup white wine
1 bay leaf
2 sprigs thyme
1 teaspoon coriander seed
1 teaspoon fennel seed
1 shallot, julienned
1 clove garlic, julienned
¼ cup heavy cream
¾ pounds sweet butter

Yogurt Walnut Dressing:
1 cup plain yogurt
⅓ cup parsley, chopped
⅓ cup tarragon, chopped
⅓ cup dill, chopped
½ tablespoon Parmesan
1½ tablespoon walnut oil
1½ tablespoon olive oil
½ tablespoon cilantro syrup
½ tablespoons toasted walnuts
Juice of 1 lemon
Salt

To Assemble and Serve:
3 cups farro, cooked al dente
1 radicchio Trevisano, tips only
1 sunchoke, peeled and sliced into ribbons
3 leaves Swiss chard, cut into 1-inch squares
4 Easter egg radishes, sliced thin

(continued)

Recipes

Method

For the Black Radish:
Cut the black radish into ⅛-inch slices. Using a ½-inch diameter ring mold, cut out rounds from each slice. Combine radish rounds with beet juice, vinegar, vegetable stock, sumac, thyme, garlic, butter and honey, and season.

For the Sweet Potato:
Coat sweet potato with olive oil and sprinkle with salt. Wrap in foil and bake at 400°F until just cooked through. Remove foil and slice sweet potato into ⅛-inch thick slices. Using a 1-inch diameter ring mold, cut rounds from each slice. Reserve.

For the Carrots:
Combine carrots, stock, butter, honey, oil, ginger juice, and season. Reduce until liquid is the consistency of a syrupy glaze.

For the Sunchokes:
Combine sunchokes, stock, butter, honey, oil, and ginger juice, and season. Reduce until liquid is the consistency of a syrupy glaze.

For the Salsify:
Combine salsify, stock, butter, honey, oil, and ginger juice, and season. Reduce until liquid is the consistency of a syrupy glaze.

For the Baby Turnips:
Combine baby turnips, stock, butter, honey, oil, and ginger juice, and season. Reduce until liquid is the consistency of a syrupy glaze.

For the Asparagus Tips:
Combine asparagus tips, stock, butter, honey, oil, and ginger juice and season. Reduce until liquid is the consistency of a syrupy glaze.

For the Beets:
Preheat oven to 350°F. Coat beets in olive oil and season. Place different colored beets with butter and water. Cover the pans with foil and bake for 45 minutes. Remove beets and peel. Trim and cut into quarters. Reserve warm.

For the Pickled Chard Stems:
Bring sugar, water, vinegar, salt, mustard seed, peppercorns, fennel seed, coriander seed, and beets to a boil. Remove from heat and strain. Add chard stems to liquid and refrigerate overnight.

For the Pickled Turnips:
Bring saffron, vinegar, water, sugar, salt, coriander seed, mustard seed, star anise, black peppercorn, and fennel seed to a boil. Remove from heat and strain. Add turnips to liquid, and refrigerate overnight.

For the Candied Lemon Zest:
Bring lemon rinds and cold water to a boil and strain. Place lemon rinds in simple syrup and bring to a simmer for 10 minutes. Remove from heat.

For the Lemon-Fennel Puree:
Sweat garlic, shallots, and fennel in olive oil until translucent. Add saffron, lemon zest, lemon juice and cook 10 minutes. Add simple syrup to taste and season. Transfer to blender and puree until smooth.

For the Lemon Vinaigrette:
Combine lemon juice, honey and vinegar. Whisk together and slowly drizzle in lemon oil. Whisk in olive oil. Add onion puree, lemon fennel puree and honey. Mix well and season.

For the Beurre Blanc:
Combine vinegars and white wine with bay leaf, thyme, coriander, fennel, shallots, and garlic. Reduce, add heavy cream and reduce again. Whisk in butter in tablespoons until melted.

For the Yogurt-Walnut Dressing:
Combine yogurt, parsley, tarragon, dill, cheese, walnut oil, olive oil, cilantro syrup, walnuts, lemon juice, and salt.

To Assemble and Serve

Toss farro with beurre blanc and lemon vinaigrette to coat and season. Place farro on a plate and arrange black radish, sweet potato, carrots, sunchokes, salsify, baby turnips, asparagus tips, beets, pickled chard stems, and pickled turnips around farro. Place radicchio, sunchoke, Swiss chard, and radishes around the plate in an artistic fashion. Drizzle yogurt-walnut dressing over the plate.

Michael Anthony's Warm Vegetable Salad

Recipes

Housemade Pork Sausage with Radishes and Salsa Verde
Chef Nate Appleman of A16 – San Francisco, CA
Adapted by StarChefs.com

Yield: 10 Servings

Ingredients
Pork Sausage:
5 pounds pork shoulder, roughly cubed
1 pound pork back fat, roughly cubed
34 grams salt
600 grams white wine
12 grams black pepper
9 grams fennel seeds
15 grams garlic
2 grams chili flakes
Natural sheep casing

Salsa Verde:
24 ounces extra virgin olive oil
3 ounces capers
6 cloves garlic
3 bunches parsley, stems removed
3-4 ounces breadcrumbs
Salt

To Assemble and Serve:
Radishes, sliced
Lemon juice, to taste
Salt, to taste

Method
For the Pork Sausage:
Mix all ingredients together thoroughly and chill overnight. Grind mixture using a ⅜-inch die and case in natural sheep casings. Portion into 4-ounce links. Wind the links into a pinwheel shape and insert a wooden skewer through the pinwheel to hold the shape.

For the Salsa Verde:
Blend 8 ounces of olive oil with garlic and capers and set aside in a bowl. Pulse the rest of the oil with parsley until it is just mixed, working quickly to avoid oxidation. Combine both mixtures with breadcrumbs in the bowl. Add salt to taste and refrigerate.

To Assemble and Serve
Grill or roast the sausage. Toss sliced radishes with a tablespoon of the salsa verde and season with lemon juice and salt. Place the radishes on the plate and spoon a small additional amount of salsa verde on top. Place sausage pinwheel beside the radishes and serve.

Grilled Watermelon with Goat Cheese, Pancetta, and Tomato Water Cloud

Chef Dan Barber of Blue Hill – New York, NY
Adapted by StarChefs.com

Yield: 4 Servings

Ingredients

Tomato Water:
2 tablespoons kosher salt
Freshly ground black pepper
2 tablespoons sugar
8 overripe tomatoes
1 ounce vodka

Tomato Cloud:
2 cups tomato water (from above)
4 sheets gelatin, bloomed
Salt and freshly ground pepper

To Assemble and Serve:
¼ pound pancetta, thinly sliced
1 tablespoon olive oil
4 ½ -inch-thick slices seedless watermelon
2 ounces goat cheese
1 pint cherry tomatoes, sliced
Salt and freshly ground pepper
Raspberry vinegar, to taste
4 leaves basil, cut chiffonade

Method

For the Tomato Water:
Add the salt, pepper and sugar to the tomatoes and marinate for 4 hours; then pulse briefly in food processor with vodka. Line a colander with 3 layers of cheesecloth and place over a bowl. Pour the tomatoes into the colander and set in the refrigerator overnight, until all the liquid is drained.

For the Tomato Cloud:
Place a whisking bowl over a bowl of ice water. In a small saucepan, warm the tomato water to around 100°F, add the bloomed gelatin, and dissolve. Pour the mixture into the bowl and whisk vigorously. As it chills, the water will begin to form a cloud and the gelatin will set. Season with salt and pepper.

To Assemble and Serve

Preheat the oven to 400°F. Place the pancetta on a rack over a baking sheet and bake in the oven for 8 minutes. Remove and drain on a paper towel. In a sauté pan over very high heat, heat the oil and sear the watermelon slices until one side is caramelized. Remove the slices and plate, caramelized-side up. Add a thin layer of goat cheese to the center of each watermelon slice, leaving a border of watermelon around the edges. Season the tomatoes with salt, pepper and raspberry vinegar, and layer on top of the goat cheese. Garnish with basil and crisped pancetta, and a spoonful of tomato water cloud.

Recipes

Tuna Tartare with Wasabi Ice Cream, Soy-Sesame Glaze, and Passion Fruit

Chef Anthony Bombaci of Nana - Dallas, TX
Adapted by StarChefs.com

Yield: 10 Servings

Ingredients

Sesame Tuiles:
3 eggs
15 milliliters water
Salt
5 spring roll sheets
Raw sesame seeds

Wasabi Ice Cream:
750 grams whole milk
100 grams heavy cream
175 grams liquid glucose
15 grams non-fat dry milk powder
25 grams ice cream stabilizer
7 grams salt
40 grams powdered wasabi

Passion Fruit Coulis:
1 cup frozen passion fruit puree
2 cups neutral pastry glaze

Soy-Sesame Glaze:
1 cup soy sauce
3 cups neutral pastry glaze
3 cups freshly toasted sesame seeds
1 tablespoon toasted sesame oil

Tuna Tartar:
1 kilogram sashimi-quality tuna loin, cut in ¼-inch dice
¼ cup finely chopped shallots
Extra virgin olive oil
Salt

To Assemble and Serve:
10 sesame tuiles (from above)
20 chive points

Method

Sesame Tuiles:
Preheat over to 350°F. Combine eggs, water, and salt in bowl to make an egg wash. Cut spring roll sheets into long triangles (1½-centimeters x 10-centimeters), dip them in the egg wash, shake of any excess egg, and dredge in raw sesame seeds. Place on a parchment-lined sheet pan in neat lines, being careful to leave space between each one. Cover with another sheet of parchment paper and place a sheet pan on top. Bake for 7 to 10 minutes until golden brown and crispy. Cool the tuiles and store them in an airtight container with silica gel so that they do not go soft.

For the Wasabi Ice Cream:
Combine milk, heavy cream, glucose, milk powder, and stabilizer in a pot and warm over medium heat. Blend mixture with a hand blender to thoroughly combine. Bring to 185°F degrees, remove from heat, and blitz with hand blender again. Strain through a fine chinoise and cool in an ice bath. Add the salt to the cooled mixture. Add 10 grams of powdered wasabi for every liter of ice cream mix. Blitz with a hand blender until mixture is completely smooth and free of lumps, and churn immediately.

For the Passion Fruit Coulis:
Combine the frozen passion fruit puree and pastry glaze, and whisk until ingredients are completely mixed. Store in a squeeze bottle.

For the Soy-Sesame Glaze:
Combine soy sauce, pastry glaze, and sesame oil in a bowl. Toast the sesame seeds in a dry skillet until golden, and add directly to the glaze. Store in a squeeze bottle (cut off the tip to avoid clogging).

For the Tuna Tartar:
Mix the chilled tuna with minced shallots and olive oil, and season with salt.

To Assemble and Serve

Squeeze a silver dollar-sized pool of passion fruit coulis in the center of the plate. Squeeze a nickel-sized pool of soy-sesame glaze directly to the left of the passion fruit coulis. Shape tuna in a ring mold and place just behind the two sauces. Place a quenelle of ice cream on top of the tuna cylinder. Place two sesame tuiles side by side on top of the quenelle. Place two chive points on top of the quenelle at opposite angles so they resemble an X.

Anthony Bombaci's Tuna Tartar with Wasabi Ice Cream, Soy-Sesame Glaze and Passion Fruit

Recipes

Sunchoke Soup with Dried Black Olives and Olive Oil Milk Foam
Chef Gabriel Bremer of Salts – Cambridge, MA
Adapted by StarChefs.com

Yield: 4-6 Servings

Ingredients
Dried Black Olives:
1 pound oil cured black olives

Sunchoke Soup:
1½ pounds sunchokes, chopped
2 small leeks or spring onions, white part only, chopped
2 Tablespoons olive oil
8 cups chicken stock
4 tablespoons butter, melted
Sea salt and white pepper

Olive Oil Milk Foam:
1 cup whole milk
¼ cup extra virgin olive oil

Method
For the Dried Olives:
Pit the olives and slice in half lengthwise. Lay the olives on a wire baking rack making sure that they are in an even layer. Place the olives in the oven set to 150°F and leave overnight to dry. Place the dried olives in a food processor and pulse in 3-second intervals until the desired texture. Store in an airtight container.

For the Sunchoke Soup:
In a medium-size stock pot combine the sunchokes and leeks, and sweat in olive oil on low heat for 2 to 3 minutes. Add the chicken stock and cook for an additional 30 minutes or until the sunchokes are soft. Transfer the soup to a blender and puree on high for 2 minutes. As the soup purées, slowly incorporate the butter. Pass the blended soup through a chinois and season to taste with fine sea salt and freshly ground white pepper.

For the Olive Oil Milk Foam:
Combine milk and olive oil in a chilled bain maire and froth liquid using a hand blender until the desired foam is achieved.

To Assemble and Serve
Serve the soup, warm, in small bowls or espresso cups. Top with the warm olive oil milk foam and finish with the dried olive powder.

Tortellono in Brodo
Chef Richard Corbo of Mecca – San Francisco, CA
Adapted by StarChefs.com

Yield: 4-6 Servings

Ingredients

Anise Spice Mix:
6 star anise
1 tablespoon coriander seed
1 tablespoon black peppercorns

Beef Sauce:
1 quart caramelized beef "bits"
1 bay leaf
1 tablespoon dry thyme
1 gram veal stock
1 cup Port
1 teaspoon granulated sugar
1 ounce butter

Beef-Maytag Blue Filling:
1 cup pulled, braised, short rib meat
¼ cup beef sauce
¼ cup finely crumbled Maytag blue cheese

Pasta Dough:
10.5 ounces fine white flour "00," or bread flour
1 egg
2 yolks
2 teaspoon kosher salt
1 tablespoon anise spice mix

Anise Brown Butter:
1 tablespoon butter
1 teaspoon rice oil
1 star anise
1 bay leaf
Salt to taste

To Assemble and Serve:
Veal stock
Shallots
Thyme
Salt
Maldon salt
Chives, chopped

Method

For the Anise Spice Mix:
Toast in a pan over low heat, grind very fine, and sift well through drum sieve.

For the Beef Sauce:
Cover the bits and spices with some of the veal stock and reduce to near sec, repeat until a rich sauce develops and all the veal stock has been pumped through the bits. Once you have reduced the liquid to approximately 1 cup, strain. In another sauce pan, reduce the port and sugar to syrup consistency, add the cup of reduced stock, and bring back to a simmer. Mount with the butter and allow the sauce to simmer for up to 5 minutes more, whisking all the while.

For the Beef-Maytag Blue Filling:
Work the braised beef and the beef sauce together in a mixing bowl until a satiny quality develops and the beef is broken down and very soft. Fold in the blue cheese so that it's evenly spread throughout the stuffing but still maintains its own shape. Chill.

For the Pasta:
Place flour on a clean, dry surface and make a hollow in the center. Add egg, yolks, salt, and spice, and incorporate little by little. When the dough is mixed well enough to form a ball, start to knead the dough until it becomes smooth and uniform. The dough should not be wet (add more flour if so). When dough is smooth, refrigerate for 1 hour.

Roll out the pasta dough to the thinnest setting, cut into squares, and add the appropriate amount of filling for the tortellono you wish to make. Fold in the style of an exaggerated tortellini – fold the square to a triangle, then marry the two opposite ends of the triangle together.

For the Anise Brown Butter:
Gently simmer the butter until a brown, nutty, buerre noisette develops. Add the oil and spices and set aside to infuse and cool. Strain and put in a squirt bottle with a fine point top.

To Assemble and Serve

Prepare a flavorful consomme with veal stock, shallots, thyme, and salt. Strain clean and hold hot. Drop the pasta into salty, boiling water, and lower the heat at the same time as to prevent the pasta from rolling around when cooking. Cook for approximately 6 minutes, allow to drip dry, then plate in a shallow soup bowl. Ladle the consomme to cover about ½ of the tortellono's body. Sprinkle the top of the pasta with Maldon salt and fresh chopped chives, and surround the pasta with droplets of anise brown butter. Serve with a fork, knife, and soup spoon.

Recipes

Parmigiano Reggiano Velouté with Prosciutto di Parma Crisps and Pink Pearl Apples

Chef Traci Des Jardins of Jardinière – San Francisco, CA
Adapted by StarChefs.com

Yield: 6 Servings

Ingredients

Parmigiano Reggiano Stock:
1 pound Parmigiano Reggiano, roughly chopped
5 ounces Prosciutto di Parma, cut into 1-inch pieces
2 bulbs fennel
2 white onions, peeled and quartered
2 heads garlic, cut in half
1 lemon, quartered
Sachet of parsley, sage and thyme
1 gallon water

Velouté:
3 ounces Prosciutto di Parma
1 teaspoon olive oil
3 onions, roughly chopped
3 leeks, roughly chopped
1 head garlic, peeled and roughly chopped
2 bulbs fennel
¼ cup all-purpose flour
1 cup dry white wine
1 lemon, thinly sliced
1 pound Parmigiano Reggiano
Sachet of parsley, sage and thyme
Parmigiano Reggiano stock (from above)
1 quart cream
1 cup crème fraiche
Juice of 1 lemon
Salt and pepper

Prosciutto Crisps:
12 grams all purpose flour
Salt and pepper
20 grams water
1 gram vinegar
2 ounces Prosciutto di Parma, rendered and finely chopped

Pink Pearl Apple Purée:
3 ounces Prosciutto di Parma rind
1 sprig sage
2 shallots, thinly sliced
4 Pink Pearl apples, peeled, cored and quartered
½ cup dry white wine
½ cup Prosciutto di Parma fat, rendered and strained
Salt and pepper

Salad:
1 Pink Pearl apple, peeled, cored and thinly sliced
½ bunch parsley, roughly chopped
½ bunch chervil, roughly chopped
Extra virgin olive oil, to taste
Lemon juice, to taste
Salt and pepper

Method

For the Parmigiano Reggiano Stock:

Combine the Parmigiano Reggiano, Prosciutto di Parma, fennel, onions, garlic, lemon, herbs and water in a large non-reactive pot and simmer, skimming off impurities, for 1½ hours. Strain and reserve, keeping warm.

For the Velouté:

In a non-reactive pot, render the prosciutto in olive oil and add the onions, leeks, garlic, and fennel and sweat for 5 minutes. Add the flour and sauté for several minutes, then deglaze with the white wine and cook off the alcohol. Add the lemon, Parmigiano Reggiano, sachet, and reserved Parmigiano Reggiano stock. Allow to simmer for 1½ hours, then remove the sachet and strain to remove Prosciutto di Parma. Blend the mixture until smooth and pass through a fine china cap. Add the lemon juice and season with salt and pepper. Reserve warm.

For the Prosciutto di Parma Crisps:

Preheat oven to 300°F. Sift the flour, salt, and pepper together. Mix the water and vinegar in a separate bowl, then whisk this mixture into the dry ingredients. Pass this mixture through a chinois and spread on a Silpat in a 1/8-inch thick layer. Season with additional salt and pepper and sprinkle with the Prosciutto di Parma. Bake for 4 minutes, then remove and slice to desired shape. Return to the oven and bake until golden brown.

For the Pink Pearl Apple Purée:

In a non-reactive pan, render the Prosciutto rind with the sage, then add the shallot and apples. Sweat the mixture until the pan begins to dry, then deglaze with the wine and cover the pot so the wine slowly evaporates. Once dry, remove the sage and blend the mixture with the rendered Prosciutto di Parma fat until smooth. Pass through a fine china cap and season with salt and pepper. Reserve warm.

For the Salad:

Combine the Pink Pearl apple, parsley, chervil, olive oil and lemon juice. Season with salt and pepper.

To Assemble and Serve

Spread a small amount of apple purée on a plate and top with the salad. Place two Prosciutto di Parma crisps to one side of the salad. Fill a warm bowl with velouté and serve.

Recipes

Charred Baby Octopus with Grilled Bread and Tomato Sauce
Chef Kendal Duque of Sepia – Chicago, IL
Adapted by StarChefs.com

Yield: 4 Servings

Ingredients
Octopus:
2 pounds cleaned and tenderized fresh baby octopus
2 lemons, quartered
1 carrot, quartered
1 small red onion, quartered
1 stalk celery, quartered
1 cup white wine
4 sprigs fresh thyme
1 bay leaf
4 cloves garlic, smashed
Kosher salt
Pepper

Tomato Sauce:
¼ yellow onion, finely chopped
10 ounces whole Italian imported plum tomatoes
¼ carrot, peeled and finely grated
¼ cup extra virgin olive oil
2 sprigs fresh basil
Kosher salt
Pepper

Lemon-Oregano Oil:
1 lemon, segmented
6 sprigs oregano
¼ cup olive oil

To Assemble and Serve:
4 slices baguette

Method
For the Octopus:
Combine octopus, lemon, carrot, onion, celery, wine, thyme, bay leaf, and garlic in a pot and cover with water. Bring to a boil, lower to a simmer, and cook 1 to 2 hours, or until octopus is tender. Remove pot from heat and let octopus cool down in the liquid until cool enough to handle. Remove from liquid, season, and reserve.

For the Tomato Sauce:
Drain tomatoes from their juice and chop finely. Sweat onion, carrot and basil in olive oil until soft. Raise heat and add tomatoes. Reduce heat to a simmer and cook, stirring often, for 20 minutes. Reserve warm.

For Lemon-Oregano Oil:
Combine lemon, oregano, and oil and mix.

To Assemble and Serve
Remove octopus form liquid and place on a hot grill until lightly charred on all sides. Remove from grill and toss in a bowl with lemon-oregano vinaigrette. Slice four thick slices of baguette and grill on both sides. Spoon tomato sauce on plate, place bread in middle, and top with octopus. Drizzle vinaigrette over and around the octopus and serve immediately.

Peekytoe Crab Canelloni with Pear, Basil, and Lemon

Chef Chef Christopher Eagle of Cielo – Boca Raton, FL
Adapted by StarChefs.com

Yield: 1 Serving

Ingredients

Peekytoe Crab:
1 Bartlett pear
8 ounces freshly picked Peekytoe crab meat
½ teaspoon finely diced yellow pepper
½ teaspoon finely diced red pepper
½ teaspoon finely diced blanched fingerling potatoes
1 teaspoon chopped chervil
Mayonnaise
Extra virgin olive oil
Lemon juice
Salt and white pepper

Pear Puree:
2 pears, peeled and diced
2 cups dry Chardonnay
1 cup granulated sugar
½ vanilla bean, scraped

To Assemble and Serve:
Pear puree (from above)
Reduced balsamic vinegar
2 tablespoons finely diced Tuscan melon
Vanilla bean-infused oil
Salt and white pepper
Lemon juice
Basil-infused oil
Prosciutto dust*
Micro arugula
Julienned yellow pepper
Julienned red pepper
Micro greens
Simple vinaigrette of your choice

*Crisped, dried, and ground Prosciutto di Parma

Method

For the Peekytoe Crab:
Place pear in a vegetable sheeter and peel 4 sheets from the pear. Take the pear sheets and cut to form four 3-inch x 3-inch squares. Cover with a damp cloth. Combine crab meat, peppers, potatoes, chervil, and chives. Season crab with mayonnaise, olive oil, lemon juice, salt, and white pepper. Place equal parts of the crab salad on the pear sheets, and roll into tight cannelloni shapes.

For the Pear Puree:
Bring all ingredients to a boil and simmer until reduced to a dense, reduced consistency. Puree and pass through a chinoise.

To Assemble and Serve
Place ½ teaspoon of the pear puree in the middle of the plate. Draw an oval around the puree with the balsamic reduction. Place one cannelloni on the pear puree. Cut the other cannelloni in half on the bias and stand on either side of the plate. Mix the melon with the vanilla bean oil and season with salt, white pepper, and lemon juice. Place on top of the center cannelloni. Top the melon salad with basil oil and prosciutto dust, and garnish with a sprig of micro arugula. Mix the julienned peppers and micro herbs, season with a simple vinaigrette of your choice, and place on the plate.

Recipes

Gratin of Nantucket Bay Scallops with Jerusalem Artichoke Puree, Parmigiano Reggiano, and Alba White Truffles

Chef Linton Hopkins of Restaurant Eugene – Atlanta, GA
Adapted by StarChefs.com

Yield: 4 Servings

Ingredients

Jerusalem Artichoke Puree:
8 Jerusalem artichokes, peeled
2 cups heavy cream
Salt, to taste

Scallops:
32 Nantucket Bay scallops, shucked
¼ cup grated Parmigiano Reggiano
¼ ounce Alba white truffle

Method

For the Jerusalem Artichoke Puree:
Combine the artichokes and cream and cook on low heat until cooked through. Puree in blender, strain, adjust the seasoning, and reserve.

For the Scallops:
Season the scallops and sauté on one side only until light golden brown. Arrange scallops in a heat proof dish, cover with Jerusalem artichoke puree, sprinkle with grated cheese, and broil until golden and heated through. Microplane the white truffle over the top and serve.

Frog "Wings" with Celery Kimchee

Chef Craig Hopson of One if by Land, Two if by Sea – New York, NY
Adapted by StarChefs.com

Yield: 12 Servings

Ingredients

Kimchee*:
2 bunches celery, finely diced
3 bunches scallions
500 grams red peppers
15 grams sambal oelek
25 grams garlic
75 grams ginger
40 grams fish sauce
15 grams sugar
10 grams salt
15 grams sesame oil
20 grams white vinegar

Sauce:
6 egg yolks
¼ cup Sherry vinegar
½ teaspoon sambal oelek
2 teaspoon salt
1 teaspoon paprika
1¼ cups grapeseed oil
½ cup peanut oil
¾ cup sesame oil
¾ cup orange juice

Frog "Wings":
24 fresh frog legs
1 cup tempura batter
2 teaspoons celery seeds
12 celery leaves

To Assemble and Serve:
2 tablespoons peanuts, roasted
and crushed

*Prepare 3 days ahead of time

Method

For Kimchee:
Blanch the celery and scallions in salted boiling water. Set aside. Purée the red peppers, sambal oelek, garlic, ginger, fish sauce, sugar, salt, sesame oil, and vinegar. Combine with the blanched celery, place in a covered non-reactive container, and store at room temperature for 3 days. Refrigerate for up to 4 weeks.

For the Sauce:
Place the egg yolks, Sherry vinegar, sambal oelek, salt, and paprika in a food processor and, with the motor running, drizzle in the grapeseed oil. Follow with the peanut oil, sesame oil, and orange juice.

For Frog "Wings":
Cut each frog leg at the top of the thigh, away from the body. Cut each leg bone at the calf muscle section and trim away excess meat. Using scissors, reach inside the remaining section of meat and cut the bone to give the legs a lollipop appearance.

Heat oil to 325˚F. Dip each leg into the tempura batter and fry at 325˚F for 3 minutes or until cooked and crisp. Drain on paper towel and sprinkle with celery seeds. Brush each celery leaf with tempura batter and fry in the same manner.

To Assemble and Serve

Spread the sauce into a pool in the middle of four plates and arrange the frog legs on each plate. Finish with a spoonful of the celery kimchee, the tempura celery leaves, and a sprinkle of peanuts.

Recipes

Kabocha Squash Tortellini with Chestnut Honey and Sage
Chef Kevin Maxey of Craft – Dallas, TX
Adapted by StarChefs.com

Yield: 4 Servings

Ingredients
1 Kabocha squash, seeds removed, roasted
2 tablespoons extra virgin olive oil
¼ cup grated Parmigiano Reggiano
¼ teaspoon freshly grated nutmeg
Salt and pepper, to taste
2 8-inch x 3-foot sheets fresh pasta dough
¼ cup chestnut honey
4 tablespoons butter
8 leaves sage
2 tablespoons Parmigiano Reggiano
Freshly cracked black pepper

Method
Combine roasted squash with olive oil, cheese, nutmeg and season to taste. Cut pasta into squares and make tortellini using about 1 tablespoon of filling per piece. Poach tortellini in salted, boiling water until cooked, then drain. Heat the chestnut honey in a sauté pan until it darkens slightly then add the butter, sage leaves and more cheese. Add the poached tortellini and gently toss to coat. Serve with additional cheese (grated on top) and fresh cracked black pepper.

StarChefs' Basic Pasta Dough Recipe

Yield: 4 Servings

Ingredients
1 pound all-purpose flour
Pinch of salt
3 eggs plus 2 yolks, beaten
1 ounce water

Method
Combine the flour and salt in a small bowl or on a flat surface and make a well in the center. Place the eggs and water in the well. Using a fork or your fingers, and working as rapidly as possible, gradually pull the flour into the liquid ingredients and stir until a loose mass forms. As the dough is mixed, adjust the consistency with additional flour or water.

Turn the dough out onto a floured work surface and knead until the texture becomes smooth and elastic. Gather the kneaded dough into a ball, cover, and let the dough relax at room temperature for 1 hour.

Kevin Maxey's Kabocha Squash Tortellini with Chestnut Honey and Sage

Recipes

New Zealand Green Lip Mussels with Ancho Chiles and Chorizo
Chef Mike Minor of Border Grill – Las Vegas, NV
Adapted by StarChefs.com

Yield: 4 Servings

Ingredients
¾ cup olive oil
10 cloves garlic, peeled and thinly sliced
2 cups diced Spanish chorizo
3 finely sliced ancho chilies
1¾ pounds New Zealand green lip mussels
Juice of 3 large limes
¼ white wine
1 cup fish stock or clam juice
1 bunch Italian parsley, leaves only, chopped
½ cup diced butter cubes

Method
Heat olive oil in a large skillet over medium-low heat. Cook garlic until tender but not brown. Add chorizo, chilies, and mussels; turn the heat to high, add white wine and lime juice (this will help the mussels open), and cook until mussels open and chilies are softened. Add stock or clam juice, butter, and parsley; let cook for a few minutes more until butter melts and is incorporated. Arrange mussels in a bowl, stir broth and check for seasoning, and ladle over top. Serve immediately.

Recipes

Shocked Tuna with Red Wine and Spicy Apple
Chef Morou Outtara of Farrah Olivia – Alexandria, VA
Adapted by StarChefs.com

Yield: 50 Servings

Ingredients
Shocked Tuna:
1 quart water
2 cups soy sauce
1 cup red wine
1 pound tuna, cut in 1-inch x 1-inch x 5-inch pieces

Spicy Apple Drink:
1 Granny Smith apple, peeled, cored and chopped
4 cups pineapple juice
2 tablespoons ginger, chopped
2 sticks lemongrass, bottoms only, chopped
¼ cup mint leaves
5 cloves
1 cup sugar

To Assemble and Serve:
50 small plastic pipettes*

*Can be found on laboratory supply sites

Method
For the Shocked Tuna:
Bring the water to a boil in a large pot. Meanwhile, prepare the brine mixture by combining the soy sauce and red wine. Drop each piece of tuna into the boiling water, separately, and cook for 10 seconds, then remove from the water and add to the brine. Allow the tuna to marinate for 2 hours, refrigerated.

Drain tuna and pat dry to remove excess brine. To finish the tuna, hold a torch to each side of the tuna piece for a few seconds. The meat should just begin to bubble and change color. Slice the tuna cross-wise into thin rectangles.

For the Spicy Apple Drink:
Place the apple, pineapple juice, ginger, lemongrass, mint, and cloves in a high-speed blender, and blend until smooth. Strain through a chinois, add the sugar, and reserve chilled.

To Assemble and Serve
Fill a small plastic pipette with the spicy apple drink and skewer a slice of tuna on one end. Instruct diners to bite off the tuna and squirt the apple drink into their mouths.

Morou Outtara's Shocked Tuna with Red Wine and Spicy Apple

Ceviche of Bronzini with Vanilla-Roasted Fennel and Almond Gazpacho

Chef Stephan Pyles of Stephan Pyles – Dallas, TX
Adapted by StarChefs.com

Yields: 4 Servings

Ingredients

Aji Mirasol Purée:
8-10 Aji Mirasol chiles
Water

Almond Gazpacho:
8 ounces blanched almonds
1 clove garlic
4 cups filtered or spring water
2 ounces white bread, crust
removed, diced
½ cup extra virgin olive oil
1 tablespoon Sherry vinegar
2 teaspoons salt

Vanilla-Roasted Fennel:
2 cups orange juice
½ vanilla bean
1 fennel bulb, quartered
2 tablespoons olive oil
Salt

Bronzini Ceviche:
14 ounces Bronzini, skin removed,
flesh sliced into 1-inch x ¼-inch
strips; reserve 2 ounces to puree
½ cup ice cubes
4 teaspoons key lime juice
Salt
1 tablespoon Aji Mirasol Purée
2 tablespoons reserved fennel-
orange-vanilla cooking liquid

To Assemble and Serve:
1 mango, peeled, pitted, cut into
¼-inch dice, frozen
Extra virgin olive oil

Method

For the Aji Mirasol Purée:
Preheat oven to 475°F. Wash and thoroughly dry the chiles, then cut off the stems, slit chiles open, and remove the seeds. Place the chiles on a baking sheet and roast in the oven for 60 seconds. Alternatively, the chiles may be dry-roasted over high heat in a skillet or on a comal until they puff up, approximately 45 seconds. Transfer the chiles to a bowl and cover with warm water. Keep the chiles submerged for 30 minutes to rehydrate, then strain the chiles, reserving the liquid, and place the chiles in a Vita-Prep. Puree the chiles, adding just enough of the liquid to make a thick paste. Strain the puree through a medium sieve. Reserve.

For the Almond Gazpacho:
Place the almonds and garlic in a saucepan with one cup of the water and bring to a boil. Strain the mixture, then pour a fresh cup of water into the pan with the almonds and garlic and bring back to a boil. Strain again. Place the garlic and almonds in a blender and add the remaining 2 cups of mineral water, white bread, olive oil, vinegar and salt. Blend the mixture until smooth, approximately 1 minute. Place a colander over a large bowl and line with cheesecloth. Pour the pureed almond mixture into the cheesecloth-lined colander and allow most of the liquid to pass through, then gather the cheesecloth and squeeze to extract as much of the remaining liquid as possible. Discard the solids and reserve the liquid; chill for at least 30 minutes.

For the Vanilla-Roasted Fennel:
Preheat oven to 375°F. Place the orange juice in a small saucepan and scrape in the vanilla bean pulp. Reduce over medium heat by half. Place the fennel in a small roasting pan and cover with the orange-vanilla mixture. Drizzle the olive oil over the fennel and season with salt. Roast until the fennel is soft, approximately 20-25 minutes. Remove the fennel and cool and reserve the fennel-orange-vanilla cooking liquid. Remove the core from the fennel, then cut the fennel into a small dice.

For the Bronzini Ceviche:
Place the reserved 2 ounces of Bronzini filet in a Vita-Prep with the ice cubes and blend until very smooth, approximately one minute. Chill. Place the sliced Bronzini in a glass or stainless steel bowl, add the lime juice and season with salt. Stir to combine thoroughly and let the ceviche marinate for 5 minutes, then add the icy fish puree and the Aji Mirasol puree; combine thoroughly. Add the reserved fennel-orange-vanilla cooking liquid and 3 tablespoons of the chopped fennel. Incorporate completely.

To Assemble and Serve
To serve, divide the ceviche among 4 shallow bowls and ladle ½ cup of the almond gazpacho around it. Drizzle with a small amount of olive oil and garnish each bowl with a few pieces of frozen diced mango.

Antoinette Bruno

Stephan Pyles' Ceviche of Bronzini with Vanilla-Roasted Fennel and Almond Gazpacho

Recipes

Foie Gras Terrine with Citrus Textures and Flavors
Chef Ken Oringer of Clio — Boston, MA
Adapted by StarChefs.com

Yield: 4 Servings

Ingredients

Foie Gras Terrine:
4 pounds foie gras, cleaned
1 ounce salt
3/8 ounce pink salt
3/8 ounce white pepper
¾ ounce sugar
1 dash Chartreuse
Duck fat

Candied Buddha's Hand:
1 teaspoon fresh yuzu
1 Buddha's Hand, sliced and blanched
Simple syrup

Kaffir Lime Sauce:
½ cup kaffir lime juice
1 teaspoon agar agar

To Assemble and Serve:
¼ teaspoon Maldon salt
¼ teaspoon Grains of Paradise pepper
¼ teaspoon chives
1 grapefruit, segmented
1 orange, segmented
1 lime, segmented
1 lemon, segmented
1 teaspoon blood orange puree
1 orange, thinly sliced and dehydrated

Method

For Foie Gras Terrine:
Season the foie gras with salt, pink salt, white pepper, sugar and Chartreuse. Using cheesecloth, roll into a torchon and hang in walk-in for 8 hours (or overnight).

The next day, heat duck fat to 120°F. Pour over torchon and let sit 8 hours (or overnight) until cooled. Remove torchon from cheesecloth and pack into a terrine mold, making sure to eliminate all air pockets. Press with weights and chill 8 hours (or overnight).

For Candied Buddah's Hand:
Steep yuzu and blanched Buddha's Hand in simple syrup for approximately 20 minutes, then remove and dry.

Kaffir Lime Sauce
Bring kaffir lime juice to a boil. Whisk in agar agar and boil again. Remove from heat and set aside.

To Assemble and Serve
Cut two slices of chilled terrine. Top with Maldon salt, Grains of Paradise and chives. Arrange citrus segments and candied Buddah's hand on plate. Garnish with kaffir lime sauce and blood orange puree. Top with a crumble of dehydrated orange.

Lobster-Cauliflower Bisque with Wisconsin SarVecchio Cheese and Tarragon Oil

Chef Kevin Rathbun of Rathbun's – Atlanta, GA
Adapted by StarChefs.com

Yield: 8 Servings

Ingredients

Soup:
1 head cauliflower, chopped
2 shallots, chopped
1½ cups lobster stock
1½ cups heavy whipping cream
¾ cup Wisconsin SarVecchio cheese*
2 tablespoons lemon juice
2 tablspoons honey
1 tablespoon kosher salt
½ tablespoon black pepper
*sub: Parmigiano Reggiano

Tarragon Oil:
Tarragon
Spinach
Extra virgin olive oil
Salt

To Assemble and Serve:
2 6-ounce lobster tails
Lobster stock
Butter

Method

For the Soup:
Place cauliflower, shallots, lobster stock, and cream in a pot and bring to a bowl, then simmer until cauliflower is tender. Transfer to a blender and puree until smooth. While soup is blending, add cheese and continue to blend until smooth. To finish, add lemon, honey, salt, and pepper.

For the Tarragon Oil:
Bring water to a boil, and prepare an ice bath. Blanch equal parts tarragon and spinach for 1 second and shock in ice bath. Squeeze dry in a paper towel, blend leaves with oil until emulsified, and season with a pinch of salt.

To Assemble and Serve
Poach lobster tails in equal parts lobster stock and butter. Chop meat and distribute among bowls of soup, and finish with tarragon oil.

Recipes

Maine Crabcake Corn Dogs

Chef Chris Santos of The Stanton Social – New York, NY
Adapted by StarChefs.com

Yield: 6 Servings

Ingredients

Crabcakes:
2 ounces butter, softened
½ cup of aioli
1 pound picked lump crabmeat
4-6 dashes of Tabasco
¼ bunch chives, minced
½ cup panko
Salt and pepper

Corn Dog Batter:
1⅓ cups cornmeal
2 cups buttermilk
⅔ cups all-purpose flour
⅔ teaspoon salt
1⅓ teaspoons sugar
2 small egg yolks, beaten
Salt and pepper

Corn Vinaigrette:
1 cup corn, roasted
4 ounces chicken or vegetable stock, chilled
2 egg yolks
⅛ cup mustard
1 teaspoon lemon juice
1 tablespoon cider vinegar
2 cups light olive oil
Salt and pepper

Corn Vinaigrette:
Wooden skewers

Method

For the Crabcakes:
Whisk together butter and aioli and gently fold in remaining ingredients. Refrigerate for at least 1 hour.

For the Batter:
Combine cornmeal with 1½ cups of the buttermilk and let thicken for 45 minutes. Mix remaining ½ cup of buttermilk with flour, salt, sugar, and yolks, and whisk into cornmeal mixture. Season with salt and pepper.

For the Corn Vinaigrette:
Purée corn and stock in blender until smooth. Add yolks, mustard, lemon juice, and vinegar and blend. Gradually drizzle in oil and emulsify. Season with salt and pepper.

To Assemble and Serve

Mold crabcakes around a stick and dip in corn dog batter. Fry until golden brown and plate 3 crabcake corn dogs per serving, standing up in a small, deep bowl. Finish with corn vinaigrette.

Antoinette Bruno

Santos' Maine Crabcake Corn Dogs

Recipes

Spiced Kanpachi Tartare with Chilled Cucumber, Cantaloupe Gelée, and Osetra Caviar

Chef Alessandro Stratta of Alex – Las Vegas, NV
Adapted by StarChefs.com

Yield: 8 Servings

Ingredients

Dehydrated Melons:
3 cantaloupes, peeled
1 red seedless watermelon

Cantaloupe Juice:
¼ cup ginger, juiced
10 ripe cantaloupes

Cantaloupe Gelée:
1000 grams canteloupe juice
(from above)
7 sheets gelatin

Cucumber Pearls:
500 grams cucumber juice
4 grams algen powder
5 grams calcium chloride
1 liter water
1 gram fleur de sel
250 grams cucumber juice

Brick Dough Crisps:
4 sheets brick dough
1 cup egg whites
Oil vegetable spray

Yuzu Vinaigrette:
¼ cup yuzu juice
¾ cup extra virgin olive oil
Salt and pepper

To Assemble and Serve:
1 pound fresh Kanpachi,
diced into ¼-inch cubes
2 Tablespoons yuzu-lemon vinaigrette
(from above)
12 grams Persicus caviar
1 cup dehydrated melon, diced
(from above)
8 slices radish
1 tablespoon togarashi
1 tablespoon chives, minced
2 tablespoons dried Bonito flakes
Micro cilantro

Method

For the Dehydrated Melons:
Dice melons into ¼-inch slices and seal in seperate Cryovac® bags. Let compress overnight in the refrigerator. The following day, remove from the bag and arrange on a dehydrator tray. Dehydrate at 115°F for 5 hours, and refrigerate.

For the Cantaloupe Juice:
Add juiced ginger to the melon and puree in a blender until smooth. Strain for 8 hours (or overnight) through a coffee filter in the refrigerator. Place the strained juice in a container and set aside at room temperature.

For the Cantaloupe Gelée:
Bloom sheets of gelatin in cold water and add to 150 grams of the canta-loupe juice. Dissolve over heat. Once dissolved, add to the remaining juice and mix well. In a pot over low heat, bring mixture up to 170ºF and pour ¾-ounce portions of the juice into small ramekins, filling them ¾ of the way full.

For the Cucumber Pearls:
Strain cucumber juice and blend with algen for 2 or 3 minutes. Allow mixture to rest at room temperature for 1-1½ hours. Add calcium chloride to water, stirring to dissolve. Keep at room temperature. Place the cucumber-algen mixture in a small-tipped squeeze bottle and squeeze small pearl drops into the calcium chloride solution. Allow the spheres to set for 45-60 seconds and gently remove with a slotted spoon. Reserve in a container with cucumber juice and chill.

For the Brick Dough Crisps:
Preheat a convection oven to 325ºF. Place brick dough sheets between damp towels to soften. Cut the brick dough into 2-inch x 4-inch long rect-angles then place back under damp towels. Spray 1-inch cannoli molds with vegetable spray and brush both sides of dough with egg whites. Triple roll the sheets tightly around the sprayed molds and spray the finished rounds with more vegetable spray. Place the molds on a flat baking sheet fitted with a Silpat, assuring that the seams are on the bottom. Bake in a convection oven with the low fan at 325ºF for 5 minutes, then turn pan for an additional 5 minutes, or until light golden brown. Reserve crisps at room temperature for up to two days.

For the Yuzu Vinaigrette:
Combine yuzu and oil, mix well, and season with salt and pepper.

To Assemble and Serve

Toss Kanpachi with yuzu vinaigrette. Fill the brick dough tubes with Kanpachi and top with caviar. Place the filled tube in the center of the canta-loupe gelée and garnish with cucumber pearls, dehydrated melons, radish, togarashi, chives, bonito flakes and cilantro.

toinette Bruno

Alessandro Stratta's Spiced Kanpachi Tartare with
Chilled Cucumber, Cantaloupe Gelée and Osetra Caviar

Recipes

Foie Gras and Caramelized Eel Millefeuille

Chef Yosuke Suga of Joël Robuchon – New York, NY
Adapted by StarChefs.com

Yield: 8 Servings

Ingredients

Espelette Whipped Cream:
500 grams heavy cream
60 grams Piment d'Espelette
Salt and pepper

Smoked Foie Gras:
Woodchips, heated to smoking point
1 lobe foie gras*
Salt and pepper
½ cup Brandy

Eel Liason and Millefeuille:
2 pieces prepared Japanese eel
200 grams prepared Japanese eel sauce
500 grams veal stock
White truffle oil
Black pepper

To Assemble and Serve:
Brown sugar
1 bunch chives, finely sliced

*Chef Suga recommends Rougie Foie Gras

Method

For the Espelette Whipped Cream:
Whip the cream to soft peaks and season with Piment d'Espelette, salt, and pepper. Reserve in the fridge until assembly.

For the Smoked Foie Gras:
Heat woodchips until smoking and place in the bottom of a hotel pan. Place a perforated pan on top, lay foie gras on the pan, and wrap in plastic to seal in smoke. Refrigerate container for 15 minutes, then remove foie gras and season with salt, pepper, and Brandy. Vacuum seal and cook sous vide at 80°C until the core reaches 60°C. Chill in ice water, cut into ⅓-inch-pieces, and lay out on parchment paper until ready to use.

For the Liason and Millefeuille:
Caramelize the eel in some of the eel sauce under the salamander. Mix the remaining eel sauce with veal stock and reduce until sauce consistency. Season with truffle oil and reserve. Line a terrine mold with parchment paper and place the trimmed foie gras on the bottom of the mold. With a basting brush, lightly brush the foie gras with the sauce, season well with black pepper, and place the eel on top. Brush with the sauce again, season with black pepper, and place another layer of foie gras. Repeat the process and finish with a layer of eel. Place a sheet of parchment paper on top of the terrine and press for 8 hours (or overnight) in the fridge. Unmold the terrine and slice into 8 portions.

To Assemble and Serve

Sprinkle brown sugar on the top of each slice and caramelize the portions one-by-one. Spoon a small amount of Espelette cream on the plate, place the millefeuille beside it, and garnish with chives.

Foie Gras Shabu Shabu with Truffle, Bartlett Pear, Candied Hazelnuts, and Watercress Purée

Chef Eric Ziebold of CityZen – Washington, DC
Adapted by StarChefs.com

Yield: 4 Servings

Ingredients

Poached Pears:
1 cup water
1 cup white wine
1 cup sugar
1 Bartlett pear, peeled, cored and quartered

Candied Hazelnuts:
1 cup powdered sugar
12 hazelnuts
Oil for frying

Watercress Puree:
1 bunch watercress
Salt

Truffle Stock:
Périgord truffles, to taste
1 liter mushroom stock

To Assemble and Serve:
4 ¼-inch foie gras slices

Method

For the Poached Pears:
Heat the water, wine and sugar until dissolved, then add the pears. Keep the syrup at 150°F and poach the pears until tender. Remove the pears from the liquid and allow to cool. Slice the pear in half lengthwise and dice into ½-inch pieces, yielding 16 pieces.

For the Candied Hazelnuts:
Sift the powdered sugar into a medium-sized stainless steel bowl and evenly coat it. Drop the hazelnuts into a pot of boiling water and remove immediately. Drain them very well but do not dry. Immediately toss them in the powdered sugar, stirring to coat evenly. Deep fry at 350°F until golden brown. Spread the hazelnuts out on a baking sheet to cool.

For the Watercress Puree:
Blanch the watercress in a large pot of boiling, salted water until tender. Shock in an ice bath and squeeze out most of the water. Purée in a high-speed blender and pass through a chinois. Season with salt if necessary.

For the Truffle Stock:
Scrub the Périgord truffles to remove any dirt, then cover with mushroom stock and simmer until tender.

To Assemble and Serve

Bring the truffle stock to a boil, turn off the heat, and add the foie gras. Paint two stripes of watercress purée in the bottom of a bowl and top with pear and hazelnut pieces. After the foie gras has cooked for 30 to 40 seconds, remove and place in the bowl. Ladle 50 milliliters of stock over the foie gras, and serve.

Recipes

Chile-Dusted Catfish with Tomato Chutney and Lemon Emulsion

Chef Hugh Acheson of Five & Ten – Athens, GA
Adpated by StarChefs.com

Yield: 6 Servings

Ingredients

Tomato Chutney:
4 tablespoons minced garlic
4 yellow onions, finely minced
4 tablespoons minced ginger
6 jalapeños, minced
½ cup corn oil
1 tablespoon mustard seed, toasted
1 tablespoon cumin
1 tablespoon ground fenugreek seed
20 Roma tomatoes, coarsely chopped
Salt
3 cups packed cilantro, cleaned and coarsely chopped

Lemon Sauce:
2 cups white wine
1 sprig thyme
1 shallot, finely minced
Zest of 2 lemons
Juice of 2 lemons
2 cups fish stock or clam juice
1 tablespoon cream
¼ pound butter
Salt

Chile-Dusted Catfish:
2 pounds catfish fillets, about 1-inch thick
1 cup panko breadcrumbs
1 tablespoon chile powder
Salt and pepper
2 tablespoons vegetable oil

Method

For the Tomato Chutney:

In a large pot over medium heat, fry garlic, onion, ginger, and jalapeños in oil for 1 minute. Add spices and continue cooking for another minute. Add tomatoes and a dash of salt and bring to a boil. Cook for 15 minutes, or until almost reduced to a coarse paste. Remove from heat and add chopped cilantro.

For the Lemon Sauce:

Combine wine with thyme, shallot, and lemon zest and juice. Reduce over heat by two-thirds. Add fish stock. Reduce liquid mixture by half. Add cream, and reduce new liquid mixture by half. Slowly whisk in butter. Season and place saucepan in a large, shallow pan of warm water to keep warm until ready to serve.

For the Chile Dusted Catfish:

Cut each catfish fillet into 3 pieces. Mix the panko with chile powder and a touch of salt and pepper. Dredge catfish in panko mixture. Set aside. Heat oil over medium-high heat. Add catfish and cook 3 minutes per side, and then finish for 2 minutes in hot oven.

To Assemble and Serve

Pool lemon sauce on each plate. Place catfish on top of sauce and spoon 1 tablespoon of spicy tomato chutney onto each portion.

Chef Hugh Acheson's Chile-Dusted Catfish with Tomato Chutney and Lemon Emulsion

Recipes

Barramundi with Artichoke-New Potato-Basil Nage, Provençal Condiment, Fried Anchovy, and Lemon Aioli

Chef Zach Bell of Café Boulud – Palm Beach, FL
Adapted By StarChefs.com

Yield: 8 Servings

Ingredients

Provençal Condiment:
4 Roma tomatoes, peeled and diced
4 shallots, minced
¼ cup chopped Nicoise olives
Salt and pepper

Aioli:
¼ cup fresh Meyer lemon juice
3 egg yolks
½ teaspoon Piment d'Espelette
¾ cup canola oil
Salt and pepper

Basil Puree:
2 bunches basil leaves
½ clove garlic, de-germed and blanched
½ cup extra virgin olive oil
Salt and pepper

Nage:
½ cup olive oil
16 pearl onions
4 globe artichokes, quartered
2 cloves garlic
1 sprig thyme
Salt and pepper
¼ cup white wine
1 pound new potatoes
2 cups chicken broth

Barramundi:
½ cup olive oil
1 onion, julienned
1 head fennel, julienned
1 lemon, thinly sliced
1 cup white wine
4 pounds Barramundi fillet, portioned into 8 pieces

Fried Anchovies:
½ pint ice cold soda water
1½ cups tempura flour
½ teaspoon baking soda
8 white unsalted anchovies

To Assemble and Serve:
16 grape tomatoes, peeled
1 zucchini, cut into 1-inch lozenges

Method

For the Provençal Condiment:
Mix the tomato, shallots and olives. Season and reserve, covered in plastic, at room temperature.

For the Aioli:
Combine egg yolks, lemon juice, and pepper and whisk until pale. Slowly incorporate the canola oil while whisking the mixture into an emulsion. Season and reserve in refrigerator.

For the Basil Puree:
Blanch basil in salted water and shock in an ice bath. Drain and squeeze the basil dry, and roughly chop with a knife. Combine the basil, garlic and olive oil in a blender and puree until smooth. Season and reserve warm.

For the Nage:
Heat olive oil in a pot over medium heat. Add pearl onions, artichokes, garlic, and thyme and cook for 2 minutes. Season, cook for 2 more minutes, and deglaze pot with white wine. Add potatoes, cover the vegetables with the chicken broth, and bring to a simmer. Re-season the liquid and cook until vegetables are tender. Remove from heat and cool. Reserve chilled.

For the Barramundi:
Preheat oven to 350˚F. Combine olive oil, onions, fennel, and lemon in a pot over medium heat and sweat until translucent, approximately 8-10 minutes. Add the white wine and reduce by half. Spread the mixture onto a half sheet tray and reserve warm. Season the Barramundi and place on top of the vegetables. Tent sheet pan with foil and place in oven for 7 to 10 minutes or until cooked through. Brush with olive oil and squeeze lemon over the top. Reserve warm.

For the Fried Anchovies:
Preheat a fryer to 375˚F. In a bowl, mix soda water, tempura flour and baking soda and reserve on ice. Dip anchovies into batter and fry in oil for 30 seconds. Remove with a slotted spoon and drain on paper towels.

To Assemble and Serve

Reheat the nage. Add tomatoes and zucchini and cook 2 minutes. Add basil puree. Spoon a layer of nage in the bottom of a small pre-heated bowl. Place a portion of Barramundi in the center of the plate, and top with provencal condiment and a dollop of aioli. Garnish with a fried anchovy.

Zach Bell's Barramundi, Artichoke-New Potato-Basil Nage,
Provençal Condiment, Fried Anchovy, Lemon Aioli

Recipes

Wood Pigeon Dressed in Leeks with Espresso-Hazelnut Risotto

Chef Dante Boccuzzi of Dante – Cleveland, OH
Adapted by StarChefs.com

Yield: 2 Servings

Ingredients

Leeks:
2 leeks, trimmed and washed
2 tablespoons butter
2 sprigs thyme

Pigeon:
2 whole wood pigeon breasts on the bone
3 tablespoons butter
Salt and pepper
¼ teaspoon ground nutmeg
4 cloves garlic

Risotto:
1 small white onion, minced
4 tablespoons extra virgin olive oil
2 cups Arborio rice
½ cup dry white wine
2 quarts roasted chicken stock, hot
½ cup toasted ground hazelnuts
2 teaspoons ground espresso
½ cup grated Parmesan cheese
Salt and pepper

Mushrooms:
4 bluefoot mushrooms, halved
¼ cup Madeira wine
2 tablespoons butter
1 shallot, minced
Salt and pepper

Method

For the Leeks:
Pull leek leaves apart and vacuum pack with butter and thyme sprigs. Place in a pot of boiling water for 8 minutes. Transfer to an ice water bath and cool. Remove from vacuum pack and reserve.

For the Pigeon:
Spread butter on all sides of pigeon breasts and season with salt, pepper and nutmeg. Wrap leek leaves around breasts. Vacuum pack breasts with garlic. Cook in a 65˚C (149˚F) water bath until internal temperature of pigeon reaches 62˚C (144˚F), about 25 minutes.

For the Risotto:
In a large pot, sweat onions in 2 tablespoons of olive oil until translucent. Add rice and cook gently, stirring often, without adding color for a few minutes. Deglaze pan with white wine and reduce until liquid has evaporated. Slowly add chicken stock to cover the rice while stirring. Repeat this process until rice becomes firm to the bite. Add hazelnuts, coffee, cheese, butter and the rest of the olive oil. Adjust consistency with more chicken stock. Season with salt and pepper.

For the Mushrooms:
In a small sauté pan, sear mushrooms until golden brown. Deglaze with Madeira wine and cook until liquid evaporates. Add butter and shallots; stir and turn off heat. Season with salt and pepper.

To Assemble and Serve

Spoon risotto into center of a soup plate. Lay pigeon slices on top. Arrange mushrooms on top of pigeon and around risotto.

Fresh Ricotta and Maine Lobster Ravioli with Louisiana Crawfish Étoufée

Chef Scott Boswell of Stella! – New Orleans, LA
Adapted by StarChefs

Yield: 10 Servings

Ingredients

Crawfish Étouffée:
¼ pound margarine
1 pound crawfish tails, peeled
1 onion, chopped
2 ribs celery, chopped
½ bell pepper, chopped
1 tablespoon paprika
½ teaspoon salt
¼ teaspoon black pepper
Pinch of thyme
1 bay leaf
1 cup chicken broth

Dough:
½ pound flour
2 whole eggs
⅛ teaspoon salt
½ teaspoon extra virgin olive oil

Filling:
3 cups ricotta cheese
1 egg
1 cup grated parmesan cheese
Salt and pepper, to taste
1 Maine lobster

Method

For the Étouffée:
Melt margarine in deep, heavy frying pan (avoid using cast iron). Add crawfish and cook 2 to 3 minutes, then remove crawfish with slotted spoon and set aside. Add onion, celery, bell pepper, and seasonings. Sauté at least 10 minutes (and be sure to remove bay leaf after 10 minutes). Return crawfish tails to pan and add chicken broth. Cook slowly, covered, for about 40 minutes, stirring occasionally.

For the Dough:
Combine all ingredients in food processor and pulse until a ball forms. Add a bit of flour or water to adjust texture if necessary. Wrap dough in plastic and rest 30 minutes.

For the Filling:
Combine ricotta, egg and parmesan cheese in a bowl. Season with salt and pepper to taste. Steam lobster 4 to 5 minutes and set aside to cool. Cut into small medallions.

To Assemble and Serve

Flour work surface. Set pasta rolling machine to highest number. Flatten pasta dough and lightly flour both sides. Roll through pasta machine and fold in half. Repeat several times to knead dough. Lower setting on machine one level at a time, and roll to desired thickness. Measure dough into sections with ravioli press. Cut with knife into sheets. Flour base of ravioli press generously. Place one section of dough over ravioli base. Fill each section with ricotta filling by piping with pastry bag. Place one lobster medallion on each dollop of filling. Top with a sheet of ravioli and lightly press with hands to remove air. Use rolling pin to roll over ravioli. Press between dollops of filling, and cut ravioli. Bring 1 gallon salted water to boil, add ravioli, lower heat, and cook until done. Serve 3 raviolis per person atop Étoufée.

Recipes

"Dead Man's Fingers" with Vadouvan
Chef Michael Cimarusti of Providence – Los Angeles, CA
Adapted by StarChefs.com

Yield: 4 Servings

Ingredients

Fingers:
1 large spiny lobster
Court bouillon

Mint Gel:
700 grams water
4 grams salt
400 grams mint leaves, picked,
blanched in salted water, squeezed dry
70 grams sugar
50 grams glucose
Ultra-tex, as needed

Vadouvan Espuma:
100 grams vadouvan, lightly toasted
1600 grams filtered water
500 grams sugar
5 grams turmeric
Lemon juice, to taste
Salt
.4 grams methyl cellulose
.4 grams guar gum
.4 grams xanthan gum

Vadouvan Sorbet:
110 grams vadouvan, lightly toasted
1700 grams filtered water
200 grams lemon juice
5 grams turmeric
100 grams Trimoline
480 grams sugar
12 grams sorbet stabilizer

To Assemble and Serve:
Maldon salt
Piment d'Espelette
Olive oil
Lime juice
Powdered vadouvan
Mint leaves

Method

For the Fingers:
Cook the spiny lobster for three minutes in simmering court bouillon. Remove the legs from the lobster and place the remaining lobster body back in the bouillon, cooking until it reaches desired doneness. Meanwhile, chill the legs of the lobster in an ice bath, then remove them and dry well.

Score the legs with a sharp knife, being careful not to cut all the way through. Snap the shell of the legs just before each joint and pull slowly. The meat should come free from the shell easily, leaving you with tender, cylindrical pieces of lobster flesh. Be sure to remove the tendon which runs through the legs of the lobster.

For the Mint Gel:
Place the water in a stainless sauce pan and bring it to a boil with the salt. Blanch mint and squeeze dry. Place the mint in a Vita-Prep with the sugar, glucose, and a pinch of salt, and purée until smooth. Strain the mixture through a chinois and weigh. Add ultra tex (4% of the total weight) to the mixture to achieve a fluid gel that will stand up on the plate; it shouldn't be runny.

For the Vadouvan Espuma:
Combine the vadouvan, water, sugar, turmeric, and lemon juice, to taste. Season the mixture with salt and strain through a chinois. Weigh out 400 grams of this mixture, then add the methyl cellulose, guar gum, and xanthan gum, and place in the bowl of a Hobart mixer with the whisk attachment. Mix on high speed until a light stable foam is achieved.

For the Vadouvan Sorbet:
Combine the vadouvan, water, lemon, turmeric and inverted sugar. Mix the sugar and the sorbet stabilizer together is a separate bowl. Whisk the dry mixture into the wet mixture and heat to 85°C, then cool over ice and strain before spinning in an ice cream machine.

To Assemble and Serve
Line up four of the "Fingers" and trim them to the same length. Season them with the Maldon, Piment d'Espelette, olive oil, and lime juice to taste. Line the "Fingers" in the center of a plate like Lincoln logs and top with a quenelle of the vadouvan sorbet. Spoon a bit of the vadouvan espuma over the sorbet and finish the plate with a few scattered drops of the mint gel. Garnish with powdered vadouvan and mint.

Truffled Heirloom Potatoes, Crispy Pork Belly, Garlic Cream, and Juniper-Infused Sea Salt

Chef RJ Cooper of Vidalia – Washington, DC
Adapted by StarChefs.com

Yield: 4 Servings

Ingredients

Juniper-Infused Salt*:
1 part roasted and ground juniper
3 parts sea salt

All Blue and Peanut Potatoes:
½ pound All Blue potatoes
Olive oil
Juniper-infused salt (from above)
2 small bay leaves
4 sprigs thyme
2 sprigs rosemary
1 garlic clove
½ pound Peanut potatoes
1 tablespoon duck or pork fat

Garlic Cream:
½ pound Yellowfin potatoes, peeled
1 teaspoon roasted garlic puree
1 cup heavy cream
Salt and white pepper
Fresh nutmeg

Fingerling Potatoes:
1 Banana Fingerling potato
Oil for frying
Juniper-infused salt (from above)

Pork Belly:
½ pound pork belly
1 quart ham hock stock

Garnish:
2 ounces chicken glace
1 ounce fresh shaved truffle (Alba White, Périgord or Burgundy)

*salt to be made 1 month ahead of time

Method

For the Juniper-Infused Salt:
Mix juniper and salt together. Infuse for one month.

For the All Blue and Peanut Potatoes:
Preheat oven to 375°F. Make two aluminum foil pouches. Toss the All Blue potatoes in olive oil and juniper salt. Place in one pouch with 1 bay leaf, 2 sprigs thyme, 1 sprig rosemary and one garlic clove. Seal the pouch.

Toss the Peanut potatoes in the melted duck or pork fat in the second pouch. Add the remaining herbs and seal.

Roast both pouches for 45 minutes, or until potatoes are cooked through.

For the Garlic Cream:
Simmer yellowfin potatoes, garlic purée and cream in a heavy-bottom pot until the potatoes are thoroughly cooked. Strain the potatoes and garlic and reserve the cream. Blend the potato mixture in a Vita-Prep on medium speed and slowly add the reserved cream, taking care not to break the emulsion. Season with salt, pepper, and nutmeg, to taste. Pass through a fine mesh sieve and set aside, keeping potatoes warm.

For the Fingerling Potatoes:
Slice the fingerling potato very thinly on a mandolin. Place the slices, one at a time, into a deep fryer. Fry until golden brown and season with juniper salt.

For the Pork Belly:
Preheat oven to 200°F. Cover the pork belly in ham hock stock and braise for 4 hours, or until tender. Cut into 2-ounce cubes. In a heavy-bottom sauté pan, pan-roast the pork belly over medium heat until golden brown on all sides. Keep warm until ready to plate.

To Assemble and Serve

Place garlic cream in the center of the plate, using the back of a spoon or a small palette knife to spread the cream to desired thickness. Top the cream with pork belly, then place the All Blue and Peanut potatoes on either side. Top belly with the Fingerling potato chips. Drizzle chicken glace on either side and shave truffles over the entire plate.

Recipes

Moroccan-Style Lamb: Lamb Bastilla, Harissa, Smoked Eggplant, Cucumber, Feta

Chef Clay Conley of Azul – Miami, FL
Adapted By StarChefs.com

Yield: 4 Servings

Ingredients

Lamb Racks:
¼ bunch mint leaves
¼ bunch parsley
30 grams garlic
30 grams rosemary
75 milliliters blended oil
¼ meter cheesecloth
4 lamb racks

Lamb Shank:
1 lamb shank
30 milliliters oil
15 grams rosemary
15 grams thyme
20 grams anchovies, chopped
1 carrot, chopped
1 onion, chopped
¼ bunch celery, chopped
¼ fennel, chopped
15 grams garlic, chopped
5 grams red chili flakes
200 milliliters red wine
30 milliliters balsamic vinegar
150 grams tomatoes, peeled
1 liter chicken stock

Bastilla:
15 grams golden raisins
1 pint lamb shank braising liquid (from above)
12.5 grams chopped shallots
5 grams cumin powder
5 grams coriander powder
5 grams curry powder
2 grams paprika
2 grams ginger powder
2 grams turmeric powder
1.5 grams cayenne powder
1.5 grams cinnamon powder
2 milliliters Cointreau
20 grams chopped scallions
Salt and pepper
1 sheet phyllo pastry dough
30 grams butter

Harissa Sauce:
1.5 grams coriander seed
1.5 grams cumin seed
1.5 grams caraway seed
¼ Calabrese chili
1 clove garlic
2 teaspoons extra virgin olive oil
2 tablespoons tomato paste
1 red pepper, roasted and peeled
Water

Smoked Eggplant Puree:
2 eggplants
15 grams minced garlic
120 grams tahini
60 milliliters extra virgin olive oil
30 milliliters lemon juice

Feta Cream:
240 milliliters heavy cream
120 milliliters feta cheese

Raita:
1 cucumber
60 milliliters Greek yogurt
60 grams Bulgarian feta cheese
2 table spoons chopped mint
2 tablespoon chopped cilantro
2 tablespoon minced red onion
3 tablespoon extra virgin olive oil

Pepper Salad:
45 milliliters extra virgin olive oil
15 grams chopped garlic
20 grams chopped cilantro
5 milliliters lemon juice
1 red bell pepper
Salt and pepper

Method

For the Lamb Racks:
Blend mint leaves, parsley, garlic, rosemary, and blended oil until smooth. Pour marinade into a hotel pan and cover with cheesecloth. Lay lamb racks on top and marinade for 8 hours (or overnight).

For the Lamb Shank:
Season lamb shank and sear in a cast iron pan over high heat. Transfer to a pan and reserve. In a heavy bottomed pot, heat oil and add rosemary and thyme. Add the anchovies, mirepoix, fennel, garlic, and chili flakes, and sauté until the vegetables are translucent. Add red wine and reduce by half. Add balsamic vinegar and reduce by half. Add tomatoes and cook for 10 minutes. Add the chicken stock and bring to a boil. Transfer liquid to reserved pan with lamb shanks and cover with foil. Bake in an oven at 350˚F for 3 hours, then remove from oven and let lamb shanks rest in the liquid for half and hour. Reserve 1 pint of braising liquid. Remove shanks and separate meat from the bones; reserve four small portions of the braised lamb for plating.

For the Bastilla:
Simmer raisins in reserved braising liquid. In a heavy bottomed pan, sauté the shallots and add cumin, coriander, curry, paprika, ginger, turmeric, cayenne, and cinnamon. Deglaze pot with Cointreau and add lamb shank meat to the pan. Add raisins and braising liquid to the pan. Once braising liquid has been absorbed by the meat, add chopped scallions and season. Transfer onto a sheet pan and let cool. Roll the mixture in cling film into a 1½-inch diameter thickness and freeze. Place the phyllo sheets on a cutting board and cover with a damp cloth. Melt butter and apply to phyllo dough using a pastry brush. Remove the lamb rolls from the cling film and roll with the phyllo sheets. Cut into desired size and refrigerate.

For the Harissa Sauce:
Sauté coriander, cumin, caraway, chili, garlic, and oil over medium heat. Cook until spices are toasted, and then transfer to a blender and puree. Cool and reserve. Heat spiced olive oil over medium heat and sauté with tomato paste. Add roasted red peppers and cook for a few seconds. Transfer to blender and puree, slowly adding water until smooth.

For the Smoked Eggplant Puree:
Heat a cast iron pan over extremely high heat. Place whole eggplants in the hot, dry pan, and allow skin of eggplant to completely burn all the way around until exterior is charred and pulp is very soft. Remove from pan, allow to cool, cut in half, and scoop pulp into a blender. Add all remaining ingredients and puree until smooth.

For the Feta Cream:
Reduce the heavy cream by half. Transfer to a blender, combine with cheese, and puree until silky.

For the Raita:
Finely dice cucumber. Combine the remaining ingredients and let it sit for an hour.

For the Pepper Salad:
Combine the olive oil, cilantro, garlic, and lemon juice. On a grill, char the pepper over direct flame until the skin turns black. Cover with plastic wrap and let sit for 30 minutes. Peel the skin off the pepper, remove seeds, and julienne. Add roasted pepper to the olive oil mixture, season, and reserve.

To Assemble and Serve
Preheat oven to 350ºF. Bake bastilla until phyllo dough is golden, crispy and flaky. Remove lamb racks from marinade and grill (or pan-roast) to desired temperature. On the left side of a rectangular plate, place a small pool of feta cream. Place the bastilla on top and spoon some of the pepper salad over the roll. In the middle of the plate, towards the top, place a spoonful of eggplant puree. Top with the grilled lamb chop. To the right of the plate place a spoonful of lamb braise, and top with a spoonful of raita. On the front of the plate place a swoop of the harissa sauce.

Recipes

Backyard Lavender-Fried Rabbit with Romano Beans and Yellow Carrots

Chefs John Stewart and Duskie Estes of Zazu and Bovolo - Sonoma, CA
Adapted by StarChefs.com

Yield: Serves 4 to 8

Ingredients

Braised Rabbit:
¼ cup olive oil
2 rabbits, each cut into 8 pieces
Kosher salt and freshly ground black pepper
3 ribs celery, roughly chopped
2 carrots, peeled and roughly chopped
1 onion, roughly chopped
2 bay leaves
1 teaspoon black peppercorns
1 teaspoon lavender
1 sprig lemon thyme
3 cups Riesling
5 cups chicken stock

Fried Rabbit:
Peanut oil, for deep frying
4 cups panko
1 Tablespoon lavender
1 Tablespoon chopped fresh lemon thyme
4 cups all-purpose flour
3 cups buttermilk
Kosher salt and freshly ground black pepper

Romano Beans and Carrots:
1 pound romano beans, trimmed
1 pound yellow carrots, peeled and roll cut
2 tablespoons unsalted butter
Kosher salt and freshly ground black pepper

To Assemble and Serve:
Buttermilk mashed potatoes
Braising liquid (from above)
Lavender sprigs, for garnish

Method

For the Braised Rabbit:
Preheat oven to 350°F. Heat olive oil in a large, lidded saute pan (a sautoir) over high heat. Season rabbit pieces with salt and pepper and sear on both sides until browned, about 10 minutes. Remove rabbit and set aside. Add celery, carrots, and onion to the rabbit pan, and saute until browned (about 5 minutes). Add bay leaves, peppercorns, lavender, thyme, and Riesling, and return rabbit to pan. Bring to a simmer and cook for about 5 minutes. Add stock, cover, and place in oven, braising until tender and falling off the bone (about 1 hour). Remove rabbit and set aside. Strain braising liquid and discard solids. Return rabbit and braising liquid to pan and cool.

For the Fried Rabbit:
Preheat deep fryer with peanut oil to 350°F. Blend panko with lavender and thyme and set aside in a bowl or dish; put flour and buttermilk each in a separate bowl or dish. Remove rabbit from braising liquid and let drain a bit (but reserve braising liquid); toss pieces in flour, coat in buttermilk, and then dredge in panko to cover. Fry until golden, about 4 minutes. Let drain on paper towels and season with salt and pepper.

For the Romano Beans and Carrots:
In a large sauté pan on high heat, bring 2 cups of rabbit braising liquid to a simmer, and add romano beans and carrots. Cook until beans and carrots are tender, about 3 minutes. Whisk butter into sauce and season with salt and pepper.

To Assemble and Serve

Spoon pile of mashed potato onto plate, add carrots and beans, and drizzle with braising liquid. Top with pieces of fried rabbit and garnish with lavender sprigs.

Slow Baked Alaskan Salmon with Peppermint Cider-Braised Carrots

Chef Mohammad Islam of Aigre Doux – Chicago, IL
Adapted by StarChefs.com

Yield: 6 Servings

Ingredients

Braised Carrots:
2 sprigs thyme
½ sprig rosemary
2 bay leaves
1 tablespoon dried peppermint
4 cups apple cider
6 cloves garlic
1 tablespoon caraway seed
4 bunches knob carrots
2 tablespoons butter
Salt and pepper
Fresh peppermint

Salmon:
1 tablespoon softened butter
6 filets of fresh Alaskan King salmon (approximately 6 ounces each)
Salt and black pepper

Spinach:
2 tablespoons chopped shallot
1 tablespoons chopped garlic
1½ pounds spinach
Salt and white pepper

Method

For the Braised Carrots:
Put thyme, rosemary, bay leaves and peppermint into a sachet. Combine with apple cider, garlic, caraway seed, carrots, butter, salt and pepper, and cook for 20 minutes, until soft. Remove from liquid and slice into thick slivers. Garnish with fresh peppermint.

For the Salmon:
Preheat oven to 250°F. Cover a sheet pan with foil and spread evenly with softened butter. Season salmon with salt and pepper, place the salmon on the foil, and bake for 15 minutes.

For the Spinach:
Sautée shallot and garlic until fully cooked. Add the spinach and season with salt and white pepper. Cook until the spinach leaves wilt but not bleed (approximately 1 minute).

To Assemble and Serve

Place salmon on the right third of a rectangular plate. Place spinach in the center and carrots to the left.

Recipes

Slow-Poached Sturgeon with Roasted Beets and Horseradish-Celery-Red Radish Salad

Chef David LeFevre of Water Grill - Los Angeles, CA
Adapted by StarChefs.com

Yield: 8 Servings

Ingredients

Roasted Beets:
3 large red beets
Sprig of thyme
Salt and pepper
1 ounce olive oil

Horseradish Vinaigrette:
2 tablespoons horseradish, freshly grated
1/3 cup fresh lemon juice
1 cup extra virgin olive oil
Salt and pepper to taste

Celery Salad:
½ cup celery, peeled, destringed, and thinly sliced on the bias
16 celery leaves, cleaned
½ cup smoked sturgeon, diced
12 red radishes, cleaned and finely julienned
¼ cup mustard sprouts
Horseradish vinaigrette (from above)
Salt and pepper

Horseradish Sauce:
½ cup white wine
3 ounces shallot, minced
½ ounce garlic, minced
1 cup heavy cream
½ cup horseradish, freshly grated
1 tablespoon olive oil
1 tablespoon white wine vinegar
Salt and pepper to taste

Slow-Poached Sturgeon:
3 cups court bouillon
8 (6-ounce) portions fresh sturgeon fillets

To Assemble and Serve:
Chive oil
Radish
Mustard sprouts
Caviar (optional)

Method

For the Roasted Beets:
Preheat oven to 400°F. In a large bowl, toss the beets with thyme, salt, pepper, and olive oil. On a sheet pan, roast the beets until knife-tender. Peel and cut into 1¾-inch disks. Save scraps and puree; strain through a chinois and reserve for garnishing. At service, warm up the beet disks in a hot oven.

For the Horseradish Vinaigrette:
Whisk all ingredients together until completely emulsified.

For the Celery Salad:
Toss the salad ingredients together with the horseradish vinaigrette. Season with salt and pepper to taste.

For the Horseradish Sauce:
In a saucepan, reduce the white wine, shallots, and garlic until the wine is almost completely evaporated. Add the heavy cream and horseradish and continue to cook, reducing by half. Add olive oil and vinegar to the above mixture, whisking thoroughly to combine. Season with salt and pepper to taste. Set aside.

For the Slow-Poached Sturgeon:
In a large shallow pot, heat the court bouillon until barely simmering. Place the sturgeon fillets inside the pan and cover. Slowly poach in the court bouillon until just cooked.

To Assemble and Serve

Place a small amount of horseradish sauce on each plate. Cover with 2 slices of beets. Layer the celery salad on top of the beets. Place the the sturgeon fillet on top. Drizzle the beet puree, horseradish sauce and chive oil decoratively on the plate, and garnish with additional radish slices, mustard sprouts, and caviar, if desired.

Lemon and Apricot Roasted Chicken with Sardinian Couscous "Risotto"

Chef Jeff McInnis of The DiLido Beach Club – Miami, FL
Adapted by StarChefs.com

Yield: 10 Servings

Ingredients

Preserved Lemon*:
5 pounds salt
30 sticks cinnamon
1 cup star anise
1 cup Szechuan peppercorns
¼ cup diced fresh ginger
1 cup lemongrass
1 quart lemons, quartered
1 quart lemon juice

Brown Chicken Jus:
20 pounds chicken bones
4 onions, chopped
4 carrots, chopped
4 sticks celery, chopped
4 leeks, chopped
8 cloves garlic, chopped
2 bunches scallion, chopped
8 pieces ginger, sliced into coins
1½ cups tomato paste
3 sprigs thyme
4 bay leaves
2 tablespoons black peppercorns
1 bunch parsley stems

Slow Roasted Tomato:
15 Roma tomatoes, cored, peeled and quartered
¼ cup extra virgin olive oil
60 sprigs thyme
Salt and pepper

Apricot Glaze:
2 cups white wine
2 dried arbol chiles
1½ cups Turkish apricots
2 cups chicken stock
½ lemon, juiced
1 teaspoon salt

*Preserved lemons to be made 30 days in advance

Chicken:
4 small chickens
1½ tablespoons fresh chopped thyme
1 tablespoon salt
1 teaspoon pepper
4 lemons, halved
2 heads garlic, halved

Couscous "Risotto":
10 shallots, finely diced
1 carrot, finely diced
4 cloves garlic, finely diced
1½ quarts Sardinian couscous
2½ cups white wine
1½ gallon brown chicken jus (from above)
1½ cups roasted salted pistachios
2 tablespoons finely diced preserved lemon
2 cups thin strips of Manchego cheese
Salt and pepper

To Assemble and Serve:
Fresh thyme
Manchego cheese shavings
Pistachios

(continued)

Chef Jeff McInnis' Lemon and Apricot Roasted Chicken
with Sardinian Couscous "Risotto," Pistachio, Manchego

Antoinette Bruno

Jeff McInnis' Lemon and Apricot Roasted Chicken (continued)

Method

For the Preserved Lemon:

Combine salt, cinnamon, star anise, peppercorns, ginger, and lemongrass. In a bucket, layer the salt mixture with the lemons, and add lemon juice to cover. Place a weight over the top to ensure lemons are fully submerged. Reserve at room temperature for 30 days.

For the Brown Chicken Jus:

Roast bones at 350˚F until golden brown. Sauté onions, carrots, celery, leeks, garlic, scallions, and ginger over medium heat in a deep pot until starting to color. Add tomato paste. Add chicken bones, cover with water, and bring to a boil. Lower heat, skim, add thyme, bay leaves, peppercorns, and parsley, and simmer for 10 hours. Reduce jus until flavor has reached desired concentration.

For the Slow Roasted Tomato:

Preheat oven to 150˚F. Combine tomatoes with olive oil, thyme, salt, and pepper, and roast for 3 hours.

For the Apricot Glaze:

Bring white wine and chiles to a boil. Add apricots, chicken stock, lemon juice, and salt and reduce by half. Remove from heat, transfer to blender and puree until smooth. Reserve in a cool place.

For the Chicken:

Preheat oven to 350˚F. Rub chickens with apricot glaze and thyme, and season. Stuff the inside cavity with lemons and garlic. Truss chickens and place on a wire roasting rack breast side down and roast until done (time will vary by size). Remove from oven and reserve at room temperature. Using gloves, shred chicken into bite size pieces.

For the Couscous "Risotto":

Sweat shallots in olive oil over medium heat until translucent. Add carrot and garlic. Add couscous, stirring constantly, until lightly toasted. Add wine, stirring until reduced by half. Add brown chicken jus 1 cup at a time while stirring until couscous is cooked al dente. Add the pistachio, preserved lemon, Manchego cheese, chicken, roasted tomatoes, and season.

To Assemble and Serve

Place couscous into a Tajine or bowl. Garnish with thyme, Manchego shavings, and pistachios.

Recipes

Grilled Veal, Fava Beans, Polenta Cake, Caper-Sage Reduction
Chef Sven Meade of Nob Hill – Las Vegas, NV
Adapted by StarChefs.com

Yield: 10 Servings

Ingredients

Veal Loin:
2½ pounds veal loin
Salt and pepper
5 ounces red wine compound butter

Caper-Sage Reduction:
½ bottle Pinot Noir
10 ounces veal reduction
3 ounces capers
2 springs sage, leaves julienned

Fava Beans:
1 pound fava beans, blanched and shelled
2 ounces butter
3 ounces vegetable stock
5 leaves basil, chopped
3 leaves mint, chopped
6 leaves tarragon, chopped
Salt and pepper

Polenta:
2 cups milk
2 cups chicken stock
¼ pound butter
½ pound polenta
2 egg yolks
2 tablespoons chives, sliced
¼ pound mascarpone
Salt and pepper
Olive oil, for frying

Method

For the Veal Loin:
Season the loin with salt and pepper and grill, brushing with red wine compound butter, for about 20 minutes or until medium rare. Set aside to rest.

For the Caper-Sage Reduction:
Reduce the wine by ¾ then add the veal reduction and simmer gently for a few minutes. Finish with the capers and sage.

For the Fava Beans:
Sweat the beans in butter without coloring them. Deglaze with the vegetable stock and reduce slightly. Finish with chopped herbs, salt, and pepper to taste.

For the Polenta:
Bring the milk, stock, and butter to a boil. Whisk in the polenta and cook for 5 minutes on low heat, or until cooked. Finish with yolks, chives, mascarpone, salt and pepper. Spread onto a sheet pan and allow to cool. Cut in small squares and fry in olive oil until golden brown (approximately 1 minute).

To Assemble and Serve
Place a square of polenta on each plate and top with fava beans and veal loin. Finish with sauce and a few more fava beans.

Roasted Veal Sweetbreads with Spanish Chorizo and Potatoes

Chef Chris Nugent of Les Nomades – Chicago, IL
Adapted by StarChefs.com

Yield: 6 Servings

Ingredients

Veal Reduction:
2 tablespoons olive oil
½ cup diced onion
¼ cup diced carrot
¼ cup diced celery
½ cup sliced cremini mushrooms
1 clove garlic, sliced
1½ cups Merlot
3 sprigs thyme
5 peppercorns
2 cups veal stock
½ cup chicken stock
Salt

Spanish Chorizo:
¼ cup olive oil
¼ cup finely diced Spanish onion
¼ cup peeled and finely diced red pepper
1 teaspoon minced garlic
⅓ cup finely diced Spanish chorizo (preferably raw)
1 teaspoon smoked paprika
1 bay leaf
2 sprigs thyme
2 cups hot chicken stock
⅓ cup finely diced Idaho potato
Salt and pepper

Pommes Puree:
1 Yukon gold potato
½ cup heavy cream
4 ounces room temperature unsalted butter
Salt

Pommes Soufflé:
1½ quarts canola oil, for frying
1 Idaho potato
Salt
1 teaspoon smoked paprika

Confit Potato Rings:
2 large Yukon gold potatoes
2 cups clarified duck fat
3 cloves garlic, sliced
3 sprigs thyme
Salt

Sauce Foyot:
1 large egg yolk
1 teaspoon warm water
4 ounces warm clarified butter
2 tablespoons finely chopped tarragon
1 teaspoon tarragon vinegar
1 teaspoon tomato paste
½ teaspoon lemon juice
3 tablespoons warm veal reduction
(from above)
Tabasco sauce
Salt

Sweetbreads:
1½ pounds veal sweetbreads
1 cup white port
3 cups chicken stock
¼ cup diced carrot
¼ cup diced celery
¼ cup diced onion
3 sprigs thyme
5 peppercorns
2 bay leaves
Salt and pepper
3 tablespoons clarified butter
¼ cup all-purpose flour
Fresh herb leaves, to garnish

(continued)

Chris Nugent's Roasted Veal Sweatbreads with Spanish Chorizo and Potatoes

 Heather Sperling

Chris Nugent's Roasted Veal Sweatbreads (continued)

Method

For the Veal Reduction:
Add olive oil to a medium saucepan over medium-high heat. When hot, add onion, carrot, and celery and caramelize vegetables (about 8 minutes). Add cremini mushrooms and garlic and cook for 3 minutes. Deglaze with Merlot and reduce by 80%. Add thyme, peppercorns, and veal and chicken stocks. Simmer until reduced by 70%. Season with salt. Pass through a fine-mesh sieve lined with cheesecloth and set aside.

For the Spanish Chorizo:
In a heavy-bottom medium saucepan over medium heat, add olive oil, onions, red pepper, garlic and chorizo. Cover and cook, stirring occasionally, until vegetables are softened, about 5 minutes. Stir in smoked paprika, bay leaf, and thyme sprigs. Cook for 1 minute, and then add hot chicken stock and diced potatoes. Simmer, stirring often, until reduced by half, and potatoes are broken down and thickening the liquid. Remove bay leaf and thyme sprigs. Season with salt and pepper and set aside.

For the Pommes Puree:
Put potato in a pot and cover with cold water. Bring to a simmer and cook until fork tender (about 35 to 40 minutes). Peel potato and press through a fine sieve into a bowl. Fold ¼ cup cream into potatoes until smooth. Add butter, remaining cream, and season with salt.

For the Pommes Soufflés:
Heat 2 cups canola oil to 275° F in a medium saucepan; heat remaining canola oil to 350°F in another medium saucepan. Peel potatoes and trim into a long oval shape. Use a mandoline to cut into 1/8-inch thick slices. Dry potato slices well. Fry potato slices in batches in 275° F oil until slices begin to bubble, swirling occasionally and maintaining the oil temperature, about 4 minutes. Use a slotted spoon to carefully transfer slices from the 275° F oil to the 350° F oil; fry until they puff and become golden brown and crispy. Drain on paper towels, season with salt and smoked paprika, and set aside.

For the Confit Potato Rings:
Preheat oven to 350° F. Use a mandoline to cut potatoes into ¼-inch thick slices. Use a 3-inch cutter to cut potato slices into circles; use a 2½-inch cutter to cut out the centers out, creating rings. Heat duck fat to 200° F in a medium saucepan; add garlic, thyme, and season with salt. Put potato rings in duck fat and cook in oven for 8 minutes or until tender. Set aside.

For the Sauce Foyot:
In a small saucepan bring an inch of water to a simmer. Put egg yolk in a small bowl and place over the simmering water. Use a whisk to whip yolk until ribbon stage is reached. Remove from heat, add 1 teaspoon warm water. Continue to whip while slowly drizzling in warm clarified butter to create an emulsion. Add tarragon, tarragon vinegar, tomato paste, lemon juice, and veal reduction. Season with Tabasco and salt and set aside.

For the Sweetbreads:
Remove outer membrane from sweetbreads. In a medium saucepan, add white port and reduce by half. Add chicken stock, carrot, celery, onion, thyme, peppercorns, and bay leaves, and season with salt to taste. Bring to a boil and simmer for 6 minutes. Add sweetbreads and poach for 5 minutes on each side, and then remove and cool in refrigerator. Cut sweetbreads into 6 portions, season with salt and pepper and dredge in flour. In a large sauté pan over medium-high heat, add clarified butter. When hot, add sweetbreads and lightly brown on all sides (about 4 minutes).

To Assemble and Serve
Place a line of pommes puree across plate; put confit potato ring in center and fill with Spanish chorizo mixture. Top with crispy sweetbreads and add a tablespoon sauce Foyot. Place pommes soufflé on top and garnish with herbs. Drizzle veal reduction on plate.

Recipes

Jumbo Shrimp with Sweet Corn Succotash, Seared Polenta, and Barbecue Butter

Chef James Richardson of Nook – Los Angeles, CA
Adapted by StarChefs.com

Yield: 4 Servings

Ingredients

Barbecue Spice:
12 Ancho chilis, toasted, seeded, and ground
1 cup dark chile powder
8 tablespoons coriander
4 tablespoons cumin
3 tablespoons sweet paprika
4 tablespoons garlic powder
1 teaspoon cinnamon

Barbecue Butter:
1 cup shallots, thinly sliced
2 cups dry white wine
1 tablespoon black peppercorns
1 bay leaf
2 cups cream
1 pound cold butter, cut into pieces
2 tablespoons barbecue spice (from above)

Succotash
2 ears corn, kernels cut from the cob
1 red bell pepper, julienned
1 poblano pepper, julienned
1 bunch green onion, sliced thin on bias
1 teaspoon minced garlic
Juice from ¼ lemon
Pinch barbecue spice
Salt and pepper

To Serve:
Polenta
Butter
8 shrimp, tails on, peeled and de-veined
Canola oil

Method

For Barbecue Spice:
Combine all ingredients.

For Barbecue Butter:
Add shallots, wine, peppercorns, and bay leaf to a sauce pan and reduce until wine is almost gone. Add cream and cook until cream is reduced by half, and mixture is thick enough to coat a spoon. Strain into another sauce pan and whisk in cold butter a piece at a time until incorporated. Add barbecue spice and adjust seasoning to taste. Keep warm until use.

For Succotash:
Sauté corn, peppers, and onion until cooked through. Season with salt, pepper, barbecue spice, and lemon juice.

To Assemble and Serve

Cook polenta and spread on a half sheet tray to cool. Cut into portions with a 2½-inch ring. Melt butter in a pan over medium-high heat and brown polenta rings on both sides. Place in the center of plate and keep warm. Sauté the shrimp in canola oil until pink. Add ½ cup succotash. Top polenta with shrimp and succotash mixture and garnish with 2 ounces of the barbecue butter.

Pork Belly with Grilled Bok Choy and Tamarind Sauce

Chef Giuseppe Tentori of Boka – Chicago, IL
Adapted by StarChefs.com

Yield: 4 Servings

Ingredients

Pork Belly:
2 pounds pork belly
2 carrots, chopped
2 Spanish onions, chopped
2 celery stalks, chopped
1 head of garlic, chopped
1 tablespoon tomato paste
1 stalk lemongrass, chopped
1 piece ginger, diced
4 Thai chilies, seeds removed, chopped
1 cup rice wine vinegar
Fresh thyme
Chicken stock

Tamarind sauce:
1 Spanish onion, chopped
2 teaspoons oil
4 ounces tamarind paste
2 cups water
1 cup orange juice
1 Tablespoon sugar
1 teaspoon salt
Salt and pepper

Buckwheat Noodles:
8 ounces soba noodles
Extra virgin olive oil
Salt and pepper

To Assemble and Serve:
8 pieces bok choy
Salt and pepper
8 ounces Cipollini onions
Reduced pork stock (from above)

Method

For the Pork Belly:
Preheat oven to 350°F. Sear pork belly in a hot, dry pan and place in roasting pan with all other ingredients. Add enough chicken stock to cover and roast for 2-2.5 hours. When done, trim fat and cut to desired portions. Transfer stock to sauce pan and reduce and reserve.

For the Tamarind Sauce:
Sweat the onion in oil over medium heat. Add the tamarind paste, water, orange juice, sugar, and salt. Continue cooking for 10-15 minutes – the resulting sauce should be quite thick. Pass through chinois, and season to taste.

For the Buckwheat Noodles:
Cook noodles in water; when soft, transfer noodles to parchment paper-lined sheet pan. Spread noodles evenly and the cover with another sheet of parchment paper. Place second sheet pan on top to weigh down paper and help set noodles. Allow to cool and then cut into 2-inch squares. Prior to serving, crisp the noodle squares in olive oil for added crunch and season to taste.

To Assemble and Serve
Preheat oven to 375°F. Blanch, shock and grill bok choy. Season to taste. Whole roast the onions for 25-30 minutes, and then cool, clean, and dice. Sear pork belly in pan for crispiness. Place slice of pork belly just left-center on the plate. "Swoosh" spoonful of Tamarind Sauce around meat. Lay two pieces of bok choy along pork belly. Balance plate with one or two buckwheat noodle squares, and spoon Cipollini onions around plate to garnish. Drizzle reduced pork belly jus over meat and season.

Recipes

Braised Rabbit Pappardelle with Seasonal Vegetables

John Toulze of The Girl and The Fig – Sonoma, CA

Adapted by StarChefs.com

Yield: Serves 6

Ingredients

Braised Rabbit:

1 2½- to 3-pound whole rabbit
Salt and pepper
2 ounces canola oil
1 large carrot, peeled and chopped
2 stalks celery, chopped
1 large yellow onion, chopped
4 cloves garlic, peeled
3 Roma tomatoes, chopped
1 cup Syrah wine
2 bay leaves
1 bunch thyme
10 black peppercorns
5 cups veal or chicken stock

To Assemble and Serve:

¼ cup whole grain mustard
6 ounces pancetta, diced and cooked
Braising liquid (from above)
1 pound pappardelle
2 tablespoons extra virgin olive oil
½ cup English peas, blanched
½ cup fava beans, blanched and peeled
8 ounces Sweet 100 tomatoes, halved or quartered
3 yellow squash, sliced horizontally
2 cloves garlic, sliced
Salt and pepper
4 tablespoons butter
Arugula pesto, for garnish
Sliced almonds, for garnish
Dried pepper threads, for garnish

Method

For the Braised Rabbit:

Preheat oven to 350°F. Break down rabbit into front and hind legs and saddle, reserving trimmings and rib bones. Put bones and trimmings on a sheet tray or roasting pan and roast until golden brown; set aside. Heat a heavy-bottom pan or similar oven-proof pan over medium-high heat. Season rabbit legs and saddle generously with salt and pepper. Add oil to pan and sear rabbit pieces on all sides until golden brown; remove from pan and set aside. Add carrot, celery, onion, garlic, and tomatoes and cook until caramelized. Deglaze with wine. Add bay leaves, thyme, peppercorns, and stock; return rabbit, as well as roasted bones and trimmings, to pan. Bring to a simmer, cover, and place pan in oven. Cook until meat begins to pull away from bone (approximately 2 to 3 hours). Remove pan from oven and let cool until rabbit is cool enough to handle. Pull meat from the bones and set aside. Strain braising liquid and skim off any fat. Return liquid to pan and reduce by half. Reserve for sauce.

To Assemble and Serve

Bring a large pot of salted water to a boil. Stir mustard and pancetta into braising liquid, add rabbit meat, and bring to a simmer, cooking until the sauce begins to thicken slightly. Cook pappardelle until al dente; drain and toss with olive oil. Add peas, favas, tomatoes, squash, and garlic to pan, and cook until vegetables are just tender. Add pasta and cook until heated through. Season with salt and pepper and finish with butter. Pile pasta into middle of bowl and garnish with arugula pesto, sliced almonds, and pepper threads.

Cervena Venison Couscous Waffle with Fresh Herbs and Mushrooms

Chef Bart Vandaele of Belga Café – Washington, D.C.
Adapted by StarChefs.com

Yield: 4 Servings

Ingredients

Cervena Venison:
Olive oil
2 pounds Cervena venison leg
Salt and pepper, to taste
½ teaspoon parsley, chopped
½ teaspoon sage, chopped
½ teaspoon rosemary, chopped
½ teaspoon thyme, chopped
½ teaspoon mint, chopped
½ teaspoon cilantro, chopped
½ teaspoon basil, chopped

Valrhona Xocopili-Venison Sauce:
2 shallots, finely sliced
1 slice bacon, chopped
1 sprig thyme, stemmed
1 bay leaf
1 tablespoon sage leaves, chopped
1 teaspoon black peppercorns
1 teaspoon juniper berries
1 teaspoon coriander seeds
1 cinnamon stick
250 grams dark Belgian ale
1 liter venison stock
200 grams heavy cream
100 grams Valrhona Xocopili chocolate, chopped

Mushrooms:
2 cloves garlic
1 shallot
Olive oil, to cover
500 grams fresh wild mushrooms
1 tablespoon butter
Salt and pepper
¼ teaspoon curry powder
1 tablespoon fresh sage, chopped
1 teaspoon hazelnut oil

Couscous:
200 grams chicken stock
200 grams couscous
1 teaspoon fresh basil
1 teaspoon fresh parsley
1 teaspoon fresh chives
1 teaspoon fresh thyme
1 teaspoon fresh rosemary

To Assemble and Serve:
1 liter waffle batter

Method

For the Venison:
Rub olive oil all over the venison, season liberally with salt and pepper, and roll in in herbs. Cover the venison and refrigerate for 8 hours (or overnight). Preheat oven to 350ºF. Heat a large sauté pan over high heat and add enough olive oil to coat the bottom of the pan. Once smoking slightly, sear the tenderloin on all sides. Roast for approximately 30 minutes or until it reaches desired temperature. Allow to rest for at least ten minutes then slice into four portions. Reserve warm.

For the Valrhona Xocopili-Venison Sauce:
Brown the shallots and bacon then add the herbs and spices and sweat for about a minute. Deglaze with the beer and reduce to a syrup consistency. Add the stock and reduce heat. After a few minutes, add the cream and allow to reduce. Once the sauce is reduced (to taste), strain through a chinois and emulsify with chopped chocolate using a hand blender. Keep warm until serving.

For the Mushrooms:
Confit the garlic and shallots by cooking in olive oil at a very low temperature for two hours. Meanwhile, sauté the mushrooms in butter and season with salt, pepper, curry and sage. Add garlic, shallot confit, and hazelnut oil, and reserve warm.

For the Couscous:
Bring the chicken stock to a boil and add the couscous. Remove from the heat and let swell for five minutes. Add the fresh herbs.

To Assemble and Serve

Mix the waffle batter, mushrooms, and couscous together until smooth. Bake mixture in a waffle machine and top with warmed, sliced venison and Xocopili-venison sauce. Serve hot.

Recipes

Toasted Gingerbread with Apples, Juniper, Sheep's Milk Yogurt, and Cider Sorbet

Pastry Chef Tim Dahl of Blackbird – Chicago, IL
Adapted by StarChefs.com

Note: The cider broth recipe below creates more broth than is needed for the gingerbread. Dahl makes enough for a few batches, and makes a fresh gingerbread cake every day. He uses Honey Crisp apples because of their large cell structure.

Yield: 12 Servings (with extra sorbet, broth, sauce)

Ingredients

Cider Broth:
4 grams green cardamom pods
12 grams cinnamon sticks
8 grams green coriander
4 grams grains of paradise
8 grams juniper
8 grams star anise
16 grams fresh ginger
2 grams lemon zest
2000 grams apple cider

Gingerbread Sponge:
255 grams all purpose flour
30 grams rye flour
140 grams sugar
200 grams brown sugar
12 grams ground Korintji cinnamon
16 grams ground ginger
12 grams baking powder
4 grams salt
120 grams rice bran oil
240 grams cider broth (from above)
85 grams egg yolks
285 grams egg whites
115 grams sugar

Cider-Yogurt Sorbet:
738 grams sugar
162 grams atomized glucose
10 grams ice cream stabilizer
6 grams salt
1206 grams apple cider
900 grams sheep's milk yogurt

Apple Sauce:
225 grams sugar
250 grams water
4 grams juniper, toasted
Juice of 1 lemon
1000 grams honey crisp apples

Juniper Syrup:
200 grams water
400 grams sugar
30 grams juniper
500 grams Bombay Sapphire gin
1000 grams Honey Crisp apples

To Assemble and Serve:
Butter
Crumbled feta cheese
Micro cilantro

(continued)

Heather Sperling

Tim Dahl's Toasted Gingerbread with Apples,
Juniper, Sheep's Milk Yogurt and Cider Sorbet

Recipes

Pastry Chef Tim Dahl's Toasted Gingerbread (continued)

Method

For the Cider Broth:
Toast the spices until they become fragrant. Add the cider and bring to a boil. Steep the mixture for 8 hours (or overnight) and strain through a chinois.

For the Gingerbread Sponge:
Preheat oven to 375°F. Line a half-sheet pan with a Silpat. Sift the flours, sugars, spices and baking powder together and reserve. Combine the oil, broth and yolks and mix until well incorporated. Gradually add the dry ingredients and mix until smooth. Whip the egg whites with the remaining sugar to soft peaks. Fold the whipped egg whites into the yolk and flour mixture. Spread the batter evenly over the half-sheet pan and bake for 25 minutes.

For the Cider-Yogurt Sorbet:
Combine all of the dry ingredients. Heat the cider to 40°C. Mix in the dry ingredients and heat the mixture to 85°C. Cool rapidly to 20°C and let mature, refrigerated, for 8 hours or overnight. Mix the syrup into the yogurt with an immersion blender. Freeze in an ice cream maker according to instructions.

For the Apple Sauce:
Prepare a syrup with the sugar, water, juniper, and lemon juice. Peel, core, and poach the apples in the hot syrup until tender. Remove the apples from the liquid and puree in a Vita-Prep, adjusting the consistency with additional syrup if needed.

For the Juniper Syrup and Apples:
Bring the water, sugar and juniper to a boil. When the syrup is cool, add the gin. Cut the apples into a uniform dice. Vacuum seal the apples with the juniper syrup and let rest for a minimum of 4 hours.

To Assemble and Serve

Cut gingerbread into serving portions and toast in a pan with butter. Spread the warm apple sauce across the plate and place the gingerbread on top. Place the apples to the side of the gingerbread and garnish with crumbled feta and micro cilantro. Finish with a quenelle of the cider sorbet on top of the cake.

Aged Pecorino and Walnut Financier with Roasted Clementine Jam

Pastry Chef Nicole Krasinski of Rubicon – San Francisco, CA
Adapted by StarChefs.com

Yield: 12 Servings

Ingredients

Roasted Clementine Jam:
5 clementines, washed, dried, sliced, and deseeded
½ cup fresh orange juice
6 tablespoons light muscovado sugar
100 grams granulated sugar
Water as needed
½ cup fresh grapefruit juice

Financier:
224 grams butter, browned and cooled
227 grams sifted powdered sugar
71.25 grams cake flour
2 grams salt.
114 grams almond flour
42.75 grams coarse cornmeal
224 grams egg whites, room temperature
250 grams clementine jam (from above)

Candied Walnuts:
150 grams walnuts
200 grams sugar
Water, as needed
2 grams salt

Fennel Citrus Salad:
1 bulb fennel
1 cup citrus segments (grapefruit, cara cara oranges, and navel oranges)
Watercress
Olive oil
Sea salt

To Assemble and Serve:
Aged Pecorino cheese, shaved with a vegetable peeler

Method

For the Roasted Clementine Jam:
Preheat oven to 325°F. Place clementines in a hotel pan, cover with orange juice, and sprinkle with 2 tablespoons of the muscovado sugar. Cover clementines with foil and roast for 60-90 minutes until they begin to soften. Remove pan from oven and bring oven temperature up to 375°F. Remove foil, sprinkle with remaining muscovado sugar, and roast for 45 minutes. Cool to room temperature. Place clementines in a food processor and pulse until well combined, adding a little orange juice if needed. In a sauté pan, cook granulated sugar and water as needed until it just begins to color. Add clementines and grapefruit juice and cook until thickened, stirring often. Cool.

For the Financier:
Heat butter in a sauce pan until bubbly and browned, about 5 minutes. Transfer to a bowl to cool. Sift the powdered sugar, flour and salt together. Whisk almond flour and cornmeal in to the dry mixture, transfer to a mixer bowl and paddle at low speed to combine. While mixer is on low speed add egg whites and browned butter, then bring mixer to medium speed to and paddle until mixture is well combined. Coat 1 full sheet pan plus ¼ of another sheet pan with cooking spray, place 320 grams of batter in pan, and freeze for 30-45 minutes until batter is just starting to set.

Preheat oven to 350°F. Spread 250 grams roasted clementine jam on top of the frozen batter in an even layer. Top with an even layer of 320 grams batter. Bake (with the fan on) for 12-15 minutes until golden. Cool and flip onto a cutting board and cut into 4-centimeter x 9-centimeter rectangles. Wrap in plastic until ready to serve.

For the Candied Walnuts:
Preheat oven to 250°F. Place the walnuts on a Slipat-lined sheet pan and toast until golden brown. In a sauce pan heat the sugar and water (just enough to moisten) to a medium-light caramel. Add salt and toasted walnuts and stir to combine. Transfer nuts back to sheet pan, cool, and chop.

For the Fennel Citrus Salad:
Slice fennel paper-thin and toss with citrus segments, watercress, olive oil, and sea salt.

To Assemble and Serve
Place about ½-ounce shaved aged Pecorino in the center of the plate and place a slice of financier cake on top. Place a small pile of tossed fennel citrus salad on the left side of the cake and sprinkle candied walnuts on the right.

Recipes

Coconut Tapioca, Lemongrass Ice Cream, Red Thai Tea Foam, Kaffir Emulsion

Pastry Chef Joel Lahon of Nobu Miami Beach – Miami Beach, FL

Adapted by StarChefs.com

Yield: 10 Servings

Ingredients

Lemongrass Ice Cream:
1220 grams milk
1 bunch lemongrass
120 grams butter
260 grams caster sugar
70 grams glucose powder
100 grams milk powder
4 grams stabilizer
160 grams egg yolk

Kaffir Emulsion:
250 grams milk
5 kaffir leaves
3 grams lecithin

Coconut Tapioca:
200 grams tapioca pearls
580 grams coconut milk
100 grams sugar

Red Thai Tea Foam:
250 grams milk
20 grams red Thai tea
105 grams sugar
2 gelatin sheets
250 grams cream

Method

For the Lemongrass Ice Cream:
Combine milk and lemongrass and reserve, chilled, for 8 hours (or overnight). Remove the lemongrass; combine milk with butter, sugar, glucose powder, milk powder, and stabilizer. Add the egg yolk and cook until mixture reaches 85˚F. Strain and cool for 4 hours. Freeze in an ice cream maker according to instructions.

For the Kaffir Emulsion:
Combine milk and kaffir leaves and reserve, chilled, for 8 hours (or overnight). Sprinkle the mixture with lecithin and mix with a hand blender. Use a spoon to collect the foam on top and reserve.

For the Coconut Tapioca:
Add tapioca pearls to boiling water and cook until translucent. Remove pearls and reserve. In a separate pot, heat the coconut milk and sugar. Add the tapioca pearls and let cool. Reserve in a chilled place.

For the Red Thai Tea Foam:
Warm the milk, add red Thai tea, and infuse for 15 minutes. Add the sugar and gelatin sheets until dissolved. Add cream, and place mixture in a siphon bottle.

To Assemble and Serve

Ladle coconut tapioca on bottom of the plate or bowl. Place a spoonful of lemongrass ice cream in the center. Using the siphon, place red Thai tea foam on one side of the lemongrass ice cream. Spoon the kaffir emulsion on the other side.

Yogurt Panna Cotta with Greengage Plums, Rhubarb Blood Orange Compote and Apple Gelée

Pastry Chef Michael Laiskonis of Le Bernardin – New York, NY
Adapted by StarChefs.com

Yield: 12 Servings

Ingredients

Yogurt Panna Cotta:
12 grams (6 sheets) gelatin
750 grams heavy cream
300 grams granulated sugar
Zest of 2 oranges
750 grams plain whole milk yogurt

Rhubarb Blood Orange Compote
150 grams granulated sugar
Water, as needed
250 grams rhubarb, washed, peeled, and chopped
Zest and juice of 1 blood orange

Apple Gelée:
4 grams (2 sheets) gelatin
20 grams water
1 grams agar agar
Sugar
200 grams apple cider

To Assemble and Serve:
12 greengage plums
Granulated sugar

Method

For the Yogurt Panna Cotta:
Bloom gelatin in water. In a saucepan over medium heat, combine cream, sugar, and zest, and gently warm. Remove from heat and stir in gelatin until dissolved. Temper into yogurt and strain through a chinois. Spoon into molds and refrigerate for at least 2 hours or until set.

For the Rhubarb Blood Orange Compote:
In a medium non-reactive sauté pan, combine sugar and just enough water to moisten. Cook to a light caramel over high heat. Add rhubarb to pan and toss. Allow juices from rhubarb to dissolve bits of sugar. Cook until mixture is fairly dry. Add orange zest and juice; cook until liquid is absorbed. Remove from heat, cool, and chill.

For the Apple Gelée:
Bloom gelatin in water. Combine agar agar with sugar and sprinkle into liquid. Bring to a gentle boil; reduce heat while maintaining a simmer for 2 to 3 minutes. Remove from heat and whisk in bloomed gelatin. Allow to cool slightly for a few moments and pour into a plastic-lined half sheet pan. Refrigerate until set; then cut into 4 centimeter squares.

To Assemble and Serve

Split plums and remove pits; sprinkle cut sides with sugar and lightly caramelize with a blowtorch. Arrange 2 plum halves on each panna cotta, along with a spoonful of rhubarb-blood orange compote. Lay squares of apple gelée over top and serve immediately.

Recipes

Meyer Lemon Cheesecake with Beurre Blanc and Lemon Rosemary Sorbet Soda

Pastry Chef Elissa Narow of Custom House and Spring – Chicago, IL
Adapted by StarChefs.com

Yield: 20 Portions

Ingredients

Cheesecake:
1 pound soft cream cheese
½ cup plus 2 tablespoons sugar
Zest of 3 Meyer lemons
2 eggs
1 egg yolk
1 ounce crème fraiche
1½ ounce Meyer lemon juice
1¾ teaspoons flour
8 ounces butter
2/3 cup powdered sugar
¼ teaspoon salt
Zest of 2 lemons
2 cups all purpose flour

Rosemary Dust:
Rosemary leaves
Powdered sugar

Lemon Rosemary Sorbet:
2 large sprigs rosemary
1 quart lemon juice
2 cups water
½ cup simple syrup
1 egg

Beurre Blanc Sauce:
1 cup Meyer lemon juice
¾ cup sugar
4 ounces butter

To Assemble and Serve:
Sugared Meyer lemon segments
Candied Meyer lemon zest
Soda water

Method

For the Cheesecake:
The night before, beat cream cheese, sugar, and lemon zest in an electric mixer with a paddle attachment until sugar is dissolved. Add eggs and yolk one at a time until incorporated, scraping down the bowl between each addition. Add crème fraiche and lemon juice. Mix in flour. Let set for 8 hours (or overnight) in a chilled place.

Prehat oven to 300°F. Combine butter, sugar, salt, zest, and flour, spread on a sheet pan, and bake until set. Transfer to food processor and crumble. Press into a thin layer in a tart ring and bake in oven for 6 minutes or until light brown. Remove ring from oven and fill to the top with the cheesecake filling. Transfer to oven with a hotel pan filled with water at the bottom. Bake for 12-15 minutes, remove from oven, and chill.

For the Rosemary Dust:
Grind rosemary with powdered sugar in a spice grinder.

For the Lemon Rosemary Sorbet:
Combine rosemary, lemon juice, and water in a blender. Strain and mix with simple syrup. Add egg to adjust consistency and taste as necessary. Freeze in an ice cream maker according to instructions.

For the Beurre Blanc:
Combine juice with sugar and reduce by half. Remove from heat and whisk in butter. Reserve warm.

To Assemble and Serve

Plate cheesecake and top with beurre blanc, sugared Meyer lemon segments, candied Meyer lemon zest, and a sprinkle of rosemary dust. Fill a shot glass with lemon rosemary sorbet and top with soda water. Serve dish with shot glass on the side.

Chocolate Pecan Torte with Cinnamon Ice Cream

Pastry Chef Shannon Swindle of Craft – Dallas, TX
Adapted by StarChefs.com

Yield: 12 servings

Ingredients

Cinnamon Ice Cream:
3¼ cups milk
3¼ cups heavy cream
8 crumbled Ceylon cinnamon sticks
1¼ cups sugar
¼ teaspoon salt
15 egg yolks

Pecan Torte - Pecan Layer:
4 ounces organic Texas pecans
2 ounces all purpose flour
4 ounces soft butter
1 teaspoon ground sea salt
½ scraped Mexican vanilla bean
½ cup sugar
1 egg

Pecan Torte – Chocolate Layer:
6 tablespoons heavy cream
½ scraped Mexican vanilla bean
7 ounces Valrhona Manjari chocolate, chopped
3 eggs
1 teaspoon ground sea salt
4 tablespoons sugar

Method

For the Cinnamon Ice Cream:

In a heavy sauce pan, scald the milk, cream, cinnamon, sugar, and salt, and set aside to steep for 1 hour. Re-scald the mixture, and temper the yolks with the hot cream. Incorporate the yolks into the mixture, and put back on the heat, stirring until the mixture thickens and coats the back of a spoon. Immediately place the custard in an ice bath to cool, stirring occasionally. Refrigerate the cooled custard overnight in a covered container. The next day, strain the base through a chinois and freeze in an ice cream freezer according to the manufacturer's directions. Allow the ice cream to set up for at least 2 hours before serving.

For the Pecan Torte – Pecan Layer:

Preheat oven to 300°F. Place the pecans and the flour in the bowl of a food processor, and process until finely ground. Set aside. In the bowl of an electric mixer fitted with the paddle attachment, cream the butter, salt, vanilla bean, and sugar. Add the egg and mix until incorporated. Spread the mixture in to 12 3-inch buttered, parchment-lined baking rings, and bake for about 15 minutes. Allow to cool before proceeding with the chocolate layer.

For the Pecan Torte – Chocolate Layer:

Increase the oven to 350°F. Place the cream and vanilla bean in a small sauce pan, and scald. Set aside and allow the vanilla to steep for 30 minutes in a small bowl, then re-scald the cream and pour the hot cream over the chocolate. Allow the chocolate to melt for a couple of minutes, then whisk in the center of the bowl until all the chocolate is melted and a smooth ganache forms. Place the eggs, salt, and sugar in a bowl over another bowl of steaming water, and hand-whisk the eggs until the mixture reaches 110°F. Transfer to the base of an electric mixer and whip (with the whisk attachment) on high speed until the mixture triples in volume. Gently fold the chocolate ganache into the whipped eggs. Divide the batter among the 12 rings on top of the pecan layer, and bake for about 12 minutes, or until the mixture is puffed and cracked, but still the consistency of custard in the center. Allow the tortes to cool for 1 minute, then carefully run a knife around the baking rings and lift the rings to un-mold.

To Assemble and Serve

Top tortes with a quenelle of cinnamon ice cream, and serve immediately.

Recipes

Banana Pecan Bread Pudding with Rum Sauce
Pastry Chef Joe Truex of Repast – Atlanta, GA
Adapted by StarChefs.com

Ingredients
Banana Bread Pudding:
2 ounces unsalted butter
3 ripe bananas, diced
5 ounces sugar
2 cups heavy cream
5 ounces dark rum
4 large eggs
1 teaspoon vanilla extract
8 ounces brioche, crusts removed and diced

Rum Sauce:
2 ounces unsalted butter
4 ounces heavy cream
4 ounces dark brown sugar
Salt
2 ounces dark Jamaican rum

To Assemble and Serve:
1 cup all-purpose flour
4 eggs, beaten
3 cups pecan pieces (or 1 cup fine-ground or 2 cups coarse-ground)
Canola oil
Butter
Salt
Vanilla, banana or rum raisin ice cream
Powdered sugar

Method
For the Banana Bread Pudding:
Melt butter in a skillet over medium heat. Add bananas and 2 ounces of sugar and cook several minutes, stirring to cook evenly. Remove from heat and cool to room temperature. Combine the heavy cream, rum, eggs, vanilla, and remaining 3 ounces of sugar in a bowl and whisk to blend. Add bananas and bread and let this mixture soak for at least 1 hour.

Preheat oven to 300°F. Line a rectangular terrine mold with plastic and pour banana bread pudding mixture inside. Cover and cook in a water bath until bread pudding reaches 175°F. Remove from oven and cool completely (preferably overnight).

For the Rum Sauce:
Melt butter in a saucepan over medium-high heat. Add cream, sugar, and salt. Bring to a boil, stirring until sugar dissolves. Remove from heat and stir in rum.

To Assemble and Serve
Remove pudding from mold and slice into ½-inch slices. Coat each piece evenly with flour, egg wash, and pecan pieces. Fry each piece to order using equal parts oil and butter until golden on each side. Sprinkle with a bit of salt and top with a scoop of ice cream. Drizzle with rum sauce and sprinkle with powdered sugar.

"Tiramisu"
Pastry Chef Tom Wellings of Fiamma – New York, NY
Adapted by StarChefs.com

Yield: 6 Portions

Ingredients
Sorbet Syrup:
3 liters water
700 grams sugar
600 grams glucose
100 grams trimoline
30 grams sorbet stabilizer

Mascarpone Sorbet:
400 grams sorbet syrup (from above)
500 grams mascarpone cheese

Coffee Soil:
500 grams sugar
200 grams cocoa powder
170 grams coffee grounds
30 grams Maldon salt
350 grams butter, softened

Amaretto Jelly:
3 grams gellan gum
150 grams water
300 grams Amaretto
200 grams sugar

Espresso Sauce:
500 grams espresso
400 grams sugar
100 grams Kahlua
2 grams agar-agar

Cocoa Tuile:
100 grams flour
100 grams sugar
100 grams egg whites
100 grams cocoa powder
100 grams butter

Method
For the Sorbet Syrup:
Bring all ingredients to a boil then strain and chill.

For the Mascarpone Sorbet:
Combine the sorbet syrup and mascarpone and blend with an immersion blender. Spin in an ice cream machine according to instructions, and reserve in freezer for later use.

For the Coffee Soil:
Preheat oven to 200°F. Combine the sugar, cocoa powder, coffee grounds, and salt then slowly add the butter and incorporate. Spread the mixture onto a sheet pan and bake for 1½ hours. Process in a high-speed blender until very fine.

For the Amaretto Jelly:
Hydrate the gellan gum in the water. Heat the amaretto and sugar; combine both mixtures and cool. Pour into a half sheet pan and allow to set. Cut into cubes and reserve.

For the Espresso Sauce:
Bring the espresso, sugar, and Kahlua to a simmer then add the agar-agar and boil for 2 minutes. Once set, puree in a blender.

For the Cocoa Tuile:
Preheat oven to 350°F. Combine the flour, sugar, egg whites, cocoa powder, and butter in a mixer and allow to rest for 1 day. Return to room temperature and spread onto a Silpat. Bake for 3 to 5 minutes. Cool and break into large shards.

To Assemble and Serve
Place a small amount of espresso sauce in a bowl. Top with the coffee soil and a quenelle of mascarpone sorbet. Garnish with the amaretto jelly and a cocoa tuile.

Elissa Narow's Chocolate Chip Sassafrass Ice Cream Sandwich (foreground) and Candy Bar with Walnut Sable, Meringue, and Cranberry Jelly (background) at Custom House, Chicago

Antoinette Bruno

Meg Galus' Roasted Pineapple, Coconut Sorbet, Cashew
Frangipane, and Sourwood Honey at Tru, Chicago

Kamel Guechida's La Framboise: Fresh Raspberry Surprise Inside White
Chocolate Sphere, Yuzu Ice Cream at Joel Robuchon, Las Vegas

Antoinette Bruno

Antoinette Bruno

Elizabeth Dahl's Hazelnut and Sage Brown Butter Crepes with Ricotta, Pear Butter, Candied Hazlenuts, Hazlenut Ice Cream, and Sherry Brown Butter at Boka, Chicago

Amanda Gager's "Sun Burst" Cocktail at Stripsteak, Las Vegas

Thomas Buckley's Steamed Snapper with Ginko Nuts, Matsutake
Mushrooms, Yuzu, Sake, and Soy at Nobu, Miami Beach

Will Blunt

Antoinette Bruno

Bob Iacovone's Cured-Smoked Duck Breast, Confit Leg, Walnut-Bleu Risotto, Hudson Valley Foie Gras, and Pear Glace at Cuvee, New Orleans

Sam Ross at Milk & Honey, New York City

Sandro Micheli's Dark Chocolate Sorbet, Coffee Granita,
Caramelized Brioche Croutons at Adour, New York City

Hugh Acheson's Pork Belly with Citrus Salad and Grits at Five and Ten, Athens

Joe Isadori's Short Rib Tortellini with Fava Beans,
Mascarpone and Black Truffle at DJT, Las Vegas

Antoinette Bruno

John Kinder Flaming Orange Zest over a Cocktail, Chicago

Uncooked Egg Purse at Adour, New York City

Neil Ferguson's Pickles, Leaves, Fruits, Herbs, and
Vegetables at Allen & Delancey, New York City

Eben Freeman Finishing a Cocktail at Tailor, New York City

Heather Sperling

Malika Ameen's Berry Crisp at Aigre Doux, Chicago

Anthony Alba's "The Big Easy" Cocktail, Las Vegas

Antoinette Bruno

Restaurant Charlie, Las Vegas

Toby Maloney Doing "La Brujita - The River of Fire" at The Violet Hour, Chicago

Donald Link's Gumbo at Herbsaint, New Orleans

The Kitchen at Morimoto, New York City

Tony Esnault's Sweetbread Meunière, Egg Purse, and Wild Mushrooms at Adour, New York City

Antoinette Bruno

Foie du Gras
Passionfruit $9
Sazerac $9

Chefs specials

SPECIAL 1$

"Rising sun" Foie Gras
Southern Valley foie gras w/ a
"Fish" crust on sticky black rice
Orange + pepper jelly sauce $16

SPECIAL #2 Yellow Tomato + Asp...
...ced yellow tomato w/ macadamia crust,
...bo asparagus + citrus aioli

Crawfish
Kracha...
filled un...
feta, ta...

Oyster Fennel St...
Yellowfin Tuna
slightly

Cleaning the Kitchen at the End of Service at Norman's, Orlando

Index

Index

Chefs by Last Name

Index

Chefs by State/City

Index

Index

Index

Index

Index

Index

Favorite Tools

Index

Index

Index

Index

Index

Index

Index

Index

Rising Stars Award Winners

Index

Index

Index

Index

Index

Index

CULINARY SCHOOLS

Index

Index

Index

Affiliation Abbreviation Guide

ACCC	The Association of Community Cancer Centers
ACF	American Culinary Federation
AIWF	The American Institute of Wine and Food
AmFar	The American Foundation for AIDS Research
CCAN	Chef's Club about Nothing
C-CAP	Careers through Culinary Arts Programs
CCC	Chef's Charity for Children
CCRRP	Crescent City Restaurant Re-Birth Project
CHS	Certified Humane Society
CIA	Culinary Institute of America
COB	Children of Bellevue
CUESA	Center for Urban Education of Sustainable Agriculture
DiRona	Distinguished Restaurants of North America
FCI	French Culinary Institute
GCM	Green City Market
GGRA	Golden Gate Restaurant Association
HRA	Hawaii Restaurant Association
IACP	International Association of Culinary Professionals
IAFOC	Italian-American Federation of Chefs
IFT	Institute of Food Technologists
JBF	James Beard Foundation
JLPF	Jean-Louis Palladin Foundation
LDE	Les Dames d'Escoffier
LRA	Louisiana Restaurant Association
MCC	Macy's Culinary Council
MOFGA	Maine Organic Farmers and Gardners Association
MOW	Meals-on-Wheels
NECI	New England Culinary Institute
NRA	National Restaurant Association
NTFB	North Texas Food Bank
NYWCA	New York Women's Culinary Alliance
OCA	Organic Consumers Association
RAMMY	RAMW's yearly chef/restaurant awards
RAMW	Restaurant Association of Metropolitan Washington
RCA	Research Chefs Association
SFA	Southern Foodways Alliance
SFBM	Southern Food and Beverage Museum
SOS	Share our Strength
TAP Project	A Unicef water project
UNICEF	United Nations Childrens Fund
WCR	Women Chefs and Restauranteurs
WRA	Washington Restaurants Association